Internet Marketing
INTEGRATING ONLINE AND OFFLINE STRATEGIES

THIRD EDITION

Internet Marketing
INTEGRATING ONLINE AND OFFLINE STRATEGIES

Mary Lou Roberts
Retired Professor of Marketing

Debra Zahay
Northern Illinois University

SOUTH-WESTERN
CENGAGE Learning

Australia • Brazil • Japan • Korea • Mexico • Singapore • Spain • United Kingdom • United States

Internet Marketing: Integrating Online and Offline Strategies, Third Edition

Mary Lou Roberts and Debra Zahay

Vice President of Editorial, Business: Jack W. Calhoun

Publisher: Erin Joyner

Executive Editor: Mike Roche

Developmental Editor: Sarah Blasco

Editorial Assistant: Megan Fischer

Marketing Manager: Gretchen Swann

Senior Marketing Communications Manager: Jim Overly

Marketing Coordinator: Leigh Smith

Media Editor: John Rich

Rights Acquisition Director: Audrey Pettengill

Senior Rights Acquisition Specialist, Image: Deanna Ettinger

Rights Acquisition Specialist, Text: Sam Marshall

Manufacturing Planner: Ron Montgomery

Design Direction, Production Management, and Composition: PreMediaGlobal

Senior Art Director: Stacy Shirley

Cover Designer: Craig Ramsdell

Cover Image: ©iStock Photo

For product information and technology assistance, contact us at **Cengage Learning Customer & Sales Support, 1-800-354-9706.**

For permission to use material from this text or product, submit all requests online at **www.cengage.com/permissions**. Further permissions questions can be e-mailed to **permissionrequest@cengage.com**.

Library of Congress Control Number: 2012932722

ISBN-13: 978-1-133-62590-2

ISBN-10: 1-133-62590-8

South-Western
5191 Natorp Boulevard
Mason, OH 45040
USA

Cengage Learning is a leading provider of customized learning solutions with office locations around the globe, including Singapore, the United Kingdom, Australia, Mexico, Brazil, and Japan. Locate your local office at **www.cengage.com/global**.

Cengage Learning products are represented in Canada by Nelson Education, Ltd.

For your course and learning solutions, visit **www.cengage.com**.

Purchase any of our products at your local college store or at our preferred online store **www.cengagebrain.com**.

Printed in the United States of America
5 6 7 16 15

The third edition is dedicated to students and practitioners of all forms of Internet and interactive marketing around the globe who have enhanced our knowledge and understanding of these continuously evolving marketing disciplines.

MLR/DZ

BRIEF CONTENTS

BRIEF CONTENTS

CONTENTS

15   Social and Regulatory Issues: Privacy, Security, and Intellectual Property   408

16   Mobile Marketing and Related Developments   439

INTRODUCTION

Since *Internet Marketing: Integrating Online and Offline Strategies* was first published in 2003, the Internet has continued to undergo rapid, and often revolutionary, change. The increasing global penetration of the Internet and the improving skills of marketers in using this new medium have made the Internet pervasive in the lives of both consumers and businesses. The question is no longer whether any commercial, nonprofit, or governmental organization should make use of the Internet. The question is how to develop a strategy that makes the Internet and digital technology increasingly the focal point of marketing effort. It is predicted that in a few short years, Internet technologies will comprise 35 percent of all advertising spending. It can be said that all marketing is becoming Internet marketing because we are now at the point where even those firms engaging primarily in traditional forms of marketing cannot ignore what is happening on the web.

The strategy paradigm used in the book is based on customer acquisition, lead conversion, customer retention, and growing customer value. All these subjects are given extensive treatment either in a specific chapter or integrated into discussions of tools and techniques that are most appropriate for executing the particular strategy.

Strategy considerations are accompanied by in-depth coverage of the ever-increasing array of tools and services that support marketing program execution. Search is where most consumers start the purchasing process on the web and search engine marketing that incorporates both optimization for natural search and pay-per-click is essential. Email remains a key part of the marketing programs of B2C, B2B, as well as nonprofit marketers, even as consumers continue to migrate to mobile communications and text messaging. Display advertising, for branding and for direct response, is undergoing a renaissance as new formats become available to better engage the viewer.

While "traditional" channels for Internet marketing have been evolving, entirely new channels have emerged. Consumers spend a large percentage of their Internet time on social networks—communicating, obtaining peer-based information, and occasionally purchasing a good or service. B2B customers are also enthusiastic users of social media for collaboration and for obtaining information. Marketers are expending a great deal of effort in learning how to use the social media channel effectively for marketing purposes. The same is true of the emerging mobile channel. A growing number of people have mobile-only Internet connections, and smartphones and tablets have become essential to the lifestyles of many of us. Mobile apps have opened up a whole new way to push information, with permission, to the consumer. Mobile commerce is demonstrating viability in countries throughout the world.

In the midst of this ongoing change, there is discussion about the future shape of the Internet. Web 3.0 is only dimly perceived at this point, but marketers need to be alert to change from whichever direction it emerges.

UNIFYING THEMES

This book is uniquely positioned to take advantage of the innovation that is inherent in the Internet. The Internet itself is no longer a stand-alone medium, if indeed it ever was. Internet marketing is most effective if strategies and messages are integrated across media. That viewpoint is pervasive throughout this book; Internet marketing is considered in the context of overall marketing strategy executed in multiple channels. Throughout, examples show the integrated use of online and offline channels by B2C and B2B to achieve business and marketing objectives.

This book also recognizes the Internet as the global phenomenon it truly is. Coverage of global issues is integrated into the appropriate subject areas. Global data are presented when appropriate, and examples of programs in various countries are seamlessly woven into content coverage. Where Internet-readiness, regulations, or culture affects Internet marketing activities, they are treated separately and specifically.

It is impossible to understand Internet marketing without having a layperson's appreciation of the technology that makes it possible. Technology also is covered in the context of the marketing activities affected by it, not as a separate issue. Complex technological subjects are explained in a manner that can be successfully grasped by those with only introductory or user-level familiarity with computer technology.

The book retains a strategic emphasis throughout as it discusses the planning, development, execution, and evaluation of marketing campaigns across multiple channels.

NEW AND UPDATED IN THIS EDITION

The third edition of *Internet Marketing: Integrating Online and Offline Strategies* has been completely rewritten to incorporate the changing Internet environment faced by marketers. It has entirely new chapters on social media marketing and lead generation and conversion in business markets. A new section on video marketing has been added.

The essential tools of search engine marketing and email have been given expanded coverage with a separate chapter devoted to each of them. The chapter on mobile marketing is entirely new, reflecting the growing reach and power of the mobile channel.

The book is divided into four sections:

1. Part 1: "Foundations of Internet Marketing" introduces the topic and profiles the Internet audience. It has chapters on the value chain, evolving business models, and direct and database marketing.
2. Part 2: "Essential Internet Marketing Tools" covers branding and video, display, email, and search marketing. It concludes with the new chapter on social media marketing.
3. Part 3: "Developing Internet Marketing Strategies and Programs" begins with the new chapter on lead generation and management and contains the chapters on CRM, website development, and customer service.

4. Part 3: "Evaluating Performance and Opportunities" has completely updated chapters on metrics, social and regulatory issues, and the convergence of media that we call mobile.

The importance of social media and mobile marketing is such that illustrations have crept into chapters throughout the book. The focus on providing both B2B and B2C examples has been continued with limited coverage of non-profit marketing and e-government efforts.

ACKNOWLEDGMENTS

Reviewers of both the first and second editions contributed materially to the soundness and readability of the book. Academic users of the book and practitioners alike have made informal contributions that have been helpful throughout. We are especially grateful to the many firms in the Internet space that have made their content available to us. This information has contributed immeasurably to keeping the book relevant and timely.

There are many people involved in publishing a book. Mike Roche, Executive Editor at South-Western, was responsible for the authorization of the third edition and has provided a steady guiding hand throughout. Sarah Blasco is the Developmental Editor at South-Western who has shepherded the book through its day-to-day creative activities and answered our many questions. To them and to others who have assisted in this book, the authors express their appreciation.

Mary Lou Roberts is particularly indebted to students in Internet Marketing and Social Media Marketing courses for introducing her to issues and developments she would never have otherwise recognized.

Debra Zahay wishes to acknowledge the support of her husband, Edward Blatz, and her parents, Joyce and Albert Zahay, and their unswerving belief in her. She also is indebted to the insightful comments and contributions of her colleagues at Northern Illinois University, Dr. Lauren Labrecque and Mrs. Sandy Domagalski, and the insights from her students.

MARY LOU ROBERTS has been a tenured professor of marketing at the University of Massachusetts Boston and held a number of administrative positions there including Director of Development. She currently teaches Internet marketing and social media marketing to a global cadre of students at the Harvard University Extension School. She has a Ph.D. in marketing from the University of Michigan. She is the senior author of *Direct Marketing Management*, 2e, available on her website www.marylouroberts.info. She has published extensively in marketing journals in the United States and Europe. Dr. Roberts is a frequent presenter on programs of both professional and academic marketing organizations and has consulted and provided planning services and management training programs for a wide variety of corporations and nonprofit organizations. She has been an active member of many professional organizations and has served on a number of their boards.

DEBRA ZAHAY is a tenured Associate Professor of Marketing and holds the title Professor of Interactive Marketing at Northern Illinois University, where she has run the Interactive Marketing Area of Study since 2003. She holds her doctorate in marketing from the University of Illinois, her master of management from Northwestern University in Evanston, Illinois, her juris doctor from Loyola University in Chicago, and her undergraduate degree from Washington University in St. Louis. Dr. Zahay researches how firms can facilitate customer relationships, particularly using customer information. Some current and recent research topics include customer information management for competitive advantage, information use in new product development and particularly crowd-sourcing, data warehousing in CRM environments, email personalization, and other aspects of interactive marketing. Some of the journals in which she has published include *Journal of Product Innovation Management, Decision Sciences, Industrial Marketing Management, Journal of Advertising Research, Journal of Business and Industrial Marketing, Journal of Interactive Marketing, Interactive Marketing, Journal of Database Marketing*, and in the working paper series for the Marketing Science Institute. She has presented her work at many academic and practitioner conferences. Prior teaching experiences include North Carolina State University in Raleigh, North Carolina and DePaul University in Chicago, Illinois. Dr. Zahay has been the president of her own database and relationship management consulting firm since 1993 and has extensive experience in helping companies identify and develop customer relationships using various marketing technologies. Her prior business experience includes senior marketing management responsibilities at MCI Telecommunications and Dun & Bradstreet. She has also served as a vice president on the Executive Board of the Chicago American Marketing Association and currently serves on the Board of the Chicago Association of Direct Marketing and the editorial board of the Journal of Database Marketing.

PART 1

Foundations of Internet Marketing

CHAPTER 1

Internet Marketing as Part of the Marketing Communications Mix

Key Terms

acquisition (10)
ARPANET (4)
business model (11)
cloud computing (15)
conversion (10)
GPS (Global Positioning
 System) (9)

hosting (14)
HTML (HyperText Markup
 Language) (5)
infrastructure stack (13)
retention (10)
scalability (7)
server (14)

SaaS (Software as a
 Service) (14)
telecommunications (13)
Web 2.0 (6)
Web 3.0 (8)
Web Services (14)

LEARNING OBJECTIVES

By the time you complete this chapter, you will be able to:

- Briefly describe how the Internet originated and what makes it unique as a communications and transactions medium.

- Describe the implications of Web 2.0 and Web 3.0.

- Discuss the business benefits of using Web 2.0.

- Understand the generic marketing objectives that form the basis for Internet marketing strategies.

- Discuss the Internet marketing channels that can be used for Internet communications and commerce.

- Describe the basic technical infrastructure of the Internet including computing in the cloud.

- Identify some of the sites where up-to-date Internet statistics can be found.

- Explain the advantages of using the Internet for consumers and for businesses of all kinds.

- Identify the strategic and economic drivers of the Internet.

- Suggest some potential best practices in acquiring, communicating with, and retaining customers on the Internet.

Mobile apps, social media, advertising networks, video streaming, broadband, Flash, optimization! These are only a few of the Internet-related terms that have entered the marketing vocabulary in recent years. They suggest, although only scratching the surface, how complex the marketing job has become in the Internet age.

Marketers are caught up in revolutionary change that began with the commercialization of the Internet in 1991 and continues today with the buzz that focuses on social media. In just two decades, the Internet has fundamentally altered the operations of businesses around the globe. The business changes include, but are not limited to, the way marketers do their jobs. It is important that we understand the deep-seated changes in business processes and strategy before we attempt to specify marketing's roles and responsibilities in dealing with the new milieu. In order to do that, it will be helpful to understand how the technology got us to where we are today.

The Evolution of the Internet[1]

The origins of the Internet date back to 1957, when Russia launched the *Sputnik* satellite and thereby the space race. In the Cold War era, the fact that Russia led in this race was cause for great concern. In order to close the gap, President Eisenhower created ARPA, soon DARPA (Defense Advanced Research Projects Agency), to fund scientific research under the direction of the Department of Defense. The planners at ARPA believed they could use the research mandate to develop an attack-proof communications structure for national defense purposes.

Precursors of the Internet

Two computer science breakthroughs were necessary to support the system the government envisioned. First came time-sharing, the ability to run programs of multiple users at the same time on the same computer, thereby using the scarce computing resources to its fullest capacity. The user would not be aware that there were multiple programs executing at the same time because the computer moved back and forth between jobs without user intervention. The second breakthrough was the linking of computers at participating institutions into a network called the **ARPANET**.

Much of the inspiration for the ARPANET came from J. C. R. Licklider who envisioned an "Intergalactic Network" of interconnecting communities of scientists who could share computer resources, exchange ideas, and cooperate on scientific projects (see Figure 1.1). The ARPANET enabled human communication in a time- and distance-independent manner that was completely new and that remains the core legacy of this military system. By the early 1970s, there were over 20 participating institutions, universities, and government agencies linked by telephone lines and satellites in the continental United States, Alaska, and Hawaii. In 1973, it became international with connections to University College in London, England, and the Royal Radar Establishment in Norway.

The original ARPANET was the province of a few scientists who needed to interact with one other and were willing to learn the arcane job control language that was required to operate the system. The system had the capacity to handle a large volume of traffic, but it had few users in its early days. To the dismay of some of the originators of the network, it quickly became the first digital post office. The volume of email was far greater than the volume of long-distance computing, and the scientists were enthusiastic about their ability to engage in research collaboration and even gossip over great distances. The ARPANET, now under the auspices of the National Science Foundation (NSF), would remain the domain of a select few users until the widespread adoption of the personal computer in the mid-1980s.

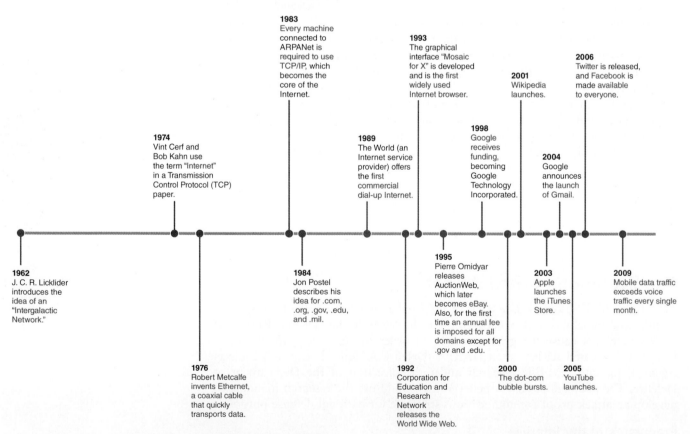

FIGURE **1.1** A Brief Graphic History of the Internet

Source: "History of the Internet," Social Media Graphics, http://socialmediagraphics.posterous.com/the-history-of-the-internet.

The Internet Goes Mainstream

Between 1982 and 1987, the foundations of the modern Internet were laid and growth accelerated. In 1984, there were 1,000 Internet host computers; by 1987, the number had grown to 10,000 and to 300,000 by 1990 (in 2010, it was estimated to be 575 million[2]). The rapid growth of the Internet contributed to the decommissioning of the ARPANET in 1990, although the NSF continued to operate the telecommunications backbone for the network. NSF banned commercial traffic on the Internet until 1991.

Even without ecommerce in the years prior to 1991, the rapid growth of the Internet was making it difficult for users to find information. In 1991, there were two important developments. The first was the release of "gopher," a text-only Internet search tool distributed free over the Net. That same year, the first computer code for the World Wide Web was posted on a relatively unknown newsgroup by Tim Berners-Lee of the European Particle Physics Laboratory (CERN) in Switzerland. Berners-Lee's system included a simple hypertext language called **HTML (HyperText Markup Language)**. HTML is easy to learn in comparison to programming languages and can be created on any word processor. In time, HTML was expanded to allow not only words but also pictures and sound to be posted as files onto the Internet.

When Mosaic (the forerunner of Netscape) was introduced as the first graphical browser in 1993, the ordinary computer user could move around the web in point-and-click mode instead of having to learn cumbersome search terms. Then in 1995, Yahoo! was commercialized as an Internet directory, and for the first time, the user could locate information on the web with relative ease. The rate of growth of the Internet, by any metric, took off and has not looked back.

The growth of the Internet during the late 1990s was phenomenal by almost all measures—the number of households and businesses connected, number of websites, and growth in ecommerce were only a few. As Figure 1.1 suggests, many of the names, from Mosaic to Google, were new. Some were well-known brands, like Pizza Hut, that were taking advantage of the new channel to extend their brand's reach.

The Bubble Bursts

Not growing as quickly—in fact, often nonexistent—were profits from the many enterprises that blossomed as part of the Internet economy. Investors around the world bought the hype surrounding the Internet and ebusiness models that appeared to have no hope of a profitable future. Let us look at three quick examples:

1. Flooz was a digital currency that existed between 1999 and 2001. Users could buy "flooz" and give it like a gift certificate. It could only be used at a limited number of participating retailers. Celebrity Whoopi Goldberg was a visible corporate spokesperson, but flooz suffered from the softening economy. Another blow was struck by a spectacular hack when a ring of thieves operating out of Russia and the Philippines charged $300,000 in flooz to stolen credit cards. The company exhausted over $50 million in venture capital before it declared bankruptcy in August 2001.[3]
2. Pets.com was established to sell pet food over the Internet. It is best remembered for its spokesperson—a sock puppet. The sock puppet stole the hearts of the American public, being interviewed on TV shows, having a balloon made in its image in the Macy's Thanksgiving Day parade, and being featured in an expensive SuperBowl ad in 2000. In spite of its visibility, the company lost $147 million in the first nine months of 2000[4] and is reputed to have spent $4 in advertising for every $1 in sales before it declared bankruptcy in late 2000.[5]

3. Boo.com has been described as Europe's largest dot-com failure. It was established to sell designer sports brands to 18- to 24-year-olds in Europe and the United States. The site featured a 3D shopping experience and a "Miss Boo" spokesperson who conducted visitors around the site. Advertising hype did produce visitors; one source estimated that there were 50,000 visitors to the site on the first day but that only one-fourth of 1 percent placed orders. The source goes on to quote a disgruntled visitor, "Eighty-one minutes to pay too much money for a pair of shoes that I still going to have to wait a week to get?"[6] Dave Chaffey says that over $2 million was spent on an elaborate online catalog for spring 2000. The catalog required download of a special reader and was slow to load in an era when most users had dial-up connections. The business failed in May 2000 after less than a year in business[7] amid reports of unrestrained spending that included elegant offices in several European cities and lavish parties fueled by champagne and caviar. The company had burned through over £100 million in its brief existence.[8]

These three dot-com failures have one thing in common: they were introduced at a time when the market size for total ecommerce was too small to support their business models. Today there are any number of successful online enterprises that include payment systems, pet supplies, and fashion apparel. While their basic business concepts may have had potential, their business models were, at best, inappropriate to the early days of the commercial Internet when only a small portion of the population was online and even fewer were comfortable purchasing goods and services there. According to *USA Today*, there were four misconceptions that led to the bursting of the dot-com bubble:

1. It is okay to sell products for less than what they cost you, because that will bring you lots of customers.
2. Internet-based companies are immune to economic cycles.
3. Internet companies cannot spend too much on advertising.
4. Internet companies that carry no inventory are infinitely profitable.[9]

Looking back, those assumptions seem laughable. However, in the wake of a new channel for communications and commerce that seemed to offer limitless possibilities, many businesspeople and investors lost all objectivity. As the preceding examples show, venture capitalists and investors also lost a lot of money when the dot-com bubble burst, which cast a pall over the entire industry for several years.

The inevitable upheaval took place beginning in mid-2000 and gained velocity through 2001, Venture capital became unavailable and many unprofitable pure-play Internet firms could not survive without it. Stock market values of even leading Internet firms dropped manyfold. As a result, major suppliers of Internet products and services, telecommunications carriers, and the burgeoning wireless market were all seriously damaged in the eyes of investors. High prices paid for licenses for wireless spectrum by European firms worsened their financial position. The public euphoria disappeared and media pundits speculated that the Internet was a short-term phenomenon that had run its course.

Events since 2002 have proven critics wrong, but a clear business vision and a business model with a clear path to profitability are now required. Internet-related businesses have remained a hotbed of innovation, even through the recession that began in 2008. This innovation is often lumped under the all-encompassing description of **Web 2.0**. This "second generation" of the Internet features companies that are creations of the web, like Facebook, and much older companies that have learned to take advantage of the Internet, like Sabre.

Take a minute to read through the time line for Sabre Holdings (see Table 1.1), and you will probably find one or more brands that are familiar to you. Even more important, you will see a company that far predates the Internet with a parent company (American Airlines) that has an even longer history. This is a company whose internal information system, SABRE, became an information

TABLE 1.1   Sabre Time Line

1957: IBM and American Airlines team up to form SABRE, the Semi-Automatic Business Research Environment. It is based on SAGE, the Semi-Automatic Ground Environment—the first major system to use interactive, real-time computing—which IBM helped develop for the military.

1960: The first SABRE reservation system is installed in Briarcliff Manor, New York, on two IBM 7090 computers. It processed 84,000 telephone calls per day.

1964: The SABRE system, and its nationwide network, is completed at a cost of $40 million and becomes the largest commercial real-time data-processing system in the world. It saves American Airlines 30 percent on labor costs.

1972: The SABRE system is upgraded to IBM S/360 and moved to a new consolidated computer center in Tulsa, Oklahoma. It is used for all of American Airlines' data processing facilities.

1976: The SABRE system is installed in a travel agency for the first time, triggering a wave of travel automation. By the end of the year, 130 locations have the system.

1984: Sabre introduces BargainFinder, the industry's first automated low-fare search capability. Competitors sue American Airlines, saying its SABRE system unfairly gives its flights priority on the displays seen by travel agents. American Airlines agrees to discontinue any preferential treatment of its flights.

1985: Sabre introduces easySabre, allowing consumers with PCs to tap into the SABRE system to make airline, hotel, and car rental reservations.

1989: On May 12, the ultra-reliable SABRE system goes down for 12 hours. The cause: a latent bug in disk-drive software that destroyed file addresses.

1996: Sabre launches Travelocity.com.

2000: AMR Corp., the parent of American Airlines, spins off the Sabre Group as an independent company.

2001: Sabre purchases a travel distribution business in the South Pacific. It introduces *Sabre*® *Aerodynamic Traveler*™, which improves passenger service by functions like curbside check-in, roving agents, and self-service kiosks.

2003: Travelocity introduces Travelocity Business™ to serve corporate travel agencies and business travelers and offers Total Trip travel packaging services.

2007: Sabre Holdings is taken private as the result of an acquisition by private equity firms, Silver Lake and TPG.

2010: Sabre Holdings consists of four companies:

- Travelocity, an online travel company serving consumers and businesses.
- Sabre Travel Network, which provides services to the retail travel industry.
- Sabre Airline Solutions, which provides products and services for the air transportation industry.
- Sabre Hospitality Solutions, which provides services for the hospitality industry.

These companies own more than ten brands that included holidayautos.com, Moneydirect, and World Choice Travel with acquisition of new brands continuing.

Source: From Gary Anthes, "Sidebar: Sabre Timeline," Computerworld, Inc. (May 31, 2004). © 2004 Computerworld, Inc. Used with permission. All rights reserved.

product sold and licensed to other companies even before the Internet. Sabre learned to take advantage of the Internet for its own business and began to establish and invest in Internet-based businesses like Travelocity. It is not one of the glitziest pieces of Internet history, but it has survived and prospered in the face of both economic cycles and technological change.

Web 2.0 and Web 3.0

"Web 2.0" is a term that has been widely used since Tim O'Reilly wrote a seminal article on his blog in 2005.[10] According to his seven principles, the characteristics of Web 2.0 products and businesses are the following:[11]

- *Services, not packaged software, with cost-effective **scalability***. Cloud computing, discussed later in this chapter, is the current manifestation of this principle.

- *Control over unique, hard-to-recreate data sources that get richer as more people use them.* User activities on the web create databases of information that are the basic resource of Internet marketing strategies. We return to this topic in Chapter 4.
- *Trusting users as co-developers.* This is the open-source business model, for example, the Firefox browser. It is also the co-creation of content in social media discussed in Chapter 9.
- *Harnessing collective intelligence.* Through applications like blogs and wikis, users are actively encouraged to contribute to the development of knowledge.
- *Leveraging the long tail through customer self-service.* The "long tail" is a search marketing term that implies niche markets. These small, underserved markets can become exceedingly profitable, especially when customers help keep costs down by serving themselves.
- *Software above the level of a single device.* A recent example is the many mobile applications that provide the same basic functions as their desktop counterparts. Apps are discussed in Chapters 11 and 16.
- *Lightweight user interfaces, development models, and business models.* Translating the technical terminology into layman's language, that means applications that are easy to use, flexible, and portable between different computing environments. Applying that same criterion to business models, the subject of Chapter 3, is a pointed reference to the need for flexible business models.

What is loosely called "Web 2.0" is the model that most often describes the current Internet. In a recent survey by the McKinsey Global Institute, the term "social technologies" was used. Responses from over 1,700 executives from around the world identified significant benefits, many of which can be directly traced to cost savings and indirectly or even directly to revenue increases.[12] Another study by Jive Software asked the users of their social business software a more detailed set of questions.[13] Figure 1.2 shows numerous productivity and revenue elements that can increase as a result of using a social business software. The ones that decrease can also be characterized as improving productivity and decreasing costs. These data provide strong business justification for the importance of technology to today's enterprise, whether it is called social technology, social business, or simply IT.

Web pundits, of course, cannot resist speculating about what comes next—**Web 3.0** presumably! The two words that seem to be most often used to characterize Web 3.0 are "semantic" and "personal." *Semantic* suggests an Internet that understands user intent and makes it easier to find information. Google's Instant Preview tool,[14] which gives a visual preview of search results, can be considered a step in that direction. The information can be organized into *personal* arrays, for example bookmarking services such as Delicious and the Firefox Bookmarks add-on. CNN suggests that Web 3.0 will have the following characteristics:[15]

- *Real-time.* Search results are often displayed in near-real time. So are Tweets. The "Trending" display on many sites today is a way of displaying what is going on at that moment.
- *Semantic.* As described earlier, semantic is the property of understanding user intent to make web activities, especially search, easier.
- *Open communication.* This complex element refers to linked data sets that allow communication across boundaries. One author described this as a "massive freely accessible knowledge base."[16] This open concept is hard to wrap one's head around, but the implication is to be able to find information without reference to where it originally resided. For example, if you are currently researching a term paper on the influence of 17th century

What Increases	What Decreases
Communication with customers	Time to find information and experts
Employee connectedness	Number of customer support calls
Project collaboration and productivity	Number of emails sent
Ideas generated inside the firm	Time needed for meetings
New business win rate	Need for travel

FIGURE **1.2** Selected Business Improvements Attributed to Social Business Software

Source: © Cengage Learning 2013

culture on the architecture of the period, you are probably going to have to put a lot of effort into matching the information you find on culture of the period to the information on architecture of the period. Maybe Web 3.0 will do that for you!

* *Mobile and Geography.* Almost everyone who reads this will have at least one device with **GPS (Global Positioning System)** capability nearby. Those devices, depending on how you configure the settings, can make location part of any communication you send. That service leads to location-based marketing, which is discussed in Chapter 16. The privacy implications are covered in Chapter 15.

The Landscape at the End of the Decade

Survivors of the shakeout included both Internet-based businesses, like Amazon and eBay, and enterprises that were in existence long before the Internet but that quickly learned to take advantage of it. IBM and GE are both good examples of the latter, along with Sabre. Almost a decade later, a list of the most valuable global brands (see Table 1.2) emphasizes that point. This is only one of several "top brands" lists, but they all contain many of the same brands, even though different criteria often put them in a different order.

This top 20 list in Table 1.2 from British consultancy Millward Brown[17] gives an interesting perspective. Millward Brown points out that technology firms—services, software, and hardware including mobile phones—dominate the list. Google and Amazon are the only ones that are purely creatures of the Internet. The remainder—whether manufacturers like Coke, service suppliers like UPS, or retailers like Walmart and Tesco—are heavy users of the Internet in ways that are appropriate to their various brands. We will use many of these companies throughout the text as examples of businesses that have used the Internet in a variety of ways to increase their reach and productivity.

INTERACTIVE EXERCISE **1.1**   Points of Control

O'Reilly and his colleagues have attempted to visualize the complexity of Web 2.0 in a global map of the competitive landscape called Points of Control. As the Points of Contact map illustrates, the large players on the Internet frequently try to occupy the same space.

Read about the concept behind the map at http://bit.ly/u0Vlha.

Visit the interactive version at http://map.web2summit.com.

TABLE 1.2	Top 20 Most Valuable Global Brands 2010, by Estimated Dollar Value		
#	Brand	Brand Value 2010 ($M)	% Brand Value Change 2010 vs. 2009
1	Google	114,260	14
2	IBM	86,383	30
3	Apple	83,153	32
4	Microsoft	76,344	0
5	Coca-Cola	67,983	1
6	McDonalds	66,005	−1
7	Marlboro	57,047	15
8	China Mobile	52,616	−14
9	GE	45,054	−25
10	Vodafone	44,404	−17
11	ICBC(Asia)	43,927	15
12	HP	39,717	48
13	Walmart	39,421	−4
14	BlackBerry	30,708	12
15	Amazon	27,459	29
16	UPS	26,492	−5
17	Tesco	25,741	12
18	Visa	24,883	52
19	Oracle	24,817	16
20	Verizon	24,675	39

Source: "The Top 100 Most Valuable Global Brands 2010," April 28, 2010, Social Brand Value.

The Internet Marketing Paradigm

The milieu in which Internet marketing takes place is seen as a complex environment (see Figure 1.3) in which marketers attempt to achieve four distinct generic goals:

- *Customer **acquisition*** is a foundation goal of all marketers. In order to grow and thrive, all businesses must attract a continuing stream of new customers. Internet marketing adds other communications channels and a variety of techniques to the customer acquisition effort.
- *Customer **conversion*** is the process of persuading visitors, shoppers, or prospects to become actual customers. It requires persuading the customer who has simply made contact, say by visiting a website, to make a purchase or to persuade him to engage in a set of interactions, often beginning with subscribing to a newsletter, that will eventually result in a purchase.
- *Customer **retention*** involves turning the newly found customer into a loyal one who will remain with the enterprise over an extended period of time. Marketers have learned that it is cheaper to retain customers than to acquire them, and must therefore focus some of their activities specifically on retention.

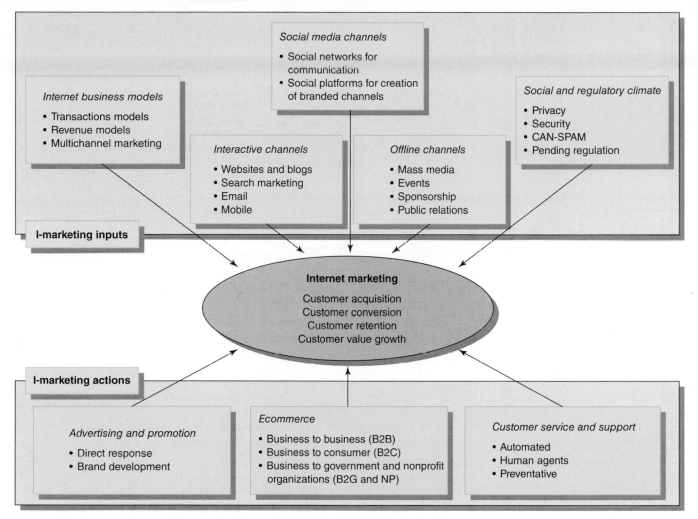

FIGURE **1.3** The Internet Marketing Paradigm

Source: © Cengage Learning 2013

- *Growth in customer value*, by which we mean the equity that exists in the enterprise's customer base, is the end goal of the acquisition, conversion, and retention process. Marketers have discovered that not all customers are equally profitable. Internet marketers can track customer behavior, calculate the profitability of individual customers, and improve the value of the overall customer base.

The actions that permit marketers to achieve these generic goals take place in an increasingly complex environment. It is made up of an external environment that affects marketing activities of all kinds and of the actions that marketers themselves take. These can be characterized as the inputs and actions of Internet marketing.

The inputs include the following:

- *Business models* that are prominent on the Internet:
  - *Transactions* models are the way in which Internet businesses organize to carry out exchange whether it be content or commercial transactions. Examples of businesses and nonprofit organizations engaged in successful ecommerce are used throughout the text.
  - *Revenue* models are the various streams of revenue that businesses can employ to support their activities. The importance of online in the development of supplier/manufacturer/customer value chains are discussed

in Chapter 2. Both transactions and revenue models are discussed in Chapter 3.

- *Multichannel* marketing is the driving force behind many business models. As it affects customer acquisition, it is discussed, with many examples, throughout Chapters 5 through 9. Multichannel marketing requires the integration of both offline (physical world) and online (interactive) channels and is also important in customer conversion (Chapter 10) and retention (Chapter 11).

- *Interactive channels* that permit Internet communication and commerce:
  - *Websites and blogs* on the Internet have become channels of communication for many businesses, especially in B2B (business-to-business) markets, where they are an essential means of customer communication for many firms. They are, of course, part of the social media landscape and are discussed in Chapter 9. The creation of websites that produce satisfying customer experiences is discussed in Chapter 12.
  - *Search marketing*, which includes search engine optimization (SEO) and pay-per-click (PPC) advertising, is the single most important way that marketers drive visitors to their websites. It is discussed in Chapter 8.
  - *Email marketing* is a key tool of the Internet marketer (Chapter 7). It can be used in customer acquisition programs, but is especially important in customer retention campaigns (Chapter 11).
  - *Mobile marketing* over the Internet is a well-developed channel in Europe and Asia and rapidly growing in the United States. It is discussed in Chapter 16.
  - There are a number of *other interactive channels and activities* like kiosks and events that are discussed in connection with customer acquisition in Chapter 6.

- *Social media channels* that include both the networks on which people communicate and platforms that permit the construction of communities that house both content and communications. The three largest networks, Facebook, Twitter, and LinkedIn, are used by people for personal communications and by businesses for communication and brand development. Social platforms like the Ning community platform or the WordPress platform for blogging allow marketers (or individuals) to establish communities around a particular brand or a subject of mutual interest. Not only have these channels become important for personal expression, they are also being integrated into the marketing communications of many marketers, large and small. Social media channels are discussed in Chapter 9.

- *Offline channels*—including the mass media of print and broadcast, marketer-created events, sponsorships, and public relations—represent an important part of the integrated communications process. As they impact online channels and multichannel marketing, they are discussed throughout the book.

- *Social and regulatory issues* have become increasingly important as the Internet has achieved a place among the major communications channels. Issues including consumer data privacy, security of customer data, and intellectual property rights have a great deal of impact on marketer actions. They are discussed in Chapter 15. Other social and regulatory issues, such as email spam and the efforts to combat it, will be discussed in the context of the channel or technique.

The actions that marketers can take to take advantage of the Internet as a powerful channel for communications and transactions include the following:

- *Online advertising and promotion* that can be used to incite the viewer to immediate action or to build the image of the brand. The Internet has become established as an effective channel for brand development efforts (see Chapter 5). It is inherently a direct response channel and is effective in activities ranging from coupon distribution to ecommerce.

- *Ecommerce*, which refers to commercial transactions on the Internet. Consumer, business, nonprofit, and governmental marketers are all using the Internet for transactions ranging from purchase of goods and services to renewal of drivers' licenses to contributions to charitable causes. Ecommerce issues will be discussed in various contexts throughout the text.
- *Customer service and support*, which is taking its place as a key marketer activity largely as a result of the emphasis on customer retention. The quality of customer service can be improved at the same time the cost to deliver it can be decreased by judicious use of the Internet. Customer service and support is the subject of Chapter 13.

The focus of this text is on developing and executing strategies using carefully selected channels and activities both on and off the Internet. In order to understand the environment in which this marketing effort takes place, it is important to understand the basics of the technical infrastructure that supports them. This is often referred to as the "Internet **infrastructure stack**" because it is, in fact, a set of interrelated technologies that build and depend on one another to create the network we know as the Internet.

The Internet Infrastructure Stack

The technical infrastructure of the Internet is portrayed in Figure 1.4. Forming the backbone of the stack is the **telecommunications** connection, either narrowband or broadband. What is commonly referred to as the "Internet backbone" is actually a series of networks run by various carriers.[18] It is a redundant system that rarely experiences problems that are visible to the average user and therefore remains essentially invisible. The average computer user gains access to the

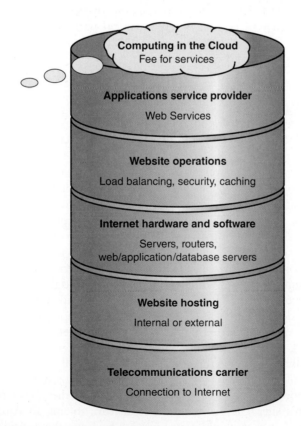

FIGURE **1.4** The Internet Infrastructure Stack

Source: © Cengage Learning 2013

Internet via an Internet Services Provider (ISP), who in turn accesses the services of the backbone itself. The user of mobile devices must subscribe directly to a mobile telecommunications service, so those carriers and the services they provide are highly visible. Wireless telecommunications are especially competitive as a result of deregulation efforts around the world.

A website must be housed on a server, an operation commonly called **hosting**. The **server** that hosts the site must be connected to the network and is dedicated wholly or in part to performing the functions needed to operate the site. That process begins, but by no means ends, with serving the files that are requested as visitors access the website. Many organizations, primarily those with either high levels of technical expertise or small websites, perform this function internally using dedicated servers. It is possible to host a website on a personal computer, but there are many problems associated with that approach. Many organizations choose to outsource this highly technical function to external services firms that provide the hosting function. Specialized software is needed for blogging, so blogs are most often created on hosted services.

One reason for the increasingly common decision to outsource website hosting is the large investment required in specialized *Internet hardware and software*. The hardware includes computers needed to serve web pages to visitors (servers) as well as increasingly large amounts of either computer or network-based storage required to hold the content and databases that drive website activities. It also includes a great deal of specialized telecommunications hardware—items like fiber-optic cables, routers, and bridgers, for example.[19] Both the computer and telecommunications hardware are driven by specialized software necessary to connect to the Internet and to run the specific applications programs that drive the functionality of the site.

The next level on the stack is the *operation* of the site—the day-to-day work of keeping the system running and of fine-tuning it to provide a high level of uptime and fast and dependable downloading of pages to users. Maintenance and operation of a website is a purely technical part of the web infrastructure, and marketers do not need specialized knowledge of the daily operational issues. They do, however, need to exhibit consistent concern about the efficient operation of the site since it is a necessary element of providing a good visitor experience.

The next part of the stack is the *applications services provider, Web Services solutions, or other outsourcing options*. When software is made available on a fee-for-usage basis, it is often referred to as **Software as a Service (SaaS)**. Applications services providers (ASPs) provide network access to the software applications that are needed for website functionality. These applications include data warehousing and personalization, both of which are discussed in Chapter 4 as important parts of Internet marketing programs. Organizations can choose to purchase or license applications like these and run them internally, but they are expensive and require a great deal of technical skill to integrate with other software and to run effectively. ASPs, who essentially "rent software," are discussed as a business model in Chapter 3. If you use a tax preparation service that is available over the Internet instead of buying the software and annual updates yourselves, you understand this concept.

Web Services solutions involve making codes available to developers (programmers who develop applications) so they can develop functions on the website that makes use of sophisticated (and expensive) proprietary software. For example, a marketing consulting company might employ several consultants who have written best-selling books. If the company wants to sell those books on its own site, it might use the codes made available by Amazon to allow visitors to purchase the books, using Amazon technology, while the visitor remains on the consulting firm's site. They could choose, instead, to link to Amazon's site for book purchase, but that would cause visitors to leave the consulting site. Since visitors who leave often do not return, keeping them on the site is preferable.

Amazon Web Services (AWS), a service platform provided by Amazon, is used by sellers of many products in addition to books. Some are small firms who choose not to maintain their own sites and some use it as an additional sales channel. The AWS site maintains a Business Managers page that covers a number of subjects that concern them, like cost savings and security. There is also a Developers page, which gives them the information and codes they need to integrate the services into the website.

Over the past few years, a new level of services has evolved. What was known as "Web Services" five years ago has taken on the additional dimension of **cloud computing**. Activities like computing and data storage now take place "in the cloud."[20] Amazon was an early mover in Web Services and, more recently, in the evolution of cloud computing. Another firm well-known for its emphasis on cloud computing is salesforce.com, an acknowledged leader in the SaaS space, providing CRM services to both B2B and B2C marketers. The screen shot of its home page in Figure 1.5 shows the emphasis it places on providing services "in the cloud." The company's argument is basically that the cloud-based services increase its clients' productivity and, at the same time, reduce costs.

Salesforce.com offers a host of services in the cloud which they call the "Social Enterprise." Salesforce.com services include:

1. *Connect and Sell:* A sales cloud that gives salespeople access to essential information about their accounts, contacts, leads, and sales opportunities (discussed in Chapter 10). It also integrates with their email. Salesforce.com also gives sales and marketing professionals the ability to find new prospects and connect with customers with data.com. Data.com gives sales and marketers access to customer data stored in the cloud (discussed in Chapter 4).
2. *Service and engagement:* Deliver next-generation customer service with the Service Cloud.
3. *Collaboration:* Through Chatter (a private social network) teams use social media to communicate internally and collaborate on projects to get things done.
4. *Automate and extend:* Build custom employee apps for the business on Force.com, or use the AppExchange to find the app you need.
5. *Social marketing:* Build mobile and social marketing apps—like Facebook pages—with Heroku.

FIGURE **1.5** salesforce.com Home Page

Source: Salesforce, http://www.salesforce.com.

6. *Listen and analyze:* Listen, connect, and engage with Radian6.
7. *Products and partners:* Connect customers, products, and enterprise data with help from Database.com.

These applications are mobilized to be used by the salesperson anywhere and anytime (discussed in Chapter 16.)

The Wall Street Journal online quotes a study by Forrester that estimates cloud computing sales at $41 billion in 2011, increasing to $241 billion in 2020.[21] Experts generally agree that the essence of this rapid growth is improved IT performance at lower cost. Cloud computing applications can also improve the customer experience by providing smoothly-functioning data-driven services of many kinds.

So all these are B2B issues and not relevant to you as a consumer, right? How many of the consumer categories do you fit into?

- 56 percent of Internet patrons who use webmail such as Gmail or Hotmail
- 34 percent of Internet users who store photos online
- 29 percent who use Internet applications such as Google Docs or Photoshop Express
- 7 percent who store personal videos online
- 5 percent who pay to store files online
- 5 percent who back up their hard drive on another site[22]

Cloud computing services have become ubiquitous without most of us even realizing we are using them! That is likely to change, however. In November 2010, Microsoft announced its plan to spend millions of dollars on a campaign called "Cloud Power" to convince business users of the benefits of cloud computing.[23] Consumers would not be able to avoid the message; one of the first ads was aired on *Monday Night Football*.[24] Besides the Internet and television, ads will appear in print, outdoor, and other out-of-home venues like the Sea-Tac airport, one of the first places the ads were seen.[25] This is another example of the importance of consistent messaging across multiple communications channels—the essence of integrated marketing communications. Yes, there is some waste reach in reaching consumers with what is essentially a B2B message. But keep two things in mind:

1. Business people watch *Monday Night Football* in large numbers.
2. Internet users are taking advantage of cloud-based services whether they know it or not, so think of reaching them as good public relations.

There are two important issues swirling around in the cloud. One issue is the economics of cloud computing and of private versus public clouds. It seems reasonable to assume that shared resources in public clouds will be less expensive for the user who avoids many fixed costs.[26] That is the argument of salesforce.com whose clouds are public in the sense they are available to many clients. Private clouds are built for the benefit of a single user. For instance, IBM has a special product that is used to build private clouds for government agencies. These clouds are built for individual agencies; the nature of the cloud products is said to make it easier to pass data between government agencies when the need arises.[27] It is easy to assume that some businesses will find it desirable to protect their data in this manner.

INTERACTIVE EXERCISE **1.2**   In the Cloud

To see background on Microsoft's cloud campaign, links to the ads, and a link to its main cloud page, visit http://bit.ly/sp1gn7.

Apple has its own cloud. Visit http://www.apple.com/icloud.

Best Buy has a music cloud. Visit http://www.bestbuymusiccloud.com.

The second issue is the "greenness" of cloud computing. The basic argument is that a few large server farms can be run more efficiently than many small ones. In particular, they will use less energy and their carbon emissions will be lower. There seems to be evidence in support of this argument,[28] but not all industry experts agree.

The Microsoft Cloud Power example suggests both the potential and the problems of reaching specific target markets over the Internet. For each campaign, marketers must identify their target audience(s) and the media to use in order to reach them efficiently. Broad statistics about Internet use are of value as background, but they are not sufficient for planning and executing campaigns.

For that reason, it is important to get a brief snapshot of Internet usage at a particular point in time. It will help to ground you in the realities of the Internet and to give some guidance on sources of statistical data. In Chapter 4 and succeeding chapters, a strong argument is presented that brands will find the best data on their own websites and in other channels they use. This argument includes the subjects of database development and use (see Chapter 4), the metrics for various tools and channels (see Chapters 5 through 9), and the Internet metrics (see Chapter 14).

Constant change, most of it evolutionary with the occasional revolutionary development, is the norm on the Internet. It is hard to paint a picture of the Internet itself and of its users. The data are often old by the time the ink hits paper.

With that in mind, we will present a snapshot of the Internet at the time of this writing. The reader should place emphasis on where and how to find business data on the Internet, as well as on the numbers themselves. The numbers represent only a static picture of a moving target.

A Profile of the Internet and Its Users

This section focuses on data sources that are free to all Internet users. As you use these sources and others like them, there are several things to keep in mind:

- Some of the data are free for a limited time only and then become accessible only to paid subscribers. Sites that specialize in data are careful to describe their usage policies.
- Summary data are often provided free of charge in order to promote the sale of full reports.
- Much of the data on the web is copyrighted and all the rules of attribution and citation apply. Your college or local library is a good source of guidelines for correct use.
- Some data are published under a Creative Commons license that specifies rules for its use. Creative Commons is discussed in the section on intellectual property in Chapter 15.

The essential point is that the Internet has not invalidated the basic rules for using resources, which can now be either printed or electronic, in your research and writing. The rules you learned in your first writing course still apply! There are different cultural standards in different parts of the world when it comes to the ideas of others, and you need to know about and be sensitive to them. However, copyright law is international and violations can have serious consequences.

The Size and Scope of the Internet

There are many technical measures of the size of the Internet. They include number of systems, number of servers, speed of networks, and many others.[29] Marketers are interested in the people who use the Internet; how many, where, how often, for what purposes, and so on. Internet World Stats.com quotes data from the Miniwatts Marketing Group that estimates over 2 billion Internet users worldwide in March 2011. Figure 1.6 shows the distribution of those users by region. Other data not shown indicates that the rate at which the Internet has penetrated

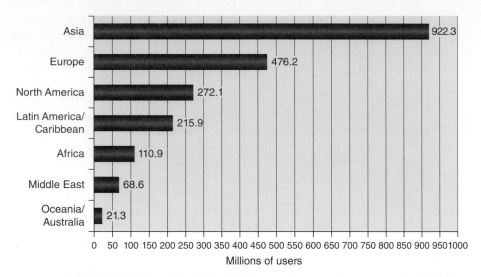

FIGURE **1.6** Size of the Internet by Region

Source: Copyright © 2000–2011, Miniwatts Marketing Group. All rights reserved.

the regions is vastly different. It ranged from a high of 78.3 percent in North America to a low of 11.4 percent. The low Internet penetration rate in developing regions and countries is a source of concern to economic development experts.

Broadband is required to access much of the content on the web, especially the Web 2.0 features. Figure 1.7 shows that the gap in broadband access between the developing countries and the developed ones is actually increasing. Lack of access to broadband makes the Internet less useful to people in the developing countries. The mitigating factor, however, appears to be the growth in cell phone penetration, especially in developing countries. According to the ITU report:

- In developed countries, the mobile market is reaching saturation levels with an average 116 subscriptions per 100 inhabitants at the end of 2010 and a marginal growth of 1.6 percent from 2009 to 2010.
- At the same time, the developing world is increasing its share of mobile subscriptions from 53 percent of total mobile subscriptions at the end of 2005 to 73 percent at the end of 2010.
- In the African region, cell phone penetration rates will reach an estimated 41 percent at the end of 2010 (compared to 76 percent globally) leaving a significant potential for growth.[30]

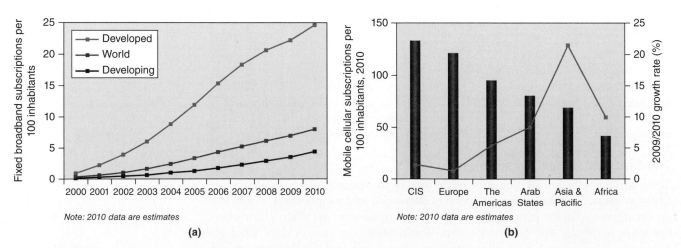

FIGURE **1.7** Global Broadband and Mobile Access

Source: "The World of 2010: ICT Facts and Figures," International Telecommunication Union, pp. 2, 6. Reprinted with permission.

U.K. Wireless Internet Users, by Access Device and Gender, 2010

	% of respondents in each group		
	Male	Female	Total
Mobile phone	37%	25%	31%
Handheld computer	5%	2%	4%
Laptop via wireless connection away from home/work	30%	22%	26%
None of the above	48%	60%	54%

Note: ages 16+ who have accessed the internet in the past three months

FIGURE **1.8** Internet Access in the United Kingdom
Source: eMarketer Inc., November 18, 2010.

These global statistics alone present serious food for thought for marketers. How likely are cell phone sales to show substantial growth when there is already more than one cell phone per person in the developing countries? The answer is "not very likely" in the absence of a major innovation like smart phones. Such innovations occur infrequently and unpredictably, so marketers cannot count on them.

The data about mobile growth in developing countries also send a strong signal. Global enterprises may have to revise some of the promotional campaigns used in developed countries for mobile delivery elsewhere. On the other hand, if their target audience is young people, who now are the primarily mobile users in the United States[31] and around the world, they may be able to use the same basic campaign in many countries, after making adjustments for cultural differences. More important, they cannot continue to focus on a single delivery channel. Recent data from the Office for National Statistics of the United Kingdom shows that almost 70 percent of consumers there had broadband connections, including wireless, in 2010. Many are now accessing the Internet wirelessly on various devices, as shown in Figure 1.8. According to the eMarketer analyst, "internet users of all ages are increasingly adept at multitasking, connecting with brands on multiple platforms and responding directly to campaigns, promotions and other offers online or via mobile."[32] Marketers must communicate with customers wherever they are, on the device they prefer. Customers have many choices and marketers must satisfy their preferences.

Who Uses the Internet, for What: Consumers

Marketers use various types of data to segment their target markets and to study their target segments in depth. Demographic data are necessary but not sufficient. Behavioral data are key to understanding the Internet consumer, from information search all the way through to purchase.

Demographics

When the researcher goes beyond the aggregate statistics presented in the preceding section, it is usually necessary to look for sources that specifically cover that nation or part of the world. The Internet World Stats site[33] has a summary table of Internet use in each region of the world. Clicking on a region brings up a list of countries and clicking on a country displays data about that country. The site also provides sources where you can find additional, and perhaps newer, data.

It is helpful when you find a compilation of data like the demographic profile of American Internet users shown in Table 1.3. It is updated frequently on the Pew Internet and American Life site[34] where you will find a variety of studies on demographic and usage patterns. The demographics of the Internet in the United States show a racially and ethnically diverse Internet population with men and women participating at the same rate. The population groups that are

TABLE 1.3	Demographic Profile of U.S. Internet Users	
		% who use the Internet
Total adults		**77**
Men		78
Women		76
Race/ethnicity		
White, non-Hispanic		80
Black, non-Hispanic		69
Hispanic (English- and Spanish-speaking)		66
Age		
18–29		90
30–49		84
50–64		76
65+		46
Household income		
Less than $30,000/yr		63
$30,000–$49,999		78
$50,000–$74,999		92
$75,000+		96
Education attainment		
Less than high school		40
High school		69
Some college		89
College and beyond		93
Community type		
Urban		78
Suburban		80
Rural		68

Note: The Pew Research Center's Internet & American Life Project, November 23–December 21, 2010 Social Side of the Internet Survey. N = 2,303 adults, 18 and older, including 748 reached via cell phone. Interviews were conducted in English and Spanish.

Source: Figure "Demographics of internet users" from The Pew Research Center's Internet & American Life Project's Spring Tracking Survey conducted April 26–May 22, 2011. Reprinted with permission of Pew Internet & American Life Project.

less likely to be Internet users include older, poorer, less educated, and rural segments.

For marketers, such information is a good beginning, but it only suggests the type of specific data they need about the target market for their own brand. It may, however, suggest to some marketers that large portions of their target audience are not online and will have to be reached by other media channels. Demographic data are only part of the picture, and an increasingly small part in the Internet environment where behavioral data are readily available.

Behaviors

Every mouse click on the Internet represents a potential data point in some database. How marketers collect and use that data is discussed in Chapters 4 and 14. The Pew Internet Project has been tracking the online activities of adult Internet users for almost a decade. During that time, the types of activities engaged in during an average day have changed as a result of the tremendous growth of social media activity. Nevertheless, the two top activities remain the same. Over 90 percent of Internet users use their email and engage in search activity on a daily basis. Engaging in an activity is a different metric from time spent on that activity. Figure 1.9 shows email and search virtually tied in frequency of engaging in the behavior. However, one email activity is likely to take longer than one search activity. Therefore, time spent on email is greater than time spent on search in the United States[35] and in other Internet-using nations as seen in Figure 1.10a.

Because Internet data come from the individual levels of activity, they can be broken down into very specific categories and activities. Figure 1.10 shows some examples. For instance, a large percentage of worldwide Internet users check their email daily, but users actually spend more time each week on social networks than they do on their email. When you look at just mobile Internet use in the United States social networking is by far the fastest growing activity, but mobile users still make greater use of practical applications like weather and maps. Search is also a rapidly-growing mobile application, and it far exceeds other types of information, except email, about new products for all age groups. The youngest two groups of adult Internet users are the only ones who get a significant portion of their information about new products from social networks. These patterns of use produce what TNS Marketing calls "digital lifestyles." They range from people who use the Internet for purely instrumental purposes (functionals) to those who use it in various ways as a means of self-expression (networkers, influencers).

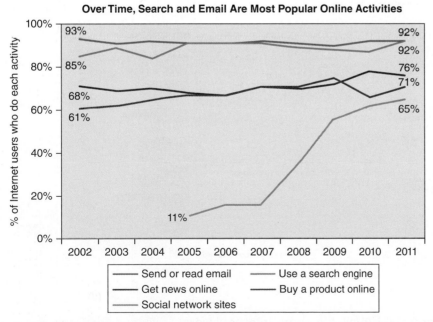

FIGURE **1.9** Top Online Activities 2002–2011

Source: Kristen Purcell, "Over time, search and email are most popular online activities," Findings: Search and email remain the top online activities, Pew Internet & American Life Project, August 9, 2011. Retrieved from http://www.pewinternet.org/Reports/2011/Search-and-email/Report.aspx.

Time Spent on Online Activities, by Type, 2010

	% of internet users worldwide	
	% doing activity daily	**Hours per week spent on activity**
Email	72%	4.4
News	55%	2.7
Social	46%	4.6
Interest	46%	3.9
Knowledge	39%	3.1
Multimedia	37%	3.7
Gaming	27%	2.9
Browsing	24%	2.3
Admin	21%	1.7
Organize	19%	1.6
Shopping	12%	1.8

Note: n = 48,804

(a)

Fastest-Growing U.S. Mobile Application Categories, 2009 & 2010

	thousands of unique users		
	April 2009	**April 2010**	**% change**
Social networking	4,270	14,518	240%
Weather	8,557	18,063	111%
News	4,148	9,292	124%
Sports information	3,598	7,672	113%
Bank accounts	2,340	4,974	113%
Maps	8,708	16,773	93%
Movie information	3,296	6,359	93%
Online retail	1,416	2,701	91%
Search	5,434	10,315	90%
Photo- or video-sharing service	3,131	5,950	90%
Total application users*	**54,414**	**69,639**	**28%**

Note: ages 13+; three-month average for period ending April 2009 and April 2010; *excludes games preloaded on device

(b)

Introducing the Digital Lifestyles

 INFLUENCERS
The internet is an integral part of my life. I'm young and a big mobile Internet user and generally access everywhere, all of the time. I'm a blogger, a passionate social networker with many social network friends. I'm also a big online shopper, even via my mobile. I want to make sure as many people as possible hear my online voice.

 COMMUNICATORS
I just love talking and expressing myself, whether that's face to face, on a fixed line, mobile or on social networking sites, instant messaging or just emailing people. I really want to express myself in the online world in the way that I can't in the offline one. I tend to be a smart phone user and I'm connecting online from my mobile, at home, at work or at college.

 KNOWLEDGE-SEEKERS
I use the internet to gain knowledge, information and to educate myself about the world. I'm not very interested in social networking but I do want to hear from like-minded people especially to help me make purchase decisions. I'm very interested in the latest thing.

 NETWORKERS
The internet is important for me to establish and maintain relationships. I have a busy life whether it's my profession or managing the home. I use things like social networking to keep in touch with people I wouldn't have time to otherwise. I'm a big home internet home user and I'm very open to talking to brands and looking for promotions. That said I'm not really the kind of person to voice my opinions online.

 ASPIRERS
I'm looking to create a personal space online. I'm very new to the Internet and I'm accessing via mobile and internet cafes but mostly from home. I'm not doing a great deal at the moment online but I'm desperate to do more of everything, especially from a mobile device.

 FUNCTIONALS
The internet is a functional tool. I don't want to express myself online. I like emailing, checking the news, sports & weather but also online shopping. I'm really not interested in anything new (like social networking) and I am worried about data privacy and security. I am older and have been using the internet for a long time.

(c)

What are the Most Common Ways You Discover a New Online Product? (Select up to Five)

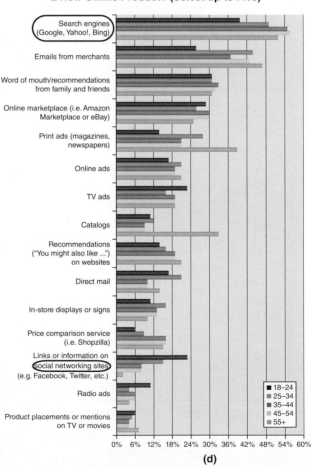

(d)

FIGURE **1.10** Examples of Behavioral Data Available about Internet Users

Sources: eMarketer Inc., November 4, 2010; eMarketer Inc., September 15, 2010; Reprinted with permission of Taylor Nelson Sofras, from http://discoverdigitallife.com/downloads/pdf/The_Digital_Lifestyle.pdf; and "Search Dominates Social Networking for Product Discovery, Study Says," by Matt McGee, Art Technology Group, October 29, 2010, Reprinted with permission of Oracle Corporation.

There are, of course, other types of data that the individual marketer may need in order to understand his target audience. One of those is motivations. The segmentation data in Figure 1.10 describes motives for using the Internet. Motives are something the marketer can only find out by asking people. Notice that all the other data presented in this section are behavioral data from the Internet clickstream. The Internet itself produces the data required to understand *what people do there*. Other types of data, including *why they do it*, are only available from marketing research. *The preponderance of data used by Internet marketers is the behavioral data produced by daily Internet activity.*

Who Uses the Internet, for What: Businesses

Businesses around the world use the Internet to attract new customers, to sell their products and services, to retain existing customers, and to deliver customer support and service. Comprehensive data from a single source are hard to find, but here are some revealing factoids:

- Borrell Associates projected total U.S. advertising expenditure to reach $238.6 billion in 2011.[36] Total U.S. advertising expenditures had peaked at $234.7 billion in 2007 and declined in 2008 and 2009 as a result of the recession. They began slow growth in 2010.[37]
- Growth in global online advertising spending has exceeded that of traditional media for several years. Figure 1.11 shows that this trend continued through the recession in advertising spending of 2008 and 2009 and returned to double-digit growth in 2010.[38]
- 2010 was forecast to be the first year that U.S. marketers spent more on digital media than on print media,[39] which represents a huge change in the marketing communications mix.
- In the United States, all types of online advertising show continued growth (see Figure 1.11a). The growth in video advertising continues to be explosive. Formats showing steady growth include search and email (see Figure 1.11b).
  - Localized online advertising is becoming a bigger part of total online advertising in the United States (see Figure 1.11c).

What do businesses spend this money for? The correct answer is, "To achieve their marketing objectives." The chart in Figure 1.12a gives a perspective on that for business marketers: they spend online dollars first on lead generation, then on customer retention, with generating awareness coming last. Across all marketers—B2B and B2C (business-to-consumer)—a majority planned to increase their 2010 budgets for social media, mobile marketing, email marketing, and paid search advertising (see Figure 1.12b). Notice that traditional print and broadcast media continue to lose out in the struggle for share of the marketer's budget.

This section has presented a brief snapshot of the Internet and its users at various points in time. It is only the tip of the data iceberg that confronts marketers. The point here is that there are many sources of aggregate Internet data, much of them free at least in summary fashion. Marketers need to choose which data sources or series they find relevant and follow them in order to keep up with general Internet trends. The data that affect actual marketing decisions are data about specific industries, products, and target markets. In the coming chapters, we will explore how marketers obtain data that are directly relevant to specific marketing decisions.

Taken overall, these data paint a picture of an Internet that continues to grow and evolve. Let us end the chapter by looking at reasons the Internet has become such a powerful force in our personal and business lives.

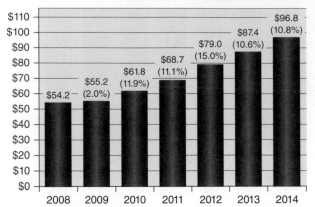

Online Advertising Spending Worldwide, 2008–2014
(in billions and % change)

(a)

Note: includes banner ads, search, rich media, video, classifieds, sponsorships, lead generation, and email; excludes mobile ad spending

U.S. Online Advertising Spending, by Format, 2008–2013
(in millions)

	2008	2009	2010	2011	2012	2013
Search	$10,691	$12,285	$13,880	$15,552	$17,686	$19,530
Display ads	$4,629	$4,933	$5,448	$6,182	$7,175	$7,958
Video	$587	$850	$1,250	$1,850	$3,000	$4,600
Rich media	$1,888	$2,030	$2,252	$2,560	$2,960	$3,360
Classifieds	$3,139	$2,956	$2,936	$2,944	$2,960	$2,982
Lead generation	$1,605	$1,645	$1,682	$1,792	$1,998	$2,268
Sponsorships	$590	$514	$542	$576	$629	$672
Email	$472	$488	$513	$544	$592	$630
Total	**$23,600**	**$25,700**	**$28,500**	**$32,000**	**$37,000**	**$42,000**

(b)

Online Ad Spending Forecast
(in billions)

National $31.8 / Local $13.7 (2010)
$35.7 / $16.1 (2011)

(c)

FIGURE **1.11** Double-Digit Growth on Online Advertising Spending

Sources: eMarketer, Inc., June 2010; eMarketer, Inc., November 2008; and Figure from "Borrell Associates' 2011 Ad Forecast Memo," Copyright © 2001–2012 Borrell Associates, Inc., Reprinted with permission.

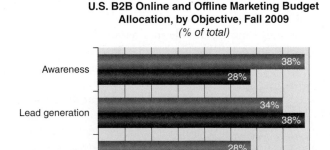

U.S. B2B Online and Offline Marketing Budget Allocation, by Objective, Fall 2009
(% of total)

- Awareness: 38% / 28%
- Lead generation: 34% / 38%
- Customer retention: 28% / 34%

■ Online and offline ■ Online only

(a)

- 70% of responding companies plan to increase their budgets for off-site social media (i.e., Facebook and Twitter).

- Only 17% of respondents are increasing their print media budgets, compared to 41% who are decreasing spending. 15% of companies are increasing their radio budgets, but 36% are spending less.

- More than half of companies plan to increase their budgets for mobile marketing (56%), email marketing (54%), and paid search (51%).

(b)

FIGURE **1.12** Marketing Budget Allocations, B2B and Overall

Sources: eMarketer, Inc., March 4, 2010; and Research Brief: "More Money, More Channels: Marketing Budgets in 2010," Exact Target.

Strategic Drivers of the Internet Economy

Table 1.4 summarizes ten strategic drivers of the Internet economy. Some are different from those of the traditional economy only in degree—the importance of people and demand forecasting to the enterprise, for example. The others tend to be the polar opposite of their traditional economy counterpart, like the issue of distance, or to have no counterpart in the traditional economy, like the network. This is what is meant by "breaking the rules of traditional economics," and it is true. Companies have a whole new economic and marketplace reality to deal with. Just remember that the basic rule of business has not been invalidated. Businesses must still produce a profit in order to sustain themselves.

TABLE 1.4 Drivers of the Internet Economy

1. *Information creates the greatest added value for products and services of all kinds.* Many products and service products are essentially at parity with their competitors in terms of product features. Information that helps users acquire products easily and get more benefits from product use is a key part of the competitive landscape.

2. *Size and distance do not matter in many types of communications and transactions.* Information is available all over the world essentially simultaneously today, whether the information is news, product availability, or customer service. In that sense, distance does not matter and the web gives small businesses the ability to have a presence similar to that of a gigantic enterprise. Digital products can be downloaded, but physical products still have to be shipped to purchasers in a timely fashion. In the case of product fulfillment, distance does still matter. In the case of resources to publicize the activity, size is still an issue.

3. *Speed and flexibility are of the essence.* Since information flows across the world are often close to real time, businesses must be able to react in an equally timely fashion. If they do not, in a connected world, communications will often be taken over by customers or others, with negative consequences for the brand. Flexibility is required in everything from ways of responding to customers to business models themselves.

4. *People are the key assets in Internet enterprises.* Companies that are successful in the Internet era are characterized by innovation and creativity. These are actually attributes of well-educated and highly motivated people, not companies themselves. The job of the organization is to create an environment in which openness and innovation can flourish.

5. *Growth in the network causes exponential increase in value.* This statement has been part of the technology culture since Robert Metcalf, the developer of the Ethernet, first articulated it in 1994.[38] While it has been true throughout the development of the Internet, the growth of social networks has made this a key phenomenon to be tapped by marketers.

6. *Marketers can deal with customers on a one-to-one basis.* The Internet is not a one-to-many network like, for instance, television in which one marketer talks to many viewers. The Internet is many-to-many; many businesses talking to customers and many customers talking to each other. This represents a radical change in the marketing landscape. Marketers can use personalization of content to create communications that are perceived as being one to one.

7. *Demand can be predicted with greater accuracy.* The marketer is closer to the customer than before and this allows better forecasting. Behavioral data, what customers are actually doing, are available to the marketer long before conventional marketing research could be completed.

8. *Cost patterns change as transaction and coordination costs shrink for businesses and consumers recognize that switching costs are low.* The Internet has fundamentally changed the nature of transactions in both the B2B and B2C markets by shortening supply chains and making them more efficient. Communications costs have also been lowered by Internet advertising and email.

9. *Customers have power in information-rich channels.* Customers—consumer and business alike—have found their voice on the Internet, and they are using it to the benefit or detriment of businesses as the situation warrants.

10. *An information economy is characterized by choice and abundance.* Information is not a scarce resource; it is not even a renewable resource. It is a resource that becomes more valuable as more people use it. Information is freely available on the Internet, although some content has a purchase price associated with it.

Sources: Adapted from "10 Driving Principles of the New Economy," *Business 2.0*, March 2000, pp. 198–284; and "Our 10 Principles of the New Economy, Slightly Revised," *Business 2.0*, August/September 2001, p. 85.

This rule applies to the nonprofit organization also, although the accounting term is "surplus" not "profit." Most other issues are similar. Just as businesses must satisfy investors, nonprofits must conduct their activities in a manner that satisfies their donors. Businesses have customers who must be satisfied. Nonprofits have clients whose needs must be met and donors whose aims must be fulfilled. There is more similarity than differences in the way for-profits and nonprofits operate, and the two marketspaces can learn from one another. Most of the material in this text is applicable to nonprofit marketers as well as product marketers and marketers of services.

Internet Marketing Best Practices for Strategic Drivers

There is a nonprofit organization that illustrates Internet best practices in terms of virtually all the strategic drivers. It is also a role model that for-profit businesses can follow in terms of communicating with and relating to their customers. With that in mind, let us conclude the chapter with a brief case history of one Internet-based nonprofit, Charity:water.

Charity:water was founded by New York City nightclub entrepreneur Scott Harrison in 2006. His story in text and video are on the founder's story page of the website. Scott's personal odyssey is compelling; the more important point is that this has been a very personal effort from the beginning, including the way the organization deals with donors.

I first heard of Charity:water when a student sent me a Mother's Day ecard that represented a $20 donation in my name.[41] That is the Internet equivalent of word-of-mouth advertising! I matched the donation because I thought it was a nice thing to do and selected a specific water project I wanted to fund. The ecard would have been enough to put me on the organization's email list, but now I was being informed about the progress of the specific water project in the country I had chosen. In the early days, the emails tended to be rough, but they provided relevant information that included a lot of pictures and videos from the field. Since then, the emails have become more polished and a blog has been added, but the emphasis on timely content from people who are actually drilling wells in the field has not changed. The emphasis on the people served is also still front and center.

One of the early promotional campaigns was a bottle of water—with an appropriate label of course—for $20, which was highly visible in the locations where it ran. Since then, $20 has become something of a standard contribution for the organization. This is from their home page (see Figure 1.13a): "Just $20 can give one person clean water for 20 years. An average water project costs $5,000 and can serve 250 people with clean, safe water."[42] This campaign puts contributions within the range of almost everyone. It also makes each contribution a personal effort. The donor has the opportunity to choose the country where the contribution will be used or to let the charity select. Whether the donor selects a specific project affects the content of the retention emails that follow—reports on the specific project or generic content.

Charity:water is a quintessential Internet enterprise. Many things it does would not be possible—or at least cost efficient—in an ink-on-paper world. The personalized email content is one good example, as is the rich media with which it is populated. Even the $20 contributions are marginal if the solicitation involves the higher donor/customer acquisition costs of mail or telephone.

However, Charity:water does not operate only in the virtual world. From the beginning, Scott Harrison's connections in New York City have been important, leading to successful fund-raising events, for example. With the

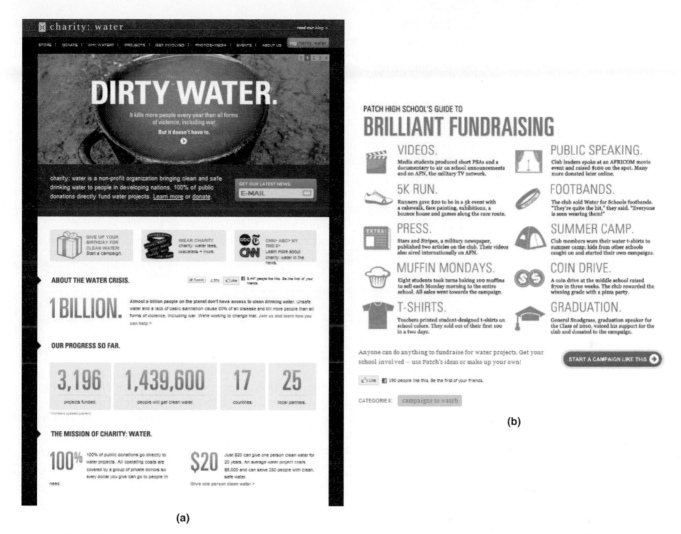

(a)

(b)

FIGURE **1.13** The Charity:water Home Page and High School Fund-Raising Project
Source: Charity Water, http://www.charitywater.org and http://www.charitywater.org/blog/ctw-patch.

help of supporters, the organization has led the way in innovative fund-raising events, including the first Twestival.[43] Using Twitter as the main channel of communications, the organizers aimed for real world events in 100 cities and $100,000 in contributions to Charity:water. The record keeping on this first effort seemed a bit rough but it appeared that there were events in over 200 cities all over the world and approximately $250,000 raised by the single event, including both real world and online contributions. Since that event in 2009, there have been various Twestivals around the world for a variety of charities.

The organization also does more traditional kinds of fund-raising. The types of fund-raising carried out by students at Patch High School for military dependents in Stuttgart, Germany (see Figure 1.13b), is a good example of both reach and a menu of fund-raising techniques, most of them real world in nature.

Perhaps Charity:water's business model is the greatest contribution of all. One hundred percent of all donations go to water projects. What about the expenses of running an organization? Scott Harrison raises all the funds for administrative expenses, both money and in-kind services. It takes a network of accomplished people to provide that kind of support.

This is the kind of charitable activity that fires the imagination of all sorts of people, from the New York glitterati to professional fund-raisers to high school students. It is the intimate, personal involvement with the projects—made possible through the website, blog, and emails—that keeps the donor/customer retention fires blazing. This represents the potential of the Internet.

Throughout this case history is the power of the strategic drivers. Some examples are:

- Content (information) is fresh, relevant, and posted without regard to the location of the contributor. It makes use of powerful web tools from video to blogging.
- The online equivalent of word of mouth is used to acquire new donors, often at little or no cost to the organization.
- People from many walks of life, in many parts of the world, have been drawn into its orbit and remain there because of a compelling mission and consistent, meaningful communications.
- It creates a constantly expanding network of people all over the world who are reached in a cost-effective fashion.
- Donors are given choice in the way in which even small contributions are used and are informed about how they benefit people who need clean water.
- In spite of the number of people and their geographical distribution, it remains a highly personal endeavor in which each person is made to feel a valued contributor.
- It has a business model that encourages contributions. The donations go directly and fully to identified projects. The donor is kept informed about the progress of the specific well to which he has contributed, creating an unusual level of transparency in the organization's operations.
- The organization continues successful fund-raising and expansion of its efforts in terms of geographical areas, suggesting a business model that is also scalable both online and offline.

Throughout this book, we will describe the marketing activities of pre-Internet enterprises that have learned to take advantage of the strategic drivers, as well as Internet-based enterprises that were founded on the new economic principles they embody. We will also emphasize the theme that the Internet is not a stand-alone channel. *It must be integrated with other channels of communications and commerce, both electronic and physical.* All must be driven by clear marketing objectives and monitored for effectiveness. Those are themes we will pursue even as we explain tools and strategies that are unique to the interactive environment.

SUMMARY

Over the past two decades, the Internet has grown from an esoteric network serving only a limited audience to an integral part of life for billions of people around the globe. In the beginning, the benefits and limitations of the new channel were not well understood, and growth has not been consistently smooth. However, it survived the flawed business models of the 1990s to emerge in the 2000s as an indispensable tool for individuals and businesses alike. Companies like Amazon and Google are creatures of the Internet itself. Old-economy companies like Sabre, General Electric, and IBM have integrated the Internet into virtually every aspect of their businesses.

Web 2.0 is already in evidence with phenomena like social networks, employee collaboration, and device-independent communications. There may be a Web 3.0 in the offering that has greater ability to understand the intent of users and consequently to make their experiences more personal and valuable.

Marketers take advantage of the Internet in various ways to perform the three basic marketing activities—customer acquisition, conversion, and retention. The data-driven nature of Internet activities makes it possible for marketers to understand the value of a single customer and to engage in marketing programs, including customer service, that will increase customer value. Ecommerce transactions are part of this picture, but so are offline sales and marketing activities.

The Internet itself can best be understood as a stack, each level of which is based on the one beneath. Each level of the stack represents a set of activities, mostly technical in nature, that are enabled by a particular set of technologies. At the lowest level is the network that allows Internet communications to travel around the world. Intermediate layers support the existence of websites, blogs, and other platforms like social networks. Currently, the top layer of the stack is called "cloud computing" in which software, computing, and communicating reside on the Internet itself and are used by customers on a fee-for-service basis.

This chapter provides a snapshot at one point in time of the Internet itself and the people and companies that use it. The picture it portrays is one of rapid growth and evolution in the ways in which both people and businesses use the web. Change is universal in the Internet milieu and any snapshot is quickly outdated. This requires the Internet marketer to understand sources of information that are relevant to her specific business and/or marketing function and to track that information, usually using the Internet itself.

The Internet provides to business an environment that is different from the natural-resource–based traditional economy. It has ushered in an information-based economy in which speed, flexibility, and customer centricity are paramount. In this economy, size and distance are often less important than they once were. However, it is still essential for businesses to engage in profitable operations in order to perpetuate themselves.

The Internet has not altered the basic requirements of successful marketing—to acquire, convert, retain, and increase the value of customers. To long-standing marketing activities in the physical world, the Internet has added another layer of online activities. Although the online activities have the same generic goals, they are driven by customer data and technology that change the way marketers communicate with their customers.

This text is premised on the need to understand how technology-driven marketing works and how it can be integrated with traditional channels and activities in order to achieve marketing success. Understanding Internet marketing is, and will continue to be, something of a moving target. At the same time that we wrestle with understanding of complex, technology-driven activities, it is important to remember that good marketing puts the customer front and center, whether online or offline. The communications channels change, but people remain much the same.

DISCUSSION QUESTIONS

1. The origins of the Internet are unusual in the history of commercial media. What makes it unusual and what qualities does that impart to the medium?

2. What do you believe are reasons for the highly visible failures of some of the early Internet enterprises? Do you see any parallels in more recent years? Are there any currently popular Internet sites that you think may not be sustainable?

3. Discuss the characteristics of Web 2.0 and give an example of each.

4. What are the broad outlines of Web 3.0?

5. "The most powerful global brands are now enterprises that were founded in the Internet era." True or False?

6. The Internet marketing paradigm includes both marketing inputs and marketing actions. Discuss the major components of both the inputs and the actions.

7. What is the *Internet infrastructure stack*? What is the relevance of this technological concept to marketers? Why does it now have a cloud at the top?

8. Discuss the role the Internet plays in the lives of consumers and businesses. Has it changed the lives of consumers in any meaningful way? Has it changed the way businesses operate in any significant fashion? Can you give examples of the impact of the Internet in B2C, B2B, or nonprofit markets?

9. Best practices represent business activities that consistently produce good results. What is an example you have seen that might be a best practice in customer acquisition? In customer retention?

10. The chapter emphasizes throughout that business and marketing processes are changing in fundamental ways as a result of the Internet. Discuss in considerable depth one specific driver of change and identify ways in which it is altering the way businesses conduct their daily and strategic activities.

INTERNET EXERCISES

1. Internet Career Builder Exercise

   There are many Internet marketing positions available at the entry level and for experienced marketers. The opportunities generally exist in specific areas like search marketing or content creation and many more. You will become familiar with positions and resources in the chapters to follow.

   Throughout the text you will be encouraged to identify specific areas of Internet marketing that interest you and prepare your credentials for applying for positions in one or more areas.

   In order to prepare for the exercises in subject-specific chapters, you should do the following:

   • Based on the advice of your instructor, establish a free account on VisualCV® or LinkedIn if you do not already have one.

   • Develop a chronological list of your work experience and outline your experience from classes, internships, full- or part-time jobs, and volunteer work that is relevant to Internet marketing.

   As you progress through the text, you will be encouraged to make this basic information more detailed and applicable to specific Internet marketing positions.

2. Select an organization (corporate or nonprofit) with which you are somewhat familiar that uses both online and offline channels. Discuss two or three specific examples of how it is taking advantage of the Internet in general and the drivers of strategic change in particular.

3. Select three different websites that you will follow for the semester. Your instructor may make several different assignments based on these sites, so you should choose sites of substance though they do not have to be large. Each should, however, be a brand site, not a site for a mega corporation with many different brands. Following at least one nonprofit site can add to the learning experience.

   Signing up for free newsletter from the sites you select will help you understand the various elements of their online strategies and may also give you insight into how their multichannel marketing is carried out.

   If the company has retail outlets nearby, you should also consider a visit to the retail site, looking for ways in which the firm is integrating marketing activities on and off the Internet.

4. Consider creating a blog to record your insights and discoveries as you move through the Internet marketing course. Blogs will be discussed in Chapter 9. Directions for creating your own blog can be found on free blog sites like Blogger or on the free version of WordPress.

5. Consider getting together with several of your classmates to create a Facebook page to share resources and insights as you progress through the course. You might consider making it a closed page in order to gain experience in work-related collaboration on a social network.

NOTES

1. Material in this section was taken from "Timeline: PBS Life on the Internet," http://www.pbs.org, nd; Michael Hauben, "History of ARPANET," http://www.dei.isep.ipp.pt/docs/arpa.html, nd; PBS Home Video, "A Brief History of the Internet, Vol. One, Networking the Nerds," 1998; and Jeffrey Veen, "The History of HTML," http://hotwired.lycos.com/webmonkey.

2. http://www.pcworld.com/article/185768/10_ways_the_internet_will_change_in_2010.html.

3. http://online.wsj.com/article/SB114424637699117715.html.

4. http://money.cnn.com/galleries/2010/technology/1003/gallery.dot_com_busts/index.html.

5. http://ezinearticles.com/?Advertising-Is-Dead.-Long-Live-PR&id=593.

6. http://www.davechaffey.com/E-commerce-Internet-marketing-case-studies/Boo.com-case-study.

7. Ibid.

8. http://www.guardian.co.uk/technology/2001/aug/26/internetnews.theobserver.
9. http://www.usatoday.com/money/dotcoms/dot039.htm.
10. http://oreilly.com/pub/a/web2/archive/what-is-web-20.html?page=1.
11. http://oreilly.com/pub/a/web2/archive/what-is-web-20.html?page=5.
12. https://www.mckinseyquarterly.com/High_Tech/Strategy_Analysis/How_social_technologies_are_extending_the_organization_2888.
13. http://www.jivesoftware.com/resources/whitepapers/access-social-business-results.
14. http://www.google.com/landing/instantpreviews/#utm_campaign=launch&utm_medium=ha&utm_source=bkws.
15. http://scitech.blogs.cnn.com/2009/05/25/what-is-web-3-0-and-should-you-care.
16. http://www.readwriteweb.com/archives/web_of_data_machine_accessible_information.php.
17. http://www.social-brand-value.com/2010/04/28/the-top-100-most-valuable-global-brands-2010.
18. http://itlaw.wikia.com/wiki/Internet_backbone_provider.
19. Routers are specialized computers or software that transfers data on a network. Bridgers work within local area networks (LANs) to connect various parts of the network, regulate traffic, and switch data. Both fall under the heading of specialized telecommunications devices.
20. http://aws.amazon.com.
21. http://blogs.wsj.com/digits/2011/04/21/more-predictions-on-the-huge-growth-of-cloud-computing.
22. http://www.cloudtweaks.com/2010/11/cloud-hypermarket-on-the-future-of-cloud-computing-and-microsofts-cloud-power-campaign/
23. http://www.microsoft.com/en-us/cloud/cloudpowersolutions.aspx?CR_CC=200010704&WT.srch=1&WT.mc_id=7061F68B-608F-4AB6-B3F9-56A1F203FF1B&CR_SCC=200010704.
24. Probably this ad: http://www.youtube.com/watch?v=Lel3swo4RMc&CMXID=2120.win7_02D5932A-A88A-4133-BD31-90A1142AEF21&WT.srch=1.
25. http://news.cnet.com/8301-13860_3-20021283-56.html.
26. http://www.microsoft.com/presspass/presskits/cloud/docs/The-Economics-of-the-Cloud.pdf.
27. http://news.cnet.com/8301-13846_3-20022353-62.html?part=rss&subj=news&tag=2547-1_3-0-20.
28. http://www.greenbiz.com/sites/default/files/Cloud%20Computing%20and%20Sustainability%20-%20Whitepaper%20-%20Nov%202010.pdf.
29. http://ccr.sigcomm.org/drupal/files/p5-carpenter.pdf.
30. http://www.itu.int/ITU-D/ict/material/FactsFigures2010.pdf, p. 6.
31. http://pewinternet.org/Reports/2010/Teens-and-Mobile-Phones.aspx.
32. "UK Consumers Are Doing More Online, More Often, with More Devices," eMarketer newsletter, November 18, 2010.
33. http://www.internetworldstats.com/stats.htm.
34. http://pewinternet.org.
35. http://blog.nielsen.com/nielsenwire/online_mobile/what-americans-do-online-social-media-and-games-dominate-activity/.
36. http://www.borrellassociates.com/component/content/article/45-general-reports/195-borrell-associates-2011-ad-forecast-memo.
37. http://www.marketingcharts.com/television/ad-spending-continues-2009-spiral-forecasts-slightly-better-for-2010-8306.
38. eMarketer newsletter, July 3, 2010.
39. http://www.forbes.com/2010/03/07/advertising-web-ads-digital-business-media-outsell.html.
40. http://www-ec.njit.edu/~robertso/infosci/metcalf.html.
41. http://diy-marketing.blogspot.com/2008/05/mothers-day-card-from-charitywater.html.
42. http://www.charitywater.org.
43. http://beth.typepad.com/beths_blog/2009/01/twestival-here.html.

CHAPTER 2

The Internet Value Chain

Key Terms

LEARNING OBJECTIVES

By the time you complete this chapter, you will be able to:

- Distinguish between the following concepts: supply chain, value chain, and virtual value chain.

- Explain lean processes and greening the supply chain.

- List the business processes that are necessary to manage the supply chain.

- Identify the desired outcomes of an efficiently functioning supply chain.

- Identify the core marketing processes.

- Discuss the concept that all goods are services.

- Define EDI, ERP, and Web Services and explain their roles in integrating the value chain.

- Explain the nature of cloud computing and its relevance to supply chain management.

- Discuss the potential benefits and negative consequences of RFID technology in supply chains.

The Transformation of Herman Miller

In 1995, furniture maker Herman Miller was a business in trouble. The closely held company had prospered for over 70 years as a manufacturer of high-end office furniture systems. Its products were marketed to large corporations through a sales force of 300 and over 240 contract office furniture dealers. But in spite of its trophy case of design awards and its reputation as one of the most agreeable employers in the country, lead times to fill customer orders were long, delivery was haphazard, and customer service was poor. There was a measurable decline in customer satisfaction, and expenses were out of control. Sales were up slightly, but profits fell by nearly 90 percent in a single year. The disarray led to the exodus of almost 200 employees that year, including the CEO.

The nature of its products increased the complexity of the situation. Herman Miller processed over 3,000 orders for office furniture and accessories each week. The furniture was sold as a system; if a single item was missing, the order could not be shipped. The required coordination between eight separate manufacturing plants was missing. Mark Douglas, project manager at Herman Miller, explained the situation at that time:

> a lack of synchronization created a three- to-four-week lag time between when the first and last components of an order were completed. "We'd get in one item one day, then the panels would come in the next day, then a few days later the chairs would come in. This meant we had three or four weeks of finished goods waiting for the rest of the order. This was driving high inventory in both our warehouses and our plants.
>
> "When all this waiting time was factored in, we were looking at very extended internal lead times of 8 to 12 weeks," the project manager notes. Add at least another month on the end of that in the distributor network (80% of Herman Miller's sales move through a dealer network), and you get a very slow product pipeline.

As the first step in resolving the problem, Herman Miller implemented planning software to improve production scheduling and delivery with the specific goal of improving customer satisfaction through better, faster service. The software allowed creation of a firm completion date for each project by querying each plant about when it could build the ordered items. Each item was then synchronized to the longest production date, with a rule of not building any item more than three days before that date.

Within 18 months, Herman Miller had increased its number of on-time shipments to 99 percent and saw a 100 percent increase in inventory turns.[1] Five years after the transformation began Herman Miller had a fully integrated, Internet-based division, initially designed to serve the small business market it had previously ignored. They were able to install the customer's order in a time frame ranging from three days to two weeks with a 99 percent on-time record and virtually no order errors. Other benefits of the system included an inventory turn of 40 times a year as compared to the industry average of less than 20.[2]

The next step was to fully integrate dealers and customers into the system. Herman Miller office systems are manufactured in four countries. They are sold and installed through a system of dealers in more than 40 countries supported by design centers and regional sales offices. At the beginning, the company's goal was to support the dealer channel, not compete with it. It now sells through the dealer network, physical retail stores, authorized online retailers, and its own Herman Miller Store online.[3] Customers can set up their own custom web page to simplify ordering and service. As a result, Herman Miller provides customers anywhere in the world the convenience of online ordering of office solutions designed to meet their unique needs, coupled with the necessary installation and support services of its local dealers.

The changes in their customer-facing processes were paralleled by internal changes in both production systems and also in the ability and willingness of Herman Miller employees to adjust to change.

"Lean Thinking" at Herman Miller

Like other businesses, Herman Miller was affected by the series of economic shocks that included the bursting of the Internet bubble, as discussed in Chapter 1, the aftermath of 9/11, and the recession that began in 2008. Their ability to weather these macro events is credited to the implementation of the Herman Miller Performance System, a lean manufacturing system modeled on Toyota's well-known production system. Herman Miller's CEO Brian Walker explains that the system results in rapid inventory turns and, in general, fewer and more liquid assets. This has allowed the company to remain cash flow and operating income positive, even in poor economic times.

Lean processes are not quick or easy to install, and individual changes often seem insignificant or even counterintuitive. Ken Goodson, Herman Miller's executive vice president of operations has a good explanation. He boils the company's entire HMPS effort down to the "simple elimination of touches." Lean processes reduce handling and therefore movement of materials. That reduces the number of people that are needed. "You eliminate space in the plant, you eliminate inventory clogging your system, and you free up cash." An example is seen in Herman Miller's growing ability to ship products directly from the manufacturing facility to the customer, bypassing the dealers' warehouses and showrooms. This requires not only coordination in the supply chain; it requires a high level of trust between its members.

This example captures the essence of the Internet-based **supply chain**. On the demand side, supply chain focuses on customer needs, going so far as to customize products and information resources for them. Needs are determined and then products are manufactured, not the reverse. In fact, as in the Herman Miller example, often the order is placed before manufacturing begins, a far cry from the build-to-inventory model of the old economy. On the supply side, vendors

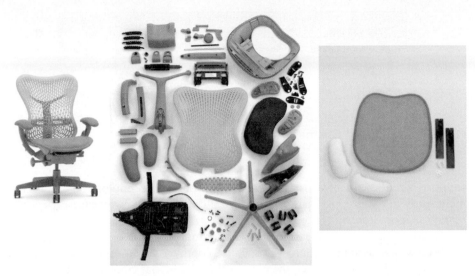

FIGURE **2.1** Herman Miller's 96 Percent Recyclable Mirra Chair
Source: Herman Miller. Used with permission.

and distributor become an integral part of the process, acting on information from electronic manufacturing and distribution systems, not on the basis of paper orders. The system completely integrates the activities of both dealers and suppliers with those of the manufacturer, and, at its best, focuses all activities on value creation for the customer. It wrings costs out of the process at every possible point, and process improvement is ongoing at Herman Miller.[4]

Greening the Supply Chain

The emphasis in recent years has been the "**greening**" of the supply chain, and Herman Miller has been recognized as a leader in that movement since the early 1990s. In January 2010, the company's executive committee approved a vision statement that includes zero landfill, hazardous waste generation, air emissions, and process water use. It also envisions 100 percent green energy use[5] and 100 percent of sales from Design for the Environment (DfE) approved products.[6]

This vision is expected to be achieved by 2020. The company's statement adds that, "Herman Miller is committed to sustainable business practices in everything we do."[7] Its progress is represented by the 96 percent recyclable Mirra chair shown in Figure 2.1. In addition to being produced with recyclable parts, the chair is produced without the PVCs that cause environmental damage.[8] CEO Brian Walker observes that, "Our company, our customers, and our industry in general are moving inexorably toward more transparent reporting when it comes to the environment."[9]

These goals are typical of companies that are attempting to implement environmentally sustainable business process. Herman Miller's 15-year journey is outlined here; many other successful businesses have gone through similar, lengthy processes. As the green movement of recent years suggests, supply chain optimization is indeed a journey that never ends. As you will see in the next section, sustainability is one of the goals of what has been called *outcomes-driven supply chain design*, a driving vision of current supply chain improvements.

Strategic Value Chain Concepts

Michael Porter popularized the concept of the value chain in the early 1980s. The familiar graphic that identifies primary activities as inbound logistics, operations, outbound logistics, marketing and sales, and service, and recognizes the

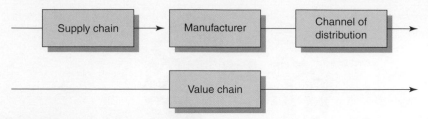

FIGURE **2.2** Value Chain Concept
Source: © Cengage Learning 2013

support activities of infrastructure, human resources, technology, and procurement provides a useful basis for understanding *how the enterprise produces value for its customers.*

Unfortunately for our ease of understanding, in the last few years the term has been widely used in a different way. In the context of the automation of business processes and later the Internet, the term "**value chain**" has come to mean the *seamless, end-to-end integration of activities throughout the channel of distribution.* In essence, this value chain concept incorporates two familiar business processes—the supply chain and the **channel of distribution** (see Figure 2.2). Companies are moving, first, to integrate the supplier-facing side of their channels—the supply chain. Fewer have moved to integrate on the customer-facing side—the channel of distribution.

Otis Elevator, however, has been integrating with customer infrastructure for many years. In 1988, it introduced the first Remote Elevator Monitoring (REM®) system. REM is a diagnostic system that monitors the performance of Otis elevators and other brands with which Otis has service contracts. It monitors both the usage level and individual systems within the elevator. The system schedules regular maintenance calls based on the level of usage. If it detects a problem, it reports the condition to a 24-hour communications center, which determines the severity of the problem, prioritizes service calls, and dispatches a repair person with the required tools and parts. According to Otis, the system identifies most problems before they occur, minimizing elevator downtime. By analyzing all the hundreds of systems in an elevator, the company also maintains that the number of service calls are minimized and performance is optimized. Reports covering both scheduled and REM-based service calls are available to the customer online. The remote monitoring of elevators is an example of the machine-to-machine business model discussed in Chapter 3.[10]

Core Marketing Processes

Figure 2.3 blends several concepts that help to clarify some of these issues by focusing on the manner in which an enterprise creates value. The primary business processes are those identified by Porter and take place at the corporate level. As you can see, the marketing and sales function represents one of several fundamental business processes.

Marketing itself has three core processes—supply chain management, product development and management, and customer relationship management.[11] Supply chain management is discussed later in this chapter. The Internet does not change the basic product development and management process, although it adds to the information sources available for success in that endeavor. Customer relationship management is the subject of Chapter 11.

This conceptualization emphasizes the importance of information in value creation. In early stages, information fosters integration between members of the value chain. In later stages, it permits the development of a **virtual value chain** and the creation of new types of value.

Taken together, all the elements of the process determine the margin realized by the firm. Using ebusiness techniques can increase margins in a number of ways.

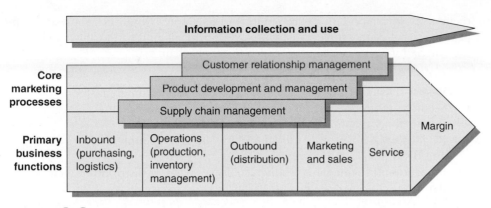

FIGURE **2.3** Value-Creating Activities
Source: Adapted from Debra L. Zahay.

Enterprises have generally focused on the supply side first, because there are large savings to be realized from streamlining the procurement process. These savings can be passed on to customers in the form of price reductions or they can increase margins and therefore profitability. Turning to the demand side, many of the same ebusiness techniques can increase the speed and decrease the cost of fulfilling customer orders. This too may decrease operating costs. Better servicing of customer orders may also strengthen the brand and provide an opportunity to charge premium prices.

Whether it focuses on physical products, services, or information products, a value chain should no longer be viewed as a simple linear entity. In its linear form, it is made up of a complex set of interlocking activities. While it is not often specified, the assumption is that the majority of the activities are carried out internally by a somewhat self-contained business entity interacting with an external environment. This is known as an "old economy" perspective, one that leads to vertical integration. As the contemporary value chain evolves, it becomes a network of fluid partnerships that constantly rearrange themselves to accomplish necessary tasks in the most economical manner. This is known as a "new economy" concept in which overall value is optimized, not the value of one link in the chain, and information flows across corporate boundaries.

It is also important to recognize that businesses in a network are not simply free-floating entities, in constant motion like tiny fish in a pond. They move with a purpose, each to accomplish the task at which it is most proficient. Therefore, we need to understand the tasks that must be accomplished, not at the high level of a Porter-like value chain, but at the granular level of daily business tasks that must be understood, automated where possible, and integrated into a chain that seamlessly delivers value to the customer. In order to do this, we need to explore three separate but related concepts:

- The supply chain
- The value chain
- The virtual value chain

These are not separate entities. They are more like a developmental hierarchy that is focused on satisfactory outcomes for both suppliers and customers.

Outcomes-Driven Supply Chains

As we examine these concepts, it is important to recognize these supply chains as an evolutionary hierarchy in which firms like Herman Miller need to begin, first by getting their supply chain in order and then moving on to higher levels of customer integration and system-wide effectiveness. Supply chains, however, are outcomes driven. They are a means to an end—business profitability—not ends in themselves. It is important to keep in mind the six criteria by which successful supply chains can be measured. Melnyk, Davis, Spekman, and Sandor have identified the criteria for a successful outcome-driven supply chain as:

- Cost: minimize cost while ensuring customer service
- Responsiveness: respond to changes in demand in a timely fashion
- Security: protect against external threats to the supply chain
- Sustainability: minimize environmental impact
- Resilience: be able to identify and react quickly to supply chain risks and disruptions
- Innovation: provide new products and new ways of distributing them that meet customer needs

Melnyk and colleagues point out that these criteria are not mutually exclusive. The management challenge is to balance all six of them in creating the most effective possible supply chain on both the supplier-facing and the customer-facing sides.[12]

If this were not already sufficiently challenging, writer Steve New adds that customers, especially ultimate consumers (who are environmentally concerned consumers), are demanding supply chain transparency to ensure that products are sourced in a way that corresponds with their values. They want products that are made from sustainably harvested materials, produced in factories that do not use child labor and meet at least minimum labor standards, and are manufactured and transported in a way that minimizes environmental impact.[13]

Outdoor equipment and clothing supplier Patagonia has a web page that allows consumers to track the "footprint" of a specific product. As of this writing, there are 16 products that can be tracked with the option to obtain further information. In the case of its Chacabuco backpack, shown in Figure 2.4, the

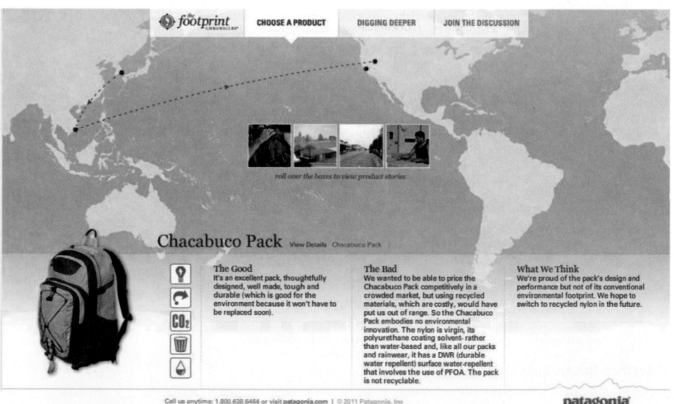

FIGURE **2.4** A Transparent Supply Chain

Source: Patagonia, http://www.patagonia.com/us/footprint/index.jsp.

Patagonia—the outdoor equipment and clothing company used as an example in this section—has a home page filled with interesting cause-related interactive elements. Visit http://www.patagonia.com.

Patagonia's website also boasts an interactive map that documents the construction of various products. Visit the interactive site at http://bit.ly/sdex1J.

company's website provides information about the plant in South Korea that weaves the fabric for the backpack and the plant in Vietnam where the backpacks are constructed. Patagonia's website uses a Flash page to present content in a way that corresponds with both its traditional corporate values and the compelling visuals present in other areas of its website. Other firms are using verification codes that link to pages on their sites where similar content is available. Still others are experimenting with RFID technology (discussed later in this chapter) to make content available on mobile phones at the point of purchase. For more details on transparent supply chains and the technologies that support them, see New's online article.[14]

The Supply Chain

A supply chain maps the physical movement of goods from initial production through assembly to the distribution process to the customer in the same way but with more detail than the map in Figure 2.4. Table 2.1 lists the business processes that are involved in managing the supply chain. As you look at the processes, which have an operations management flavor, keep in mind that a single enterprise may have dozens or even hundreds of suppliers whose activities must be coordinated.

Because supply chain management is such a complex task, enterprises can realize large cost savings from integrating and improving it, with best-in-class companies spending 5 to 6 percent less of their total revenue on supply chain costs than their median industry counterparts. They can also realize major

TABLE 2.1   Supply Chain Management Processes

1. Selecting and qualifying desired suppliers
2. Establishing and managing inbound logistics
3. Designing and managing internal logistics
4. Establishing and managing outbound logistics
5. Designing work flow in product-solution assembly
6. Running batch manufacturing
7. Acquiring, installing, and maintaining process technology
8. Order processing, pricing, billing, rebates, and terms
9. Managing (multiple) channels
10. Managing customer services such as installation and maintenance to enable product use

Source: Rajendra K. Srivastava, Tasadduq A. Shervani, and Liam Fahey, "Marketing, Business Processes, and Shareholder Value: An Organizationally Embedded View of Marketing Activities and the Discipline of Marketing," *Journal of Marketing*, 1999, Vol. 63, p. 170.

improvements in process elements ranging from inventory (25 to 60 percent improvement) to overall productivity (10 to 16 percent improvement).[15] The classic example of a tightly integrated value chain is Dell Computers, which is discussed later in the chapter. Zara, the European clothing chain, provides an example of combining customer information with supply chain integration to succeed in the ever-changing world of fashion.

Zara—Fast Fashion

Zara, a division of Spanish conglomerate Inditex Group, had over 1,400 stores in 77 countries in 2010.[16] Its growth and financial results have captured the attention of investors in recent years because they have far outstripped those of other fashion retailers. In the still-struggling global retail economy of 2010, Zara announced first-half increases in both sales and profits. In addition, it continued its global expansion and, for the first time, offered customers in some countries the opportunity to purchase online.[17]

Zara's success comes from two key drivers. First is its fashion appeal. Customer trends are constantly monitored. Store employees using handheld devices roam the stores, asking customers what they like, do not like, and are looking for but do not find. That information is transmitted to the design team at headquarters, which immediately begins to sketch new items. At the end of each day, store managers provide sales reports to headquarters, giving constant updates on what merchandise is and is not selling.

The second driver is the ability of Zara's supply chain to produce new items and get them into stores in just two weeks. Competitive fashion chains like Swedish-based H&M and Chicos in the United States often take as much as six months to spot a trend and react to it by producing more of desired items and disposing of unpopular ones.[18]

How has Zara designed a supply chain that supplies desired merchandise so quickly and so effectively? First, it owns many production facilities, making about 40 percent of its own fabric in highly automated factories in Spain. It also makes about 60 percent of the garments it sells. Most are produced in small workshops throughout Spain and Portugal instead of being outsourced to lower-cost-of-labor countries. Inventory reaches stores quickly, by truck in Europe for short distances and by air for more distant locations.[19] Its marketing effort includes a website that is carefully localized for the various countries in which it operates and what appears to be a single Facebook page with over 8 million fans globally.

The importance of supply chain excellence in the fashion industry is well summarized by Jani Friedman of FreeBorders, a San Francisco software firm that serves the retail outsourcing trade. According to Friedman, "Speed to market is the Holy Grail. Retail companies that figure it out will have a significant increase in revenue because they'll sell more trend items at full price, which drives profitability."[20] Zara's unusual supply chain approach continues to be of great interest and generates considerable visibility for its business practices.[21]

By following this approach, both supplier and customer win. But it requires that the supplier take a broader perspective, looking at the customer's demand chain as well as its own supply chain. This is another example of managing business processes beyond corporate boundaries, and moves us toward the concept of a value chain.

The Value Chain

In order to create optimal value, a company must examine the entire supply chain, from initial production to final consumption, in order to understand where costs are incurred in the process. Consultants at Bain & Company liken it to a Swahili game called the game of Jenga. In this game, each player must remove as many blocks as possible from a tower, using them to build additional structures, all without causing the original structure to come crashing down. This seems an apt analogy.

Bain's consultants identify four key factors in this effort:

- Information search costs
- Transaction costs
- Fragmentation of the customer marketplace
- Standardization of products

Information and transaction costs together typically account for over 40 percent of total costs. Economists characterize these costs as "friction" in channels of distribution, and they offer ripe targets for cost reduction in value chains.[22]

Integrated value chains represent an important step in managing both the supply-facing and the customer-facing sides of the business. Dell's integrated value chain operates extensively in Internet space, hence the term "virtual value chain."

Dell's Direct Model

Dell Computers is one of the classic examples of creating a value chain in Internet space, one that is not a series of links but a network of interconnected enterprises, both supplier and customer. Before Dell's direct model became a force in the industry, personal computers had major issues in all four of the categories established by Bain. Search and transaction costs were high, especially for the small business or individual customer. The fragmented market ranged from the individual customer buying a single unit to the very large corporation that might purchase several hundred computers each month. Even very large customers tended to settle for a standard product because it was cheaper to buy in a large, standardized lot until Dell.

In its early years, Dell enjoyed great success as a result of its build-to-order model that featured a streamlined supply chain (see Figure 2.5) and careful financial control of manufacturing and distribution operations. Touting Dell's success in 2004, *Fast Company* magazine stated that "Dell has replaced inventory with information, and that has helped turn it into one of the fastest, most hyperefficient organizations on the planet."[23]

Dell also uses information to create customer value. One primary mechanism for doing this is its Premier Pages. Dell was one of the first companies to provide each business customer—from a Fortune 500 enterprise to a small local business—its own secure page on the Dell site. This page includes the products that have been approved for purchase by the firm and support information for those specific products. Products not approved for purchase are not even seen, making life easier for the purchasing department. In addition, employees with purchasing authority can simply log on and make their purchase without going through purchasing, saving time for both. Dell also wins because purchases are driven to the website, where transactions are cheaper. This service is feasible for even a small business because Dell's telephone representatives have easy-to-use templates that allow them to set up a page by simply entering information provided by the customer over the phone. Other firms copied this customer personalization approach, from Herman Miller's eZConnect to the customer account pages of some of Dell's direct competitors.

Beginning in about 2005, Dell suffered a number of issues, both public and strategic. The company that prided itself on customer service ignored the complaints of a customer who was a well-known blogger[24] until it became a media firestorm.[25] The next year, a Dell laptop exploded in flames while sitting alone on a conference table. The event transfixed the Internet.[26] In response to the customer care issues, Dell established, first, a blog (see Figure 2.6a) and later a wiki-like site to solicit customer ideas and opinions (see Figure 2.6b) and supported both with a branded customer community (see Figure 2.6c) and various product-specific product

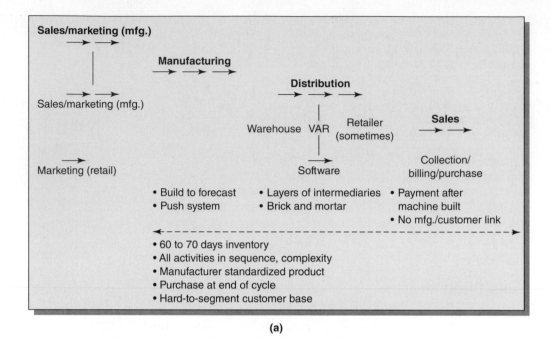

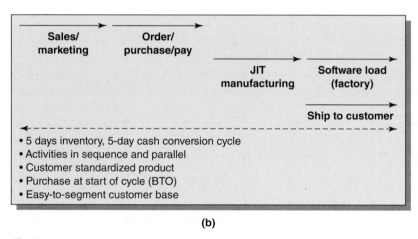

FIGURE **2.5** Traditional Computer Manufacturer versus Dell
Source: © Cengage Learning 2013

forums. In December 2010, Dell launched one of the early social media listening posts.[27]

While it was getting its marketing house in order, Dell also reevaluated its build-to-order business model, which had become unsustainable.[28] An announcement to the Dell community in 2010 that publicly launched a program called Client Reinvention signaled an end to that model. According to the post:

> Client Reinvention is primarily a COGS [cost of goods sold] initiative to improve our forecasting, streamline the supply chain model, and ultimately reduce costs in the client (primarily desktop, mobility and workstation products) value chain. We are establishing a segmented supply chain that delivers either lean fixed configuration products or configurable for customization products with slight derivatives of each.[29]

This move seems to signal fewer models and customization and value chain services that depend on customer segment needs and potential profitability.

If you wish, you can read this as a case history covering more than 15 years of making mistakes and correcting them. You can also think of it in terms of the outcomes-driven supply chain model described earlier in the chapter. At the very least, it demonstrates close control of costs and responsiveness to a changing competitive environment.

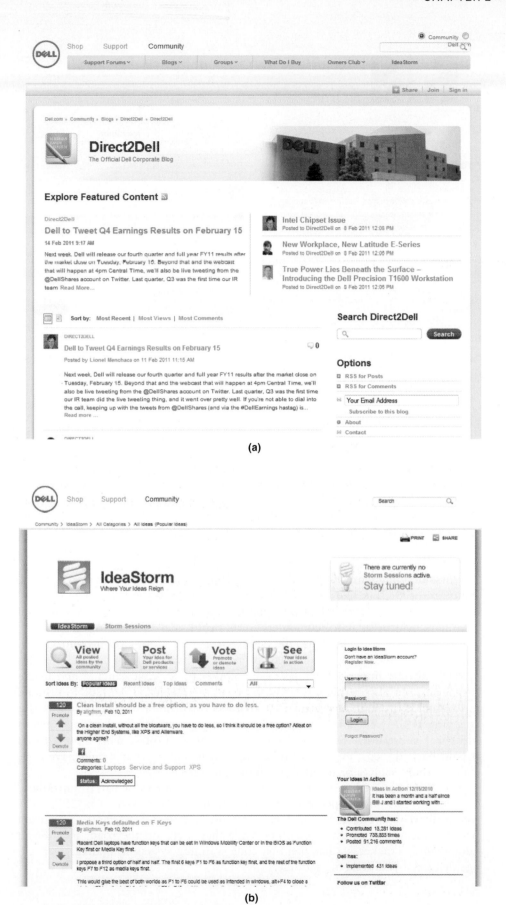

(a)

(b)

FIGURE **2.6** Dell Customer Communications Sites

Source: Dell Inc., http://en.community.dell.com.

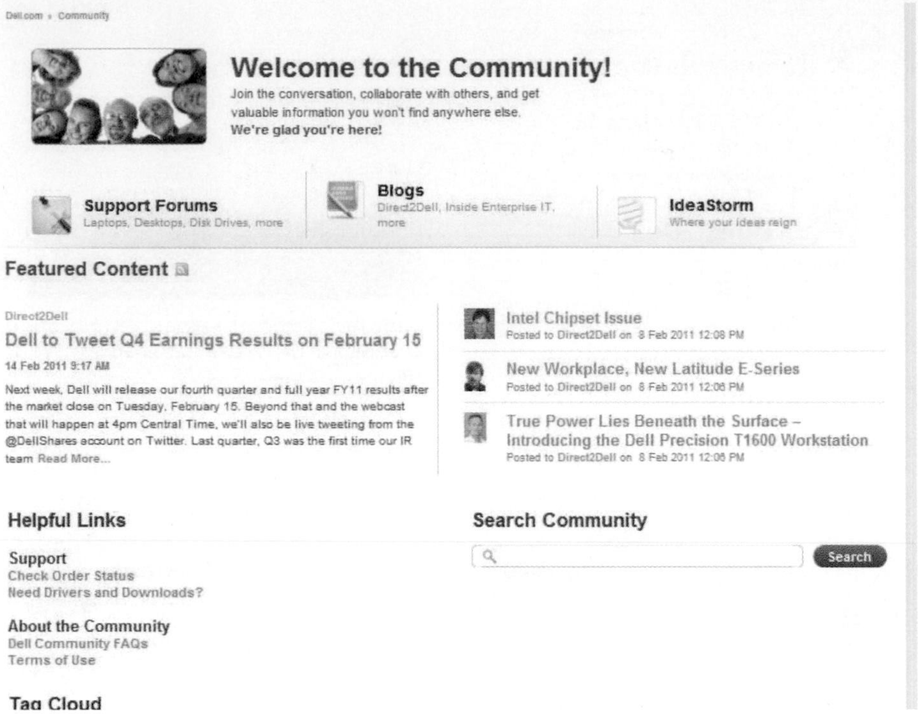

(c)

FIGURE **2.6** (Continued)

Creating a Virtual Value Chain

As the Herman Miller, Zara, and Dell examples illustrate, integrating the complex value chain process and moving it onto the web is a formidable task. The three steps shown in Figure 2.7 represent basic steps in the process. Highlights from the value chain development of consumer snack maker Frito-Lay and business services provider FedEx help to illuminate the process.

Visibility

The first step in creating a virtual value chain is for the enterprise to provide visibility (translate that relevant information) of all activities in the supply chain to all employees who need it. Frito-Lay created visibility for its supply chain when it gave handheld order-entry computers to its route salespersons. Inside the retail store, the reps were able to use the devices to record store-level inventory data, which were immediately transmitted to Frito-Lay headquarters by satellite. This system not only improved management's ability to forecast demand and inventory levels, but also permitted reps to make price changes in the field to respond to local market conditions. Data about competitor promotional activity was also collected in the field and transmitted to headquarters. While the initial investment was substantial, Frito-Lay's director of information systems reported that it paid back the cost every year in savings on inventory that would have gone stale on retail shelves or in the distribution pipeline.

FedEx pioneered visibility for its service operations when it introduced COSMOS (Customer Operations Service Master Online System) in 1979. The following year it added DADS (Digital Assisted Dispatch System) to transmit package pick-up requests to couriers while they were on the road. In 1986, it added Super Tracker®, a handheld barcode scanning system to manage its package delivery operations in real time.

Mirroring

The second step is called "mirroring," the ability to create information systems that provide a complete picture of the supply chain at a given point in time. Leading-edge companies like Frito-Lay and FedEx have not only created systems

Frito-Lay		
Late 1980s—Gives handheld computers to route salespeople and builds data warehouse; store-level data transmitted daily to central information system	Late 1990—With parent company PepsiCo and Tropicana Products unit, has consolidated system to monitor and maintain store-level inventory and to develop common promotions	2000—Builds knowledge management portal to make customer knowledge consistent and available and to foster collaboration among employees 2004—Prepares to incorporate radio frequency identification (RFID) tags into its supply chain systems 2008—Announces $55 million annual energy savings from ten-year sustainability program 2010—Uses store-level merchandise plans (planograms) to optimize products based on available shelf space Improves security throughout distribution chain to protect food safety
 **Visibility** Enterprises are able to "see" supply chain processes more clearly through their information systems.	 **Mirroring** Enterprises create a parallel system in which information "mirrors" the physical activities of the supply chain.	 **More value to customers** Enterprises use information to deliver value to customers in different ways and to create new value.
FedEx		
Early 1980s—Launches digital assisted dispatch system (DADS) to transmit information to couriers on the road	Middle 1990s—Introduces software that allows customers to manage shipping from desktops and follows with a variety of ebusiness tools	2002—Announces ability to track FedEx shipments from wireless devices 2004—Purchases Kinko's, creating the "File, Print, FedEx Kinko's" service 2008—FedEx Kinko's rebranded as FedEx Office® 2010—Releases 2009 Citizenship Report and announces EarthSmart initiative 2011—FedEx Office® Print & Go, mobile and flash drive activation of in-store printers

FIGURE **2.7** Creating a Virtual Value Chain
Source: © Cengage Learning 2013

that provide a complete real-time view of their supply chains, but have also shared this data with their customers.

In 1992, FedEx began providing free software that allowed customers to schedule shipments and track packages using dial-up connections. In 1994, it debuted http://www.fedex.com, its corporate website on which customers could access many services, including real-time package scheduling and tracking. Customers were able to see the FedEx information in real time, providing a degree of control that lead to increased customer satisfaction. For FedEx, it greatly decreased the number of routine inquiries to the telephone call center and substantially reduced the cost of that function.

At Frito-Lay, mirroring takes the form of electronic sharing of store-level inventory and pricing data with the retailer. By ensuring that the manufacturer and the customer have precisely the same data, the system substantially reduces procurement costs and errors.

Enhancing Customer Value

The direct customers of Frito-Lay are, of course, retail grocery outlets of various kinds. Beyond the cost and time savings its information-driven store replenishment system is able to offer, Frito-Lay is able to offer both data and promotional services. By 2010, point of purchase data allowed Frito-Lay to create individual planograms[30] for each store, often reducing the number of SKUs (stock-keeping units) by 20 to 30 percent, which actually increased consumer convenience and satisfaction. Being able to merchandise on an individual store basis increased the growth of store sales between 2 and 4 percent.[31]

The company's ongoing environmental sustainability effort[32] took a hit in 2010 when customer complaints caused it to pull noisy SunChips bags that were compostable and to return to older style packaging.[33] At the same time, it was engaging in a major effort to protect the safety of food and packaging products in its supply and distributions chains.[34] Both efforts suggest continuing outcomes-driven improvement in its value chain.

FedEx also delivers new types of value to customers in various ways. In recent years, it has become an integral part of many websites through Web Services applications that allow customers to schedule shipments or offer FedEx services to customers[35] without leaving their own sites. In addition, the acquisition of Kinko's in December 2004 created new options for serving customers. The division was rebranded FedEx Office® in 2008. It has continued to expand its online service offerings, and in 2011, it introduced a mobile application called Print & Go.[36] FedEx also has an ongoing sustainability initiative, and in 2010, it added the first electric parcel delivery trucks to its alternative-energy fleet.[37]

Benefits of an Integrated Value Chain

The kind of integrated value chains exemplified by Frito-Lay and FedEx have five key characteristics:

- They are customer-centric, focusing on the customer demand chain as well as supply chain and logistics issues.
- They encompass both the demand chain and the supply chain, from customers' customers to suppliers' suppliers.
- They are designed to compete as an extended enterprise, bringing customers and suppliers into the system through real-time information flows.
- They increase customer value added by provision of information and customer service and support.
- They offer the opportunity to create specialized value propositions for individual customers or customer segments.[38]

In the Internet economy, customer value has taken on a special meaning. The quality of products is still unquestionably important. However, the stark truth is that many companies have mastered the art of product quality. They spent much of the last 10 to 15 years learning to produce products at or near the **Six Sigma** level of quality (no more than 3.4 defects per million according to the American Society for Quality). This kind of quality has become expected and even standard in many applications. It is necessary, but no longer sufficient. Bix Norman, the originator of the SQA concept at Herman Miller, says:

> A product's a product….It isn't about product, it's about simplicity and how fast you can get it….If you looked at our industry from a customer's viewpoint of what it was like to buy and get office furniture, you'd find that it was just a big, huge pain.[39]

It is customary to point out that customers want performance, reliability, speed, and convenience, both in products and in the distribution of those products. That is true, but Vargo and Lusch, searching for a way to integrate the subdisciplines of product marketing and services marketing, take that reasoning a step further. Their concept, which is nothing less than a new paradigm for marketing itself, has occasioned much discussion. They state that:

> the service-centered dominant logic represents a reoriented philosophy that is applicable to all marketing offerings, including those that involve tangible output (goods) in the process of service provision.[40]

Are all goods—tangible and intangible—actually services? While that may sound like a revolutionary idea, advertisers have long known that they must sell product benefits, not product features. For the most part, people do not purchase products just to possess them; they purchase them to derive benefits of some sort, even if the benefit itself is something intangible like "status."

There are more points in Vargo and Lusch's argument, but these are especially relevant to Internet marketing in general, and value chains in particular. Their hypotheses include:

- Goods Are Distribution Mechanisms for Service Provision
- All Economies Are Services Economies
- The Customer Is Always a Cocreator of Value
- The Enterprise Can Only Make Value Propositions
- A Service-Centered View Is Customer Oriented and Relational[41]

Customers are looking for value, whether that value is delivered by a tangible product or by a service product. A key task of the enterprise is to create that value. Articulating a value proposition is the first step in creating value, and it is an integral part of business models. Value propositions are discussed in Chapter 3.

As companies improve their supply chains and make them virtual, they are looking for meaningful improvements in how they work. A late 2010 survey by McKinsey asked supply chain executives around the world what their priorities had been and how they were changing as the world began to emerge from recession. The results are shown in Figure 2.8.

The time-honored goals of reducing overall operating costs and reducing inventory levels remain important, but they are less so as executives look to the next five years. Assuming almost equal importance are improving customer services, speeding products to market, and improving product quality. These are external, customer-facing challenges, not external or supply-chain facing challenges.

There are three enabling technologies that have been deployed over the years to achieve both those outcomes, as well as a newer entry in the field. We will look briefly at EDI, ERP, and Web Services, and its newest manifestation, cloud computing.

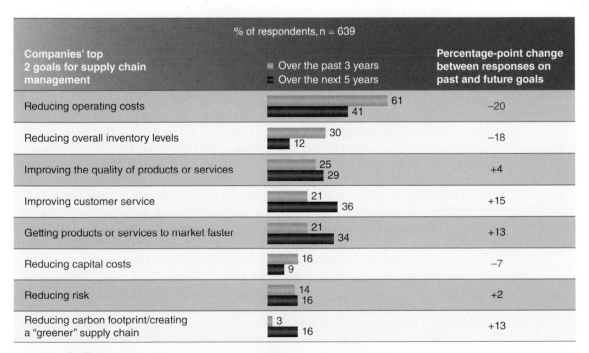

Companies' top 2 goals for supply chain management	■ Over the past 3 years ■ Over the next 5 years	Percentage-point change between responses on past and future goals
Reducing operating costs	61 / 41	−20
Reducing overall inventory levels	30 / 12	−18
Improving the quality of products or services	25 / 29	+4
Improving customer service	21 / 36	+15
Getting products or services to market faster	21 / 34	+13
Reducing capital costs	16 / 9	−7
Reducing risk	14 / 16	+2
Reducing carbon footprint/creating a "greener" supply chain	3 / 16	+13

% of respondents, n = 639

FIGURE **2.8** Shifting Priorities in Supply Chain Outcomes

Source: Excerpted Exhibit 2 from "The challenges ahead for supply chains: McKinsey Global Survey results," 2010, *McKinsey Quarterly*, www.mckinseyquarterly.com. Copyright © 2010 McKinsey & Company. All rights reserved. Reprinted by permission.

Enabling Value Chain Technologies

Electronic data interchange, the oldest of the processes, provides a way of automating the supply chain. *Enterprise resource planning* is a broader term that describes systems stretching back into the production process and forward into the order processing and distribution systems with the objective of integrating all business processes into a seamless network. Web Services, as described in Chapter 1, is a newer entry into the process automation space that relies on outsourced services that replace capital investment with pay-as-you-go services. Cloud computing—an extension of Web Services—is rapidly being adopted in channels of distribution and has potential to become a way of delivering Internet-based supply chain services on a fee-for-service basis. Let us briefly discuss each.

EDI: Paperless Transaction Processing

EDI (electronic data interchange) has been available and in use by large corporations and their suppliers for at least three decades, which makes it a pre-Internet technology. The term is representative of the process; essentially EDI enables paperless transaction processing. In spite of the benefits of speed, error reduction, and lowered costs that it offers, the cost and difficulty of implementing the technology have slowed its adoption. In particular, the cost of an EDI installation puts it out of the reach of small businesses in the early years.

In general, the steps in an EDI transaction are:

- The order is entered into the system and an electronic purchase order is generated instead of a paper purchase order. This electronic purchase order contains all the information of a paper purchase order. In addition, the purchase order may contain information required by the purchaser, such as stocking information needed by a retailer.
- The order is sent to the seller, either directly or through a proprietary network.
- The order enters the seller's order entry and processing system.
- An electronic acknowledgment is sent to the purchaser.
- The seller's system generates fulfillment instructions to its warehouse, which fills the order and prepares it for shipping.
- An electronic invoice is prepared by the seller and transmitted to the purchaser.
- Payment for the goods is transferred by means of a secure electronic payments system.

One supplier of services estimates that over 80,000 companies use EDI systems.[42] Because large firms can require that their suppliers use EDI to deal with them, this multiplies the number of users manyfold.

Walmart has always required that its suppliers do business with it electronically, originally using its own proprietary networks and software. In 2002, it mandated that suppliers use an Internet-based platform, successfully replacing the older and more expensive proprietary networks. In 2003, it launched a program to require RFID (radio frequency identification) tags on product shipments, but the initiative has been less successful. Walmart has a supplier diversity program that focuses on local suppliers, small businesses, and minority- and women-owned enterprises.[43] Like other enterprises described in this chapter, it has an active environmental sustainability program.[44] More uniquely, it has free supplier training program available to its U.S. suppliers[45] and similar training has been deployed in India[46] and China.[47] All these activities are necessary to support a far-flung supplier network.

In the early days of EDI, software packages alone cost tens of thousands of dollars. Their use required extensive and expensive systems integration as well as skilled technicians to operate the system. Today, there are many hosted EDI applications that are more affordable to the small and medium-sized business without an extensive IT workforce. In fact, a small industry has grown up by providing EDI services for Walmart alone. One of the suppliers estimates that it costs $70 or more and takes up to ten days to process a paper order while an

EDI order can be processed for a dollar or less and requires only one day. Quality of delivery is improved because manual and repetitive order entry is eliminated. Faster order processing also decreases inventory cost for suppliers.[48] These factors make EDI a component technology of Walmart's supply chain and those of other enterprises. It is, however, no longer a unique competitive advantage. *CIO Magazine* has a succinct statement of the reason:

> Two decades ago, the world's number-one retailer used IT to reinvent global supply chains. The world caught up and now Web 2.0 technologies are forcing retailers to pay more attention to customers.[49]

In Walmart's case, reinventing its supply chain has included working to improve its website, its customer service, and its ability to communicate with customers in ways that range from email newsletters to programs driven by its Facebook page. Walmart, whose supply chain has for many years been the one all tried to emulate, now sees the world as do executives in the McKinsey study (see Figure 2.8). Emphasis has shifted to activities that create pleasing customer experience that, in turn, results in customer satisfaction.

With an EDI system and a more efficient supply chain in place, firms can shift emphasis to smoothly functioning internal and customer-facing processes. Enterprise resource planning is the technique most often used to achieve information integration inside the organization

ERP: Information Integration Across the Enterprise

ERP (enterprise resource planning) is the name given to modular software systems that attempt to "integrate all departments and functions across a company onto a single computer system that can serve all those different departments' particular needs."[50] Such a system requires nothing less than creating a digital record of every business transaction in a totally integrated enterprise-wide system.

The goal of ERP is to tie together systems that have formerly run independently, often on mainframe computers, into an integrated system that gives a complete view of corporate activity from the perspective and desktop of the relevant decision maker. The human resources professional needs one view of personnel data; the operations planner needs to see the same data through a different lens. The marketer needs access to enterprise data, including personnel availability, as well as access to a wealth of marketing-specific customer and promotional data.

According to the ERP Resource Center, there are five basic reasons for an organization to embark on an ERP project:

- To *integrate financial information* so that all users work from a single information source.
- To *integrate customer order information* so that it moves seamlessly between all functions from order intake to customer fulfillment to inventory monitoring. This also presents the opportunity to make this information visible to the customer.
- To *standardize and speed up manufacturing processes* in an effort to increase productivity and decrease costs.
- To *reduce inventory* by speeding up the internal movement of work-in-process and finished goods inventory. An ERP system, however, is not a substitute for supply chain management software, which links both internal and external systems.
- To *standardize human resources information*, especially important for merged companies where the previously independent firms used different HR systems.[51]

If you are able to enroll for classes online or to check your grades online at the end of the semester, the enabling system is most likely the result of an ERP initiative. It has not all been smooth sailing at many institutions, however. A decade ago, many schools faced the same situation:

> By the mid-1990s, most college administrative systems were a disconnected mess of legacy applications. Forward-thinking administrators knew that they needed to

graduate their aging, mostly homegrown systems. College administrators loved the idea of having an HR management, financial and student administration system that could unite offices and departments.[52]

Colleges and universities almost universally opted for ERP software to replace legacy systems that were often either homegrown or built on commercial software that had been substantially modified over the years. Few found the transition easy. Students and staff sometimes found themselves unable to access systems that provided key information, like room assignments or financial aid awards. IT administrators were faced with system malfunctions or crashes at peak load times, such as when students return to campus in the fall. Administrators were confronted with longer time frames and higher costs than they originally anticipated.[53] You may have also experienced difficulty with some of the student-facing systems yourself, but you cannot imagine a college or university without electronic access to critical systems and services. You can be assured that the higher education experience has not been substantially different from that of many corporations; the path to ERP success is often long and difficult.

The need for integration is compelling, but the difficulties are substantial. It may take several years for an integration project to be completed. A study of 63 corporations by the Meta Group estimated the average TOC (total cost of ownership) of an ERP installation to be $15 million, with an astounding range of $400,000–$300 million. A later study by the Aberdeen Group found that a large enterprise could spend as much as $6 million. The Meta Group study found that it took eight months after system completion to see any financial benefits. At that point, the median annual cost saving was estimated at $1.6 million.[54] It is even harder to measure the benefits to staff and customers—ranging from a student's ability to register for classes online to a corporate customer's ability to track an order from his desktop PC. To put it in another way, integrating internal systems is a necessary precursor to providing customer value through visibility of value chain processes.

However, the costs and difficulties of implementing EDI and ERP have given rise to another set of technologies aimed at the same issues. This set of technologies has come to be known by the entirely nondescriptive name of Web Services.

Web Services: Software as a Service

Web Services is a constantly evolving discipline, and there are many companies eager to sell software and services into this market. Consequently, there is a great deal of hype and considerable confusion over just what the term means. The basic idea, however, is to enable different computer systems—including those that power supply chains—to communicate with one another without the expensive software and systems integration required by EDI and ERP.

A definition from an article with the perhaps questionable title "Understanding Web Services" says:

> Web services technology represents an important way for businesses to communicate with each other and with clients as well. Unlike traditional client/server models, such as a Web server or Web page system, Web Services do not provide the user with a GUI [graphical user interface]. Instead, Web Services share business logic, data and processes through a programmatic interface across a network. *The applications interface with each other, not with the users* [emphasis mine].[55]

If you think the definition needs an explanation, it is understandable. The field of Web Services is a labyrinth of technical terms and different programming languages. A trained applications developer is required to navigate the technical complexity and develop custom applications. There are many applications, however, that can be implemented by a nonprogrammer. Whichever approach is taken, it is essential that marketers understand the general outlines of Web Services and the functionality they offer.

eBay is one of the largest purveyors of Web Services, and eBay Marketplace Services gives insight into one way that Web Services work. You may see the eBay icon (see Figure 2.9a) on other companies' websites. If you click on it, it takes you to one of two locations where you can buy the advertised product:

1. To a *listing* on eBay itself where you can buy the product immediately at a fixed price or participate in the classic eBay auction process. That is the *affiliate model*, discussed in detail in Chapter 3, which allows a website owner or blogger to sell products on another site and obtain a percentage of the proceeds (see Figure 2.9b).
2. To an eBay *store* that features a broad offering of the website's products. Figure 2.9c shows the Tommy Hilfiger store on eBay. The brand sells its own products there while eBay takes care of all the ecommerce details from providing a secure shopping cart to accepting secure payments to fulfilling the order. Tommy Hilfiger has its own ecommerce site, http://usa.tommy.com/tommy, but it uses the eBay store as another way to extend its reach to customers and sell its products.

Both the affiliate program and storefront can be implemented by following point-and-click applications on the eBay website. Fashion brands like Tommy Hilfiger are likely to use professional programmers to make the storefront adequately represent the brand, but the applications are designed to be implemented by the owner herself.

Web Services can be provided from the website itself as shown in the eBay example. Amazon is also a major supplier of Web Services and has chosen to deliver its services "in the cloud."

Cloud Computing—Software as a Service, Platform as a Service, and Infrastructure as a Service

The newest addition to this set of technologies (at the top of the infrastructure stack portrayed in Chapter 1) is cloud computing. Two editors of InfoWorld agreed in July 2010 that there was no commonly accepted definition of what cloud computing actually is. They said:

> Some analysts and vendors define cloud computing narrowly as an updated version of utility computing: basically virtual servers available over the Internet. Others go very broad, arguing anything you consume outside the firewall is "in the cloud," including conventional outsourcing.[56]

The Gartner Group has a simpler definition, which may or may not be more understandable, that is quoted in a Microsoft document.

> A style of Computing where scalable and elastic IT capabilities are provided as a service to multiple customers using Internet technologies.[57]

Microsoft considers cloud computing so important that it aired a series of commercials beginning in late 2010 to explain cloud computing to a broad audience.[58] The importance of the concept is also emphasized by the fact that the European Union has issued its own definition and call for standards and potential regulation.[59]

Why is cloud computing viewed as being so important? The key reason for users to adopt cloud computing is clearly the expectation of savings in IT costs, especially the high capital costs of IT installations. In addition, cloud computing is flexible, allowing users to migrate to different software or platforms without the time and cost of developing and installing their own systems. Cloud computing is easy to use since the development and maintenance are handled by the services provider.[60] As you might imagine, IT and top managers often express concern about outsourcing mission-critical operations to service providers.

Two brief examples are helpful in understanding the concept and its uses.

1. Amazon is known as one of the premier retailers of the Internet. Just like eBay, when Amazon began, there was no robust ecommerce software available. Both firms had to develop their own in the beginning, and over

(a)

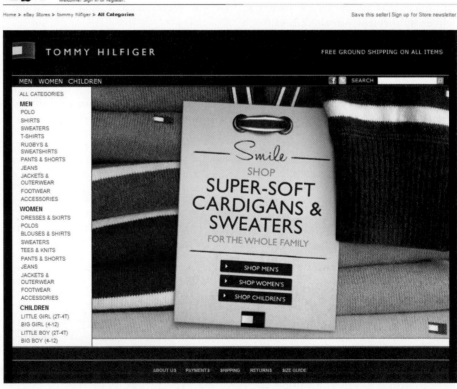

(b)

(c)

FIGURE **2.9** eBay Marketplace Services

Source: eBay, http://pages.ebay.com/api/index.html, https://publisher.ebaypartnernetwork.com/files/hub/en-US/aboutEbay.html, and http://stores.ebay.com/tommyhilfiger.

time, both began offering their own platforms as services. In 2006, Amazon began offering its Web Services "in the cloud." It has a huge suite of products. In terms of ecommerce alone, Amazon can provide the following:

• Web Services that allow a business to develop an ecommerce site and deploy it in the cloud. In other words, easy-to-use tools facilitate website development; Amazon handles hosting and operations.

- A checkout solution that provides a shopping cart and secure payment. Because the system is handled by Amazon, the customer can use the information stored in her Amazon account (shipping and payment information) to complete the purchase without creating a new account and entering information.
- A simple payment solution that implements just the use of Amazon account information described earlier.
- Fulfillment services in which Amazon stocks products and ships out customer orders. This is an important ecommerce activity that is discussed in detail in Chapter 4.
- A web store, similar to the eBay application described earlier, by which the user can set up an Amazon storefront.
- Advertising services that allow the marketer to advertise on various pages in the Amazon site.
- Amazon Mechanical Turk, an expert system that facilitates back-end ecommerce applications like pricing and marketing merchandise.

If your eyes have glazed over a bit at this list, consider that the ecommerce applications suite described here is only 1 of 13 Amazon Web Solutions listed on its website![61] You should also recognize that each of the bullets represents modular services that can be adopted with or without the others.

2. Netflix has been a direct competitor of Amazon and others in the business of providing DVDs to households all over the world. In 2007, Netflix announced it would begin streaming movies direct to personal computers,[62] a major change in its business model. By 2008, subscribers could stream movies to their television sets,[63] and Netflix announced unlimited streaming without a physical DVD rental option.[64]

   Netflix had made major capital investments to service the physical DVD rental business. In 2010, it decided to move most of its streaming operations to Amazon's Web Services cloud, ignoring their competition in physical rentals.[65] Commenting on this development, the Motley Fool site commented that, "Strange times make strange bedfellows." Editors of the site went on to say, "And so Netflix moves into the cloud. It did not *have* to be Amazon's cloud, since there are credible alternatives to the Amazon EC2 cloud-computing service from well-respected vendors like Microsoft and Rackspace Hosting. But Amazon operates its service on a scale that blows everybody else out of the water."[66] The implication was that if Netflix wanted to continue to grow the streaming business it needed services on a massive scale and Amazon could provide those in a reliable manner.

   In early 2011, Amazon announced that it would begin its own movie streaming service,[67] soon adding that it would offer a large set of movies free of charge to its prime customers.[68] That puts Netflix both in the position of being a major user of Amazon's cloud and a direct competitor to another service of Amazon. Strange bedfellows indeed!

You will notice that both these examples are channel of distribution examples; they are not complete value chain applications. Supply-side applications have been slower to "take to the cloud." That appears to be because many supply chain applications are heavily customized, and users are wary of cloud applications that they see as "one size fits all."[69] Because enterprises have to integrate hundreds, perhaps thousands, of suppliers into their supply chain, the move to cloud computing may not be as rapid as in other business, and even marketing, functions.

The case for supply chain cloud computing is well made by a U.K. expert.

"We don't compete as individual businesses any more; we compete as supply chains," says Martin Christopher, emeritus professor of marketing and logistics at the Cranfield School of Management in Cranfield, England. The winners, he says, aren't necessarily the companies that have the best products and services, but the ones that have the most efficient supply chains.

Thanks to the cloud, Christopher notes, even companies that operate on a modest technology budget can collaborate with their suppliers to make more accurate delivery forecasts, minimize excess inventory build-ups and avoid nasty last-minute surprises for their end users.[70]

As in all other aspects of Internet marketing, you can expect further developments in terms of supply chains "in the cloud." A technology with a different place in the value chain world that continues to increase the number and scope of its applications is RFID tags.

The RFID Future

Increasing the speed and reducing the cost of supply chain operation continues to be the focus of both business and technological innovation. According to the METRO Group RFID Innovation Center in Neuss-Norf, Germany:

> RFID is a key technology for the automation of business processes in retail. It enables the unique identification of items along the entire supply chain. This means that the movement of goods and accounting procedures along the supply chain can now be registered and documented automatically.[71]

RFID Tags

RFID (Radio Frequency Identification) technology is not new. It was used by the British in World War II to identify friendly aircraft. Figure 2.10 shows the basic workings of an RFID tracking system in a supply chain environment.

An RFID system begins with a **tag**, which contains a chip with a unique identifying code called an *electronic product code*. The format of the code and the number of characters it contains permit an almost infinite number of IDs. Consequently, the manufacturer can give each individual product its own identifier including all the data needed throughout the supply chain right down to the retail SKU. The tag also contains a tiny antenna. As the product moves from one place to another, a reader captures the data on the tag. The tag reader (or interrogator) captures data from as far as 20 feet away without the intervention of a human operator. The data are passed to a host computer, which can process and transmit the data into a tracking database.[72]

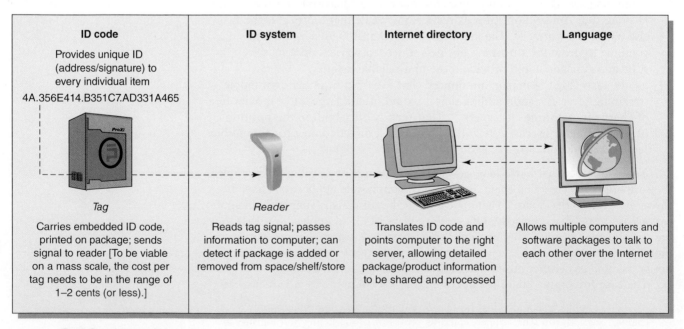

ID code	ID system	Internet directory	Language
Provides unique ID (address/signature) to every individual item			
4A.356E414.B351C7.AD331A465			
Tag	*Reader*		
Carries embedded ID code, printed on package; sends signal to reader [To be viable on a mass scale, the cost per tag needs to be in the range of 1–2 cents (or less).]	Reads tag signal; passes information to computer; can detect if package is added or removed from space/shelf/store	Translates ID code and points computer to the right server, allowing detailed package/product information to be shared and processed	Allows multiple computers and software packages to talk to each other over the Internet

FIGURE **2.10** RFID Schema for Transportation and Storage of Goods

Source: © Cengage Learning 2013

Theoretically, it is possible to attach RFID tags to each individual product in a shipment. Most applications now tag shipping pallets, not individual products. That means that shipments can be tracked while in transit or in the warehouse, and orders of pallet quantity can be identified for outbound shipment to distribution centers or stores.

Tests of RFID technology have been carried out at the store level with varying results. In 2003, a British supermarket chain tested "smart shelves" in selected stores in the United Kingdom. Chips were embedded in both shelves and products, which were able to scan inventory and alert store personnel when stock needed replenishing.[73] Tesco (and other potential users like Gillette and Walmart) tried to educate consumers about the use of the chips and the fact that the chips were deactivated (like a library book, for example) when purchased. Consumers were not convinced. They quickly labeled them "spy chips" and in some cases actually demonstrated against their use.[74]

On the other hand, Walgreens and a supplier of RFID systems have carried out a successful eight-year test using RFID to manage promotional displays in Walgreens stores. RFID tags are embedded in the promotional displays—end-aisle or rack displays, for example—and a series of readers interrogate the displays from time to time. The data are transmitted back to a data center where it is combined with product movement data from the store POS (point of sale) system to measure promotional effectiveness.[75] According to the *Supply Chain Digest*, "Walgreens is said to have ultimately found that by achieving better execution based on RFID data, sales from promotional displays from 200–400%."[76]

Why has there not been a customer uprising over Walmart's use of RFID? It is easy to hypothesize that the reason is that it elected not to embed tags in products themselves (although it does use RFID tags on larger packing units in its transportation and distribution system). Consumers had no reason to worry about the privacy issues of RFID tags going home with them and potentially tracking their movements! This represents a huge difference that marketers must take into account for the foreseeable future.[77]

There are, however, many potential applications for RFID technology that do not bring issues of customer privacy into play. Owners of expensive livestock or pets—animals like racehorses and champion dogs—have long embedded chips in their animals to deter theft. In fact, the Canadian government has a national program that sets standards for the tagging of cattle like the charmer shown in Figure 2.11 and, more recently, sheep.

FIGURE **2.11** Cow with Canadian Cattle Identification Program-Compliant RFID Tag

Source: Canadian Cattle Identification Agency, http://www.canadaid.com.

INTERACTIVE EXERCISE **2.2**   **The Future Store Initiative**

To better understand the marketing implications of RFID technology, major corporations support a developmental project in Germany called the METRO GROUP Future Store Initiative. See what the future supermarket or mass merchandiser may look like at http://bit.ly/vxPLs3.

In 2010, one industry analyst said that RFID chips were priced at as little as 5 to 7 cents per unit, bringing them within the range of many applications from tracking runners in marathon races to finding lost children in amusement parks. The article reports one of the more innovative uses in August 2010 as follows:

> A three-day summer camp in Israel brought Facebook to the real world. Using bracelets equipped with radio-frequency identification tags and programmed with their Facebook log-ins, teenagers could "Like" objects and activities by holding their arms close to readers throughout the camp.[78]

That sounds like fun, although the marketing implications may not be entirely clear at the moment. However, it is quite clear that consumers find some uses of RFID technology threatening while others do not set off privacy concerns. This must be a guiding concern going forward.

The Benefits of Business Integration

Moving from a linear supply chain to a web of interlocking partnerships that work together to lower costs and create maximum customer value is essential to success in the Internet economy. The dominant characteristics of these new organizational modes can be summarized as the "four V's" of business integration:

- *Velocity*. Customers demand better products and services and expect to receive them more quickly and with complete accuracy. They expect a seamless, satisfactory experience.
- *Visibility*. Transparency of information between customers and all value chain members creates a self-service model that speeds flows and improves customer satisfaction.
- *Variability*. Customers want products manufactured and delivered according to their individual requirements. This is true of B2B customers who order customized products and/or order in large volumes. It is increasingly true of consumers who expect everything from media on demand to customized products, both of which will be discussed in succeeding chapters.
- *Volume*. Achieving profitable scale and scope in an environment that requires marketing to individual customers is essential. This requires systems that are scalable—that is, systems that can grow as the business grows without the large disruptions inherent in replacing old systems with new ones.[79]

Technology is essential to achieve the benefits of organizational integration, but technology alone does not present a solution. Achieving the desired outcomes requires relentless focus on the needs of the customer, achieving internal efficiencies of time and cost and managing across organizational boundaries to achieve maximum impact.

The supply chain of the past cannot meet the requirements of the Internet economy. Neither can a "one size fits all" product that is pushed through channels using conventional marketing promotional and pricing techniques. In some cases, such as configuring internal and external networks, the final product is inherently a custom proposition. In others, such as office furniture systems, prospering in a competitive marketplace requires using a set of products to meet customer needs in an individualized manner. Marketers are required to achieve these outcomes in a changing business environment that has recently increased emphasis on a green supply chain.

SUMMARY

The traditional linear supply chain has evolved into a virtual value chain made up of interconnected relationships. Each member contributes its core capability, and the final product is delivered to the customer as a single strong and recognizable brand, one that has a strong value proposition. This represents a revolution in business organization and management that few enterprises have yet fully achieved. As examples throughout this chapter have emphasized, it is an achievement that can be years in the making.

Enterprises will often begin by creating information systems that allow them to visualize all aspects of the value chain, first as a snapshot in time and then in real time. They can then progress to the creation of information systems that fully mirror the activities of the value chain. This information will first be of use to management in controlling, forecasting, and planning. It will generate additional value if it is shared with customers. That will be the first step in delivering value to customers in ways that are faster and more convenient. It can be followed by the creation of entirely new kinds of customer value. One way of looking at the process is through the lens of service-centered dominant logic—the marketing concept that says all products deliver services and the job of the enterprise is to create value propositions.

None of this is easy. It is likely to require reengineering of existing business processes and major projects to integrate internal systems and to communicate across organizational boundaries with both suppliers and customers. Existing technologies like EDI and ERP will be part of this process. Web Services offer the potential for achieving the benefits of value chains without time-consuming and costly integration projects. The applications that are needed in supply chains and channels of distribution can potentially be delivered "in the cloud," making their implementation even faster and smoother and offering services on a fee-for-usage basis.

RFID technology is being used in a variety of ways to increase visibility in supply chains. On the customer-facing side, RFID tags give rise to concern over violations of individual privacy that has retarded their adoption in some retail environments. When the privacy concerns can be overcome, or where they do not exist, RFID tags can significantly increase the efficiency of operations.

The activities required to create value chains and then virtualize them are many and often complex. They require changes on both the supplier-facing and the customer-facing sides of the business. Some firms that are far advanced in making their supply chains more efficient have found it necessary to turn to activities that will improve product and customer service quality and provide satisfactory customer experience. This increases the competitive requirements on all firms.

DISCUSSION QUESTIONS

1. Differentiate between three key concepts: supply chain, value chain, and integrated value chain.
2. Marketing has three core processes: one of which is supply facing, one of which is essentially internal, and one of which is customer facing. Do you agree with this statement? Be prepared to explain why or why not.
3. What are the business outcomes that are the result of a successful supply chain?

4. Do you agree with the concept that all goods are essentially services? Why or why not?
5. What are the business practices used by Zara that have made it responsive to customer needs and successful financially?
6. What stages is an enterprise likely to go through en route to a virtual value chain?
7. Discuss integrative elements Dell has employed on (a) the supply side and (b) the customer side.
8. How does the combined use of EDI and ERP facilitate the development of an integrated value chain?
9. What potential advantages does Web Services have to offer over EDI and ERP?
10. What is meant by Web Services? Cloud computing?
11. What is RFID technology? In what ways can it improve supply chain functioning?
12. What are the four benefits of business integration?

INTERNET EXERCISES

1. Select an industry (e.g., automotive) or a specific company (e.g., Ford) or even better a specific product model (e.g., Ford Focus) and identify elements of its value chain. Where can information be used to decrease costs or increase customer satisfaction or both?
2. Think about how you bought the text and other material for this class. It might have been through the college bookstore, a local supplier, over the Internet, or some combination of all three. Identify the elements of the value chain that were necessary to get these products to you, the final customer.
3. Spend some time on the website of your school, college, or department. How does that organizational unit use its website to help students visualize institutional processes, mirror activities carried on in the physical world, and increase the strength of relationships with students and potential students? What more could it do in each of these areas?
4. Locate a news article on a marketing application of RFID technology different from those described in the chapter. Discuss the application in class, being specific about how it is improving a supply chain or other marketing process.
5. Locate a nontechnical article about Web Services in general or cloud computing in particular and discuss the implications of this way of delivering technology.

NOTES

1. Lisa H. Harrington, "A Tale of Two Planners," April 3, 2000, http://www.industryweek.com, pp. 3–4.
2. David Rocks, "Reinventing Herman Miller," Business Week e.biz, April 3, 2000, p. 90.
3. http://store.hermanmiller.com/Home.
4. http://www.jda.com/file_bin/casestudies/HermanMiller_casestudy_112310.pdf.
5. http://www.usgbc.org/DisplayPage.aspx?CMSPageID=222.
6. http://www.epa.gov/dfe.
7. http://www.hermanmiller.com/About-Us/Environmental-Advocacy/Our-Vision-and-Policy.
8. http://www.lean.org/admin/km/documents/07EADBDF-A03A-4B27-AAEC-03C614B610B0-LEI%20Herman%20Miller%20Success%20Story2_final%20%284%29.pdf.
9. http://www.hbrgreen.org/2008/02/you_are_only_as_green_as_your.html.
10. http://www.otis.com/site/us/Pages/REMElevatorMonitoring.aspx?menuID=4.
11. Rajendra K. Srivastava, Tasadduq A. Shervani, and Liam Fahey, "Marketing, Business Processes, and Shareholder Value: An Organizationally Embedded View of Marketing Activities and the Discipline of Marketing," *Journal of Marketing*, 1999, pp. 168–179.
12. Steven A. Melnyk, Edward W. Davis, Robert E. Spekman, and Joseph Sandor, "Outcome-Driven Supply Chains," *Sloan Management Review*, Winter 2010, Vol. 51, No. 2, pp. 33–39.
13. Steve New, "The Transparent Supply Chain," *Harvard Business Review*, October 2010, pp. 1–6.
14. http://www.scribd.com/doc/38810400/Transparent-Supply-Chain.
15. Scott Stephens, "Supply Chain Council & Supply Chain Operations Reference (SCOR) Model Overview," PowerPoint presentation, May 2000, http://www.supply-chain.org.
16. http://www.inditex.es/en/who_we_are/concepts/zara.
17. http://www.thisislondon.co.uk/standard-business/article-23880826-zara-taps-into-fashion-for-internet-shopping.do.
18. http://www.businessweek.com/globalbiz/content/apr2006/gb20060404_167078.htm.
19. http://www.docstoc.com/docs/8390917/Zara-Clothing.
20. Susan Reda, "Retail's Great Race Getting Fashion to the Finish Line," *Stores*, March 2004, http://www.stores.org. Other sources for this section: Robert D'Avanzo, "The Reward of Supply-Chain Excellence," December 2003, http://www.optimizemag.com; and Eric Wahlgren, "Fast, Fashionable—and Profitable," *Business Week*, March 10, 2005, http://www.businessweek.com.
21. See the video at http://www.supplychainer.com/50226711/supply_chain_video_the_way_zara_operates_its_supply_chain.php and a shorter one at http://www.youtube.com/watch?v=zUkCuzQjOio&feature=related.

22. http://www.bain.com/bainweb/PDFs/cms/Public/BB_Jenga_phenomenon.pdf.

23. "Living in Dell Time," November 2004, p. 86, http://www.fastcompany.com.

24. http://www.buzzmachine.com/2005/08/17/dear-mr-dell.

25. http://www.buzzmachine.com/archives/cat_dell.html.

26. http://gizmodo.com/#!182257/dell-laptop-explodes-in-flames.

27. http://www.youtube.com/watch?v=w4ooKojHMkA.

28. http://www.wired.com/wired/archive/10.07/dell.html.

29. http://en.community.dell.com/dell-blogs/dell-shares/b/dell-shares/archive/2010/03/11/client-reinvention-building-the-most-flexible-and-effective-value-chain.aspx.

30. http://retail.about.com/od/planograms/a/planogramming.htm.

31. http://logisticsviewpoints.com/2010/04/20/frito-lay-drives-shelf-level-demand.

32. http://www.environmentalleader.com/2008/10/08/frito-lay-sustainability-efforts-save-55-million-on-water-energy.

33. http://www.npr.org/blogs/thetwo-way/2010/10/06/130382547/noise-from-consumers-prompts-sunchips-to-go-back-to-traditional-packaging.

34. http://www.securitydirectornews.com/?p=article&id=sd2010O6ttvg.

35. http://www.fedex.com/us/web-services/index.html.

36. http://americanprinter.com/digital-presses/news/fedex-office-launches-mobile-0120.

37. http://fedex.com/us/promo/sustainability/environment.html.

38. John H. Dobbs, "Competition's New Battleground: The Integrated Value Chain," Cambridge Technology Partners, nd, http://www.ctp.com, p. 5.

39. David Bovet and Joseph Martha, *Value Nets: Breaking the Supply Chain to Unlock Hidden Profits*, New York: John Wiley & Sons, 2000, p. 171.

40. Stephen L. Vargo and Robert F. Lusch. "Evolving Toward a New Dominant Logic for Marketing," *Journal of Marketing*, Vol. 68 (January 2004), p. 2.

41. Stephen L. Vargo and Robert F. Lusch. "Evolving Toward a New Dominant Logic for Marketing," *Journal of Marketing*, Vol. 68 (January 2004), 1–17; and Robert F. Lusch and Stephen L. Vargo. "Service-Dominant Logic, Reactions, Reflections, and Refinements," *Journal of Marketing Theory*, Volume 6(3): 281–288(2006), 282–288.

42. "Overview of EDI," Covalent Networks, nd, http://www.covalentworks.com/overview-of-edi.asp.

43. http://walmartstores.com/Diversity/247.aspx.

44. http://walmartstores.com/Sustainability.

45. http://www.8thandwalton.com.

46. http://www.newsindia-times.com/newsindiatimes/20101116/5192247699132368238.htm.

47. http://walmartstores.com/Suppliers/10337.aspx.

48. Hanna Hurley, "EDI Takes to the Internet," *Network*, October 1, 1998, http://www.cma.zdnet.com; "EDI Legacy Systems: Make the Old Work With the New," June 11, 2003, http://www.techrepublic.com; and "Overview of EDI," "How EDI Works," Covalent Networks, nd, http://www.covalentworks.com.

49. http://www.cio.com/article/143451/How_Wal_Mart_Lost_Its_Technology_Edge?page=1&taxonomyId=3066.

50. http://www.cio.com/article/40323/ERP_Definition_and_Solutions.

51. Christopher Koch, "The ABCs of ERP," ERP Resource Center, *CIO Magazine*, http://www.CIO.com; and http://www.cio.com/article/40323/ERP_Definition_and_Solutions?page=2&taxonomyId=3009.

52. Thomas Wailgum, "Big Mess on Campus," *CIO Magazine*, May 1, 2005, http://www.CIO.com.

53. Ibid.

54. Christopher Koch, "The ABCs of ERP," ERP Resource Center, *CIO Magazine*, http://www.CIO.com; and http://www.cio.com/article/40323/ERP_Definition_and_Solutions?page=3&taxonomyId=3009.

55. http://www.webopedia.com/DidYouKnow/Computer_Science/2005/web_services.asp.

56. http://www.infoworld.com/d/cloud-computing/what-cloud-computing-really-means-031?page=0,0.

57. http://blogs.gartner.com/daryl_plummer/2009/01/27/experts-define-cloud-computing-can-we-get-a-little-definition-in-our-definitions.

58. http://www.youtube.com/watch?v=-HRrbLA7rss.

59. http://www.information-age.com/channels/data-centre-and-it-infrastructure/news/1147048/european-union-defines-cloud-computing.thtml.

60. http://www.cio.com/article/662605/Cloud_Onomics_101?page=1&taxonomyId=3000.

61. http://aws.amazon.com/ecommerce-applications.

62. http://www.nytimes.com/2007/01/16/technology/16netflix.html.

63. http://gizmodo.com/#!389698/first-netflix-streaming-box-review-100-and-unlimited-downloads.

64. http://www.informationweek.com/news/internet/ebusiness/showArticle.jhtml?articleID=205604459.

65. http://www.nytimes.com/2010/04/19/technology/19cloud.html.

66. http://www.fool.com/investing/general/2010/04/21/netflix-gets-on-amazons-cloud.aspx.

67. http://latimesblogs.latimes.com/entertainmentnewsbuzz/2011/01/amazon-netflix-hulu-streaming.html.

68. http://www.pcmag.com/article2/0,2817,2380711,00.asp.

69. http://blogs.apics.org/intl/2011/02/06/cloud-based-supply-chain-systems.

70. http://knowledge.wharton.upenn.edu/arabic/article.cfm?articleid=2610.

71. http://www.future-store.org/fsi-internet/get/documents/FSI/multimedia/pdfs/broschueren/WISSB_Publikationen_Broschueren_RFID-Innovation-Center_E.pdf, p. 6.

72. RFID, nd, http://www.techweb.com/encyclopedia/defineterm.jhtml?term=RFID; RFID, nd; and http://en.wikipedia.org/wiki/RFID.

73. http://news.cnet.com/2100-1017-979710.html.

74. http://www.boycotttesco.com/spychips.html.

75. http://www.rfidjournal.com/article/articleview/2031/1/1.

76. http://www.scdigest.com/assets/On_Target/09-03-10-2.php.

77. http://www.rfidjournal.com/blog/entry/7835.

78. http://articles.sfgate.com/2010-09-06/business/23990796_1_alien-technology-rfid-technology-rfid-tags.

79. Kevin P. O'Brien, "Value-Chain Report," April 3, 2000, http://www.industryweek.com.

CHAPTER 3

Business Models and Strategies

Chapter Outline

Understanding Business Models

eToys: Failing to Control Costs and Create Value
Functions and Elements of Business Models

The Value Proposition

Identifying Business Models

The Evolving Business Models of Restaurant.com
Brokerage Model: Bringing Buyers and Sellers
  Together
Advertising Model: Delivering Messages with
  Content
Infomediary Model: Reselling Useful Data
Merchant Model: Providing Goods and Services
Manufacturer (Direct) Model: Reaching Buyers
  Directly

Affiliate Model: Offering Incentives to Partner Sites
Community Model: Connecting Individuals and
  Groups
Subscription Model: Delivering Services and Content
  for a Set Fee
Utility Model: Delivering Services or Content
  "Pay as You Go"

The Future of Business Models

SUMMARY
DISCUSSION QUESTIONS
INTERNET EXERCISES
NOTES

Key Terms

LEARNING OBJECTIVES

By the time you complete this chapter, you will be able to:

- Explain the concept and functions of a business model.
- Discuss the concept of the value proposition and its importance in developing marketing strategies.
- Name and describe the business models that are most prominent on the Internet.
- Give examples of each of the business models.

Our examination of value chains made it clear that organizations that existed prior to the advent of the Internet (traditional brick and mortar firms) can and have been taking advantage of the opportunities the Internet presents just as pure-play Internet firms can. They may, however, do so in different ways. A set of business models is emerging, most of which meld the best of both the Internet and physical worlds.

Understanding Business Models

A Google search for the term "business model" returns over *130 million hits*. The discussion of business models was at its height during the Internet bubble when start-up companies were largely funded on venture capital and an idea. Many of these firms did not survive as they had no viable way to make money or to provide revenue. Still, there is no commonly accepted definition of the term "business model." Professor Michael Rappa's definition is one of the most often quoted: a "business model is the method of doing business by which a company can sustain itself—that is, generate revenue. The business model spells out how a company makes money by specifying where it is positioned in the value chain."[1]

A more detailed definition is set forth by Professors Ethriraj, Guler, and Singh. They define a "business model" as "a unique configuration of elements comprising the organization's goals, strategies, processes, technologies, and structure, conceived to create value for the customers and thus compete successfully in a particular market." The professors go on to say that a business model describes the core value proposition, sources and methods of revenue generation, the costs involved in generating the revenue, and the plan and trajectory of growth.[2]

In other words, a **business model** is how a company *makes money* or a not-for-profit organization *achieves its revenue objectives, how an entity sustains itself.* Before starting any business, Internet or otherwise, it is advisable to think how the revenue will be realized and processed. Sites of all kinds, whether it is their major objective or not, are mainly earning revenue from *transactions.* Websites may be selling products ranging from clothing to computers or services that vary from employment listings to credit cards. Sites may be selling their own products or services; they may be affiliates of large sites like Amazon, or operate from a larger site like eBay. Sites may also be community-based or ask for donations to survive, like Wikipedia. However, they are all processing revenue from transactions.

Ecommerce describes the most common type of revenue production on the Internet and refers to an economic exchange in which a purchaser pays the seller for the goods or services. Ecommerce is ubiquitous in B2C (business-to-consumer), B2B (business-to-business), governmental, and nonprofit markets. The Internet also provides an opportunity for firms to charge for services that complement their primary offering in terms of *value-added services revenue*. For example, a B2B auction site may offer credit verification services to support transactions that take place on its site.

eToys: Failing to Control Costs and Create Value

While it is true that how revenue is obtained on the web is important, it is a great mistake to ignore the cost side of the business equation. An example of an Internet company that did not know how to produce revenue or control costs is Pets.com, as illustrated in Chapter 1, which opened up in 1999 and closed in November of 2000. Another prime example of a company that failed to control costs versus revenue is that of eToys.com, a retail website that sells toys via the Internet. It was launched in 1997, went public in 1999 and went through Chapter 11 bankruptcy and closed its U.S. site in March 2001.

The eToys site was expensive to get going and at the time the company went public, it had only $30 million in revenue but was worth $7.7 billion on paper![3] In spite of its "first mover" advantage and being the first toy retailer on the Internet, the company miscalculated the costs of running a retail business. It also suffered greatly after Toys "R" Us teamed up with Amazon.com.[4] After another failed attempt to operate on its own, the website was eventually acquired by Toys "R" Us in February 2009.

Many of these early Internet businesses actually had a viable way to make money but were unable to control costs and articulate a clear value proposition at the time. Another early company that could not control costs is Webvan, an Internet grocery delivery service, which has also been resuscitated as part of Amazon.com. Webvan was highlighted by CNET as the number one .com flop of all time, along with eToys.com (number five) and Pets.com (number two).[5] CNET wisely says, "A core lesson from the dot-com boom is that even if you have a good idea, it's best not to grow too fast too soon."

Functions and Elements of Business Models

Professors Henry Chesbrough and Richard Rosenbloom explain that the functions of a business model are to:

- Articulate the value proposition, that is, the value created for users by the offering based on the technology.
- Identify a market segment, that is, the users to whom the technology is useful and for what purpose.
- Define the structure of the value chain within the firm required to create and distribute the offering.
- Estimate the cost structure and profit potential of producing the offering, given the value proposition and the value chain structure chosen.
- Describe the position of the firm with the value network linking suppliers and customers, including identification of potential partners and competitors.
- Formulate the competitive strategy by which the innovating firm will gain and hold competitive advantage over rivals.[6]

Similarly, consultant and author Alex Osterwalder suggests that business models are an evolving process that should be tested. He suggests that there are nine key elements of preparing a business model:[7]

1. Who are your customer segments?
2. What is your value proposition?
3. What is the customer relationship?
4. What are your revenue streams, how much do they generate?
5. What are your key resources?
6. What are your key activities
7. Who are your key partners?
8. What is your cost structure?
9. What are your distribution channels?

It is important to note that a *business model and a business plan are two distinctly different entities*. A business model is a conceptual description that may have been given a name like "advertising." A business plan is a detailed document that is prepared for strategic guidance and to aid in the acquisition of resources, either internal or external. There is some similarity of content between the two, but they are not synonymous. Recognizing this issue, Chesbrough and Rosenbloom go on to specify the differences between a business model and a strategy:

- A business model focuses on creating value for the customer and delivering that value to the customer to a clearly defined market segment.
- It focuses on creating business value that can be translated into value for the shareholder.
- It requires that managers use technical inputs to create economic results in a context of technological and market uncertainty.

Chesbrough and Rosenbloom's final point puts the business model concept firmly in the arena of business innovation including Internet-based businesses. It also reinforces the focus on value creation by the firm as a key element of an Internet business model. Using this explanation of the function of a business model, we can see that Pets.com (see Chapter 1) had not articulated a clear value proposition of why customers should purchase pet supplies online, failing to create a better alternative to what they already had. The company had also not defined a clear target market ready for its services and did not fully understand the cost/revenue structure to profitably run such a business or the value chain for distribution. A bad business model can often mean just bad business. And if you do not have a product people want at a price people are willing to pay, no business model in the world will save your business.

The Value Proposition

This discussion leads us squarely to another term that is used frequently but not defined with any degree of precision. In this case, it seems to be because marketers follow the definition of "economic value," which is essentially the value of ownership and use, minus the cost of the item. The term **value proposition** has come to mean the value delivered by the firm to a specific, targeted customer segment. From that rather simple beginning, marketers can study the drivers of value in a particular market. Professors Osterwalder and Pigneur have a simple framework that is useful in that process (see Figure 3.1). It combines consideration of the needs of the target customer, which define the nature of the value desired, with an understanding of the core capabilities of the enterprise, which determines the value that can be delivered.[8] Data can be obtained and used to understand both target customer and organizational capabilities, making developing a value proposition an information-driven marketing activity.

It is also important to remember that the value that the enterprise is able to deliver is dependent on its own core capabilities. Having developed a value

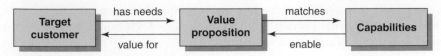

FIGURE **3.1** The Value Proposition

Source: Adapted from Alexander Osterwalder and Yves Pigneur, "An e-Business Model Ontology for Modeling e-Business," 15th Bled Electronic Commerce Conference, Bled, Slovenia, July 17–19, 2002.

proposition, the firm must then understand how it can obtain revenue from the proposition to "monetize" the offering in Internet terms. Pets.com lacked the competencies to operate profitably in the Internet space, having a poor understanding of the economics and processes of running what was essentially a direct marketing company. Pandora, which delivers Internet radio services, went public in June of 2011 but is yet to figure out how to monetize its offering. Most of Pandora's subscribers take the free version and the company has yet to make a profit; the company lost 1.8 million in its latest fiscal year ending January of 2011. The story of Restaurant.com (see the following section) illustrates how a company needs to change to create a business model that creates value for customers.

Identifying Business Models

Now that we understand the basics of business models, it is time to look at Internet business models. Here again, we face the problem that there is no commonly accepted set of models. Worse, various authors have given different names to the same model. Table 3.1 gives an overview of the nine models suggested by

TABLE 3.1 Business Models*

Business Model	Quick Description	B2C Examples	B2B Examples	Nonprofit/ Government Examples
Brokerage Model	Bringing buyers and sellers together	Orbitz, eBay, Priceline, Restaurant.com	Alibaba, ChemConnect, eBay, Bizydeal	
Advertising Model	Delivering messages with content	Google, Facebook	LinkedIn	
Infomediary Model	Reselling useful data	*Wall Street Journal*	InfoUSA	Cancer.gov, Upromise.com
Merchant Model	Providing goods and services	Amazon.com, Barnes & Noble	Grainger Industrial Supplies	Redcross.org
Manufacturer (Direct) Model	Reaching buyers directly	Dell Computer	Dell Computer, Salesforce	
Affiliate Model	Offering incentives to partner sites	Amazon.com	Restaurant.com	Kommen.org
Community Model	Connecting individuals and groups	Threadless, Etsy	CrowdSPRING, Linux.org	Wikipedia.org, Craigslist.org
Subscription Model	Delivering services and content for a set fee	Netflix, Angieslist	Salesforce, LinkedIn (higher levels of membership)	WCPE.org
Utility Model	Delivering services or content "pay as you go"	Skype, Google Voice, Audible	Slashdot.org	

*Many thanks to Professor Rappa for allowing us to use his basic structure of nine business models and some of his examples.

Source: Professor Michael Rappa, updated by Roberts and Zahay.

Professor Michael Rappa. The table gives examples of each in B2C, B2B, and nonprofit/government sectors. We will spend more time and give more detail on the more common business models but cover all nine business models: brokerage, advertising, infomediary, merchant, manufacturer, affiliate, community, subscription, and utility.

The Evolving Business Models of Restaurant.com

Business models are constantly evolving as companies react to changes in the environment. Restaurant.com (RDC) is an example of a company that used several different business models before it found success with the main model that it has now. The company is also a good example of using multiple business models in one firm. The company started in 1999 following a *manufacturer* business model, trying to sell websites to restaurants for $1,200 a year. Sales people hit the streets, but restaurants were not ready for this concept, which had not been field tested. Nine months after start-up, the company's initial business model was a resounding failure.

CEO and President Cary Chessick, who had left a successful law career to pursue his Internet dreams, along with his board and executive team, sought to develop a profitable business model. The company did not have to go into bankruptcy but had little money, no business model, and only a domain name. For several years, the company survived selling restaurant gift certificates on eBay. The Restaurant.com domain name was a redirect to eBay. However, as eBay's environment evolved to be less friendly to these types of arrangements, Restaurant.com shut down the eBay auction business and started all over again.

The company moved to its current B2C *brokerage* business model, bringing together restaurants with empty tables and future customers, selling $25 gift certificates for $10 online to drive traffic to restaurants and help fill seats. The restaurants pay nothing for the company's innovative marketing program, which includes a custom Restaurant.com website, free online reservations, and customer feedback. The company makes its money selling the certificates.

On the B2B side, the company relies on the *affiliate* model, using affiliates to drive traffic to its site and providing incentives to do so. For example, Threadless.com might offer a gift certificate to incent someone to purchase a t-shirt. Restaurant.com opened another branch of the company operating under the *community* business model, which allows nonprofit organizations to do fund-raising for their organizations. Restaurant.com also started its Incentive and Loyalty Solutions division for companies to reward and retain clients, customers, and employees.

Today, the company has several million unique visitors per month and thousands of restaurant partners nationwide. In addition, Restaurant.com pioneered a "Feed It Forward" program that allows consumers to give free gift certificates to family, friends, coworkers, community, and charities during the holiday season. The company's customers rallied in support and gave away more than $30 million in certificates the first three years.

Brokerage Model: Bringing Buyers and Sellers Together

Brokers make markets: the function of a broker is to bring buyers and sellers together and facilitate transactions. Brokers play a frequent role in B2B, B2C, or C2C (consumer-to-consumer) markets. Usually, a broker charges a fee or commission for each transaction it enables, but not always. The formula for fees can vary.

Subcategories of the **Brokerage Model** include

- *Marketplace exchanges* (Orbitz, Alibaba) operate independently or through a consortium and cover the entire transaction. Marketplaces have been part of the human experience for thousands of years. Given the pervasiveness and longevity of the physical business model, it is perhaps not surprising that the emarketplace has become an important business model on the web in both B2C and B2B spaces.

- *Demand collection systems* (Priceline) refer to the patented "name-your-price" model pioneered by Priceline.com. Prospective buyer makes a final (binding) bid for a specified good or service, and the broker arranges fulfillment.
- *Auction brokers* (eBay) conduct auctions for sellers (individuals or merchants). The broker charges the seller a listing fee and commission, on a scale with the value of the transaction. Auctions vary widely in terms of the offering and bidding rules. The traditional auction, in which many buyers compete for the product of a single seller, is commonly seen in the physical world for products as diverse as fine art to agricultural commodities. The reverse auction, in which many sellers compete for the business of one buyer, is an important facet of B2B activities on the Internet.
- *Transaction brokers* (PayPal) provide a third-party payment mechanism for buyers and sellers to settle a transaction.
- *Virtual marketplaces* (Merchant Services at Amazon.com) provide a virtual mall—a hosting service for online merchants that charges setup, monthly listing, and/or transaction fees. It may also provide automated transaction and relationship marketing services.
- *Coupon promotion sites* (Restaurant.com, Groupon, Bizydeal) offer a "daily deal" such as Groupon, LivingSocial, or, most recently, Bizydeal in the B2B arena; these sites are noted for bringing buyers and sellers together for a one-time transaction. Sellers hope to convert newly acquired customers to long-term customers this way. Restaurant.com offers a slightly different model whereby the company makes its money through the sale of discount coupons, which the participating restaurants honor to fill tables and create future repeat customers. Some of these sites also follow a group buying format.

eBay: Bringing Buyers and Sellers Together Worldwide

One of the most famous examples of the brokerage model is certainly eBay. Referred to as the "The World's Online Marketplace," this site has been used by more than 223 million people worldwide. The company has more than 94 million active users globally, and there are millions of items listed for sale at any given time. eBay connects not only individual buyers and sellers but small businesses, and over $2,000 in transactions take place every second. In 2010, the impact of eBay was $62 billion worth of goods sold.[9]

How and why has eBay evolved from a tiny site, which Pierre Omidyar, the company's founder, started as a hobby to solve the technical problem of direct person-to-person online auctions, to a force in the global economy?[10] On the emotional side, eBay seems to speak to a human need to meet and trade items of interest. On the practical side, it provides a place for many small businesses to offer their wares. In order to do that, eBay has been required to build an extensive infrastructure, not only of technology, but also of services.

When eBay was founded, it offered only the auction model of transactions. The company learned that some buyers did not want to participate in auctions and began to offer a "Buy It Now!" option. It also realized that customers were actually selling used cars on eBay by listing them in the Toy Cars section. Subsequently, eBay Motors was launched, which now accounts for a substantial amount of the dollar volume of sales on the site. Among its other skills, eBay has become a master at listening to its customers and reacting quickly to their wants and needs. eBay has grown through acquisitions such as PayPal and Skype (eBay still holds an interest in that company even though it has divested itself of the acqustion) and partnerships in China, Latin America, and Taiwan. However, overall company growth has slowed and the basic business model and business plans need to be reexamined to ensure future prosperity. For example, two-thirds of the company's sales over the 2010 holiday period were conducted over mobile device. The company over the last few years has developed a strong partnership with ChannelAdvisor to help its members create a complete ecommerce solution and improve the checkout process.[11]

B2B Marketplaces

B2B marketplaces are a subset of the brokerage model and provide their own challenges. Since the B2B buying process tends to be somewhat long and often complex, and since the process of locating suppliers can be onerous and expensive, marketplaces quickly took hold in the B2B space. The marketplace is able to reduce information search costs for buyers by maintaining a selected set of potential vendors that have been prequalified for expertise and reliability. It is able to provide sales leads for sellers because it has a set of member firms, usually in a vertical market, that need particular kinds of goods and services.

Three different kinds of B2B marketplaces exist:

- Public marketplaces serve any qualified purchaser or supplier.
- Private exchanges serve only a single firm.
- Industry exchanges, often called consortia, serve several competitor firms a particular industry. There are many of these exchange serving various industries, for example, Exostar or ChemConnect in the airline and chemical industry, respectively.

Most B2B marketplaces offer the opportunity for participating sellers to post their online catalogs for simple ecommerce transactions. The primary transaction mechanism, however, is the reverse auction.[12] In the early days, B2B marketplace sites loudly trumpeted huge savings realized by purchasers on their sites. Buyers' savings, however, translated into decreases in margin on the part of sellers. Marketplaces tried to compensate by trying to get most of their own revenue from buyers in the form of commissions on purchases, membership fees, and value-added services. However, it appears that the pressure on sellers created an unsustainable situation because most of the sites of the Internet bubble days have quietly gone out of business or have been acquired by and their technology integrated into other sites. There are new sites such as Alibaba.com that take advantage of the globalization of industry and brings buyers and sellers together across distances, facilitating trade with China, Indian, Malaysia, and other up-and-coming world trade countries. B2B marketplaces may be reinventing themselves and offer opportunities for growth and profitability across the globe.

An exception to the slower growth of marketplace sites has been in egovernment, which has the purchasing power and perhaps an appeal to corporate citizenship, that makes reverse auctions a continuing presence in that marketspace. The government of Australia has an online and reverse auctions resource center that gives links to government auction and reverse auction in the United States and United Kingdom. The British government has a site that provides information and services for government agencies that want to set up eauctions. This trend suggests that one of the key motivators for egovernment around the world is access to low-cost procurement, using the reverse auction as one key component.

Advertising Model: Delivering Messages with Content

The web **Advertising Model** is an extension of the traditional media broadcast model. Content on a website or in an email can be sponsored, providing another type of advertising opportunity. In the typical model, the broadcaster—in this case, a website—provides content (usually, but not necessarily, for free) and services (i.e., email, Instant Messaging, blogs) mixed with advertising messages in the form of banner ads. The banner ads may be the major or sole source of revenue for the broadcaster. The broadcaster may be a content creator or a distributor of content created elsewhere.

TABLE 3.2	Top Five Advertising Sites' Market Share			
	2009 (%)	**2010 (%)**	**2011 (%)**	**2012 (%)**
Google	34.9	38.5	40.8	44.9
Yahoo!	16.1	13.3	11.0	9.7
Facebook	2.4	4.6	7.0	7.8
Microsoft	5.2	5.7	6.1	7.2
AOL	4.4	3.4	2.7	2.3
Total top five	63.0	65.6	67.7	72.0
Total Internet (in billions)	$22.66	$26.04	$31.30	$36.80

Note: Net ad revenues after companies pay traffic acquisition costs to partner sites.

Source: eMarketer, Inc., Net U.S. Online Ad Revenues at Top 5 Ad-Selling Companies as Percent of Total Online Ad Revenues, 2009–2012.

The advertising model works best when the volume of viewer traffic is large or highly specialized. In Chapter 1, we discussed the explosive growth of advertising on the Internet. Nevertheless, few sites can sustain themselves on advertising revenue alone. As a general rule, the more the reach, the more likely the website is to be sustainable as an advertising business model for a particular company. Almost from the beginning, those models supported by advertising are also large information portal sites, such as Google, Yahoo!, AOL, Microsoft, and now Facebook.

Not surprisingly, these top five advertising sites are predicted to capture 72 percent of all advertising revenue by 2012, with Google taking the lion's share of the market at 44.9 percent (see Table 3.2). Most of Google's advertising revenue growth is attributed to the growth of its search advertising. Needless to say, it is quite difficult to compete in terms of the advertising business model facing such strong competition from existing portals and intense industry consolidation.

Advertising content can be targeted contextually and also target ads based on customer demographics. Some portals, such as AOL, offer network connectivity and related services on a monthly subscription. These firms are also making money with the *subscription model* by offering access to the Internet, either through a dial-up connection or, most frequently, through a broadband connection.

In May 2011, comScore reported that Google Ad Network led the May AdFocus ranking with a reach of 92.3 percent of Americans online, followed by Yahoo! Sites with an 87.3 percent reach. AOL Advertising captured the number three spot with 85.3 percent reach. The effect of community sites on advertising reach can be seen through the rise of Facebook in advertising reach and revenue (see Table 3.3). FT Analysis, based in London, forecasts that Facebook's advertising revenues will rise 95 percent from $1.8 billion to $3.5 billion in 2011, a rise of 95 percent. At the same time, Google's display ad business, including YouTube and DoubleClick (its ad-serving and campaign management network), is expected to rise from $2 to $2.6 billion.[13]

Some categories of the advertising model are:

- *Portal* (Yahoo!, AOL) includes a search engine and varied content or services. A high volume of user traffic makes advertising profitable and permits further diversification of site services. A personalized portal allows customization of the interface and content to the user. A niche portal cultivates a well-defined user demographic. Some portals also charge a monthly subscription fee and operate simultaneously under the subscription model.
- *Classifieds* (Monster.com, Craigslist) list items for sale or wanted for purchase. Listing fees are common, but there also may be a membership fee.

TABLE 3.3   comScore AdFocus Ranking (United States)

Rank	Property	Unique Visitors (000)	% Reach
	Total Internet: Total Audience	*216,250*	*100.0*
1	Google Ad Network**	199,648	92.3
2	Yahoo! Sites	188,763	87.3
3	AOL Advertising**	184,357	85.3
4	Yahoo! Network Plus**	184,094	85.1
5	ShareThis	177,213	81.9
6	Turn Media Platform**	176,023	81.4
7	Google	173,982	80.5
8	ValueClick Networks**	171,704	79.4
9	Specific Media (unified)**	170,883	79.0
10	24/7 Real Media Global Web Alliance**	167,019	77.2
11	AdBrite**	159,762	73.9
12	Facebook.ccm	157,219	72.7
13	Collective Display**	156,224	72.2
14	Tribal Fusion**	152,690	70.6
15	Vibrant Media**	145,303	67.2
16	Burst Media**	144,144	66.7
17	AudienceScience**	142,975	66.1
18	Microsoft Media Network US**	142,159	65.7
19	FOX Audience Network**	140,188	64.8
20	Traffic Marketplace**	139,861	64.7

*Entity has assigned some portion of traffic to other syndicated entities.
**Denotes an advertising network.

Notes: % Reach denotes the percentage of the total Internet population who viewed a particular entity at least once in May. For instance, Yahoo! Sites was seen by 87.3 percent of the 216 million Internet users in May.

Source: comScore, http://ir.comscore.com/releasedetail.cfm?ReleaseID=600220.

- *Query-based paid placement* (Google, Overture) sells favorable link positioning (i.e., sponsored links) or advertising keyed to particular search terms in a user query, such as Overture's trademark "pay-for-performance" model.

We now take a closer look at web-based portals with a focus on Yahoo! and how that company's model has evolved, along with that of other web portals.

Yahoo!: The Evolution of Web Portals

The definition of "a portal" is straightforward: a portal is a gateway, often an imposing one. On the Internet, the term has come to mean a site that serves as an entrance ramp onto the Internet through a search engine and links to content. There are many sites that describe themselves as portals. Some serve particular interests, like health or sports information. Others serve vertical business markets as was suggested earlier in the chapter. Still others serve particular technologies, for example, portals that give access to wireless services and content.

Yahoo! was the brainchild of two graduate students working out of a trailer at Stanford University. Soon the directory outgrew the capacity of the university network. The name Yahoo! stands for "Yet Another Hierarchical Officious

Oracle," but Filo and Yang insist they selected the name because they liked the dictionary definition of a Yahoo!: "rude, unsophisticated, uncouth."

Whatever the name stands for, the site quickly added other services, transforming it from a directory of sites to what is generally regarded as a portal, including news services, financial information, and a fantasy sports league. Soon Yahoo! was offering free email, personalized pages, and a free trial of a Yahoo! store.

The content, the services, and the localized websites add up to one of the most globally recognizable sites on the web. By 2011, Yahoo! had over 600 million unique visitors per month worldwide,[14] and its search engine served 243 million unique visitors each month worldwide.[15] Every month, 6.6 million visitors visit Yahoo! for travel information. Thirty percent of revenue comes from outside the United States, and the brand is often considered one of the most recognizable global brands on the Internet.

Advertising revenue alone was insufficient to maintain the site from the time it was commercialized and the firm has experienced several years of negative growth. However, the firm is still profitable. It seems clear, however, that Yahoo! is not only an Internet survivor, but has prospered as a portal that offers a vast array of Internet-based services. Today, more people get their news from Yahoo! than from any other source (see Figure 3.2).

However, the competition is stiff in this area. Not only does Google continue to expand its services, but AOL, with its merger with the *Huffington Post* and the development of its local news service Patch, clearly wants to differentiate itself as a top local and other news provider. AOL has poured $40 million into its Patch sites—33 new sites with local focus.[16]

Although, as indicated above, Yahoo! has had several years of negative growth, it still has a strong customer base that is attractive to advertisers, as well as a popular advertising portal that helps perspective customers target specific markets and provide industry insight (see Figure 3.3). The company touts itself as "the world's most visited homepage" and in 2009, Yahoo! hired a new CEO, Carol Bartz. She made significant changes, such as signing a deal with Microsoft making Bing the search engine for its sites, and putting Yahoo! in charge of search ads. However, revenue continued to plummet, and after a short time on the job, the company fired Bartz. Tim Morse was named as interim CEO

1 | Yahoo! News
30 - eBizMBA Rank | **80,000,000** - Estimated Unique Monthly Visitors | ***29*** - Compete Rank | ***30*** - Quantcast Rank | **N/A** - Alexa Rank.
Most Popular News Websites | Updated 5/10/2011 | eBizMBA

2 | CNN
44 - eBizMBA Rank | **65,000,000** - Estimated Unique Monthly Visitors | **35** - Compete Rank | **40** - Quantcast Rank | **58** - Alexa Rank.
Most Popular News Websites | Updated 5/10/2011 | eBizMBA

3 | MSNBC
45 - eBizMBA Rank | **62,000,000** - Estimated Unique Monthly Visitors | **40** - Compete Rank | ***50*** - Quantcast Rank | **N/A** - Alexa Rank.
Most Popular News Websites | Updated 5/10/2011 | eBizMBA

4 | Google News
51 - eBizMBA Rank | **51,000,000** - Estimated Unique Monthly Visitors | ***60*** - Compete Rank | ***42*** - Quantcast Rank | **N/A** - Alexa Rank.
Most Popular News Websites | Updated 5/10/2011 | eBizMBA

5 | New York Times
64 - eBizMBA Rank | **38,500,000** - Estimated Unique Monthly Visitors | **49** - Compete Rank | **60** - Quantcast Rank | **84** - Alexa Rank.
Most Popular News Websites | Updated 5/10/2011 | eBizMBA

FIGURE **3.2** Most Popular Websites, May 2011

Source: eBizMBA, "The Top 15 Most Popular Websites," May 2011, http://www.ebizmba.com/articles/most-popular-websites.

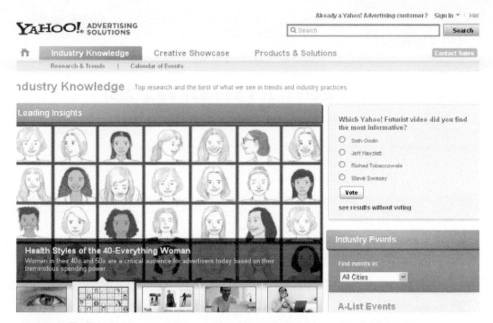

FIGURE **3.3** Yahoo!'s Advertising Solutions Network Provides Industry Knowledge

Source: Reproduced with permission of Yahoo! Inc. ©2011 Yahoo! Inc. YAHOO! and the YAHOO! logo are registered trademarks of Yahoo! Inc., http://advertising.yahoo.com/industry-knowledge.

to try to reposition the company for future growth. Morse was later replace by Scott Thompson, formerly of PayPal, as CEO, and it is said that co-founder Jerry Yang resigned from the Board to make way for Thompson to revitalize the company. The company is also currently considering merger and purchase offers.

Infomediary Model: Reselling Useful Data

Some firms function as **infomediaries** (information intermediaries) assisting buyers and/or sellers to understand a given market. An **Infomediary Model** on the web is a website that gathers and organizes large amounts of data and acts as an intermediary between those who want the information and those who supply the information.[17] The term is used broadly to cover virtually any third party that manages and distributes data on the Internet.

Data about consumers and their consumption habits are valuable, especially when that information is carefully analyzed and used to target marketing campaigns. Independently collected data about producers and their products are useful to consumers when considering a purchase. Some types of infomediaries are listed here:

- *Advertising networks* (Google, Sharethis) feed banner ads or social media messages to a network of member sites, thereby enabling advertisers to deploy large marketing campaigns. Ad networks collect data about web users that can be used to analyze marketing effectiveness.
- *Audience measurement services* (Nielsen/NetRatings) function as online audience market research agencies.
- *Incentive marketing* (MyPoints, Upromise) sites operate customer loyalty programs that provide incentives to customers such as redeemable points or coupons for making purchases from associated retailers. Data collected about users are sold for targeted advertising. Sallie Mae helps members get money back from everyday spending through Upromise. Figure 3.4 illustrates the incentive marketing program at MyPoints.
- *B2B infomediaries* (InfoUSA) provide information about companies that is important in marketing efforts such as company size and contact information.
- *Metamediaries* (Edmunds) facilitate transactions between buyer and sellers by providing comprehensive information and ancillary services, without being involved in the actual exchange of goods or services between the parties.

FIGURE **3.4** Incentive Marketing at MyPoints

Source: MyPoints, http://www.mypoints.com/emp/u/what-is-mypoints.vm.

Merchant Model: Providing Goods and Services

Web merchants are wholesalers and retailers of goods and services. Sales may be made based on list prices or through auction. Merchants have pioneered many of the innovations that have come to be associated with marketing on the web. Several types of **Merchant Models** are as follows:

- *Virtual merchant* (Amazon.com) operates as a merchant or etailer solely over the web.
- *Catalog merchant* (Lands' End) operates a mail-order business with a web-based catalog and combines mail, telephone, and online ordering.
- *Bit vendor* (Apple iTunes Music Store) deals strictly in digital products and services and, in its purest form, conducts both sales and distribution over the web.
- *Click and mortar, aka multichannel/bricks n clicks* (Best Buy) operates as traditional brick-and-mortar retail establishment with web storefront. The terms "bricks n clicks" and "clicks and mortar" are frequently used to describe the business model that includes a physical retail store (or stores) and an ecommerce Internet site. That is not, however, a complete description of the business models of these firms. For example, Abercrombie & Fitch has stores, a transactional website, and a magazine, and issues seasonal catalogs. Other retailers include a telephone call center as part of the mix. Whatever the exact components of the channel mix, "multichannel" seems like the most accurate term. Most retailers today operate a multichannel environment.
- *Aggregator* (Overstock) organizes and choreographs the distribution of goods, services, and information. It intermediates transactions between producers and consumers, creating value for both and for its shareholders. The value proposition of such companies depends on six complementary variables: selection, organization, price, convenience, matching, and fulfillment.[18] Aggregation is a familiar way to make money, not unlike the path

taken by direct catalog marketers. Most retailers, both online and offline, are aggregators who combine merchandise from a variety of suppliers into an edited selection for their customers. Some companies, like Overstock.com, have made a business of bringing unsold goods together in one place.

Innovation and Value at Amazon.com

One company that has done a good job of articulating and implementing its value proposition is Amazon.com. The company was first known as an etailer, first with books, videos, and DVDs, and in later years, with many diverse product lines. In fact, Amazon.com has the immodest vision of being the place "where people can come to find and discover anything they might want to buy online,"[19] suggesting that it views itself as the ultimate web merchant. As the number of merchandise lines has increased beyond books, the site has been carefully organized by product category in a way that is simple to decipher and use.

One of Amazon.com's early innovations was the use of customers to provide some of the content on the site. Amazon.com was also one of the first to give personalized recommendations based on the customer's purchase pattern using a technique called **predictive modeling**. Predictive modeling is really a series of statistical techniques known as predictive analytics to identify underlying patterns in data. An identified customer who has shopped at Amazon before is greeted by name on a personalized home page when she visits the site. If, for example, the customer buys several books on advertising and marketing communications, the recommendations for other advertising and marketing communications books are usually quite accurate.

Amazon also uses *collaborative filtering* technology (software that performs statistical analysis to determine patterns of activity) to generate personalized recommendations for products on its site. The user gets an individualized recommendation, the "My Store" feature that includes recommendations, new product releases, and bargains, all based on the customer's purchase history. The customer may also log in and have the option of editing his purchase history, selecting favorite Amazon stores or products, or rating products that he owns to improve recommendations.

From the beginning, Amazon offered a huge selection of books, so a good search engine for the site was important. The Amazon.com search engine is based on Google functionality, but it displays a much richer set of information. Amazon has also innovated in a number of services unique to the web. One service that has been widely emulated is its patented 1-Click® process that "remembers" the customer's purchasing information and mailing list, eliminating the need to fill out lengthy forms. The books and many of the products Amazon.com sells are standardized; its customer-friendly services make the customer experience nonstandard and encourage repeat transactions.

The company continues to expand and to add goods and services for sale. The new Kindle Fire tablet computer, based on the Android operating system, became available in November of 2011 and allows users to access Amazon's rich sources of content. There are now daily deals and coupons as well as expanded features for individuals and small businesses to sell their wares on Amazon.com. Although the company is profitable, its emphasis on continued growth and expansion means that it has sacrificed some profitability (see Figure 3.5).

Figure 3.5 illustrates relative profitability and growth for two of the different business models discussed so far. Amazon.com and Barnes and Noble represent the Merchant Model, Ebay the Brokerage Model. As can be seen from the figure, just choosing a particular business model is not a guarantee of success. Amazon started as a click-only retailer while Barnes and Noble had to transform its existing brick and mortar operation to compete with online merchants. EBay is able to be more profitable than Amazon by taking advantage of the lower cost structure of the Brokerage model.

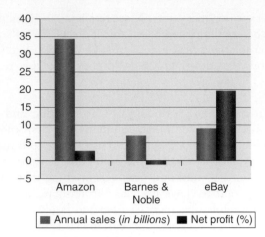

FIGURE **3.5** 2010 Profitability and Sales Growth for Three Different Firms Representing Two Different Business Models
Source: Hoover's, Inc.

Manufacturer (Direct) Model: Reaching Buyers Directly

The **Manufacturer,** or **"Direct Model,"** is predicated on the power of the web to allow a manufacturer (i.e., a company that creates a product or service) to reach buyers directly and thereby compress the distribution channel. This model relies on the concept of *disintermediation*, or eliminating the middleman and going direct to the consumer. In the beginning of the Internet, it was thought that the Internet would eliminate all middlemen, but as we see with Amazon and other business models, one of the key benefits of the Internet is to create efficient places for exchange, and those who create those places for exchange, such as Amazon, have thrived on the Internet.

The manufacturer model can be based on efficiency, improved customer service, and a better understanding of customer preferences. Dell Computer is a good example of the manufacturer model as the company not only sells directly but also engages in mass customization. The product can be purchased, leased, licensed, or syndicated (property rights remain with the manufacturer). **Proprietary systems** may become an important source of competitive advantage, and some firms will guard them closely. Others, however, will find additional revenue opportunities in sale or licensing of specialized software. It is important to remember, though, the example from Chapter 2 of Amazon's free provision of Web Services to other software developers.

Several examples of the manufacturer model include

- *Direct selling* (Dell) sells goods and services directly to consumer or business customer.
- *Syndication or licensing of content* (*New York Times*) is the marketing of content by physical-world publishers. Content can be actively marketed to other sites through RSS feeds. Software firms may choose to license their products to users instead of selling them outright. They may collect revenue based on the number of users, as the creators of most B2B software products typically do, or they may charge on a usage basis as search engines often do.
- *Software-based services* (Salesforce) sell software to firms in hosted solutions, so firms avoid owning and maintaining their own software. Software as a service is referred to as the "cloud" or "cloud computing." Salesforce is a good example of such services—database services for mobile sales professional that is delivered in the cloud—and more and more companies are gravitating to this model.

Affiliate Model: Offering Incentives to Partner Sites

In contrast to the generalized portal, which seeks to drive a high volume of traffic to one site, the **Affiliate Model** provides purchase opportunities wherever people may be surfing. It does this by offering financial incentives (in the form of a percentage of revenue) to affiliated partner sites. The affiliates provide purchase-point click-through to the merchant. It is a pay-for-performance model—if an affiliate does not generate sales, it represents no cost to the merchant.

The affiliate model is inherently well-suited to the web, which explains its popularity. Variations include banner exchange, pay-per-click, and revenue sharing programs. Many nonprofits such as the Susan G. Komen for the Cure use affiliate programs to their advantage, partnering with various companies so that a portion of the proceeds of transactions will benefit breast cancer research. Amazon began its affiliate program in 1996 and has over one billion affiliates currently. When the links are activated, the affiliate site begins to earn revenue from referral sales made on Amazon. However, the automated system makes it possible to handle a large number of affiliates in a cost-effective fashion. Amazon does not disclose the proportion of sales that are achieved through associate referrals—neither does it attempt to estimate the advertising value derived from the presence of the Amazon logo on over *one billion* websites! There are people who make a living explaining how to make money on the Amazon.com affiliate network. However, a number of states, including California, have passed laws requiring that sales tax be collected on Amazon.com's sales, resulting in the company canceling its affiliate program in affected states rather than lose its low-cost advantage that is has currently by not charging sales tax to its customers. It remains to be seen whether this tactic will be effective in the long term for Amazon.com. The following is a list of different types of affiliate sites:

- *Banner exchange* trades banner placement among a network of affiliated sites.
- *Pay-per-click* sites pay affiliates for a user click-through.
- *Revenue sharing* (Amazon.com) offers a percentage-of-sale commission based on a user click-through in which the user subsequently purchases a product.

Community Model: Connecting Individuals and Groups

The Internet is based on network principles, which means the ability to connect not only nodes and computers on the Internet but also individual Internet users to each other. From the beginning, users of the Internet saw the ability to connect virtually based on common levels of expertise and interest. Initially, these connections were in chat rooms and forums, and then through community-based websites such as Facebook. The Internet is inherently suited to community business models, and today, this is one of the more fertile areas of development, as seen in the rise of social networking.

Using a **Community Model** as a business model is to create a business based on user loyalty and repeat engagement. Users have a high investment in both time and emotion. Revenue can be based on the sale of ancillary products and services or voluntary contributions; or revenue may be tied to contextual advertising and subscriptions for premium services.

The Internet public became aware of the community business model in terms of **peer-to-peer (P2P)** computing applications in early 2000 when the popular download software for music files, Napster, became a media event. P2P applications allow for file sharing from one computer to another, and Napster's members were sharing music with each other through their computers without paying fees or royalties to the music industry. The site was already well known to a dedicated following mostly composed of teens and young adults but emerged from the shadows when colleges began to filter Napster from their networks. The music files that students were downloading in computer labs and dorm rooms were clogging networks and devouring storage space. The music industry's unwavering opposition to Napster forced the company to transition to a paid subscription model and Napster was owned by Best Buy and recently purchased by Rhapsody.[20] More recent entries into the P2P arena, such as Kazaa.com, offer file sharing of multiple types of files for a monthly subscription fee.

Although the application is much less newsworthy, P2P is alive and well—legally—in business markets. Sharing of supply chain information was discussed in Chapter 2. B2B marketplaces provide a forum for users to exchange ideas and information. Corporate **intranets** host busy traffic in files moving around the world. **Extranets** link corporate information resources to those of strategic partners and suppliers. Sharing information within the enterprise and with external partners is a key part of the networked economy, and it will support the continued growth of P2P in the business space. Several specific types of community models are listed next:

- *Open source* (Linux, Firefox) is carried out by a group of volunteers and at least the basic product is available free to all users. These sites recall the early freewheeling days of the Internet where commercialism was suspect. From a practical point of view, they also contribute to the constant innovation that is the nature of the Internet. Many of them are sold by businesses that provide the free source code but also include proprietary software utilities and a technical support package. For example, Linux, a popular operating system, is available both free of charge on its website or for a fee from a number of software developers. Firefox is an open source browser that has evolved from the original Netscape browser. It allows users to extensively customize their browsers and actively recruits software developers to assist in maintenance and in developing new functionality.
- *Open content* (Wikipedia, dmoz) is openly accessible content developed collaboratively by a global community of contributors who work voluntarily. For Wikipedia, the content is provided by volunteers, and donations are solicited to purchase and maintain the system necessary to provide it.
- *Crowdsourcing* (Threadless, CrowdSPRING, Local Motors) involves a community of members to design and vote on products that will be produced.
- *Fund-raising* (American Red Cross) relies on a community of users to support the site through voluntary donations. In the early days of the commercial Internet, it was considered highly improbable that nonprofit organizations would be able to raise money on the Internet. Time, a relatively short amount of it, has proven that early prediction to be incorrect. Fund-raising is particularly effective online in regard to emergency response, such as to an earthquake or a tsunami, as news spreads quickly online and responses follow quickly as well. Nonprofit marketers raise substantial sums of money through their websites. There are also a number of large sites that exist on services donated by the Internet community. Two-thirds of President Barak Obama's successful online fund-raising campaign in 2008 was a combination of email and web efforts.[21]
- *Social networking services* (Flickr, Facebook) provide individuals with the ability to connect to other individuals along a defined common interest (i.e., profession, hobby, romance). Social networking services can provide opportunities for contextual advertising and subscriptions for premium services. Therefore, a social networking site or service can still employ an advertising or subscription business model to raise revenue. Although community-based, LinkedIn uses both an advertising and subscription model.

Subscription Model: Delivering Services and Content for a Set Fee

In the early days of the Internet, most content was free. Much content is still available for free, but because companies need to make money with their business models, some content-oriented sites are charging for the content they provide. In the **Subscription Model**, users are charged a periodic—daily, monthly, or annual—fee to subscribe to a service. It is not uncommon for sites to combine free content with "premium" (i.e., subscriber- or member-only) content. Subscription fees are incurred irrespective of actual usage rates. Subscription and advertising models are frequently combined. Several specific types of subscription models are listed here:

- *Content services* (Listen.com, Netflix) provide text, audio, or video content to users who subscribe for a fee to gain access to the service.
- *Person-to-person networking services* (Classmates) distribute user-submitted information, such as individuals searching for former schoolmates.
- *Trust services* (TRUSTe) provide membership associations that abide by an explicit code of conduct, and in which members pay a subscription fee.
- *Membership organizations* (WCPE The Classical Station.org) provide services for free but encourages contributions and provides special services for ongoing support. Many nonprofit organizations are encouraging monthly giving to provide a steady revenue stream.
- *Application services providers (ASP)*, (Adobe, Corio) offer Internet services to access software applications and other services. ASPs range from large to small and from general business/ecommerce to specialized software applications for vertical markets. They may also offer various services like domain name registration, website hosting, Internet access, and submission to search engines. Their customers are both small businesses that cannot afford to own or manage the software and large enterprises that prefer to outsource some technical services. For example, Corio, a division of IBM, is one of the largest ASPs, focusing on enterprise applications and high-end ecommerce solutions for Global 1000 firms. For consumers, Adobe offers a service that allows subscribers to create .pdf files online instead of owning the Adobe Acrobat software themselves.

Utility Model: Delivering Services or Content "Pay as You Go"

The **Utility Model**, or "on-demand," is based on metering usage, or a "pay as you go" approach. Unlike subscriber services, metered services are based on actual usage rates. Traditionally, metering has been used for essential services (e.g., electricity, water, long-distance telephone services). Internet services providers (ISPs) in some parts of the world operate as utilities, charging customers for connection minutes, as opposed to the subscriber model common in the United States.

- *Metered usage* (Skype, Google Voice) measures and bills users based on actual usage of a service. Voice calls are charged per minute called.
- *Metered subscriptions* (Slashdot) allow subscribers to purchase access to content in metered portions (e.g., numbers of pages viewed).

The Future of Business Models

There has been significant upheaval in the Internet business model landscape over the past few years. When the changing landscape is carefully examined, two major patterns appear. First, the basic nature of the models present has not changed a great deal. The same models are in evidence now that were present in the earlier days of the Internet. However, the prominence of various models has changed. For instance, when Internet use was growing at a spectacular rate, simply providing access, the ISP by itself was considered a viable business model. Now ISPs have become components of many other business models. Likewise, in the early years, the web was home to hundreds of B2B marketplaces, far too many to gain sustainable market share. The number of marketplaces has greatly decreased, although the model is viable in both B2B and B2C markets, as evidenced by eBay.

Second, in the halcyon days, there was widespread belief that sufficient quantity of website content would draw sufficient number of visitors to produce advertising revenue sufficient to support the business. This has proven not to be true, and sites have found it necessary to develop multiple revenue streams in order to achieve and maintain profitability.

The evolution continues, with community-based models gaining strong footing and producing spectacular earnings for their investors in the form of IPOs (initial public offerings) such as those by LinkedIn and Facebook. Community models will continue to expand and even to produce new business models as time goes on. Some may be counterparts of physical world business models, as are many of the current Internet models. Some may actually be new models, ones that take advantage of the unique characteristics of the Internet. The example of Restaurant.com in the "Identifying Business Models" section speaks to the evolving nature of business models.

SUMMARY

Internet business models are how enterprises are configured to create value for customers and to deliver that value in a profitable way on the Internet. A business model is a conceptual description of the business. Business models on the Internet have been given a set of names, although there is no commonly accepted set of names or classifications of types of business models. The emphasis on the value proposition, however, is characteristic of all discussions of Internet business models. The drivers of value are customer wants and needs. It is up to the business to uncover the relevant wants and needs and design products and services that meet those needs and fit with its core expertise. This is a customer-centric, not a product-centric, approach. There are a number of commonly accepted business models—*brokerage, advertising, infomediary, merchant, manufacturer, affiliate, community, subscription and utility*—and some others not discussed here. Most of them can be found in both B2C and B2B marketspaces and are also used by nonprofits and governmental agencies.

There are a number of ways that Internet businesses can generate revenue within these models. Few Internet businesses find it possible to sustain themselves on a single revenue stream; most find it necessary to employ several revenue-generating approaches in order to achieve sustained profitability. The evolution of business models on the Internet continues. It is likely that different models may achieve prominence at different periods of time and possible that entirely new models may emerge as the Internet matures.

DISCUSSION QUESTIONS

1. Why is the concept of the business model important? In what ways is it useful?
2. Why did some early Internet firms such as eToys fail?
3. How does the value proposition change a firm's approach to creation of new products and new marketing strategies?
4. Can a company have more than one business model?
5. How do business models evolve?
6. Would you start a business today driven by the advertising model?
7. How has the approach to content changed over the life of the commercial Internet?
8. Some firms choose to generate revenue by selling or licensing their proprietary software. Others choose an open systems approach and distribute it free of charge. What do you think drives the decision?
9. The example of eToys.com suggests that multichannel retailers are more likely to experience long-run success in the Internet economy than are pure-play Internet retailers. Take a position on this conjecture and defend your position. Is there anything to learn from the profitability and sales growth chart in Figure 3.5 in this regard?
10. Consider Figure 3.5 and the differences in profitability and sales growth between the three firms. Are there any other factors other than those mentioned in the text that explain the differences in profitability and sales growth between these companies?

INTERNET EXERCISES

1. Internet Career Builder Exercise

    Select a company that markets on the Internet that you think you would like to work for after graduation and assume you are preparing for an interview. Lynn Hazan, a marketing recruiter based in Chicago, recommends the "WOW" project on an interview. She suggests that students come to an interview having studied the company and prepared to make recommendations for improvements.

    • What is the company's business model, that is, the primary way it makes money?
    • Has the company's business model evolved over time?
    • What recommendations would you make on an interview in your "WOW" project in terms of other business models the company could use to make money? For example, can the company use the community model to increase sales from its business as an Internet merchant?

2. Choose one of the websites you are following for a detailed study of the business model it represents. Carefully examine the way(s) in which obtains revenues, and try to find out from its own reports or from industry sources what its current revenue is and what weight is given to each of its revenue streams. Then make your assessment of the manner in which the enterprise (both the website and any physical-world business components) creates value for its target customers. Present your analysis in class.

3. Choose a business that you believe fits into one of the business models in Table 3.1. Research the elements of its business model and examine the site in considerable detail. Discuss both the revenue and cost models of your chosen business and explain how it creates value for its target customers. Explain how the company has changed business models and evolved over time.

4. Think again about the retail entity from which you bought the material for this class (see Internet Exercise 2 in Chapter 2). Analyze all of the ways in which that enterprise attempts to create value for its customers. Also consider the nature of its revenue model and whether it has only a single revenue stream or multiple sources of revenue.

5. Choose one of the business models from Table 3.1. Search for an article about an Internet business that is representative of the model. Discuss how the business implements the chosen model.

6. Choose one of the business models from Table 3.1. Construct your own hypothetical business around the model. Use some of functions and elements of business models discussed above to organize your model. How would you go about developing a value proposition for the business? What would the viable revenue streams be? Why?

7. The Yahoo! example explores how web portals have evolved. Based on your knowledge of business models and what is going on currently, describe how you think the web portal space will evolve and why? Which portal will dominate and how will each develop its own market niche?

NOTES

1. Michael Rappa, "Business Models on the Web," http://digitalenterprise.org/models/models.html.
2. Sendil Ethiraj, Isin Guler, and Harbir Singh, nd, "The Impact of Internet and Electronic Technologies on Firms and Its Implications for Competitive Advantage," Working Paper, The Wharton School, University of Pennsylvania, 18–19.
3. http://www.funginguniverse.com/company-histories/EToys-Inc-company-History.html, retrieved July 11, 2011.
4. http://news.bbc.co.uk/2hi/buinsess/1208079.stm, retrieved July 11, 2011.
5. http://www.cnet.com/1990-11136_1-6278387-1.html, retrieved July 11, 2011.
6. Henry Chesbrough and Richard S. Rosenbloom, "The Role of the Business Model in Capturing Value from Innovation: Evidence from Xerox Corporation's Technology Spin-off Companies," *Industrial and Corporate Change*, Volume 11, Number 3, 2002, 533–534.
7. http://thebln.com/2011/10/alex-osterwalder-building-competitive-advantage-through-business-model-thinking, retrieved October 30, 2011.
8. Alexander Osterwalder and Yves Pigneur, "An e-Business Model Ontology for Modeling e-Business," 15th Bled Electronic Commerce Conference, Bled, Slovenia, July 17–19, 2002.
9. http://www.ebayinc.com/who, retrieved July 12, 2011.
10. http://www.achievement.org/autodoc/page/omi0bio-1, retrieved, July 12, 2011.
11. http://www.channeladvisor.com/e-commerce-products, retrieved July 12, 2011.
12. See Sandy D. Jap, "An Exploratory Study of the Introduction of the Online Reverse Auction," July 2003, *Journal of Marketing*, Vol. 67, 96–107.

13. http://www.ft.com/cms/s/2/d4f537d2-7a65-11e0-af64-00144feabdc0.html#ixzz1PpYwqgFZ.

14. https://www.google.com/adplanner/#siteDetails?uid=d%252Byahoo.com&geo=US&lp=false, retrieved July 12, 2011.

15. http://advertising.yahoo.com/products-solutions#product=DisplaySolutions, retrieved July 11, 2011.

16. http://techcrunch.com/2011/05/16/as-2012-election-season-ramps-up-aols-patch-will-launch-33-sites-in-key-primary-states.

17. "Infomediary," http://www.webopedia.com/TERM/I/infomediary.html.

18. Don Tapscott, David Ticoll, and Alex Lowy, *Digital Capital: Harnessing the Power of Business Webs*. Boston, MA: Harvard Business School Press, 2000, 67.

19. http://www.company-statements-slogans.info/list-of-companies-a/amazon-com.htm, retrieved October 30, 2011.

20. http://www.pcworld.com/article/241114/rhapsody_buys_napster_as_it_battles_spotify.html, retrieved October 30, 2011.

21. http://www.epolitics.com/2009/08/27/two-thirds-of-obamas-online-fundraising-was-via-email, retrieved July 12, 2011.

The Direct Response and Database Foundations of Internet Marketing

Key Terms

A/B split (96)
back end (88)
CLV (customer lifetime value) (90)
customer service (88)
customization (110)
data (82)

data mining (106)
database (101)
front end (88)
fulfillment (88)
information (82)
interactive (82)
NPV (net present value) (92)

personalization (110)
predictive model (105)
profile (104)
sales promotion (85)
testing (96)

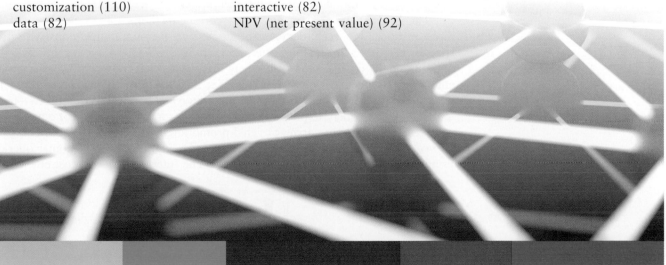

LEARNING OBJECTIVES

By the time you complete this chapter, you will be able to:

- Explain the ways in which the Internet is a direct response medium.

- Distinguish between acquisition, conversion, and retention strategies.

- Identify the elements of a direct response marketing strategy.

- Explain the concepts of offer, customer lifetime value, and testing.

- Explain the role of a customer database in the development and execution of Internet marketing programs.

- Describe a data warehouse and how it is used by marketers.

- Define data mining and explain why it is important in making marketing decisions.

- Discuss how strategies can become more customer focused by using information-driven marketing.

The Internet as a Direct Response Medium

The Internet is the ultimate direct response medium. Why? Certainly it is an **interactive** channel, allowing two-way dialog between marketer and prospective customer using direct response techniques or social media. It is also a sales channel, with ecommerce growing at a rapid rate from the early days of the Internet to the present. The Internet is also a powerful branding medium, as we discuss in Chapter 5. However, it is difficult to do successful Internet marketing without understanding the basics of direct marketing. This chapter will focus on direct response principles and execution on the web.

The Internet presents powerful opportunities to the shrewd marketer. From the consumer's perspective, it permits a seamless purchase process. From the marketer's perspective, the Internet allows fine-tuning of marketing programs in ways previously unimaginable. There are four important characteristics—call them the "four Is"—that describe the ways in which marketing efforts are powerfully affected by the capabilities of the Internet (see Figure 4.1).

The Internet, more than any other current medium, allows *interactivity*. In direct response mode, marketers can initiate two-way communications with prospective customers by sending offers to them and tracking their responses or by initiating direct communications by way of surveys, chat rooms, or other Internet-enabled techniques. All marketing activities on the web have the potential to be **information**-driven. Every move a website visitor makes, every action taken—from sending an email query to purchasing a product—is a potential piece of **data** for the marketing database that drives targeted promotional activities. The Internet fosters *immediacy* in a variety of ways. Marketers can reply directly to customer queries, using human agents or automated systems. The Internet makes it cost-efficient to

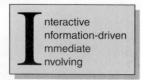

I nteractive
I nformation-driven
I mmediate
I nvolving

FIGURE **4.1** The Four Is of Internet Marketing
Source: © Cengage Learning 2013

construct offers that appeal to a specific market segment or to make offers that are seasonal or that are triggered by a particular event, say the NCAA basketball finals. Internet promotions can also be *involving*. Marketers are increasingly using streaming video, games, and other types of rich media in Internet advertising to attract and involve prospective customers. A good direct response offer incites prospects to take action—either to request information or to make a purchase on the spot.

Some marketers have learned to combine brand marketing, discussed in the online context in Chapter 5, with direct response marketing. Procter & Gamble, best known for its use of mass media and mass distribution channels, was a user of direct response long before the advent of the Internet. Figure 4.2 shows one product in its Cheer brand family, Cheer Free & Gentle, which does not contain perfumes and dyes. This is important to the small segment of people who are allergic to those additives and can have intense reactions to products washed with detergents that contain them; the segment is small, but within it, the customer need is great. When Cheer Free was introduced more than two decades ago, P&G knew that mass market techniques would not be cost-efficient. Consequently, it used promotional techniques like free samples and coupons to build a mailing list of households that needed this product. Using this list, the company was able to promote directly to these households by mail, a targeted and cost-effective solution.

Fast forward to the present when the web is now the hub of P&G's marketing strategy. It is still necessary to use traditional techniques—in this case, often coupon offers in Sunday supplements or shared coupon mailings—in order to drive new prospects to the Cheer Free & Gentle web page. Because this product is targeted at people with a medical issue, the page is more focused on information—including encouraging customer reviews—than the other Cheer pages. It is possible to purchase the product directly from this page, but that is not the primary purpose of the site, and is easy to assume that few sales are actually made. The objectives are twofold: brand development and driving traffic to retail stores. Note the store locator on the home page.

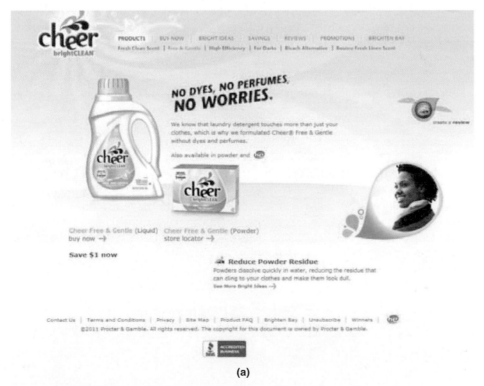

(a)

FIGURE **4.2a** Cheer Free & Gentle Home Page

Source: The Proctor & Gamble Company, http://www.cheer.com/laundry-detergents/free-gentle-detergent.shtml.

(b)

FIGURE **4.2b** Cheer Branded Soap Opera Page
Source: The Proctor & Gamble Company, http://www.cheer.com/brighten-bay/index.shtml.

(c)

FIGURE **4.2c** The Sign Up Box
Source: The Proctor & Gamble Company, https://www.pgeverydaysolutions.com.

The visitor can choose to view P&G's branded "Brighten Bay" soap opera (see Figure 4.2b) without registering. However, if she wants to download a coupon or to enter a sweepstakes and select her own preferred prize, she must register (email address and create password only). If she goes from the home page to the Everyday Solutions page, which offers coupons and samples for many brands, she will also have to register (or sign in) to download a coupon (see Figure 4.2c). P&G offers value to the customer in return for her email address, which will, of course, be used for continued promotion. Consider the fact that email to a person who has already expressed interest in the product is a much more cost-efficient marketing approach than mailing coupons to undifferentiated audiences with the associated low redemption rate. P&G provides additional value by allowing consumers to load coupons directly to a grocery store shopping card for paperless shopping convenience.

Whether the offers are for coupons, free samples, or contests, all are **sales promotions** that have the objective of inducing consumers to take immediate action. One action is sign-up that provides an email address for further promotion. Each succeeding promotion invites action. Action taken—or not taken—provides additional information for the customer database, allowing the company to more precisely target its email promotions. P&G's ability to seamlessly integrate multiple channels of communications and sales to take full advantage of the cheap and effective communications abilities of the web is an important part of its ongoing global success.

This example illustrate that many of the time-honored tools of direct marketing can be transferred onto the web in fairly straightforward ways. It is critical for marketers to understand direct marketing methodology so they can develop and refine successful Internet marketing programs.

In order to understand the importance of this methodology, we should look first at the basic types of direct marketing strategies. Then we will follow with specific techniques that form the basis of successful direct marketing programs.

Generic Direct Marketing Strategies[1]

Essentially, there are three types of direct marketing strategies that parallel a basic customer life cycle (see Figure 4.3). First, a customer is acquired. This state represents trial of a product or a service. In the acquisition stage, the customer has made a single purchase, or perhaps engaged in free use as a result of a sample or a demonstration, but is not yet committed to the brand. The second stage is conversion, so called because in this step the prospect converts to customer. This may require one to three purchases, or enough to form a habitual purchasing pattern. The final stage is retention, in which the customer continues to make purchases, a situation we might call behavioral loyalty. Even better, in this stage, the customer begins to exhibit loyalty in an attitudinal sense, which may result in behaviors ranging from rejecting competing offers to becoming an advocate for the product.

Each of the basic strategies requires a different type of effort on the part of the marketer. *Acquisition* is roughly equivalent to the awareness stage of general advertising with an action component added. It requires a conscious attempt to get

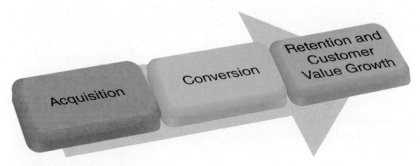

FIGURE **4.3** The Basic Direct Response Strategies

the attention of the prospective customer through media placement and creative execution. Direct marketers often add an incentive to clinch product trial. We discuss customer acquisition on the Internet in detail in the chapters of Part 2.

The *conversion* step is focused on getting the customer to make additional purchases, often the three that psychologists recommend to establish a habitual behavior. Product and service satisfaction is critical to achieving this goal. Customer contact, through media ranging from personal selling to newsletters, is often useful. Sequential incentives have also been used with good results. For example, a bank that wanted its customers to make more deposits at ATMs sent them a series of three checks, each of which could be used only with a series of ATM deposits. The first check was for $5, the second was for $3, and the third was for $1. The incentives were not only sequential, they decreased in value as the presumed habit formation was taking place. It is hard to prove habit formation, but in this case, it seems reasonable to assume that many customers, after three successful deposits, recognized that it is safe to make deposits through ATMs. This was a sensible, low-cost conversion program aimed at achieving a worthwhile business goal. Its only visible drawback was that the bank did not make good use of its customer database. It sent the checks to customers who regularly made ATM deposits as well as to those who never deposited through an ATM! We discuss conversion marketing in Chapter 10.

Finally, it is important to *retain* customers in order to create the highest possible customer lifetime value (CLV). Retention is most often the result of adding value to the customer purchase and use experience and superior customer service. A planned program of customer contact, carried out at appropriate points in the purchase cycle, can also be a useful component of retention programs. We discuss retention in detail in Chapter 11.

Critical Strategy Elements

The marketing mix that supports direct marketing programs uses slightly different terminology from the 4Ps of traditional marketing. They are:

- The offer—product, price, positioning, and any other product-related elements that make up the complete proposition presented to the prospective customer
- The list—the targeting vehicle
- The media used—with the understanding that any medium can be a direct response medium with the proper implementation
- The creative execution—which tends to play a secondary role in this action-oriented context
- The service and support—long recognized as a key element in this environment where the shopping experience and many sensory stimuli are not present

These elements are all required to implement any direct response program. It is, however, especially important to understand the role of the offer in developing Internet marketing strategies.

Offers That Incite to Action

The first rule of direct marketing is that the offer must include a call to action. Put another way, it must tell the viewer exactly what the marketer wants her to do and must make it easy for her to take that action. This sounds like a simple notion, but it is easy to let the call to action become buried in website pyrotechnics. It also happens all too frequently that the visitor is willing to take action but cannot find a response form, finds that the form does not work, or finds the questions on the form to be intrusive or simply too onerous. Action that is not taken when the impulse burns strong will probably never be taken.

A particular Internet marketing program has one of three generic action objectives:

- *To get the visitor to remain on the site longer,* exploring more of what it has to offer. This is referred to as site "stickiness," and it has a direct bearing on the CPM (cost per thousand) rates that sites are able to charge for their advertising space. If the site does not have a transactional component, this may be a terminal objective. In the more common situation, in which sites are trying to achieve transactional as well as advertising revenue, it may be a first-stage objective with one of the other two objectives as the primary objective.

* *To cause visitors to request additional information about a product or service.* This is the conventional lead-generation objective long used in both B2C (business-to-consumer) and B2B (business-to-business) markets. When automobile manufacturers send to a carefully selected mailing list inviting consumers to come to their nearest dealership and test drive a new model, they are engaged in a multiple-step B2C lead generation and conversion program. When a software firm offers a free online demonstration of its new release, it is engaged in a B2B lead generation program. If the site requires the visitor to register and provide an email address in order to get the desired information, it is building an email list of people who have qualified themselves by indicating their interest in the product. These are clearly more qualified prospects than individuals who have the correct demographics with known or unknown buying habits that the car manufacturer or software developer obtains from a list rental firm.
* *To achieve a sale.* When the product and the purchasing situation are appropriate for a one-step sales effort, the actual sale becomes the objective.

One of the key tools for achieving offers that compel action is the incentive. Different objectives call for different incentives. The hair care ad in Figure 4.4a offers a sample to back up its claim of increasing hair strength. Netflix, in Figure 4.4b, offers a free trial for nonmembers and access to a current film that members could access. In both these cases, the incentive is inherently related to the product itself: the mark of a good incentive. It might not be in good taste to offer an incentive with a cause-marketing appeal, but Toyota in Figure 4.4c does offer an informative video.

(a)

(c)

(b)

FIGURE **4.4** Offers with Calls to Action

Source: Yahoo.

Internet marketers have learned in recent years that free shipping is another compelling incentive.

Another tool that is a key part of the offer is the brand. We discuss building online brands in greater detail in Chapter 5, but in designing the offer, the marketer must consider how strong the brand is. The stronger the brand, the easier it is to get the prospect to accept a good offer. If the brand is unknown, it may be harder to compel action. A bigger incentive is one option. Another is to make use of another important tool—risk reduction. Risk is reduced when a strong guarantee is offered. Customer reviews and third-party endorsements are also useful. However, the best way to reduce potential buyers' perceived risk is to build a strong and trusted brand.

Much has been written about the issue of trust on the Internet. There is no doubt that marketers need to build trust in the relationship between their company and brands and their prospective customers. In the longer term, trust is going to be achieved by the way the marketer does business—prompt and accurate fulfillment, satisfying returns and service practices, and guardianship of the customer's privacy. The immediate issue for the marketer without an established brand, however, is how to create a sense of confidence that will make the prospect feel reasonably comfortable about conducting a transaction. In the early days, Amazon recognized that, even though it was making Herculean efforts to establish its brand, many customers were still reluctant to give their credit card numbers over the web. It posted a prominent guarantee that promised to reimburse any losses customers incurred as a result of transmitting their credit card information to Amazon. This was appropriate for its time, but it has been replaced with a free shipping offer for many Amazon purchases.

A good offer is designed to compel immediate response from the prospective customer and lays a strong foundation for future marketing efforts to a targeted, identified customer. To do this cost-effectively, the marketer must understand front-end versus back-end issues.

The Front End versus the Back End

Direct marketers have long used these terms although no precise definition exists. It is useful to think of the **front end** as being all the activities that are employed in making the sale. The **back end** is all the postsale activities, primarily order fulfillment and customer service. Marketers understand the front end well; that is their historical domain.

Internet marketers, however, have tended to ignore the importance of the back end. They have concentrated on what customers see—the acquisition activities on the front end—to the exclusion of what they do not see—the back-end functions. The problem with that perspective is that it is the back-end activities that create lasting customer satisfaction and lead to customer retention.

It is also worth noting that this is an arena in which established direct marketing firms had an initial advantage over established bricks-and-mortar retailers. Established direct marketers have the infrastructure and the processes for effective order **fulfillment** and **customer service** in place. Established bricks-and-mortar businesses have infrastructure and processes that are precisely the opposite of what is needed on the web. Their back ends are designed to meet the needs of a series of stores, not to fulfill the orders of individual customers. As an Internet-only retailer, Amazon understands the importance of quick and accurate fulfillment. It has dozens of fulfillment centers around the world, employing over 30,000 people.[2] This makes it possible for it to act as a contractor for firms that do not want to establish their own fulfillment operations. It offers fulfillment as one of the Web Services described in Chapter 3.[3]

Many direct marketers have long concentrated on establishing superb customer service, recognizing the importance of this element in the absence of the store shopping experience. The extent to which many established retailers have slighted customer service functions is well recognized although an outstanding few like retailer Neiman-Marcus and cataloger L.L. Bean have systems that have transferred well into the web environment. Customer service must be experienced, but there is often visible evidence of commitment to providing exceptional service, as discussed in Chapter 13. (Figure 13.8 shows the customer service page at Eddie Bauer, which offers many types of and channels for customer service and a strong promise that excellent service will be forthcoming.)

The line between customer service and customer experience is somewhat blurry, but it is clear that customer service is one element of overall customer experience. The luxury hotel chain Ritz-Carlton is famous for both. While home pages for its various properties emphasize the experience element, its corporate home page has a perspective on the pervasiveness of customer service culture at the Ritz (see Interactive Exercise 4.2). Like manufacturer P&G, they had learned their direct marketing lessons prior to the Internet. The established brick-and-mortar retailer that has no experience in direct marketing will not only require a different infrastructure to be successful at Internet marketing, but will also need a change of mindset in several important areas.

There are a number of other perspectives that are important in the direct marketing environment that must be adopted in order to achieve long-term success in the Internet space. One is the concept of lifetime value of a customer.

The Role and Importance of Customer Lifetime Value[4]

It has long been a truism that the role of marketing is to create a customer, not just a sale. That is true, but it has been an elusive goal for many mass media marketers. Being unable to identify their end customers, they could not interact directly with them and engage in specific attempts to retain them and to increase their long-term value. This represents another direct marketing technique that is now available to all marketers who make informed use of their Internet marketing activities.

The basic idea of **CLV** (**customer lifetime value**) is that, if the marketer understands what it costs to acquire, maintain, and service a customer, then he can make a reasoned decision about how much to spend to market to that customer. The underlying model is simple:

$$\text{Net Customer Revenues}$$

$$\text{Less}: \frac{\text{Cost of goods sold}}{\text{Gross margin}}$$

$$\text{Less}: \frac{\text{Cost of servicing}}{\text{Customer Revenue}}$$

$$\text{Times}: \frac{\text{Cost of capital}}{\text{Net present value of customer revenue stream}}$$

The calculation takes into account the amount of time the customer is likely to persist with the firm. It usually takes as much as three years of data to calculate CLV with a reasonable degree of accuracy. After five years, the discount for the cost of capital becomes so high that future revenue streams have little value, so three to five years is usually satisfactory. Notice that data must be collected for as much as three years in order to begin developing CLV and marketing programs based on it.

Professors Venkatesan and Kuman use a graphic (see Figure 4.5) that helps make the issues clear.[5] Characteristics of the customer that include switching cost, involvement with the product category or brand, and the customer's purchase history are used to predict his future purchasing frequency and the profit obtained from it. The cost of communicating with the customer determines

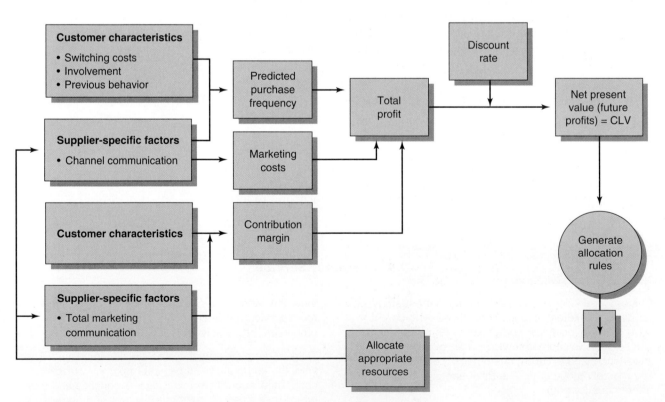

FIGURE **4.5** A Conceptual Framework for Measuring and Using CLV

Source: Adapted from Rajkumar Venkatesan and V. Kumar, "A Customer Lifetime Value Framework for Customer Selection and Resource Allocation Strategy," *Journal of Marketing, 68,* 2004, p. 110.

marketing costs. The contribution margin from each customer is determined and the amount of communications with the customer across all channels is taken into account. The profit from the customer is based on the frequency of purchasing at a particular contribution margin (revenue times contribution percent) less the costs of marketing to the customer. The discount rate is applied and the NPV of a future stream of profits—CLV—is computed. Then the marketer determines actions that can be taken to increase CLV.

A CLV Example

The implementation is less straightforward than what the basic model may suggest. There are a number of questions even after the necessary customer-level data has been confirmed. What is the typical life span of a customer in this particular situation? What is the time period required to achieve a reasonable level of accuracy in predicting purchase frequency and contribution margin across multiple purchases in multiple time periods? Even identifying the relevant revenues and costs is not as easy as it sounds.[6] The following example will help to explain the concept and its application.

Consultant Arthur Hughes[7] gives an example that is based on the experience of the Safeway supermarket chain. Supermarkets have notoriously thin gross margins, and Safeway was concerned that it spends its scarce promotional resources in the most effective way. It turned to a CLV analysis for guidance. Table 4.1 presents the first stage of that analysis.

Assume that the firm acquires 5,000 new customers in year 1 and that the goal is to track their value over three years, generally considered a minimum for calculating customer value. These customers make 0.64 visits per week, purchasing an

TABLE 4.1   Baseline Consumer Lifetime Value Calculation

Lifetime Value Before New Programs			
	Year 1	Year 2	Year 3
Customers	5,000	3,500	2,590
Retention rate	70.0%	74.0%	80.0%
Visits/week	0.64	0.69	0.78
Average basket	$33	$45	$55
Total sales	**$5,280,000**	**$5,433,750**	**$5,555,550**
Cost percentage	83.0%	80.0%	79.0%
Direct costs	$4,382,400	$4,347,000	$4,388,885
Labor + benefits 11%	$580,800	$597,713	$611,111
Card program $16, $8	$80,000	$28,000	$20,720
Advertising 2%	$105,600	$108,675	$111,111
Total costs	**$5,148,800**	**$5,081,388**	**$5,131,826**
Gross profit	$131,200	$352,363	$423,724
Discount rate	1.00	1.20	1.44
NPV profit	$131,200	$293,635	$294,253
Cumulative NPV profit	$131,200	$424,835	$719,088
Lifetime value	$26.24	$84.97	$143.82

Source: Arthur Middleton Hughes, "Building Successful Retail Strategies Using Customer Lifetime Value," Database Marketing Institute, September 7, 2011 (http://www.dbmarketing.com/articles/Art181.htm).

average of $33 each trip. Direct costs are 83 percent of total sales, and labor and benefits for marketing personnel are another 11 percent. Safeway spends $16 on a shopper loyalty card program for each customer in the first year and $8 in succeeding years. Advertising is 2 percent of total sales. The calculations that follow are:

Total sales	$5,280,000
Less: Total costs	$5,148,800
Equals: Gross profit	$ 131,200
Times: Discount rate	1.0
NPV of first year revenue	$ 131,200
Lifetime value of a customer in year 1	$ 26.24

The item that needs particular attention—both in terms of computation and of meaning—is the discount rate. A discount rate is necessary because a future stream of revenue is worth less than revenue received in the current year. Consequently, in year 1, the discount rate is 1.0. For subsequent years, the rate is calculated using the formula

$$D + (1 + i)^n$$

Where D is the discount rate, i is the current interest rate plus a risk factor, and n is the number of years that will elapse before the revenue is realized. When the gross profit for any given year is multiplied by the discount rate for that year, the result is the **net present value (NPV)** of the gross profit for that specific year.

Looking back at the baseline table, the retention rate of these customers is 70 percent in the first year. This means that, of the 5,000 customers acquired in the first year, 3,500 will persist as customers into year 2. As presumably satisfied customers, they will visit the store somewhat more frequently, buy a bit more, and cost a bit less to serve. Following through to the end of year 2, the value of an original customer in year 2 is $84.97 (the cumulative NPV of the profit stream, $424,835, divided by 5,000). Using the same reasoning, the customer value is $143.82 when a customer acquired in year 1 persists to year 3.

The first step in working with CLV is usually to identify additional marketing efforts that can be used to increase customer value. Activities that come under this heading include upselling and cross-selling. Upselling means activities designed to persuade customers to buy more, either in volume or in higher-priced items or both. Cross-selling refers to programs that attempt to sell other products to the customer; for example, a bank that markets certificates of deposit (CDs) to high-value checking account customers. This type of program is, in fact, particularly attractive in industries such as financial services where customers frequently have a number of financial products scattered among the offerings of many financial services providers. The attractiveness of persuading customers to consolidate their holdings with a single provider is obvious. This phenomenon has come to be known as "share of wallet" in the financial services industry or, more generally, "share of customer." Many marketers would argue that this is a better metric of marketing success than the more commonly used "share of market." Other types of retailers like supermarkets are also testing programs to increase customer value.

Returning to Arthur Hughes's example, he points out that Safeway had determined that it could spend a maximum of $2 per customer per month on customer relationship management. That is not a great deal of money, and it is imperative that it be used wisely. Safeway, for example, tried giving targeted customers an ice cream cone on their birthdays and measured incremental sales that resulted from that trip to the store. Retailers have also experimented with programs including:

- Customer specific pricing, where members get cheaper prices on certain items
- Rewards for larger total purchases
- Rewards for frequency of purchase

TABLE 4.2	Increase in Customer Value Using Targeted Programs

Lifetime Value Before New Programs

	Year 1	Year 2	Year 3
Customers	5,000	3,750	2,963
Retention rate	75.0%	79.0%	85.0%
Visits/week	0.68	0.73	0.82
Average basket	$38	$50	$61
Total sales	**$6,120,000**	**$6,843,750**	**$7,409,213**
Cost percentage	83.0%	80.0%	79.0%
Direct costs	$5,079,600	$5,475,000	$5,853,278
Labor + benefits 11%	$673,200	$752,813	$815,013
Card program $16, $8	$80,000	$30,000	$23,700
Customer-specific marketing	$61,200	$66,438	$74,092
Advertising 1%	$61,200	$66,438	$74,092
Total costs	**$5,955,200**	**$6,394,688**	**$6,840,176**
Gross profit	$164,800	$449,063	$569,037
Discount rate	1.00	1.20	1.44
NPV profit	$164,800	$374,219	$395,165
Cumulative NPV profit	$164,800	$539,019	$934,183
Lifetime value	$32.96	$107.80	$186.84

Source: Arthur Middleton Hughes, "Building Successful Retail Strategies Using Customer Lifetime Value," Database Marketing Institute, September 7, 2011 (http://www.dbmarketing.com/articles/Art181.htm).

- Rewards for shopping on slow days
- Personal recognition and relationship programs

What if the company took the major step of cutting its advertising budget in order to divert money to the customer relationship program? In Table 4.2, Hughes presents some possible results.

Assume that the company has cut advertising to 1 percent from the 2 percent in Table 4.1. That money is shown in the "Customer Specific Marketing" line in Table 4.2. All the rest of the cost and CLV calculations are the same. Notice, however, that the top portion of the table changes. In year 1, the retention rate goes from 70 percent to 75 percent. Visits per week increase from 0.64 to 0.68. The average basket (sale) increases from $33 to $38. As a result of the increase in number of visits per week and average sale, the CLV for year 1 goes from $26.24 to $32.96. Because the retention rate has gone up, the company starts year 2 with 3,750 customers instead of 3,500. This increases the revenue stream. Visits per week and average sales go up as compared to year 2 without the targeted programs. The same reasoning follows for year 3. At the end of year 3, the NPV of the net revenue stream is $934,183. Divided by 5,000—the original cohort of customers who have now been tracked through three years—the CLV is $186.84.

Table 4.3 shows the increase in CLV that results from the targeted programs. Since the cost of the targeted programs came out of the amount previously budgeted for advertising, there is no increase in marketing cost. The gain is therefore incremental profit.

TABLE 4.3	Gain in Customer Value from Using Targeted Programs		
Effect of Adoption of New Programs			
New lifetime value (CLV)	$32.96	$107.80	$186.84
Previous lifetime value (CLV)	$26.24	$84.97	$143.82
Gain	$6.72	$22.83	$43.02

Source: Arthur Middleton Hughes, "Building Successful Retail Strategies Using Customer Lifetime Value," Database Marketing Institute, September 7, 2011 (http://www.dbmarketing.com/articles/Art181.htm).

Uses of CLV

The Safeway case study is simple compared to the reality of customers being acquired and leaving at various times, a multiplicity of marketing programs occurring at the same time or in sequence, and the activities of competitors, all of which may have important effects on variables like retention rates. It also assumes that all customers are equally desirable prospects for targeted programs. That is usually not true. Banks, for example, sometimes find that their highest value customers are not desirable targets for additional marketing effort because they are already giving the bank as much of their business as they are likely to give. At the other end of the scale, many enterprises find that their lowest value customers are unlikely to upgrade enough to make the marketing expenditures worthwhile. An overriding issue becomes, "How much should I spend to acquire customers who fit a certain profile?"

The acquisition problem is commonly stated as, "Who are my best customers and how can I acquire more like them?" To that we should add, "And how much should I spend on the acquisition?" Identifying best customers is another time-honored direct marketing technique based on a simple RFM (recency × frequency × monetary value) model. This model does a good job of segmenting a customer database according to value in many industry sectors.[8] The issue of acquiring more customers like the best ones can be as simple, in the traditional direct marketing environment, as renting lists with similar characteristics and mailing to them. As we build databases of customer activities on the Internet, the same principles will apply. To speed the process of acquiring many years of customer data, marketers have increasingly turned to predictive modeling to profile the best potential customers and to estimate a suitable acquisition cost target. We will give a brief introduction to predictive modeling in the last part of this chapter.

Many CLV-based marketing approaches are directly transferable onto the web where their value is often magnified. What if, based on available data and models, the marketer could know within seconds what the prospective value of a

INTERACTIVE EXERCISE 4.3   Calculating CLV

There are several interactive tools available for calculating CLV. Look at the sample problem on the Harvard Business School site at http://bit.ly/vJm4MU.

Then try changing assumptions in the data on the Tools tab to see how sensitive the results are to different

operational data, like gross margin, customer data, and number of purchases per year. Think about how marketing decisions could be affected by this type of information.

site visitor is and consequently could generate an offer that is both optimally cost-effective and attractive to the prospect—all done on the fly, so quickly that the viewer is unaware of the background mechanics? In fact, this is exactly what happens when a customer applies for a credit card online.

On the other hand, CLV analysis will invariably show some customers to be unprofitable. That presents two basic options. If additional analysis indicates that there are one or more subsegments that have the potential to become profitable, marketing programs should be developed with this objective. If there are, as if often the case, other subsegments that appear to have little probability of becoming profitable, one of two actions must be taken. The first is to cut costs— either by cutting the costs of acquiring customers in this segment or by reducing costs to serve them. For example, these customers may be offered only self-service options via telephone or web, with personal service options reserved for profitable customer segments.

Some of these applications raise the specter of overstepping the bounds of customer privacy, a subject that is covered in detail in Chapter 15. As long as we can manage issues of customer privacy, however, strategies based on knowledge and enhancement of CLV provide exciting prospects for Internet marketers. This also includes the social net, where marketers are struggling to quantify the return on investment of their social media marketing investment. One aspect of that is trying to understand the value of a customer on a specific platform. Because of its dominance of the social media space, there is great interest in Facebook, which has led to a recent assessment of the value of a Facebook customer (see Figure 4.6).

The survey by Syncapse found that across the 20 consumer brands studied:

- Facebook fans spend an average of $71.84 more on the brand than nonfans.
- They are 28 percent more likely to continue using the brand than nonfans.
- They are 41 percent more likely to recommend a fanned product than are nonfans.
- Fans were more likely to report favorable attitudes toward the brand than were nonfans.

The model also includes the value of "earned media," essentially favorable commentary by customers, a social media concept that is discussed in Chapter 9. When these five model elements were quantified, Syncapse estimated the average value of a Facebook fan to be $136.38. Nike has the highest "best fan" value of all brands studied at $380.16. Oreo cookies have the lowest "average fan" value at $60.60.[9] That is a striking example of how the difference in product margins affects customer value. It also suggests that some people eat a lot of Oreo cookies! You can be confident that there will be many other attempts to quantify the value of customers based on their use of social networks. That is an important application of CLV concepts that is in its infancy.

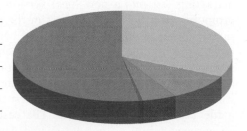

Spend	$ 71.84
Loyalty	$ 43.71
Recommendations	$ 13.57
Earned Media Value	$ 6.79
Cost Offset for Fan Acquisition	$ 0.47
Sum	$ 136.38

FIGURE **4.6** The Estimated Value of a Facebook Fan

Source: "The Value of a Facebook Fan: An Empirical Review," p. 14, June 2010, Syncapse Corporation (www.syncapse.com). Reprinted with permission.

The almost limitless marketing options presented by this type of information-based marketing strategy development and execution[10] call into play another important direct marketing technique, that of testing.

Testing Direct Response Programs

Testing in a timely and statistically valid manner is another advantage that direct marketing has traditionally held over mass media marketing. Direct marketers are able to track each response and therefore to know whether programs are performing satisfactorily. In addition, some direct response media, mail for example, have lent themselves well to controlled testing of different offers or different creative executions. On a broader scale, offer placement in different media can also be tested. Again, this set of direct marketing tools is directly transferable to the Internet space, which offers even greater potential for evaluating and refining marketing efforts on a timely basis. Rick Fernandes of webloyalty.com describes the comparison as follows:

> In an offline campaign, a fortunate marketer can create and launch a new campaign in eight to 10 weeks. Orders begin to trickle in and maybe 80 percent of orders are in 90 days later. So a baseline is established five to six months after the idea is crystallized.
>
> To improve the baseline performance, you can try to improve the quality of the list to determine if the offer was effective. Perhaps you could improve the order process. You can systematically test variables to determine critical paths, but it's hard, costly and time consuming. You basically drop the mail and hope for the best.
>
> Now consider an email marketing campaign. There's not that much left to chance. Did your message get delivered? How many opened it? Which version of your email was most effective? Did those graphics in the email help or hurt? Once they got to your site, did they go past the home page? Where else did they go? How long were they there?
>
> You receive answers immediately, and if the test is not meeting expectations, you can drop it or do major surgery on it before you do yourself any real economic damage.[11]

The simplest kind of direct marketing test is an **A/B split**. There are two key aspects of an A/B split test:

1. *Change only one element.* That can be a specific element of the promotion like an offer—"15% Off" versus "Free Shipping," for example. Or it can be a promotion that is completely different in some major respect—the creative execution, for example. If only one element is changed, any differences in response can be attributed to that element and that element only.
2. *Test the big things.* Test only changes that are likely to make a substantial and profitable difference in response to the promotion.

There are also two different ways of executing the test. The classic direct marketing test pits a new (test) version against a control, which would be the promotion that has worked best in the past. It is also possible to test two versions, neither of which has been used before.

In the traditional print environment—mail or magazines, for example—testing requires different physical versions of the direct mail piece or magazine ad. Although good direct marketers tested consistently, it was slow and cumbersome compared to testing on the Internet where changes to a promotion can be made with a few mouseclicks. The ease and speed of testing on the Internet encouraged products that automated new test versions and placement in online media or on the website. An early entrant into this space was a firm called Offermatica; think about the name! It offered an automated approach to testing that was an important component of overall marketing optimization. Offermatica was purchased by Omniture, a metrics firm. Omniture was subsequently purchased by Adobe, whose products are familiar to anyone who has ever read a PDF file. Adobe had been using the Omniture product line in its own testing prior to acquiring the company. It was the case of "liking the products so much we purchased the company." It was also a case of understanding that testing is essential to Internet marketing success.

Figure 4.7 shows two homepage promotions for Adobe's Lightroom product—software for digital image editing. Figure 4.7 Recipe A shows the control for this test and Figure 4.7 Recipe B shows the new creative execution (the test). The fact that Recipe A is specified as the control for this test indicates that it had been successfully used in the past. However, the product managers at Adobe though it could be improved.

Adobe wanted to test an updated page template with a shorter hero (main) image on the page and smaller Learning/Help thumbnails in order to move content higher on the page above the fold, as well as wanting to test a black versus white backgrounds. Their hypothesis was that these changes would make it more likely that visitors would find what they were looking for and therefore be less likely to abandon the page. You can see (Recipe B) that the slightly smaller hero image and smaller supporting images helped condense the page, allowing visitors to consume the content on the homepage at a greater rate without scrolling down or instead, abandoning the page.

The test execution produced a revenue per visitor 15.82 percent higher and an average order value 13.3 percent higher than that achieved by the control version. Notice the metrics that were chosen to measure success. It was not a simple response measure like click-throughs. It was a measure of actual revenue by the number of visitors to the page, a comparison of success to the marketing effort required to achieve it. We will return frequently to the issue of selecting the most appropriate and powerful metric to measure Internet marketing success throughout the text.

The statistical question is whether the 15.82 percent improvement is a statistically significant difference over the control. It is a notable improvement and the number of visitors to the page over the duration of the test is probably large, so the likelihood that it is statistically significant is high. In any event, the difference is enough that Adobe planned a follow-up test before making the decision to use only the winning page (Recipe B). This is also standard direct marketing procedure; do not make important decisions on the basis of a single test.

Notice that this is precisely the statistical testing process taught in basic statistics courses. As this example suggests, there are now software packages that have testing options, alternative marketer objectives, and statistical decision making built in.

Direct marketing testing, whether it uses a simple A/B split or a complex experimental design, is both a marketing and a statistical process. Table 4.4 summarizes the marketing approach. Paralleling the marketing activities is a set of statistical activities—establishing hypotheses, choosing the significance level, computing the sample size, and specifying the decision rule—that the student recognizes as the classical hypothesis testing process from statistics and marketing research courses. Both the marketing and the statistical activities are necessary in order to have a valid test on which to base decisions.

Some marketers test some variable on every marketing program they run. *Fast Company* magazine profiled the credit card issuer Capital One and described, "Its mission: Deliver the right product, at the right price, to the right customer, at the right time. Its method: Never stop testing, learning, or innovating."[12] Others test only when a marketing problem is evident. Whatever the corporate policy on testing, it is a powerful tool to show marketers what actually works best in a natural setting.[13]

(a)

(b)

FIGURE **4.7** A/B Split Test of Adobe Lightroom Home Page Promotion Versions

Source: Courtesy of Adobe. Used with permission.

TABLE 4.4	The Testing Process

Reasons for Conducting a Test
- Standard practice ("We test all marketing programs.")
- Strategy questions ("Which subset of lapsed customers can be reactivated?")
- Tactical questions ("Which incentive works best with this offer?")

Design the Test
- What marketing variables to test (New offer, different creative execution, new list, or others.)
- Type of test (Against control, A/B split, complex experimental design)
- Sample (Entire population or random sample; sample size)

Establish Test Metrics
- Test criterion (variable on which test is judged)
- Decision rule (the values of the variable on which the decision will be based)
- Cutoff date
- Ranges for success/failure/continued testing
- Timing and nature of reporting (Online, on demand, formal report)

Execute and Monitor the Test
- Ensure that test is conducted according to specifications
- Record results
- Monitor competitive/environmental activity that might affect results
- Record any deviations from testing plan

Analyze and Report Test Results
- Which version performed best?
- Was the difference
  - Statistically significant?
  - At an acceptable level of risk?

Make Marketing Decisions
- What changes, if any, should we make to our marketing efforts?
- Should we repeat the test? Should we test new variables?

Source: A statistical approach to marketing testing is described by Paul Berger in a chapter from *Direct Marketing Management* at http://marylouroberts.info/images/dir.mark.man.ch10.pdf.

A More Complex Online Test

In the A/B split example, we pointed out that, in order to have a valid test, only one element of the promotion can be changed. In that case, it was the featured product offer.

Figure 4.8a shows the bare bones of another example, a test conducted by MarketingExperiments for an unidentified client. It represents another traditional direct marketing type of test. In this case, three different "treatments" are compared to a "control" in the classic experimental protocol covered in marketing research courses. In the case of marketing experimentation, the control treatment is the promotion that has been most successful in the past—implying ongoing testing. It is also a careful approach in which the historically most successful promotion (the control) is not discarded until something clearly better (i.e., a statistically significant better experimental treatment) is found.

The other difference from the simple A/B split is that the entire promotion, or major elements of the control promotion, can be revised. In this case, there were three experimental treatments. Treatment 1 was almost entirely text, as opposed to the control, which has prominent graphical elements. Treatment 2 has similar text but more graphics. Treatment 3 has the same elements, but smaller graphics.

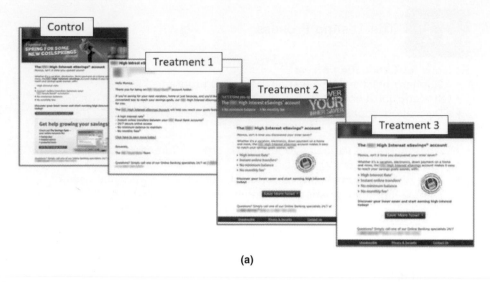

(a)

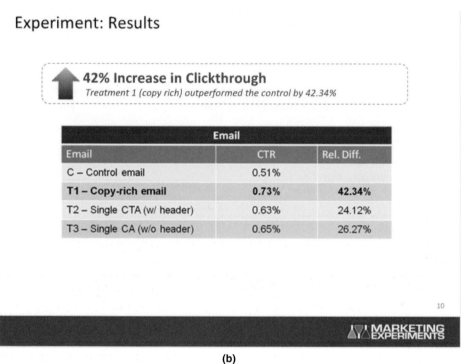

(b)

FIGURE **4.8** Email Experiment with Control and Three Experimental Treatments

Source: Marketing Experiments, http://www.marketingexperiments.com/email-marketing-strategy/the-five-best-ways-to-optimize-email-response-part-3.html.

Figure 4.8b shows that all three experimental treatments (different emails) performed better than the control. The copy is simpler and more "chunked," so that may be one explanation. However, and be honest, would you have guessed that the straightforward and not visually appealing Treatment 1 would have performed substantially better than the treatments with graphics? While many of us would not have assumed so, the hypothesis may be that there is less distraction in the text-only email, which leads to a higher click-through rate. Direct marketers would add that if you really do not believe the results, repeat the test. In the online environment, repeat testing is quick and inexpensive, and it should usually be done before the marketer adopts a "new control" on the basis of one test to replace one that has performed well over time.

Traditional direct marketers would also make a strong case for experimentation over marketing research to identify most successful promotional approaches. Testing permits the marketer to find out what people actually do when faced with an offer or another type of communication. Marketing research has to rely on what people say they will do. Online testing can be set up quickly by experienced personnel, and the conduct of the test is also quick, even compared to online marketing research.[14]

No discussion of online testing would be complete without a mention of Google Website Optimizer.[15] This Google service uses the principles just described to allow marketers to develop tests of web pages to improve their performance. The service is easy to use and it is well explained in a good video tutorial on their site.[16] It is an excellent place to start for any marketer who wants to test promotional executions but is not familiar with the process.

Testing various direct response options is one way in which traditional direct marketing has carried over onto the Internet. Far and away, the most important transplant, however, is the use of a customer database. From the beginning, this text has pointed out that every mouse click on the Internet represents a possible data point. Only marketers who capture and use this data to make better marketing decisions can tap the full power of the interactive web.

The Database Imperative

The distinctive tools and techniques of direct marketing all have a great deal to offer in the interactive marketing setting created by the Internet. The foundations of virtually all the capabilities that differentiate direct response marketing from mass media marketing reside in the marketing **database**. It is the repository of all customer-related knowledge and the source of data for analytical activities. It is the knowledge resource that to some extent can compensate for the churn of human resources in many contemporary firms.

Correctly conceptualized, however, it is not "the marketing database." When marketers refer to "the marketing database," they are generally referring to the customer database. However, there are actually numerous databases that should all be linked through some type of a central repository such as a data warehouse so information can be provided on demand to decision makers and operational personnel. Figure 4.9 provides a hypothetical mapping of a typical marketing database system indicating the nature of the data in each and its primary source.

From the marketer's viewpoint, the data warehouse, which contains multiple individual databases, can be conceptualized as having four basic components. The marketing management databases drive marketing programs, and the marketing support databases provide additional data that are important for decision-making purposes. Other functional areas of the business supply databases that are crucial to the functioning of marketing programs and customer service. These include the order-processing database and the inventory database, both of which are essential to good customer service. The sales force management and project databases also provide important marketing-related information. Finally, externally purchased or linked databases provide additional valuable data. This includes commercial

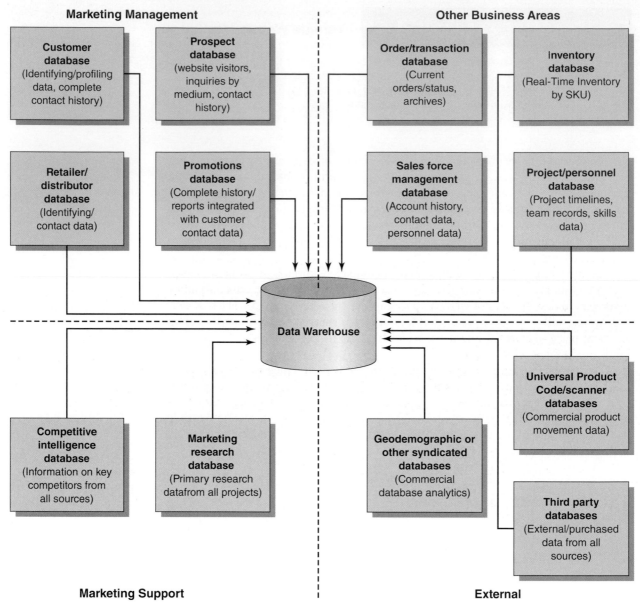

FIGURE **4.9** Marketing Database System
Source: © Cengage Learning 2013

scanner databases that track product movement. There are numerous database products that marketers can overlay onto the customer database to increase its predictive power. The Prizm geodemographic products of Nielsen's Claritas division[17] are a good example of this type of external data product. There are a variety of other databases available from third parties that are important information resources to specific industry sectors. For example, the data of the large credit bureaus are used in proprietary credit scoring models by banks and other credit issuers.

Some marketers may require fewer databases for effective decision making and operations, but in reality, a large company may have dozens of databases that need to be integrated to give a full view of the customer. And the technological reality is that the individual databases are often not neatly interconnected through a data warehouse. Instead, they are sitting on various desktops, connected to one individual or unit, and essentially acting as isolated islands of information. If this is the situation, marketers will be unable to make effective use of the information resource for marketing or customer service.

The difficulty of integrating many databases that have a variety of data structures and that reside on a variety of different platforms can hardly be understated. However, integrating the databases into a data warehouse is a technical task. The job of the marketer is to determine what data need to be in the central repository and to champion its creation. In order to do this, the marketer must ask what accessible database information can accomplish for the business. In answering that question, let us focus for the moment on the database of actual and prospective customers.

Benefits of Using a Customer Database

The profile and customer transactions data contained in the database are captured from the clickstream created by customer activity. The challenge is to capture the data and use that data effectively for marketing decision making. Even before the Internet, some companies that were not traditional direct marketers began to build and use customer databases in ways that improved their marketing programs. One interesting example is Harrah's Hotels and Casinos, the gambling and entertainment mecca.

In the mid-1990s, Harrah's made a far-reaching strategic decision. While its casino competitors were pouring money into lavish physical facilities in Las Vegas, Atlantic City, and other prime gambling venues, Harrah's decided to place its bets on a customer loyalty program backed by superior customer service and satisfaction at all its properties. In 1997, it rolled out its "total rewards" program, based on airline frequent-flyer programs. Its player card tracked all the activities—gambling, entertainment, dining, and hotel stays—of a customer who was visiting a Harrah's property. The company used this data to build a comprehensive database of individual patronage of all 12 Harrah's properties.

MIS professor Hugh J. Watson has visualized Harrah's system from both the marketing and IT perspectives (see Figure 4.10). Many marketers use the term "closed loop" to describe a process in which data are collected in a database and used to execute programs, with data from those programs being added to the customer database. With each program, the marketer has better data with which to create better programs. From the IT perspective, all data, from whatever source, are lodged in a data warehouse in which data analysis can be carried out. The analysis identifies key marketing elements like best offers and best market segments—the better data the marketer needs to create the better programs. This is not only a good portrayal of the Harrah's system, but also an excellent example of how marketing and IT must work together to create a data-driven decision system.

Harrah's found that building the database across properties and their differing IT platforms was a technological challenge. Persuading property managers to cooperate and to make use of the data for cross-property promotions was even more challenging. All casinos assumed that players were loyal to specific properties, and on this assumption, each of the 12 Harrah's locations had run their marketing programs independently. Their independence even included having their own individual player's cards and separate databases. Headquarters had to convince the property managers of the merits of a centralized database and marketing programs to encourage cross-property visits. The system represented a different way of thinking about how each manager marketed the casino in a general sense. More specifically, the idea of cross-marketing with other casinos suggested cannibalization of an individual casino's business. It may have represented a perceived loss of control over the casino's marketing and therefore its success.

A positive outcome, however, was quickly evident. In two years, Harrah's cross-market revenues increased by 72 percent and almost 10 percent of its profits could be traced to cross-market visits.[18] This was an impressive short-term result, but more success was to come as Harrah's began to mine the database of information it was capturing about its customers (discussed later in this chapter).

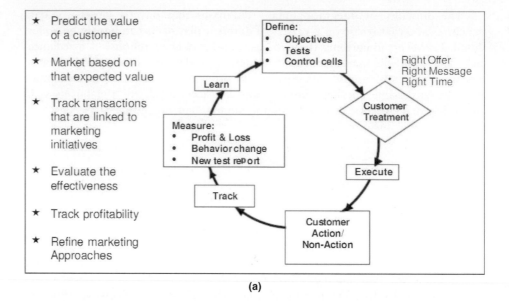

(a)

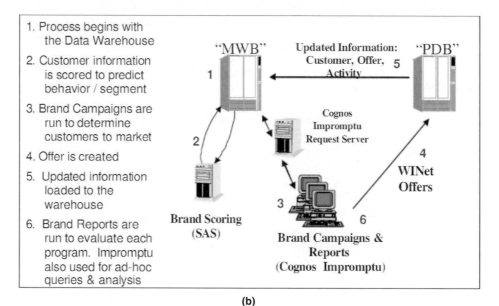

(b)

FIGURE **4.10** Marketing and IT Views of Harrah's Closed-Loop Marketing System

Source: "Harrah's High Payoff from Customer Information," pp. 10 (Figure 5), 12 (Figure 7). Reprinted with permission of Caesars Entertainment.

Using a Customer Database for Program Execution and Marketing Analytics

There are two different ways to approach database use. One involves *analytics*—any statistical technique that compresses the vast amount of data into summary statistics that are useful either for managerial decision making or for program execution. The second approach involves using individual data items or summary statistics to *execute marketing programs.* Figure 4.11 presents an overview of both types of use in a hierarchical format. The programmatic activities portion is not absolute; it is rather a suggestion of the types of uses at each analytical level that are generally more appropriate.

While it is possible to develop marketing programs around a single data item—an offer to all women in the database, for example—it would be unusual for this to be an optimal use of the database. It is more likely that a **profile**, using either RFM or a special-purpose data model, will produce more precise marketing action. This action is

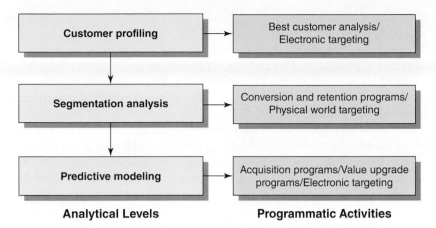

Analytical Levels   **Programmatic Activities**

FIGURE **4.11** Analytical Database Hierarchy
Source: © Cengage Learning 2013

most likely to take the form of targeting individuals who have been identified as potential best customers for a particular marketing program. It is described as "electronic targeting" because the capabilities of the web allow customers to be identified and targeted with individualized content. One type of individualized targeting is "event-triggered" targeting. Some event in the customer's life—anything from purchase of a new car to a birthday—triggers an automated system to communicate with that specific customer.

At the second level of complexity in analytical terms is statistical analysis, which has an important use for segmentation purposes in a database environment. When the application requires selection of a group of potential best customers out of the larger database, this will be the approach to take. Because this leads to segmentation marketing, it is an approach that is highly appropriate for the physical world in which targeting customers individually is usually cost-prohibitive. In addition, because the focus is on existing customers who reside in the database, it is particularly suitable for conversion and retention programs, which can be executed either offline or online. The most often used analysis at this level is some form of regression ranging from simple linear regression to more complex nonlinear models. Cluster analysis is also used for segmentation purposes. It is worth noting that these commonly used statistical techniques are often described as models, and they produce results that aid in understanding the relationships between variables that affect customer behavior and hence are a necessary precursor to formal model building.

The line between segmentation analysis and **predictive modeling** often seems blurry in actual practice, but the conceptual distinction is clear. Segmentation analysis uses statistical models to group customers on the basis of characteristics (demographic and lifestyle) and product-related behaviors. Predictive modeling uses this data to build models that predict future customer or prospect behavior. The most commonly used type of predictive modeling is response modeling in which the statistician constructs a model that predicts the likelihood of response to a given program on a customer-by-customer basis.

Capital One has used the results of its continuous testing to develop an extensive set of predictive models that are used to make an additional offer to almost anyone who calls Capital One for almost any reason. For example, if you call to activate a credit card, you are offered an associated service like balance transfer. Capital One views every call as a selling opportunity and uses models to predict which callers are most likely to buy something and what they are likely to buy. Calls are routed to call center reps who are specially trained to handle particular types of calls. According to Joey Berson, who directs cross-sell offers at Capital One:

> Every one of the three dozen non-credit-card products that Capital One offers has a statistical model behind it that outlines which kinds of customers will find it most appealing, and under what circumstances. A specific "product offer" comes to a customer-service rep in the same data burst as a caller's account information. So the decision about what to offer is made the instant someone calls.

He adds that if "you're calling because you lost your card, I'd be a fool not to sell you credit-card registration."

In practice what happens is that information about the customer plus the offer the customer is most likely to accept shows up on the rep's screen while the call is being routed through the system (a "data burst"). By the time the rep answers, she has all the information in front of her to service the customer well and to make an offer that is likely to result in a sale.[19] That is the ultimate goal of predictive modeling. Note, however, that this kind of modeling is based on extensive testing to determine which offers work for which customers as well as a database that contains the customer data, results of thousands of tests, and many predictive models, all of which can be linked together in real time. It is a complex process but nothing less would allow a company to link service calls to sales opportunities in real time.

The Power of Data Mining

The opportunities presented by the customer database are great, but you may have seen a recurring theme running through the preceding sections. The traditional approach to database marketing requires that data be captured, housed in a database, analyzed, and modeled. For databases of moderate size, this approach, using simple tools like Excel macros or multiple regression, works well. However, data warehouses like Harrah's, which contained about 300 gigabytes of customer transactions and preferences data as early as 2003,[20] quickly become unwieldy, and more powerful tools are needed.

The solution to a problem like Harrah's and other large-scale collectors of data like Capital One is a set of statistical tools that has become known by the catch-all name of **data mining**. Kurt Thearling writing on Thearling.com gives a deceptively simple definition of data mining. He says it is "*the automated extraction of hidden predictive information from databases.*"[21] He goes on to say that this includes "*automated prediction of trends and behaviors.*"[22] For instance, all three of the test emails for savings accounts in Figure 4.8 performed well. Did, for example, current investment customers respond better to one email while customers with only a checking account responded better to another? Knowing this would be the next step in developing more customer-centered communications. Data mining also enables the "*automated discovery of previously unknown patterns.*" Patterns that exist in data are often not intuitively obvious. Witness the often quoted finding that people who purchase diapers at the supermarket are also likely to purchase beer. The reason for patterns like this is often not known, nor may the reason even be important to the marketer. As it stands, it suggests a promotional opportunity and that is sufficient.

In other words, data mining is used to produce customer information not previously known, or perhaps even previously hypothesized, from large databases. How is it done? The simple answer is that data mining produces new knowledge because it looks for patterns in data that might not be revealed by traditional statistical analysis. Techniques like decision trees and neural networks may be used as well as techniques commonly used in marketing research like regression and cluster analysis.

One of the important aspects of data mining is that marketing managers do not have to deal directly with the complex analytics. They also do not have to request programming assistance from the IT department in order to get information from the data warehouse through the data mining routines. The software includes easy-to-use interfaces that permit managers to ask questions, often in natural language, like "What were sales yesterday in the northeastern region?" The manager can specify how the information is to be provided—a numerical report or a graphic are common options.

Data Mining at Harrah's

In the case of Harrah's, management made a conscious decision to let customer data suggest marketing strategies, instead of developing strategies and then looking for data to execute them. It already knew from its marketing research that customers who carried their loyalty card only spent about 36 percent of their annual gaming budget at Harrah's.[23] Extensive mining of its enterprise data warehouse revealed more useful information:

- 26 percent of its patrons generated 82 percent of the revenue.
- These patrons were not the "high rollers" portrayed in books and movies. They were more likely to be middle class or professional, and middle aged or retired, to have discretionary time, and to prefer playing slot machines.
- They responded better to an offer of free chips than to the more traditional casino offers of free rooms, meals, and entertainment.
- Customers who were satisfied with the Harrah's experience increased their spending by 24 percent per year. Those who were dissatisfied decreased it by 10 percent.

Using the results of its data mining, Harrah's was able to construct and test a predictive model of "customer worth," a theoretical forecast of how much a customer could be expected to spend over the long term. This is CLV by a different name. The company used the estimate of customer worth to create three tiers of rewards. The highest level Diamond cardholders, for example, were assigned personal hosts and rarely if ever had to stand in line for anything from checking into the hotel to visiting a restaurant for a meal. Platinum customers stood in visibly shorter lines. Gold cardholders (the lowest level) or customers without a player's card stood in lines and watched the Diamond and Platinum customers sail on by. Harrah's dubbed this "aspirational marketing" and it worked to give customers an incentive to spend more in order to move up to a higher service level.[24]

Data Mining in the NBA

A final example illustrates data mining used in a different context. Would you believe that the NBA (National Basketball Association) has a sophisticated application based on data mining for both operations and marketing? The Orlando Magic was one of the first teams to begin using statistical software to look for patterns in the huge amount of game data. An average game has about 200 possessions and there are about 1,200 NBA games each year. The sheer volume of data was so overwhelming that initial efforts provided only the basic kind of stats that could be found in any newspaper.

Enter an IBM strategic partner by the name of Virtual Gold and a data mining application called Advanced Scout, specifically tailored for the use of NBA coaches and scouts. After two devastating losses to the Miami Heat in the 1997 finals, the coaches of the Magic turned to Advanced Scout. According to Virtual Gold press material:

> Advanced Scout showed the Orlando Magic coaches something that none of them had previously recognized. When Brian Shaw and Darrell Armstrong were in the game, something was sparked within their teammate Penny Hardaway—the Magic's leading scorer at that time. Armstrong received more play-time and hence, Hardaway was far more effective. The Magic went on to win the next two games and nearly caused the upset of the year. Fans everywhere rallied around the team and naysayers quickly replaced their doubts with season ticket purchases for the following year.[25]

The software application is used in tandem with video recording of games to help coaches uncover patterns they otherwise might miss. A technology note from UCLA's Anderson School of Management explains a bit more about how it works:

> An analysis of the play-by-play sheet of the game played between the New York Knicks and the Cleveland Cavaliers on January 6, 1995, reveals that when Mark Price played the Guard position, John Williams attempted four jump shots and made each one! Advanced Scout not only finds this pattern, but explains that it is interesting because it differs considerably from the average shooting percentage of 49.30% for the Cavaliers during that game.[26]

IBM, whose software provides the basis for the application, said that 25 NBA teams were using the application by 2001.[27]

With that level of adoption, it is not surprising that NBA teams have turned to mining of their customer database as one way of dealing with the declining game attendance in the last several years. Group 1 Software consultant Jim

Stafford has a case study of an NBA team that was moving into a larger arena, in the face of declining game attendance. The team needed to upgrade existing season ticket holders and identify new season ticket prospects from the ranks of single-game ticket purchasers.

After careful processing of the available ticketing data and choice of statistical models, the analysts identified patron segments that had the highest likelihood of responding to ticket offers. In addition to demographic profiles from its own data, Group 1 overlaid Prizm[28] cluster data on its segments. Using its response model and all this data, it ranked each member of the database according to his probability of responding positively. That produced a list ranked from 1 (the patron who has the highest probability of responding) to the total number of database members, in this case, about 3,000 customers (the patron in this data set who has the lowest probability of responding). In this kind of predictive modeling, *each member of the database receives a score and those scores are rank ordered from highest to lowest*. Admittedly, there are some special techniques for handling large databases—perhaps a million or more members—but the principle of ranking each member holds.

The yellow bar in Figure 4.12a shows the result of the ranking—the 5 percent who had the highest probability of responding favorably to a season ticket

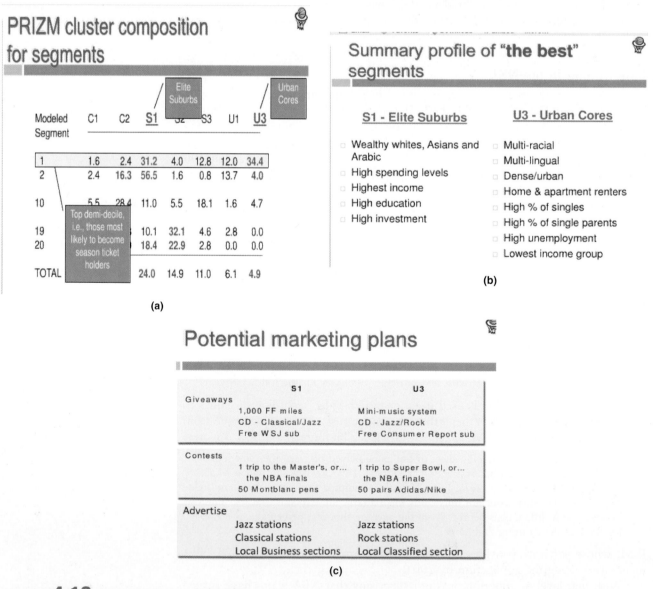

PRIZM cluster composition for segments

Modeled Segment	C1	C2	S1 (Elite Suburbs)	S2	S3	U1	U3 (Urban Cores)
1	1.6	2.4	31.2	4.0	12.8	12.0	34.4
2	2.4	16.3	56.5	1.6	0.8	13.7	4.0
10	5.5	28.4	11.0	5.5	18.1	1.6	4.7
19			10.1	32.1	4.6	2.8	0.0
20			18.4	22.9	2.8	0.0	0.0
TOTAL			24.0	14.9	11.0	6.1	4.9

Top demi-decile, i.e., those most likely to become season ticket holders

(a)

Summary profile of "the best" segments

S1 - Elite Suburbs
- Wealthy whites, Asians and Arabic
- High spending levels
- Highest income
- High education
- High investment

U3 - Urban Cores
- Multi-racial
- Multi-lingual
- Dense/urban
- Home & apartment renters
- High % of singles
- High % of single parents
- High unemployment
- Lowest income group

(b)

Potential marketing plans

	S1	U3
Giveaways	1,000 FF miles CD - Classical/Jazz Free WSJ sub	Mini-music system CD - Jazz/Rock Free Consumer Report sub
Contests	1 trip to the Master's, or... the NBA finals 50 Montblanc pens	1 trip to Super Bowl, or... the NBA finals 50 pairs Adidas/Nike
Advertise	Jazz stations Classical stations Local Business sections	Jazz stations Rock stations Local Classified section

(c)

FIGURE **4.12** Data Mining in the NBA

Source: SlideShare Inc., http://www.slideshare.net/jrstafford/ncdm-datamining-case-study-2010-3563095, slides 28, 33, 40.

offer. When you aggregate the top two rows, segments S1, Elite Suburbs in Prizm terminology, and U3, which Prizm calls Urban Cores, are clearly the most desirable segments; that is, they have the highest probability of responding to a season ticket offer. Analysis of demographic and behavioral data produced the profiles in Figure 4.12b. With this information, the team could devise a separate marketing approach for each of the two segments.

Even without segmentation, the analysis suggested the team could cut marketing costs substantially by just promoting to the top 50 percent of the season ticket prospects. That would produce 70 percent of the likely responses.[29] A published literature review suggests that other NBA teams have been successfully using data mining applications in their marketing programs for a number of years.[30]

All the examples described in this chapter point to the detailed data collection and analysis that must take place in order to enable data-driven marketing. This is not something that happens over night. Both the Harrah's and the NBA examples showcase programs that have evolved over a decade or more. With that in mind, we close the chapter with a brief discussion of a hierarchy that can help to guide marketers through this process, providing a return on the investment of money and time at each step.

The Hierarchy of Interactive Strategies

Marketing on the Internet offers many possibilities for data analysis and strategy development that marketers have only been able to wish for in the past. At the same time, it presents many demands, both technological and strategic. Successful Internet strategies appear to be moving up a hierarchy in which each stage allows more persuasive communication with the prospective customer and more compelling ways in which to create value for that customer. Each stage also places increasingly rigorous requirements on marketing strategies and operations as well as on the associated technology. The hierarchy is shown in Figure 4.13.

The underlying rationale is that as marketers learn more about their customers, they can develop more focused strategies and more targeted promotional efforts. Take as an example the new website of a hypothetical start-up business that is just beginning to develop a customer database for marketing purposes. The firm undoubtedly has some *informational* marketing material that it can make available to customers as it begins to work on a corporate site. A B2C firm might adapt advertising material, especially from print media, as site content. A B2B firm is likely to have sales support material that will provide initial content—hence the derogatory term "brochure ware." A rather static, informational site may be a viable beginning, but the business needs to have a plan to move beyond that in order to tap the power of the Internet.

A reasonable next step is to add some *interactivity* to the site, both to engage the visitor's attention and to provide reasons for the visitor to return. The P&G

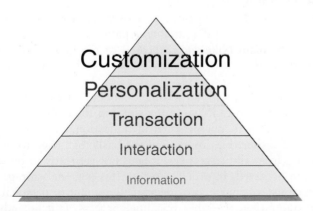

FIGURE **4.13** Hierarchy of Customer-Focused Marketing Strategies
Source: © Cengage Learning 2013

pages shown in Figure 4.2 are good examples in a B2C context. B2B companies provide valuable information like product demonstration videos and real-time order tracking to increase their level of on-demand customer service. Egovernment sites allow citizens to handle many of the details of everyday interaction with government agencies like renewing driver's licenses. Nonprofits allow people to join or renew memberships, to donate, or to request information or services.

At some point in the informational or interactive stages, the business needs to begin to collect the names and email addresses of visitors as it looks ahead to personalized communication. That is the beginning of the customer database.

Every organization needs to think about how it can capture the email addresses of visitors who are genuinely interested in their product and are willing to receive additional communications. This step is the beginning of the conversion and retention processes, discussed in more detail in Chapters 10 and 11. Before an organization begins to collect data, it needs to think carefully about how the data will be used to add value to the customer experience as well as to provide data for better marketing decisions. Put another way, it needs to collect useful data that visitors are willing to provide.

Moving to a *transactional* site is a big step. Transactional sites require specialized technology like shopping carts. They require the integration of back-end data—inventory databases for in-stock status, for example. The site must be sure that effective security software and procedures are in place before any transactional features are activated. These and other possible requirements are demanding in terms of both technical complexity and smoothly functioning internal business processes. This is a good point for the business to stop and recognize that any process that is not smooth, error-free, and customer-friendly in the physical should be reengineered *before* it is moved to the Internet where its flaws are likely to be magnified many times over. It is also a point at which the business can turn to Web Services instead of developing all the applications on its own.

Once solid transactional functionality is in place, the site may turn to **personalization** as a reasonable next step in its attempts to attract and, especially, to retain customers. Specific personalization techniques are discussed in Chapter 11 in the context of customer relationship management. The options range from a simple greeting of a return visitor by name to the construction of individualized pages with content and functionality specified by the customer. Personalization, a technique long used by traditional direct marketers, is one way in which the Internet vastly expands the opportunities for meaningful marketing actions.

Another step a site might take is to offer **customization**. At this point, the site might have so much information about individual customers that individualized products or services can be created. For example, sites like Netflix that can amass a huge set of customer preference data can customize recommendations for the next rental that are often highly satisfactory.

A Customization Example

Some websites can allow the customer to customize his own product in a way that takes advantage of the web's unique capabilities. NIKEiD, for example, is a companion to the main Nike site dedicated to the task of helping customers design and purchase their own versions of Nike styles made popular by their celebrity endorsers.[31]

The customer can start with an available model and change elements or start with a plain shoe. He then can choose the size and the color for each part of the shoe. He has the option to put personal identification, in a color of his choice, on the tongue of the shoe. Having created the basketball shoe to fit his game, he can then look at it from all perspectives. If he is not yet ready to purchase, the customized shoe can be saved. In order to set up this personal storage space on the NIKEiD site, he must, of course, provide a small amount of personal information.

This is an interesting, perhaps appealing, process. Is it an indication of the type of customized products we will see more of in the next few years? Probably. Does it create real value for customers? You decide.

These stages of data-driven marketing development are reasonable and observable in current Internet space. At the same time, the order is not fixed. Personalization may be interchangeable in order with the transactional stage on the website. Content-rich sites—portals, for example—may choose to personalize the visitor experience in order to retain them and build the critical mass for transactional activities. On the other hand, eretail or B2B sites may transact first and then create personalized shopping experiences for consumers or accounts to encourage repeat purchases. A site like NIKEiD may even be a vehicle for new customer acquisition if the offer is sufficiently compelling.

Companies need to carefully consider, and rigorously test, the various options that are available for bringing customers to their sites and persuading them to transact or to identify themselves as sales leads for a future transaction.

SUMMARY

Good Internet marketing has an existing marketing discipline—direct marketing—from which to draw tools and techniques that have been developed and honed in other media. The web permits faster, cheaper, and more precise execution of many existing direct response marketing techniques, and it often allows the development of other approaches that would not be cost effective in physical-world media. The Internet marketer can profit from the knowledge of both front-end and back-end marketing requirements that successful direct marketers have accumulated over several decades. This is truly a "do not reinvent the wheel" situation in which marketers who recognize the direct response foundations of Internet marketing can enjoy a very steep learning curve on the Internet.

A number of tools and techniques of direct marketing find direct applicability on the Internet. The offer, which is made up of product, positioning, price, and incentives, is one. A compelling offer is necessary in any marketing environment and is especially important on the web where the contact is impersonal and the time devoted to any marketer-initiated communication is usually minimal. Customer lifetime value (CLV) is becoming increasingly important in both acquisition and retention programs as Internet marketers make use of their ability to capture detailed customer activity and purchase data. Testing is becoming more widely used as marketers understand the opportunities offered by the Internet to test alternative marketing approaches in a speedy and reliable manner. All of this is made possible by the existence of "the marketing database," actually a complex system of databases with customer, promotional, and marketing operations data, often contained in a data warehouse.

Some marketing programs will be driven by single pieces of marketing data like "registered on baseball website." Still others will be driven by profiles or the results of complex analytics, for example segmentation by CLV, or predictive modeling. Many, if not most, of these marketing programs will be driven by the goal of increasing CLV as the most direct route to increasing the effectiveness of the marketing effort.

DISCUSSION QUESTIONS

1. Why is it important for the marketer to distinguish between customer acquisition, conversion, and retention when developing marketing strategies?
2. How does "the offer" differ from "the product" of traditional mass media marketing?
3. In addition to the offer, what are the elements of a direct marketing strategy?
4. How do direct marketers distinguish between the "front end" and the "back end" of a transaction? Why is this important?
5. Explain the "customer lifetime value" concept. Thinking about a specific firm, how could it use the concept of CLV to increase the overall profitability of its customer base?

6. How is testing different from marketing research?
7. Why and how does testing offer opportunities to Internet marketers?
8. What are some types of analytics that are supported by the customer database?
9. Distinguish between the concepts of customer profiles, market segments, and predictive modeling.

10. Explain the related concepts of data warehousing and data mining.
11. What do you think the future is for customized products? Think of an example of a product that could reasonably be customized and explain why the target customer would find value in the customization.

INTERNET EXERCISES

1. Internet Career Builder Exercise
   a. These are some of the jobs that are available in direct marketing. You can find others on sites recommended by your instructor or through search.

      Account manager

      Copywriter

      Creative director

      Video/Infomercial producer

      Customer service representative

      Digital media planner

      Ecommerce manager

      Data analyst

      Development officer (annual fund, planned giving, other)

      Director (assistant, associate) of development, annual giving, alumni relations

      and many more

   b. Select a direct marketing job from the list in 1a or from your own search. Outline the responsibilities of that position. You may find it useful to locate job postings on the web in order to understand the job requirements.
   c. Outline knowledge and experience from classes, internships, full or part-time jobs, and volunteer work that prepare you for this specific position.
   d. Prepare five questions you could ask at a job interview. The questions should exhibit your understanding of the position requirements without lecturing the interviewer about what she already knows.
   e. Update your VisualCV® or LinkedIn profile with this information.

2. Register at a B2C website—one of those you chose to track for the semester if one is appropriate. If not, choose another site for this exercise.
   a. Carefully consider the potential value of the data captured on the registration form. If the option is presented, you may want to configure a personal page, especially if you have not done so before. Then spend a few minutes getting acquainted with the site. What other customer data of value could the site have added to its database as a result of the time you spent there? Would you have been willing to provide that data?
   b. Keep a log of contacts that result from this registration. Bear in mind that contacts may come from the sponsor of the site itself and others may come from marketers with whom the site shares its lists, depending on the options you choose in the registration process.
   c. Consider the four Is of Figure 4.1. Locate a site that makes good use of each, some, or all of the Is. How do these characteristics affect customer experience on the site?

3. Choose a website that permits personalization—portals or large content sites are a good choice. Personalize your own page on the site. Think about the kinds of customer data that are produced as you use your personalized page on this site. How can the site use this data to engage in targeted marketing? Also think about the benefits to you, the user, of having a personalized page on the site you have chosen.

4. Visit a website that you patronize frequently, one from which you have purchased something, if possible. Identify two marketing elements that could usefully be tested. How would you go about setting up one of these tests?

NOTES

1. Concepts in this chapter are based on Mary Lou Roberts and Paul D. Berger, *Direct Marketing Management*, 2nd ed., available for free download at http://www.marylouroberts.info.

2. http://www.amazon.com/Locations-Careers/b?ie=UTF8&node=239366011.

3. http://www.amazonservices.com/content/fulfillment-by-amazon.htm.

4. For an extensive discussion and computational appendix, see "Profitability and Lifetime Value," in Mary Lou Roberts and Paul D. Berger, *Direct Marketing Management*, pp. 179–201, http://www.marylouroberts.info.

5. Rajkumar Venkatesan and V. Kumar, "A Customer Lifetime Value Framework for Customer Selection and Resource Allocation Strategy," *Journal of Marketing*, Vol. 68, 2004, p. 110.

6. Details can be found in other articles in journals that deal with issues of data manipulation. A classic article is Robert Dwyer, "Customer Lifetime Valuation to Support Marketing Decision Making," *Journal of Direct Marketing*, Vol. 8, no. 2 (1989), 73–81. Other publications in relevant journals include Paul D. Berger, Bruce Weinberg, and Richard Hanna, "Customer Lifetime Value Determination and Strategic Implications for a Cruise-Ship Company" *Journal of Database Marketing and Customer Strategy Management*, Vol. 11, no. 1 (2003), 40–52; and Wernar J. Reinartz and V. Kumar, "The Impact of Customer Relationship Characteristics on Profitable Lifetime Duration," *Journal of Marketing*, Vol. 67 (January 2003), 77–99.

7. This example is based on Arthur Middleton Hughes, "Building Successful Retail Strategies," Database Marketing Institute, February 5, 2002, http://www.dbmarketing.com.

8. For more detail and an example, see Arthur Middleton Hughes, "How to Succeed with RFM Analysis," nd., http://www.dbmarketing.com/articles/Art106.htm.

9. http://www.syncapse.com/media/syncapse-value-of-a-facebook-fan.pdf.

10. For another detailed CLV example, see http://www.kaushik.net/avinash/2010/04/analytics-tip-calculate-ltv-customer-lifetime-value.html.

11. Rick Fernandes, "Reap the Web's Testing Capabilities," *iMarketing News*, April 10, 2000, p. 28.

12. http://www.fastcompany.com/magazine/24/capone.html?page=0%2C0.

13. For a more detailed discussion, see Chapter 10; "Testing Direct Marketing Programs" in Mary Lou Roberts and Paul D. Berger, *Direct Marketing Management*, http://www.marylouroberts.info/images/dir.mark.man.ch10.pdf.

14. http://diy-marketing.blogspot.com/2008/09/testing-to-make-im-fast-and-simple.html.

15. https://www.google.com/analytics/siteopt/exptlist?account=5607410&hl=en.

16. http://www.google.com/websiteoptimizer/tour.html.

17. http://www.claritas.com/MyBestSegments/Default.jsp.

18. Jill Griffin, "How Customer Information Gives Harrah's a Winning Hand," 2003, *CEO Refresher*, http://www.refresher.com/!jlgharrahs.html.

19. http://www.fastcompany.com/magazine/24/capone.html?page=0%2C4.

20. Gary Loveman, "Diamonds in the Data Mine," *Harvard Business Review*, May 2003, p. 2.

21. http://www.thearling.com/index.htm.

22. http://www.thearling.com/text/dmwhite/dmwhite.htm.

23. Gary Loveman, "Diamonds in the Data Mine," *Harvard Business Review*, May 2003, p. 3.

24. Gary Loveman, "Diamonds in the Data Mine," *Harvard Business Review*, May 2003, pp. 1–5.

25. IBM in partnership with Virtual Gold helps NBA coaches score big with IBM data mining application, nd., http://www.virtualgold.com/customers_sstories.html#success_AdvancedScout.

26. Bill Palace, "Data Mining: What Is Data Mining?" nd., http://www.anderson.ucla.edu/faculty/jason.frand/teacher/technologies/palace/datamining.htm.

27. http://www-03.ibm.com/press/us/en/pressrelease/1190.wss.

28. http://www.tetrad.com/demographics/usa/claritas/prizmne.html.

29. http://www.slideshare.net/jrstafford/ncdm-datamining-case-study-2010-3563095.

30. http://www.thesportjournal.org/article/new-market-research-approach-sport-data-mining.

31. http://nikeid.nike.com/nikeid/index.jsp.

PART 2

Essential Internet Marketing Tools

CHAPTER 5

Online Branding and Video Marketing

Chapter Outline

Marketing Effectiveness in the Age of New Media

Consumer Media Habits in the Internet Age

The Effectiveness of Online Advertising and Promotion

Building Internet Brands
Brand Equity and Brand Image
Creating a Strong Brand on the Internet
Building and Developing an Online Brand
What about a Brand Community?

Video Marketing
The Reach of Video

Video Marketing Strategy
Publishing
Optimizing for Search and Sharing
Promote
Analyze

Video Marketing for Small Business

Video Marketing Best Practices

SUMMARY
DISCUSSION QUESTIONS
INTERNET EXERCISES
NOTES

Key Terms

By the time you complete this chapter, you will be able to:

- Describe ways in which consumer media habits are changing.
- Discuss how and why online advertising and promotion is effective.
- Define major branding concepts.
- Understand how marketers are using online techniques to build and reinforce brands.
- Describe ways in which consumers are consuming video.
- Identify the types of videos businesses can use to reach both consumers and business customers.
- Discuss the elements of video marketing strategy.
- Identify key video marketing metrics.
- Explain why video marketing is valuable to small as well as large businesses.

Marketing Effectiveness in the Age of New Media

The way we think about the use of Internet tools in customer acquisition, conversion, and retention has matured in recent years, as have other business elements discussed in Chapter 1. The current management environment for online marketing can be described as:

- Management pressure for return on investment (ROI), really for return on promotional investment (ROPI), for all expenditures.
- Increasing knowledge about the power of the integrated marketing communications mix that includes the Internet as one component.
- Understanding the power of the Internet as a branding medium.
- Understanding the power of other tools, including video, online advertising, email, and search as part of integrated marketing campaigns.
- Increasing interest in social media marketing.

In this chapter, we will discuss Internet branding and video marketing as an important part of the digital marketer's arsenal.

Consumer Media Habits in the Internet Age

The Internet has helped consumers become accustomed to on-demand media that is available 24/7/365. It is not, however, the only factor. Consider, for example, the phenomenal popularity of Apple's iPod and iPad. They, along with the growing number of other smartphones and readers, allow consumers to download music, videos, and all kinds of electronic media content. Apps[1] of all kinds push content to mobile devices so consumers can access content at their convenience. Will consumers who become accustomed to controlling their media content and use to this degree ever again be satisfied with an inflexible schedule of offerings from any medium? Probably not.

There are many media alternatives in addition to mobile apps that are responding to consumer desire for on-demand content. Consider the following developments:

- DVDs that offer large amounts of storage for entertainment and gaming applications.
- Digital video recording that allows viewers to watch programming at the time of their choice.[2]
- Pay-Per-View and Video On Demand television content.
- Video streaming that replaces physical rental of movies.
- A proliferation of sites offering online video games.

Has the new media landscape affected consumer media habits? Figure 5.1 indicates that it has had an impact. Traditional media—radio, newspapers, and magazines—are experiencing consistent year-over-year declines as measured by

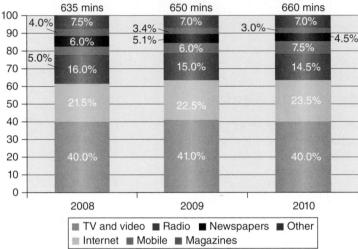

Share of Time Spent per Day with Major Media by U.S. Adults, 2008–2010
(% of total)

Note: Time spent with each medium includes all time spent with that medium, regardless of multitasking; for example, 1 hour of multitasking on the internet and watching TV was counted as 1 hour for TV and 1 hour for internet

(a)

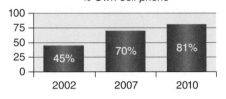

Cell Phones, Computers Increasingly Common
% Own cell phone

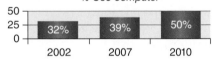

% Use computer

Based on median % across the 16 nations where 2002, 2007, and 2010 data are available.

(b)

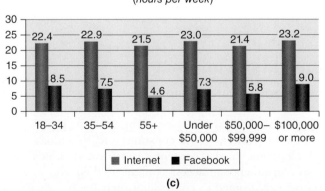

Internet/Facebook Time Spent by Age and Income
(hours per week)

(c)

FIGURE **5.1** Perspectives on Consumer Media Use

Sources: eMarketer, Inc., December 28, 2010; "Global Publics Embrace Social Networking: Computer and Cell Phone Usage Up Around the World", December 15, 2010, the Pew Global Attitudes Project, a project of the Pew Research Center; and Morpace Omnibus Report, June 2010, p. 2. Reprinted with permission of Morpace, Inc.

consumer time spent (see Figure 5.1a). Television is neither growing nor significantly declining, perhaps because of on-demand video access. Time spent on the Internet continues to increase but mobile is clearly the growth star. Other data from the Pew Foundation show that television continues to be the largest provider of national and international news, unless you are under 30, in which case you are more likely to obtain news from the Internet. Overall, the number of Americans accessing news over the Internet has increased by over 20 percent in just six years.[3]

Marketing Charts headlines a post by pointing out that both cell phones and computers are becoming more prevalent around the world (see Figure 5.1b). Note that internationally, the penetration of cell phones is greater than that of computers, signaling another media shift in the making. Morpace surveyed American consumers about how much time they spent on the Internet in general and Facebook in particular (see Figure 5.1c). The general answer is that consumers spend more than 20 hours each week on the web. No one will be surprised that younger users spend more time on Facebook than do the 55+ age group, although some observers continue to be surprised that older consumers use Facebook at all. They are in fact online, and their use is growing.[4] Less intuitive is the finding that consumers with higher incomes spend slightly more time on Facebook than do even those with incomes under $50,000, who would most likely be young people.

The Effectiveness of Online Advertising and Promotion

Some of the most careful, early studies on adding interactivity to the media mix are part of the Cross-Media Optimization Study (XMOS) of the Internet Advertising Bureau (IAB), the industry trade association. The research project, cosponsored with the Advertising Research Foundation, began in 2002. Studies conducted in cooperation with leading national brands used a variety of research approaches. One year later, they had conducted four studies and found that all the brands would benefit from increasing online advertising expenditures. The results were:

	Current Online Expenditure (percent)	Recommended Online Expenditure (percent)
Colgate	7	11
Kleenex	3	10
Dove Nutrium Bar	2	15
McDonalds	1	13[5]

The most far-reaching study in this series was that of the Ford F-150 launch in 2004. According to the IAB:

> The 2004 all new Ford F-150 marketing launch was the largest and most comprehensive marketing launch in the history of Ford Motor Company. The XMOS research examined branding and sales impact from television, magazine, Online Roadblocks, online ads, Internet Search, Auto Websites, Ford's website, Spanish language online advertising and offline events sponsorships.
>
> Ford's online efforts were unprecedented, launching a massive reach program including "Online Roadblocks"—ads that took over AOL, MSN and Yahoo! home pages[6] and email sections in a coordinated fashion. This effort resulted in Ford's reaching over 40% of males aged 25 to 54 in a single day.

ClickZ describes other elements of the campaign. In addition to the road-blocks, there were:

> … in-market ads that ran on Yahoo Autos, and other focused sites, such as Kelly Blue Book and Edmunds.com. The in-market ads—given that moniker because visitors to those sites were presumably "in the market" for a car—directed users to a comprehensive personal walk-around of the vehicle when clicked. The idea was to present an experience that was contrary to what potential buyers would encounter in a show-room. It allowed individuals to perform deep dives into the elements of the vehicle they found most interesting, rather than be distracted by a salesperson's pitch.[7]

IAB listed the results as follows:

- Six percent of all sales could be directly attributed to *online advertising exposure*. Additional sales beyond 6 percent could be traced to click-through and online brochure requests.
- *TV* generates the greatest level of absolute reach and purchase consideration impact, but was significantly less cost-effective. TV was more than 20 times more expensive than the most cost efficient opportunity, the *Online Road-block*, and five times less cost efficient than online or magazines.
- Users conducting a *search* on terms such as "Truck" or "4 × 4" were three times more likely to buy an F-150 than the general population.
- Users visiting the truck section of an *auto website* were two times more likely to buy an F-150 than the general population.
- *Magazines* and in-market websites offered similar results, including selectivity and efficient delivery of in-market prospects.[8]

Briggs, Krishnan, and Borin conducted an extensive review of the campaign and added these conclusions:

- Electronic **roadblocks** are the most cost efficient, and can produce significant daily reach (40+ percent); however they are not as scalable as TV. While roadblocks delivered 40 percent reach in a day, TV can deliver nearly twice the level in a single day.
- Due to changing media habits of consumers, Ford's campaign could be fine-tuned to increase sales by 5 percent *without spending a dollar more.*[9]

The italicized entries in the preceding paragraphs provide an outline of the overall integrated communications campaign. Two points are clear:

1. Online advertising did provide a lift to the overall campaign results, even as early as 2004.
2. No single medium in isolation could have generated the results that were produced by the integrated marketing communications program.

While these early studies illustrate the complexity of advertising media planning in the current media environment, they also seemed to suggest a consistently positive outlook for online brand advertising. In 2010, the consultants at Bain found that not to be the case (see Figure 5.2). Working with IAB, they found that brand marketers were still spending about 75 percent of their advertising budgets in TV and print, and that online had become the primary venue for direct response marketing. They concluded that "marketers seeking to build brands online have become disappointed with the medium."[10] For two of the three key brand development objectives—creating awareness and generating familiarity—one or more traditional mass media perform better. Only in promoting consideration does online outperform magazines and newspapers.

A study by Professor Alex Wang conducted for Adobe, creator of digital publishing software, that was published in early 2011 gives another perspective on media evolution and its impact on advertising. He conducted an experimental study examining reactions to advertising in the May 24, 2010 edition of *Wired* magazine.[11] Participants read either the print or the digital magazine version of

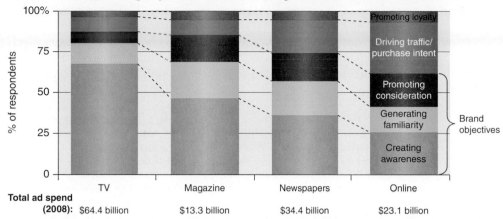

Which Marketing Objectives Are the Following Media Vehicles *Best* Suited for?

FIGURE **5.2** Brand Development Objectives and Media Effectiveness

Source: John Frelinghuysen and Aditya Joshi, "In search of a premium alternative: an action plan for online brand advertising," p. 2. Copyright © 2010 Bain & Company, Inc. All rights reserved. Reprinted with permission.

that edition. (There are other digital magazines, but this *Wired* platform is only for iPad apps.) After reading through either the print or the digital edition, respondents were asked to examine a specific ad from Qwest. The results indicated that the interactive ads in the digital magazine produced greater perceived interactivity, perceived engagement, message involvement, and more positive attitude toward the ad(s). This response was true whether the question was about the specific ad or interactive ads in general.[12]

Never far behind when it comes to new media developments, the *Martha Stewart Living* magazine launched its iPad app in November 2010 with an entire issue created especially for the iPad. On her blog, Martha Stewart posted a cover shot and a demonstration video (see Figure 5.3). Of the cover shot she says, "This is the cover of the Special Digital Issue of *Martha Stewart Living*. You

FIGURE **5.3** Cover Page of the Digital *Boundless Beauty* Magazine

Source: Martha Stewart, http://www.themarthablog.com/2010/11/the-launch-of-boundless-beauty.html.

can actually watch this peony unfurling, as the image is made up of 180 time-lapse photos over a 10-hour period taken in my garden."[13] This interactive ability showcases the power of the visual display and interactivity itself, which had everyone from app critics[14] to CNBC[15] gushing over its beauty. By February 2011, the magazine itself was being published digitally. The future may be summed up in this question and answer from the support page on the MarthaStewart.com website:

> 6. *If I don't have an iPad, how can I view the Boundless Beauty special issue?*
> Boundless Beauty was created especially for the iPad—its interactive content and special layouts were meant to be viewed on that device. However, we're considering other formats and would like to know what devices you use. E-mail us at customersupport@marthastewart.com.

The emergence of easy-to-use and engaging digital magazines, and corresponding response from advertisers, supports a key recommendation of the Bain/IAB study. They say that it will be necessary to make premium engagement opportunities available to advertisers and to keep those opportunities from becoming cluttered with run-of-the mill advertising.[16] The iPad digital magazines represent a new online publishing format that offers that premium opportunity. Only the future will tell whether publishers can implement a premium strategy on existing content sites.

Engaging **ad formats** will not be optimally effective unless marketers develop strategies that have impact at the appropriate stage in the brand development process. The consultants at McKinsey studied both online and offline marketing efforts, and found different effectiveness, depending on the stage in what they call "the consumer journey"—or the consumer decision process.[17] Writing in the *McKinsey Quarterly*, Edelman reported on a global study that showed the impact on the consumer's initial consideration set, active evaluation, and closure. Figure 5.4 reveals that company-driven marketing such as advertising has the most effectiveness in the initial consideration stage. Past experience has the most impact on the evaluation stage, while word of mouth and in-store interactions are most effective in the closure stage.[18]

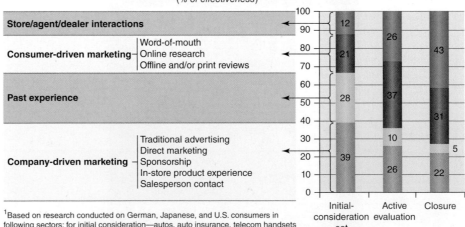

The Consumer Decision Journey: Where it Counts

Most-influential touch points by stage of consumer decision journey, for competitors and new customers (*% of effectiveness*)[1]

[1]Based on research conducted on German, Japanese, and U.S. consumers in following sectors: for initial consideration—autos, auto insurance, telecom handsets and carriers; for active evaluation—auto insurance, telecom handsets; for closure—autos, auto insurance, skin care, and TVs; figures may not sum to 100%, because of rounding.

FIGURE **5.4** Impact of Various Activities on Stages of Consumer Decision Making

Source: Excerpted Exhibit 4 from "The consumer decision journey," June 2009, *McKinsey Quarterly*, www.mckinseyquarterly.com. Copyright © 2010 McKinsey & Company. All rights reserved. Reprinted by permission.

INTERACTIVE EXERCISE **5.1**	**The Consumer Decision Journey**

Based on their global studies of brand marketing, McKinsey has reorganized the traditional consumer decision process model. See their interactive presentation here.

Visit http://bit.ly/tPK64d.

The multitude of different marketing options and the varying needs of consumers as they proceed on their "decision journey" require a focused and disciplined process of building and developing brands on the Internet.

Building Internet Brands

While there is much controversy swirling around issues relating to building brands on the Internet, there is no disputing one simple point. *Having a strong and trusted* **brand** *is essential to success on the web*. Visitors surf in from a variety of sources ranging from search engines to affiliate links to offline promotions. They are reluctant to give their money to an entity with which they do not have an established relationship. A known and trusted brand gives the greatest possible reassurance that they will have a satisfactory purchase and use experience. This leads us to the concept known as brand equity.

Brand Equity and Brand Image

The strength of a brand is measured by *brand equity*. Professor Kevin Lane Keller presents a number of definitions of **brand equity**. The definition attributed to the Marketing Science Institute is comprehensive. They define brand equity as:

> The set of associations and behaviors on the part of the brand's customers, channel members, and parent corporation that permits the brand to earn greater volume or greater margins than it could without the brand name and that gives the brand a strong, sustainable, and differentiated advantage over competitors.[19]

Brand equity is a concept that describes a financial asset as well as a competitive advantage. The issue for marketers is what activities and results are necessary to create a brand that becomes a source of both competitive and financial advantage.

The marketing issues are encapsulated in two concepts: *brand awareness* and *brand image*. **Brand awareness** has two levels. If consumers remember seeing/hearing about a brand, that is evidence of **brand recognition**. Recognition is measured by showing a representation (product, ad, etc.) and asking if members of the target group remember having seen or heard of it. Brand recognition is most likely to be achieved through repeated exposure to brand-related messages and images. *Recall* is considered a higher level of branding than is mere recognition. It involves being able to remember information about the product or brand. Notice that the research summarized in Figures 5.2 and 5.4 uses different terms for what are essentially the same stages in the branding process. This is an area of marketing in which there is little standardization of terminology, and that can be confusing if you are not paying close attention.

Marketers do agree, however, that brand awareness alone is not sufficient to drive behavior when the product or service in question requires any significant level of involvement and information processing. The purchase of **high involvement** products—which can be equated with high risk purchases whatever the price—generally requires a **brand image** with strong and positive brand associations. Powerful incentives can compensate for some lack of strength in brand image, but not all. A strong brand image is essential for consumer comfort in an unfamiliar purchasing situation like the Internet.

Low involvement products, on the other hand, require less effort and involvement on the part of the customer who may take action on the basis of awareness alone. Low involvement items can usually be equated to low margin (convenience) products. Whether the brand is low involvement or high involvement, creating a trusted brand is a lengthy and expensive process, but it creates a lasting competitive advantage, especially in the nonpersonal environment of the web.

A recent study of brand trust by marketing agency Cone found that consumers still place trust in the recommendations of family (63 percent) and friends (31 percent). However, they discovered an additional step in the process. Consumers were going online to do additional research after getting a recommendation from a trusted personal source; they called this step *verification*. The report found consumers, especially those in the 25-to-34 age group, looking for online recommendations to verify their brand choices.[20]

Creating a Strong Brand on the Internet

Advertising executives Larry Chiagouris and Brant Wansley identify four stages in the brand building process (see Figure 5.5) that are reminiscent of the advertising hierarchy of effects and use terms that are understandable in any discussion of branding.[21]

Awareness represents a nodding acquaintance with the brand and, as noted, is measured by ability to recognize the brand or to recall being exposed to it. Familiarity suggests some knowledge of the product, its features, and services offered. It is measured by asking about recall of message points from the ad.

The next stage is the creation of a positive brand image. According to Keller:

> A positive brand image is created by marketing programs that link strong, favorable, and unique associations to the brand in memory. The definition of customer-based brand equity does not distinguish between the source of brand associations and the manner in which they are formed; all that matters is the resulting *favorability*, *strength*, and *uniqueness* (emphasis mine) of brand associations.[22]

The final stage in this model, the transaction itself, should be the beginning of a relationship, not the end of a process. Traditional brand building, however, has been done in the mass media where the maintenance and deepening of relationships is difficult because of the inability of those media to address consumers based on their stage of relationship development. *The best brand building on the Internet will fuse the attention-getting power of the web's interactive environment with the targeted relationship techniques of information-driven direct marketing. It will be tightly integrated with offline brand development activities.*

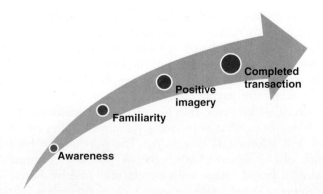

FIGURE **5.5** Brand Development Hierarchy
Source: Adapted from Ciagouris and Wansley.

Building and Developing an Online Brand

There are a number of contexts in which online brand building occurs. The marketer of a start-up company has a clean slate, and that represents a great opportunity to build a strong brand using all contemporary marketing tools. There are well-known online companies, from Amazon to Facebook to Groupon, that have successfully established their corporate brand solely online. In all cases, it takes considerable resources of both time and money, especially since none of these companies have made significant use of offline paid media to build awareness.

The brand marketer of an established product has the job of integrating online into the existing marketing strategy and media execution. This integration represents its own challenge, especially if the business is not particularly web savvy or oriented. It may require a lot of internal marketing, as well as external marketing. Even if the brand already uses the Internet well, it often makes sense to keep a campaign separate—its own microsite, Facebook, and/or Twitter pages, for example—instead of reconfiguring the corporate brand page and messaging. That is especially true if the campaign is aimed at only one of several market segments served by the brand.

There is an intermediate situation in which an entirely new product or brand is added to the corporate portfolio. In that case, the brand itself has a clean slate but it must be configured within the overall context of the corporation and its product portfolio. Personal care products often provide good examples of frequent brand extensions and additions. There is also the situation in which an existing brand comes into the business through acquisition and may have to be tweaked to fit comfortably into the corporate brand image.

Most marketers find themselves working in some sort of existing context. Here are considerations they must keep in mind:

- Ensure the best possible *product and customer experience*. Trying to successfully brand a poor-quality product or one that has bad experience elements like customer service is a thankless and ultimately unproductive job.
- Learn about your *target audience*, especially their online media use. Remember that demographics of offline media use may not be predictive of online media activity.
- Set *branding objectives*. Specific and measurable objectives are essential for any marketing strategy development, including branding.
  - Establish policies for corporate, affiliate, and other uses of your brand content if they do not already exist. Even if corporate policies are well spelled out, review them for adequate coverage of Internet issues. What if one of your channel partners wants to use your brand logo on its site? You have to ask if it is allowed, not allowed, or what the conditions are for usage.
- Establish your message; give your brand a *voice and personality*. These are basic elements of any branding program in any medium. What additional opportunities does the Internet offer? The *Martha Stewart Living Boundless Beauty* edition is simply not possible in any other communications channel. The fact that it is beautiful and appeared to work seamlessly from the time it was released can only add luster to the Martha Stewart brand.
- Develop the necessary *creative elements* to convey the desired message and personality. Again, this is standard practice, but the web may offer additional opportunities. Did you know that the Travelocity Roaming Gnome has his own "Home," a web page of his own? It has some cute content and, of course, a flight search box.[23]
- Balance *online and offline media mix*. This too is standard practice. However, as the XMOS study results suggested, most firms did not, and evidence is that they still do not,[24] use the optimal media mix for reaching their target audience with the greatest effectiveness.
  - Ensure that the *brand website* provides a satisfactory and engaging customer experience. Some of the tools for engaging customers on the

site include rich media, including video, personalization, co-creation of content (blogs, brand community), purchase-process streamlining (forms with saved information), self-service on demand, customization of content or even products, and dynamic pricing (last-minute offers on hotel and travel sites).[25]

- Integrate *social media* based on target audience, brand objectives, and corporate readiness and expertise. As discussed in Chapter 9, social media marketing is less a matter of the appropriate tools and platforms than it is a matter of educating and configuring the business to use social media effectively.

- Create relevant content and distribute it across the web. Content marketing, which is discussed in more detail in Chapter 10, is the practice of creating relevant, informational content—not advertising—and distributing it across the web for inbound marketing purposes.

- *Engage* with customers and prospects. Whether on the website or in social media, people want information and support—and the occasional apology—from companies with which they do, or contemplate doing, business. The brand that ignores customer communications in any channel is simply throwing its brand development money away.

- *Monitor* online conversations and use of your brand to protect its integrity. Brands like Gatorade[26] and Dell[27] have set up formal "mission control" rooms to monitor brand-related conversations online. They will engage with customers as necessary and collect and analyze data to improve their brands and marketing.

- Continue to *grow and evolve* the brand. Obviously brands cannot stand still when the world is moving so rapidly around them. Whether it is adding the latest in social media components to the program of a successful brand, like Pepsi's Gatorade brand, or the Pepsi brand returning to 2011 Super Bowl advertising[28] after a year of successful cause marketing,[29] brands must continue to grow in ways that parallel those of their target audiences.[30]

What about a Brand Community?

The word "community" is often used loosely to refer to like-minded people who congregate somewhere on the web. A brand community is something more limited and precise. Muniz and O'Guinn have advanced a universally accepted definition:

> A brand community is a specialized, non-geographically bound community, based on a structured set of social relations among admirers of a brand.[31]

In a subsequent publication, they add that:

> These consumers are drawn together by a common interest in, and commitment to, the brand and a social desire to bond with like-minded others. New modes of computer-mediated communication facilitate and flavor communal communication (p. 19).[32]

Building a brand community is not an activity to be undertaken lightly.[33] It takes time, resources, and experience in successful social media marketing. If the marketer is extremely lucky, there is an existing brand community that can be gently co-opted by the corporation. Such was the case with the Harley Owners Group® (HOGs) who, as early as the 1920s, banded together in the physical world to enjoy motorcycle rides together. Harley Davidson recognized the value and assigned executives to go along on the rides long before the Internet. The Internet gave them an opportunity to "support" the HOGs with an Internet site. The site facilitated many subtle marketing activities, including support of local chapters and women's activities.[34] The brand community is also alive and well on Facebook.[35] Whenever you look, there are numerous posts from members and some from local chapters, promoting events. There are, however, few comments from page administrators (i.e., corporate social media marketers). Members are doing it all for them! That is truly a vibrant brand community. It started with an experiential product that owners were passionate about, and that is why there have been HOG groups from the brand's early days.[36] This relationship gives Harley Davidson a rich history on which to build a modern community, but it also evokes great caution to not "take over" what is essentially a customer activity.

It is not uncommon for companies to build brand communities on the basis of existing customer relationships. Fiskars is a Finnish company that parlayed strong relationships with scrapbooking and gardening customers into a lively brand community.[37] Most enterprises, however, will not have the advantage of a functioning offline community as a basis for building an online branded community. They must decide whether their customers would find a community appealing and whether it is worth the time and expense of building one. Advertising agency Universal McCann, in Wave 5 of its Socialization of Brands surveys, interviews brand community members around the globe. The agency found that:

- 72 percent said they thought more positively about the brand as a result of joining the community.
- 71 percent said they were more likely to buy the brand.
- 66 percent said they felt more loyal to the brand as a result of being a community member.
- 63 percent said they would recommend joining a community to their friends.[38]

As you read this, you should realize that this is a more limited view of brand community than the sociological perspective presented by Muniz and O'Guinn. It describes a commercially mediated brand community, whether built from scratch or on the basis of existing customer relationships. Both perspectives are correct, depending on the context. Exercise care to understand which type of community is under discussion.

Whatever branding tools and channels are chosen, it is essential in today's media environment to support brands with appropriate Internet brand development techniques. A brand that is strong and trusted, both offline and online, is an important asset in all stages of the customer cycle—acquisition, conversion, and retention.

In the same sense, every contact with the customer must be viewed as an event in the brand development process. Every customer interaction—at whatever customer touchpoint, online channel, or offline channel—has an impact on the brand. While recognizing the power of each interaction for positive or for negative brand associations, we must acknowledge that some tools have special impact. Online display advertising, discussed in Chapter 6, is important in customer acquisition and can have great impact on brand perceptions. Email, the subject of Chapter 7, is most useful in customer retention where it continues to build brand favorability and purchase action. Video is a tool that is valuable in both acquisition and retention and that can have a powerful and lasting impact on brand perception. With the advent of broadband in both the wired and wireless Internet environments, video has come into its own as a marketing tool, and we conclude this chapter with a discussion of effective video marketing.

Video Marketing

We are all aware of the communications impact of video. We have been amazed to see videos of a building collapsing, a tornado approaching, or an overpowering tsunami wave all because an ordinary citizen had the presence of mind to grab a video camera and record the event as it happened. The impact of video on the social and political scenes and its impact on the reporting of news can hardly be overstated. These are important developments, and they will continue to influence the way we see the world and live our lives.

User-created video is an important social phenomenon, but our focus is narrower. Marketers must learn to create and deploy effective videos, and the effective use of video as an online marketing tool is our sole focus. At the same time, we should learn from effective videos in other contexts and examples will be given with the objective of stimulating marketing creativity as we learn how to use the powerful video tool to its best advantage.

The Reach of Video

Video has permeated virtually every aspect of our lives, both as consumers and as businesspeople. In his vook™,[39] *Winning the Zero Moment of Truth*, Google's Jim Lecinski says that the second-most-used search box is the one on YouTube. He often asks managers at all kinds of enterprises to try to stump him with a search term. Whether it is an esoteric technical subject like "semiconductor diodes" or a subject that cuts across business and consumer activities like "mixing cement," Lecinski says that "10 out of 10 times we find a bunch of videos about it."[40] Try it yourself!

Consumer Use of Video

Consumers watch a lot of television and a lot of video on a variety of devices. The shifting patterns of what they watch, when they watch in, and on what devices have intrigued marketers for a number of years. Video watching has skyrocketed, while television viewing has continued to increase, resulting in an increase in total video viewing.[41] In July 2011, Nielsen reported that:

- 86 percent of the U.S. Internet audience viewed online video.
- The duration of the average online content video was 5.3 minutes, while the average online video ad was 0.5 minutes.
- Video ads accounted for 12.4 percent of all videos viewed and 1.2 percent of all minutes spent viewing video online.[42]

Table 5.1 shows that all people over 2 years of age watch more than 35 hours of television each week, with the figure for age cohorts ranging from a low of more than 26 hours each week for teens to over 49 hours each week for people over age 65. Overall, people watch over 30 minutes of video on the Internet with the highest being 57 minutes for adults aged 25 to 34. Table 5.1 makes it clear that there are many ways to consume video content, an important marketing consideration.

Clearly people spend a great deal of time watching videos. For marketers the key question is, "Do marketing videos have an impact on customer purchasing behavior?" Video marketing services firm Invodo have a video statistics page that focuses on the impact of video on purchase intent and behavior. Recent headlines indicate that videos do influence purchasing behavior in a variety of contexts. Some of the headlines include:

TABLE 5.1	Time Spent Watching Video									

Weekly Time Spent in Hours:Minutes

	K 2–11	T 12–17	A 18–24	A 25–34	A 35–49	A 50–64	A 65+	P 2+	Hispanic 2+	African American 2+
Traditional TV	26:31	24:21	26:28	30:34	36:23	44:54	49:17	35:37	30:42	47:37
Timeshifted TV	1:49	1:31	1:30	3:11	3:11	2:48	1:40	2:25	1:34	1:42
Using Internet on a computer	0:40	1:45	5:31	8:29	8:34	7:20	3:55	5:43	4:10	4:54
Watching videos on the Internet	0:07	0:20	0:48	0:57	0:38	0:25	0:12	0:33	0:32	0:30
Mobile subscribers watching videos on mobile phone	NA	0:20	0:15	0:10	0:05	0:02	<0:01	0:07	0:12	0:13

Note: Data is uniquely based on the total population (over age 2) in the United States.

Source: Table 1, "The Cross-Platform Report., Quarter 1, 2011," page 6. Copyrighted information of The Nielsen Company, licensed for use herein.

- Viewing of retail videos increased by more than nine times at the start of the 2011 holiday season (MediaPost, January 2012)
- Visitors who viewed product videos were 85 percent more likely to buy than visitors who do not (Internet Retailer, April 2010)
- Visitors who viewed videos on the product pages of home retailer Stacks and Stacks were 144 percent more likely to add products to their shopping cart (Internet Retailer, March 2011)
- Visitors who view videos remain on the site for two minutes longer than other visitors and are 64 percent more likely to purchase (comScore, August 2010)[43]

IT services firm CMIT Solutions adds:

- Retail sites that include video increase conversions by 30 percent and boost their average sales by 13 percent (L2 Specialty Retail Report, September 2010)
- Visitors who viewed videos at OnlineShoes.com converted at a rate of 400 percent greater than those who did not, and the site has experienced a year-over-year increase in video views of 359 percent.[44]

These examples provide strong support for video marketing on websites. Video advertising can help drive traffic to those sites.

Figure 5.6 presents an interesting picture of global video use from the GlobalWebIndex study conducted by Trendstream. It shows, as expected, younger Internet users being more active consumers of all types of video than their older counterparts, sometimes by a large margin and sometimes by a very slim one. All video viewers are consuming more professionally produced content. They are not rushing to view ads and corporate videos; they are watching movies and television programs on all types of devices. Other data reflects greater willingness on the part of younger users to pay for content. All users want their brands to keep them informed; younger users want to be entertained in the process. The study concludes that the Internet is becoming a "transmitter economy" and less of a place where consumers create their own content. It reaches another interesting conclusion on media evolution, "The Internet will not replace traditional media, traditional media will distribute through Internet channels."[45]

Mass Video Consumption Is Diversifying into Multiple Internet Platforms

	16 to 24	25 to 34	35 to 44	45 to 54	55 to 64
Visited a video sharing site	69%	57%	43%	30%	23%
Visited a film site	61%	55%	44%	35%	26%
Watched a full length film	51%	39%	29%	25%	17%
Downloaded free TV shows/film	49%	44%	33%	29%	20%
Visited a Digital content store e.g. iTunes	47%	43%	35%	27%	19%
Stream Personal home videos	42%	31%	22%	16%	10%
Watch on demand TV shows online	40%	35%	29%	27%	24%
Stream Film trailers	31%	25%	17%	11%	7%
Stream Music videos	31%	25%	17%	11%	7%
Listened/Watched a podcast	31%	27%	22%	18%	15%
Streamed a LIVE TV show	25%	20%	16%	11%	9%
Watched a sports program	23%	20%	15%	14%	11%
Download TV show/film via P2P	22%	19%	12%	7%	5%
Watched on demand video clip on a mobile	19%	18%	13%	7%	4%
Paid TV show/film download	14%	13%	9%	6%	4%
Watched live streamed TV on a mobile	9%	8%	6%	3%	2%

- Globally, younger internet users are much more active in consuming content online.

- However, most of the content that they and older users are enjoying is not user-generated content but is professionally produced content such as full-length movies and TV shows.

- These same consumers are also willing to pay for this content, but the hurdle has been the slow development of digital content distribution channels and models.

- This is changing, however, and promises huge rewards for content owners as consumers consume more and more content online.

Which of the following have you done online in the past month? *(% of internet users globally by age group, Wave 5)*

FIGURE **5.6** Global Video Trends

Source: GlobalWebIndex 5, June 2011.

Business Response

Figure 5.7 chronicles the rapid growth of video advertising. Expenditures on video ads are expected to show especially strong growth in 2012 as a result of the London Olympics and the presidential election in the United States. An IAB study predicted that marketers would spend 17 percent of their online display advertising budgets on video advertising in 2011.[46]

The data on the growth of video advertising begs the larger question, "How much are marketers spending to produce and deploy marketing videos?" There are so many types of marketing videos that it's a hard question to answer.

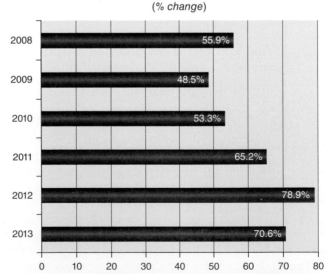

U.S. Online Video Advertising Spending Growth, 2008–2013
(% change)

Year	% change
2008	55.9%
2009	48.5%
2010	53.3%
2011	65.2%
2012	78.9%
2013	70.6%

Note: Online video advertising includes in-stream (such as preroll and overlays), in-banner and in-text (ads delivered when users mouse over relevant words)

FIGURE **5.7** Video Advertising Expenditures

Source: eMarketer, Inc., August 2008.

Consider the basic types suggested by Search Engine Watch:[47]

- Slideshows
- Product demonstrations
- How-to and tutorials
- Case studies and testimonials
- Social videos (branded videos designed to promote viewer sharing[48])
- Vignettes or series
- Scribing (animated storytelling using cartoon-like graphics, also called RSA animation and whiteboard animation.[49])
- Branching videos (essentially links embedded in videos that open new videos upon mouseover[50]

This list may have some terms that are unfamiliar to you, but if you follow the links, you will find that you have seen all of them. And if this list is not sufficiently extensive and detailed, another marketer lists 51 ways to use video to grow a business![51] His list is divided into categories including customer references, public relations, and events.

There are many ways to use videos for business and marketing purposes. There is also a wealth of information about how to produce them and many video production companies. In this discussion, we will concentrate on developing effective marketing strategies that include video. One word about video quality is in order, however. While slickly produced and visually impressive commercial videos clearly have their place, there has long been a belief that an authentic voice and compelling content is more engaging than technical quality alone. Recent studies at Rice University provided data for marketers to ponder. Across four experiments, Professor Philip Kortum and his colleagues showed 100 participants two-minute videos that were encoded at levels of quality ranging from low to high. The correlation they found was between desirability of the content and perception of quality. Kortum said:

> At first we were really surprised by the data. We were seeing that low-quality movies were being rated higher in quality than some of the high-quality videos. But after we started analyzing the data, we determined what was driving this was the actual desirability of the content.
>
> If you're at home watching and enjoying a movie, we found that you're probably not going to notice or even concern yourself with how many pixels the video is or if the data is being compressed.[52]

Kortum went on to say that the relationship holds true outside the laboratory setting when subjects view longer videos in more natural settings. This is not an argument for poor quality, but it is an argument for authentic voice. A video clip of a successful marketer speaking about his or her specialty at a conference may be a little pixelated and jerky, but it is his or her passion and experience the viewer is seeking. In addition, these videos filmed on site are often posted immediately, giving the content the added advantage of timeliness.

Although authenticity is essential, marketers need to consider the quality issue. Much of what they offer, especially in B2C markets, falls under the heading of **branded content**. That refers to content that is obviously produced by the brand but that is not overtly promotional in nature. In other words, branded content needs to be entertaining and that often suggests professional production

INTERACTIVE EXERCISE **5.3**   The Online Video Market

Ad Age has an interactive video poster that gives more data on the pervasiveness of video in our lives and how business is using the channel. See the poster and click through on issues that interest you to get more detailed data.

Visit http://bit.ly/vMZ73s.

quality. A 2011 study by Yahoo! found that professionally produced video advertising achieved better recall on both the ad and the brand. The study also found that consumers were more receptive to video that was featured in connection with an article, with the video plus text presentation being regarded as more professional by 61 percent of the respondents.[53] The conclusion is that brand image matters, in video marketing as in all other types of brand marketing.

Video Marketing Strategy

Video marketing has become an important part of Internet marketing strategy for B2C, B2B, and nonprofit marketers. Like any other marketing communications effort, business videos need to be produced and deployed in a strategic manner that fits in with the remainder of the Internet marketing strategy. Figure 5.8 shows a four-step process for developing video marketing programs that meet strategic business and communications purposes.

The first step is to publish compelling, customer-relevant video material. Whatever type of video you choose, it needs to tell a story that shows the benefits of the product to the consumer or business. The best video with the most compelling story line, however, has no value if no one sees it. Consequently, the second step is to optimize the video, on whatever channel or channels are appropriate for your target audience, for both search and sharing. The next step is to promote it by using your business channels and those of other publishers with whom you have partnerships or who have reason to value your content. Finally, the marketer needs to be sure this effort has been productive by analyzing the metrics produced by the channels and platforms or with metrics provided by third-party metrics suppliers or both. We will briefly discuss each of these steps in turn.

Publishing

There are many technical issues involved in making a good video and much good content that covers the technical issues. Our concern is solely with the issue of marketing effectiveness, not the technical quality issues.

What Makes a Marketing Video Effective?

We all know what videos we like and have our own personal favorites. That is fine, but it is not the marketing issue. The marketing issue is, "What works for our target market?"—a much more difficult question. A video is a creative effort and there are no rules about how to make one that will work, just as there are no hard-and-fast rules about how to make an effective television ad. We do have video metrics, to be discussed later, but metrics are after the fact—after the time and money to produce and deploy a video have been expended. It is also true that, like many other

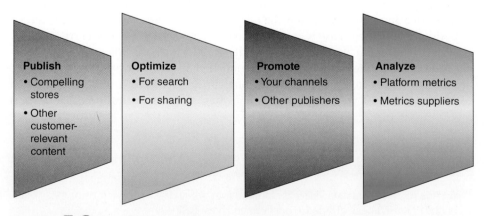

FIGURE **5.8** Elements of Video Marketing Strategy

Source: Adapted from HubSpot, http://www.slideshare.net/HubSpot/how-to-use-online-video-for-marketing-1557896.

TABLE 5.2 Examples of Successful Business, Entertainment and Viral Videos

Business/Marketing	Entertainment/Information	Viral
Nike's Write the Future	Hans Rosling's 200 Countries, 200 Years	Budweiser, Wassup
T-Mobile's Angry Birds Live	Robert Reich Solves the Economy in 2 Minutes	Burger King's Subservient Chicken
McKinsey Quarterly's Eric Schmidt on business culture, technology and social issues	Mp3 Experiment 8	Corning's A Day Made of Glass
Coremetrics' The Voice of Reason	Repower America's Video Wall	Eric Whitacre's Virtual Choir

Source: © Cengage Learning 2013

experiences, each of us knows when a video engages ourselves and when it falls flat, and this can be subjective. So there are no firm rules, but we can learn from successes. Table 5.2 lists some videos by category—branded commercial videos, general information and entertainment, and videos that have gone viral. It is worth studying what works, and whether these videos are your personal favorites; they are widely accepted as being effective examples of their type. Studying what works is a time-honored practice of successful marketing creatives, and it can only improve your ability to judge an effective video when you see one.

Marketers clearly believe that video does work as a marketing tool. Figure 5.9 contains data from both B2C and B2B marketers, both of whom find video channels effective. Notice that B2C and B2B marketers do not differ much in their evaluation of the effectiveness of YouTube and other video-sharing channels like Vimeo. Flickr is not described as a video-sharing channel, but it is also a venue for short videos.

There is more to this chart than just the effectiveness of the channels for stand-alone video. Facebook is seen as the most effective channel for reaching consumers. Businesses post a lot of videos to their Facebook pages. These marketers say that LinkedIn is the most effective way of reaching business people, and LinkedIn is great for communicating and recruiting, but it is not media intensive. However, blogs are almost equally effective in reaching the business community. Blogs are both informative and engaging. One way to increase engagement is to embed videos in blog posts. On my own blog, I can tell by the amount of time spent on the post which posts have videos or slide presentations embedded—one measure of engagement. Twitter is also very effective in reaching business people and many Tweets link to videos and others link to blog posts with videos. The content ecosystem is highly interconnected and video plays a role in many ways.

INTERACTIVE EXERCISE 5.4   Interactive Version of Write the Future

By all media accounts, Nike's "Write the Future" ad was successful. Apparently Nike agreed; they have developed an interactive version. You have to register with Nike to Write Your Future, but it is worth the free registration to try out this interactive video.

Visit http://bit.ly/sF074a.

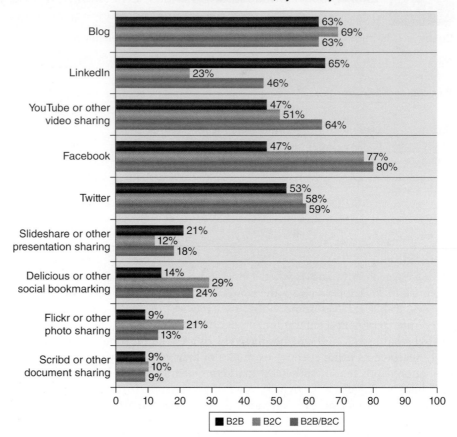

FIGURE 5.9 Effectiveness of Video as a Social Media Platform

Source: Adam T. Stutton, "Social Media Chart: Which channels are the most effective for inbound marketing?" April, 18, 2011, Marketing Sherpa, http://sherpablog.marketingsherpa.com/inbound-marketing/channels.

Figure 5.10 contains an infographic that illustrates the value of video as a marketing tool. It also highlights some of the semantic issues in this space. It correctly lists video platforms as channels for content distribution. It also identifies types of videos and places them in a three-stage buying process. These stages are:

- *Awareness stage*, where viral videos create awareness and positive attitudes since they are shared by liked, trusted friends.
- *Consideration stage*, where webinars and demonstration videos convey knowledge about the product and its benefits. Ebooks (and vooks™) and enewsletters are also useful in this state and they are frequently used to disseminate videos.
  - Customer testimonials, which can be text as well as video, help to move the prospect from consideration into the close (purchase) stage.
- *Close stage*, where hard information becomes paramount. Case studies can be videos and videos from in-person events provide information to the nonattender and reminders to attenders. Press releases often have embedded videos, partly to encourage journalists and bloggers to write pieces with embedded videos.

In other words, video can play a major role in each stage of the buyer consideration process. This infographic has a B2B perspective, but all of the roles for video are equally applicable in B2C markets.

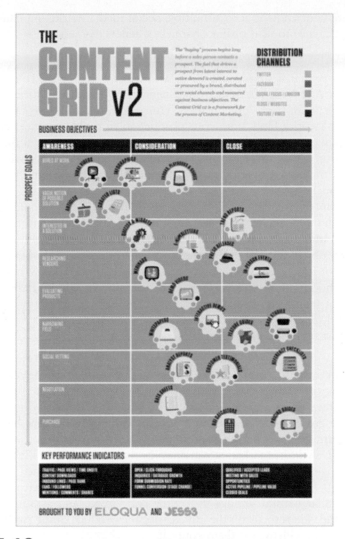

FIGURE **5.10** Video Is Both a Communications Channel and a Marketing Tool

Source: Eloqua, http://blog.eloqua.com/the-content-grid-v2.

Developing Customer-Relevant Content and Stories

Even though the creative aspect of making a video cannot be reduced to rules, it should be approached in the same way as developing any other marketing communication. The advice of one video marketer is:

- Decide which types of content you are going to use to deploy your video.
- Establish your marketing objectives. And do not forget a call to action at the end of the video that clearly tells your audience what you want them to do and makes it easy for them to do it—a link, a form, whatever is relevant.
- Identify your target audience and learn all you can about their use of your product category and their video consumption habits. Video viewing has been unplugged from the desktop. A recent study by market research firm In-Stat reports that 50 percent of tablet owners are viewing feature-length movies and television programs on their devices and they are doing so both at home and on the go. Their research also finds that by 2015 65 percent of the U.S. population will own a tablet or a smartphone. Of those, 86 percent will view video on their mobile devices.[54]
- Make the content relevant to your audience—engaging, unexpected, memorable, entertaining, or informative—depending on the nature of your product and your message.

- Integrate your content across multiple social media marketing channels. Make reference to it in offline channels whenever practical.[55]

Another video marketer adds additional pieces of advice:[56]

- Tell a story that is simple, engaging, and will resonate with your target audience. A story is different from a persuasive advertising message. It should be about how your business, your products, and your customers live in the real world. How does your product solve problems, meet customer needs, make their lives better? A good story needs to be based on fact and delivered in a way that customers can relate to. If it touches their emotions, so much the better. Stories work just as well in the B2B environment as they do in B2C.
- Show them, don't tell them. Talking heads do not do the job. Make the product the star. Jimm Fox says, "The power of video and rich media is in its ability to demonstrate the tangible benefits that a product or service can offer."
- Establish objectives first and make sure your presentation, whether it is scripted or unscripted, contributes to the desired outcomes. While you should choose the best video format to meet your needs, content is more important than technical issues.
- Above all, *the only perspective that matters is the customer's perspective.* That must permeate every aspect of your video.

Most business videos qualify as "branded content," a term that is hard to define but easy to spot. You can think of it as soft-sell advertising. You can also think of it as entertainment with obvious sponsorship. It is really a combination of advertising and entertainment in which the owner of the brand has end-to-end responsibility for the content. Energy drink Red Bull has been sponsoring athletes, often stars of extreme sports, for many years.[57] It has used video marketing extensively in its marketing activities. In the summer of 2011, the company received a great deal of favorable attention, including being listed in Ad Age's Creative 50,[58] for videos featuring parkour (free running) athlete Ryan Doyle. Using spectacular natural settings in Turkey and Greece and astounding feats of athleticism, the videos focus on the athlete, not the product. Static captures cannot do justice to these videos. See them yourself:

- Turkey: http://www.youtube.com/watch?v=IUTXXMdQnio&feature= player_embedded.
- Greece: http://www.youtube.com/watch?v=uiIgrGWRaik&feature=player_ embedded.
- For more parkour and to better understand Ryan Doyle's relationship with Red Bull, see his website www.ryandoyle.co.uk.

Think about it for a minute. Isn't this exactly how marketers want their videos to be perceived? "You have to see them for yourselves." And the company they want their product to keep—the best of the best? And in this case, the tie between the energy drink and the extreme sport is perfect, and Red Bull was smart enough and creative enough not to overdo the product tie-in. The whole series featuring Ryan Doyle, as well as much of the rest of Red Bull's content, has a story line but they are more about evoking feelings than about well-developed plots.

This section contains some guidelines for developing effective marketing videos, but all the videos listed here also make the point that creativity has a lot to do with the success of a video or a video series. The best way to know whether you have a video that is relevant and engaging is to test it with members of the target audience. Marketing testing is mentioned in basic marketing books and discussed in detail in marketing research texts. We discuss marketing testing in the context of landing pages in Chapter 10.

Once you have a video that resonates with the target audience, it is time to determine how to bring it to their attention. It is possible to advertise the availability of videos in traditional or online media, but that is rarely done. It is expensive and it tends to defeat the purpose of not being hard-sell advertising. Instead, marketers first optimize it so it will be visible and shared on the web and then they promote it, most often in media channels they control or partner with.

Optimizing for Search and Sharing

Search

The principles of optimizing content for the search engines are essentially the same, whatever the medium or channel and they are discussed in detail in Chapter 8. However, most search engines are text based and cannot actually see video. Consequently, special care must be taken in order to make videos visible to the search engines. Two factoids illustrate the importance of video visibility:

1. In August 2008, YouTube surpassed Yahoo! in number of search queries, becoming the second largest search engine behind its parent Google.[59]
2. A Forrester study in 2010 found that "any given video in the index [the database of all pages found by Google] stands about a 50 times better chance of appearing on the first page of results than any given text page in the index."[60]

Forrester's Nate Elliott adds that relatively few marketers are optimizing their videos, so that makes the odds of a video getting a first-page Google ranking even better. Those odds are too great for marketers to ignore!

In a nutshell, here are things marketers need to do to optimize their videos for search:

1. *Study relevant keywords and use them in all the other optimization activities.*
2. Whenever possible—on the website for example—include text since that is visible to the search engines. Some marketers post a transcript of the video which allows the full content to be searchable.
3. Where you cannot embed the video in a text page—on YouTube for example— tag it with keywords and write a description, using keywords, of course.
4. Have a short, catchy title.
5. Optimize video and page URLs.
6. Encourage user ratings.
7. Post your video to YouTube. The tools for optimizing video sharing on YouTube are available whenever you upload a video. You should create a title, a description, and tags, all of which are keyword rich. Choosing a category like "Pets & Animals" helps people find your content. You can also create up to three thumbnail images that will be indexed for search and therefore will lead people to your video.
8. Consider using a video platform that submits your video to many channels. Examples of platforms include Limelight, Ooyala, MobiTB, and many others. Do not confuse platforms whose primary function is to help the marketer upload and monetize videos with video advertising platforms like TubeMogul. The platform space is crowded and confusing, so the marketer needs to exercise caution.[61]
9. Keep your video brief. Two to three minutes should be the maximum length for almost all videos. Consider breaking long videos into three-minute segments.

Remember to use keywords in each step and to optimize your website itself. Both keyword identification and website optimization are major topics of Chapter 8.

Sharing

There is a lot of content sharing going on. Many of us contribute by sharing various types of content—content on our Facebook page, retweeting items that we like, emailing images or videos, and much more. The chances are that all readers of this book are part of the torrent of shared content. Mark Zuckerberg, using data from Facebook, says that the volume of sharing is doubling each year and predicts that 32 billion pieces of content will be shared *each day* by 2014.[62]

It is probably not surprising that Facebook is the primary channel for video sharing. U.K. data shows the following:

- Facebook had 30.8 million video shares in May 2010. That number rose to 58.6 million shares in January 2011. The peak during that time period was December 2010 with 62.5 million shares.
- Video sharing on Twitter remained relatively constant during this time period at over 600 thousand shares and a peak of 839 million shares in November 2010.
- Video sharing on blogs declined from 460 thousand in May 2010 to 243 thousand in January 2011.

The large increase in Facebook and decrease in blog video sharing is attributed to the rise of mobile phones, which makes consumption and sharing of content on Facebook, and also on Twitter, easy.[63]

This is U.K. data, but there is no reason to believe that the overall picture is different elsewhere since the growth in Facebook subscribers and mobile Internet use is rapidly increasing throughout the world.

YouTube also offers tools for sharing whenever you upload a video. You can automatically post your YouTube video on Facebook, Twitter, the Google Reader, Google Buzz, Orkut, and MySpace just by having an account on each platform and connecting your video to it. On Facebook, the best way to promote video sharing is to encourage your friends to share your video on whichever platforms they use, from a personal blog to a social bookmarking site like Digg, to their personal Twitter account.

Promote

Content sharing is highly desirable since it comes from a trusted source, most often a friend or family member. However, it is unlikely to create as much visibility as the marketer desires. Having optimized the content and the site for sharing, the marketer needs to turn to promotion of the content. That is, in fact, the first, and perhaps the most crucial, step in promoting your videos.

There are, however, other actions the marketer can take to see that her videos are widely deployed across the web. Post video *on the marketer's own channels*. Post or link your video to every one of your other content channels. Feature a link or embed the video on the site's home page for a reasonable period of time, then archive it to a product or another relevant page like Customer Success Stories. Write a blog post and embed the video. Post it on your Facebook page and Tweet it. Post it on video-sharing sites other than YouTube. There are many of them, and each may attract a more specialized and perhaps a more engaged audience than YouTube. You can post a link back to the original YouTube posting. Embed the video in a customer newsletter. The marketer needs to think about all the channels by which he can reach customers and make the video available in each one.

Post video *on the channels of other publishers*. One of the marketer's goals is to get the video featured, for example, by embedding it on a blog or posing it to the Facebook page or corporate website of business partners. The other goal is to get as many inbound links to the posted video as possible. The way to do this is to reach out to business partners and influential bloggers by email, informing them about the video, and encouraging them to feature it prominently in their content. Press releases should include links to relevant corporate or product videos. Post the video to social bookmarking sites like Diigo and Reddit. If there are forums or discussion groups (on LinkedIn, for example) that are frequented by your target audience, post to those groups as well. Think about the multitude of Internet venues that the target audience uses and figure out how you can draw attention to your video in those locations.

Video-sharing site Vimeo has good advice that covers both making your video visible and encouraging sharing. They suggest:

> The more you interact with the community by liking and commenting on their videos, the more they will be interested in watching your videos and getting to know you in return. To start, we recommend joining some Groups that may interest you or subscribing to some Channels. You should also think about participating in some of the many great Vimeo projects in our Projects Forum.[64]

Overall, understand that this is a social space. To be effective, the marketer needs to be social.

Analyze

Marketing videos will produce most of the general Internet metrics, like number of visitors and page views that are discussed in Chapter 14. There are also some metrics that are specific to video marketing. As with all metrics, there are two ways of obtaining them: directly from the platform or from a third-party metrics provider. Video marketing is still in its early stages, so platform metrics and specialty video metrics providers are the most common. Larger integrated metrics providers are beginning to integrate video metrics into their comprehensive metrics platforms.[65]

For example Figure 5.11 shows a YouTube Insight page provided by Greg Habermann, blogging for Search Engine Watch. Habbermann is COO of digital marketing agency, SageRock, which featured a YouTube video on its home page.

This portion of the "Views" page captured gives traffic (views) for all time for all videos in the SageRock channel, daily views over the past month, and viewership by global region and by country. Habbermann was interested in the fact that his videos were popular in Australia, but he had no explanation for why

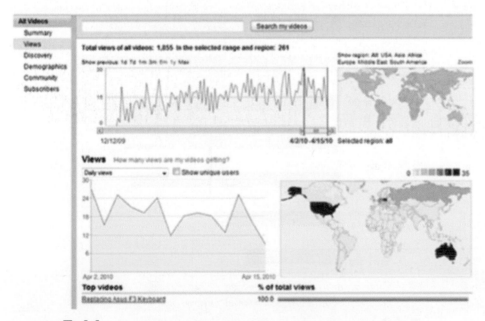

FIGURE **5.11** Video Metrics Supplied by YouTube

Source: Incisive Media, http://searchenginewatch.com/article/2066563/Online-Video-Analytics-Getting-Started-with-YouTube-Insight.

that was the case. (If you are familiar with Google Analytics, which is discussed in detail in Chapter 14, you will see the similarities.)

Visible Measures, one of the specialty video metrics providers, lists common metrics as:

- Placements, the number of videos associated with the campaign, measured by the number of videos with a unique URL. They can be broken down as:
  - Original or seeded videos, the ones uploaded by the video creator
  - Copies uploaded by others
  - Derivatives that include mash-ups (combinations with other content), spoofs, parodies, etc.
- Collection and analysis of comments and ratings posted by viewers
- Engagement, measured by individual metrics like completion rates, fast forwards, and video abandonment[66]

Figure 5.12 presents some of the most important metrics for measuring video advertising. Some of them, like purchase, are more relevant to video ads than they are to marketing videos in general. However, the chart gives a good sense of what video marketers are looking for—videos that create interaction—comments, for example—videos that impact brand metrics, time spent watching the video, and the completion rate. All the metrics listed in Figure 5.12 are useful in assessing the effectiveness of a marketing video.

Remember that **video marketing** is part of a **content marketing** strategy, and that content marketing is only one aspect of the overall Internet marketing strategy. Metrics at each level must be chosen and assessed from the perspective of achieving organizational Internet marketing objectives, not from the perspective of that channel or campaign alone.

Video is a powerful marketing tool, especially if it is approached from a strategic point of view. The good news for small business is that video marketing is accessible to the smallest of local businesses.

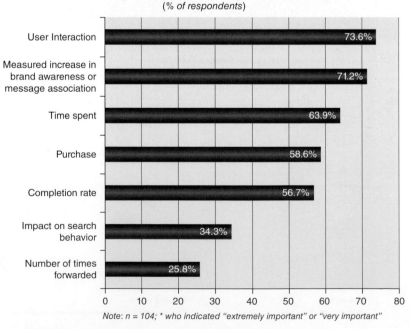

Important Engagement Metrics for Measuring Online Video Advertising According to U.S. Advertisers/Agencies*, April 2010
(% of respondents)

Metric	%
User Interaction	73.6%
Measured increase in brand awareness or message association	71.2%
Time spent	63.9%
Purchase	58.6%
Completion rate	56.7%
Impact on search behavior	34.3%
Number of times forwarded	25.8%

Note: n = 104; * who indicated "extremely important" or "very important"

FIGURE **5.12** Metrics Widely Used by Video Marketers

Source: Tremor Media and DM2PRO, "State of Online Video 2010," as cited by eMarketer, Inc., April 12, 2010.

Video Marketing for Small Business

Many experienced marketers believe that video marketing is essential for the small business. Why? First, since both video production and video marketing can be essentially free. Second, the process of creating and deploying can be fast, and it can be entirely in the control of the business owner. It is, of course, possible to bring in professional video producers and marketing consultants, but the small business owner can do it all himself, often with considerable success.

The classic case is wine retailer Gary Vaynerchuk, who retired from daily video production in early 2011 after a five-year run that made him a celebrity in New Jersey and beyond. His family immigrated from Belarus when Gary was 3. At age 8, he had a successful lemonade stand. By the time he was 35, he had revitalized his family's liquor store in Springfield, New Jersey, started a successful online wine business, written two best-selling business books, and established a social media marketing agency that numbers Fortune 500 corporations among its clients. His daily wine videos were at the heart of his social media empire. He started Wine Library TV with a flip cam and a New York Jets helmet (he tastes the wine and spits it into the helmet) from the back room of the family liquor store.[67] By 2011, when he retired from daily video with a video farewell (see Figure 5.13), his empire was valued at more than $50 million.[68]

There is much opinion about the reasons for Vaynerchuk's success. His videos demystify wine and wine tasting, and generally feature wines of moderate price. It may have a lot to do with his style, which is a take-no-prisoners approach to the often stuffy wine business. A lot of it had to do with persistence. He produced a wine video almost every business day for five years. He also kept up with developments in the video channel, offering sharing icons and mobile apps to spread his word about wine, both of which can be seen in Figure 5.13. In the process, he proved that social media in general, and video in particular, has much to offer to the small business.

There are two basic ways for small businesses—or any marketers for that matter—to use video. The first is to create a video channel, like Gary Vaynerchuk did. The second is to invest in video advertising.

FIGURE **5.13** Video Farewell and Thank You

Source: Daily Grape, http://dailygrape.com/videos/89-the-final-grape.

Marketers can create a video channel on any of the video-sharing channels. YouTube is popular with both businesses and users, which may make it easier to generate traffic. ReelSEO has a blog post that gives good examples of video use by small business. Advice to small business people for effective use of videos includes:

- Show your product in action.
- Give instructions and advice.
- Let your customers become fans by reviewing and sharing yours or even producing their own.
- Post your videos on your website as well as on your video-sharing platform of choice.
- Study the analytics provided by the platform.[69] As portrayed in Figure 5.11, robust analytics are provided by the platforms and website analytics for pages with videos can provide additional insight.

Video advertising, carefully chosen, is accessible to even the smallest business. Ads on YouTube are self-service and creating one is similar to the step-by-step process for a creating Facebook ad that is discussed in Chapter 6. Like Google AdWords (see Chapter 8) and Facebook, YouTube offers robust targeting options that include demographics, customer interests, and keywords,[70] as well as several video ad formats.[71] In addition, the YouTube advertising site allows you to insert your videos into Google AdWords campaigns.[72] Some YouTube advertising, like an ad on the home page, can be very expensive but a Search Engine Journal experiment found YouTube ad bids as low as 28 cents.[73] Keyword bidding is discussed in Chapter 8. This type of ad also allows the marketer to cap daily expenditures, ensuring that the budget will not be exceeded.

There is a second way to advertise on YouTube—promoted videos. With a budget of a few dollars per day, video owners can have their videos featured with relevant search terms which puts them next to relevant content. You see promoted videos just about every time you conduct a search on YouTube, but you may not have thought about how these particular videos are selected. Interactive Exercise 5.5 will enable you to see this kind of advertising from the consumer's perspective. If you are familiar with Google Adwords, discussed in Chapter 8, you will recognize the format. Across the top are the two videos that had the highest keyword bids and down the right side there may be more. The ad also entitles the marketer to what YouTube calls an overlay ad. This is clickable text that appears below the video while it is running. This allows the marketer to drive the viewer to the website for more information and a potential transaction.

There are two important aspects of this discussion that should be kept in mind:

1. All the techniques and tools in this discussion of video marketing for small businesses apply in just the same way to large corporations, as illustrated by the promoted videos example. However, the reverse is not true. Video marketing in general, and video ads and promoted videos in particular, are

---

INTERACTIVE EXERCISE **5.5**   Search YouTube

http://www.youtube.com.

Try a search for just about anything on YouTube. Chances are that you will see two promoted videos in a box above your search results and more on the right hand bar. (If there are not any or many, you will see some featured videos and probably a YouTube ad promoting the advertising program.). Play one of the featured videos and see if it includes an overlay ad.

Try your search several times, on subjects you think might be quite popular or subjects you do not think many people search for. See how your results differ and pay attention to the number of times the various videos have been viewed. Also think about how many people are searching for videos on all kinds of subject matter and the opportunities that offers to marketers.

available to the small business in ways and at prices that are not true of most mass media channels.

2. This discussion is specific to the video marketing channel. You will find that the same principles apply to other Internet media channels like picture sharing (Flickr, Photobucket,), social bookmarking (Digg and Reditt,) document sharing (Scribd), webcasts (BrightTalk), and presentation sharing (Slideshare). These and other Internet media channels give businesses large and small a rich set of options for deploying and promoting their content.

Video Marketing Best Practices

Since video marketing engages viewers and is relatively inexpensive, it has the potential to be an important tool for all marketers. Let us end this chapter with a brief discussion of video marketing best practices. The final installment in an eight-part series on video marketing (well worth reading in its entirety) includes the following recommendations:

- Set social goals, not financial ones. Videos are one part of a content marketing strategy and, as such, are impossible to link to specific financial goals like sales.
- Have a marketing plan.
- Have a social media presence, which gives you channels to distribute your video content.
- Include sharing options in your video posts and marketing campaign activities like emails.
- Encourage commentary and respond as needed.
- Measure results.
- Look at video as a relationship building tool more than as a direct sales generation tool.
- Monitor what people say about the campaign in other channels (Facebook, Twitter, trade industry publications, for example).
- Have a formal debriefing at the end of the formal campaign to assess effectiveness and pinpoint things learned that will make future campaigns better.[74]

These recommendations are good advice for marketing in all social media channels. YouTube is the dominant video channel and Awareness has a brief ebook that details best practices specifically for YouTube.[75] We will return to the discussion of social media channels in Chapter 9.

SUMMARY

In its early days, the Internet was regarded as essentially a direct-response medium with capabilities that exceeded other direct response media. However, as the Internet has matured, marketers have learned that it is also an effective branding medium. The legacy of the early days tends to persist, with many brand marketers finding Internet advertising most effective for generating a direct response. However, research shows that Internet ads can be effective in brand building, especially in the purchase consideration step. Online advertising is most effective when used in integrated programs using both online and offline channels. All channels must work together to ensure a satisfying customer experience.

Online brand marketing takes place in an ever-expanding content ecosystem. Marketer must create compelling content and optimize and deploy it in ways that make it visible to the desired target audience. The purpose of making the content widely available is to drive target customers to the website or blog for further information and, ultimately, a transaction. Using this content-focused type of marketing approach has become known as content marketing or inbound marketing. Content that is controlled by and associated with a brand, although it lacks overt persuasive content, is branded content. Branding activities are facilitated by the existence of branded communities of the faithful.

One tool that is especially valuable to the marketer for creating brand favorability and purchase intention is the marketing video. Watching videos of various lengths on various devices has become a major type of content consumption for the majority of Internet users. Even though most of the videos consumed are not marketing videos, a marketing video can be not only engaging but also relatively inexpensive compared to other types of content. As such, it is accessible to both large and small businesses in business, consumer, and nonprofit markets.

Video marketing needs a planned strategy, just like any other type of marketing communications campaign. It is important to publish videos—on video-sharing platforms and business websites and blogs—that customers find compelling, to optimize them for both search and sharing, to actively promote viewership and sharing, and to measure and analyze the results.

There are numerous aspects that are important in creating an effective marketing video. One of the keys is to tell a story in which the brand is the star—meeting customers' needs and delivering benefits that exceed what they find elsewhere. Marketers produce videos themselves, with or without the assistance of professional production houses, and they can also encourage their customers to create and post video content.

Video advertising is a separate marketing tool. Videos can be embedded in various types of online display advertising. Marketers can advertise their videos on the video-sharing platforms. They can also avail themselves of promoted videos that are similar to other pay-per-click ads.

Video marketing is already a useful marketing tool and its importance will continue to grow as Internet users increasingly have access wherever they are through mobile devices.

DISCUSSION QUESTIONS

1. Think about your own Internet use habits. Have you changed your use of traditional media? Why or why not? How do your own habits fit the media use attitudes and patterns described in this chapter?
2. A businessperson who is not an Internet expert asks you whether the Internet is useful for branding. What answer would you give and how could you support it with examples?
3. What are special tools and techniques that enterprises can use in their brand-building process on the web?
4. Do you believe that online advertising has more potential to engage viewers than mass media advertising? Why or why not?
5. What is a branded community? If you are a member of one or more branded communities, what has your experience been? If you are not, why have you not joined communities for products or services you like?
6. Think about your own consumption of video. What kinds of entertainment and informational videos are you most likely to view? Why? Do you often find yourself viewing marketing videos? Why or why not?
7. Add some of your favorite videos to the business/marketing, entertainment/information, and viral videos shown in Table 5.2. Is there another category that would be useful for marketers studying the video space?
8. What are the elements of video marketing strategy? Why is it important that marketers have a strategy for their use of videos?
9. What is meant by "branded content?" Are you aware of recently seeing branded content on the Internet? How much and what kinds?
10. What makes a marketing video effective?
11. Why are optimizing for search and sharing important parts of a video marketing strategy?
12. What are some of the key metrics that are used to measure the effectiveness of marketing videos?

INTERNET EXERCISES

1. Internet Career Builder Exercise
   a. These are some of the jobs that are available in brand marketing and video marketing, on both the client side and the agency side. You can find others on sites recommended by your instructor or through search.

Brand marketing manager

Marketing manager

Associate product manager, Product manager

Product development manager

Content strategist

Media planner, buyer, supervisor

Digital media planner

Video assistant, producer

Videographer

Video editor

Multimedia production specialist

Director of video services

Video manager

and many more

b. Select a brand or video marketing job from the list in 1a or from your own search. Outline the responsibilities of that position. You may find it useful to locate job postings on the web in order to understand the job requirements.

c. Outline knowledge and experience from classes, internships, full- or part-time jobs, and volunteer work that prepare you for this specific position.

d. Prepare five questions you could ask at a job interview. The questions should exhibit your understanding of the position requirements without lecturing the interviewer about what he or she already knows.

e. Update your VisualCV® or LinkedIn Profile with this information.

2. Visit one or more of the websites you have been following. Think about the nature of their brand, whether it is a tangible product, a services product, or a nonprofit organization, in which case the brand is likely the organization itself. How are they going about brand-building on the site itself?

3. Do several searches on YouTube, some using very popular topics or products, some using more unusual, even esoteric, ones. Do you ever fail to come up with videos? What do you see in terms of promoted videos in these searches?

4. EyeView Digital is a producer of personalized video advertising. It has a quiz that tests your ability to determine which videos are likely to be more effective. Try the quiz and see how you fare: http://www.eyeviewdigital.com/video_marketing_quiz.htm.

NOTES

1. http://www.digitaltrends.com/mobile/uk-woman-helps-apple-reach-10-billion-app-downloads.

2. http://blog.nielsen.com/nielsenwire/media_entertainment/do-americans-watch-more-dvrd-commercials-than-you-think.

3. http://pewresearch.org/pubs/1844/poll-main-source-national-international-news-Internet-television-newspapers.

4. http://www.istrategylabs.com/2010/01/facebook-demographics-and-statistics-report-2010-145-growth-in-1-year.

5. http://www.iab.net/about_the_iab/recent_press_releases/press_release_archive/press_release/4623.

6. Roadblocks are ads that appear on two or more sections of the same page at the same time. For instance, one ad might be a banner at the top of the page and another a skyscraper on the side. The point is that for the duration of the viewer's stay on that page he is exposed to advertising of that one brand only. Roadblocks are offered by large portals and content sites; they represent a media buy, not an advertising format.

7. http://www.clickz.com/clickz/news/1712283/ford-f-150-drives-away-with-online-success.

8. http://www.iab.net/about_the_iab/recent_press_releases/press_release_archive/press_release/4725.

9. http://www.marketingevolution.com/downloads/industry_related/me_multichannel_communication.pdf.

10. http://www.iab.net/media/file/BAIN_BRIEF_Digital_Advertising_4-19-10_FINAL.pdf.

11. Posted online, without the ads from the print version at http://www.wired.com/magazine/18-06. Throughout, there are house ads for the Wired iPad app.

12. http://blogs.adobe.com/digitalpublishing/files/2011/01/digital_magazine_ad_engagement.pdf.

13. http://www.themarthablog.com/2010/11/the-launch-of-boundless-beauty.html.

14. http://www.padgadget.com/2010/11/13/martha-stewart-living-boundless-beauty-app-review.

15. You can see a demonstration and discussion with CNBC anchors at http://www.cnbc.com/id/15840232?video=1639574734&play=1.

16. http://www.iab.net/media/file/BAIN_BRIEF_Digital_Advertising_4-19-10_FINAL.pdf, p. 6.

17. David C. Edelman, "Branding in the Digital Age." *Harvard Business Review*, December 2010, pp. 1–9.

18. https://www.mckinseyquarterly.com/The_consumer_decision_journey_2373.

19. Kevin Lane Keller, *Strategic Brand Management* (Upper Saddle River, NJ: Prentice Hall, 1998), p. 43.

20. http://www.coneinc.com/consumers-confirm-recommendations-online.

21. Larry Ciagouris and Brant Wansley, "Branding on the Internet," *Marketing Management*, Summer 2000, pp. 35–38.

22. Kevin Lane Keller, *Strategic Brand Management* (Upper Saddle River, NJ: Prentice Hall, 1998), p. 51.

23. http://www.travelocity.com/Promotions/0,,TRAVELOCITY%7C6473%7Cmkt_main,00.html.

24. http://www.iab.net/media/file/IAB_WHITE_PAPER_FINAL_AUGUST-3-2010.pdf.

25. Based on Mary Lou Roberts, "Interactive Brand Experience," in Irvine Clarke III and Theresa Flaherty, *Advances in Electronic Marketing*, 2005, Idea Group, Inc., 109–116.

26. http://link.brightcove.com/services/player/bcpid 1543292789?bctid=619312676001.

27. http://mashable.com/2010/12/08/dell-social-listening-center.

28. http://www.pepsico.com/PressRelease/PepsiCos-Doritos-and-Pepsi-MAX-Turn-Over-Unprecedented-Six-Super-Bowl-Ads-to-Con09152010.html.

29. http://www.refresheverything.com.

30. Based on http://www.tmcatoday.org/MembersOnly/Archives/PDFs/2007/TMCA_Online_Branding.pdf; http://blog.hubspot.com/blog/tabid/6307/bid/5178/The-Secret-to-Social-Media-Brand-Building-Cultivation.asp; and http://searchengineland.com/5-key-strategies-to-build-your-brand-online-39420.

31. Albert M. Muniz, Jr., and Thomas C. O'Guinn, "Brand Community." *Journal of Consumer Research* 27 (March 2001): 412.

32. Thomas C. O'Guinn and Albert Muniz, Jr., "Collective Brand Relationships," in *Handbook of Brand Relations*, eds. Joseph Priester, Deborah MacInnis, and C. W. Park (N.Y. Society for Consumer Psychology and M.E. Sharp).

33. http://diy-marketing.blogspot.com/2010/12/what-are-branded-community-best.html.

34. http://www.cyrilhuzeblog.com/2010/10/03/harley-davidson-scoring-high-after-intensively-courting-women.

35. http://www.facebook.com/pages/Harley-Owners-Group/112424855438821#!/pages/Harley-Owners-Group/112424855438821?sk=wall.

36. http://www.ultimatemotorcycling.com/Harley_Owners_Group_HOG_History.

37. http://diy-marketing.blogspot.com/2009/02/customer-retention-communities.html.

38. http://www.umww.com/global/knowledge/view?id=128, p. 58.

39. Defined in the vook blog as "a new innovation in reading that blends a well-written book, high-quality video and the power or the Internet into a single, complete story—all on one screen, without switching between platforms."

40. Jim Lecinski, *Winning the Zero Moment of Truth—Changing the Rules of the Game*, position 637 on the iPhone for Kindle app.

41. http://blog.nielsen.com/nielsenwire/online_mobile/what-consumers-watch-nielsens-q1-2010-three-screen-report.

42. http://www.comscore.com/Press_Events/Press_Releases/2011/8/comScore_Releases_July_2011_U.S._Online_Video_Rankings.

43. http://www.invodo.com/html/resources/video-statistics.

44. http://www.cmitsolutions.com/corporate/blog/how-powerful-video-promotional-tool.

45. http://www.slideshare.net/Tomtrendstream/wave-5-trends-master-august-2011-slideshare-version, slide 46.

46. http://www.iab.net/media/file/DigitalVideoAdvertisingStudyIABFINAL001.pdf.

47. http://searchenginewatch.com/article/2103884/Video-Marketing-to-the-T-Types-Tips-Trends.

48. http://www.reelseo.com/branded-social-video-blueprint.

49. http://machoarts.com/11-informative-whiteboard-animations-by-rsa.

50. See an example at http://imm.sheridanc.on.ca/interactivevideo/branching.html.

51. http://onemarketmedia.com/blog/2011/01/51-ways-to-use-web-video-to-help-your-business-grow.

52. http://www.sciencedaily.com/releases/2010/08/100812122615.htm.

53. http://advertising.yahoo.com/industry-knowledge/phase2-video-snapshot.html.

54. http://www.instat.com/press.asp?ID=3248&sku=IN1105139MSV.

55. http://www.reelseo.com/content-marketing-video-social-media/#ixzz1VJPP6O6X.

56. http://onemarketmedia.com/blog/2010/08/7-habits-of-highly-effective-video-marketing.

57. http://www.bloomberg.com/news/2011-05-19/red-bull-s-adrenaline-marketing-billionaire-mastermind.html.

58. http://creativity-online.com/news/creativity-50-2011-dietrich-mateschitz-and-amy-taylor/227962.

59. http://ir.comscore.com/releasedetail.cfm?ReleaseID=335556.

60. http://blogs.forrester.com/interactive_marketing/2009/01/the-easiest-way.html.

61. http://www.optify.net/seo/10-tips-optimizing-video-search; http://www.inc.com/guides/2010/05/search-engine-optimization-for-video.html; and http://www.reelseo.com/basic-tips-optimizing-video-content-search-engines.

62. http://bx.businessweek.com/social-media-marketing/view?url=http%3A%2F%2Fblog.summify.com%2F2011%2F08%2F24%2Fsocial-sharing-infographic%2F.

63. http://econsultancy.com/us/blog/7198-online-video-sharing-doubles-within-a-year.

64. http://vimeo.com/faq/pro#get_more_views.

65. http://www.omniture.com/en/products/online_analytics/sitecatalyst#fragment-5.

66. http://corp.visiblemeasures.com/video-metrics.

67. http://www.npr.org/2011/04/25/135578933/a-wine-bloggers-guide-to-social-media-for-business.

68. http://www.positivearticles.com/Article/A-Conversation-with-Gary-Vaynerchuk/47045.

69. http://www.reelseo.com/7-ways-online-video-affordable-effective-marketing-tool-small-businesses; http://www.nytimes.com/2011/03/17/business/smallbusiness/17sbiz.html?_r=3; and http://www.reelseo.com/video-small-business-advertisers.

70. http://www.youtube.com/t/advertising_audience_targeting.

71. http://www.youtube.com/t/advertising_trueview.

72. http://www.youtube.com/t/advertising_video_targeting.

73. http://www.searchenginejournal.com/youtube-channel-experiment/22322.

74. http://www.reelseo.com/social-video-blueprint-part-8. The seven earlier posts are linked on this page.

75. Download the ebook from this page http://info.awarenessnetworks.com/Youtube-Best-Practices.html

CHAPTER 6

Display Advertising and Other Customer Acquisition Techniques

Chapter Outline

Internet Customer Acquisition Tools

Online Advertising
Online Display Advertising

Online Ad Serving and Targeting
Targeting Online Ads
Targeting on Vertical Advertising Networks
Social Network Advertising Options

Miscellaneous Acquisition Techniques
Event-Driven Marketing
Affiliate Programs
Portal Relationships
Viral Marketing

SUMMARY
DISCUSSION QUESTIONS
INTERNET EXERCISES
NOTES

Key Terms

LEARNING OBJECTIVES

By the time you complete this chapter, you will be able to:

- Explain the meaning and importance of customer acquisition as a marketing strategy.

- List the major customer acquisition techniques, both online and offline.

- Identify the major online advertising formats.

- Explain ad serving and how ad serving networks are used to target online ads.

- Identify the most common methods of targeting.

- Explain the various types of behavioral targeting.

- Discuss the benefits and drawbacks of advertising on Facebook, LinkedIn, and other social media networks.

- Define event marketing, publicity, affiliate marketing, and portal sponsorships.

The Internet marketing paradigm in Chapter 1 defined the four basic marketing strategy objectives as customer acquisition, conversion, retention, and value growth. The concept of customer lifetime value (CLV), by which the marketer measures customer value, is discussed in Chapter 4. Conversion to a loyal customer and customer retention are very important marketing objectives discussed in Chapters 10 and 11, but, while trite, it is also true that the marketer must acquire a customer before creating loyalty and retention. It is also important to note that a steady stream of new customers is necessary to fuel growth in most organizations.

This chapter focuses on specific interactive marketing tools that are most often used in customer acquisition strategy. There are other acquisition tools, most importantly search marketing, that are discussed in the later chapters. Throughout these chapters, it is important to realize that virtually any of the Internet marketing tools can be used in an acquisition program, but some of them are especially well suited to acquisition efforts.

Examples also imply that there is more than one definition of *customer acquisition*. Certainly *acquisition* can be defined as "making a first purchase." However, it can also be defined as getting the customer to engage in a behavior that permits further contact—signing up for a newsletter, for example. For the social media marketer, *acquisition* may be defined as getting additional fans or followers on a social network page. We return to the issue of definitions and metrics to measure acquisition in various later chapters. For the moment, however, just try to focus on the generic concept of "new customer."

Internet Customer Acquisition Tools

While there are numerous ways to acquire new Internet customers in B2C (business-to-consumer), B2B (business-to-business), and nonprofit markets, they fall into several basic categories as shown in Figure 6.1. These tools are invariably used in combination with one another as discussed throughout this text. In order to better understand the complex issues of developing an effective media mix, it is necessary to understand the strengths and weaknesses of each tool. In this chapter, we discuss online advertising and miscellaneous acquisition techniques. In the following chapters, we discuss email promotions, search engine marketing (SEM), and social media marketing. In so doing, we will keep in mind

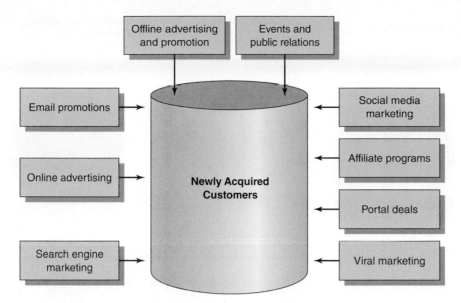

FIGURE **6.1** Customer Acquisition Techniques
Source: © Cengage Learning 2013

the fact that any and all of these techniques can and should be used in concert with the traditional tools of offline advertising and promotion, and examples will illustrate media mixes that include various online and offline channels and tools.

Online Advertising

There are a number of types of online advertising. The charts in Figure 6.2 cover total online ad spending and three of the leading types. Overall, it is clear that online advertising is growing rapidly. The growth is true both in terms of absolute dollars of U.S. spending (see Figure 6.2a) and as a percentage of ad spending globally (see Figure 6.2b). In fact, online advertising spending is growing more rapidly on a global basis than it is in the United States.[1] However it is measured, online spending is still a relatively small percentage of the total (see Figure 6.2b). Online spending continues to grow at a rapid clip, with more of the online budget going to social media (see Figure 6.2c). Social network revenues continue to grow also fueled by advertising and gaming revenues (see Figure 6.2d).

There is more than one type of online advertising. Three of the important types are:

1. **Display advertising**, which includes copy, graphics, and corporate branding elements like logos. Online displays can be static like its print advertising counterpart, or it can be dynamic, rotating several frames or making use of rich media formats.
2. Search advertising, which includes the various paid formats like pay-per-click (PPC) and expenditures for search engine optimization (SEO), which is discussed in detail in Chapter 8. Display and PPC advertising are both relatively mature formats and their growth is steady (see Figure 6.2c).
3. Social media advertising, which comprises standard display formats and platform-specific formats like Facebook ads, are discussed later in this chapter. Its growth is strong (see Figure 6.2d), even though it is hampered by disbelief on the part of many marketing executives and lack of good metrics for measuring its effectiveness.

The charts do not cover mobile advertising, discussed in detail in Chapter 16, which is currently the most rapidly growing channel for interactive advertising.[2]

The fact that online advertising expenditures are growing rapidly is indirect evidence that marketers find online ads effective. The marketer needs to use

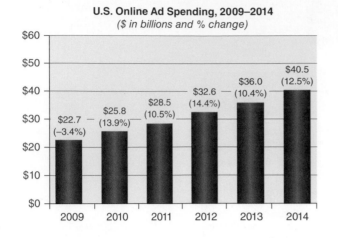

U.S. Online Ad Spending, 2009–2014
($ in billions and % change)

(a)

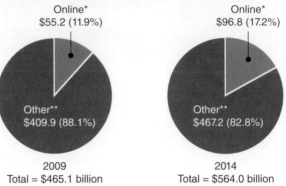

Online Advertising Spending Share of Total Media Advertising Worldwide, 2009 and 2014
($ in billions and % of total)

Online*
$55.2 (11.9%)

Online*
$96.8 (17.2%)

Other**
$409.9 (88.1%)

Other**
$467.2 (82.8%)

2009
Total = $465.1 billion

2014
Total = $564.0 billion

*Note: *includes banner ads, search, rich media, video, classifieds, sponsorships, lead generation and email; excludes mobile ad spending; **includes direct mail, magazines, newspapers, outdoor, radio, TV (broadcast and cable), yellow pages and other*

(b)

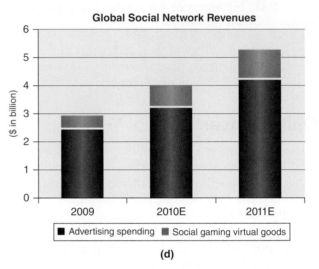

Email
19%

Social media
11%

Paid search
(PPC)
21%

Search engine
optimization (SEO)
10%

Website
27%

Online display
advertising
6%

Other online
marketing
6%

(c)

Global Social Network Revenues

■ Advertising spending ■ Social gaming virtual goods

(d)

FIGURE **6.2** Online Ad Spending and Budget Allocation

Sources: eMarketer, Inc., November 2010; eMarketer, Inc., June 2010; "New Chart: Social Media's Share of the Online Marketing Budget," Marketing Sherpa, 2010 (http://www.marketingsherpa.com/1news/chartofweek-02-09-10-lp.htm); and "Technology, Media, & Telecommunications Predictions 2011," p. 27, by Deloitte Development LLC. Reprinted with permission.

a variety of metrics like the branding metrics shown in Figure 6.3 to begin to demonstrate effectiveness. Of course, branding is not the ultimate goal—a purchase is. The purchase transaction occurs on the website, and the job of the marketer is to track the purchase back to the referral (source) that initially brought the purchaser to the site. That is a metrics challenge, and it is discussed in Chapter 14.

Dynamic Logic collects performance data so its marketing clients can compare the effectiveness of their own ads to others on a number of criteria like size of the ad and the industry of the product. The message from Figure 6.3 is that, in general, online ads are effective. However, creatively excellent ads are much more effective than ads that are not well designed and executed. Those poor performers can even damage the brand, which is not much different than in offline advertising. As discussed in Chapter 5, different types of advertising and media channels are differentially effective in different stages of brand development.

The chart in Figure 6.3 is taken from a study of creative best practices in online advertising. In addition to emphasizing the importance of a trusted brand, its other recommendations fall under the general heading of keeping the ad simple and easy to understand in the few seconds the viewer is likely to be

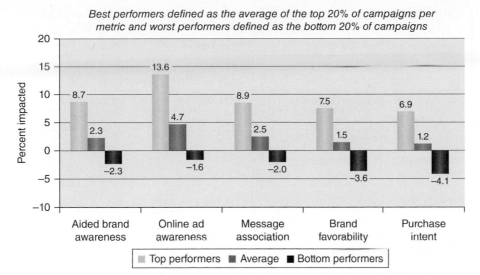

Best performers defined as the average of the top 20% of campaigns per metric and worst performers defined as the bottom 20% of campaigns

FIGURE **6.3** Online Advertising Effectiveness in Various Stages of the Branding Process

Source: "Ten Tips for Driving Online Ad Effectiveness and Maximizing Brand Impact," p. 2, by Amy Fayer, published by AAAA Research Matters. Reprinted with permission.

exposed to the ad. For instance, it is important to put the brand/logo up front, not leaving it for the final frame.[3] You might catch an implication here—most display ads today are not static. They have multiple frames or perhaps an interactive activity or a video. Online ads should use appropriate tools to engage the viewer. Otherwise, they can be lost in the clutter of content and promotion.

Online Display Advertising

It is not clear that there is a formal definition of display advertising, but it is generally understood to be an ad that can include text and images in any channel, and movement and interactivity in channels that offer that functionality. Display advertising is the creative standard to which all other types of advertising are often compared, but search advertising has historically garnered a larger share of the online ad budget. Display is gaining, as shown in Figure 6.4, and is projected to equal or slightly surpass the amount spent on search by 2015.

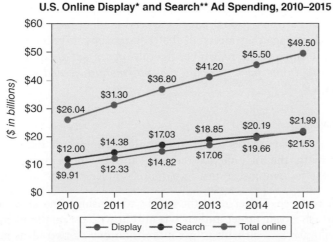

U.S. Online Display* and Search** Ad Spending, 2010–2015

Notes: *includes banner ads, rich media, sponsorships and video;
**includes contextual text links, paid inclusion, paid listings
(paid search) and SEO

FIGURE **6.4** Display Ad Spending Gaining on Search

Source: eMarketer, Inc., June 2011.

NOTE: ALL dimensions are in pixels.

Rectangles and Pop-Ups	Skyscrapers
300 × 250 IMU - (Medium Rectangle) 250 × 250 IMU - (square Pop-Up)	160 × 600 IMU - (Wide Skyscraper) 120 × 600 IMU - (Skyscraper)
240 × 400 IMU - (Vertical Rectangle)	300 × 600 IMU - (Hatf Page Ad)
336 × 280 IMU - (Large Rectangle)	
180 × 150 IMU - (Rectangle)	
300 × 100 IMU - (3:1 Rectangle) 720 × 300 IMU - (Pop-Under)	
Banners and Buttons	
468 × 60 IMU - (Full Banner) 234 × 60 IMU - (Half Banner)	
88 × 31 IMU - (Micro Bar)	
120 × 90 IMU - (Button 1)	
120 × 60 IMU - (Button 2)	
120 × 240 IMU - (Vertical Banner) 125 × 125 IMU - (Square Button)	
728 × 90 IMU - (Leaderboard)	

FIGURE **6.5** Standard Online Display Ad Formats

Source: "Ad Unit Guidelines," IAB, http://www.iab.net/iab_products_and_industry_services/1421/1443/1452.

Online Advertising Formats

There are many online display ad formats, and the IAB (Interactive Advertising Bureau) maintains standards for the industry. Figure 6.5 lists the standard online formats that are offered by most online publishers. If you go to the page on IAB, you can view an example of each, although the terms are reasonably self-explanatory.[4] This section of the site also has information about how to configure a display ad for online.

When creating an online display ad, the marketer must decide the destination for click-throughs. There are two important options. If there is need to collect information, provide information, or just to provide a logical path from the ad content to a transactional page, a special landing page will be required. If there is a product page that meets all the requirements, it becomes a satisfactory landing page. In either event, remember the rule, *never just dump the click-through onto the website home page; provide the information needed without requiring additional search.*

Rich Media Ads

There are other best practices for creating online display ads that apply to these standard formats, the rich media formats, and the new rising stars formats discussed in the following sections. Experts recommend the following:[5]

- Do your research. Understand the online advertising context, your competition, and who your target audience is and how they use the web.
- Keep it simple. It is difficult to get more than one or two ideas across in an ad, even an offline print or broadcast ad. Online ads are small in size and accommodate only a few lines of text, so it must be clear and to the point.
- Tell a compelling story. You only have a few words to work with, so make every one count.

- Have an effective call to action. That is an integral part of a direct-response ad but it is also important in a branding ad where people need to be told what action to take next.
- Make sure the landing page and the website make it easy to take the action.
- Keep the file size small so the ad will load smoothly and quickly.
- Have a strong, attention-getting headline.
- Choose colors that are appropriate for the sites on which your ad will appear.
- Choose sites that are appropriate for your target audience. Then be prepared to re-target them as they move around the web. Methods of targeting are discussed later in the chapter.
- Conduct tests of your ads on a continuous basis. One example of the improvements that can come from testing is the Adobe Lightroom ad versions discussed in Chapter 4.

In fact one expert says, "You're not buying advertising, you're buying an audience."[6]

Most online campaigns today have at least some **rich media** elements. They are not only informative, but also engage the viewer. IAB defines rich media ads as:

> advertisements with which users can interact (as opposed to solely animation and excluding click-through functionality) in a web page format. These advertisements can be used either singularly or in combination with various technologies, including but not limited to sound, video, or Flash, and with programming languages such as Java, Javascript, and DHTML.

There are also a number of **rich media** formats. Figure 6.6 lists the basic rich media formats which have been available for a number of years. There are two key things to remember about these rich media formats:

1. Not all sites make all these rich media formats available.
2. They have a lot of moving parts, and the marketer needs to be familiar with what each format can and cannot do and carefully follow the guidelines and best practices given on the IAB page.[7]

NOTE: ALLs dimension are in pixels.

In-Banner Video (file-loaded and streaming)	Expandable/Retractable
300 × 250	
180 × 150	
160 × 600	
728 × 90	
300 × 600	
Pop Up	
300 × 250	
550 × 480	
Floating	**Between-the-Page (Interstitial)**
Initial size not specified but file size important	

FIGURE **6.6** Rich Media Online Advertising Formats
Source: © Cengage Learning 2013

New "Rising Stars" Ad Units

In Chapter 5, we quoted the Bain study on creating digital brands, which found that marketers were still spending about 75 percent of their ad budgets in traditional media. The study also found that online advertising was being used primarily for direct-response advertising because marketers had become disillusioned with the ability of online to convey impactful branding messages.[8] The more recent chart from eMarketer (see Figure 6.7) shows that direct response still attracts more dollars but that display is growing more rapidly.

The reason for the upswing in display advertising appears to be new formats that allow for greater creativity and interactivity. Concerned about the implications of the Bain study for the future of online display advertising, the IAB worked with major advertising platforms to develop new formats that could offer more creative options and provide more viewer impact. In June 2011, IAB introduced six new "Rising Stars" formats that had been developed by major advertising platform owners and advertising networks. They are:

- Billboard, developed by Google/YouTube
- Filmstrip, developed by Microsoft
- Portrait, developed by AOL
- Pushdown, developed by Pictela
- Sidekick, developed by Unicast
- Slider, developed by Genex, built by MediaMind and Unicast[9]

IAB emphasized the depth of its commitment to what it called "brand-friendly" ad formats by sponsoring a Rising Stars competition for successful use of the new formats. The success of the ads was judged by how well the

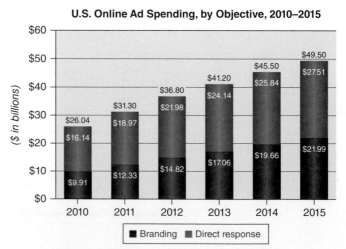

U.S. Online Ad Spending, by Objective, 2010–2015

Note: numbers may not add up to total due to rounding

FIGURE **6.7** Online Ad Spending: Branding vs. Direct Response
Source: eMarketer, Inc., June 2011.

branding message was conveyed, successful user experience, use of interactive techniques, how well the ad integrated into the page content, and how easily the concept could be adopted by other publishers.[10] You will immediately note that these are branding and marketer-use criteria that are more like the creative criteria used to judge ads in traditional media than the behavioral measures more commonly used by Internet marketers, discussed in detail in Chapter 14.

Figure 6.8 shows examples of two of the new formats, the billboard, which is being used to spotlight videos, and the slider, which features a video, images, and other types of content. On the IAB page, you can find a concept ad for each format, videos that explain their uses, and a style guide for developing these content-rich new ads.[11]

It is clear, however, that even the best ads are useless unless they reach their intended targets. Just as online advertising offers marketers a wider range of creative options, it also offers them an array of effective targeting options.

Online Ad Serving and Targeting

Just as most ads are not static today, most are served onto the web page separately from the content files. **Ad serving** is an important activity of third-party marketing services firms that match an advertiser's need for targeted ad placement with a publisher's need for revenue-generating ads on its site. *PC Magazine*'s encyclopedia page has a succinct definition of ad serving:

> The hardware, software and personnel required to deliver advertisements to Web sites and ad-supported software. It also includes the monitoring of click-throughs and required reporting to the ad purchasers and Web site publishers.[12]

This explanation is correct and helpful as far as it goes. But how are the destination websites chosen and by whom? These further queries require us to define ad networks and ad targeting. *PC*'s definition of ad networks is:

> Internet advertising organizations [that] act as a middleman between the advertiser and the Internet venues that display the ads. They sell the online campaign to the advertisers and then deliver the ads to the sites that display them. The site owners receive a royalty based typically on the number of times users click the ads.[13]

In addition to charging on the basis of clicks (CTR) publishers can charge on the basis of exposure to the ad (CPM, cost per thousand viewers) just as offline print and broadcast media do.

It is true that ads can be embedded in a web page in the same sense that they are placed on a magazine or newspaper page, but that is not common except for house ads—ads for the site's own products. It is more common to serve ads separately from content. In order to meet the needs of both advertisers and publishers, complex software and systems are required. Most marketers are happy to leave this function to third-party service providers. If you want more detail about ad serving and ad networks, Wikipedia has good articles that have a minimum of technical detail.

(a)

(b)

FIGURE **6.8** Billboard and Slider Concept Ads from IAB

Source: Interactive Advertising Bureau (IAB), http://www.iab.net/
iab_products_and_industry_services/508676/508767/Ad_Unit/risingstars#1.

When you stop to think about the fact that it is important to serve the best ad from *both* the website and the advertiser's point of view, the complexity begins to become obvious. When you consider that the decision must be made and the ad retrieved from inventory and sent to the appropriate site while the site content is loading—often in a matter of milliseconds if the user has a broadband connection—another layer is added to the complexity. Even though complex, this example represents the basic situation. If the advertiser wishes to use more complex targeting techniques, the question of which ad to serve to which viewer on which site becomes even more daunting, explaining why most sites of any size use ad serving technology of some kind.

Targeting Online Ads

It does no good to have the most creative ads with the most engaging rich media unless the advertiser can reach the right target audience. The ability to target with precision, based on data of many kinds from many sources, is the overarching advantage of advertising on the Internet.

The 2010 Display Advertising Study from ad network Collective[14] suggests that the two basic ways of targeting ads are by site or by audience. For instance, if the content and readership of MarthaStewart.com[15] is a good match with the advertiser's target audience, the advertiser can make a media placement directly with the site.[16] This simple statement, however, ignores the print magazine and the digital app discussed in Chapter 4. Each of the three audiences—website, magazine, and iPad app—will have slightly different audiences with a lot of overlap. Placing an ad, or a series of them, in all of three of the media channels can reach a specific target audience with frequency and impact. Publishers offer advertising packages that make published rate sheets—when you can find them—relatively meaningless in actual practice. While sites like MarthaStewart.com offer a specialized lifestyle audience, portal sites like Yahoo! and MSN offer greater reach, but a much less targeted audience. In addition, there are tens of thousands of sites—large and small—that offer ad space. It makes the media buying decision overwhelming and creates the need for advertising networks.

The Collective study asked what kind of targeting advertisers are actually using. The results are shown in Figure 6.9. Demographic data still leads the list, but not by much. Demographics are a weak proxy for how people actually live their lives and have been losing ground to behavioral targeting. In a general sense, **behavioral targeting** and segmentation means segmenting customers on the basis of actual behavior, in this case, their activities on the web.

Also growing rapidly according to this study is advertising targeted by channel—entertainment, politics, health, for example—and geographically targeted advertising. The latter may seen counterintuitive in the light of the worldwide reach of the Internet, but local retailers and other businesses have been moving onto the web in large numbers,[17] often through advertising opportunities offered

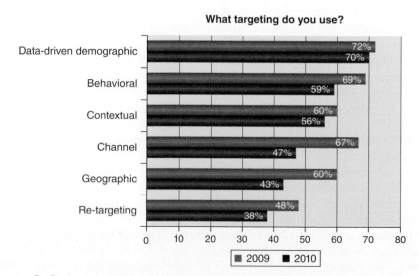

FIGURE **6.9** Targeting Methods of Online Advertisers

Source: "2010 Display Advertising Study," p. 9, Collective, an advertising technology company. Reprinted with permission.

by services like Google Places[18] and Yahoo! Local.[19] These services and others allow local businesses to advertise to a local audience in a cost-effective manner.

Growing less rapidly is **contextual advertising**. Contextual ads are targeted according to the content of the page the person is currently visiting. Visit one of the auto sites like Edmunds or a travel site like TripAdvisor, and you will find ads that are clearly based on the content. Or, if you use Gmail, take a moment and look at the PPC ads beside your emails. Some are good fits, some are so mistaken they are funny, but all have a contextual reason for being there. Of all these standard types of online targeting, behavioral is the one that draws the most attention but perhaps is also the least understood.

Behavioral Targeting

In the offline world, marketers have to ask customers to self-report what they do, which can have elements of unreliability. In the online world, marketers and third-party data collection services can collect data about what people actually do—what sites they visit, what pages on the site, what purchases, and much, much more. There are variations in the ways advertising networks actually carry out the process, but the three basic types of behavioral targeting are:

1. Targeting identified users (people who have registered on a website, for example)
2. Targeting unidentified users by using tracking tags (cookies)
3. Targeting with predictive models (also called pixel-less targeting)

Targeting Identified Users Targeting identified users is straightforward for the marketer and observable to the customer. When a customer visits Amazon, for example, she is encouraged to log in to the site. When she does, a number of Amazon services become available—the wish list, 1-Click ordering, and recommendations among them. The wish list and 1-Click ordering have been set up by the customer herself. It is obvious to even the casual observer that the recommendations are based on previous purchases. Amazon actually encourages the customer to provide additional data to improve the recommendations. Amazon is more open about what it does and how it does it than most sites,[20] but this type of targeting on the site is visible and does not arouse a lot of concern among most Internet users.

Targeting Unidentified Users Targeting anonymous users is an issue that does raise privacy concerns and we return to that aspect in Chapter 15. In this section, we discuss how it works. Figure 6.10 presents an understandable view.

This type of targeting is done by advertising networks and made available to advertisers who use the network. The hypothetical situation set up in Figure 6.10 shows an unidentified (not signed in) user visiting a website that has information about hotels in San Francisco. The user's activity suggests intended behavior, and a **cookie** is set on the visitor's browser. A cookie is a piece of code that can track visitor activity but does not necessarily last beyond a single web session or link to identifiable personal information. We discuss cookies in more detail as part of the metrics process in Chapter 14. In Figure 6.10, the cookie is simply used to track the visitor to other websites and to display an ad for a hotel supersite (a client of the advertising network) on both a site about dogs and on a social page like a blog.

The ad networks collect huge amounts of this type of behavioral data and mine the data to find patterns of behavior that constitute market segments. The hypothetical user in Figure 6.10 could be a "frequent traveler" or perhaps an "adventure traveler," which are fairly generic segments, although the targeting they represent is still valuable to the marketer. The network can drill down in the data to find microsegments, "architectural history traveler" or "garden traveler," for example. The ad networks actually configure the segment to be targeted for each individual advertiser, so you do not find much detail on their sites about the segments they offer. Collecting and using data like this also implies placing cookies that persist over a period of time, not cookies that are set for a

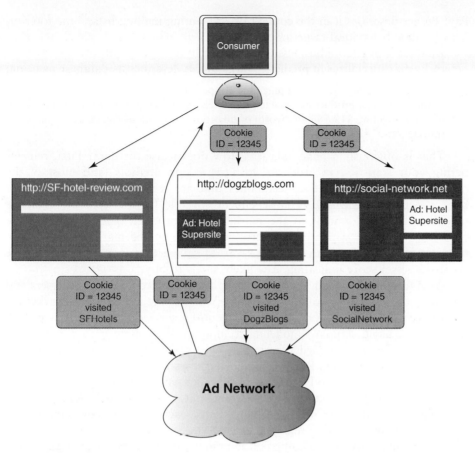

FIGURE **6.10** How Behavioral Targeting of Anonymous Users Works

Source: © Cengage Learning 2013

single user session. Tracking a user over time also allows **re-targeting** of a visitor who has left a site (one that sells shoes, for example) without making a purchase.[21] All the shoe sites would like to reach that person.

Behavioral targeting has gone far beyond simple visitor behavior—data points like websites visited, types of products examined, coupons downloaded, and so forth. A recent article in iMediaConnection listed newly available targeting databases that vastly expand behavioral targeting options.[22] They are:

- Values targeting, which the agency describes as being able to reach people on the basis of enduring human values.[23]
- Cut-and-paste content sharing, which is based on items that readers cut and paste from publisher sites. This content produces search key word suggestions, as well as behavioral profile data.[24]
- Retailer co-operative database, which identifies people who are shopping on the web for certain products. This database can be used for re-targeting.[25]
- Search re-targeting, which is the ability to purchase display advertising based on search activity.[26]
- Owner targeting, which focuses advertising based on ownership. Direct marketers have long used, for example, product registrations to confirm ownership of an article in a database. Behavioral tracking allows activity like looking at online owner's manuals or search for replacement parts for a product to be included in the database as evidence of product ownership.[27]

Targeting with Predictive Models In recent years, another type of behavioral targeting has appeared. It makes use of the kind of predictive modeling described in Chapter 4. Predictive modeling has long been a staple of direct marketing,[28] and

Paul Berger describes it in the context of segmenting mailing lists,[29] the forerunner of online behavioral targeting.

Akamai, whose core business is efficient delivery of content, owns one of the networks that specializes in predictive targeting. It describes its database as being:

> our industry's only online shopping data cooperative. It's made up of over 550 multi-channel retailers, product manufacturers, travel, and telecom websites who contribute data representing $13.5 billion worth of quarterly, anonymous consumer shopping transactions.[30]

That is obviously a huge data set. How does it use the data? First, remembering your statistics, in order to do a regression analysis (and most of the modeling is done on analytic techniques that are regression-based), you must have a dependent variable. The dependent variable for this type of predictive model is a person who is in the market for a product. The purpose of the model is to predict which of the persons who are in the market at any given time are most likely to buy. Another way of saying that is each person in the database gets a score indicating how likely she is to buy.

As Akamai explains, it has 140 million cookies placed on user browsers and each day it scores each cookie to determine whether the user is in the market for one of the industry sectors (e.g., travel, telecom) it services. It then builds predictive models, using standard modeling techniques, that allow it to compare the results of targeting standard descriptive segments[31] as opposed to the results using predictive targeting. Predictive modeling uses more and more directly relevant data, so it is likely to be more effective. Akamai correctly says that the concept is simple, but in practice, it can become quite complicated.[32] When you are working with a data set of 140 million items, each described by hundreds of variables, complicated is an understatement!

Each online advertising campaign is unique and requires its own approach. Consider the *Los Angeles Times* newspaper, which wanted to acquire new subscribers for its Sunday edition in the five county geographical area that it serves. Its key demographics included people over the age of 25 with incomes of at least $50,000. Simple demographic targeting, right? Not entirely. The offer did not require a credit card, the usual online purchasing method. Instead, it offered the subscription on a "bill me later" basis, which is not the norm for online ads. The newpaper's agency was able to add a predictive model to the basic demographic targeting that increased the likelihood of reaching customers who preferred to pay at a later date and thereby increased the overall efficiency of the campaign.[33]

When you look at behavioral targeting from a marketer's point of view, the desirability of precision targeting based on actual visitor behavior data seems obvious. When you look at it from the visitor's point of view, it quickly becomes clear that a lot of Internet firms know a great deal about Internet users. Is that good or bad? We consider that issue in Chapter 15.

Targeting on Vertical Advertising Networks

A different approach to targeting ads to is to use one of the many **vertical advertising networks**. Glam Media is a digital property of Conde Nast magazines. The website was established to service a variety of its women's fashion publications like *Vogue*, *Glamour*, *Allure*, and *Style*. Several years ago, it established its own vertical advertising network, the Glam Media Network, to take advantage of its "fashion passionista" audience (see Figure 6.11). It moved aggressively to sign up other publishers who wanted to reach the same audience of fashion-conscious women and now has over 3,000 sites in the network and has developed its own proprietary ad serving platform.[34]

Other examples of specialized vertical networks include the following:

- CBS Sports Ad Network is made up of over 200 college athletics sites, providing access to sports enthusiasts, especially followers of college teams.
- Fox Sports Ad Network reaches followers of professional sports teams.

FIGURE **6.11** Vertical Online Advertising Network

Source: Glam Media, http://www.glammedia.com/publishers/glam_publisher_network.

- Fantasy Sports Ad Network reaches players of fantasy sports.
- Haven Home Network is one of many vertical networks that target home owners and do-it-yourself-enthusiasts.
- Noir Woman Ad Network reaches African-American women, especially affluent urban residents.
- Parent Media Group reaches parents, especially those with young children.

And so it goes—endlessly, it seems. The number of advertising networks is a strong testament to advertisers' desires to target their audiences with precision.

It is hard to find sales data for ad networks because most of them are owned by large corporations, often publishers or broadcasters. In 2008, vertical networks were still fairly new; however, it was estimated that they reached over 57 percent of the U.S. Internet population.[35] Specialized vertical networks are beginning to emerge within the B2B space as well.[36]

Social Network Advertising Options

The success of vertical networks is one testament to the effectiveness of careful ad targeting. As social media has grown, it has offered marketers another opportunity to reach targeted markets—the social networks. In this space, blogs of many kinds and the specific platforms Facebook and LinkedIn are particularly important.

Targeted Advertising on Blogs

The blog search engine, Technorati, lists over 1.2 million blogs and divides them into nine categories from entertainment to science.[37] The living category is the largest with two of its subcategories, health and family, each listing over 10,000 blogs. Within that group are the blogs that have been dubbed "mommy blogs." Mommy blogs have become such big business that they now have "dozens" of ad networks[38] competing to help the bloggers monetize their blogs, their own "top 50" list,[39] and at least one mommy blogger conference.[40]

Moms represent a huge market for consumer products of many kinds, and marketers are eager to reach them. Moms also have a voracious appetite for information and for socialization, both of which the mommy blogs fulfill. Both of these factors make them an excellent context for advertising relevant products.

BargainBriana is part of an even more specialized group: the blogs that distribute coupons and other marketer incentives. Adding to its large market size

FIGURE **6.12** A Coupons Blog

Source: Bargain Briana, http://bargainbriana.com.

and the desire for information is the fact that women (mostly) come to these blogs with a specific intent—to purchase products. The women are the right target market and they are in the right mood—what more can an advertiser ask? The BargainBriana page is long and a static capture cannot get it all, but notice that Google is one of the advertisers on this site (see Figure 6.12). All together, there were seven display and PPC ads on this particular page. The value of ad networks that are able to place ads on the popular mommy blogs can hardly be overstated.

Facebook Advertising

Advertising on Facebook has grown at an astounding rate. eMarketer[41] reported that the social network is expected to have global ad revenues of $4.05 billion in 2011 and those revenues are expected to increase by 678 percent between 2011 and 2012. (These estimates do not even count the money marketers spend on social media marketing on Facebook, a subject discussed in Chapter 9). This revenue refers only to the ads that appear on the right sidebar of your Facebook page.

Facebook ads have elements of other PPC advertising, but they also have unique aspects. The PPC similarity lies in how they are constructed. It is a self-service process with three steps, which are the same irrespective of which Facebook ad type you choose.[42]

First the ad is created. It a title of 25 characters or less, body copy with a maximum of 135 characters, an image, and a destination URL. Second, you select the target audience by location (country, state, or city), demographics, and likes and interests that are drawn from user profiles. There are a few other options for advanced users, but these are the three main targeting mechanisms. *Each time a setting is entered or adjusted, the number of people who will be reached*

INTERACTIVE EXERCISE 6.3 **Facebook Advertising**

Every Facebook member (register at http://www. facebook.com) has the advertising link at the bottom of her page. Click on that link and try your hand at creating a Facebook ad. Try one for your school or student organization or choose a product. Pay special attention to the targeting options. You can work with the ad, and as long as you do not give a credit card number in the final step, you will not be charged.

by the ad is shown. This immediate change provides an opportunity to adjust the reach number of viewers reached up or down and provides immediate feedback on the targeting choices being made. In the third step, the budget and scheduling are established. When all three steps have been completed, a maximum cost per click is given. The advertiser can adjust the cost per click up, which may improve the frequency with which the ad is run, or down, which may result in less than optimum frequency or reach. This is the standard bidding system for PPC ads, which is discussed in more detail in Chapter 8. You can explore the ad creation process for yourself. An advertising text link is present at the bottom of every Facebook page.

Creating an ad on Facebook is just this simple. Creating an ad that is genuinely effective is, however, not simple. Just writing a 25-character headline and a 135-character copy block that are compelling enough to attract notice and persuade viewers to click is extremely difficult. To include the social element, which a Nielsen study conducted for Facebook has shown to be very important, is even more difficult.

The social element is not under the direct control of the marketer. All Facebook ads have the Like icon. Nielsen calls that a Homepage ad (although not Facebook's terminology). If one or more friends of the viewer has "liked" the brand's page, the version with Social Context (also not Facebook's term) is shown—meaning, the names of those friends show up in the ad. The hypothesis is that the names attract attention and credibility, which causes those ads to work better. In addition, when a friend "likes" a brand, that information can show up as an item on the user's News Feed,[43] again, attracting attention. While Facebook uses a proprietary algorithm to select items for the user's News Feed, Nielsen calls this the "organic" version. Clearly, marketers would like to know what is necessary to achieve those desirable organic ads.[44]

The lesson for the marketer is twofold. First, Facebook ads have a vast reach at relatively low cost, often $1 per click or less. Second, the more fans the brand has for its Facebook page, the more likely the ads are to be effective. Marketers are finding that a powerful combination.

Advertising on LinkedIn

LinkedIn offers opportunities to advertisers who want to reach its professional audience, which numbered over 90 million in early 2011.[45] These ads offer limited formats—squares, rectangles, and text links. They offer only demographic targeting, but their demographics—items like industry, job title, and membership in LinkedIn groups—cannot easily be matched by other sites. The screen capture in Figure 6.13 shows an ad for LinkedIn's signal service;[46] essentially a way to filter a large amount of traffic on a page. This ride-over format is not offered to outside advertisers: the rich media rectangle on the right and the text link at the top of the page are paid ads.

The creative and bidding processes for LinkedIn ads are similar to Facebook's, which in turn are similar to Google's (see Chapter 8). There is presently much controversy about how well LinkedIn ads work.[47] It is easy to hypothesize that part of the reason is the relevance of the ad to the targeted LinkedIn population. Another hypothesis may be the intent of LinkedIn users. They come to LinkedIn to engage in professional dialog or to search for jobs or hires. Purchasing most products may

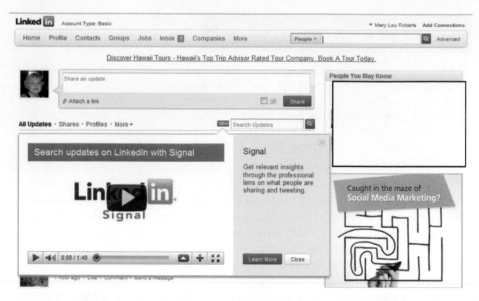

FIGURE **6.13** LinkedIn Ads: House and Display
Source: LinkedIn.

not be uppermost in their minds, and the PPC ads offered on LinkedIn are direct-response ads, not branding ads.

In addition to advertising, there are a number of other types of marketing activities that have important roles in customer acquisition and often in developing customer relationships. These strategies are explored in the following sections.

Miscellaneous Acquisition Techniques

Referring back to Figure 6.1, we now discuss other miscellaneous acquisition techniques, such as event-driven marketing, affiliate programs, portal deals, and viral marketing.

Event-Driven Marketing

Event-driven marketing is a marketing activity that can be used both to acquire new customers and to solidify relationships with existing customers. Events have been a staple in offline marketing for product launches, to reach segments that are hard to attract through mass media, and to generate awareness and "buzz" in general. The ability of the web to reach desirable market segments in a way that attracts attention has made it a natural for the staging of events. In this space, there are three related marketing terms that can cause confusion. All can be executed offline or online or using a combination of offline and online tools.

• Event-driven marketing is current terminology that encompasses the traditional marketer activities of trade shows, exhibits, conferences, and seminars. All these activities have been effective in both B2B and B2C markets. Event-driven marketing is taking on new importance as more marketers develop experience marketing programs to deepen the brand experience.

• Experience marketing is the approach about one-third of event marketers pursue, according to the EventView 2010 study. It defines experience marketing as:

> an evolved form of event marketing which goes beyond the traditional interruptive model, to create physical and digital brand experiences that serve to powerfully demonstrate the value of a brand and its product or service and its relevance to the needs, wants and expectations of the audience. Experience marketing communicates this value authentically and in a highly targeted manner with an eye towards generating specific, measurable audience behaviors.[48]

This definition echoes the International Experiential Marketing Association manifesto, which emphasizes both person-to-person interaction between marketer and customer and the importance of authenticity in all interactions.[49] The terms "experience" and "experiential" are being used synonymously.

- The term "event-triggered" is often used to describe marketing communications strategies that are based on an event in the life of the customer. Some events in the lives of each of us mark major transitions—graduation from college, the birth of a baby, purchase of a home are just a few. Events like these not only represent major changes in the way a consumer lives, and therefore the products he purchases, but are also matters of public record and therefore accessible to the marketer.

The AARP (American Association of Retired Persons) has been pursuing an event-triggered strategy brilliantly for many years. Its database is legendary. It is virtually impossible for anyone in the United States to celebrate (or to try to ignore) his fiftieth birthday without receiving a mail from AARP with congratulations on reaching the milestone and an offer to join AARP. Since AARP has a wide array of benefits to offer to the still-working population as well as to the retired, it has many reasons to continue to contact people in the target demographic with attractive offers for both products and services. Since this type of contact is automated, it tends be very cost-effective.

The more common type of event-driven marketing is made up of events that are initiated and managed by the marketer. In the B2B space, this includes activities like product introductions or demonstrations, which can often be held on the web much more effectively and economically than the equivalent physical event.

In the B2C space, marketer-initiated events take on many forms. One form is to support a nonprofit. The Twestival—begun in 2009 by social media marketers to support Charity:water, whose business model was described in Chapter 1—has become a global undertaking. It has both a global event that supports a single charity in that year and the opportunity to register and conduct local Twestivals for local charities. Its website says that, "Since 2009, over 200 cities have participated in Twestival, raising close to $1.2 million for important causes like clean water and education."[50] The basic model is to use Twitter to issue invitations, to host a physical event that is supported by Twitter activity to involve people who cannot participate in the physical event, and to continue the fund-raising buzz via Twitter and the charity's website for a time after the actual event. This campaign represents an innovative use of Twitter, to be further discussed in Chapter 9, and an excellent integration of online and offline event-driven marketing.

As another example, Kraft's DiGiorno pizza brand has successfully combined online and offline marketing to promote its image of a premium frozen pizza. In April 2009, it reached out to influential Tweeters, asking them to host tweetups. These are in-person events prearranged on Twitter—Twestivals in the consumer market, if you will. The offer was to deliver free DeGiorno pizzas to the events.[51]

In late 2010, Procter & Gamble announced an open-ended event program as part of its "Have You Tried This Yet?" campaign.[52] Early events included a pop-up experience in New York City, featuring a wide variety of products (see Figure 6.14).[53] The pop-up experience is an increasingly popular type of marketing in which a brand takes over a vacant retail location and transforms it into a brand experience for a brief time. It is possible to create pop-up stores on Facebook, further confusing terminology. Facebook pop-up stores are generally used for a short-term ecommerce activity; they are not pure event marketing.

Event-driven marketing is part of a general trend away from mass media and toward new media and more experiential kinds of promotions. As the preceding examples show, events are limited only by the imagination of the marketer, and the interplay between a physical and virtual world is a key component of success.

P&G Event "Have You Tried This Yet?" on October 21, 2010 in New York City.

FIGURE **6.14** A Pop-Up (Short Time) Store Event

Source: The Proctor & Gamble Company, https://picasaweb.google.com/112159055995233423538/
HaveYouTried ThisYet?feat=flashalbum#5535610336831962882.

Events also have a close tie-in with publicity, either online or offline, as promotion for the event or buzz surrounding it. The field of public relations has been significantly changed by the Internet.

Generating Publicity

Although public relations is a communications discipline separate from marketing, the two must work closely together. Staging events, arranging product placement in films and TV, and issuing press releases are all tools that the public relations professional uses to generate unpaid media attention for products, services, and causes. Of those, the issuance of press releases appears to have been most changed by the Internet.

Writing press releases and distributing them to the firm's own media list or through a news wire service is the stock and trade of public relations. It has always been important to write press releases well, keeping in mind the interests of the target media, and to distribute them in a timely fashion to journalists who are likely to pick them up and use them to write an article or even write a feature article around the subject of the press release. The issue has always been that journalists are deluged with press releases. This problem has only increased with the Internet, and drawing their attention to a particular one is difficult.

Making press releases visible to journalists on the Internet—optimizing press releases—assumes more importance in this environment. In addition to writing the press release well, optimization requires the use of search marketing tools including:

- Selecting relevant key words.
- Using the key word or phrase in the title of the release and in the various tags that identify the content to search engines.

- Tagging images for identification by the search engines.
- Using three anchor links: one to the home page, one to the product page, and one to the most relevant blog post.[54]

The tools of search engine marketing (SEM) are discussed in detail in Chapter 8.

The optimized press release is posted with its own URL on the business' website to facilitate search. The releases are tagged with keywords and the content itself is optimized for search, both topics covered in Chapter 8. In addition, most businesses use an Internet press service to distribute their releases to the largest possible set of relevant journalists, who will generally have all the information they need to write articles or posts without having to contact the marketer and wait for a reply.

In addition to being optimized for search, press releases can also contain rich media including images and videos, providing journalists with engaging content. Figure 6.15 displays a template for an interactive press release featuring traditional

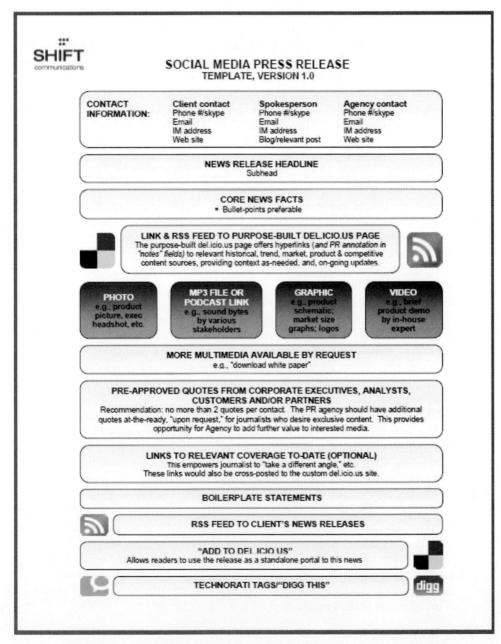

FIGURE **6.15** Social Media Press Release Template

Source: Shift Communications, http://www.shiftcomm.com/images/downloads/smprtemplate.pdf.

elements like text and contact information plus rich media elements including links to images and videos. Other links encourage writers to post their content to bookmarking sites like Delicious and news sites like Technorati. These postings add to the reach of the content and may also increase the search ranking since they represent incoming links (discussed in Chapter 8).

Event marketing and public relations are two closely related Internet promotional techniques. Now we turn to another acquisition technique, affiliate programs.

Affiliate Programs

We discussed **affiliate programs** as an Internet business model in Chapter 3. Since many of the prospects who enter a website as a result of an affiliate listing may be new customers, affiliate programs clearly qualify as a customer acquisition technique. Marketers like affiliate marketing because it is a relatively low-cost activity. It can largely be automated, and affiliates are paid on the basis of performance. Note that low cost, however, does not necessarily mean high revenue.

Affiliate programs follow the **80/20 rule**: about 80 percent of the affiliates are low volume, and 20 percent produce significant volume; meaning only a small number of the affiliates produce the most click-throughs and most profitable sales. Consequently, affiliate programs need to be actively managed. Networks have grown up to serve the affiliate marketing sector by finding appropriate affiliates for merchants and publishers and relevant sites for small businesses who wish to participate in affiliate marketing. There are also marketing services firms that will assume the management of an affiliate system. If you conduct a search on virtually any subject that includes the term "affiliate marketing," you will see many "make money fast and easy" sites and ads. That should be a *caveat emptor* signal to anyone trying to enter the business.

Well-run affiliate programs like Amazon's[55] can be a cost-effective element of the marketing and advertising strategy. On the other hand, portal deals have been criticized as unlikely to produce ROI (return on investment) on large marketing investments.

Portal Relationships

Portal placement deals generate both revenue for major portals and reach for advertisers. During the go-go days of the early Internet, marketers were paying the large portals like AOL and Yahoo! millions of dollars for the right to be their retailer of choice or even the exclusive retailer of a particular product category on the site. Think of it as negotiating for a prime location in a shopping mall; the principle is the same. When the go-go days ended, deals became more realistic, but they did not end altogether.

AOL now offers portal sponsorships different from the megadeals of the early days. The sponsorships are for a wide array of specialty pages like its seasonal pages.[56] When you combine the ability to reach a targeted market like Memorial Day travelers with the reach of AOL's own advertising network, the right marketer can find a desirable advertising opportunity. There also seems to be some portal sponsorship activity in vertical portals ranging from real estate to sports.

The common thread here appears to be targeted markets, not the huge reach of the early days. Advertisers can buy display advertising on main portal pages, but the complex and expensive portal deals of the early days seem to be history. As long as portal sponsorships provide a way to produce a satisfactory ROI, they are likely to be a part of the Internet marketing toolkit of certain marketers.

An Internet technique that clearly offers an opportunity for large return on small investments is viral marketing—if it works, that is.

Viral Marketing

Viral marketing is a promotion that, either by design or by accident, catches on with Internet users and is passed from one to the other, multiplying the effectiveness of the original distribution. The classic viral email from the early days of the web was the series of Wassup Super Friends parodies. Creators Philip Stark and Graham Robertson tried to build a business based on their success with the Super Friends clips, but it never really caught on. This example illustrates the difficulty of viral marketing. If it catches on, it can be explosive. If it does not, it sinks without a trace.

Videos are the medium most likely to go viral at present. A UK headline illustrates the difficulty of creating a viral ad. The headline in September 2010 was "Boring Product, Great Ad."[57] In the video, a hunter interacts with a grizzly bear and actually manages to make a brand connection with a stationary product called Tipp-Ex. This example is a classic instance in which description cannot do it justice, and one would need to play with the video to understand.[58]

If a piece is too obviously a sales message, it simply does not go viral. Marketers will continue to try viral marketing, and on rare occasions, one will succeed. However, the best advice seems to be not to count on any specific ad will going viral, as it is simply outside of the marketer's control.

SUMMARY

As the Internet has matured and its ability to perform as a branding channel has been recognized, online advertising has become an increasingly important Internet marketing tool as evidenced by its growing role in the marketing budget. This budget is still dominated by search marketing expenditures (direct response), but display advertising and, more recently, advertising on social networks continue to grow. The growth is primarily because of their effectiveness in branding, especially as new online advertising formats are developed to more effectively engage the viewer. Online marketing events can also contribute to brand development, as can viral campaigns. Each of these Internet marketing tools contributes to brand development and at the same time operates as an effective customer acquisition mechanism.

There are numerous formats that can be used for online display ads. Static ads are losing popularity to rich media ads, which attract attention and deliver compelling messages. Most online ads are placed on websites by an ad serving network. The system tries to balance the requirements of the site with those of the advertiser. The site wishes to sell as many spaces as it has available on its site at the best possible rates. The advertiser wishes to reach the defined target audience with the right frequency at the lowest possible cost. Ads can be served directly to large sites or within networks of sites that have been brought into an alliance for that purpose.

As both technology and databases improve, it becomes possible to target ads with more precision. Contextual targeting is based on the content being viewed by the visitor at a given time. Behavioral targeting can be based on a user activity profile, profile of either an anonymous web user or an identified user. It can also be based on more complex predictive models. Using any of these targeting approaches, the visitor is followed through the site, and ads can be served based on the visitor's segment membership without regard to the content being viewed at any given time. The visitor can be followed off the site with relevant ads being served on other websites. Both types of targeting require the compilation and use of consumer data, often without the consumer being aware that the data are being collected.

In recent years, a new advertising opportunity has arisen as a result of the large membership, frequent visits, and long periods of time spent on social networks. Blogs attract targeted audiences, some of which can be lucrative to the marketer. Facebook and LinkedIn, and by extension other social networks, have their own advertising programs. While their reach is huge, it is really the targeted advertising opportunities they offer that make them so attractive to the marketer.

In addition to online advertising, other customer acquisition techniques include the marketing stalwart event-driven marketing and techniques unique to the web including affiliate programs and portal sponsorships. Viral marketing is included in the list of acquisition techniques although its ability to perform is always in doubt.

DISCUSSION QUESTIONS

1. True or False: All businesses need to create a steady flow of new customers as part of their marketing strategy. Explain your answer.
2. Identify the main customer acquisition tools.
3. What is online display advertising, and how does it relate to offline display advertising?
4. What is an online ad format? Why must marketers be familiar with the formats and understand what creating an online ad requires?
5. What is a rich media ad? What benefits does it offer the marketer? Does it have any potential downsides?
6. Why were additional new ad formats developed? What benefits do they offer the marketer? Do any of the formats have any potential downsides?
7. How does a marketer go about placing an ad on Facebook or LinkedIn?
8. Why is ad serving an improvement over just placing an ad on a web page and just leaving it there?
9. Behavioral ad targeting is especially important on the Internet. Explain why and give a hypothetical example, perhaps based on your own experience.
10. Is demographic or behavioral or contextual advertising a better way to precisely target website visitors?
11. True or False: Marketing events are necessarily held in the physical world, but they can be promoted on the Internet. Explain your answer.
12. Discuss whether or not generating publicity is one of the few marketing communications activities that has not changed much as a result of the Internet.
13. Do affiliate programs tend to attract many websites or blogs that can generate a large volume of traffic that results in sales? Why or why not?
14. What is the importance of portal deals to Internet sites today?

INTERNET EXERCISES

1. Internet Career Builder Exercise
   a. These are some of the jobs that are available in online advertising, event marketing, and public relations. You can find others on sites recommended by your instructor or through search.

      Account manager

      Advertising operations manager

      Advertising or event sales representative

      Internet marketing analyst

      Media planner, analyst, or manager

      Creative director

      Events planner or manager

      PR account assistant, manager, or executive

      and many more

   b. Select an online advertising, an event, or a PR job from the list above or from your own search. Outline the responsibilities of that position. You may find it useful to locate job postings on the web in order to understand the job requirements.
   c. Outline knowledge and experience from classes, internships, full or part-time jobs, and volunteer work that prepare you for this specific position.
   d. Prepare five questions you could ask at a job interview. The questions should exhibit your understanding of the position requirements without lecturing the interviewer about what she already knows.
   e. Update your VisualCV® or LinkedIn profile with this information.
2. Visit a website you go to often, paying attention to the advertising this time. What kinds of ads do you see and why do you think they were placed on this particular site? Close out of the site and come back several times in quick succession. What do you see going on with the ads? How does it illustrate concepts discussed in the chapter?
3. If you have not already done so, make a contact with one of the three websites you are tracking. You could register, ask for information, or even purchase

a product if you wish. Think about the experience you have as you interact with the website. Then keep a log of contacts that are made because of your initiative. How does the site appear to be using the data from your contact(s)?

4. Visit the website of your local newspaper. Carefully examine the online media kit to understand what it offers that is the same as or different from the ad formats described in this chapter. Try your hand at developing an ad for one of the available formats.

NOTES

1. http://www.bloomberg.com/news/2010-12-06/web-emerging-markets-to-lead-global-advertising-growth-in-2011.html.
2. http://www.marketingcharts.com/television/media-ad-revenues-to-grow-3-15852.
3. http://www.aaaa.org/news/bulletins/Documents/onlinecreative.pdf.
4. http://www.iab.net/iab_products_and_industry_services/1421/1443/1452.
5. http://onlinebusiness.volusion.com/articles/banner-ads-creating-effective-banner-ad-campaigns; and http://blog.hubspot.com/blog/tabid/6307/bid/28805/3-Ways-to-Waste-Money-on-Online-Advertising.aspx.
6. http://blog.eloqua.com/8-online-ads-rules.
7. http://www.iab.net/guidelines/508676/508767/displayguidelines.
8. http://www.iab.net/media/file/BAIN_BRIEF_Digital_Advertising_4-19-10_FINAL.pdf.
9. http://www.iab.net/about_the_iab/recent_press_releases/press_release_archive/press_release/pr-060811.
10. http://www.iab.net/about_the_iab/recent_press_releases/press_release_archive/press_release/pr-022811_risingstars.
11. http://www.iab.net/iab_products_and_industry_services/508676/508767/Ad_Unit/risingstars#1.
12. http://www.pcmag.com/encyclopedia_term/0%2C2542%2Ct%3Dad+serving&i%3D37491%2C00.asp.
13. http://www.pcmag.com/encyclopedia_term/0,2542,t=Internet+advertising&i=45193,00.asp.
14. http://collective.com/insight/2010-display-advertising-study.
15. http://mslomediakit.com/index.php?/digital/marthastewart.com/audience.
16. http://mslomediakit.com/index.php?/digital/advertising_specs.
17. http://www.borrellassociates.com/home/45-general-reports/195-borrell-associates-2011-ad-forecast-memo.
18. places.google.com/business.
19. http://local.yahoo.com.
20. http://www.amazon.com/gp/help/customer/display.html/ref=pd_ys_help_iyr?ie=UTF8&nodeId=13316081.
21. http://www.nytimes.com/2010/08/30/technology/30adstalk.html.
22. http://www.imediaconnection.com/content/29257.asp.
23. http://www.resonatenetworks.com.
24. http://www.tynt.com.
25. http://www.buysight.com.
26. http://www.magnetic.is.
27. http://www.owneriq.com.
28. http://www.clickz.com/clickz/column/1716301/a-new-breed-behavioral-targeting.
29. http://marylouroberts.info/images/dir.mark.man.ch5.pdf.
30. http://www.akamai.com/html/solutions/ads_predictive_segments.html.
31. http://www.akamai.com/dl/brochures/ADS_descriptive_segments.pdf.
32. Ibid.
33. Ibid.
34. http://www.adexchanger.com/ad-networks/glam-media-glamadapt.
35. http://www.clickz.com/clickz/column/1696993/vertical-ad-network-update.
36. http://www.minonline.com/news/Business-Journals-Launches-B2B-Ad-Network_14962.html.
37. http://technorati.com/blogs/directory.
38. http://www.momcentral.com/blogs/mom-central-blogger-university/monetizing-your-blog-with-ad-networks.
39. http://www.babble.com/mom/work-family/top-50-mom-bloggers.
40. http://www.blogher.com/blogher-topics/blogherconferences/blogherconference2011.
41. eMarketer Newsletter, January 18, 2011.
42. http://www.facebook.com/adsmarketing/index.php?sk=adtypes_group#!/adsmarketing/index.php?sk=adtypes.
43. http://blog.facebook.com/blog.php?post=2207967130.
44. http://www.thedailybeast.com/blogs-and-stories/2010-10-18/the-facebook-news-feed-how-it-works-the-10-biggest-secrets.
45. http://www.linkedin.com.
46. http://blog.linkedin.com/2010/09/29/linkedin-signal.
47. http://online.wsj.com/article/SB10001424052748704698004576104032486083992.html.
48. https://www1.vtrenz.net/imarkownerfiles/ownerassets/2206/EventView_2010_NEW.pdf, p. 13.
49. http://ixma.org/manifesto.htm.
50. http://www.twestival.com/faq.
51. http://adage.com/digital/article?article_id=135876.
52. http://www.pg.com/en_US/news_views/blog_posts/2010/nov/have_you_tried_this_yet.shtml.
53. http://www.nycgirlatheart.com/2010/10/have-you-tried-this-yet-p-event-in-nyc.html.
54. http://www.toprankblog.com/2010/03/press-release-seo-tips-ses.
55. https://affiliate-program.amazon.com.
56. http://advertising.aol.com/spotlight/seasonal-packages.
57. http://www.clickz.com/clickz/news/1731120/boring-product-great-ad-tipp-ex-channels-subservient-chicken.
58. http://www.youtube.com/profile?user=tippexperience&annotation_id=annotation_820885&feature=iv.

CHAPTER 7

Email Marketing to Build Consumer and Business Relationships

Key Terms

LEARNING OBJECTIVES

By the time you complete this chapter, you will be able to:

- Discuss reasons for the growing importance of email marketing.
- Describe the various levels of permission.
- List the steps involved in developing an email marketing campaign.
- Identify the basic steps in developing an email marketing program.
- Learn the basics of email design.
- Recognize key provisions of CAN-SPAM laws in the United States and Europe.

Email Marketing

Email as promotional activity has exploded in recent years, and most forecasters believe that its growth is likely to continue for the foreseeable future. A recent survey by StrongMail showed that **email marketing** was the top area of business budget growth for marketers, with 65 percent of marketers surveyed planning to increase their spending on email marketing.[1] Why this continued growth from what has been termed the "granddaddy" of Internet mediums? After all, email started many years ago and today's focus tends to be on new media like social and mobile marketing. In the 1970s, the first email program was developed through ARPANET and was instrumental in developing the protocols to help send email messages from computer to computer. With the popularization and commercialization of the Internet, email caught on quickly as a way not only to communicate but also to communicate directly with prospective customers.

Although email was one of the first technologies to really take off on the Internet, and in spite of its early presence and the emergence of other media, the tool is not going away. According to ExactTarget, 58 percent of online consumers begin their day with email,[2] while 20 percent of consumers check a search engine or portal first thing, and only 11 percent check Facebook. So it is obvious that email plays a critical role in consumers' lives. Email offers marketers a fast, flexible, and highly controllable format. Email is essentially direct mail on steroids because not only is the customer contacted directly, but also different offers and methods of engagement can be tested to find the most effective means of communication. A deep understanding of the nature of offline mail promotions is also useful to the email marketer because of the relationship between the two media. In both direct mail and email, the marketer needs a solid offer and time deadline, and an attention-getting device (think envelope versus subject line). And in both cases, measurement is critical to gauge success.

Even better, email direct marketing offers several advantages to traditional direct mail marketing (see Figure 7.1) and was initially positioned as a cost-effective alternative to direct mail. Emails can be developed quickly, tested, revised on the fly based on almost immediate feedback, and can reach many Internet users in a short period of time. Compared to other types of Internet promotions, email is cheap on a per customer contact basis. Although email response rates differ widely by application and industry, email still has a favorable response rate compared to direct mail, with a strong return on investment (ROI). The Direct Marketing Association (DMA) projects that in 2013, email

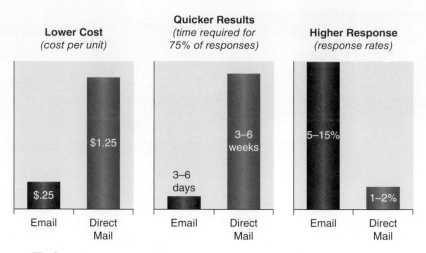

FIGURE **7.1** Email Is Cheaper, Faster, and More Effective Than Direct Mail

Source: yesmail.com, LucWathieu, Harvard Business School, March 22, 2000, 500092-PDF-ENG.

marketing will generate about $40 for every dollar spent, outperforming both traditional direct marketing and other forms of Internet marketing by several fold.[3] Forrester estimates that emails are so cost-effective that they have the ability to drive ROI two or three times higher than other forms of direct marketing, resulting in a continued increase in email spending.[4]

Additionally, email can be used by any marketer—B2C, B2B, or nonprofit—who has an acceptable way to acquire an email list of potential customers. Email, like direct mail, is also highly measurable and database-driven. Email marketing systems also offer a good way to tap into data from other internal and external systems to create meaningful and relevant communications for customers.

In fact, email has proven to be a more powerful retention tool than an acquisition tool (see Chapter 6). According to the StrongMail 2011 Marketing Trends Survey mentioned in the opening paragraph, increasing subscriber engagement tops the list of important email marketing initiatives. Figure 7.2 illustrates how email marketing has evolved to a sophisticated tool for customer engagement from a broadcast tool highly reminiscent of spam. The DMA reports that about 73 percent of businesses are focused on customer retention with their email program versus 27 percent that are focused on customer acquisition.[5]

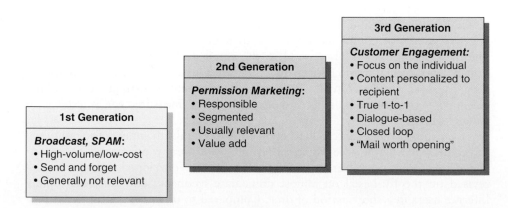

FIGURE **7.2** Evolution of Email Marketing

Source: © Cengage Learning 2013

The cornerstone of a good email marketing campaign is the concept of permission, which will be discussed in detail in the next section. Targeted emails to those customers who want to hear from you are going to get a higher response rate than a list of customers that are not familiar with your product or service. Although it is possible to conduct an email marketing campaign to those you do not know, Seth Godin's book, *Permission Marketing*, outlined the concept of permission that holds true today. Customers want to interact with companies, but on their own terms and in their own time frame. Just as you would not (hopefully) propose marriage on a first date or accept such a proposal, consumers want to see that they are doing business with the right type of company for them before revealing personal information and giving companies permission to use that information.

Scott's Turf Builder

Email is also ideally suited to event marketing campaigns, as discussed in Chapter 6.

The Scotts® company, known for its lawn and garden expertise and for the Miracle-Gro product, started a lawn care update email program in the spring of 2000 and now has over a million and a half subscribers. The company uses over 355 unique geo-demographic variations of its newsletter for a variety of purposes, customizing it for the customer. The content of these updates is based on the consumer's grass type, zip code (which indicates climate zone), and possible weed and insect problems that might abound at a particular time of year. Imagine getting an email telling you it is now time to treat your lawn for grubs! If you were in an area where grubs are a concern, you would be grateful. Email marketers have integrated their campaigns with direct mail for years. As social media has become more widely used, another opportunity for engagement has developed (see Figure 7.3). In this case, Scotts® also invites its Facebook friends to opt-in for emails, incorporating social media and developing an integrated campaign strategy. The "events" noted in this case could be, for example, times of the year for planting seeds, fertilizing, and providing other lawn care services. These event-type emails nurture the customer relationship each step of the way.

This type of approach is just one example of how email works with event marketing campaigns. However, email marketing can just as easily be applied to other major events in a customers' life, such as high school graduation, buying a first car, entering college, and so on.

FIGURE **7.3** Integrating Email and Social Media

Source: © Cengage Learning 2013

Email as a Communication Medium

Along these same lines as Scotts®, Johnston & Murphy, a high end shoe company, has highly segmented its customer base and provides offers that are relevant to the consumer based on age, gender, interests, and past purchases, resulting in an increase in open and response rates, as well as sales. Therefore, in spite of being one of the first communications mediums to "take hold" in the marketplace, email remains a vital way for businesses to communicate with their customers. In fact, during their 2010 email Summit, Marketing Sherpa reported that 75 percent of social media users said email is the best way for companies to communicate with them. The same report also stated that 49 percent of Twitter users and 36 percent of Facebook users have made an online purchase as a result of an email[6] and 78 percent of consumers shared information through email versus 22 percent on social media.[7]

Customers, for their part, are very active in the email space. Email is so prevalent that 72 percent of people check their email at least once a day.[8] Consumers receive about 44 messages per day, 12 of which are commercial messages they signed up to receive.[9] In 2010, the typical corporate user sent and received about 110 messages daily. In May of 2011, 88 percent of American Internet users reported using email daily and 37 percent reported using it "constantly."[10] Nearly three-quarters of emails received by consumers were perceived as *spam*.[11] **Spam** is unsolicited email. Consumers typically report higher open rates for permission-based emails and definitely see the value in signing up for relevant commercial messages. While the latter is good news for marketers, the existence of spam provides an ongoing problem.

A May 2009 study by the Pew Foundation found that just about half (51 percent) of all Internet users complained that spam was a big problem, down from 57 percent in 2003. In addition, fewer users than ever before are reporting spam as a problem at all. The percentage of users who say spam is not at all a problem has risen from 16 percent to 28 percent since 2003.[12]

The study also reported that:

- 37 percent of users with a personal email account say they are getting more spam than a year ago, up from 28 percent two years previous and 24 percent three years prior.
- 29 percent of users with a work email account say they are getting more spam than a year ago, up from 21 percent two years previous and 18 percent three years prior.
- 55 percent of email users say spam has made them less trusting of email, compared to 53 percent two years previous and 62 percent three years prior.
- 63 percent of email users say spam has made being online unpleasant or annoying, compared to 67 percent two years previous and 77 percent a year prior.

Those statistics could pose a problem for marketers. However, as the Pew report notes, many users are having fewer problems with email and are becoming more sophisticated in dealing with spam; 71 percent use filters offered by their email service or employers to block spam.

In spite of the negative perception that much of email is spam, consumers do value messages from commercial sources. Many marketers have come to rely on email marketing as a cost-effective tool, not necessarily for customer acquisition, but for customer development and retention. ExactTarget reports that 49 percent of research respondents have purchased as a result of an email.[13] Some purchased online immediately, others online later, and still others purchased offline at a later date. Almost 60 percent of those who redeemed online coupons did so offline.[14] These data are consistent with other research and monitoring statistics, which all testify to the power of email marketing to influence consumer behavior.

All in all, email usage is predicted to continue to grow. According to Radicari Group, Inc., the number of email accounts will increase from greater than 2.9 billion to over 3.8 billion by 2014.[15] Not only is email usage growing, but email marketing results are strong. In fact, Epsilon and the DMA's Email Experience Council Q1 2011 North American Email trends report announced a 4.2 percent increase in open rates year over year to 23.3 percent with a slight decrease in click-through rate to 5.9 percent from 6.0 percent year over year.[16]

Dreamfields Pasta

Dreamfields Pasta is a good example of a company using email marketing and permission to create demand for its products by building good customer relationships. Dreamfields is a specialty company that offers a healthy pasta that is suitable for everyone but targeted to diabetics and those with other health concerns. People with diabetes can enjoy Dreamfields Pasta and still control their blood sugar. The company uses SEO (search engine optimization), pay-per-click, online advertising, print advertising, and word of mouth to attract customers to its website, www.trydreamfields.com. Consumers register for Dreamfields email newsletter and receive a $1 coupon as a thank you. Dreamfields uses these emails to create an opt-in database, with over 500,000 consumer email subscribers. The company's offers include coupons to subscribers, as well as recipes and other cooking tips via email. Integrating social media, consumers are invited to visit the company's fan page on Facebook and participate in the Dreamfields conversation. Another email campaign targets health care professionals.

The results have been astounding. In 2009, the company sold 8.3 million pounds of pasta, a 13 percent increase over the prior year. In 2010, Dreamfields sold 9.1 million pounds of pasta, a 9.6 percent increase. The company has also significantly reduced its advertising budget by more than 50 percent since converting to digital marketing. Figure 7.4 illustrates the email sign-up page, which shows the benefits of the product, as well as the incentive provided for registering. Figure 7.5 illustrates a portion of an email sent as part of a Dreamfields campaign powered by ExactTarget. These emails are attractive and offer something a consumer might want to receive, in exchange for giving part of their consumer information.

FIGURE **7.4** Dreamfields Initial Permission Email Sign-Up Offer
Source: Dreamfields Pasta.

FIGURE **7.5** Dreamfields' Pasta Permission Emails

Source: Dreamfields Pasta, http://www.dreamfieldsfoods.com/emails/2011-June-Newsletter.html.

Levels of Permission Marketing

Dreamfields Pasta illustrates an important principle of email marketing—the issue of **permission**. In this text, we encourage the use of permission-based marketing, particularly in email messaging.

The first issue relating to permissions is that of spam. Unsolicited email is referred to as "spam," but it is not because the food product SPAM is unliked. Instead, the origins are from a Monty Python skit on SPAM in which it is offered on the menu of a restaurant many times (see Figure 7.6). The waitress' continued use of the word

FIGURE **7.6** Monty Python SPAM Skit

Source: Python (Monty) Pictures.

"spam" to describe the menu items made the word become annoying. (You can watch the video online at http://pythonline.com/youtube_archive/spam.)

No responsible marketer uses or sanctions the use of spam. Ever. Period. And as stated earlier, permission-based marketing is the only responsible way to conduct email marketing campaigns.

Direct marketers have been sending unsolicited mailings for many years. Many, if not most, consumers do not like it. However, unsolicited physical mail does not appear to arouse the same level of ire in consumers that spam email does. It seems that consumers regard spam email as more intrusive than mail. Either way, it is clear that reputable marketers do not want to be identified with spam in the minds of the consuming public.

In order not to be considered a spammer, the marketer must obtain permission from the customer or prospect before sending email. There are four levels of permission:

1. **Opt-out** means that the visitor *did not* refuse to receive further communications from the marketer. This is an improvement over spam, but it does not represent a high level of commitment on the part of the visitor. Usually there is just a check box that needs to be unchecked to opt-out.

    Opt-out email addresses are often collected via online registration forms or other methods, even face-to-face. The point is to make consumers take some explicit action in order *not* to receive further communications. The theory behind opt-out seems to be that people may not bother to take the action, or be unaware that they could take it, and will therefore, almost by default, become members of the list. This is often operationalized by an already-checked box saying in effect, "Please send me email." Even if the choice is made to precheck the box, the accompanying statement must be clear about what the visitor is agreeing to. The statement should be unambiguous and it should be located in a visible place. Under the CAN-SPAM law (described in detail at the end of this chapter), all emails must have a clear option to unsubscribe.

    Opt-out represents, at best, passive agreement to receiving email, but at present, it represents the minimum acceptable standard. Opt-in is the preferred method by many marketers and observers of the field.

2. **Opt-in** means that visitors have actively chosen to receive further communications, usually by checking a box on a registration form. It represents active acquiescence, if not enthusiasm, about receiving future communications from the marketer. Consequently, members of opt-in lists should be more receptive to messages.

3. **Double opt-in** is a technique by which visitors agree to receive further communications, probably by checking an opt-in box on a site, and are then sent an email asking them to confirm their consent by replying to the email. The visitor has taken two actions, first indicating willingness to accept email, then actively confirming it by replying to the confirmation. This response should indicate an interested, potentially well-qualified prospect.

4. **Confirmed opt-in** is somewhere in between opt-in and double opt-in. Visitors actively acquiesce to receiving email, again probably by checking a box. They are then sent a follow-up email confirming the permission, but no reply is required.

An easy way to remember the difference between opt-in and opt-out is that in opt-in, the box is checked and in opt-out, you must uncheck the box or perform some action.

The opt-in/opt-out controversy is in part the traditional direct-marketing issue of fewer, better-quality leads versus more leads of lower quality. Marketers are often wise to choose quality over quantity in lead situations. As with direct mail, the list is critical in maximizing response rate. The differences in the email context have to do with both the economics and the relationships with potential customers. The cost of incremental email is virtually zero, arguing for larger lists, even if they are less qualified. The annoyance factor is so high, however, that

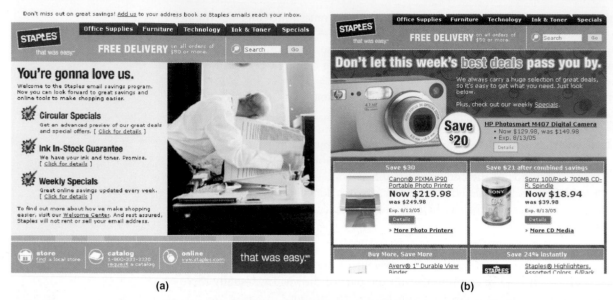

(a)   **(b)**

FIGURE **7.7** (a) Welcome Email from Staples (b) Weekly Featured Products Email

Source: Copyright © Staples the Office Superstore, LLC.

there is a strong argument for high quality opt-in lists of prospects who are genuinely willing to receive marketer-generated communications.

The one gray area is when the marketer has an email list that was obtained without use of specific opt-in or opt-out authorization by the consumer. These lists should be converted to either opt-in or opt-out by means of one carefully constructed email to confirm participation, perhaps including the use of incentives. There are relatively few email lists like this which were collected in the early days of the Internet before the permission-based protocol became something of an accepted standard. The existence of a small number of lists in this category should not be taken as an excuse for spam by other marketers. Today when email lists are rented from a list broker, the marketer does not get the emails. Rather, the list broker who owns the permission-based list sends out the emails and the marketer only gets the addresses and other personal information if there is a response, such as an order or inquiry. Once the person or business on the list moves from a customer to a prospect and the relationship is developed, then the marketer gets information about that person or company. As in direct marketing, the "house" list is most effective, which incents the marketer to provide the best offer possible to be able to gather a new inquiry or order and, hopefully, an ongoing customer.

Both the emails in Figure 7.7 are the result of a new registration on a site. Staples replied to a new registration with a welcoming sales message that linked to promotional areas on the site. Notice that at the top of Figure 7.7a, it contains a message relating to *deliverability*, asking registrants to add the address to their address books so it will not be screened out by ISP spam filters.

Developing an Email Marketing Campaign

The Peppers and Rogers Group, whose expertise is in relationship marketing, summarizes the email marketing process as it moves from analysis to action (see Figure 7.8). Their process involves four steps:

- *Gather customer data.* This includes contact information, physical address or email address, or both. The transactional data from the company's own files also include purchase history and a record of all customer interactions. It also includes the types of information (offers) they wish to receive, their

Customer Insight Drives Email Marketing Action

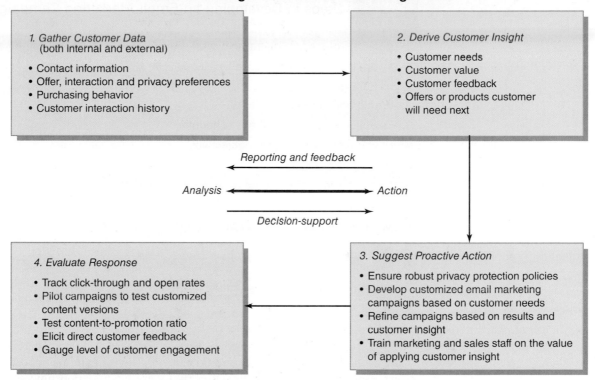

High-impact email marketing relies on leveraging customer insights throughout the email marketing campaign lifecycle. By applying customer-focused approaches to email marketing, companies can better generate the positive customer experiences driven by long-term, loyal relationships.

FIGURE **7.8** The Basics of Email Marketing

Source: © Cengage Learning 2013

preferences for receiving it (frequency and communications channel), and their privacy preferences.

- *Derive customer insight.* Using the different types of information that have been captured about the customer, begin to understand what the customer needs and values. The most valuable type of understanding is what should come next in the purchase cycle—an extended warranty program for a recently purchased appliance, for example.

- *Suggest proactive action.* This is the point at which the process moves from analysis to action. Email programs are developed, executed, and refined based on the results of the programs themselves, captured in the customer database.

- *Evaluate response.* In this step, program metrics are collected and analyzed to refine existing programs and suggest new strategies. Different approaches and content should be tested to see which perform better. It is also good to encourage direct feedback from recipients in order to further understand likes, dislikes, and desires.

Peppers and Rogers present an overview of the process that applies whether email is being used for acquisition of prospects or relationship marketing to customers. Let us now turn briefly to a detailed set of steps for developing an email campaign, which also applies to either acquisition or retention settings (see Table 7.1).

- *Build or obtain an email list.* Like Rome, email lists are not built in a day, and list development needs to be an ongoing process, one begun well in advance of an actual email campaign. Marketers who wish to be welcome in the inboxes of their customers obtain permission at one of the four levels just discussed. In direct marketing terms, this becomes their own "email house list" and it is an essential foundation for permission-based email marketing.

TABLE 7.1 Steps in Developing an Email Marketing Campaign

1. Build or obtain an email list
   a. Build a permission-based list
   b. Rent email lists
2. Profile and segment the list
3. Establish a communications schedule
4. Develop specific program objectives
5. Write compelling copy
6. Structure your email to be received and opened
7. Create links to further information
8. Make it easy for viewers to take action
9. Test and revise the email
10. Measure results
11. Integrate learning into next email program

Source: © Cengage Learning 2013

If it is necessary to rent email lists—and there are a considerable number available—the marketer should carefully investigate the source of the list, especially any privacy promises that were made to consumers as the list was constructed. Many privacy policies make it clear that lists will "from time to time" be shared with other marketers deemed acceptable to the list owner. When this is the case, both marketers are clearly within their legal rights. However, that does not mean that the consumer will be thrilled about receiving email from a company with whom she may have no relationship.

Lists for acquisition programs should be rented with care, from reputable list management agencies. Although lists are available for less, good lists will run from $100 to $400 per thousand, with established, performing lists closer to the higher end. Extremely cheap lists have been complied by software (bots) that search the Internet and snatch email addresses in public places like chat rooms. They are the source of spam and should be avoided at all costs.

- *Profile or segment the list.* The customer/prospect database should have data, the volume of which grows over time, that allows a descriptive profile (middle-aged, high-income golfer living in an upscale suburb in the Midwest) or segmentation analysis that produces typical demographic (high-income two-worker family with school-aged children) or lifestyle segments (patron of the arts). We return to the subject of segmenting the database as an element of relationship marketing strategy in Chapter 11. It is essential in order to know what communications to address to which segments of the list in order to get the best response.

- *Establish a communications schedule.* The ease of sending email makes it tempting to send email whenever the firm feels like it. With the exception of important "breaking news" types of notifications, which should be rare, the organization should establish a mailing schedule and stick to it. Better yet, it should ask the subscriber for her preferences when she signs up. Then the marketer will send content that is relevant to the subscriber on the schedule she has dictated. That is the way to make email welcome in the inbox.

- *Identify the target segment and communications objectives.* Each mailing should have its own specified target segment and specific objectives. Simply sending the same message to an entire list will not often be effective. Perhaps the business marketer is announcing a new product to users of that product line. The marketer of consumer credit cards may be delivering an offer of credit card protection insurance to new cardholders. The nonprofit marketer may wish to invite large donors and prospects to a special event showcasing the successes of the organization. The objective and the target segment must be a good fit and the single campaign must fit into the overall communications and marketing strategies. Specify the action you want the recipient to take. You may, for instance, give the prospective large donor the option of calling a special phone number or visiting a special landing page to respond to the invitation.

- *Write compelling copy.* Email copy should be only as long as is necessary to convince the recipient to take the desired action. Often this action will be to click-through on a link to go to a particular page on the website, known as a landing page or micro site specific to that campaign. The target pages should be carefully examined to make sure they are consistent with the objectives and message of the email campaign. Writing short copy that persuades is not an easy task.

- *Structure your email to be received and opened.* In their effort to control spam, ISPs have set up filters in an attempt to remove the offenders. In the process they capture many messages from legitimate marketers. The "from" header and the "subject" header are both important in this respect. The source must be clear and the subject descriptive.

- *Create links to further information.* One of the beauties of email, whether text or HTML, is that links to more detailed information, usually on the website, are easy. Copy has to be written around the concept of linking. The website and/or landing page must be examined to ensure that it is ready to receive visitors from the email.

- *Make it easy for readers to take action.* Marketers need to specify what it is they want recipients to do after the recipients click-through to the site. Do they want the recipients to send for additional information? If so, create an email link, or better, a form that requests a small amount of information about the requester. Is the objective to persuade recipients to donate to a charitable cause? If so, the links to material on the site need to make the case for the contribution, with multiple opportunities to click-through to the form that accepts the donor's information.

- *Test and revise the email.* Emails can and should be tested using the techniques discussed in Chapter 4. Important things to test include the preheader, subject line, and the offer. A test can be mailed to only a selected segment of the target list or an A/B split can be used. Testing is a powerful tool, and it should not be overlooked.

- *Measure results.* Email service providers supply the most common metrics—delivered, opened, and clicked-through, are typical. Marketers can get more detailed results by creating special landing pages to receive click-throughs and then tracking them through the site. Results will also include maintenance issues like bounce-backs and unsubscribes. Detailed reporting is usually available with most email service providers.

- *Integrate learning into the next email program.* Most organizations today will find themselves doing another email campaign rather quickly. An ongoing challenge is how to use the results of one campaign to make the next one better. Some companies have developed formal programs for doing so, a subject to which we will return in Chapter 11.

This list appears to be a rather formidable series of steps. However, the seasoned email marketer, with the support of a well-maintained database and suppliers of the necessary services, can develop and launch an email campaign in days, if not hours. The speed, the relatively low cost, and the ability to target and measure will only fuel marketers' interest in effective email marketing.

Email Design

There are many types of emails, such as email newsletters, new product announcements, general marketing and advertising, alerts and reminders, and market research emails—all of which need to be designed according to the objective for each. Since email marketing has its roots in direct marketing, an email for promotions and discounting—which is the majority of emails that companies send out—should follow the basic rules of direct marketing. In other words, the email should have a clearly defined offer or call to action, with a time deadline, and should also use good web design principles as discussed in Chapter 10.

In addition, there are basic elements of design that are unique to emails themselves. These design elements are summarized in Table 7.2. A good promotional email includes a preheader (a short text blurb; the part of the email that displays after the subject line and is above the text or html of the email) and can include many items. Successful preheaders restate and reinforce the offer provided, link to the online version of the email if the receiver cannot view the email, and perhaps include a short reminder of the relationship or an option to view on a mobile device.[17]

Although the preheader is important, the email subject line is often the determining factor in **open rates**. There is much debate over the email subject line and what is most compelling since what works most effectively depends on the product, the offer, and the customer. What might work for a retail environment might not work in B2B marketing. In general, the subject line should be short, less than 50 characters, which is usually the number of characters displayed on an email system and generates a higher open rate. The email subject line should also include as much as possible the reason for the email, including a brief summary of the offer.

The email itself should clearly state the offer—and only including one offer is best. Sometimes you might see emails that try to cram in a lot of information and refer to several different offers with different time frames. Studies have shown that people get fatigued by multiple messages in the same email and tend to click-through less as more, competing messages are provided. The offer should include the time deadline, that is, when the offer expires and by when the action is expected. The email should also use good web design principles, including the most important information (e.g., the offer) appearing in the "golden triangle,"

TABLE 7.2	Promotional Email Checklist
Email Element	**Recommended Approach**
Preheader	Link to online version of email, reminder of relationship, restates offer
Subject line	Short, include brand, call to action, urgency
Offer or call to action	Specific, clear, and meaningful
Time deadline, sense of urgency	Not only what the customer should do, but by when?
Web design principles	Above the fold, golden triangle
CAN-SPAM	Include reply-to and unsubscribe, and otherwise be compliant
Viral marketing	Include forward to a friend as well as social media links
Social media	Integrate with popular sites on social media

Source: © Cengage Learning 2013

15" monitor
640 × 480 pixels

17" monitor
800 × 600 pixels

19" monitor
1024 × 768 pixels

FIGURE **7.9** Above the Fold Viewing Dimensions
Source: © Cengage Learning 2013

the upper left triangle area where the user's eye spends most of its time. Another good web design principle to apply to email design is "above the fold." Above the fold is a simple concept adapted from newspaper publishing which suggests that the reader's eye is going to concentrate above the fold of a newspaper, which, in this case, is the area above where his web browser cuts off the email. Where the fold falls depends on the physical size of the monitor used, the resolution that the screen has been set to, and the type of browser used. As Figure 7.9 illustrates, the information available can vary greatly based on these criteria. It is a good idea to test emails on multiple web browsers before sending to ensure readability and clarity. Mobile marketing campaigns also mean that emails must be designed to be read and responded to on smaller screens on various devices.

Good promotional emails are also CAN-SPAM compliant and clearly state that the message is advertising or promotional in nature; they have a valid reply-to address and street address listed; and a valid opt-out or unsubscribe feature. (We will discuss more about CAN-SPAM at the end of this chapter.)

Finally, a good promotional email takes advantage of word-of-mouth marketing and social media, including a forward to a friend feature and the ability to post on the consumers social media accounts (which accounts depends on the consumer and where they "hang out" in social media.

Although we have focused on promotional emails, the design of other types of emails can be equally important. *Transactional emails* can be an overlooked source of marketing. *Welcome emails* typically have a higher open rate than traditional emails and can be used to up-sell and cross-sell as well as to leverage social media marketing. All these emails can benefit from the viral and social aspects of email marketing.

Figure 7.10 illustrates an email received by one of the authors that is a good example of all the elements discussed in this section. It makes good use of the preheader, provides the offer in the golden triangle space, and has pertinent information above the fold. This email also has social media integration and is CAN-SPAM compliant, although it is missing a clear time deadline in the text of the email.

Figure 7.11 clearly shows an email offer of 20 percent off if purchases are made in a certain time frame, is simple in design, and does not provide too many competing messages. Not all promotional emails illustrate the principles mentioned here. It could be that companies not using these principles are testing different approaches or it could be that they are in need of hiring people who have taken an Internet Marketing course to help them with their email design. In any case, marketers will continue to test different approaches to determine what generates the best response.

Sending Emails

There are a number of different choices in sending emails, but with any type of volume, it is usually wise to use an email service provider (see list of some major providers in Table 7.4). An email service provider does a number of things for its

Preheader reinforces offer,
gives alternative way to view

Offer in "Golden Triangle"
but no time deadline

Most information is
"Above the fold"

Social media integration

CAN-SPAM compliance

FIGURE **7.10** Email Analysis

Source: Hanes.

FIGURE **7.11** Email Offer with Time Deadline

Source: JCP Media L.P.

customers, including help with the design. First though, most standard email packages have limits on the number of recipients for an email in an effort to avoid spam filters, so most email service providers have the ability to help figure out what will trigger a spam filter and get emails delivered. For example, the tried and true direct marketing offering of "free," which historically has delivered the highest response to direct mail campaigns, will trigger a spam filter at some

ISPs. Other benefits of using a service company for email include help in tracking and measurement, easy integration with a company's internal database and other software programs such as salesforce.com, and other marketing campaigns.

One of the key benefits is usually the ability to integrate with a current database of customers and their transaction history. Integration with the database means that emails can be personalized to individuals and offers can be customized based on the data and interests of that particular customer. Dynamic content management is what allows Scotts® to send out over 300 versions of its emails or Johnston & Murphy to customize its product offerings in its promotional emails. The content and greeting change per each email, making it more personal and less like spam. When used wisely, dynamic content can increase the chances emails will be opened and responded to by the target consumer. Table 7.3 provides a summary of what an email service provider can do for a company. Some of the top email service providers, with the ranking of the strength of their offering on these and other dimensions, are included in Table 7.4.

TABLE 7.3 Advantages of Email Service Providers

Help get emails delivered through ISPs

Aid in tracking, measurement

Provide database integration

Manage content dynamically

Integrate with social marketing, other campaigns

Source: Adapted from the Forrester Wave™: Email Marketing Service Providers, Q4, 2009, Carlton A. Doty and Julie M. Katz for Interactive Marketing Professionals.

TABLE 7.4 Forrester List of Email Marketing Service Providers, 2009

Service Providers	Strength of Offering (5 is highest)
Acxiom	4.45
Alterian	2.15
BlueHornet	2.31
ClickSquared	3.12
Datran Media	3.6
E-Dialog	4.68
Emailvison	2.11
Epsilon	4.54
ExactTarget	4.53
Experian Marketing Services	4.59
Lyris	2.14
Responsys	4.45
Silverpop	3.43
Yesmail	4.72
Zeta Interactive	3.99

Source: Adapted from the Forrester Wave™: Email Marketing Service Providers, Q4, 2009, Carlton A. Doty and Julie M. Katz for Interactive Marketing Professionals.

Another major concern is timing—what time of day to send emails and on what date. The answer really depends on the customer base. The best way to determine when people will answer emails is to test a few different days and times, using some common sense about the habits of the customers. In general, for business customers Monday morning and Friday afternoon are bad times to send email, with Tuesday mornings or afternoons being preferred as people have gone through their inboxes the previous day. For consumer messages, weekends and evenings are preferred, but again, this timing depends on the targeted consumer and the product or service offered. The answer really is that "relativity" matters in the timing of email sends.[18]

For example, a 2011 study by MailerMailer[19] of 977 million emails sent by 1,600 different clients found that "Consumers are most likely to open and click on an email on Sunday," with messages generating a 12 percent open rate and 4 percent **click-through rate** on the first day of the week. The lowest open and click-through rates occur on Thursdays, at 11 percent and 2 percent, respectively. In addition conventional wisdom in the area indicates that email programs that delivered less than one message a month experienced a higher **bounce rate** than programs with at least a daily delivery. So more frequent email can mean better delivery prospects because lists are more likely to be updated.

Tracking Emails

One of the biggest benefits of using an email service provider is the ability to track metrics such as click-through and open rates, and compare metrics across different offers (known as A/B testing from the direct marketing world). Email service providers make it much easier to tell which emails were effective. Here is an example of some of the email tracking available on ExactTarget's Dashboard in Figure 7.12. As you can see, 650 emails were sent out and most of them (636) were delivered—97.85 percent, with 8 hard bounces and 6 soft bounces. A **hard bounce** means the email address is bad or truly undeliverable, whereas a **soft bounce** means the email could not be delivered at that particular time, perhaps because of a system problem. There are many ways to calculate email metrics and we describe the most common method here.

Of the 174 opened, there were 88 unique (individual) opens for a 13.84 percent open rate (calculation: 88/636). There were 13 click-throughs on 88 unique opens for a click-through rate of 14.78 percent (calculation: 13/88). Many other statistics are available on the dashboards of email service providers, and it is also possible to see who opened or did not open the email and where they clicked-through to find more information.

Figure 7.13 illustrates activity over time and we can see that this email was opened primarily within three days of delivery. In fact, most activity occurred within 48 hours of delivery. This figure illustrates again that fast email response rates are critical in developing effective programs. If something does not work, a marketer can try another offer, list, or design to get the desired response from the customer and provide the information the customer needs.

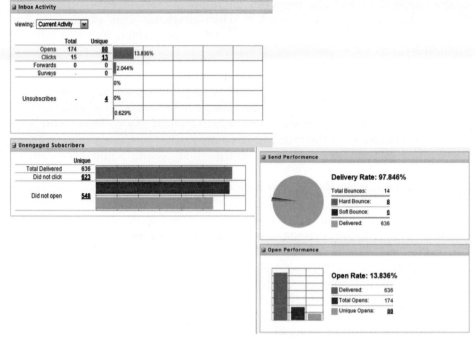

FIGURE **7.12** ExactTarget Email Dashboard
Source: ExactTarget.

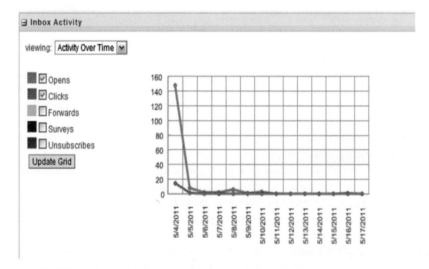

FIGURE **7.13** Open Rates Decline after 48 Hours
Source: ExactTarget.

The Golden Rs of Email Marketing and Targeting, Personalization, and Customization

As we discuss email marketing as a whole, we enter another semantic thicket: the differentiation between targeting, personalization, and customization. These three important terms are used often, in many contexts, with many shades of meaning. When defined by various authors, they often give different definitions.[20] The distinction between "personalization" and "customization" is especially fuzzy, with some authors using them interchangeably and some attempting to give more precise meanings. For the purpose of our discussion in the remainder of this chapter, we will give the terms the following meanings, which are helpful in teasing out the specific ways in which marketers can use these techniques. These definitions were presented in previous chapters and they are still applicable:

- *Targeting* refers to directing marketing communications to individuals or businesses that have been identified as valid prospects for acquisition or retention for the good or service. Targeting can be visible, as when a marketer sends an email newsletter with personalized content to a customer who has given permission for this type of communication. It can be invisible to the receiver, as when targeted ads are served onto a website without the visitor's explicit knowledge.
- *Personalization* involves the creation of specialized content for a prospect with a known profile by choosing from an array of existing content modules. In addition to the email newsletter, just described, personalization occurs when a visitor registers on a website like Yahoo! and creates a My Yahoo! page by choosing the content he wants from extensive lists presented by the site.
- *Customization* is the creation of new content, services, or even products based on the needs and wants of an individual customer—either business or consumer. Internet marketers like NikeID are offering the ability to customize products. Others like iTunes are offering customers the ability to customize their own user experience.

Note that this terminology defines customization rather tightly, calling into question the way in which the term is often used by Internet marketers. Even so, there is still a gray area in which goods or services are configured to customers' orders from a set of components or services. This is represented by manufacturing processes like Dell's and NikeID's and has been called "mass customization" in discussions in both the academic and trade press.[21]

With few exceptions, Internet marketers are not engaging in customization at this level, and we can therefore center our discussion on targeting and personalization. In so doing, we are not missing any important marketing issues since the processes used to identify and reach prospective customers with offers for truly customized products are the same as the ones used to identify customers in order to target them with personalized content.

Again, MailerMailer clients last year found little difference in click-through rate with personalized subject lines (i.e., the recipient's name), whereas there was better performance, 11 percent versus 4 percent, in terms of open rate by *not* including the recipient's name in the subject line (see Figure 7.14). However, the study also found that emails with personalized body content generated a 13 percent open rate. Emails with subject lines 4 to 15 characters in length had a 14 percent open rate, versus a 9.9 percent open rate for a 50-character subject line.[22]

Personalization research is in its infancy in academia. Some research by White, Zahay, Thorbjornsen, and Shavitt[23] indicates that although personalization can yield higher response rates (Postmaa and Brokke [2002]),[24] consumers do not react well to highly personalized messages that are given too soon in the relationship. The consumer develops a response called "reactance" in response to highly personalized messages where the fit between the offer in the message and consumers' personal characteristics is not explicitly justified by firms. In other words, if Dreamfields pasta were to make an offer based on highly personalized information, perhaps about the size of the consumer's family, too soon in the relationship, it might turn customers off. However, starting the consumer relationship with a simple dollar off coupon as they do is not threatening and is a good idea to help develop the relationship.

Email inboxes are crammed with spam, emails of dubious value to the recipient, and a small number of communications that are welcome and that have a good chance of inciting to action. There is an approach marketers can follow to

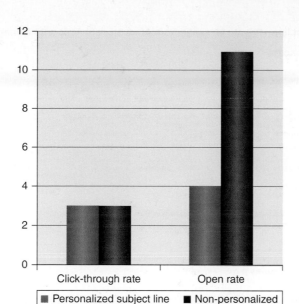

FIGURE **7.14** Click-Through Rate and Open Rates in Percentages, Nonpersonalized versus Personalized Subject Line Emails
Source: MailerMailer 2011.

give their emails the best chance of being opened and acted upon. We call this the three "Golden Rs of Email Marketing."[25] They are:

- *Relevance.* All content should be applicable to the recipient's needs and life-style. Content that is not relevant will not motivate the recipient to take action and it may tarnish the brand of the communicator.
- *Respect.* Relevant content cannot be generated without in-depth information about the recipient. In order to get the information and keep the trust of the recipient, the sender of emails must guard data from unwarranted or frivolous use.
- *Recipient control.* Go beyond simply obtaining permission to communicate with the recipient. Make the recipient an active partner in deciding what content he wants to receive and how often he wants to receive it. That gives the content a much better chance of being seen as valuable.

Following these three Rs will not only give the emails the best possible chance of success but it will also, over time, contribute to the creation of brand that is trusted by the members of its target market.

Requirements of the U.S. CAN-SPAM Act

Because email is open to abuse by spammers, phishers, and others who seek to dupe the unwary, legislation, the **CAN-SPAM Act,** has been passed in an attempt to curb the worst abuses. *Phishing* is the process of using emails to obtain or "fish" for a consumer's personal information, usually financial. There is an example of a phishing email in Figure 7.15. The subject line says that it is from Amazon.com accounts management and the text asks for the recipient's personal bank account information. When receiving emails that looks suspicious, see if the emails are compliant with the CAN-SPAM act, as discussed later. If there is a valid reply to address, a valid street address, and an unsubscribe provision, the email is less likely to be a "phishing" expedition.

The law, officially named "Controlling the Assault of Non-Solicited Pornography and Marketing Act," was passed in 2003 by the U.S. Congress in an attempt to curb unsolicited and, especially, offensive email. Although it does not use the

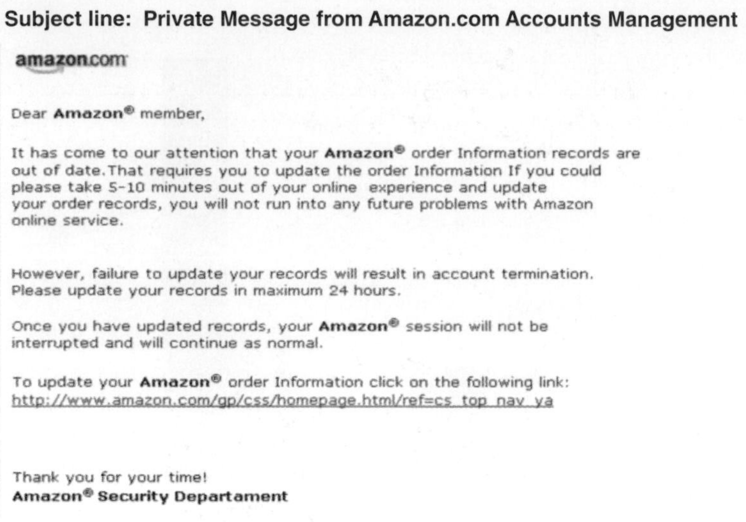

Subject line: Private Message from Amazon.com Accounts Management

amazon.com

Dear **Amazon**® member,

It has come to our attention that your **Amazon**® order Information records are out of date. That requires you to update the order Information If you could please take 5-10 minutes out of your online experience and update your order records, you will not run into any future problems with Amazon online service.

However, failure to update your records will result in account termination. Please update your records in maximum 24 hours.

Once you have updated records, your **Amazon**® session will not be interrupted and will continue as normal.

To update your **Amazon**® order Information click on the following link: http://www.amazon.com/gp/css/homepage.html/ref=cs_top_nav_ya

Thank you for your time!
Amazon® **Security Departament**

FIGURE **7.15** What Is Wrong?

Source: © Cengage Learning 2013

terms, it distinguishes between acquisition mailings by marketers and relationship mailings. Relationship mailings, or in the terms of the Federal Trade Commission, "a transactional or relationship message," are emails that facilitate a transaction or update an existing customer. As long as the content is not false or misleading, these emails are generally exempt from the provisions of CAN-SPAM. Acquisition or promotional mailings as we have been discussing here, however, come under the provisions of the law. It is wise to pay attention to the law since every separate email in violation of the law can be subject to a penalty of $16,000 so it pays to pay attention to the law:[26]

According to the FTC website, the main provisions of the law are:

- *It bans false or misleading header information.* Your email's "From," "To," and routing information—including the originating domain name and email address—must be accurate and identify the person who initiated the email.
- *It prohibits deceptive subject lines.* The subject line cannot mislead the recipient about the contents or subject matter of the message.
- *It requires that your email give recipients an opt-out method.* You must provide a return email address or another Internet-based response mechanism that allows a recipient to ask you not to send future email messages to that email address, and you must honor the requests. You may create a "menu" of choices to allow a recipient to opt out of certain types of messages, but you must include the option to end any commercial messages from the sender.
  - Any opt-out mechanism you offer must be able to process opt-out requests for at least 30 days after you send your commercial email. When you receive an opt-out request, the law gives you ten business days to stop sending email to the requestor's email address. You cannot help another entity send email to that address, or have another entity send email on your behalf to that address. Finally, it is illegal for you to sell or transfer the email addresses of people who choose not to receive your email, even in the form of a mailing list, unless you transfer the addresses so another entity can comply with the law.
- *It requires that commercial email be identified as an advertisement and include the sender's valid physical postal address.* Your message must contain clear and conspicuous notice that the message is an advertisement or solicitation and that the recipient can opt out of receiving more commercial email from you. It also must include your valid physical postal address.

Commercial email service providers as we have discussed help marketers abide by the provisions of the law. Most of them seem straightforward, but some are difficult to implement if the marketer has a large list. This is especially true of the requirements for removing "unsubscribes" from the marketer's own list as well as those of any affiliates who may have been given access. If the list is to be rented, the unsubscribes must be meticulously purged from the rental list. Software that automates this process is desirable since errors must be avoided.

There are other practices specified as unacceptable in the FTC implementation guidelines. Most are practices not used by reputable marketers in any event. These practices include so-called harvesting of email addresses from other websites, a so-called dictionary attach in which the spammer uses computer algorithms to create email addresses, using unauthorized networks, and other practices that mislead the consumer about the results of registering with a site. The last provision means, for example, that if a marketer needs to place a special piece of software on the registrant's computer so he can receive emails in the desired format, the registrant must be explicitly notified of and agree to the placement of the software on his computer. That is an issue that can trip up even a marketer whose intentions are good.

Figure 7.16 from the DMA describes how to identify an email that is not compliant with the CAN-SPAM Act.

Advocates of permission marketing argue that the requirements of CAN-SPAM are simply good business practice. In fact, many of them would argue that they represent minimal acceptable levels, not best practices. Some level of opt-in is considered more effective than opt-out. Many would go a step further, arguing that segmentation and personalization of content is a requirement for effectiveness. Permission marketers speak disparagingly of "blast" emails that are sent to all members of a list, regardless of the relevance of the content.

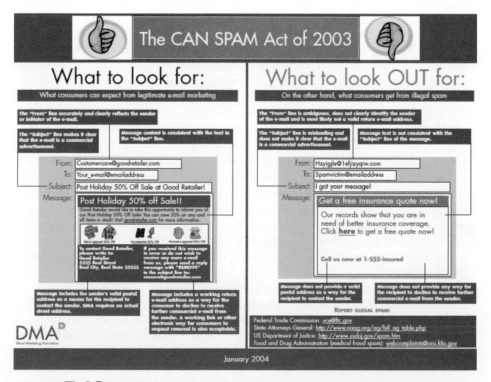

FIGURE **7.16** What to Look for in a CAN-SPAM Compliant Email

Source: Direct Marketing Association, http://www.dmaresponsibility.org/CanSpamChart.

CAN-SPAM in the European Union

The European Union's Directive on Privacy and Electronic Communications was passed in 2002 and is probably due for updates and revisions. This Directive sets out guidelines for direct marketing in all media and requires that member nations of the EU harmonize their individual laws under the umbrella of the EU Directive. Email is covered under the general policy directive and the basic requirement is that people must opt-in to receive marketer-initiated communications in all electronic media. The "technology neutral" laws resulting from the EU Directive have been criticized as being unenforceable. The very generality of laws that attempt to cover the wide spectrum of electronic media makes it hard to be specific, and therefore enforceable. The fact that the directive also covers the 27 members of the European Union also creates difficulties. Finally, the fact that much spam received in Western Europe comes from outside that geographical area makes enforcement exceedingly difficult.

However, without similar antispam rules being adopted across the globe, the EU Directive is not going to stop spam sent to European email users from beyond the region."[27] That refrain sounds familiar to email users around the globe. Many spam sites are located outside the United States, for example. A summary of the EU Directive can be found online provided by the European Commission on Information, Society and Media, along with links to other information about the data privacy laws in Europe.[28]

In both the EU and the United States, CAN-SPAM laws specify legal standards that marketers must meet. They are not, however, sufficient to assure effective email marketing.

The marketer choiceboard of customer retention techniques is rich, varied, and growing. The challenge is to use the correct ones for the correct objective at the correct time and to do so in a fully integrated online and offline communications program. Emails can be used in conjunction with other communications channels such as direct mail and social media for powerful results.

Email marketing for customer retention offers a number of legitimate benefits. Not only can marketers contact consumers in a timely and more cost-effective fashion than other response mechanisms, but response is almost immediate, and offers and campaigns can be altered to increase response rate. Permission is the key to effective email marketing since email is marketing's version of a two-edged sword. Email has genuine benefits when used as part of an integrated permission marketing program. However, the volume of spam threatens to drown the efforts of legitimate marketers. Governments around the globe are attempting to stem the tide of spam.

The secret to effective email marketing, as with all direct techniques, is a good list—and in this case, permission-based lists are superior. Levels of permission range from opt-out to opt-in to double opt-in. Generally, a form of opt-in permission is considered to be most consistent with good email marketing practices. Good lists help decrease the bounce rate and increase click-through rates. Emails need to be designed with good web design principles in mind, compelling subject lines and offers, and need to take into account in their design the limitations of the computer screen on which they will be received.

Marketers need to offer the consumer the right to opt-out or unsubscribe at any time, provide a physical address on their email and a valid reply-to email address, and to otherwise comply with good email marketing practices as outlined in the CAN-SPAM provisions. Good campaign planning is critical to success and the ability to measure many aspects of response can allow the marketer to adjust the campaign accordingly in short order. Used properly, with a concern for relevance, respect, and recipient control, email can be a highly effective marketing tool.

DISCUSSION QUESTIONS

1. Why is email still a strong tool for Internet marketers? Do you think it will be replaced by mobile applications, such as text messaging, and in what time frame?
2. What is meant by permission marketing? Do you think it is an important concept to email marketers?
3. Think about email communications from marketers, perhaps some that you receive yourself. What makes them interesting and worth your time to open and read? Do you ever take any action as a result of the emails? Why or why not?
4. What are the main benefits of using an email service provider? Say you are the head of a student organization and you need to regularly contact members, would you consider using an email service provider if the cost were within your budget? Why or why not?
5. What aspects of promotional email design would you take into account if you were designing an email to invite students to a meeting of the organization mentioned in question 4? Where would you put the most important information? What would be your call to action?
6. From your perspective, is the CAN-SPAM law working? Why or why not?
7. Assume that WilyMarketer.com is running an email campaign to acquire new customers. It is considering two options: review the following option choices. In either event, actual campaign management will be outsourced to an interactive agency. Which program would you recommend and why?
   - Option A would use a high quality rental list of 100,000 email addresses. Direct costs under this option would be the rental list at $250/m and creative, program management and reporting costs will be $10,000. If the email campaign brings in 623 new customers, what is its customer acquisition cost?
   - Option B would rely on banner advertising at $20 CPM, which has a predicted click-through rate of 1.5 percent. The campaign is designed to reach 100,000 viewers, and its creative, program management and reporting costs will be $10,000. How many customers will it bring in and what is the customer acquisition cost?

INTERNET EXERCISES

1. Internet Career Builder Exercise
   a. There are a number of resources for email marketing, which is predicted by Kiplinger to be a top ten job opportunity in the next few years.[29] The Email Marketers Club[30] indicates a number of jobs, some of which require experience. For entry-level jobs in email, here are a few titles:

      Email marketing analyst

      Email marketing producer

      Email marketing manager

      Email marketing coordinator

      Email marketing also may be included in Internet analyst or other online marketing positions

   b. Select an email job title from the previous list or from your own search. Outline the responsibilities of that position. You may find it useful to locate job postings on the web in order to understand the job requirements.
   c. Outline knowledge and experience from classes, internships, full- or part-time jobs, and volunteer work that prepare you for this specific position.
   d. Prepare five questions you could ask at a job interview. The questions should exhibit your understanding of the position requirements without lecturing the interviewer about what she already knows.
   e. Update your VisualCV® or LinkedIn Profile with this information.
2. If you have not already done so, sign up for an email newsletter from one or more of the sites you are following. Keep a log for the next few weeks of the email contacts that result. How many emails do you receive and how often? Pay special attention to how long it took for the site to confirm/welcome you and the nature of the confirmation communication. If you are already receiving email newsletters and other communications, keep a log of these communications.
3. Assume you are to design and send an email to invite students to attend a presentation on email marketing at your university. Using the suggested processes and tips in this chapter, create a plan for obtaining the list, sending the email and measuring the results.
4. Next, design the email that you have planned to send using good email design principles. Share your design with the class and get feedback.

NOTES

1. http://www.marketingprofs.com/charts/2010/4117/Email-social-marketing-top-2011-budget-growth, retrieved July 20, 2011.
2. Presentation, Joel Book, May 18, 2011, Northern Illinois University "Hot Topics in Internet Marketing."
3. *DMA Statistical Fact Book*, The Definitive Source for Direct Marketing Benchmarks, Direct Marketing Association, New York, (2009), page 87.
4. Forrester, U.S. Email Marketing Forecast, 2009 to 2014.
5. *DMA Statistical Fact Book*, 30th Edition, The Definitive Source for Direct Marketing Benchmarks, Direct Marketing Association, New York, (2008), page 115.
6. http://www.marketingsherpa.com/heap/whiteboard/EmailSummit2010Whiteboard.html.
7. http://www.marketingsherpa.com/article.php?ident=31393.
8. http://www.emarketer.com/Article.aspx?R=1008025, retrieved August 11, 2011.
9. http://www.exacttarget.com/sff, "Email X-Factors: A Research Report from ExactTarget and CoTweet."
10. http://www.exacttarget.com/sff, % per the May 2011 SFF survey. (This is of online consumers in the United States 15+—weighted by age and gender).
11. http://www.thewhir.com/web-hosting-news/062811_Symantec_Report_Finds_Spam_Accounts_for_73_Percent_of_June_Email.
12. http://www.pewinternet.org/Reports/2007/Spam-2007.aspx, retrieved July 20, 2011.
13. http://www.exacttarget.com/sff (This is of online consumers in the United States 15+—weighted by age and gender). Question wording, "Have you ever made a purchase as the result of a marketing message you received through: Email (email was one of multiple yes/no questions).
14. "DoubleClick's 2004 Consumer Email Study," http://www.doubleclick.com/us/knowledge_central/documents/RESEARCH/dc_consumer_Email_0410.pdf, 7.
15. http://Email.about.com/gi/o.htm?zi=1/XJ&zTi=1&sdn=Email&cdn=compute&tm=13&f=00&tt=12&bt=0&bts=0&zu=http%3A//www.radicati.com, retrieved August 8, 2011.
16. http://www.epsilon.com/News%20&%20Events/Press%20Releases%202011/Q1_2011_North_America_Email_Trend_Results_Open_Rates_Increase_from_Previous_Quarter_and_Q1_2010/p1095-l3, retrieved July 20, 2011.
17. http://www.lyris.com/Email-marketing/535-Email-Preheaders-Work-So-Make-Them-Work-For-You, retrieved July 18, 2011.
18. http://engage.tmgcustommedia.com/2010/11/best-time-to-send-Email, retrieved August 8, 2011.
19. http://www.dmnews.com/subject-line-personalization-doesnt-impact-click-rates-study/article/207840, retrieved July 20, 2011.
20. For a discussion of competing definitions see, "Is It Personalization or Customization?" Don Peppers and Martha Rogers, *Inside 1 to 1*, June 20, 2000, http://www.marketing1to1.com.
21. See, for example, James Gilmore and Joseph B. Pine, II, "The Four Faces of Mass Customization," *Harvard Business Review*, 1997.
22. http://www.dmnews.com/subject-line-personalization-doesnt-impact-click-rates-study/article/207840, retrieved July 20, 2011.
23. T. B. White, D. L. Zahay, H. Thorbjorsen, and S. A. Shavitt, "Getting too Personal: Reactance to Highly Personalized Email Solicitations," *Marketing Letters* 19(2008): 39–50.
24. O. J. Postma and M. Brokke, "Personalization in Practice: The Proven Effects of Personalization," *Journal of Database Management*, 9 (2002): 137–42.
25. Based on a concept suggested by Bill Nussey, *The Quiet Revolution in Email Marketing* (New York: iUniverse, Inc., 2004).
26. http://business.ftc.gov/documents/bus61-can-spam-act-compliance-guide-business, retrieved August 10, 2011.
27. "European Spam Laws Lack Bite," BBC News, April 28, 2004, http://news.bbc.co.uk/1/hi/technology/3666585.stm.
28. http://ec.europa.eu/information_society/doc/factsheets/024-privacy-and-spam-en.pdf.
29. http://finance.yahoo.com/blogs/power-your-future/10-today-hottest-jobs-184644468.html, retrieved August 10, 2011.
30. http://b2bemailmarketing.jobamatic.com/a/jbb/find-jobs.

Search Marketing: SEO and PPC

Key Terms

LEARNING OBJECTIVES

By the time you complete this chapter, you will be able to:

- Discuss the reasons why search marketing is so important.
- Explain the difference between a directory and a search engine.
- Understand how search engines work and what is a search algorithm.
- Define SEM, SEO, and PPC.
- Understand the basic process of optimizing a website for organic search.
- Identify the basic issues in keyword bidding and developing PPC ads.

Previously, we discussed online advertising and how it is used for both branding and customer acquisition. We have also pointed out that there are multiple customer acquisition techniques used by marketers in integrated programs spanning both advertising techniques and media. In this chapter, we discuss another acquisition technique that is enjoying explosive growth on the Internet and has become an integral part of how we work on the Internet—search marketing. Search marketing is in a sense a true outgrowth of the direct marketing roots of the web because it allows us to be in front of the customer at the exact moment they are researching a product or service or considering purchase. Although we may not know exactly who the customer is at the point they see our organization or firm listed on the results of a search, we do know what they are interested in at the moment. If we can encourage them to learn more about us or make a purchase, we then have the opportunity acquire them as a customer, to collect specific information about them, and develop a longer-term relationship.

The Growing Impact of Search

When the Pew Internet & American Life Project asked American consumers in 2004 about their use of **search engines**—websites that work to help users to find the things they wanted to find on the Internet—32 percent said they "couldn't live without them."[1] At that time, the average Internet user performed 33 searches per month, a total of 3.9 billion searches on the 25 most popular search engines.

The trend toward search engine usage and dependence has continued at a breakneck speed. The comScore Expanded Search Query Report from January 2010 stated that in the United States Internet users performed 75 searches per month, with an expected growth rate of 2 percent per month, for a total of over 35 billion searches per month predicted by the end of 2011.[2]

A Pew Internet report from August 2011 indicates the following:

- On any given day, more than half the users who are online launch a search (59 percent).
- 92 percent of U.S. Internet users have used search engines.
- 29 percent use search engines daily.
- Although 96 percent of the youngest adult Internet users (ages 18 to 29) used search engines, 87 percent of the oldest users (65+) also still use search engines to find information online.
- There are no significant differences by gender or race/ethnicity in terms of those who say they used search "yesterday."
- Those with higher incomes and who have attended college are, however, slightly more likely to use search engines to find information online.[3]

Web users continue to look for information on specific topics, maps and directions, news and current events, general information, shopping, and

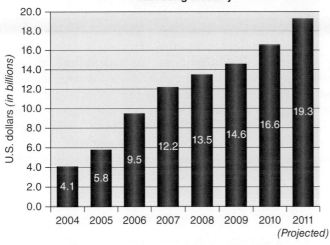

Value of North American Search Engine Marketing Industry

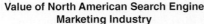

(a)

Worldwide Mobile Search Advertising Spending, by Region, 2007–2012 *(in millions)*

	2007	2008	2009	2010	2011	2012
U.S.	$34.5	$107.4	$241.8	$530.5	$910.2	$1,484.2
Asia-Pacific	$26.0	$72.0	$189.9	$372.8	$732.4	$1,160.0
Western Europe	$18.4	$52.0	$140.5	$339.7	$614.1	$968.2
Rest of World	$4.4	$12.4	$24.4	$47.0	$88.6	$160.9
Worldwide	**$83.3**	**$243.7**	**$596.6**	**$1,289.9**	**$2,345.2**	**$3,773.2**

Note: Includes spending on sponsored display ads and text links that appear alongside mobile search results, as well as spending on audio ads played to mobile phone callers making a directory inquiry; Western Europe includes France, Germany, Italy, Spain, UK; Asia-Pacific includes China, India, Japan, South Korea; numbers may not add up to total due to rounding

(b)

FIGURE **8.1** (a) Value of North American SEM Industry (b) Worldwide Growth of Mobile Search Ad Spending

Sources: Econsultancy, April 21, 2011, "SEMPO Study–US Search Spending Nears $20 Billion," Reprinted with permission; and eMarketer, Inc., February 2008.

entertainment—in other words, just about everything! All those searches everyday cover a wide range of subject matter. Search has radically transformed fields such as healthcare and real estate, with patients walking into their doctor's office armed with information and home buyers depending on real estate search sites and virtual tours to limit their possibilities before they even set foot in a home for a real world tour. No wonder marketers have found opportunities for marketing through search engines on the web medium.

Marketers are also using search engine marketing for just about everything. Web marketers use search for branding, online sales, lead generation for both manufacturers and dealers, driving traffic to websites, and simply to provide content. The Search Engine Marketing Professional Organization (SEMPO) in its first year of studying search engine marketing (SEM) stated that marketers in the United States and Canada spent over $4 billion on search marketing and advertising in 2004 and planned to increase their search spending by an average of 39 percent in 2005.[4] SEM is now valued at $16.6 billion in 2010 in North America alone. SEMPO and Econsultancy predict a 16 percent increase in 2011 to bring the total industry value to $19.3 billion (see Figure 8.1a).

About a third of budgets of survey respondents in the SEMPO survey were dedicated to local search campaigns. As we discuss in more detail later in this chapter, the respondents were also making even greater use of the integration of search and social media marketing, with 84 percent of company respondents using social media marketing on Facebook, and 74 percent of North American agencies reporting their clients run pay-per-click (PPC) campaigns on Facebook. Three quarters of companies in this report (75 percent) use Twitter to promote their companies or brand. Add to this prior amount an increase in spending from a rapidly growing worldwide mobile search sector, and we have a formidable industry (see Figure 8.1b).[5]

The World of Search

The world of search is broader than just search engines, important though they are. Search includes several types of search engines, including desktop only search, specialty search, and another major category—directories—which are aids in finding Internet websites. **Directories** create a list of sites that are usually arranged by category, and each directory has a search function.

Directories emerged early in the history of the Internet. As discussed in Chapter 3, Yahoo! began as a directory in which Jerry Yang and Paul Filo listed their favorite websites. And the essence of a directory remains the same. Yahoo! is now a paid directory service also that offers both free basic listings and paid enhanced listings that allow any local business to add business details, including photos and a link to their website, to their basic listing.[6]

Directories can also be complied from other sources. The Open Directory Project by dmoz is free and describes itself as "the largest, most comprehensive human-edited directory of the Web. It is constructed and maintained by a vast, global community of volunteer editors."[7] Online directories seem to be overtaking their offline counterparts in many market sectors, ranging from finding your former high school classmates to locating business services. However, directories have declined in importance in terms of SEM with the rise of search engines. In reality, the most important aspect in being able to be found on the Internet is to be indexed by the major search engines, which usually requires submitting the website to these engines. Like directories, search engines have both a paid aspect and a free aspect.

Search Engine Marketing

The entire process of getting listed on search engines so consumers can find you is called **search engine marketing (SEM)**. SEMPO defines SEM as "a form of internet marketing that seeks to promote websites by increasing their visibility in search engine result pages."[8] There are two basic aspects of SEM:

- **Search engine optimization (SEO)** refers to the process of designing a site and its content whereby search engines find the site without being paid to do so. SEMPO describes SEO as "the process of editing a web site's content and code in order to improve visibility within one or more search engines." The free aspect of SEM known as SEO is also called *natural search, organic search*, and sometimes *algorithmic search*.
- **Pay-per-click (PPC)**, or paid advertising, involves "text ads targeted to keyword search results on search engines, through programs such as Google™ AdWords are sometimes referred to as PPC advertising and Cost-per-Click (CPC) advertising."[9] The paid aspect of SEM is also called **paid search** and is based on an advertising model where firms seeking to rank high in specific search categories will bid on certain terms or "keywords" in the hopes of a lucrative search ranking. A lucrative ranking is one that makes money for the firm and is not necessarily the number one or two spot on the page. Sometimes a number two or three spot will be just as profitable for the firm.

Search engines used to employ paid placement or "sponsored links" to help marketers rank high on search criteria, but they have generally abandoned this effort. Yahoo! still offers sponsored links in preferred pages, but advertisers only pay when the ad is clicked upon. Therefore, in the paid aspect, most search engines' success at bidding still determines ad placement, and in the natural search aspect, other factors are taken into account. Also, there used to be products known as paid inclusion and paid placement whereby advertisers paid to be listed higher in search engine rankings or above the organic results, but these products are no longer formally offered by the major search engines.

While both paid and natural search are important, natural search brings in the majority of website visitors (about 61 percent according to Forrester) and is the "most commonly used resource to navigate websites." Paid search advertising has declined 10 percent since 2009 and only about 3 percent of adults find websites this way. It is referrals and not ads that drive traffic. Referrals and social media are playing an increasing role in helping users find websites.[10] The

TABLE 8.1   Comparison of SEM Techniques: SEO versus PPC

	Advantages	Disadvantages
SEO (Natural or Organic Search)	Better response since majority of clicks are organic	Results are not immediate
	More return traffic	Ranking is difficult to predict
	Lower cost	Initial Time Investment and time is major cost
	Long term marketing solution	Takes time for results to be displayed
	Brand recognition and loyalty	
Paid Search (PPC, Pay-Per-Click)	Immediate results based on bidding system in which there are charges for clicks received	Easy to lose ranking or spot
	Daily budget can be limited	Daily budget can be expensive depending on keywords
	Gives definite search volume	Unqualified clicks
	Easy to change focus	
	Unlimited keywords	
	Ability to test (keywords, ad copy, landing pages, etc.)	

Source: © Cengage Learning 2013

reason is that users want to trust the source that is recommending the site and organic search results or referrals from a friend or an often-used social media site are the most trusted ways to find information on the web.

Table 8.1 compares the advantages and disadvantages of the two types of SEM. Although SEO requires no out-of-pocket costs to pay for ad placement, there is a cost in terms of time to effectively design a site to optimize it for natural search. It is also difficult to predict search ranking with SEO and may take several months for the results of the efforts to be noted on search engines. PPC provides immediate results and allows the user to limit spending to a daily budget, but PPC campaigns also must be monitored on a daily (or hourly) basis because it is easy to lose a top search ranking if another firm outbids your firm in terms of keywords. Also, the impact of SEO, while it takes longer to set up and implement, if monitored properly can have a long-term effect versus the short-term effect of PPC programs, which last only for the duration of the ad campaign. (Please note we are referring to search results as "search results" or "search ranking." The specific term **"page rank"** refers to a mathematical algorithm named after Google co-founder Larry Page to indicate how important a page is on the web.)

Organic Search

Keywords are search terms, words or phrases, selected by the user when making a search in a search engine. The term "keywords" can refer to but is not limited to all of the following items:

1. Search terms, words or phrases, selected by the user when making a search in a search engine
2. Terms that are bid on in a PPC system such as Google or Bing
3. A section in the hypertext markup language (HTML) code for a website where site developers put terms that they hope search engines will classify the site when users search for those terms on the web

In other words, the same term is used in a variety of situations and contexts. If the usage seems confusing, it is. Remember that SEM is a relatively new and

```
<HEAD>
<TITLE>Pink Handbag World</TITLE>
<meta name="description" content="Pink Handbag World has a huge selection of stylish,
affordable handbags and purses for girls. Get the latest fashion trends and tips to look your
best from phw.com."/>
<meta name="keywords" content="Purses, Handbags, Purses for Girls, Pink Handbags,
Pink Purses"/>
</HEAD>
```

FIGURE **8.2** HTML Code for Title, Description, and Keywords in the Head Section of a Fictional Website for Pink Purses
Source: © Cengage Learning 2013

evolving discipline in marketing, and it is common to see the same term used in different ways.

In the case of HTML code, keywords are designated by a "meta name" also known as a **meta tag** or meta element. An example of HTML code containing keywords used by a fictional purse website is included in Figure 8.2. The HTML code listed is within the *header* portion of the website. (You can see the header data on any website by going to View → Source in your browser.) Below the beginning of the header section is the **title tag**, a useful tag that we discuss later in this chapter. Below the title tag are two meta tags; these tags are written as meta name=. The first meta tag is the "description," which often contains a sentence or two describing the site and in this example, it describes our fictional site, Pink Handbag World. The second meta tag is "keywords," which states the keywords for searches in which the site would like to be ranked.

In the past, search engines paid close attention to the description and keywords in the meta names. However, the major search engines, particularly Google, increasingly do not even refer to the keywords to rank a page. The fear with meta tags and keywords is that they may be manipulated and not refer to anything close to the content that the site actually contains. Some search engines do look at the "description" content tag, so it is probably still useful to include that tag and, following the example here, just include a few relevant terms in the keyword tag.

Search Engines

Search engines are the focus of attention in SEM because they are the heart of the search process. Search engines have the ability to organize and make accessible the vast amount of information available on the web.

When a user enters a query, the search engine looks for information on the web and returns a list of results known as a search engines result page (SERP). These results are in the form of suggested web pages, images, videos maps, or other types of files. Increasingly, they include results from the users' social contacts, as discussed later in the chapter. The inclusion of search results from multiple content sources such as videos, images, news, maps, books, and websites into one set of research results is called **universal search**. While the search results are rather instantaneous for the user, there are a multitude of processes that occur behind the scenes. Figure 8.3 illustrates the process of a web search.

First, the user initiates a query which goes to the search engine's web server. The web server then sends the query typically to an **index server**, which stores information on previously categorized websites as a best fit to certain keywords. In order to index all this information, search engines use **spiders** or "robots," which are programs that "crawl" the web and follow every link or piece of data that they see and bring this information back to be stored. The contents of each page—words extracted from the titles, headings, or the special fields (meta tags)—are

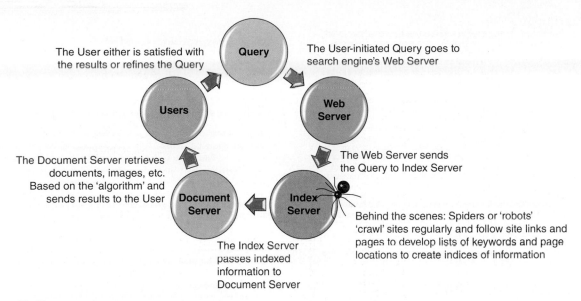

FIGURE **8.3** The Generic Search Process

Source: Adapted from "The Life Cycle of a Query" from *Marketing and Advertising Using Google: Targeting Your Advertising to the Right Audience,* Copyright © 2007 Google Inc., p. 12.

then analyzed to varying degrees to determine how it should be indexed. (Site content, inbound and outbound links, and other information are also used, which we discuss later in this chapter.)

The relevant documents are then taken from the search engine's document server based on an appropriate *algorithm*, and then displayed for the user. The word "algorithm" in the context of search does not refer to the process of solving a mathematical problem. A **search engine algorithm** displays the search engine's "best guess" at which pages are most relevant to the user's search and in which order they should be shown.

Figure 8.4a indicates how spiders looked at the ESPN website on a fall day in 2011. As the spiders move through a site, they are just looking to see what topics are covered and the order in which they are covered. The spiders do not make any particular judgment about the activity. In this case, the spider would pass information back to the index indicating each time the term "ESPN" had been used and on which page.

A "word cloud" of the site shown in Figure 8.4b illustrates the most frequently used terms in the site. In this case, "ESPN," "football," and "fantasy" are shown as larger than other terms, which indicates that they are used more often. ESPN is known for its fantasy game leagues so the prominence of this term is not surprising. As would be expected, "college" and "football" are terms that are also used more frequently on the site this time of year. A **keyword density**

INTERACTIVE EXERCISE **8.1**   How Spiders Look at Websites

Look at the ESPN site or another site of your choosing, perhaps your own college or university website. Using the tools in Figure 8.4a and b, run a spider simulator, a word cloud, and keyword density chart.

Another useful tool is from HubSpot at http://websitegrader.com.

Use the HubSpot tool to see if the site has maximized its SEO potential and run the free report. Make recommendations for improvements to get as close to a perfect score as possible in SEO.

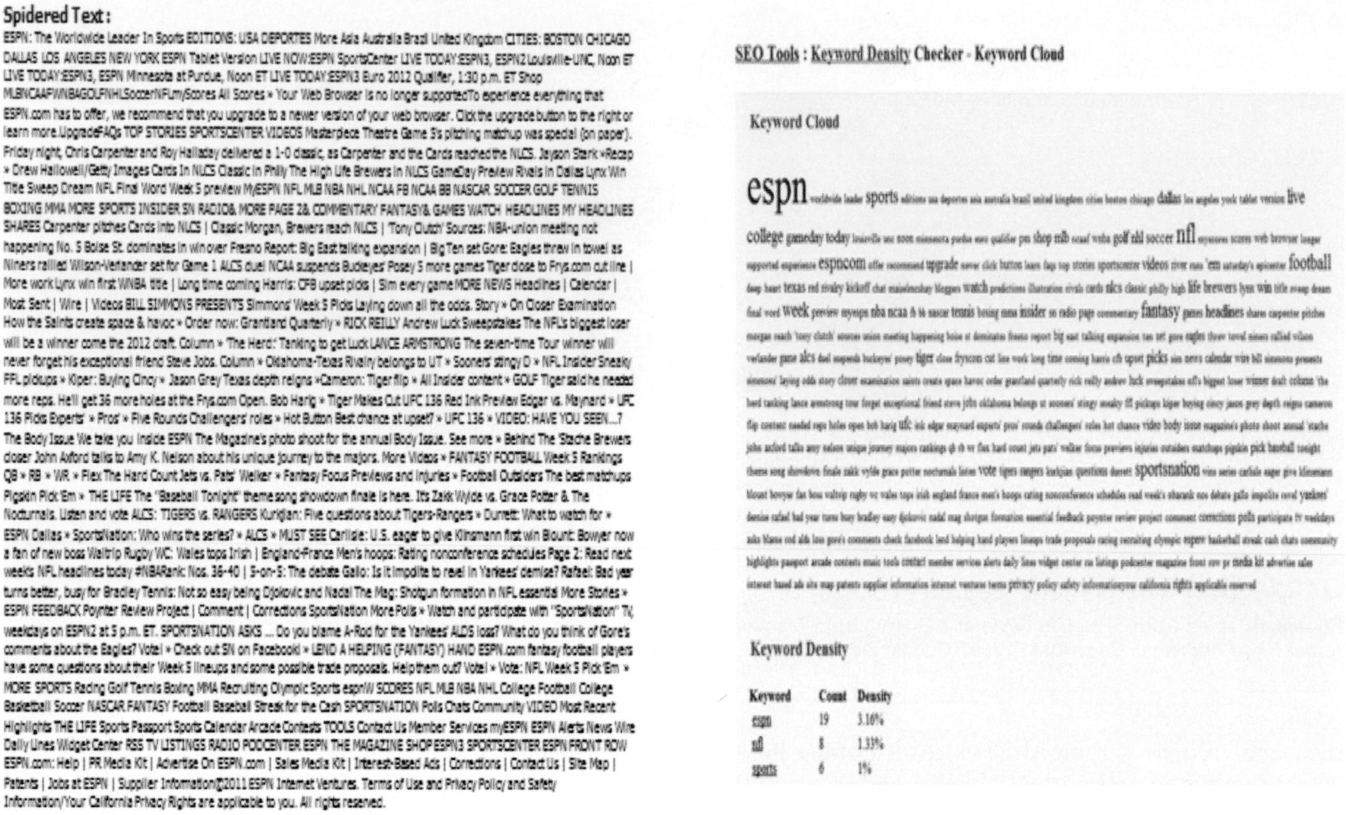

(a) **(b)**

FIGURE **8.4** (a) Search Engine Spider Simulator (b) Word Cloud and Keyword Density Chart

Source: Webconfs, http://www.webconfs.com/search-engine-spider-simulator.php and http://www.webconfs.com/keyword-density-checker.php.

chart is also shown below the word cloud. Keyword density is the percentage of times a particular word is used in comparison to the number of words on a page. The keyword density should not be too large (less than 3 percent), which in this example (3.16 percent) can indicate that the site is engaging in keyword practices that might get it in trouble with search engines. However, a density of at least 1 percent is recommended in order to be properly indexed by search engines. Although 1 percent does not seem like a lot of words from one page, it is important not to overload with keywords on the page or try to trick the search engine into indexing and ranking the page a certain way.

Search results can and do vary by search engine. Most users prefer the search engine that they believe gives them the results they want, with preferences varying depending on the searcher. Each search engine has its own algorithm for ranking entries, which is not published. There are a number of search engines with significant market shares, as measured by the number of searches conducted (see Figure 8.5). Google has dominated the search market for many years, although it is down from its peak of over 70 percent. Yahoo! has been losing market share over time, primarily to Microsoft's Bing.

Figure 8.6a and b provide the results of two separate searches for "pink purses" on two separate search engines, Google and Yahoo!. The results of organic search show up in the main area of the search page on the left-hand side. Exactly how the results are displayed varies from one search engine to another, but the intention is that organic search results are always ranked by relevance based on the keyword or phrase chosen and provide the majority of the content on the page. Down the right-hand side of the page, the searcher will generally see boxes with text images and links. Those links are paid ads (PPC). There may also be a band of color across the top of the page that displays the highest-ranking paid ads.

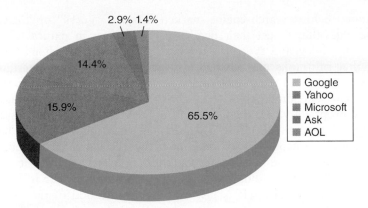

FIGURE **8.5** Search Engine Market Share, June 2011

Source: Adapted from comscore, http://searchenginewatch.com/articlc/2094160/June-2011-Search-Engine-Market-Share-from-comScore-Hitwise.

As shown in Figure 8.6a the "organic" or "natural" search rankings appear to the left of the page underneath paid search terms, which also can appear to the right of the organic search terms. Marketers seek to be "above the fold" or in the top four or five search terms because most users do not scroll down past the first few rankings and rarely venture to subsequent search pages.

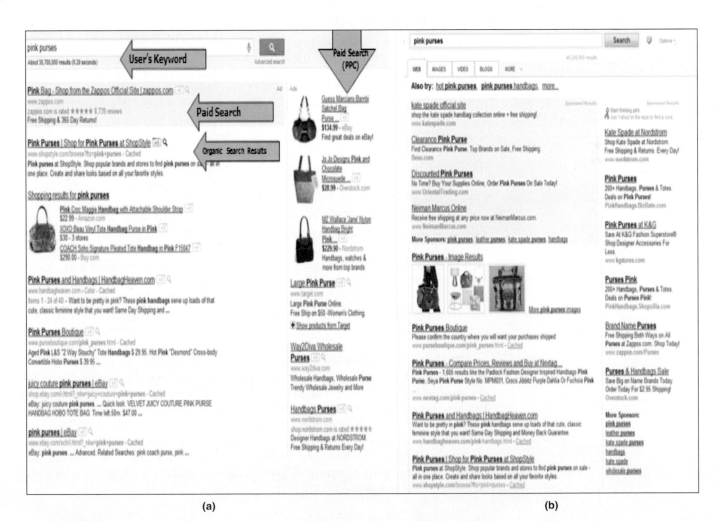

(a)   (b)

FIGURE **8.6** Google versus Yahoo! Search Results for Pink Purses

Sources: Google and Yahoo!

As stated before, search engine marketers try to "guess" or "reverse engineer" the algorithm to get their pages ranked highest in natural search. The entries to the index and the calculations of the algorithms change over time, meaning that site ranks may change just because the way of determining site ranks has changed. All the search engine ranking algorithms are different, placing different weights on different characteristics. The exact ranking algorithm of any site is proprietary, although trade sources make educated guesses at the nature of the different algorithms. The meta tag "description," as we have seen, often contains a sentence or two describing the site. Some search engines pay attention to the description. Google, for one, completely ignores it in ranking the site, although this tag and the title tag do affect how the site is displayed on the search page. This example is just one small indication of the difference in ranking algorithms among different search engines. Some items that are usually used for inclusion in the rankings are

- The location and frequency (density) of keywords on the page
- The HTML title tag (the title you see in the blue bar at the top of the page)
- Site content, including quality and relevance
- The number of other sites that link to the page
- The number of click-throughs generated by searches to that page
- Recency of mention and number of social mentions

Optimizing Organic Search

From the discussion in the last section, it sounds like it should be relatively easy to get your web page ranked highly on the major search engines. You simply choose the right keywords, then stuff your page header and content pages with those keywords, and you will get ranked accordingly. There are two problems with that reasoning. First, it does not work that way. The search engine algorithms look for items, such as undue repetition of keywords, or, even worse, putting keywords on a page in an invisible way, for example, by making them the same color as the background. Second, if the search engines identify the site as an offender in terms of practices deliberately designed to trick them, they can refuse to rank it altogether. This practice is often referred to as "black hat" search.[11]

As the definition of SEO suggests, practitioners try to work within the algorithms of the individual search engines to achieve the best possible ranking for the site or page on that particular search engine so their sites are listed at or near the top in the organic search listings. You may notice a problem here, however. Since the search engine algorithms are not disclosed, practitioners are working from what they believe the algorithms to be, based on their own experience and their own proprietary techniques for studying search engine rankings. This practice is not for amateurs, although nonprofessionals can certainly learn some of the main techniques and practice them.

Therefore, most practitioners of SEO follow the practices suggested here for maximizing their rankings. They start by understanding their target market, developing keywords to reach that market, and defining and developing their site around those keywords. In addition, it is important to use keywords you think are important in search engines and see if the type of company you are thinking of, yours or a competitor, is displayed in the search results. For example, the term "dat" can be digital audio tape, the Dental Admissions Test, or the Danish Air Transport company. A good suggested process for beginning an SEO campaign is as follows:

1. Define the target market.
2. Find out what they search for.
3. Develop a search strategy: find keywords and phrases.

4. Redesign site with those keywords in mind.
5. Register the site with search engines.
6. Implement a paid search campaign to complement or inform the organic search campaign (optional).

Starting with the customer and what they are looking for is critical and often overlooked. Sometimes search terms might be obvious and sometimes they might not. For example, there are several spray products based on Cherith Clark and Kirstin Stokes' 2008 book *Monster Spray* that produce an aroma that is supposed to convince young children that this spray eradicates or scares away monsters in their bedrooms at night. However, parents eager to allay their child's fears might not search for "monster spray" but rather "children afraid of the dark" or other related terms.

Even Coca-Cola[12] with its worldwide brand needed help with SEO strategies and worked with an agency to deploy a team that works internationally in 200 countries. The search tactics worked and thecoca-colacompany.com set a record in 2010 of over four million visits, one million more visits than in 2009, and had good results in terms of company's return on investment (ROI). By taking its time to select and mange keywords on the site over multiple countries, Coca-Cola's organic search campaign delivers media impressions, traffic, and customer connections, particularly in one of its growing markets, China. We cover some tools that can help identify relevant keywords to help fuel success later in the chapter.

Even when conducting an SEO campaign only, a number of tools exist to develop keywords. It is always a good idea to do market research and ask the customer how they search for your product. Looking at search trends and "hot keywords" is also a good way to select keywords. In addition, most search engines have keyword finder tools, and we take a look at the Google version later in the chapter. Paid search sites also have a number of useful tools for free use that can help explore and narrow down keyword selection. One great tool available is the Keyword Tool in Google, which can either be used for free or as part of the capabilities of a Google AdWords account.[13] The example in Figure 8.7a shows for "pink purses" how much competition there is for the term and the number of monthly global or local searches (local can be defined for a particular geographic area). The traffic estimator tool in Figure 8.7b then can be used to give a better idea of how many clicks might be expected from that search term and the average **CPC**, or **cost-per-click**, to the online advertiser.

Once the proper terms have been identified, the site's title tag and content must be completely redesigned with the appropriate search terms in mind. It is a good idea to think of the top five or six terms and their variations that the company would like to be ranked on and to include those terms throughout the content of the site. In addition, many companies are unaware of these common problems in organic search, and it is a good idea to make note of them:

- *Search engine spiders unable to navigate the website:* Flash is the single biggest barrier to the spiders. A Flash Player is a web browser plug-in that allows images such as videos to display on a website. The problem is that spiders cannot read these images. Opening your website entry page with a Flash video can be a problem because spiders will not know how to categorize your website. Images in general, even photos, can pose a problem for spiders and using Alt tags to describe the image can aid in SEO.
- *No site map on website:* A detailed and accurate site map provides important assistance to the spiders. Laying out the site in an easy manner means all pages can be crawled and indexed by search engines.
- *Nonoptimized navigation structure:* The spiders need to be able to move through the site, understand the HTML code, and determine how to

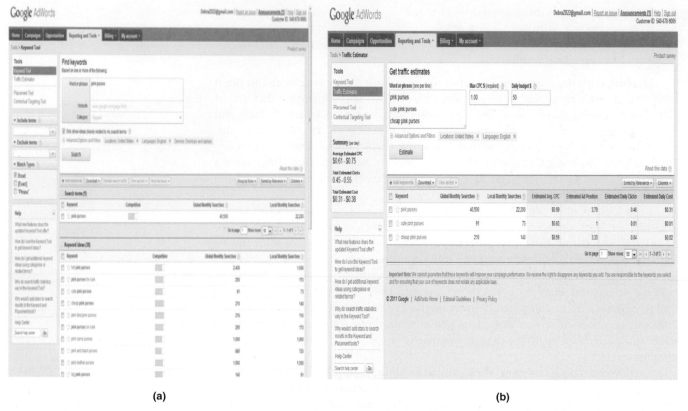

(a) (b)

FIGURE **8.7** (a) Google Keyword Selector Tool (b) Google Traffic Estimator
Source: GOOGLE AdWords™ advertising service.

best index it. Anything that makes it difficult, like the extraneous HTML code inserted by some of the website development tools, impedes their progress.

- *Diluted link popularity of key category/product pages:* Links are important to ranking. However, they need to be relevant and represent a real relationship to the topic of the main site.

Fixing these problems can improve search rankings. However, please note that improving rankings may take several months for the changes to be made and for initial results to be seen. For example, Google updated its search algorithm in March 2011. The new algorithm, called Google Panda, was an attempt to make it less easy to engage in "black hat" SEO practices. Such practices are employed by companies that resort to activity that, while not illegal, may be unethical and artificially raise organic search results. Google recently cracked down on several well-known companies who were doing such black hat practices, like paying to have thousands of links placed on hundreds of sites leading directly to their firm.[14] Another version of this practice are sites that link to one another called "link farms" that aim for search engines to perceive these links as valuable and raise the ranking of the site. Another example which Google perceived as a black hat practice was a firm that provided incentives for colleges and universities, which are typically perceived as "authority" links by search engines, to link to their site.

Items that are usually included in the rankings for natural searches are also the ones that should be targeted for SEO. These items are listed in Figure 8.8 and are considered the "low lying fruit" of SEO that can be easily added to a page:

- *The URL or domain name:* The uniform resource locator (URL) itself should be descriptive of the firm and consistent with how you want to be found. Being around for a long time and having a search history will also help.

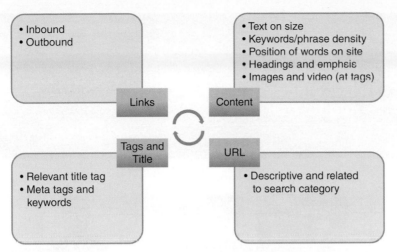

FIGURE **8.8** Basic Approach to Search Engine Optimization
Source: © Cengage Learning 2013

- *Title tag, also known as the HTML title tag* (the title you see in the blue bar at the top of the page): Many companies ignore the title tag, which should include a company description and the most important search terms or keywords. A good example to follow would be to include the keyword portion first (how you want to be found), followed by the branding portion (your firm name or description of your firm), and to keep the title page short (35 characters or less) so it can be read when it displays on search engines.
- *Content:* Content includes quality and relevance to the desired search topic as well as the location and frequency (density) of keywords on the page. Decide what terms are important and rewrite the page content to reflect those terms. Do not just focus on written content, although this content should contain relevant references to your desired keywords. Videos and blogs are likely to improve the search ranking considerably because the search engines look upon these activities favorably, presumably because of the web traffic and links that they produce.
- *Links:* The number of other sites that link to the page, the number of pages the site links to, and their relevancy to keywords and search phrases are most important for the site. Not only the quantity but also the quality of the links are significant for search engines. It is easy to create relevant outbound links and less easy to get sites to link to you (also known as a backlink). However, backlinks are more important to SEO. Authority links as previously mentioned, directory links such as Yahoo! Directory, real-time links from blogs, and social bookmarking links all increase the chances of a high search ranking.

The Econsultancy site in Figure 8.9 illustrates some of the points listed above for optimizing for natural search. The company's URL is econsultancy.com. The title tag repeats the URL and adds a tag, so it becomes "econsultancy | Become a smarter digital marketer." This title tag thus includes both a keyword piece and a branding piece, the company's "tag line." This tag line is also repeated in the site content on the first page. The site also includes links to blogs and other relevant content as well as other providers of information on Internet marketing. The keyword "econsultancy" is somewhat questionable in this context however. Are potential customers searching for the term "econsultancy" or for "econsulant" or "digital marketing consultant"? Whether this site is optimized for natural search depends on how they expect their company will be found. If Econsultancy is a strong enough keyword, then this is a site well-optimized for SEO. Otherwise, the title should be reversed with "Econsultancy" second as the brand to be reinforced and the most relevant keywords relating to the company's business placed first.

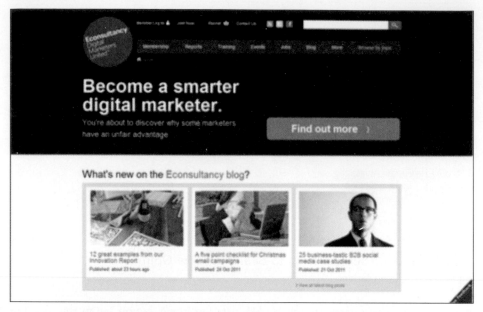

FIGURE **8.9** Optimizing the Site for SEO

Source: Econsultancy, http://econsultancy.com/us.

It is estimated that 33 percent of search ranking comes from link activity, including links to blogs and social media. It has been suggested that the second most important influencer of organic search is the on-page content, followed by the **domain name authority**, web traffic, social media footprint, and the ease of the website registration process (see Figure 8.10). Domain name authority is the extent to which that domain name is considered to be a reputable website in a particular category. Authority comes from good

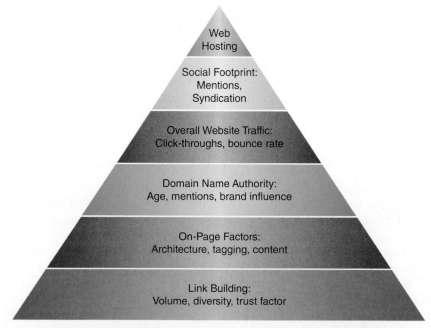

FIGURE **8.10** Organic SEO Influencers (most important influencers at bottom of pyramid)

Source: © Cengage Learning 2013

behavior over time and includes the length of time links have pointed to the site and the overall authority of those sites. For example, universities, charities, and governmental agencies are in general considered to have high authority.[15]

Once the SEO changes are in place according to our suggested process, it is a good idea to register the site with major search engines, especially if the site has never been registered before. Google's "Crawl URL Tool" says, "Google adds new sites to our index, and updates existing ones, every time we crawl the web. If you have a new URL, tell us about it here. We don't add all submitted URLs to our index, and we can't make predictions or guarantees about when or if submitted URLs will appear in our index." In other words, you can submit your site but you may not be added to the index. You can also not submit the site and if it is important as perceived by the search sites, it will still be indexed. It is most important to submit the site to the major search engines but less important to submit to the hundreds of other minor search engines. There are firms which will charge money to do so, but since organic search traffic is concentrated and some of the search sites share information anyway (like Bing and Yahoo!), submitting to hundreds of search sites is unnecessary.

Organic and Paid Search Work Together

Before we move to the discussion of paid search, we would like to discuss the role of paid search in developing an organic search campaign. It is often quite useful to employ a paid search campaign before, after, or during development of an organic search campaign to determine which keywords should be used to optimize the site for paid search. A paid search campaign can be used to finely target terms for an organic search campaign. In other words, it is useful to use paid search terms where the site is not showing up as strongly in the organic search rankings as was hoped. Equally, once the SEO campaign is successful and showing results, the terms for which the site is ranked the highest naturally can be considered as candidates for paid search. Landing page copy can also be used in paid search ads. In any case, the two campaigns should ideally work together. iCrossing found a synergy between paid and natural search. If the keywords purchased by paid search are also ranked in natural search, clicks increased by 92 percent, time on the site increased by 39 percent, and orders increased by 45 percent.[16]

It can legitimately be said that "search is search" and that both types of campaigns should work together.[17] In the prelaunch phase, the keywords can be used to develop a consistent site message. A consistent message and the intelligent use of keywords on the site help improve the quality score during the campaign execution phase. During the reporting and analysis phase, the results of each type of search should be compared and paid keywords should be refined based on input from both the paid and organic search campaigns.

PPC or Paid Search

The paid search process revolves around bidding on keywords that are entered in when a user searches the web. The keywords that are bid on may or may not be the same keywords that are entered into the HTML code in Figure 8.2. The term "keyword" is the same, but the purpose is quite different. In paid search, the company or individual engaged in paid search selects a number of keywords, usually at least 20 for each ad that will then be displayed in the paid search results above or to the right of the organic search results, as shown in Figure 8.6a and b. The hope of the paid search advertiser is that enough searchers will click on the ad to more than make up the cost of paying for the advertisement.

Each keyword will have a separate price that is based on its popularity. Some keywords may be priced out of the range of smaller marketers. Some categories dominated by larger companies, such as insurance, may have keywords on some days that cost over $10 per click. Other categories may, however, appear to be quite cheap and have a minimum bid of 25 cents. On some search engines, the minimum bid will actually be the lowest amount paid. Google, however, may set a higher minimum based on the popularity of the word, and often times the minimum bids suggested in AdWords is not the final minimum bid in the campaign.

In this section, we use Google for our paid search examples because the company is the largest search firm and dominates paid search. Another reason to focus on Google is because the company has a number of programs that benefit undergraduate students hoping to make a career in interactive marketing. However, there are a number of other companies offering paid search, and sites such as Facebook also offer paid search advertisement and have separate tools to manage their campaigns.

Google's tool for placing and managing PPC advertising programs is called Google AdWords. The first of the programs run by Google, which may be of interest to students is a program known as the Google Online Marketing Challenge,[18] which is an international challenge. Students work with real companies or nongovernmental organizations that have never used paid advertising from Google before and receive a $250 advertising budget. Over a three-week period, they work to optimize the PPC campaign of these organizations. The overall winners, who are judged not only by their campaign results but also by pre- and post-campaign reports submitted to Google, get to travel to California to Google headquarters to meet the AdWords team. Google is able to expose its AdWords program to companies that have never used it before, the companies receive some free advertising, and the students earn valuable experience that they can use on their resumes. The second program of interest to undergraduates is the ability to obtain certification in the AdWords tool itself. Individuals may learn about the tool in-depth and take certification exams that will also help them improve their chances of finding and doing well in a job in paid search.[19]

When embarking on a paid search campaign, remember that the steps that we listed for organic search are good steps to follow for paid search in terms of first making sure that you know who your customer is and what they want from the site. These steps are (1) define the target market, (2) find out what they search for, and then (3) develop a search strategy in terms of keywords and phrases. Good keywords for paid search advertising reflect the products/services that are offered, match what the audience is looking for, and target the audience without being too general.

The overall process for a paid search campaign is similar to an organic search strategy, but the execution is different. A good process for paid search campaigns is as follows:

1. Investigate broad search categories and trends.
2. Narrow down keywords.
3. Determine traffic and cost.
4. Select terms and match criteria.
5. Design ads.
6. Run campaigns.
7. Measure and refine.

From the information in the investigative phase, the advertiser narrows its keyword search and determines if it can afford to bid on the most appropriate keywords, adjusting its strategy if necessary. Next, the advertiser can make the final selection of keywords to bid on and must also decide on match types.

TABLE 8.2	Types of Keyword Matches	
Types of Match Terms		**Example**
Broad match: reaches widest audience and not in same sequence		**sale purse = purse sale** and ad will appear
Phrase match: must be in exact sequence, enclosed in quotes		**"pink and purple purses"** in that order will trigger an ad
Exact match: most precise method, enclosed in brackets		**[pink purse]** will trigger an ad but not **pink purse store**
Negative match: uses a minus sign and prevents ads from appearing		**-handbags** and your add will not appear

Source: © Cengage Learning 2013

A **broad match** searches all volumes for that keyword idea, including synonyms and related words, whereas a **phrase match** must include that entire phrase. An **exact match** will return the search volume for that particular keyword, and a **negative match** is a term that you do not want to be considered (see Table 8.2). Another option when developing ad campaigns is to consider the Contextual Targeting Tool, which will also give you ideas of keywords and themes of keywords, as well as ad group names that can run on the Google Display Network. Google has two networks for advertising: the broader Search Network, which includes sites like AOL, CompuServe, and Ask; and the more targeted Display Network with sites like business.com and nytimes.com available for PPC campaigns.

Contextual targeting allows for advertisings on a list of websites that have partnered with a search engine to display its advertising on their site. Contextual advertising, discussed in Chapter 6, is considered a leading-edge Internet advertising tactic because it allows for a more refined targeting of display ads. In Google AdWords, the Contextual Targeting Tool will serve up advertising on particular sites as deemed relevant. For our "pink purses" example, it could be a web page or it could be an email, particularly Gmail in the case of Google, or a discussion group about fashionable purses. PPC ads on Google AdWords are priced on a CPC basis, with the cost determined by the keyword as described previously.

Using the Display Network allows the advertiser to choose specific sites on which to display PPC ads. Choice of sites will be based on the product offered and the characteristics of the target market. For "pink purses," we might choose accessory or other types of shopping sites. Site placement targeting also allows you to pick specific sites or categories that match your products and services and to select matching demographic characteristics of those you would want to see your ad. The pricing for site targeting is based on **CPM**, the **cost-per-thousand** of impressions.

Of course, whether your ad does get served up to users when they put in a particular match term is dependent on cost, how much you actually have bid for that term, and the quality of your ad. Google not only ranks PPC ads by the amount the advertiser is willing to pay for the keyword, but it also includes something called a quality score. In determining the quality score, Google looks at a number of factors such as click-through rates, ad text relevance, past performance, and the landing page. The idea is to create a "fair playing field" where it is not just the amount of money that is bid that determines whether the ad is served and discourage irrelevant advertising.[20]

The next step is then to design ads based on different themes known as ad groups and then test different ads within that group to determine which ones are most effective. An ad group might be handbags or purses, and then

Pink Purse Store   Title limit to 25 characters

Find Pink Purses in All Styles.   Ad limit 70 characters (each line limit 35 characters)

Free Shipping Today!
www.PurseSale.com   URL limit 35 characters

FIGURE **8.11** Sample Advertisement

Source: © Cengage Learning 2013

different types of advertisements could be created for the different types of accessories within that category, such as leather purses, pink purses, tote bags, etc. The quality score will also drop when keywords are not grouped logically together.[21]

Google allows for just three lines for the display ad plus a **display URL**, which may or may not be the same as the actual site URL. In other words, the display URL should reflect ad content and link to the relevant page on the site. A meaningful and descriptive display URL can be used to mask a landing page that has a less descriptive or appealing name. In English, the title may be no longer than 25 characters, the ad text 70 characters, with each line limit of 35 characters and the display URL 35 characters. An effective ad is persuasive, specific, and concise and distinguishes your firm from the competition. A good practice is also to include a call to action, a standard direct marketing best practice to provide an incentive for clicking-through the advertisement. Of course, including the keywords that you have bid on and that the user is searching for in the ad is also a best practice.

The sample ad in Figure 8.11 includes the search term "pink purses" and a call to action—in this case, the offer is free shipping today. It also is indented so that the ad copy on the first line is longer than the second, which has been shown in some studies to increase click-through rate. The URL is also intercapitalized to bring attention to the ad and again increase the click-through rate.

Another technique for increasing click-through rate includes using a **local search** term for ads targeted to geographic areas. Google allows for targeting of ads to countries and regions within them. In the United States, regions can be as small as metropolitan areas, allowing PPC ads to be affordable and relevant to local and regional businesses.

The final step after the ad campaign is run *measurement of the results*. Not only can the advertiser measure on a daily basis how much was spent, the number of clicks or impressions, the click-through rate, the CPC, and other key metrics in AdWords but can also sign up for conversion tracking and measurement. (A conversion is any action a visitor takes on your site that is of value, such as a purchase or a request for information.) In addition, by using Google Analytics an advertiser can also determine how traffic arrived to the site, whether from search engines or other referral sites, and which keywords have been most effective. As is discussed in Chapter 14, larger and sophisticated websites rely on other reporting tools such as the Adobe® SiteCatalyst®, powered by Omniture®, to monitor site traffic, improve conversion rates, and attribute performance to the proper marketing channel.

For PPC, Google AdWords maintains a high market share among both large and small businesses. Estimates of share vary hugely, presumably by the population chosen.[22] There are paid metrics suppliers that offer even more functionality and opportunities for customization and are included in the discussion in Chapter 14. Most larger and sophisticated websites also rely on other reporting tools to monitor site traffic, improve conversion rates, and attribute performance to the proper marketing channel.

INTERACTIVE EXERCISE **8.2**   Google AdWords

Watch the following brief Google AdWords videos and create an AdWords campaign for a specific product/service, including who you will target and ad groups you will use. Write an ad that will be used in the campaign for one of the ad groups.

AdWords Basics in 90 seconds: http://bit.ly/uOHucl.

AdWords: Create Your First Campaign: http://bit.ly/uK0JHA

Simple AdWords Tips for Success: http://bit.ly/rF6AuV.

INTERACTIVE EXERCISE **8.3**   Keyword Search

Use the keyword tool at: http://bit.ly/vbJMVe.

Alternately, create a Google Adwords account and use the keyword tool in that account. What keywords would

you bid on to drive traffic to the site you have decided you would write ads for in the Interactive Exercise 8.2? Why would you choose these keywords?

Specialty Search

Local search continues to be a rapidly growing activity. As early as 2005, one study estimated that 70 percent of U.S. households use the Internet as an information source when they are shopping locally for products or services. Of the over 35 billion unique searches a month in the United States, it is estimated that about 40 percent of these queries have a specific local intent. In addition there are the following trends:[23]

- 5 percent of the searchers use the city and/or state name
- 2 percent use informal terms, like neighborhoods when they search
- A total of 0.5 percent use zip codes on Yahoo!

According to BIA/Kelsey, "This puts the Internet on par with newspapers as a local shopping information resource, with the Internet likely to surpass the impact of newspapers in the very near future."[24] Yahoo! was among the first to offer not only local search, based on the location specified by the user, but also to allow the user to view the search results on a map. Basic listings on Yahoo! Local are free, and they have offered local businesses incentives such as a free website to encourage submission of business listings. That incentive suggests the nature of the problem with local search. Many small businesses are not active on the Internet and encouraging the millions of small firms to become active in ways that directly benefit their business and take advantage of the unique capabilities of the web is a huge task. Many users are also not aware that they can add a zip code or other local identifier to make their search more meaningful.

Optimizing local search is also providing a different challenge for search engine marketers. According to Justin Sanger, founder of an agency specializing in local search, a new type of SEO is emerging. He says it "was born as a result of major search engines Google, Yahoo!, MSN, and others segmenting their local search properties to create distinct local search engines. The major search engines' decision to create distinct local search properties came as a result of an increased understanding of **user intent**. Combining their knowledge of user intent with a basic knowledge of local consumption patterns, the engines created unique local search results based on algorithms tailored for local search."[25] The search engines have templates so local businesses can provide the necessary information easily. The search engines operate in such as way as to also encourage user creation of content including ratings of businesses and comments. The ultimate objective is to give local search a rich content base that attracts business and searchers alike. It will provide a new challenge to marketing services providers, most of whom practice the traditional types of SEM and SEO described earlier in the chapter.

Local search growth is also fueled by the growth of *mobile search*. Mobile searches are primarily going to pull their results from local search engines. BIA/Kelsey predicts mobile local search advertising revenues alone will reach $1.3 billion in 2013[26] and Efficient Frontier predicts that by the end of 2011 "somewhere between 7.0%–9.5% of search advertising dollars could be spent on mobile devices."[27] Of the mobile searches that are conducted, about 30 to 35 percent also have local intent. There are approximately 54.5 million mobile Internet users in the United States (or about 25 percent of online users) and approximately 15 percent of iPhone applications are local. Local search and mobile search will continue to grow hand-in-hand for the foreseeable future.

The mobile search market will continue to experience growing pains as marketers adjust their marketing techniques to this new medium. Mobile searches experience a 30 percent lower click-through rate than searches performed on desktop computers, with a 13 percent higher CPC and usually a lower ROI than searches made from a desktop. Marketers must learn to optimize their web pages and their search capabilities for the mobile market. Efficient Frontier also reports that specific vertical markets will benefit from mobile, including restaurants, autos, consumer electronics, finance, insurance, beauty, and personal. Companies such as Foursquare that provide searches and special offers related to local markets will also play a role in the expansion of local search.

Vertical search is another type of specialty search. According to the *San Francisco Chronicle*, "By going vertical, search engine companies hope to reduce extraneous results for users by better guessing user intent. A query for 'great white'—the name for an '80s rock band and a shark species—can get very different results on Google compared with an engine that specializes in academic material. In other words, if you are on the academic search engine, you are going to get the listings for the shark species, not the rock band. The specialty search engine attempts to narrow the user intent. The user went to the academic search engine with a purpose—or so the search engine assumes.

Vertical search engines also can ask questions more quickly. Shopping search engines, for example, can ask up front the color, size and manufacturer of what you want to buy."[28] Some of the other types of search engines are as follows:

- Topical search: such as worldwidescience.org, WebMD
- Industry search: such as business.com, chemindustry.com
- Image search: such as Picsearch, Yahoo! Image Search
- News search: such as NewsNow, onlinenewspapers.com
- Blog search: such as Technorati, blog-search.com
- Books and articles search: such as Google Scholar
- Social real-time search: such as Twitter Search

It is not hard to see that vertical search engines have sprung up all over the place. There are search engines devoted to travel and others devoted to shopping, as only a few examples. The major search engines also allow for searching on images, videos, and places, among other topics. There are other types of search being introduced into the Internet marketspace and as long as vertical search engines can meet the need for relevant search results, the market will continue to grow. YouTube as a stand-alone company from Google is the second largest search engine in the world.

The Relationship between Search and Social Media

This chapter would not be complete without a few more words about the integration of search and social media. Social media continues to capture the interest of search marketers, as shown in Figure 8.12, and for good reason. Search marketers are expanding their use of social media by driving inbound links from social media forums, expanding their profiles on social media accounts, and monitoring social media conversations to influence SEO. Marketers want to be where their consumers are and to participate in the conversation to engage and retain those customers. A study by business.com and BtoBOnline in 2010 indicated that the best performing companies in a survey of 464 business-to-business (B2B) online marketers were using social media to enhance their natural search efforts. Enhancement for these firms was accomplished by expanding the profiles on social media accounts, monitoring social media conversations to influence SEO, and driving inbound links via various social media outlets. Increasing the number of social media followers and encouraging them to share your content in all channels will also impact search rankings.[29]

Monitoring social media conversations is another great way to determine how to pick appropriate keywords to monitor both paid search and SEO. Using tools such as Radian6 and Alterian's SM2 marketers can see what and how customers and prospects are talking about it across the social web and develop search marketing campaigns based on this input. Google's social search capability means that searches you conduct while signed into Google will highlight relevant content from your social connections, including websites, blogs, images, and other contacts created by or shared by your social connections. Web content that has been recommended using the +1 button in Google plus will also be highlighted. Other search engines have or will have adopted a similar strategy regarding integrating social media "likes" into organic search results. Since marketers know that consumers trust recommendations of friends more than those of advertisers, the future will bring about an even greater integration between search and social media. Another related trend will be the integration of display advertising into the results of search campaigns.

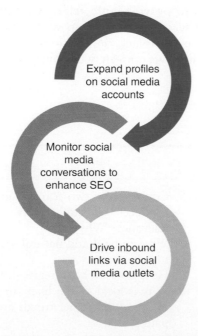

FIGURE **8.12** Use Social Media to Enhance SEO

Source: © Cengage Learning 2013

SUMMARY

Search is a key focus of Internet marketers at present. Other customer acquisition techniques, however, continue to evolve and remain an important part of the marketer's toolkit. Since the size of the web increases by many pages each day, the importance of search to users, B2C and B2B alike, can hardly be overstated. Because it is important to Internet users, marketers and advertisers are close behind. While search has a growing impact and can be confusing for marketers to understand, the basic concept is simple.

Search engines send out spiders or crawlers that look at websites and categorize them to create indices that are used in specific search queries. The marketer needs to think about what words its customers or prospects use when trying to find a product or service. There are a number of free tools that can be used to develop these keywords. Relevant keywords can be then used in both organic and paid search. Organic search is sometimes called natural search or algorithmic search, as it depends on algorithms that are developed by commercial search engines to find the most relevant web pages to display as the result of a search query.

In organic search, the relevant keywords are used in the title bar of a website and the website content to raise the ranking of the page as the result of a query. Other techniques to achieve this objective include links from and to the page and the overall authority the page commands.

In paid search, the advertiser bids on relevant keywords to gets its advertisements displayed in the top or near the top of the paid advertisements. The bidding processes can be complicated, and there are many tools to help determine which keywords to bid on and how much to pay. Organic and paid search can work together as the paid search campaign can inform the selection of organic keywords and there is evidence that having a high paid ranking can encourage more click-throughs overall.

The search process as a whole is iterative and is "never done" as the search engines are constantly updating their algorithms and the bidding for keywords changes daily, if not hourly. The field offers a good opportunity for employment and a steady prospect for growth as new aspects of search are developed.

You can expect two levels of change that affects SEM in the years to come. At a granular level, the search engines themselves will continue to tweak their algorithms to provide more relevant results. Search engine marketers will continue to scramble to keep up with those changes. At the level of the overall search marketplace, innovations like vertical, local, social, mobile search, and others yet unseen will continue to proliferate for years to come.

DISCUSSION QUESTIONS

1. Why do you think search has become such an important part of the life of Internet users?
2. What options do marketers have when it comes to developing a search marketing strategy?
3. What are the most impactful elements of a website in terms of optimizing a site for organic search?
4. How come the major search engines do not publish their algorithms?
5. Compare the two searches in Figure 8.6. Which produces the better results in terms of quality and relevance? Why?
6. Why do paid and natural search work so well together?
7. How do search strategies differ for mobile devices?
8. Why is local search likely to be important in the future? What other trends are likely in organic and paid search?

INTERNET EXERCISES

1. Internet Career Builder Exercise
   a. There are a number of resources for search engine marketing and the jobs are expected to continue to grow at double-digit rates, outpacing the rest of the economy.[30]

      Search engine marketing analyst

      SEO manager

      Marketing specialist, paid search

      Search marketing coordinator

      Search marketing also may be included in Internet analyst or other online marketing positions

   b. Select search job title from the list above or from your own search. Outline the responsibilities of that position. You may find it useful to locate job postings on the web in order to understand the job requirements.
   c. Outline knowledge and experience from classes, internships, full- or part-time jobs, and volunteer work that prepare you for this specific position.
   d. Update your VISUALCV® or LinkedIn profile with this information.

2. Choose a well-known branded product with which you are familiar.
   a. Brainstorm and identify at least 10 keywords that a person might use to search for the product or the brand.
   b. Search for the product on at least two different search engines.
      • What is the product's position in natural search?
      • What is its position in paid search?
   c. Use the Google Adwords' keyword tool[31] to learn how good your keyword choices were. Were there others that should have been in your top 10?
   d. What recommendations would you have for the managers of the product to help them improve their organic search rankings on the search engines you studied?

3. Using the branded product above, imagine that you have the opportunity to market that product through paid search. Select keywords and develop at least two different ad groups with two different ads underneath them. Design two ads and discuss in class which might be most effective.

NOTES

1. Deborah Fallows and Lee Rainie, "The Popularity and Importance of Search Engines," August 2004, http://www.pewinternet.org.
2. http://searchmarketingcommunications.com/2010/02/11/u-s-searches-per-capita-per-month-spcpm, retrieved September 24, 2011.
3. http://www.pewinternet.org/Reports/2011/Search-and-email/Report.aspx, retrieved September 24, 2011.
4. SEMPO, "The State of Search Engine Marketing 2004," http://www.sempo.org.
5. http://econsultancy.com/us/blog/7447-sempo-study-us-search-spending-nears-20-billion, retrieved October 5, 2011.
6. http://www.ecommerceoptimization.com/local-business-listing-guide.
7. http://dmoz.org.
8. http://www.sempo.org/?page=glossary#s.
9. SEMPO, "The State of Search Engine Marketing 2004," http://www.sempo.org, 4.
10. Forrester titled, "How Consumers Find Websites in 2011—Trends to Consider for Your 2011 Strategy, Shar VanBoskirk, as quoted in http://www.marqui.com/blog/how-do-consumers-find-websites-in-2011.aspx.
11. http://www.beanstalk-inc.com/tactics/black-hat.htm.
12. http://www.icrossing.com/our_work/?casestudy=coca-cola, retrieved October 9, 2011.
13. https://adwords.google.com/o/Targeting/Explorer?__u=1000000000&__c=1000000000&ideaRequestType=KEYWORD_IDEAS#search.none, retrieved October 9, 2011.
14. http://www.nytimes.com/2011/02/13/business/13search.html?_r=3&pagewanted=all, retrieved October 9, 2011.
15. http://searchenginewatch.com/article/2064461/SEO-Link-Building-The-Domain-Authority-Factor, retrieved October 29, 2011.
16. http://www.scribd.com/doc/2235975/icrossing-search-synergy.
17. http://searchenginewatch.com/article/2067308/Search-is-Search-Paid-and-Organic-Search-Synergies, retrieved October 29, 2011.
18. http://www.google.com/onlinechallenge.
19. http://www.google.com/adwords/professionals/individual.html.
20. http://adwords.google.com/support/aw/bin/answer.py?hl=en&answer=10215, retrieved October 29, 2011.
21. http://www.thewebmasterscafe.net/ppc/adwords-keyword-grouper.html, retrieved October 29, 2011.
22. http://www.quora.com/What-is-Google-Analytics-market-share-relative-to-WebTrends-Omniture-CoreMetrics-etc; and http://w3techs.com/technologies/details/ta-googleanalytics/all/all, retrieved October 26, 2011.

23. http://semwinners.com/323/online-local-search-trends-2010/2010/03, retrieved October 10, 2011.

24. "New Research by The Kelsey Group and ConStat Indicates 70% of U.S. Households Now Use the Internet When Shopping Locally for Products and Services," March 22, 2005, http://www.kelseygroup.com/press/pr050322.htm.

25. Justin Sanger, "A New Form of Local Search Optimization, Part I" July 7, 2005, http://www.clickz.com/experts/search/local_search/article.php/3517776.

26. "BIA/Kelsey Forecasts U.S. Mobile Local Search Advertising Revenues to Reach $1.3B in 2013," http://www.biakelsey.com/Company/Press-Releases/090224-U.S.-Mobile-Local-Search-Advertising-Revenues-to-Reach-$1.3B-in-2013.asp, retrieved October 10, 2011.

27. "The growth of mobile search: huge in numbers, not in CTR (research)," http://www.stateofsearch.com/the-growth-of-mobile-search-huge-in-numbers-not-in-ctr-research, retrieved October 10, 2011.

28. Verne Kopytoff, "New Search Engines Narrowing their Focus," April 4, 2005, http://www.sfgate.com/cgi-bin/article.cgi?file=/c/a/2005/04/04/BUGJ9C20VU1.DTL&type=printable.

29. http://img.en25.com/Web/BusinessCom/Search%20and%20%20Social%20Integration_2921.pdf?elqIsAgent=True%2cTrue, retrieved November 21, 2011.

30. http://tchat.universityalliance.com/media/chatv2/Default.aspx?SessionID=13416607&GUID={A9A16831-F219-48C2-8517-E3C85817C4DA}&CURL=http%3a%2f%2fwww.usanfranonline.com%, retrieved October 6, 2011.

31. https://adwords.google.com/o/Targeting/Explorer?__u=1000000000&__c=1000000000&ideaRequestType=KEYWORD_IDEAS#search.none.

CHAPTER 9

Social Media Marketing

LEARNING OBJECTIVES

By the time you complete this chapter, you will be able to:

- Define social media marketing.

- Explain why marketers find it necessary to engage in social media marketing.

- Explain why social media marketing is not free.

- Describe the ways in which marketer communications are different in social media from those in traditional mass media and online marketing.

- Identify the elements of a social media marketing strategy.

- Explain what it means to build a community around a brand.

- Discuss the differences among paid, owned, earned, and shared media.

- Identify metrics that can be used to measure the success of social media marketing campaigns.

- Understand how to build your own personal brand in Internet space.

- Discuss the potential of location-based marketing.

The Explosion of Social Network Use

Every day people across the globe—both at home and at work—log on to social networks and blogs. Nielsen finds that three-fourth of all people online visit a social site at some time. There are over 1.5 billion people online worldwide,[1] so that equates to 1.125 billion people using social sites.

They do not just visit social sites; they spend an average of 22 percent of their online time on these sites, an increase of 24 percent in a single year. Facebook is only the third largest global brand in terms of share of people visiting the site with 54 percent, but it tops all others in time spent—a whopping 6 hours per person per year. As you might expect, Google tops all other sites in visitor share.

Brazil has the largest percentage of active users who visit social sites—86 percent. Each spends just over 5 hours per year. Australia, with 72 percent of its Internet users visiting social sites, sees those users spending over 7 hours and 19 minutes on them each year.[2]

Social media has become a global phenomenon, but as these statistics suggest, there are wide variances on the amount and nature of use in different parts of the world. The world map in Figure 9.1 shows that change is the norm in the social media space. Facebook alone had over 500 million users worldwide by late 2010, with 50 percent of them logging onto Facebook on any given day.[3] Most students have a Facebook page, so its popularity and widespread use are no surprise. However, are there some of the large sites in Figure 9.1 that you do not recognize? Probably so. Some are specialized B2B sites. Others are popular in some countries, but not in others. For example, Orkut, Google's social network site, has never taken off in the United States but is wildly popular in countries such as Brazil and India. After all, most of us as individuals use only a few of the many platforms out there, but the social media marketer must have a wide knowledge of the resources available.

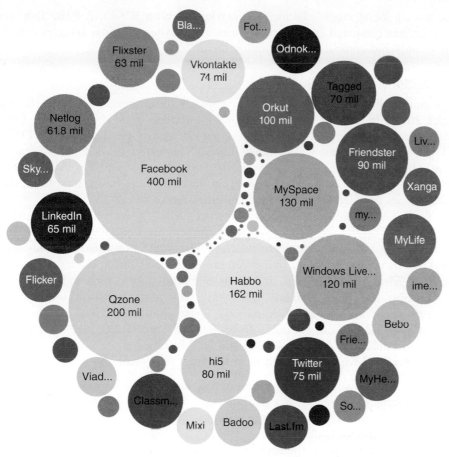

FIGURE **9.1** Number of Subscribers to Various Social Media Platforms

Source: Courtesy of International Business Machines Corporation, © International Business Machines Corporation.

Marketers "Follow the Eyeballs"

There is an old advertising maxim that says marketers must "follow the eyeballs." In other words, where their customers go for information and entertainment, marketers must follow. That necessity has prompted an explosion in

INTERACTIVE EXERCISE **9.1**   Social Media Map

Visit the interactive version at http://bit.ly/twKsqB.

This site shows a map of social media sites organized by categories that range from social networks to Twitter tools to social wikis. By including Wikipedia it gives evidence of a broad definition of social media. Some people argue, for example, that Wikipedia is an encyclopedia, not a social site. It is a collaborative encyclopedia; doesn't that make it a social site? Acquaint yourself with the diversity of social media sites by downloading the interactive version of the map and clicking through on some categories or sites that you are not familiar with.

the use of social media channels by marketers, both B2C and B2B. This new practice has presented both opportunities and challenges for marketers and for the brands and companies that employ them.

Old Spice Generates Buzz

The most talked-about social media campaign of summer 2010 was the Old Spice effort. It featured former *National Football League* (NFL) player Isaiah Mustafa, who debuted as brand spokesperson in a Super Bowl 2010 TV ad, "The Man Your Man Could Smell Like." The video quickly went viral on YouTube. In just two weeks following the Super Bowl, it had 1.6 million views. By fall, it was still going strong, closing in on 22 million views. In spring 2011, a new series of videos was launched, another sign of success.[4]

So far, this sounds like normal practice, right? Most national advertisers put their ads on the web. However, most of them are not compelling enough to be shared by users, making them go viral. The Old Spice video not only went viral but also spawned about two dozen more videos featuring the hunky spokesperson.[5] Most have achieved only 2 or 3 million views, although one called "Questions" had over 16 million in early fall. This particular social media breakthrough came in July 2010 when Old Spice announced that for two days Mustafa would answer questions from the Old Spice Facebook, Twitter, and Reddit communities.[6] Between July 14 and 16, Mustafa and the Wieden + Kennedy agency produced what has to be a record amount of content and traffic:

- Over 180 personalized videos responding to audience requests and questions. He made a voice mail message for one fan but turned down Alyssa Milano's marriage proposal.
- Over 5.9 million video views.
- 22,500 comments on the social networks.
- Number of subscribers to the Old Space YouTube channel increased to 120,000.
- Number of Facebook fans increased to 616,000.[7]

On July 16, Mustafa declared victory[8] and presumably hung up his towel, ending the questions phase of the overall campaign.

All this activity represents a tremendous creative accomplishment, but it begs the ultimate marketing question: did it increase sales? According to a Procter & Gamble representative, it did. "'Since the 'Smell Like A Man, Man' campaign broke in February, Old Spice has month-over-month strengthened its market position,' said (Michael) Norton in an email. He added that Old Spice is now the No. 1 brand of body wash and anti-perspirant/deodorant in both sales and volume with growth in the high single/double digits." Nielsen data appeared to confirm this corporate statement, although it is hard to separate what the impact was of a two-day social media campaign out of a long-term brand campaign in multiple media.[9] However, it is clear that social media marketers and technical experts worked closely together to make this campaign successful.[10] Whether they used additional technology like seeding[11] is unclear.

Cisco Fails Miserably

Social media marketers were paying attention to the Old Spice phenomenon. About a week later, Cisco launched its own version, "Ted from Accounting." This was supposed to be a tongue-in-cheek parody of the Old Spice Campaign, featuring an appropriately geeky accountant. According to Meagan O'Neill from the Social Times blog,[12] a Cisco blog post with a marketer video explaining the concept was posted in the morning. Cisco employees then Retweeted from several accounts during the day. In the afternoon the central video, "Who Is Ted from Accounting?" was posted. While the central video is amusing, as of fall 2010, it had received just under 10,500 views. What

INTERACTIVE EXERCISE 9.2   Doing What Cisco Does Well

Cisco has been using interactive media for many years to reach out to, to communicate with, and to collaborate with the IT engineers and technicians who make up its customer base. In March 2008, the company launched a new series of routers, entirely in social media. It began with an optimized press release[13] that announced the product line and linked to files, videos, and at least one podcast. Visit http://bit.ly/v33Prr, as it shows some of the content of that press release including links to content on other platforms.

The launch event was held in Second Life and was attended by 9,000 people. That is 90 *times* the number that usually attends a traditional product launch. Cisco invented a "transporter" for their audience to play with in Second Life. It also offered a widget that pushed content about the router to the customer's desktop. Visit

http://bit.ly/sFTl4r

and

http://bit.ly/swzPK4.

Cisco executives attended the one-hour launch event by video conference at corporate headquarters instead of flying to a physical location with the attendant expenditure of time, money, and effort. All indications were that they were pleased. They could not only see the presentation, but they could also see the audience in Second Life.

The virtual launch generated 3 times the usual number of articles in the trade press and over 1,000 blog posts. Over 40 million online impressions were achieved. The virtual launch achieved great reach, at the same time it cost about one-sixth the cost of a traditional, physical world, product launch—which represents a savings of about $100,000 on a single marketing effort![14]

went wrong? O'Neill says there was little Twitter activity. She suggests the following reasons:

- There was no buildup to the campaign. They just dropped in on an unsuspecting (and uncaring) public on launch day. It takes work to create buzz in anticipation of an event. Cisco did not do the groundwork necessary.
- They ran the Twitter from various existing Cisco accounts instead of using a dedicated brand or campaign account. They tried to tie it all together with a hashtag, #CiscoSPice, but it was not effective.
- They copied the "man in a towel in a bathroom" theme. That works for a body wash and fragrance collection. What does it have to do with a router? What is the appeal to an audience of engineers?

It is also an advertising maxim that copycat campaigns rarely work. In this case, both the concept and the execution were flawed, so it never had a chance—a rare failure from a company that usually does both well.

Record-Setting Fund-Raising in Social Media

On October 14, 2010, tech entrepreneur Dave Morin posted a "birthday wish" to raise money for the Benioff Children's Hospital in San Francisco on his Causes page (see his post at www.causes.com/posts/564977). This former Facebook employee and start-up CEO announced his donation goal as $10,000 for the hospital by the holiday season.[15] Instead, he raised $10,000 in a single day, with several more thousand dollars coming in after that day.[16]

Morin is hardly a novice to the Causes platform. It was the personal philanthropy platform used by Facebook, which now also operates a stand-alone website. Morin himself had done two previous birthday wish fund-raising projects. In addition, one can assume that he has numerous friends on Facebook, LinkedIn, and other platforms that can be invited to contribute. Morin's professional skills aside, the growing number of social fund-raising sites represents another aspect of the exploding social network scene.

Notice that the three successful campaigns mentioned have both skilled practitioners and a clear objective. It is also reasonable to assume that they had objectives and had identified success metrics in advance. We will discuss both

those subjects in more detail later in the chapter, but it is important to recognize social media marketing as a carefully planned and executed marketing activity, not as a bunch of people having fun posting on Facebook and Tweeting about whatever comes to mind.

What Is Social Media Marketing?

There are definitions of social media marketing (SSM) on the web, but they all seem to have a heavy emphasis on platforms. That is understandable. In the mid-1990s, when many companies were struggling to learn to use electronic media for marketing purposes, the question often heard was, "Should we have a website?" Fifteen years later the answer is a given, and there are many websites that provide excellent customer experiences, whether the customer goal is information or a purchase. Fast-forward to what is still the infancy of SMM and the question is often, "Should we have a Facebook page?" The implication is often, "Our competitors have one; maybe we should also."

The answer is that an organization—whether a B2C or B2B commercial enterprise or a nonprofit—should not have any branded social media platform without a clear purpose. A formal objective is better. There also needs to be a clear understanding of where social media marketing fits into the overall marketing communications strategy and activities of the firm.

In other words, SMM needs to be as carefully planned and executed as any other marketing activity. The choice of platform should be the *last step*, not the first. With that in mind we can attempt a definition of SMM:

> Social media marketing is business use of selected social media channels to understand customers and to engage them in communication and collaboration in ways that lead to the achievement of ultimate marketing and business goals.

Which Businesses Use Social Media Marketing?

The examples earlier in this chapter provide evidence that all types of businesses, including nonprofits, are using SMM to achieve business objectives. Still, not all businesses are adopting SMM with equal enthusiasm.

Figure 9.2 shows something of a mixed picture. According to *eMarketer*, many more B2B marketers (45 percent) have a social media presence but do no

Level of Social Media Marketing Engagement by U.S. B2B vs. B2C Marketers, March 2010
(% of respondents)

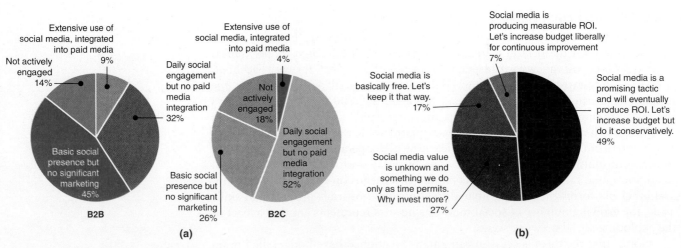

FIGURE **9.2** Adoption of SMM

Sources: eMarketer, Inc., May 27, 2010; and MarketingSherpa 2010 Social Media Marketing Benchmark Report, p. 31.

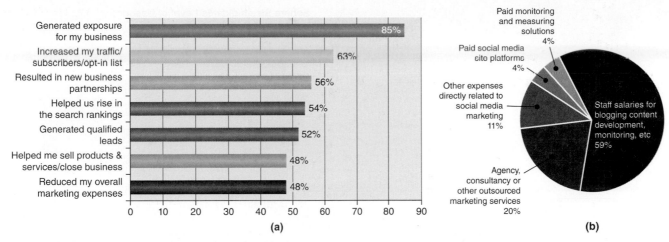

FIGURE **9.3** Benefits and Costs of Social Media Marketing

Sources: 2010 Social Media Marketing Industry Report, Michael E. Stelzner, p. 15; and MarketingSherpa 2010 Social Media Marketing Benchmark Report, p. 44.

more significant SMM than B2C marketers (26 percent). In other words, they have accounts on sites such as Facebook or Twitter, but do no significant marketing there. At the same time, more B2B than B2C firms make extensive use of SMM and integrate it into paid media campaigns. The depth of SMM use by a small percentage of B2B firms can probably be traced to their successful use in generating high-quality sales leads.[17]

MarketingSherpa's Benchmark Report emphasizes marketer focus on payback on the SMM investment and the widespread conviction that return on investment (ROI) is uncertain and is hard to measure. Consider the earlier examples. Many social media metrics are used to tout success. Even the spokesperson for P&G could only say that sales increased while the Old Spice campaign was active. He could not, or would not, give a direct link among traditional broadcast advertising, much less social media, and increased sales.

Users are convinced that SMM increases their visibility and, in the process, brings more visitors to companies' websites (see Figure 9.3). SMM helps firms generate qualified sales leads and increases their search engine rankings. SMM contributes to search engine visibility in a number of ways but the most straightforward is generating incoming links. Well-written SMM content includes multiple links to product information on the company website or blog (which is, in turn, linked to the website) and incoming links is one input to search engine rank.

A popular misconception is that SMM is free. True, most of the popular social platforms offer free services. However, even pages on popular sites such as Facebook and Twitter can be customized, often at substantial cost. By far the greatest cost, though, is staff time to perform the myriad of tasks associated with effective SMM. Social media marketing is not free!

Figure 9.4 sheds interesting light on that statement. Look at these highly effective platforms. They include the social networks themselves, microblogging (e.g., Twitter), blogging, and sharing content across communications channels. Blogging requires a lot of effort. Blogger relations require the greatest level of effort. It takes a lot of work to identify influential bloggers, often in terms of a specific product category, and to reach out to them in an effort to get them to write about products or services. When the blogger relations effort is successful, however, it results in communications from third parties who are often viewed as highly trustworthy. That is true even though ethical bloggers are careful to reveal payments and gifts of any kind. In fact, in the United States they are required to do so.[18]

Marketers are beginning to use SMM, although many are new to it and most still lack confidence in its effectiveness. With that in mind, there are two other ways in which social networks are being used that deserve mention.

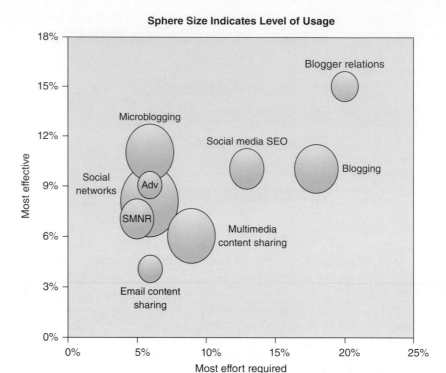

Sphere Size Indicates Level of Usage

FIGURE **9.4** SMM Platforms by Effectiveness and Effort
Source: MarketingSherpa.

The Use of SMM by Small Businesses

It should come as no surprise that small businesses are interested in the opportunities offered by SMM. The traditional broadcast and print media have always presented obstacles to use by small businesses. They are expensive and they often have a wide reach, not the local audience that many small businesses need. The free social networks consequently have great appeal and small businesses are beginning to make use of them.

eMarketer reported in September 2010 that about one quarter of all small business are now using social media, although the increase in participation seems to have plateaued.[19] A recent study by the American Express OPEN credit card finds that small businesses that use social media report that SMM increases exposure and website traffic. It is also important in retention of current customers (see Figure 9.5). A significant minority does not, however, see any value from social media use. The potential for the small business, whose market is presumably local, is highlighted in this quote:

> For business owners, social media ultimately should be a two-way street. It's about business owners connecting with customers and customers connecting with businesses," said Susan Sobbott, president of American Express OPEN, in a statement. "More than 10% of consumers we surveyed reported posting a review of a small business through social media channels such as Facebook, Twitter or LinkedIn, and of these posts, two-thirds say the reviews have been positive.[20]

The point about consumer reviews is especially important. Study after study has indicated that managers are worried about engaging in social media activities because they are afraid customers will say bad things about their product or service. Social media marketers respond with two crucial points:

1. The majority of reviews posted are positive.[21] Why? There is some element of wanting to compliment people or products that are doing a good job. The reason that generally comes through, however, is that shoppers want to be helpful to other shoppers.

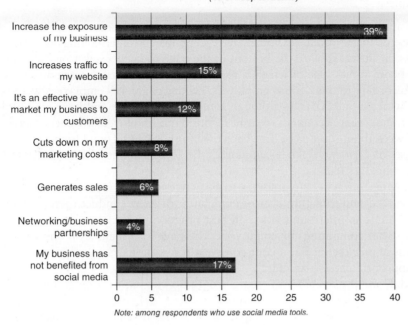

**Leading Benefits of Using Social Media Tools
According to U.S. Small Business, Sep 2010**
(% of respondents)

Increase the exposure of my business — 39%
Increases traffic to my website — 15%
It's an effective way to market my business to customers — 12%
Cuts down on my marketing costs — 8%
Generates sales — 6%
Networking/business partnerships — 4%
My business has not benefited from social media — 17%

Note: among respondents who use social media tools.

FIGURE **9.5** Small Business Accomplishments with SMM
Source: *eMarketer*, October 18, 2010.

2. If there are people saying unfavorable things, shouldn't the business know it? Only by knowing what is being said (listening!) can the business solve customer problems (the most common requirement) or, occasionally, replace misinformation with correct information.

Careful monitoring of all customer posts is especially important for the small business that relies heavily on word-of-mouth recommendations. You might say that word of mouth is in the process of becoming "web of mouth."

In spite of the popularity of SMM with businesses, large and small, it is important to note that across all age groups, email is still the preferred means of communication, although the margin appears to decrease with every new study. Email is the preference of older age groups[22] while millennials prefer text messaging and short message service (SMS) to email.[23] It is really not an either/or question, however. The important marketing skill is using email to leverage communication in social networks, not choosing one communications channel over the other. Small businesses, in particular, find both communications channels within their reach.

Using Social Media to Engage and Motivate Employees

The second issue is internal use of social media. This represents use of social channels in an attempt to create employee engagement and motivation. While it is admittedly a human relations issue more than a marketing one, it is worth mentioning briefly here for two reasons:

1. The expertise for this type of communication currently seems to reside primarily in the marketing department.
2. Social media use is blurring the lines among traditional business functions. Consider the Cisco press release in which many of the SMM product launch marketing efforts were featured. This sort of optimized press release also uses the same set of techniques to create visibility[24] that are used by marketers.

The ways that enterprises use social media to engage and motivate employees are as many and as varied as the firms themselves. Consider just a few examples:

- Zappos has generated a great deal of buzz in recent years for its wide ranging use of social media. Its home page[25] contains customer comments about its products. Toward the bottom of the page there is a link to its statement of core values, one of which is to encourage employees to learn and grow. According to the Zappos employees Twitter page, 499 employees were on Twitter in fall 2010[26]—although some are very active and have many followers, other accounts appear to be dormant. Employees are encouraged to Tweet about subjects of their choice.[27] Zappos CEO Tony Hsieh is an avid user of Twitter.[28] Like his employees, he Tweets about both business and personal issues.
- IBM encourages its employees to be active in social media and provides a detailed and thoughtful set of guidelines for their conduct there.[29] The page includes an interesting video on best practices in social media use (they call it social computing) by employees. The page also includes a link to report abuse in these media, a common way of asking users to help monitor the appropriateness of content.
- McDonald's has a social media program aimed at making employees feel good about it.[30] It has its own site[31] where McDonald's crew members from all over the globe can participate in activities that include exchanging ideas, playing games, and winning prizes.

A recent study suggests that activities such as these can be effective in engaging employees. According to the Melcrum study, the greatest benefits perceived by firms that use social media internally are:

- Improved employee engagement: 71%
- Improved internal collaboration: 59%
- Creating two-way dialogue with senior executives: 47%[32]

Developing a Social Media Marketing Strategy

We cannot say it too often: Good SMM results from a carefully planned strategy, not from a series of random activities. It must also be carefully integrated into the firm's overall marketing communications strategy and activities, as case histories throughout this chapter emphasize. The first question we ask should be, "How does a business go about developing a social media marketing strategy?"

Although different authors use different terminology, there is general agreement on the steps needed to develop an SMM strategy (see Figure 9.6). Following this process leads to a deeper relationship with the customer. That kind of relationship takes time and effort—an upfront investment, if you will—but the end result is well worth the effort. Let us take a brief look at each of the steps.

Listening to the Target Audience

Whether they are your customers or whether they are people you want to attract as customers (prospects), the marketer must listen before she speaks. A good way to think of it is the way in which a socially savvy individual behaves at a party. He does not just walk up to a group of people and start talking. He listens to the content and tone of the conversation before joining in. That is exactly what savvy marketers do in the initial stages of developing an SMM strategy.

Marketers must first identify the social habitats of their defined target market. For example, young males can be found in large numbers on gaming sites

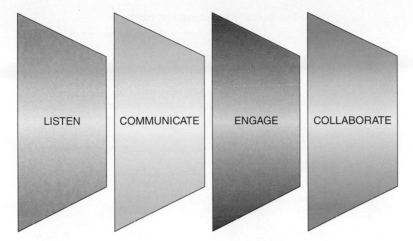

FIGURE **9.6** Steps in Developing a Social Media Marketing Strategy

Source: Adapted from Jeremiah Owyang, "Social Media Marketing," Awareness, Inc. Webinars, http://www.awarenessnetworks.com/learning/webinars, December 9, 2008.

and young mothers have an extensive system of "mommy blogs" that traffic in everything from coupons to parenting advice. Both women and men are sports fans these days and can be found on league and sports commentary sites. The list could go on and on, but it is important to realize that the key issue is lifestyle and interests, not demographics *per se.*

It is also important to pay attention to what people do when they are visiting social sites. Here we are also using a broad definition of any site that allows inter-activity (e.g., product reviews), not just the social networks. Forrester Research has been conducting research on that subject for several years; they call it the Social Technographics® Ladder (see Figure 9.7).

First you should note that people can be a member of various categories over time and for various reasons, so the numbers add to much more than 100 per-cent. Notice, though, that there are not many people who classified themselves as totally inactive in 2010. There are, however, huge numbers of people who can be best described as consuming content or simply joining sites; but they do not con-tribute. There are a substantial number of people in the critics category, driven by the desire to post product and service ratings and reviews online. Likewise, there are numerous conversationalists who socialize online. There are relatively few collectors, but those are people who carefully search the web for content and aggregate it on third-party sites or on their own websites. The proportion of creators is even smaller. These are the influentials of the social web, the people who create and distribute content. Forrester points out that this group has pla-teaued between 2009 and 2010, while the proportion of joiners continues to increase.[33] Forrester offers an online tool to help marketers evaluate the techno-graphics of their chosen target audience (see it at www.forrester.com/empowered/tool_consumer.html).[34] Go online and give it a try!

Listening Tools

It is a big web out there; how can a business possibly keep track of what people are saying about it on the Internet? There are tools to track it, the best known of which is undoubtedly Google Alerts. It is free and easy to turn on and off.[35] As part of their personal branding program (discussed at the end of the chapter), many people have an alert on their names; it is nice to know who is saying what about you! Do you have a research paper assignment this semester? Consider setting up an alert for news on the subject. This alert system will give you links to current content, but it will not research past events for you. *Hint:* be sure to check what types of Internet content is acceptable for your assignment in a particular course. While you are on the Google Alerts page, note that there are examples of how Google

The Social Techonograhics* ladder

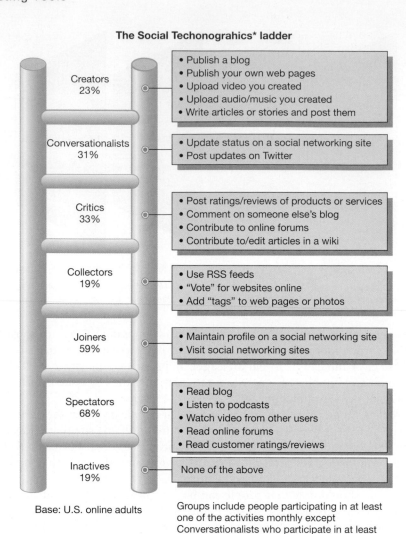

Creators 23%	• Publish a blog • Publish your own web pages • Upload video you created • Upload audio/music you created • Write articles or stories and post them
Conversationalists 31%	• Update status on a social networking site • Post updates on Twitter
Critics 33%	• Post ratings/reviews of products or services • Comment on someone else's blog • Contribute to online forums • Contribute to/edit articles in a wiki
Collectors 19%	• Use RSS feeds • "Vote" for websites online • Add "tags" to web pages or photos
Joiners 59%	• Maintain profile on a social networking site • Visit social networking sites
Spectators 68%	• Read blog • Listen to podcasts • Watch video from other users • Read online forums • Read customer ratings/reviews
Inactives 19%	None of the above

Base: U.S. online adults

Groups include people participating in at least one of the activities monthly except Conversationalists who participate in at least one of the included activities at least weekly.

FIGURE **9.7** Forrester's Social Technographics®

Source: Forrester Research, Inc., The Latest Global Social Media Trends May Surprise You (Jackie Rousseau-Anderson), September 2010 http://blogs.forrester.com/jackie_rousseau_anderson/10-09-28-latest_global_social_media_trends_may_surprise_you.

Alerts works—which are straightforward but helpful to the novice user. For most of its other products, Google offers one or more videos giving detailed instructions on how to use the product effectively. That is definitely an Internet best practice!

One recent list of best reputation monitoring tools[36] has eight tools, including Addictomatic, which allows the user to create a custom page on any subject of his choice; HowSociable? which creates a brand visibility rating based on 32 different metrics; and Trackur, which is a paid reputation monitoring tool that offers a user-friendly dashboard. This list includes tools that are either free or low cost. There are also social media metrics platforms that include listening tools that will be discussed in the metrics section.

Communicating with Your Audience in Social Space

This one is easy, right? After all, communicating is what marketers do! The problem is that both the landscape and the rules of the road change in social media. It is no longer a one-marketer to many-audience-members type of communication. It is many-to-many. Even more difficult, marketers no longer establish the rules of communication. Audience members do.

Seven Behaviors

Embrace and Navigate the Complexity	• Identify and understand the landscape/audiences
Listen with Intelligence	• Conduct comprehensive research
Participate in the Conversation	• Find, listen, and join the conversations
Create and Co-Create Content	• Use content to attract/retain attention and built credibility
Socialize Media Relations	• Understand and utilize online influences/channels
Champion Open Advocacy	• Be open and honest about agenda, goals, intent, and motives
Build Active Partnerships	• Develop third-party relationships

FIGURE **9.8** Rules of the Road for Marketer Communications in Social Media

Source: Richard Edelman, "PR to Public Engagement: The Opportunity for the Industry," June 10, 2009, p. 17. Copyright © 2009 Edelman. All rights reserved. Reprinted with permission.

Public relations firm Edelman has a set of behavioral guidelines for public engagement (see Figure 9.8) that give marketers good guidelines for communicating in the social space. Important themes that emerge from their guidelines include:

- Marketers must understand their target audience(s), listening and communicating in ways that meet the needs and suit the values of their audiences.
- Marketers must be responsive and trustworthy in all their communications. If they are not, audience response is likely to be swift and scathing.
- Relationships with external partners, especially influentials can be helpful in guiding the conversation.

All companies need to think of themselves as creators and communicators of content, a subject to which we discuss in Chapter 10. This is a tall order, especially for marketers who are used to trying to put their products in the best light, not to being responsive to what customers are saying and doing. One marketer puts it well when he says that, "No One Cares About Your Products." Sage Lewis argues that people care about what other people say, and that they care about experiences more than the products themselves. This quote captures the essence of his argument:

> People don't care what you say about your products. They want to know what other people say about your products.
> *If we don't realize this, I believe our Web sites will become obsolete.*
> People simply won't go to your site because they know it's just filled with puffery, marketing-speak, and straight-up meaningless content.[37]

This short article is worth reading for its content. It is also worth reading the comments; Lewis' arguments attracted the attention of other marketers—the mark of an influencer. His key point is painful but important. Marketers cannot go on social media and talk about their products. People want to hear about things that are meaningful in their lives. If your product offers meaningful benefits and experiences, they will listen. But if you talk about products themselves, they will simply tune you out.

Engaging Your Audience

First, let us admit that the line between "communicate" and "engage" is blurry. The marketer communication needs to be relevant and engaging, or it will not

INTERACTIVE EXERCISE 9.3   Mountain Dew Flavor Contest

Visit http://www.dewmocracy.com.

As early as 2007, PepsiCo's Mountain Dew used a variety of digital platforms, including its branded Facebook page, to challenge users to create the next Mountain Dew flavor. This campaign, called DEWmocracy, included many events and the creation of a private online community, Dew Labs, for its most dedicated brand loyalists. Mountain Dew fans collaborated in-person and on social media sites to create three new flavors and vote for their favorite. The winner, Mtn Dew White Out, is now a permanent part of the Mountain Dew line-up. To create the flavor fans could vote on Mountain Dew's website or text a vote. Voting was heavily promoted on the Xbox Live Site. Note the interactivity of the web page and the continuing push to engage fans on its main facebook page, which had over 2.3 million fans by the fall of 2010. You might enjoy going to the brand's main Facebook page (www.facebook.com/mountaindew) and checking out the network of related Facebook pages. It is the epitome of a complex campaign with a long-term commitment by the sponsoring brand.

attract attention. However, remember the Forrester ladder. It is nice to have people who simply consume your content. It is even better to have people who post favorable reviews (while having a response strategy for those whose opinions are unfavorable) and people who actually cocreate content.

Think about the examples at the beginning of this chapter. If no one had asked questions of the Old Spice Guy, the campaign would not have been successful. A lot of bloggers wrote about the Cisco router, and in this case, also its novel product launch. Friends and acquaintances, such as those of Dave Morin, often contribute to a cause at the request of someone they know, which is facilitated by the social networks. All this is engagement.

Pepsi is another enterprise that has worked in social media in a number of ways over the past few years and has seen a lot of success. One example is that of its contests for Super Bowl advertisements. According to Wikipedia, Pepsi first launched this promotion in 2007[38] for its Doritos brand and has continued it with variations in the years since. The Pepsi brand, long a major advertiser on the Super Bowl, chose not to advertise in 2010. Instead it launched the Pepsi Refresh program, which has given away over $10 million so far, to causes that received the most fan support.[39] Pepsi returned to the 2011 Super Bowl with another "create the best ad" campaign. This type of contest invariably attracts some contestants and a much larger number of viewers who vote on their favorites. This is engagement at two levels.

What is not as readily apparent is that Pepsi has organized its marketing department for social media success. Its executives often talk about its efforts, including a conference speech[40] by Bonin Bough[41] who is PepsiCo's director of Digital and Social Media. Ford's social media head, Scott Monty,[42] is also a vocal proponent of strategic social media use[43] by global brands.[44]

The Pepsi campaigns also provide an example of two other related issues of SMM:

1. A social media campaign is unlikely to thrive in a single channel. Multiple channels can include combinations of social media channels with Twitter and Facebook often being used to reinforce one another.
2. Campaign for national or global brands usually also requires paid media, whether online display advertising or traditional media advertising or both.

No, SMM is not free!

You may also note that this section does not attempt to define customer engagement, although metrics including engagement will be discussed later. The material here implies that engagement is defined by the customer taking some action as desired by the marketer. The action is often the outcome of an attitude—possibly brand loyalty. That, however, revives a long-unsettled marketer controversy about the measurement of brand loyalty. Exhibiting the marketer-induced behavior, however, is probably a good surrogate for a positive attitude toward the brand.

Collaborating with the Brand

By now you are probably braced for another fuzzy boundary, this time between engagement and collaboration. The Pepsi brands provide a good example of an engagement strategy that causes customers to collaborate in various ways. The outcomes of this collaborative engagement include consumer-created ads, donations to worthy causes, and even new products.

There are many opportunities for collaboration and cocreation of content. Let us take a brief look at some of the major ones.

Corporate Blogs

eMarketer predicts that 43 percent of all corporations will be blogging by 2012. It continues by saying that growth in corporate blogs continues, although the growth in number of personal blogs seems to have slowed down.[45] Even so, Technorati's annual State of the Blogosphere report shows that 72 percent of its sample blog as a hobby and only 4 percent report blogging for corporations.[46]

One blog lists the benefits of business blogging as follows:

1. It helps the business establish expertise and credibility. Remember the importance of being open and honest in all content in order to build, over time, a trusted blog.
2. It makes the business a resource for important information. That leads to visibility on and off the Internet.
3. It creates a dialog, primarily between businesses and their customers, although prospects will also find a well-written blog. Dell has done this well with its Direct to Dell and IdeaStorm blogs. It did not happen overnight or without consistent effort and attention from Dell employees and managers.
4. It develops new relationships, not only with customers, but also with potential business partners.
5. Blogs increase the visibility of the brand. Blog entries often rank high in search engine results because of both their content and their recency. They also generate incoming links to the blog content itself and to the corporate website.

There are paid services that work to increase the visibility of blogs, but good writers can do a great deal without cost or much effort by learning to write web-friendly content and by tagging their posts, which all blog platforms facilitate. HubSpot (on its corporate blog, of course) gives a set of steps for setting up a blog and offers an on-demand webinar on how to create a successful business blog.[47] Writing for search has many facets, but the most important are generally agreed to be:

* Select the best keywords.
* Study search results to see which competitive sites rank highest and what keywords they are using.
* Use keyword(s) in title tags.
* Use keywords in site meaningful, well-written site (or blog) pages. Images are nice, but it is textual content that drives search engine results.[48]

Are you getting a message here? Locating and using keywords well is a critical activity, in searchable social media such as blogs, as well as in website content. There are useful tools that can help with the all-important activity of keyword research, which is discussed in detail in Chapter 8.[49]

Twitter

Much has been said, pro and con, about business use of Twitter. It is hard to argue, however, that you can successfully incorporate Twitter into SMM without having experience in using it. Both Bonin Bough and Scott Monty are regular users of Twitter, as one example. However, examples is all we have, because even Twitter itself does not attempt to estimate how many use it primarily for personal reasons and how many for business. Twitter does have a TwitterBusiness page that gives tips for business users.[50] Even more important for novice business users, they have a Twitter 101 page that includes a best practices link.[51]

Consulting firm Gartner lists four benefits of business use of Twitter as follows:

1. Using Twitter as a marketing or public relations channel. Gartner's report points out that uninteresting or self-serving Tweets can do more harm than good. The report also warns against engaging in arguments with viewers.
2. Employee use of Twitter to enhance the company's reputation. Zappos is a good example of this type of use.
3. Employee use of Twitter for internal communications. Gartner points out that the platform may not be sufficiently secure and suggests that there is proprietary software that provides secure microblogging platforms for businesses.
4. Gartner calls it "inbound signaling." We have described it as listening to the business' customers and broader audience. Whatever you choose to call it, the importance of listening to the voice of the customer in today's connected world cannot be overstated![52]

Product Reviews

Product reviews have become an important part of online shopping for most customers, both B2C and B2B. A recent study by ChannelAdvisor[53] reported that 92 percent of all U.S. Internet users read product reviews with 46 percent being influenced positively, 43 percent being influenced negatively, and only 3 percent not being influenced at all. The data in Figure 9.9 reinforces the importance of

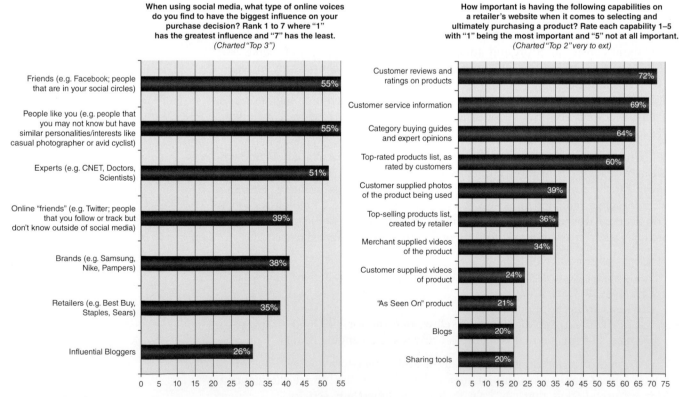

FIGURE **9.9** The Importance of Consumer Product Reviews

Source: "5 Social Shopping Trends Shaping the Future of Ecommerce," pp. 21, 23. Reprinted with permission of Power Reviews, Inc.

customer product reviews, but it also makes another key point. Product reviews are not the starting point for a purchase; search engines are. Fully 57 percent of shoppers start their research with a search engine, while 20 percent start with the brand's own site, and only a handful start on a social site (Facebook 3 percent, Twitter 2 percent). It seems that consumers use search to develop the evoked set of brands from which they plan to choose and then look for recommendations.

In the choice stage, personal recommendations—from their own friends or from people perceived to be like them—assume primary importance. Have you referred to a consumer review in making an online purchase? Informal observation suggests that most consumers answer "yes, sometimes" or even "yes, almost always." Brands themselves or the retailers who sell them are considerably less important according to the study. Influential bloggers are at the bottom of the list. The less important sources of information also appear to be the least trustworthy. Given the importance of reviews, it make sense that consumers want ecommerce sites that offer reviews, ratings, and even consumer-supplied images.

Product reviews are one of the important ways in which marketers can encourage customer collaboration. Have you purchased a product online recently and experienced a follow-up that inquires about your satisfaction with the product and encourages you to post a review online? This is another best practice of successful online retailers! It provides content that is not only important to shoppers but to which social media marketers must listen, paying attention to both positive and negative reviews.

Social Sharing

A report entitled "Social Is the Next Search" (think about that title!) has an excellent summary of the social sharing challenge: "To drive quality referral traffic from social networks, site owners should focus on optimizing the quality and quantity of content and activity shared by users." How does a marketer do this? Basically, marketers do this by adding social media icons such as those shown in Figure 9.10a. You are accustomed to seeing those on websites and blogs; how many of them do you recognize? Probably only a few—and there are many others—although these represent some of the most powerful.

Overdrive Interactive calls them "chiclets" and says: "Chiclets are those little logos/buttons you see all over the web ... that give individuals the ability to share web content with their friends, families, and colleagues through their choice of social media sites and applications."[54] The white paper explains how each of these icons works; sadly for the social media marketer each one has a slightly different purpose and method of operation. Fortunately, there are sharing icons such as the popular open source, ShareThis. Figure 9.10b expresses the issue

(a) (b)

FIGURE **9.10** Social Media Sharing Icons and Avoiding "Icon Overload" with ShareThis

Source: Overdrive Interactive, "Chiclets: The Social Glue of the Web," http://www.ovrdrv.com/chiclets/pdf/Chiclets. pdf; and Copyright © 2006–2011 ShareThis Inc. All Rights Reserved.

well. Instead of having to use separate icons and develop a strategy for each, the website owner or blogger can use ShareThis and customize a set of icons to be presented when the visitor clicks on the green ShareThis icon. Clearly, that is much easier for the publisher.

How should the site or blog owner choose a reasonably small set of icons to present to visitors? The issue is which sites will be most effective in attracting user attention and in encouraging users to click through to the site. Consider two important issues:

1. The size of the social media site matters. A study reported on ReadWriteWeb shows that Facebook leads other social networks with 68 percent of all referrals to websites, while number two Twitter sends only 25 percent, and no other site has more than a 4 percent share of referral traffic.

   However, comparisons are difficult. Here is what the author of the study says:

   > "referrers have been segmented into different categories in order to more easily compare traffic. For example, there is no use in comparing Google to Flickr since they are not categorically related. If we're making a determination which search engine to focus on, Flickr would not be in the mix—and if we're looking for a photo hosting site, Google would not be in the mix. The four main referral categories that drive virtually all traffic are: Search Engines, Media, Social Bookmarks and Social Networks."[55]

   It is hard to argue with that logic, but it adds another layer of complexity. The good news, though, is that each category is skewed toward one or a few sites. The social networks category, for example, finds YouTube creating 84 percent of the referrals while number two Flickr creates only 9 percent. Perhaps only one per category is enough for most sites.

2. The target audience of the website or blog also matters. Social bookmarking is not as pervasive an activity as having a Facebook page or a Twitter account. However, sites such as Digg and Delicious, which are arguably the best known, are not the largest referrers—Digg 30 percent and Delicious only 2 percent. StumbleUpon leads viewers to sites similar to the one being viewed and consequently provides the largest share of referrals, 51 percent. Reddit is a smaller service reputed to be especially popular with the IT crowd and it drives 5 percent of referrals. The original post has a lot more interesting details.[56]

The moral of this rather complicated story is as follows: the social media marketer should include the large sites in the social sharing options in the absence of any information to the contrary. Then she should carefully examine the behavior of the target audience for patronage of niche sites, which might also be effective. It is essential to follow the website metrics to see where the referrals are actually coming from and make any strategy adjustments that appear to be necessary. Finally, it should go without saying that, in order for any of this to work, you must have content that engages the audience and makes them want to share it with other people!

A social sharing strategy should also take the Facebook Like application into account. When a viewer "likes" a piece of content, that item is added to the viewer's Facebook feed and thereby shared with her network of friends. The friends see it as being recommended by one of their friends, which should increase its trustworthiness. In addition, the behavior of "liking" adds to the user's Facebook profile. The profile is key in targeting Facebook advertising as will soon be discussed. Using both "Share" and "Like" gives visitors an opportunity to contribute and share in whatever way they choose.[57]

Creating Community

There is one important SMM activity that does not find an easy place in the strategy steps. Perhaps that is because creating community is both an outcome and an activity of social media use.

It is an outcome when a group of people, of their own volition, began to congregate around one or more platforms that deal with subjects of interest to them. The interests can be very broad, such as sports or entertainment news. They can be niche, such as a blog about golf or a site that answers income tax questions. Sites that attract even a small number of regular users can be referred to as a community.

Businesses and nonprofits may decide against waiting for a community to develop and decide to build their own. The Pickens Plan is a prime example (see Figure 9.11). In July 2008, Texas oilman Boone Pickens announced his intention of building an online community to support his personal plan for U.S. energy independence. He was not coy about his willingness to spend from his own personal fortune in order to accomplish this—$58 million according to Forbes.[58] According to two of the original developers, less than a year later the Plan had 1.5 million members, a social network[59] with 200,000 members, and produced over 1.1 million emails to Congress.[60] The author of this text was an early member and even wrote about her own experiences, including the fact that the Plan achieved a million members in less than four months[61]—powerful testimony to the importance of traditional media in promoting social media activities. She became a "featured member" on the network site for a few days when she wrote a favorable post about the Plan's community guidelines,[62] which provide a good model for any firm planning to build a public community. Giving active members a public thank-you is another best practice way to reward them for effort and support.

Nonprofits and small businesses can build branded communities, even though they may lack the resources of Boone Pickens. There are many good examples in the nonprofit world. A somewhat unique small business effort is Bella of Cape Cod.[63] This business run by two young mothers in a resort community suffers from the normal problem of resort retailers—about two months of frenzied business, four or so "shoulder" months of decent business, and a winter

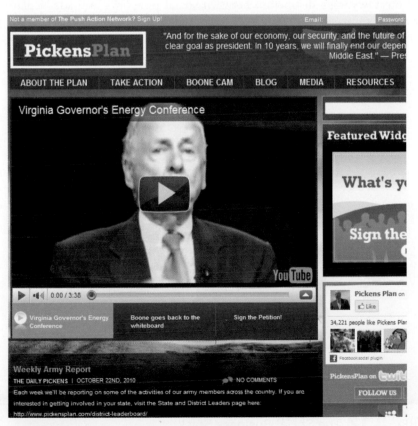

FIGURE **9.11** The Pickens Plan Home Page

Source: http://www.pickensplan.com.

INTERACTIVE EXERCISE **9.4** Nonprofit and eGov World

Visit http://my.nature.org.

Check out the My Nature Page at the Nature Conservancy, which offers conservation information personalized to the member's interests,

Visit http://1.usa.gov/xxrBa8.

NASA originally developed its app to provide updates on space missions. It has become a broad information resource. View the video on this page and look at other resources NASA provides.

season where business is totally dormant. Bella is actually able to close the retail store for several months in the winter, keeping the business going on its website and, more important, through eparties.[64] Each eparty, held entirely online, builds the email list for future eparties, and both the fun and the fund-raising make them popular among the Bella customer base. This model might not work for every retailer, but it is a great example of a business model that is based on community and interactivity.

If by now you are shaking your head over the number of activities that can be incorporated into a social media strategy and the complexity of some of them, you are not alone. This is the challenging issue that social media marketers face on a daily basis. It is also one reason they often find it difficult to communicate the nature and benefits of an SMM strategy to top management, a subject which we will return to at the end of this chapter.

This section also emphasizes that there are free tools and paid services that can assist the marketer in various activities necessary to developing and executing an SMM strategy. This aspect of the social media landscape was recently examined in research from the Altimeter Group (see Figure 9.12).

Note Owyang's distinction between social networks and social platforms. In general, the networks are places for people to communicate, while the platforms provide opportunities for people and companies to build their own

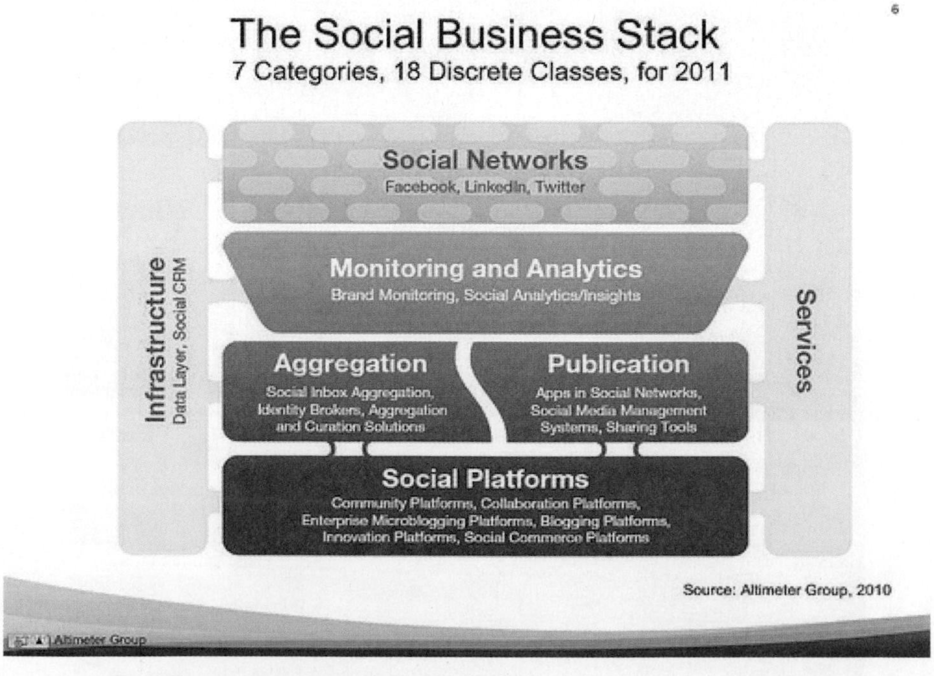

FIGURE **9.12** The Social Business Stack

Source: "Industry Reference: The Social Business Stack for 2011" by Jeremiah Owyang, Altimeter Group, November 5, 2010. Reprinted with permission.

virtual spaces, including the content and the types of communications they choose.

Executing SMM Strategies

Nokia, a global brand, has used various types of customer interaction over the years. Forums and clubs were prominent in earlier years; customers like to talk about their phones and what they do with their phones. In recent years, Nokia has made SMM a key part of its marketing communications strategy.

Nokia's Vision: Moving Beyond Paid Media

When any endeavor is as complex as developing and executing a social media strategy, it helps to have a simple vision of what it aims to accomplish. Nokia has done an excellent job of conceptualizing its social media vision and, along the way, has been willing to talk about both achievements and campaigns that fell short. Nokia's description of traditional marketing communication as "big bang campaigns" is interesting and apt (see Figure 9.13). Its vision of the new opportunity as being continuous engagement in a networked world, stimulated by campaign activities in social media, is thought-provoking. It also brings up the subject of paid versus earned media, one that has become important in the social media world.

In the social media world, marketers are faced with several new types of media. *Paid media* has been the foundation of advertising efforts both on and

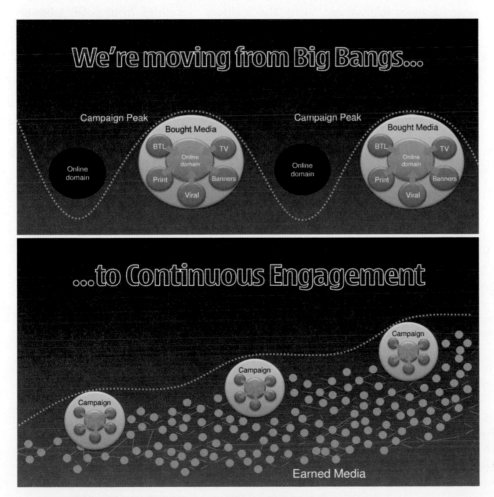

FIGURE **9.13** Nokia's Vision for Social Media Marketing

Source: http://www.slideshare.net/chriss/social-media-at-nokia-social-media-marketing conference.

off the web. Online display ads, as discussed in Chapter 6, are a major component of paid media on the Internet. It also includes various kinds of advertising and sponsorships including paid ads on Facebook, LinkedIn, and on Twitter in the form of Promoted Tweets. The common theme in all these types of advertising is that the marketer must pay for the media exposure.

Owned media might be considered the foundation of social media marketing efforts. Owned channels include websites, blogs, and email newsletters, as well as branded social media channels like Facebook pages, Twitter accounts, and YouTube channels. These channels are clearly identified as carrying marketer-initiated content, although customers are invited to engage with marketers in all these channels.

Earned media is unpaid presence in channels other than those owned by the brand. Earned media happens in various ways. It includes formal marketing efforts like reaching out to bloggers in an attempt to persuade them to make blog posts about the brand. It may be primarily customer initiated as when a video goes viral and customers share it among themselves without marketing intervention. It can also result from PR efforts, both offline and online. Marketers can provide the platform, for example the Facebook Like button or a product ratings page, but it is up to the customer to create the content.

That brings us to *shared media* in which customers become the primary creators and distributers of content. Shared media includes marketer-sponsored activities, such as the Super Bowl contests of the past several years in which customers have created ads for the specific brands.[65] Another example is Coke's Expedition 206 campaign in which three winners traveled the world for one year and video-blogged about it.[66] Shared media also includes everything from posting brand-related content and images on Facebook, to Tweeting about a sports event or a shopping experience, to uploading photos of your wedding to a local news channel, or Tweeting about local weather on Weather.com. In each of these examples—and many others—marketers have given customers an opportunity to create or share meaningful content that is brand related but not the persuasive messaging that characterizes paid media. Shared media usually comes from friends and family, which adds an element of credibility.

The differences in the types of media are described in Table 9.1. Chip Griffin, writing in the CustomScoop blog puts it this way:

- Paid and owned media can stimulate shared media.
- Shared media can inspire earned media.

TABLE 9.1 SMM Expands Types of Media Available to Marketers

Media Type	Media Vehicles/Platforms	Advantages and Disadvantages
Paid	Traditional online advertising – Display ads, PPC, sponsorships, paid ads on social networks	Marketer controls Often non-engaging Cost
Owned	Media created and controlled by marketer – Websites, blogs, email newsletters, social media accounts	Content primarily marketer-initiated Can be informative, entertaining Platforms can be free or low cost
Earned	Unpaid media presence – Results of PR efforts including articles, blog posts, WOM, buzz, viral	Highly credible Marketer does not control content Can persist in media environment
Shared	Brand and customer interact and co-create content on social media sites	High level of engagement Platforms free or low cost Marketer does not control content

Source: © Cengage Learning 2013

- Shared media can propagate across social networks to friends, colleagues, and other social networks.[67]

Social media has created a media ecosystem in which the marketer is a player—an important one but certainly not the only or even the most important one. This media evolution validates Nokia's decision to abandon "big bangs" for ongoing engagement with customers in multiple communications channels.

Executing Nokia's Social Media Vision

In a nutshell, Nokia's strategy has been to develop robust internal social media communications, using what it learns there, in external social media programs. This effort appears to have begun in 2006 with a formal social media communications team established in 2008. They have three key internal tools:

- BlogHub[68] pulls together employee blogs from all over the world and makes it easy to find information that other employees are looking for.
- VideoHub is open source software that permits the development of apps for the various Nokia models. The app makes it easy to search for video clips on the mobile phone.[69]
- Infopedia is an internal wiki application for internal collaboration and knowledge sharing.[70]

These internal tools were part of the inspiration for Nokia's successful external blog "Conversations."[71]

Nokia executives, including Mark Squires, Director of Social Media, openly talk about their experiences. Squires was asked how difficult it was to convince top management of the value of social media. Here is part of what he said:

> The problem is not engaging with customers via social media, but in bringing the rest of your company along with you...
>
> I wrote a paper on it which helped make the argument internally, then it took time, starting with Nokia's internal blogs. We already had around 1,300 blogs on Nokia's intranet.
>
> We drew up a set of guidelines, using best practice examples from companies like Sun Microsystems. We also changed the rules and allowed employees to blog about our products in company time.[72]

Squires also admitted that the public relations agency hired by Nokia for a blogger outreach program did not fulfill its promises to blogger/marathoner Muireann Carey-Campbell. It is worth reading the original post;[73] note the October 12, 2010, comment by Mark Squires. He admitted that Nokia did not get it right but he was neither defensive nor confrontational; that is, both effective listening and responding! When you look at the dates, it is apparent that the favorable interview with Squires (November 1, 2010) was a result of effective response by Nokia to the unfavorable post about the blogger (October 12, 2010). That is the way good social media works—an ongoing conversation. Just keep in mind that an unfavorable conversation can be perpetuated just like a favorable one can. It is the job of SMM to behave and react in such a way that there is more favorable than unfavorable buzz in social media space.

Social Media Marketing Metrics

Throughout this chapter, you have seen examples of the metrics social media marketers use to measure the effectiveness of their campaigns. We have also pointed out that these are behavioral metrics, which most marketers consider more desirable than merely asking people what they did or are likely to do via marketing research. One advantage is that these are behaviors they have actually exhibited, not just reported. The other main advantage is that these metrics are available in almost real time without additional costs of data collection. This is the reason that many marketers now argue that customer listening and behavioral metrics[74] should be a precursor to marketing research and, in many instances, it can be a substitute.[75]

The example of the Facebook ad highlights several important issues about social media metrics themselves. The issues can be summarized as follows:

- Social metrics may include traditional advertising metrics such as reach and impressions.
- There are interactive metrics that are applicable to social media. Click-throughs and time spent on a page are two examples out of many.
- In social media, each channel has invented its own terminology. For instance, we talk about views on YouTube, which is akin to an advertising impression—exposure to the message.
- Each social media channel may have metrics that are somewhat unique but are often related (e.g., Facebook fans and Twitter followers).
- Each platform provides its own metrics dashboard. While this provides essential metrics, it creates a bewildering array of data for the marketer to follow and analyze. Hoffman and Fodor present a detailed list of social media metrics, organized by stage in the branding process.[76]

Figure 9.14 shows the ideal marketing situation. All media—traditional, digital, and social media—would be measured and the results fed into a single metrics platform. It would provide the marketer with a customizable dashboard that presents key metrics chosen by the marketer in close to real time, by campaign, by channel, or by product line. This is the ideal, but it is not a reality today.

Figure 9.14 refers to only three of the metrics platforms available—Google Analytics, because it is free and comparatively easy to use; WebTrends, because it is one of the commercial metrics platforms for large enterprises; and HubSpot,[77] because it specializes in small business marketing and offers a robust social media metrics platform. HubSpot focuses on visibility in social media and via email marketing (it calls this "inbound marketing"), not detailed website metrics such as number of visitors, page views, and the many other website

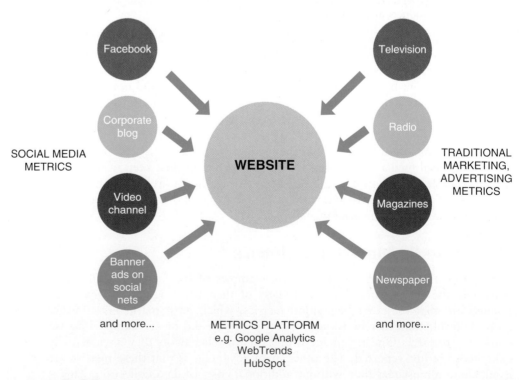

FIGURE **9.14** Ideal Web Metrics Concept

metrics that owners need to access to assess the effectiveness of their websites or blogs.

On the other hand, Google Analytics[78] offers a complete set of website metrics, discussed in detail in Chapter 14. The platform is able to integrate metrics from email, online advertising, and various types of offline advertising. For a business with a website of moderate size in terms of pages and moderate activity in terms of marketing communications, this provides a deluge of data. It is another example of a platform that is free but that requires an investment in employee time and expertise in order to provide meaningful analysis for decision making.

At this point, any thoughtful person asks how marketers at any level can possibly make sense of all the data available on the various platforms. There is one critical rule:

> Establish clear objectives for your campaign and choose the appropriate metrics before the campaign begins.

Why is this setting objectives so important? It is critical because setting objectives is essential, not only to guide the campaign, but also to identify the metrics that are necessary for its success. Otherwise the marketer will be trying to make sense of the torrent of data with no guidelines to follow. If metrics are selected after the fact, the likelihood that they will be objective measures is essentially nonexistent. They will be measures chosen to support whatever thesis the presenter wants to support, and that is not a prescription for good decision making!

Table 9.2 gives a hypothetical example of how this can be done. It shows four reasonable, specific objectives for a small business blog. It also shows the corresponding metric for each objective. In this simple example, only one metric is needed for each objective; often multiple metrics are required. Setting them up in a matrix like this makes it clear what metrics are needed and whether anything is missing to measure the achievement of campaign objectives. What even this simple example also makes clear is that it may take four different tools to provide four essential metrics. That is the metrics dilemma of the social media marketer today.

This table is a simple example. If you want a detailed tutorial by one of the undisputed metrics gurus, see this post by Avinash Kaushik. It includes not only mapping to objectives but also metrics for key performance indicators.[79]

The strategy development, execution, and measurement process is a complex one, although it follows the basic process that marketers have long used in traditional and digital media.

We end this chapter with two issues that are of personal interest to most students and then conclude with a final word on making SMM acceptable in

TABLE 9.2	Mapping Metrics to Objectives for a Small Blog
Objective	**Metric**
Increase average visits per day	Average number of visits per day from Google Analytics
Increase number of comments	As long as small, can count. May need comment feed
Increase number of shared posts	Provided by ShareThis icon

Increase number of incoming links	Will use GoRank.com tool as long as free tool is sufficient
	    May need to measure different types of links (other blogs, websites, etc.)
	    A different tool/report *for each*

Source: © Cengage Learning 2013

the overall marketing communications strategy of any organization. First, let us consider an issue that has become increasingly important as the Internet pervades all aspects of our personal and work life. The first issue is building your own personal brand on the Internet.

Building Your Personal Brand in Social Space

If you are a student or young professional reading this text and you have already begun a planned effort to build your personal brand, congratulations! If you have not yet begun, it is never too late. The Internet Career Builder exercises at the end of most chapters are part, but by no means all, of that effort. There are many resources on the subject that you will find helpful as you build your brand. There is an Internet TV channel,[80] and there are many books and countless blogs. Here is a brief summary of steps to get you started or to evaluate your progress:

1. Be real before being virtual. You must speak with an authentic voice. It is not easy to be objective about ourselves, so this takes effort.
2. Know your baseline. What do hiring managers find when they Google you? It is an established practice these days, and you should be sure what they find is positive. For a social media position, they are likely to look at how many friends you have on Facebook or how many connections you have on LinkedIn. For a position in any business field today, you should have a good LinkedIn profile. That is where most human relations people turn first when looking for a person to fill a particular slot.
3. Start with the basics. According to the MarketingProfs blog:
    a. Buy your own domain name even if you do not plan to use it right away. That keeps someone else from using it.
    b. Establish yourself on LinkedIn, including getting recommendations there.
    c. Establish a Google Alert for your name.
    d. See what is out there. Follow newsletters and blogs that keep you updated on events in your chosen profession.[81]
    e. And here is advice from another personal branding expert:[82] Keep your name and your photo constant across your platform profiles. That makes you recognizable.
    f. And here is more advice from a long-time professor: If you do not already have an "adult" email address, get one, and use it for all professional correspondence.
4. Connect the real world with the virtual world. Think about building an online portfolio beginning with a great PowerPoint presentation you made in a class or a video clip of a key part of a presentation. The Visual CV® site facilitates this process.
5. Enhance and maintain. Continue to add relationships and content, or even to create content by doing something such as starting your own blog.[83]

LinkedIn is a very popular site for online profiles, but your school may have other recommendations that are based on the advice of recruiters. Take your online profile seriously, whichever site you choose. Social media guru Chris Brogan has pithy advice for developing a good profile.[84] There are also a number of good posts on optimizing your LinkedIn profile for search.

You should find personal branding resources that appeal to you and follow them. The search engines can be helpful. You can also access the Blog Directory at Technorati.com and search for "personal brand" to get an extensive list of blogs.

Also find out if companies you wish to work for have any standards in terms of social media activity. If you want to work in social media and have only two Facebook friends and no profile on LinkedIn, your chances are slim!

Bringing Top Management into the Social Media Fold

Earlier in this chapter, it was noted that 59 percent of B2B and 44 percent of B2C marketers have yet to become heavily engaged in SMM (recall Figure 9.2). The conventional wisdom of marketing says that reluctance is because they cannot be sure that SMM will produce measurable RO(promotional)I. The 2010 MarketingSherpa Benchmark Survey confirms the importance of ROI in the context of other challenges faced by SMM (see Figure 9.15). While measurable ROI leads the list of challenges, converting social followers to paying customers is a close second; clearly generating revenue from SMM leads the list! Note also that most of the marketers surveyed found the challenges becoming more important in 2010 than in 2009. This confirmation is testimony to the newness of the field and also to continuing resistance on the part of top management to accept and fund SMM initiatives in many organizations.

There is no quick and easy solution to the problem of top management's resistance to SMM, especially if managers themselves are not users of some of the social channels. If they see it as just something that their teenage children do, marketers must brace for a process of making SMM acceptable in their organizations. It helps if they recognize it as a process of change management, which is a topic in both the general management and the quality management[85] literature. Internet marketing was a revolutionary change for most marketing organizations, and SMM, as another revolutionary change, has come along before many businesses have completely integrated Internet marketing into their strategic thinking.

When marketers think about gaining acceptance for SMM in that way, a set of steps emerge. They fit the quality management paradigm of starting small with

Challenges Becoming Increasingly Important in the Year Ahead

Challenge	Increase	Not change	Decrease
Measuring and proving the ROI of social media programs	77%	22%	1%
Converting followers, fans, etc. into paying customers	71%	27%	2%
Getting target audiences to engage and participate	71%	27%	2%
Finding the time to perform social media programs	62%	34%	4%
Lack of an effective social media marketing strategy	62%	31%	7%
Getting the budget and resources social media deserves	58%	37%	5%
Finding experienced and proficient social media marketers	50%	43%	7%
Management resistance to sharing information online	30%	45%	25%

■ Importance will increase ■ Importance will not change ■ Importance will decrease

FIGURE **9.15** Challenges Faced by Social Media Marketers
Source: MarketingSherpa.

projects that can demonstrate success and thereby earn acceptance and funding for larger projects. A reasonable set of steps are:

- Educate yourself. The footnotes in this chapter open the door to extensive resources on the current state of social media marketing. It is essential to follow a selected few that best fit your needs. Other resources such as podcasts and webcasts (usually free) and conferences are important in keeping up to date.

- Start small and test. This step is critical for a number of reasons. In this chapter, you have seen that an effective SMM campaign often has a lot of moving parts. They can quickly spiral out of control, and keeping them on track requires practice. Sadly, not all will succeed. It is important to learn from failures. It is also important to keep failures small!

- Analyze all campaigns so you can document successes. According to one author, "Anecdotal wins are great, but hard data is what is going to resonate with the most senior of audiences."[86] Use the metrics referenced in this chapter and remember the advice about mapping metrics to campaign objectives.

- Communicate your results across the company. In the beginning you may find it necessary to persuade key stakeholders within the organization on a one-to-one basis. As buzz builds, it will be possible to build groups for reporting and brainstorming.

- Assemble an interdepartmental team, informally at first if necessary. Not only are various skills and expertise needed (e.g., public relations skills and brand management expertise), but SMM requires a team with depth. If it relies on a single person, it cannot outlast that person's tenure with the organization.

- Enlist outside experts, but do not give up your brand. Agencies and consultants can be important in sustaining an SMM effort. However, it is important that they be carefully supervised by an involved SMM team. Better, they should become working members of the internal team.

- Focus on SMM projects that will lead to measurable results. In B2C markets, it is often useful to focus on increasing the value of a customer through retention and loyalty efforts. In B2B markets, the key issue is often generating qualified customer leads. For nonprofits, it may be social fund-raising or it may be building a larger audience base for your fund-raising efforts.

As a social media marketer, whatever you do, keep your eye on the ROI target.[87]

SUMMARY

A few intrepid marketers—large and small, B2C, B2B, and nonprofit—are finding success in social media space. In order to thrive it is likely that most businesses will have to incorporate some elements of SMM into their marketing communications mix in the not-too-distant future. If customers are in social space—and they are—marketers must be there also.

The authors of this text have defined SMM as follows: Social media marketing is business use of selected social media channels to understand customers and to engage them in communication and collaboration in ways that lead to the achievement of ultimate marketing and business goals. SMM is carefully planned, and that includes the establishment of specific, measurable goals. Program execution is monitored carefully and evaluated with the social media metrics currently available.

All good marketing begins with customer knowledge. The acquisition of customer knowledge is facilitated in social media space where good listening is a precursor to development of SMM strategy. The steps in developing a strategy are:

- Listening
- Communicating
- Engaging
- Collaborating

There are numerous tools that can be used to support marketer efforts in each stage.

There are also important metrics that are used to evaluate the effectiveness of each step. They include membership metrics such as Facebook fans or subscribers to a branded YouTube channel, engagement metrics such as commenting on blog posts or posting product reviews, performance metrics such as number of sales leads generated, or ultimate measures such as sales or cost savings. It is important to link social media campaigns to actual sales results whenever possible, but that is often difficult.

The social media space continues to change on an almost-daily basis and will continue to do so for some time. Current developments include location-based marketing and social couponing. The young social media marketer is wise to pay attention to the subject of personal branding in Internet space.

In spite of rapid change and fascinating new developments, the social media marketer must retain focus on two important issues:

1. SMM is not yet fully accepted by management in many business and non-profit organizations.
2. SMM is one part of the overall marketing communications mix and must be carefully integrated into it, in both strategy development and execution.

The world of social media is a fascinating one, and it offers marketers an ever-increasing array of tools and techniques by which they can advance their brands.

DISCUSSION QUESTIONS

1. Why do you think social networks have grown so quickly in countries all over the world?
2. Be able to explain why social media marketing is useful to small businesses as well as large corporations. Are there differences in executing an SMM strategy in a small business and a large corporation?
3. How do the steps in developing an SMM strategy differ from those you have seen in other aspects of marketing, for example, developing a brand marketing plan or an advertising campaign strategy?
4. Why do marketers consider earned media especially desirable?
5. What potential values do blogs and Twitter have for B2B marketers?
6. What are some ways in which Facebook can be used by B2C marketers?
7. Thinking just of corporate content, do you often share, write product reviews, or comment or like? Why or why not?
8. Do you receive any coupon or other deal offers by email or mobile app? Do you like them? Do you use them?
9. In case histories throughout this chapter, the metrics that were used to measure the success of the program have been given. Make a list of metrics and the platforms to which they apply and be prepared to discuss their value to the marketer.
10. Do you see any value to having a "personal brand" on the Internet?
11. Why do you think some managers are resistant to the idea of engaging in social media marketing? What could you do or say to convince your reluctant boss that SMM could be a good idea in a specific business setting?

INTERNET EXERCISES

1. Social media marketing career builder.
   a. There are many different types of marketing positions available in the social media field. Ones that may be available to graduates with little prior experience include:

      Content coordinator

      Social media marketing analyst

      Social media account coordinator

      Social media monitor

      Online events specialist

      Community development coordinator

      and many more

      In addition to management positions in each of the specialties listed earlier, experienced marketers may find opportunities including:

      Creative services director

      Director of social media, online marketing, marketing communications or corporate communications

      Strategy and/or planning director

      Project manager

      Director of customer engagement

   b. Select a social media marketing job from the list above or from your own search. Outline the responsibilities of that position. You may find it useful to locate job postings on the web in order to understand the job requirements.
   c. Outline knowledge and experience from classes, internships, full or part-time jobs, and volunteer work that prepare you for this specific position.
   d. Prepare five questions you could ask at a job interview. The questions should exhibit your understanding of the position requirements without lecturing the interviewer about what she already knows.
   e. Update your VisualCV® or LinkedIn Profile with this information.

2. Study the Forrester Social Technographics® Ladder in Figure 9.7. Develop a short questionnaire to determine the segment into which a consumer fits and the specific platforms he uses and what he does on those platforms. Administer the questionnaire to a sample of your friends, family, and colleagues as directed by your instructor. Be prepared to discuss your findings about social media activities in class.

3. Choose a business (B2C or B2B) or nonprofit organization that could benefit from a social media campaign and develop a campaign outline. Include the following elements in your outline:
   • Specific campaign objectives
   • Identification of the target audience
   • Detailed description of the social media marketing activities
   • Metrics to be used to judge campaign success
   • Timeline for the specific campaign
   • Budget for direct costs incurred

   Now that you have thought about what you want to do, write an Introduction for your plan outline that explains why the social media initiative is important and how it integrates into the overall marketing activities of the business.

NOTES

1. http://www.google.com/publicdata?ds=wb-wdi& met=it_net_user&idim=country:USA&dl=en&hl= en&q=number+of+internet+users#met=it_net_user &idim=country:USA&tdim=true.
2. http://blog.nielsen.com/nielsenwire/online_mobile/social-media-accounts-for-22-percent-of-time-online.
3. http://www.facebook.com/press/info.php?statistics.
4. http://www.youtube.com/watch?v=qt6iEGzLPjg& feature=relmfu.
5. http://www.youtube.com/watch?v=owGykVbfgUE& feature=channel.
6. http://www.gossipjackal.com/entertainment/2010/07/16/who-is-isaiah-mustafa-obviously-perfect-old-spice-guy.
7. http://mashable.com/2010/07/15/old-spice-stats/ and http://johnbell.typepad.com/weblog/2010/07/how-to-reproduce-the-old-spice-video-phenomena.html.
8. http://www.youtube.com/watch?v=nFDqvKtPgZo& feature=player_embedded and http://johnbell.typepad.com/weblog/2010/07/how-to-reproduce-the-old-spice-video-phenomena.html.
9. http://www.adweek.com/news/advertising-branding/old-spice-campaign-smells-sales-success-too-107588. You can see a detailed case study with additional metrics at http://wearesocial.net/blog/2010/07/social-media-buzz-advantage-spice.
10. http://www.readwriteweb.com/archives/how_old_spice_won_the_internet.php.

11. http://www.brandweek.com/bw/content_display/news-and-features/direct/e3i45f1c709df0501927f56568a2acd5c7b.

12. http://www.socialtimes.com/2010/07/cisco-old-spice-campaign.

13. http://newsroom.cisco.com/dlls/2008/prod_030408b.html.

14. http://www.socialmediaexaminer.com/cisco-social-media-product-launch; see a Cisco presentation at http://www.slideshare.net/lasandra5/leveraging-social-media-and-web-20-in-a-product-launch.

15. http://apps.facebook.com/causes/posts/564977?m=.

16. http://www.worldtech24.com/business/new-features-help-birthday-wish-set-new-causes-record-10k-24-hours.

17. "B2B Online Marketers Focus on Lead Gen," *eMarketer*, March 4, 2010.

18. "FTC Publishes Final Guides Governing Endorsements, Testimonials," http://www.ftc.gov/opa/2009/10/endortest.shtm.

19. *eMarketer*, September 29, 2010.

20. *eMarketer*, October 29, 2010.

21. http://www.bazaarvoice.com/resources/stats.

22. http://pewresearch.org/pubs/1711/older-adults-social-networking-facebook-Twitter.

23. http://www.accenture.com/Global/Research_and_Insights/By_Role/HighPerformance_IT/CIOResearch/Jumping-Boundaries.htm.

24. http://www.marketingprofs.com/8/writing-search-engine-optimized-press-releases-cornwall-malseed.asp.

25. http://www.zappos.com.

26. http://Twitter.zappos.com/employees.

27. http://myadengine.com/blog/index.php/2010/08/case-study-how-zappos-achieved-social-media-success.

28. http://Twitter.com/zappos.

29. http://www.ibm.com/blogs/zz/en/guidelines.html.

30. http://www.employeefactor.com/?p=2658.

31. https://www.stationm.com/entrance.

32. http://www.melcrum.com/offer/socialmedia/07a.

33. Forrester Research, Inc., The Latest Global Social Media Trends May Surprise You (Jackie Rousseau-Anderson), September 2010 http://blogs.forrester.com/jackie_rousseau_anderson/10-09-28-latest_global_social_media_trends_may_surprise_you.

34. http://www.forrester.com/empowered/tool_consumer.html.

35. http://www.google.com/support/alerts/bin/static.py?hl=en&page=guide.cs&guide=28413&rd=1.

36. http://www.subhub.com/articles/reputation-monitoring-tools-subhubs-top-picks.

37. http://www.clickz.com/clickz/column/1707550/no-one-cares-about-your-products.

38. http://en.wikipedia.org/wiki/Doritos.

39. http://www.destinationcrm.com/Articles/CRM-News/Daily-News/What-Makes-Pepsis-Digital-Marketing-So-Refreshing-70567.aspx.

40. http://socialmediainfluence.com/2010/07/14/how-pepsico-formulated-an-organization-wide-social-media-strategy.

41. http://www.linkedin.com/in/boninbough.

42. http://www.linkedin.com/in/scottmonty.

43. http://www.slideshare.net/scottmonty.

44. http://www.scottmonty.com/2010/03/how-ford-uses-social-media-video.html.

45. *eMarketer*, August 17, 2010.

46. http://technorati.com/blogging/article/state-of-the-blogosphere-2009-introduction.

47. http://blog.hubspot.com/blog/tabid/6307/bid/6240/how-to-create-a-successful-business-blog-in-minutes.aspx.

48. http://www.clickz.com/clickz/column/1711845/seo-dynamic-field-surebut-some-things-never-change.

49. http://www.clickz.com/clickz/column/1828523/keyword-competitive-intelligence-101.

50. https://Twitter.com/TwitterBusiness.

51. http://business.Twitter.com/Twitter101.

52. http://www.gartner.com/it/page.jsp?id=920813.

53. *eMarketer*, November 2, 2010.

54. http://www.ovrdrv.com/chiclets/pdf/Chiclcts.pdf, p. 3.

55. http://www.readwriteweb.com/archives/analysis_what_are_the_webs_top_sources_of_referral_traffic.php.

56. http://www.readwriteweb.com/archives/analysis_what_are_the_webs_top_sources_of_referral_traffic.php.

57. http://info.gigya.com/WP.SBP.html?s=g.

58. http://www.forbes.com/2008/07/11/pickensplan-wind-energy-tech-science-cz_af_0710pickens.html.

59. http://push.pickensplan.com/index.php.

60. http://personaldemocracy.com/audio/how-pickens-plan-recruited-15-million-volunteers-nine-months-todd-zeigler-bivings-group-and-he.

61. http://diy-marketing.blogspot.com/2008/10/best-practices-for-community-building.html.

62. http://diy-marketing.blogspot.com/2008/12/monitoring-community.html.

63. http://www.bellaofcapecod.com/#.

64. http://www.bellaofcapecod.com/parties.php.

65. http://diy-marketing.blogspot.com/2011/01/social-media-lines-up-for-super-bowl.html.

66. http://diy-marketing.blogspot.com/2010/01/tracking-coke-on-social-media.html.

67. http://www.toprankblog.com/2011/07/online-marketing-media-mix.

68. http://blogs.forum.nokia.com/summary.php?op=BlogList.

69. http://www.n97i.com/nokia-5800-applications/open-video-hub-symbian-s60-5th-edition-review-4330.

70. http://www.simply-communicate.com/case-studies/company-profile/nokia%E2%80%99s-internal-communication-driven-social-media.

71. http://conversations.nokia.com.

72. http://econsultancy.com/us/blog/6782-q-a-mark-squires-director-of-social-media-at-nokia.

73. http://econsultancy.com/us/blog/6715-nokia-screws-blogger-due-to-marathon-pr-failure.

74. http://diy-marketing.blogspot.com/2009/03/still-thinking-about-social-media.html.

75. http://diy-marketing.blogspot.com/2010/01/listening-for-customer-understanding.html.

76. Hoffman, Donna L. and Marek Fodor, "Can You Measure the ROI of Your Social Media Marketing?" *Sloan Management Review*, Fall 2010, pp. 41–49.

77. http://www.hubspot.com.
78. http://www.google.com/analytics.
79. http://www.kaushik.net/avinash/2010/11/web-analytics-maturity-structure-models-process.html.
80. http://www.personalbranding.tv.
81. http://www.marketingprofs.com/9/social-media-and-your-personal-brand-arruda.asp.
82. http://www.personalbrandingblog.com.
83. http://www.marketingprofs.com/9/social-media-and-your-personal-brand-arruda.asp.
84. http://www.chrisbrogan.com/make-your-linkedin-profile-work-for-you.
85. http://asq.org/learn-about-quality/change-management/overview/overview.html.
86. http://smartblogs.com/socialmedia/2010/04/01/five-steps-to-build-a-company-wide-social-media-plan.
87. http://smartblogs.com/socialmedia/2010/03/01/selling-social-media-upstairs and http://smartblogs.com/social-media/2010/04/01/five-steps-to-build-a-company-wide-social-media-plan.

PART 3

Developing Internet Marketing Strategies and Programs

CHAPTER 10

Lead Generation and Conversion in B2B Markets

Key Terms

buy(ing) cycle (260)
content marketing (265)
demand generation (257)
hard lead (262)
inbound marketing (264)
inquiry (261)

KPI (key performance indicator) (273)
landing page (279)
lead distribution (271)
lead generation (255)
lead qualification (270)

microsite (or minisite) (279)
permission marketing (264)
persona (276)
QR (quick response) code (268)
scenario (278)
soft lead (263)

LEARNING OBJECTIVES

By the time you complete this chapter, you will be able to:

- Define and explain the importance of a sales lead.
- Explain the difference between sales lead generation and demand generation.
- Describe the B2B buying cycle.
- Discuss the steps in the sales lead generation and management process.
- Identify channels that can be used to generate sales leads.
- Discuss the issues in defining conversion.
- Explain the meaning and use of customer personas and buying scenarios.
- Discuss the use of landing pages and the importance of testing them.

The Internet marketing paradigm introduced in Chapter 1 suggests that all marketing activities fall into one of four generic categories:

1. Customer acquisition
2. Customer conversion
3. Customer retention
4. Customer lifetime value (CLV) growth

In Part 2, we discussed a number of Internet marketing tools that can be used for customer acquisition. Some, like display advertising and search marketing, are primarily used for acquisition. Email marketing is primarily used for customer retention. Social media marketing falls in between, with its value for acquisition or retention depending on platform and marketer objectives.

Customer conversion is the second level of marketing activity. In its broadest sense, conversion is generally equated with making the first sale to a particular customer. This is a good place to start, but this chapter will show that conversion is a more complex process. It is not a simple activity with a clear beginning and an equally clear termination. It is more like a river, with many tributaries entering it that eventually empties into the sea, which is, in this case, a customer database. If this seems a bit abstract, we will illustrate the concept in many ways in this chapter.

Before we do that, however, it is necessary to specify where the practice of lead generation and management originated, why, and where it is applicable today. In the process, we must also distinguish between two terms that are often loosely used—"lead generation" and "demand generation," and understand them in the context of the B2B (business-to-business) buy cycle.

What Is Lead Generation?

Traditional offline direct marketers have used the process of sales **lead generation** and management since the 1950s at least. Over time, the process has taken advantage of customer databases and marketing automation software and has become a highly disciplined and cost-effective marketing technique of the business marketer.[1] The process focuses on getting individuals to self-identify as a potential decision maker in the purchase of a product or service—a sales lead.

Why was this process developed by business marketers? Business marketers traditionally have large field sales forces that call on customers, which is an expensive process. It is especially costly in the technology and high-ticket industrial spaces where closing a sale may require a year or more and necessitate multiple customer calls from a sales representative supported by engineers and designers. Multiple sales calls by multiple expensive personnel add up to a very expensive process! This costly process is true even if the customer has a defined need for the product and is ready to purchase.

If the customer is early in the sales cycle—just collecting information for a possible purchase in the indefinite future, for example—personal selling is simply not cost-effective. If personal sales calls represent the only option, the company risks losing contact with a customer who may eventually make a purchase. The other option is to maintain communication in nonpersonal channels—originally by mail, now primarily in interactive channels—until that potential customer is ready to make a purchase decision. It is a simple concept that is surprisingly difficult to implement for reasons that are organizational, not technological. We will return to that topic later in the chapter.

Generating high quality sales leads was perceived as the greatest challenge by B2B marketers surveyed by MarketingSherpa in 2010. A large volume of leads was important, but much less so than *high quality* leads. We will consider the reasons why in the following section. Figure 10.1 also implies that the sales cycle is becoming longer, which increases the key role of good sales leads. Note that no other issue even approaches the importance of generating high quality sales leads as far as these business marketers are concerned.

It is important to understand that sales lead generation and management is a marketing tool that is used for high-ticket sales with a long purchase cycle. By now, you may have realized that some consumer purchases also fit that description. The purchase of a car usually fits into that category; so does the purchase of a condo or a house. In consumer behavior terms, these are situations in which the consumer goes through the entire purchase process—triggering cue, information search, selection of alternatives, purchase decision, product use, and information feedback. This type of situation is ideal for identifying someone in the initial stage of the purchase process, communicating as the process unfolds, and making an effort to close the sale when the time is appropriate. All you have to do is look at the websites of any major automobile brand to see this process in

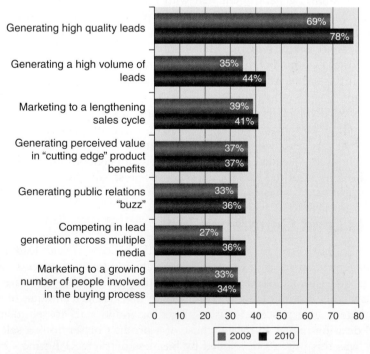

FIGURE **10.1** Top Challenges for B2B Marketers in 2010

Source: "New Chart: Top Challenges for B2B Marketers from 2009 to 2010," by Jen Doyle, October 12, 2010, Marketing Sherpa (http://www.marketingsherpa.com/article.php?ident=31726).

FIGURE **10.2** The BMW USA Home Page

Source: BMW of North America, LLC, http://www.bmwusa.com.

operation. You will not get far into the site before you are required to give an email address in order to proceed. You will also notice that behaviorally targeted ads, as discussed in Chapter 6, immediately begin to appear as you surf the web.

BMW has long been good at identifying potential customers and nurturing them. Its USA home page shown in Figure 10.2 offers exclusive features and the ability to "build your own" car to people who sign up. These offers of information and special functions encourage people to sign up, which means providing their email address. Have no doubt that BMW will be in touch once you register! This is a classic example of the use of the lead process in a consumer market. We will focus on B2B applications in this chapter, but remember that there are also important applications in B2C (business-to-consumer) markets, and they work in the same way.

What Is Demand Generation?

In recent years, the term **demand generation** has also entered the marketing lexicon. It has generated more heat than light,[2] partly because marketers often use the two terms—lead generation and demand generation—as if they are interchangeable. When they stop to think about it, though, there is general agreement that lead generation is a subset of the broader activity, demand generation. One marketer described it this way:

Demand Generation = Awareness + Lead Generation + Lead Nurturing + Customer Development[3]

That conceptualization is helpful because it takes us back to the advertising/branding hierarchy (see Chapter 5), which encompasses the entire process. What it suggests is that much of this text—especially the tools covered in Part 2—represent demand generation activities. In this chapter, we will concentrate on the more specific, and much less well understood, process of lead generation and management. Before we go further, let us look at a B2B lead generation campaign that successfully borrows ideas from B2C marketing.

Juan Eloqua Generates Sales Leads

Do you remember commercials for Columbian coffee in the 1980s and 1990s that featured Juan Valdez[4] picking "the world's best coffee"? The campaign lasted for many years and was viewed as a successful primary demand stimulator.

Fast forward to the present day when a marketing automation[5] firm, Eloqua, needed to generate sales leads. Playing off the Juan Valdez concept, it invented a character, Juan Eloqua, who helps firms grow revenue. It made videos, one showing Juan drinking a Grande cup of coffee and the other showing him having dinner with his precocious son Diego, who is confused about the concept of growing revenue. All these are aimed at getting business marketers to download one of two Grande Guides on lead scoring (to be discussed later in the chapter) and sales enablement, which this chapter refers to as readiness on the part of the customer. It used email for the initial customer contact (see Figure 10.3a). The email and the Juan Eloqua video both led to a landing page specifically designed for the campaign (see Figure 10.3b).

So, the association is a bit strained. According to the comments on a blog post by Howard Sewell about the campaign,[6] some recipients of the email liked

(a)

FIGURE **10.3a** The Eloqua Email

Source: Eloqua, http://www.eloqua.com/grande.

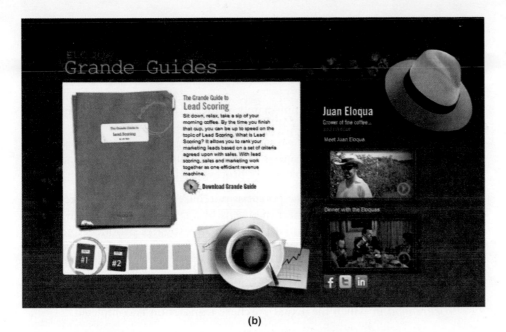

(b)

FIGURE **10.3b** The Original Grande Guides Landing Page
Source: Eloqua, http://www.eloqua.com/grande.

it and some did not. It did, however, get three of them sufficiently engaged to comment on the post. More importantly, in best social media marketing fashion, Joe Chernov, director of content marketing at Eloqua, was monitoring the blog and commented on the post and reactions. He admitted in a separate blog post[7] that the execution was a bit complex, but he gave data that seemed to validate the approach as follows:

- We activated well over 1,000 inactive contacts.
- We generated 250 marketing qualified leads.
- We have four [sales] opportunities in the pipeline as a direct result of this campaign.

His conclusion was that it was a successful effort and the target audience can expect to see more of Juan Eloqua and Grande Guides in the future.

Chernov's metrics make another point about business markets: You have to get used to small numbers. Often, the total market size is rather small, perhaps a few thousand firms. Each sale can be quite large—in the hundreds of thousands or even millions of dollars. Consequently, each sales lead is indeed something to be nurtured.

Howard Sewell, the author of the original blog post, had another conclusion: B2B marketing does not have to be dull, although frankly a lot of it is! B2B marketers, though, tend to be focused on results, not fun. Will that mindset evolve in the era of social media marketing and customer engagement? Only time

INTERACTIVE EXERCISE 10.1   **Get Acquainted with Juan Eloqua**

Meet Juan Eloqua on YouTube at http://bit.ly/uBxCU7.

Visit the Eloqua Channel on YouTube at http://bit.ly/sUKAtf.

Explore the Grande microsite at http://bit.ly/s3FQvF.

As you view these sites and videos, think about how this is an example of an ongoing content marketing campaign and how that differs from the typical persuasive marketing campaign.

will tell. What is clear, however, is that B2B buying is done by people. It is done as part of a process called the *buy(ing) cycle* that has both similarities with and differences from the process as carried out in consumer markets.

What Is the B2B Buy Cycle?

Looking at Figure 10.4, it is immediately evident that the concept known as the **buy cycle** is a restatement of the consumer decision process familiar to all students of marketing. Whether you use the term "B2B" or the older descriptor, industrial, it is the set of stages business buyers go through as they make a purchase. Using business marketing terminology, the process is as follows:

- *Needs awareness* in which the potential purchaser recognizes the need for a product or service to meet the needs of a specific business activity.
- *Research* in which the potential purchaser investigates products and vendors.
- *Consideration and comparison* in which the potential purchaser studies potential vendors and their products, arriving at a short list from which the purchase will be made.
- *Procurement* in which the actual purchase transaction is completed.

There are two issues that make the B2B purchase process different from that of the typical consumer purchase process, even though the steps are essentially the same. The first is the length of the purchase cycle. A recent study was conducted by GlobalSpec, a specialty search engine, about the length of the purchase cycle. The findings supported what business marketers have long known: the length of the purchase cycle increases as the price and/or the risk inherent in the purchase go up. Eighty-one percent of its respondents stated that their buying cycle was less than one month long for purchases under $1,000. When the purchase amount is over $10,000, the purchase cycle is five months or longer.

An equally important differentiator from the typical consumer purchase is the number of people involved in the buying decision. The same survey found only 7 percent of buyers making all purchase decisions alone while another 50 percent make less than half of their company's purchase decisions alone.[8] These results suggest that a majority of B2B purchase decisions are made by a group, not by a single person. That phenomenon has long been[9] called the buying center or the decision-making unit. Whatever it is called, it is not a single purchasing agent making the majority of purchases for a business, but a team.

FIGURE **10.4** The B2B (Industrial) Buy Cycle

Source: Marketing Maven Blog: "The Industrial Buy Cycle: Part 1," February 4, 2010, GlobalSpec. Reprinted with permission.

Both the length and the number of people involved in the business purchasing process complicate the task of the marketer. These factors also enhance the importance of lead generation and management in order to understand who the information researcher (gatekeeper) for the business buying center is and to access the current stage of the buying process.

The Lead Generation and Management Process

Whether offline or online communication channels are employed, the basic lead generation and management process follows the steps in Figure 10.5. *Generating* leads means to identify people or businesses that are potential customers (prospects) for the product. *Qualifying* leads is establishing whether the prospects have both the ability and willingness to purchase the product. *Distributing* leads is essentially segmenting or categorizing the leads based on their readiness stage. Leads that are nearing a purchase decision are distributed to a sales force, internal or external, for follow up and closing (*conversion*). Leads that are not yet ready to purchase are distributed to a communications system for nurturing, to be followed up when they near a purchase decision.

Each of these steps represents a distinct set of marketing activities. We take a brief look at each step.

Generating Sales Leads

The first step in the process is to get a person to self-identify as a potential sales lead. Whatever the channel, this process requires producing and distributing content that induces the reader or viewer to ask for more information. This initial stage is called an **inquiry**. In other words, the marketer does not yet know whether that person—the inquiry is made by a single person, whether in a B2B or a B2C market—is actually considering a purchase.

The download of the chart in Figure 10.6 is a good example of thoughtful execution of the inquiry generation step. I went to the author's website to get the current version of the chart. I found it easily and downloaded it—no

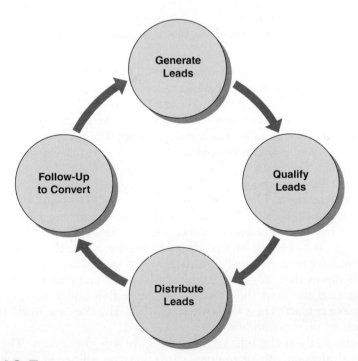

FIGURE **10.5** The Lead Generation and Management Process

Source: © Cengage Learning 2013

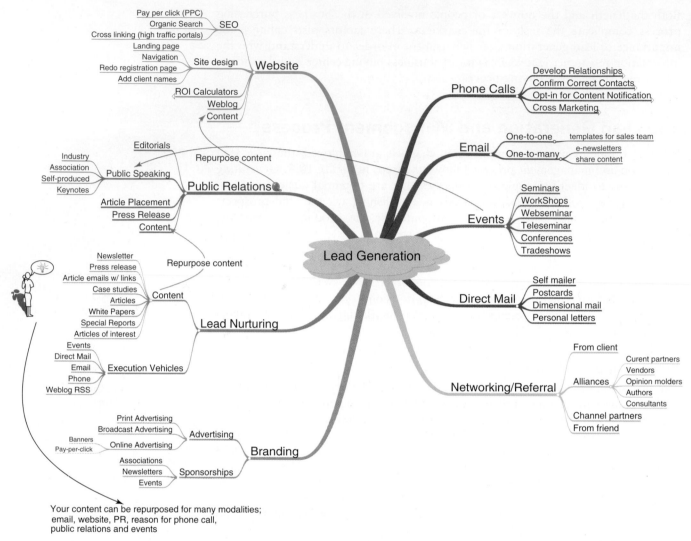

FIGURE **10.6** Online and Offline Lead Generation Channels

Source: "Lead Generation," InTouch, http://www.leadgenerationbook.com/downloads/lead_generation_modality_map.pdf.

personal information, no registration required. Does that risk losing a sales lead? Technically, yes, although in this case it makes sense. InTouch is a marketing services firm that focuses on helping the client's sales force "convert highly qualified leads into revenue" in a complex sales process.[10] As an author and educator, I have a zero probability of ever becoming a client. The content I produce, however, is reaching people who may need to purchase lead management services, now or in the future. This reach creates awareness, and while it is useful, it does not mean that the inquirer has any potential to be classified as a sales lead.

What if you are looking for lead management services and you find your way to the InTouch website? There is a lot of content readily available, including its corporate brochure. The brochure has every possible contact channel listed on the back page, but nowhere on the site is registration needed to get information. Instead, you have to contact InTouch directly if you are interested in becoming a client. This means that only people who work with a complex sales process and have recognized the need for assistance in generating and nurturing leads are likely to make contact. These leads are **hard leads**, and they are worth the follow up to check on their qualifications.

Consider leads at the other end of the hard/soft continuum. The "bingo" cards (many offers on a single response card) that you still see in some magazines tend to produce a large volume of highly unqualified prospects. So does any offer that includes a sizeable free gift, especially one that is unrelated to the product itself. "Soft offers" produce **soft leads**, which in turn produce major marketing expenses as the (few) good are sorted from the (many) bad.

The question is not really whether a marketing department can produce leads. Anyone can produce inquiries if the marketing budget is large enough! The question is how to produce a desired quantity of leads that are worth careful qualification and potential distribution to the sales force. When you put the issues of quality and quantity together, lead generation becomes a serious marketing activity.

Now take a look at the actual content of the chart in Figure 10.6. Most of the lead generation channels are traditional in nature—telephone calls, direct mail, events (which can be virtual as well as physical), word of mouth (networking), public relations, and the various demand generation activities included under the heading of branding. The only two generation channels (we will return to nurturing in a moment) that are directly attributable to the Internet are email and websites. However, all channels have been profoundly affected by the Internet. Much of the contact activity that was once done by mail or by phone is now done by email, and offline channels are often used to drive prospects to the corporate website for in-depth information. Events now include activities like webinars. Press releases that are an important part of public relations are now posted on the Internet and optimized for search (see Chapter 6).

The connection between corporate events and public appearances by corporate personnel at industry events is a traditional one. The activity of "repurposing content" is not entirely new, but this ungrammatically titled effort has become essential in view of the endless appetite of the web for relevant new content. The corporate website and its associated corporate blog have become the hub of all this content, which needs to be widely distributed across the web in order to produce the greatest level of awareness and the largest volume of leads.

The study of B2B purchasers, which Figure 10.7 depicts, tried to find which of these many information sources potential purchasers used most often. The three top sources—search engines, supplier websites, and online catalogs—are

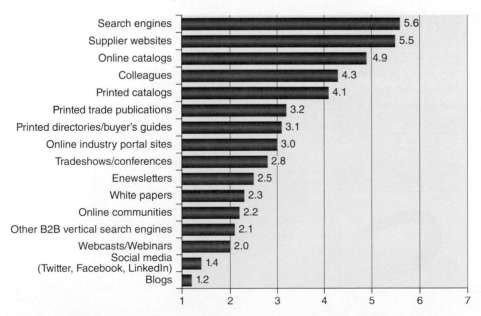

Sources Used When Searching for Products/Services to Purchase
(mean score on scale 1–7, 1 = Rarely use, 7 = Always use)

Source	Score
Search engines	5.6
Supplier websites	5.5
Online catalogs	4.9
Colleagues	4.3
Printed catalogs	4.1
Printed trade publications	3.2
Printed directories/buyer's guides	3.1
Online industry portal sites	3.0
Tradeshows/conferences	2.8
Enewsletters	2.5
White papers	2.3
Online communities	2.2
Other B2B vertical search engines	2.1
Webcasts/Webinars	2.0
Social media (Twitter, Facebook, LinkedIn)	1.4
Blogs	1.2

FIGURE **10.7** Sources Most Often Used by Business Marketers When Researching a Product

Source: "Understanding the Buy Cycle: Align Your Marketing with Customers' Behavior," p. 10, GlobalSpec. Reprinted with permission.

all online sources. The fourth in order of frequency consulted is colleagues, reinforcing the importance of word of mouth in the B2B purchasing process. The critical question is "How do potential customers find these online sources?"

In spite of the importance of online information, marketers cannot just put content on a website and expect people to find it and respond to it in large numbers. People have to find content in places, physical and virtual, that they commonly frequent—which usually does not include corporate websites as a first step. Content distribution that aims to drive traffic to the website can be described as "inbound marketing."

Inbound Marketing for Lead Generation

The concept of **inbound marketing** has been popularized by marketing services firm HubSpot, although concepts like "interruption marketing" and "permission marketing" were originally used by other marketers (see Figure 10.8). Most notable among them is Seth Godin, who has been preaching the doctrine of permission marketing since the early days of the Internet.[11]

It has already been discussed that most potential customers turn to *search* as the first step in the purchase process, even before they consult personal sources (see Chapter 8) or corporate sources of information (see Chapters 5, 6, and 7). This association makes having all content optimized for search a top priority for Internet marketers. It is also important to have content in places frequented by potential customers since they generally see corporate websites as a last stop, not a first one.

HubSpot says succinctly that "Inbound Marketing is marketing focused on getting found by customers."[12] It is not the traditional "marketer talking to customer" approaches characterized in Figure 10.8 as outbound marketing (also described as "interruption marketing"). Instead, inbound marketing involves making content available to customers when and where they want it. It also involves getting customers' permissions to push desired content to them through feeds or newsletters of various kinds. This marketing method has been called **permission marketing** since the early days of the Internet.

However, none of these marketing approaches takes place without content—and lots of it! That is why Figure 10.6 refers to repurposing content for various

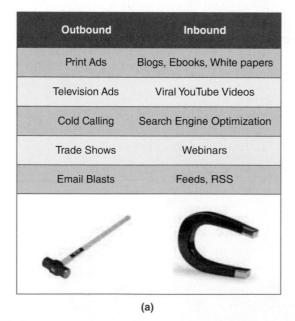

Outbound	Inbound
Print Ads	Blogs, Ebooks, White papers
Television Ads	Viral YouTube Videos
Cold Calling	Search Engine Optimization
Trade Shows	Webinars
Email Blasts	Feeds, RSS

(a)

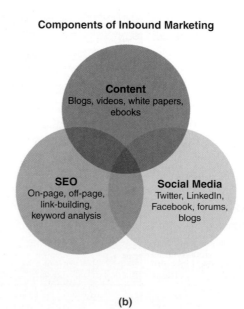

Components of Inbound Marketing

Content
Blogs, videos, white papers, ebooks

SEO
On-page, off-page, link-building, keyword analysis

Social Media
Twitter, LinkedIn, Facebook, forums, blogs

(b)

FIGURE **10.8** The Differences between Outbound and Inbound Marketing

Source: Rick Burnes, "Inbound Marketing & the Next Phase of Marketing on the Web," November 18, 2008, HubSpot, Inc. Reprinted with permission.

channels. This can mean something very simple, such as posting a video on YouTube as well as on the corporate website. It can also take more effort—using corporate material to develop a webinar, for example. Corporate content can be optimized for search in whatever channel it exists. For instance, corporations might establish YouTube channels to group their content and make it easier to locate—the Gillette Old Spice channel discussed in Chapter 9 is a good example. In addition, an individual YouTube video can be tagged to make it easier to find. Businesses can also reach out to customers in other ways on social media as discussed in Chapter 9. Social media encourages the creation of content by customers, which can be a huge asset to the content-creation effort. Any platform like a blog that encourages customer comments also creates an opportunity for customer co-creation of content.

Content Marketing in B2B Markets

We discussed content marketing in B2C markets in Chapter 5. B2B marketers have always done a certain amount of content marketing. Informative content in traditional B2B marketing is generally described as "collateral material." This includes things like brochures or other "leave behinds" that salespeople use as part of the personal selling process. Collateral material has been almost an afterthought as compared to advertising, even in B2B markets. Talking about **content marketing** shifts the focus from traditional advertising, in offline or online media, to marketing that depends on marketer-created and customer-created content that is either informative or entertaining or both.

There are many types of content that are appropriate for the web. The infographic seen in Figure 10.9 characterizes types of content versus channels—an

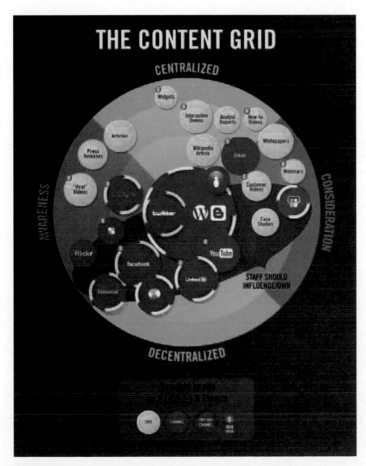

FIGURE **10.9** The Content Grid

important distinction. It also categorizes types of content according to whether they are best used in the customer awareness stage or when the customer is actively considering a purchase. It identifies content and channels, Facebook, for example, which should be the province of the entire staff as opposed to those like whitepapers and press releases that are authored by an individual or a small group. Finally, it indicates types of content that can be rich in useful data.

Notice that many of the content types in this figure were also listed earlier in Figure 10.6, especially under the headings of Events and Content. One recent publication lists 42 different types of content and says that is not all! No single firm can or should use all these techniques to repurpose content and distribute it across the web. The authors suggest that companies start with only a few options that make sense for them and make it easy to repurpose important content (a feed from your Facebook page to your Twitter account, for example). The marketer should test efforts and solicit customer feedback and contributions. This must all be done in a context of understanding the information needs and media habits of the target audience while producing content that conveys a consistent corporate message.[13] In other words, take a strategic approach to producing and distributing content; it is the essence of being visible on the web. Being visible is the necessary forerunner to attracting people to the corporate website from which they can be identified, nurtured, and eventually converted to customers.

It is no longer about fluffy or even persuasive advertising messages. It is about informational content in the brave new world of Internet marketing.

Cost of Lead Generation

The ultimate question is always, "How much does it/should it cost to generate a sales lead?" The answer, as usual, depends on the nature of your product and the competitive environment in your industry. Here are some generalizations. The 2010 study of lead generation by HubSpot found that companies that used mostly outbound marketing (e.g., trade shows, telemarketing, and direct mail) incurred an average cost of $332 per lead, while companies that used mostly inbound techniques incurred an average cost of $134. Within these figures, there are huge variations by firm and by industry. Compared to the firm's average cost per lead, 63 percent of respondents said that social media and blogs produced leads at a lower than average cost. The best performing outbound media were direct mail and telemarketing, producing leads at 37 percent and 34 percent, respectively, below the firm's average.[14] Again, industry sector and individual company variance is huge, but so are the costs to generate a sales lead, whether qualified or not.

Pontiflex, a marketing services company that produces leads for B2C and nonprofit firms, finds the cost of leads in those markets varying from $0.88 (minimal information collected) to $1.47 (more information collected), and gives an understanding of the difference in different vertical markets. In consumer packaged goods, a premium (more information) lead averages $1.16 while in the travel industry, it averages $2.00.[15] This is a significant difference in the cost of consumer leads between consumer packaged goods products and travel products and services. Why the difference? Think about the average price (more precisely the gross margin) of the two types of sales. In general, the travel package will be more expensive and will produce a higher gross margin to cover the costs of lead generation and other marketing activities.

When the same reasoning is applied to the cost of generating a B2B sales lead, the business marketer can accept a higher cost per lead. Also, the large differences in the costs and gross margins of various B2B products means there will be large variations in lead costs between industry segments in business markets.

This discussion of generating sales leads assumes that the firm, whether B2B or B2C, is generating its own sales leads, alone or with the support of a specialty marketing services firm. There are thousands of firms that advertise sales leads at a low cost for virtually any business. On one end are the traditional providers of direct marketing lists, which can loosely be described as sales leads. Hoover's[16] and InfoUSA[17] are both traditional purveyors of business databases and lists to the direct marketing—and now the Internet marketing—industry, for as little as a few cents per lead. The source of the leads is the business and consumer directories compiled by these firms. These are business leads that are qualified only by industry membership; the "lead" does not necessarily have a need for the marketer's product. A survey by Chief Marketer shows that "targeted lists" are still popular among B2B marketers,[18] although its list of direct marketing tools used for prospecting did not appear to include either PPC or search optimization.

There are also marketers who offer a set of "free leads" for little or nothing as an incentive for purchasing more leads. Many of these leads are of extremely poor quality and have been obtained in questionable ways like hacking. Purchasing sales leads is a "buyer beware" activity! The poorer the initial lead quality, the more it will cost to qualify them and the fewer good leads will come out the end of the lead funnel.

How Marketers Generate Sales Leads

B2B marketers do not talk a great deal about their lead generation and management campaigns. Competitors are listening and marketers do not like to give away campaigns that work. This is especially true for lead generation campaigns because many of them continue for a long time with ongoing improvements learned from the campaign itself.

On the other hand, marketing service firms that offer lead generation and management services like to talk about success brought to their clients by their products. Be a bit careful of what you find and what you believe, especially when the aim is to sell a product or a service. Here are two recent examples told from the marketer perspective:

1. Cloud Marketing Labs helps small and mid-sized businesses generate sales leads using inbound marketing. In early 2010, it realized that it needed to "drink its own Kool-Aid," follow the advice it gave to clients. Founder Greg Digneo described the company's situation as: *"How can a business that does not have many hits on their website, has no followers on Twitter, and no Fans on Facebook, generate sales leads using inbound marketing in only 30 days?"*

   Cloud Marketing Labs is a small start-up and it cannot do everything described in the previous discussion. It focused on three marking activities.

   - One was blogging. You need a story, a mission, and a perspective on what your business marketing firm does. The story that Cloud Marketing Labs wanted to dispense was "sales leads in 30 days using social media." Because it already had good content on its blog, it made use of that content by sending links to friends and customers and asking them to share it with their friends. Many people will retweet good links; some will post them on their Facebook pages; and a few will email them to their friends and colleagues. However, Digneo warns that you should not abuse your friends by doing this often.
   - Second was a focus on public relations. It used blogger relations strategies to offer guest posts on other blogs. (For instance, I read its post on the Real Time Marketer blog,[19] not on the Cloud Marketing Labs corporate blog.) It also developed a webinar on the subject and publicized it using the PRWeb Services, which optimizes press releases for web search.
   - Third was the use of PPC advertising. It used Facebook ads, not Google AdWords for two reasons. The first is that Facebook PPC ads are

cheaper. Second is related to the visibility about the target audience that Facebook offers.[20]

Did it work? According to Greg Digneo, writing on its corporate blog:

> At the start of this plan we started with exactly one visitor to our website. When we presented our webinar at the end of the 30 days, we had over 1,200 visitors to our landing page, website and blog. There were 107 registrants to the webinar and we have already given out four proposals. Finally, due to our PR efforts, we've been featured on 2 blogs, and contributed to an article on Entrepreneur.com.[21]

Cloud Marketing Lab focused on online communications with fairly conventional lead generation approaches: writing for trade publications (in this case, blogs), public relations (optimized for web search), and advertising (PPC online). Doyenz used an even more high-tech twist on a traditional approach—generating sales leads at trade events.

2. Doyenz offers cloud-based disaster recovery systems for IT networks. Under content strategist Adriana Dunn, Doyenz set out to increase its followers on Facebook and Twitter. It wanted to use two conferences in November 2010 to create more followers. It used a QR code provided by a specialty firm called Likify.

A **QR (quick response) code** is a small symbol that works on the same general principles as a bar code (see Figure 10.10). A QR code can be scanned by smartphones that have downloaded the appropriate reader. The Likify system, as the name suggests, allows users to "like" a Facebook page, in this case, Doyenz's page.[22] It is a new technology and does require interested parties to (easily) download a reader, but someday, it just might replace the time-honored lead generation technique of asking people to drop business cards in a fishbowl at the event. Doyenz does appear to be adding likers on Facebook and followers on Twitter and has an active Facebook page full of content. Time will tell whether electronic techniques like this catch on. What cannot be denied, however, is that whether attendees drop business cards in a fishbowl or scan a QR code, any inquiry has to be followed up to determine whether it is a real sales lead and if the person is sales-ready.

FIGURE **10.10** A Likify QR Code

Source: Boondoggle-Life Labs (www.likify.net), http://boondoggle-lifelabs.prezly.com/likify–enables-people-to–like-real-world-products-on-facebook-through-qr-code.

Purchasing Sales Leads

No discussion of generating sales leads would be complete without a mention of the "make or buy" decision that businesses constantly face. Our coverage of sales lead generation has intentionally focused on the "make" aspect—a company generating and managing its own sales leads. However, there are a plethora of companies who are eager to sell sales leads in virtually any quantity the marketer desires. These purchased leads are almost always cheaper per lead than the ones internally generated. Some come from highly reputable sources—the business directories and financial ratings firms, for example. At the other end of the quality spectrum are leads that are collected by bots that search the web for any business mention. In between is a huge quality range, from very good to very bad.

Whatever the quality of the collection process, purchased leads tend to have one thing in common; there is no indication whether the so-called lead is in the market for the product or not. There are exceptions, like firms that specialize in sales leads that are gleaned from sources like paid search, where clicking on an ad is an indicator of customer interest. There is, however, no question that internally generated sales leads are generally of better quality than purchased leads. That said, there is great pressure on marketing managers to keep the sales force supplied with leads, and this often results in the purchasing of leads, even by companies with excellent lead generation and management programs. There are two warnings: purchased leads need to be qualified just like internally generated ones; and, second, buyer beware!

Qualifying Sales Leads

Once an inquiry has been generated, the next step is to qualify in order to determine whether it actually represents a sales lead. Direct marketers have a time-honored model of issues that must be included in the qualification process. These issues can be stated as:

- Desire: for the product or service
- Authority: to make the purchase decision
- Money: for making the purchase
- Need: for the benefits the product will deliver

A moment's reflection suggests that these issues are easily translated into specific questions that can be asked to try to qualify an inquirer as a lead. For instance, "Do you have money in this year's budget to make the purchase?" The inquirer will generally know the answers to the qualifying questions and will be willing to provide them. This process saves time for both the marketer and the prospective purchaser.

Prior to the Internet, qualification was almost entirely conducted by telephone. It is a process that works, but it is relatively expensive. Today, firms try to get as much qualifying information as they can in the inquiry process as shown in the HubSpot information request form (see Figure 10.11).

Deciding how much information to request requires a delicate balancing act. Think of it in customer relationship terms. There really is no relationship yet, so prospects are reluctant to give up much information. The more information the marketer can get, the less it will cost to identify real leads and qualify them. The minimal amount of information is name and email address. On the HubSpot qualifying form, each box below the email request represents a specific decision that the information is worth the risk of losing the inquiry. This set of information is moderate in size—not minimal but also not detailed. The comments box is useful however and allows the inquirers to further qualify themselves, saving time and money for everyone concerned. (For instance, they could note something like, "I'm a marketing student, not a buyer.") It is also a smart idea to use empty space on the page for more content offers.

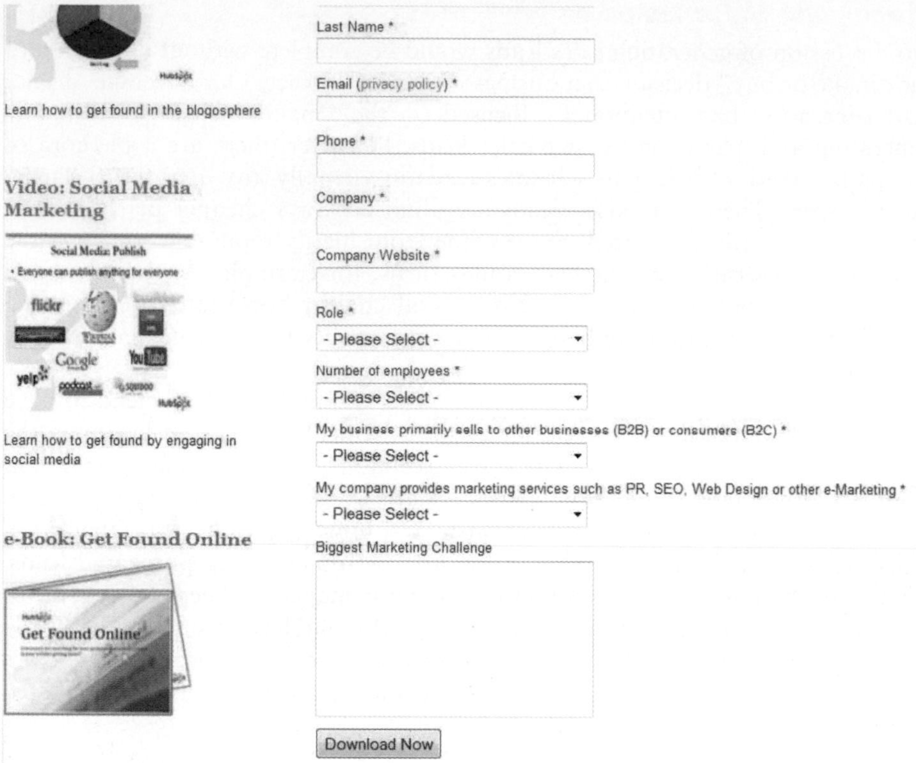

FIGURE **10.11** A Qualification Form for Information Download

Source: HubSpot, http://www.hubspot.com/lead-generation-using-inbound-marketing-kit.

How does the marketer know how much information is too much? First, you test, as will be described later in the chapter. Second, you review the web metrics to determine how many people start to fill out the form and exit the page before completing it. It is even better if the analytics allows you to see at which line in the form the visitor stops.

Cost of Lead Qualification

The higher the lead quality, the less it will cost to qualify it; this is the underlying rationale for getting as much information as possible in the inquiry process.

David Green, director of best practices at MECLABS, has a hypothetical example of **lead qualification**, which is drawn from wide experience. The ratio of 70 valid leads per 100 shown in Figure 10.12 is reasonable and can be affected up or down by the desirability of the offer and the amount and intrusiveness of the information requested on the inquiry form.

Green assumes that the cost of a sales rep, including salary and fringes, is $200,000, and the rep has 1,960 productive hours available after vacation, training, and so on. If she can make 10 qualification calls per hour, that will amount to 19,600 phone calls per year. If she takes 4.2 minutes to make a qualification call, it will take a total of 40 hours to qualify all 100 leads. If only the 70 valid leads enter the qualification process, the number of hours is reduced to 34. If only sales-ready leads are called, the number of hours is less than 3, reducing the total cost from $4,082 to $286.

Decreasing qualification costs by acquiring more valid and sales-ready leads is a matter of degree, not of absolutes. It is reasonable to strive for a high proportion of valid leads, but a firm is unlikely to ever get only sales-ready leads. In fact, such a scenario would not be desirable. The lead pipeline needs to be kept stocked with leads in various stages of readiness to keep sales stable and sales costs at a minimum. Remember that these figures are hypothetical. Any good

	Annual cost	Hourly cost
Loaded cost/Sales rep	$ (200,000)	$ (102)

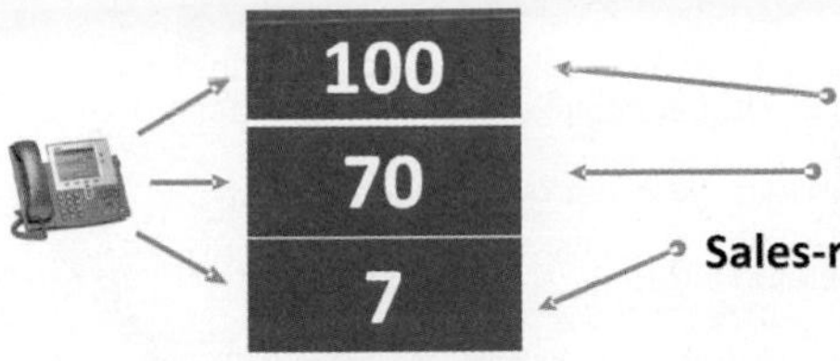

	Leads	Hours	Cost/Hour
New leads	100	40	$ (4,082)
Valid leads	70	34	$ (3,469)
Sales-ready leads	7	2.8	$ (286)

Assumes 1,960 hours per year and 19,600 dials.

FIGURE **10.12** Lowering the Cost of Lead Qualification

Source: J. David Green, "2011 Lead Generation Trends and Challenges," p. 20, November 15, 2010. Reprinted with permission of MECLABS.

marketer tracks the success of individual lead generation programs using metrics like number of leads, cost per lead by medium, and number of qualified leads. *Past performance is the best measure of success, not general or hypothetical industry metrics.*

Lead Scoring and Distribution

The essence of **lead distribution** is to categorize leads for immediate closing efforts or nurturing them with a view to future closing. There is also a delicate balance between giving salespeople only well-qualified leads that are worthy of their efforts and keeping them supplied with a target number of leads.

Lead scoring requires a model that requires data that includes:

- Online activity: number and frequency of visits to site, multiple visitors from same firm, time spent, clicks on email newsletters, and more (negative: time spent on job openings page)
- Current or previous customer relationship
- Title; role in buying center: purchasing agent may be a negative, depending on product in question
- Ideal customer profile: industry, size of firm, annual revenue, and more[23]

It should be noted that most of these criteria are not simple "yes/no" questions. It may be sufficient to score them on a simple scale—1 to 3, for example. In that case, a set of categories needs to be developed for items like "number of visits to site: 1 visit in past six months, 3–5 in past six months, 6 or more in past six months." This categorization suggests that the marketer is rescoring leads every six months. It is often better to assign points for each item instead of using a scale. A point system allows the marketer to build in weights for important or negative items. For example, the VP of procurement title may be heavily weighted positively; whereas a prospect in a region where the firm does not have sales representation may be heavily weighted negatively.

There are automatic scoring applications available from CRM (customer relationship management), metrics, and lead suppliers. These applications make operations easier, but they do not solve the basic problem. The marketer must ensure that he has a scoring system that genuinely expresses the lead quality, and he must revisit the items and associated scores at frequent intervals to make certain that they still accurately reflect the firm's situation and needs.

The outcome is a set of lead categories. Figure 10.13 shows the minimum number of categories—leads ready for distribution to sales force, leads for

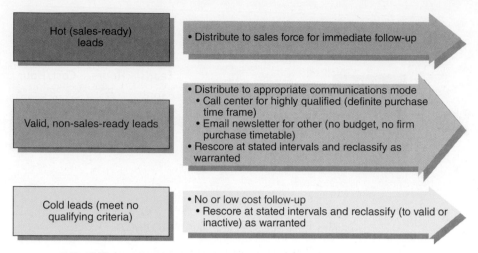

FIGURE **10.13** A Sales Lead Distribution System
Source: © Cengage Learning 2013

nurturing, and leads to receive no attention at present. Even this simple system has subcategories—telephone call versus enewsletter for non-sales-ready leads, for example. A scoring system can become much more complex, but it is wise to start as simply as possible and add to the complexity of the scoring only as experience clearly demonstrates the need.

Lead Generation and Scoring at EDGAR Online

Lead scoring is an area in which business marketers often seek the assistance of a marketing services firm. Silverpop, originally a supplier of email services, is one firm that offers lead scoring as part of its marketing automation software.[24]

The experience of financial services firm EDGAR Online as a client of Silverpop represents several of the issues. EDGAR Online's basic problem was one shared by many marketers: it needed to increase the quality of the leads distributed to the sales force; in other words, to make sure they were indeed sales-ready. It began by better promoting its content—white papers and newsletters and by offering free product trials as an incentive. This promotion actually increased the number of leads generated, which could have compounded its problem. Instead, it refined its lead scoring criteria and developed a careful, automated lead distribution process. According to Bill Shaughnessy, director of online marketing:

> We score every single lead that comes through our online registration. As a result, the quality of those leads passed over to sales has gone up tremendously. Those that meet the criteria are automatically routed to the appropriate sales division. For those leads that do not meet the criteria, the team is now able to effectively nurture these leads until they are ready to buy.

The Silverpop case study recounts the following outcomes:

- Attraction of new customers and better communication with existing ones led to a 400 percent increase in sales leads.
- The lead scoring system led to "tremendous increase" in quality of warm leads.
- The rate of sales closure is more than double the average for EDGAR Online's industry sector.[25]

This technique makes such good sense that all good B2B marketers do it, right? Sadly, that is not the case. A 2008 study by consultancy Aberdeen found only 57 percent of marketers using lead management technology (a part of larger marketing automation systems) at that point in time. Only 40 percent of its respondents were using lead scoring and prioritization (distribution).[26] The low usage of these systems is usually the result of an organizational disconnect between marketing and advertising, who produce the sales leads, and sales, who are responsible for following them up and closing the sale. All too often lead qualification falls into the organizational crack between marketing/advertising and sales, and is simply not followed up. Marketing is spending money to generate leads. Sales complains that the leads received are of poor quality. If no one in the organization is responsible for fixing the crack, the organizational return on its marketing and sales investment suffers. In fact, Aberdeen estimates that 70 percent of all sales leads *are never acted upon* and that 45 percent of the leads the company generates will eventually buy the product, but *from a competitor, not from the company itself.*[27]

To sum up, the activities leading up to the closing step are of great importance, even though the point of the entire process is to close the sale.

Lead Conversion

While "lead conversion" can generically be defined as closing a sale, it too can be a deceptively simple concept. Omniture, a metrics and process optimization firm, says:

> In general, most organizations spend more time and money promoting their websites through acquisition channels such as search or affiliate marketing than they do optimizing existing conversion rates.
>
> In addition to neglecting the conversion process, we tend to think of conversion too narrowly as only converting existing site visitors in the, "here and now." We often overlook applying marketing fundamentals such as identifying and defining profiles that comprise our larger target audience, developing the right offer and corresponding message, and delivering it to them at the right time in their purchase cycle.

Omniture goes on to say that this is all about relevancy—the right content and offers at the right time—the customer's right time, not the marketer's! It lists seven steps in an optimized conversion process:

1. *Identify Conversion Goals and KPIs.* **Key performance indicators (KPIs)** are internal benchmarks for performance at each stage: number of advertising impressions, number of click-throughs to the site, and number of lead forms completed, for example.
2. *Define and Acquire Target Profiles—Apply 40/40/20 Rule.* Chapter 4 discusses the direct marketing rule that 40 percent of success can be attributed to targeting and another 40 percent to the offer with 20 percent being attributable to creative execution.
3. *Organize and Optimize Site Structure.* It is important to have a site that makes it easy for visitors to find and purchase what they want.
4. *Develop a Compelling Message.* The importance of the message seems to go without saying, but in this context, it must be a message that is relevant to each specific audience segment.
5. *Place Effective Calls to Action.* Chapter 4 notes that specific and compelling calls to action are a key part of any direct-response effort. That notion applies to conversion as well.
6. *Enhance Shopping Cart and Lead Capture Processes.* A visitor with a product interest has only two action options while on the website: he purchases the product at that moment using the shopping cart function; or alternatively, he can fill out a form requesting more information or to be kept informed via newsletters. A third option, of course, is to leave without doing either. It is the job of the marketer to ensure that few qualified prospects as possible leave the site without taking positive action of some kind.
7. *Test, Measure, and Refine.* There are many steps in the conversion process that can be tested. We will discuss testing landing pages later in this chapter. Both test results and the metrics produced by the program can and should be used to improve future conversion programs.

These steps also seem to follow a commonsense approach, and they do. However, they only mention the thorny problem of defining exactly what a conversion is so appropriate goals can be set.

How to Define Conversion

Traditional direct marketers are responsible for the term "conversion," and its original definition is making the first sale to a prospect—converting the lead to a sale. As the importance of CRM became evident in the 1980s, direct marketers were heard to speak of "converting to a loyal customer." That sounds like exactly what marketers are trying to do, but it begs the question of exact metrics. Is it the second or maybe the third sale? Is it obtaining a growing share of the customer's expenditure on the product in question? It could be either, or both! It could be another performance indicator that is more closely tied to the company's strategy.

As time has gone on, even more groups inside the organization have taken some responsibility for generating sales leads. Marketing is responsible for the branding aspect of demand generation. Advertising is responsible for various types of advertising, some of which may have a direct call to action. If direct response is an important part of the company's strategy, it is likely to have a direct marketing department that is responsible for that portion of the overall advertising.

Recently, companies have begun to report success in generating sales leads through social media marketing. Ed Linde II of IBM's online marketing team says his company has "uncovered millions of dollars worth of sales leads" through social media so far, using a program called Listening for Leads, and expects continued growth. Again, the lead generation is part of a careful process, which he describes as follows:

> We try to identify those leads, get them to a lead development rep who is a telephone sales rep who has been trained to have a conversation with the lead to qualify and validate the opportunity. They'll qualify and validate it and then pass it to the appropriate sales resource to follow up.[28]

His statement suggests two important conclusions:

1. There is no "one size fits all" definition of a sales lead, much less a sales conversion. *Each company should customize its own definition of a conversion, arriving at one that reflects its goals and processes.*
2. There may be multiple "conversion" points. For example, you often hear social media marketers saying they have "converted" a Facebook fan to a sales lead when the fan clicks on a link and provides contact information on the website in return for desired information. From the standpoint of the social media team, it seems to be a conversion, because the team has passed on the responsibility to another group. However, using conversion that way is a loose application of the term. *Measurable objectives should be established for each team at each stage of the lead generation and management process.*

In most firms, there are many internal teams involved in various stages of the lead process, and each should have its own target to reach for that stage. The "sales funnel" is the concept commonly used to describe this process. The funnel in Figure 10.14 is typical and has some useful additional strategy guidance.

The customer is correctly portrayed as the centerpiece of the process with the funnel itself representing the stages of the B2B buying process and the categories on the right representing the generic stages of lead qualification. Media channels on the left are paired with the appropriate customer readiness stage. Various internal teams—marketing, advertising, online marketing, direct marketing, the internal call center, and more—are implied by the media channels. Promotional programs (a webinar, for example) and ongoing marketing activities (lead qualification in the call center, for example) *must each have specific targets.*

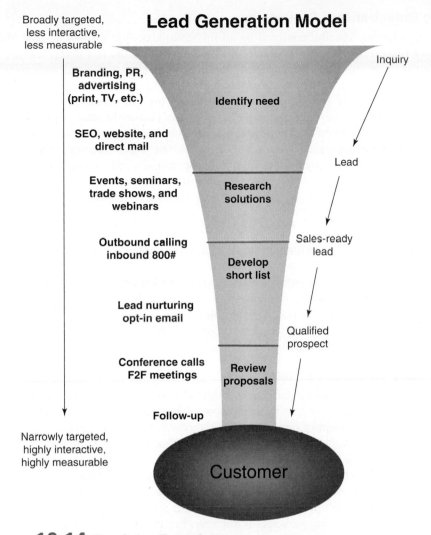

FIGURE **10.14** The Sales Funnel

Source: "Start with a lead: Eight Critical Success Factors for Lead Generation," ebook by Brian J. Carroll, p. 7 (http://www.startwithalead.com/ebooks).

A webinar should have a specific lead goal for its program; the call center should have specific time-based goals.

All leads from whichever channel go into a central database, which identifies each lead by media source. Each lead should be tracked through to a sale or lack thereof. As data throughout the chapter has indicated, leads generated from different sources tend to have different acquisition costs. To further complicate the matter, they also tend to have different conversion rates, making the cost per converted lead vastly different from one channel to another. This is an important input into planning future marketing strategy.

INTERACTIVE EXERCISE 10.2   **Calculate ROI for Lead Generation**

Sales lead generation and management is a time-consuming and expensive process. Marketers need to be prepared to demonstrate that it is worth the cost. The basics of the ROI (return on investment) calculation are laid out in an interactive spreadsheet provided by one leading consultant in sales lead generation. Try some

assumptions in it to get a sense of issues facing the marketer and how sensitive outcomes are to some of your assumptions.

Download the spreadsheet at http://bit.ly/tSBXl2.

The Organizational Conundrum

Are you feeling lost and confused by all this complexity? If so, you are not alone! Senior marketing managers recognize the complexity and the fact that it will require an investment in process improvement and marketing automation software to resolveit. This may take some time, postponing the ROI until sometime in the future.

Even worse, all this occurs in the context of organizational politics in which the leader of each internal team may be trying to maximize his team's performance, even at the expense of performance in other stages of the process—generating a large number of low-quality leads, for example. The organizational context represents a serious management issue that will take time and effort to resolve. Sadly, it is often easier just to ignore the issue of an optimal lead process.

Lead Generation and Management Issues

B2B marketing can be a complex activity. However, there are approaches that help clarify strategic options, making the process more straightforward. There are four important ones that are especially relevant in the context of this chapter. Please keep in mind that although the illustrations are B2B, they are also techniques that are widely used in B2C marketing. The four methods are creation of customer personas, development of scenarios, creation of conversion paths through the website, and testing of landing pages and other marketing activities.

Creating Customer Personas

Every marketing student is familiar with the concept of market segmentation and knows how important it is to select the appropriate target segment for a marketing campaign. The concept of **personas** takes the concept one step further. It puts flesh on the bones of a typical segment profile, which describes a customer (or perhaps a customer firm in B2B) on a series of business demographic, product use, and buying behavior items. The items are straightforward quantitative measures: "yearly revenue between $50 and 100 million," for example. A persona weaves a textual description around the set of quantitative data, making it qualitative and humanizing it.

The idea of creating personas is not new, but it has become newly popular in the context of the Internet. Personas are helpful to everyone involved with customers, but they are especially helpful with the interface between marketing and IT. It is the job of marketing to select segments around which to develop marketing strategy and to profile those segments for strategy execution. It is the job of IT to design websites and landing pages that reflect the strategy and support the execution. If marketing can give IT a written depiction of a specific customer who represents a specific segment, IT will have a human image to which it can design. Such a specialized strategy should result in a better product from both the marketing and IT standpoint.

In its ebook entitled *Persuasion Architecture Future Now*, a consulting group defines personas as "archetypical fictional characters who represent your buying audience." In describing how this group creates personas for its clients, it goes on to say:

> When we design personas for persuasive systems, we are primarily interested in understanding how they initiate relationships, how they gather information, how they approach the decision-making process, what language they use and how they prefer to obtain agreement and closure. These are the principal factors that influence how we choose and connect prospects to content that helps them buy in a manner comfortable to them.[29]

Personas are created on the basis of detailed marketing research—both qualitative and quantitative—and website and other online metrics.[30] Consultant Patty Seybold cataloged the many methods that Staples used in creating personas for its website design that ranged from conventional marketing surveys to the less conventional observation of customers in its own offices.[31] Use of these personas in the actual website redesign will be discussed in Chapter 12.

Digital marketer Paris Danielle describes a B2C persona created for Yellow Tail wine. The persona is a young wife and mother named Andrea who is deeply engaged in the lives of her young son and her military husband. The persona describes her on several dimensions:

- *Needs* that include connection to family and friends and time balance between family and her own routine.
- *Fear* of disconnection to family and friends and to her own creative self.
- *Aspirations* that include serenity in her life and seeking cultural influences that will help her grow her career as a photographer.

The persona statement also describes her connectedness to other young moms, her online activities, and her purchasing behavior.

How does Yellow Tail wine fit into the picture? Andrea is quoted as saying, "Wine accompanies the times when I mellow out. It's artful and puts me in a beautiful place." Why Yellow Tail wine? She chooses her own lifestyle and Yellow Tail's tag line, "Play by your rules" fits her well. What kind of wine? Pino Grigio, which she enjoys and which saves her family money.[32]

This is a warm and engaging portrait of a consumer who undoubtedly represents a Yellow Tail segment. The persona helps everyone who is planning campaigns and developing content for the brand to understand the target audience and create appeals that work.

Figure 10.15 is a graphical representation of a customer persona that was developed in the specific context of lead generation and management in a B2B market. It describes a CIO (chief information officer) who is in the category of transformational leader, one of the three types identified by CIO magazine.[33] It contains a great

	Technical Decision Maker: The Transformational Leader
	• CIO • Technical decision maker • Develops IT strategy and roadmap • Leads technology team that evaluates technology options
Key Attributes	40-55 years old; Masters in Science, Executive MBA; at least 1 leadership roles
Attitude	Leader, business savvy, frugal, skeptical of vendor claims
Reputation	Visionary, decisive, well regarded within industry, egotistical
Job Focus	Creating enterprise-wide change, shifting perception of techno
Pain Points	• Identifying most promising technology • Getting company-wide buy-in for new software initiatives • Finding ways to make measurable impact
Keywords Used to Search for Information	enterprise software ROI, strategic software investments, breaki enterprise-wide productivity
Values	• **Leadership:** Ability to see and convey the "big picture" • **Knowledge and expertise:** Broad IT knowledge but not inte • **Innovation:** Follows latest trends; seeks proof of how others • **Expectations:** High expectations of IT team and vendors/so
Fears	Making bad purchase decision, tarnishing reputation
Pet Peeves	Self-serving vendors who don't do their homework to understa implementation
Internal influences	Board of directors, CEO, CFO
Motivators	Bonus structure, ego, industry recognition
Information Sources	Peers; online search; Gartner, Forrester; Gartner CIO Leaders magazine
Content Preferences	In-depth white papers, podcasts

FIGURE **10.15** Persona for a CIO in the Transformational Leader Segment

Source: http://www.findnewcustomers.com/buyerpersonas.

deal of detail on what this type of CIO does and how he does it. It includes data that are specific to B2B marketing like pain points. It also includes important characteristics like values and motivators and critical details like keywords used in searches and favorite information sources.

The questions a marketer needs to answer in order to develop a persona like this are laid out by Jeff Ogden, President of Find New Customers, a B2B lead generation firm. His questions are:

- What pressing issues keep this person up at night?
- What motivates her to take action?
- What sources does he turn to for information and daily news?
- How does she go about making business decisions?
- What type of organizations does he belong to and what events does he attend?
- Does he seek advice from colleagues, industry peers or unbiased third parties?
- What specific words or phrases does she use to describe the problems she is facing? (This is almost always missed!)
- What might prevent her from selecting your company or product?
- What are his content preferences throughout the buying cycle?[34]

He argues that it is important to know your target buyer in as much depth and detail as possible in order to sell effectively,[35] and this persona is a good example of that kind of knowledge.

Developing Purchasing Scenarios

The term **scenario** may be familiar to you from a strategy course. Here are two definitions from the corporate strategy literature:

1. Michael Porter defines a scenario as "an internally consistent view of what the future might turn out to be—not a forecast, but one possible future outcome."
2. Peter Schwartz describes scenario analysis as "a tool for ordering one's perception about alternative future environments in which one's decisions might be played."[36]

Marketers use scenarios in at least two ways. The first is to understand the customer purchasing process for uses such as developing a content strategy. The second is more specific: to understand how the customer uses the website in making a purchase. We will discuss conversion paths in a coming section.

The GrokDotCom blog defines a marketing (persuasion) scenario as follows:

> A scenario consists of persuasive components that lead a visitor segment to participate in a conversion action. Some of these components will be linear; others will be non-linear. All must be customer-focused—based on how each segment approaches the decision to buy—rather than business-focused.[37]

Consultant Patricia Seybold, writing about the use of scenarios by her consultancy, describes the kind of revelations marketers can find when they get the customers' perspective on the purchase process. Two of her examples are:

- Monster, the job search website, is an important tool for corporate recruiters. Monster prided itself on providing a large number of qualified candidates for each job that recruiters were trying to fill. What it found was that the large number of candidates it was returning caused the recruiters to spend too much time screening. According to Seybold, "They wanted the best three candidates and they wanted them within 24 hours."
- Merck's Medco consumer prescription management service deals with a long value chain—doctors, insurers, and pharmaceutical companies to name only some. Consumers care about getting their prescriptions refilled quickly and accurately. Other members of Medco's value chain had policies and procedures in place that interfered with or slowed down refilling of prescriptions on the site. By working with the members of the value chain to align refill

policies, Medco was able to eliminate 30 percent of pharmacists' and patients' telephone calls that had been coming in to its call center.[38]

The Irish consultancy iQ Content has an example of a complete scenario written for website design use. It calls it sales call back (variant 1), which reads as follows:

> The Sales Prospect sees an offer on the site that they'd like to avail of but they'd like more information before deciding to buy. There's a link that says you can have a member of the Vodafone customer care team call you about the offer at a time of your choosing. They click that link and because the offer is open only to existing Vodafone customers the system checks to see if they are logged in. They aren't, so they are taken to the log in screen. This also offers them the option of registering if they do not have log in details already. The Sales Prospect logs in and is taken to the call back scheduling form. The query title, relating to the specific offer the Sales Prospect expressed interest in, has already been entered on the form by the system and their personal details are already entered in the relevant form fields. The Sales Prospect schedules a call using the form controls and submits the form.[39]

Notice that this scenario works fine if the prospect is a Vodafone customer. What if she is not? One good solution would be variant 2 in which there is a different offer for noncustomers and/or a call to action to become a customer. That is a primary benefit of a scenario; it allows the marketer to see what is working or not working and what else may be needed.

Personas put life into market segment descriptors, and scenarios map out the path to conversion, which can be website-specific or more general in nature. This process is, however, aimed at getting prospects onto the website and converting them to customers there. The next step then is a landing page.

Designing and Testing Landing Pages

The **landing page** refers to the page customers encounter when they click through from any channel to a business website, which sounds simple enough, correct? It is correct as stated, but there are two possibilities:

1. There is a product page already on the website that will fill the information needs promised in the channel content. This may meet the visitor's needs quite well, but it does not allow the marketer to identify the person or to obtain any qualifying information.
2. A landing page is constructed that is specific to the content or offer in one or more channels. This type of landing page is housed on a server but is not part of the website itself. It allows the marketer to get contact and qualifying information like that in Figure 10.11. This is much more useful in the context of lead generation and management and it is the type of landing page we will describe in this section.

There is another alternative and a huge mistake that is often made. First, the mistake. The click-through from the external channel simply plops the visitor down on the corporate home page that requires the visitor to locate the information he expected, often on a large and complex site. That is a perfect recipe for immediately losing a visitor. Ask yourself this: why does a company spend good money to create content or to place advertising only to fail to meet the needs of what might otherwise be a prospect? *There is no good reason for simply dumping click-throughs on the corporate home page.* There must be a landing page, whether it already exists on the website or whether it must be constructed specifically for the ad or lead generation campaign.

There is another option that was exemplified by the Juan Eloqua lead generation campaign shown in Figure 10.3b. The click-through from the email landed prospects on a **microsite**. The term "microsite" is often used rather loosely, but it is properly used to refer to a page or set of pages with a URL different from the homepage of the website. The information on it is usually temporary and therefore can be removed without redesigning navigation paths on the main site. It can also be referred to as a "minisite."[40] This description perfectly fits the Juan Eloqua site. It has videos and offers that would be hard to include on a single landing page without it becoming very busy. The microsite can also be expanded for other Grande Guides, videos, and additional offers, again without interfering with the main site.

Since the corporate product pages that may be identified as satisfactory landing pages already exist on the website, our discussion will focus on landing pages that are constructed for a specific promotional program.

There is a great deal of useful advice on the Internet about best practices for creating landing pages[41] and landing page mistakes.[42] A good summary comes from MarketingExperiments, which, as the name suggests, conducts extensive testing of marketing activities throughout the sales funnel, using the techniques described in Chapter 4. It uses the term "marketing optimization," which has become popular to describe data-driven improvements at any stage of the sales funnel. From its extensive testing experience, it has settled on three criteria for landing pages that work—*simplicity, continuity*, and *relevance*.

Figure 10.16 shows the second stage in an optimization process, testing and improving a landing page. The company had already tested and improved the PPC ad for this unidentified business software company, improving the click-through rate by 21 percent.[43]

The next step was to make changes in the landing page to increase its simplicity, continuity, and relevance. The changes were:

- To improve the layout by eliminating the left-hand navigation bar and reducing the number of call to action buttons to just one. Taking off the website navigation bar from the landing page may seem counterintuitive, but look at it this way: the marketer wants the reader to click on the call to action button, following the conversion path the marketer has designed. Clicking on anything

Landing Page Experiment

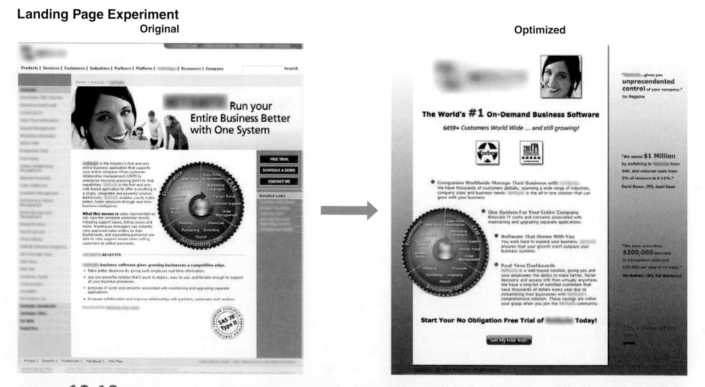

FIGURE **10.16** Testing a Landing Page to Optimize Click-Throughs

Source: Marketing Experiments, http://www.marketingexperiments.com/journals/3rd%20Quarter%20%282010%29%20-%20MEx%20Research%20Journal.pdf.

else—any one of the links on the navigation bar—interrupts and probably destroys the conversion path. The changes created a *simpler* page.

- To "chunk" the copy into smaller bulleted units. The headline, subhead and the award symbols directly below the subhead mirrored the "we're number 1" promise made on the PPC ad, thereby improving the *continuity* from one element of the path to another. MarketingExperiments points out that the information was already there; it just rearranged it.
- To improve the *relevance* of the landing page, it included customer testimonials. Though brief, the testimonials included numbers that demonstrated improved outcomes from use of the software.

Taken together, these changes improved the click-throughs from the landing page to the forms page by 54 percent.

MarketingExperiments also optimized the forms page using both design and messaging that reflected the landing page. The form looked simpler, but it actually asked for the same amount of information. And the number of forms submitted increased by 97 percent. That growth was not all the result of the improved form; more people arrived on the landing page and more people clicked through from the landing page. That meant there were many more people who arrived at the forms page where the completion rate improved by just over 7 percent from the original to the optimized form.

An improved landing page helped a great deal in this particular test. However, *it was the optimization of each page as part of a three-step process* that created the final outcome—an improvement of 272 percent in overall conversion. According to MarketingExperiments, this "272% increase in conversion led to 268% more projected revenue and, when combined with the corresponding 66% reduction in cost-per-acquisition (fewer unqualified searchers clicked on the optimized ad), the optimized path produced more than four times the monthly profit (302% increase)."[44] This data demonstrates the value of testing in the Internet marketing environment.

Personas, scenarios, and learning from testing and research all contribute to the creation of effective paths through the site that will allow visitors to obtain the information they need to convert to customers.

Conversion Paths

By now, you understand that visitors take various routes (paths) through a website. One job of the marketer is to ensure that as many of them purchase (convert) as possible. Of course, there is one further complication. Figure 10.17 shows a set of paths through an unrealistically simple video games site that explains the issue.

The complication is that different market segments take different paths through the site. Would you expect the person who comes to a video games site to purchase the latest Star Wars game to take the same path through the site as a person who came to purchase a game but did not know which specific one? Would either one of those segments take the same path as a person who just dropped by the site to see what they stocked? No; these three and other segments would take different paths, and the marketer needs to satisfy the information needs of each and provide a call to action at the appropriate time.

Figure 10.17 shows that 100 visitors enter the site, and some visitors apparently came to look at games while others came to look at gaming devices. Of the 60 who came to look at games, more (40) went to the Star Wars page than to the PacMan page (20). Of those who went to the Star Wars page, half purchased while the other half was evenly split between leaving the site and going on to the product demonstration page. A majority of those who saw the demonstration purchased the game and the rest exited the site; although it is possible that they could have looped back and looked at another game. The marketer has now accounted for the 40 people who went to the Star Wars page. In order to account for all 60 who went to the games page, it is necessary to find out what happened to the

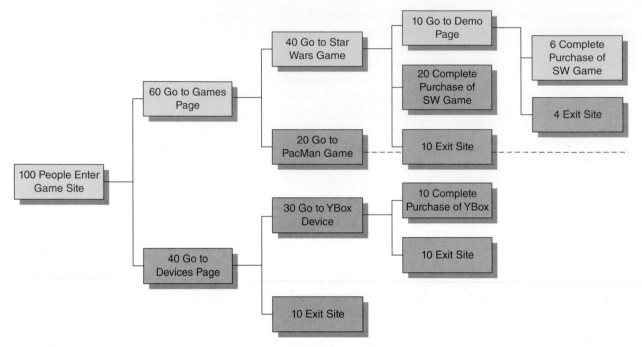

FIGURE **10.17** Conversion Paths through a Hypothetical Video Games Site
Source: © Cengage Learning 2013

20 who went to the PacMan page. Forty went to the devices page and the chart shows that outcome. The point is that the marketer has to account for all 100 of the people who came to the site, study the actions of each segment, and locate points where the conversion outcomes might be improved. On a site of any size, this is a monumental task, which can be lessened by concentrating on target segments (some people got here by accident) and on the few target segments that are large enough to be worth the effort of improving outcomes. Still it is a large task. It is also an important one because this is another instance in which it is cheaper to convert more of the target audience once they reach the site than to engage in acquisition marketing to get more people to the site in the first place.

That last point actually applies to this entire chapter. It is less expensive in the end to generate reasonable quality leads, to manage them well, and to convert a significant portion of them than it is to engage in endless acquisition campaigns, only to ignore or mismanage the sales leads that are produced.

SUMMARY

The sales lead generation and management process is a key element of B2B marketing and is important in certain product categories in B2C marketing. It is a complex process full of sometimes mind-numbing detail. In large part, that is because market sizes are often small and unit sales can be quite large, making each contact important. The chapter has emphasized throughout that there are many points in the process where marketing strategy or execution can be improved—improvements that can substantially raise revenue, cut marketing costs, or both.

The business buyer goes through a buying cycle process characterized by needs awareness, research, consolidation and consideration of potential vendors, and a purchasing decision. Since this process can take a year or more for a high-risk purchase, business marketers have a major challenge in keeping up with the potential customer's progress, providing the right content at the right time, and attempting to close the sale when the time is right. This leads to a formal process of sales lead generation (one of the most important activities of the business marketer), lead qualification, lead distribution, and follow-up to close the sale.

Many media, both online and offline, can be used to generate sales leads. They include traditional outbound channels such as direct mail and email. Leads are often cheaper when generated by inbound marketing, being visible on the web in a way that draws potential customers to the website for further information. The request for information can become the beginning of the lead generation and management cycle.

Qualification typically begins with an information form filled out on the website in return for content. The purpose of the information is to determine which state of the buying cycle the prospect is in and what kind of communications are appropriate. As the process goes on, more information is obtained, and when the prospect is deemed ready, the lead is distributed to internal or external sales reps for closing (conversion). This often-lengthy communications process leads to the concept of content marketing in which the right content is provided at the right time.

Conversion is not a "one size fits all" concept. Each organization is likely to have its own definition and metric for conversion. A well-managed process combines that metric with clear objectives at each stage for each team involved in the lead generation and management process. It is, indeed, a complex process that involves many groups within the organization. This makes its implementation and execution problematic in many companies for reasons that are purely organizational, not technological.

There are marketing techniques that can improve the process. They include creating customer personas, building conversion scenarios, building and optimizing landing pages, and creating clear conversion paths through the website. This whole process of better understanding customer market segments, developing segment-specific strategies, and testing to optimize the process can result in major improvements in ROI in the B2B marketing process.

DISCUSSION QUESTIONS

1. The chapter states that the discipline of sales lead generation and management was developed by direct marketers and later adapted to the Internet. Why do you think direct marketers, and not traditional advertisers, originated the practice of sales lead generation and management?

2. True or False: Sales lead generation and management is a discipline practiced only by B2B marketers. Why or why not?

3. Why do you think B2B marketers consider producing an acceptable quantity of high quality sales leads one of their most important challenges?

4. True or False: The B2B buy cycle has roughly the same steps as the consumer purchase decision process, is carried out in much the same way, and takes about the same length of time. Explain your answer.

5. What is your understanding of content marketing as a strategy? How does it differ from the kind of marketing or marketing communications that you are accustomed to?

6. Describe the four steps in the lead generation and management process.

7. Identify two or three online and two or three offline channels in which sales leads can be generated. Which channels do you think are likely to be most effective in generating leads? Which are likely to be the most expensive to use?

8. What are the basic criteria that are used to qualify a sales lead?

9. Explain what is meant by sales lead distribution and why it is important.

10. What are some of the issues marketers should consider when trying to make the conversion process on their websites as effective as possible? How can personas and purchase scenarios be helpful?

11. Why do you think it is hard to come up with a single, concise definition of conversion? Can you give at least two examples of different definitions of conversion and explain why the different definitions are needed?

12. What is the importance of the landing page in a marketing campaign?

INTERNET EXERCISES

1. Internet Career Builder Exercise
   a. These are some of the jobs that are available in online B2B marketing. You can find others on sites recommended by your instructor or through search.

   Sales (usually of a specific product or service category, e.g., enterprise software sales, advertising sales)

   Sales training program

   Telesales representative

   Sales lead analyst

   Account manager/executive

   Online marketing coordinator/manager

   Communications manager

   Events coordinator

   Media coordinator/manager

   Director, online marketing

   and many more

   b. Select a B2B marketing job from the list in 1a or from your own search. Outline the responsibilities of that position. You may find it useful to locate job postings on the web in order to understand the job requirements.
   c. Outline knowledge and experience from classes, internships, full or part-time jobs, and volunteer work that prepare you for this specific position.
   d. Prepare five questions you could ask at a job interview. The questions should exhibit your understanding of the position requirements without lecturing the interviewer about what he or she already knows.
   e. Update your VisualCV® or LinkedIn profile with this information.

2. Using the four steps in the lead generation and management process, develop a scenario that describes how a company of your choice might go about a lead development marketing campaign.

3. Go to the website, blog, or Facebook page of one of the companies you are following. Think about how conversion might be defined on this platform. Then identify the steps in a path that would lead from your entry point to the defined conversion activity. Can you think of any ways to make the progress along this path more persuasive?

NOTES

1. Mary Lou Roberts and Paul D. Berger, *Direct Marketing Management*, 2nd edition. See Chapter 9, B2B Direct Marketing, available for free download at http://www.marylouroberts.info/chaptersfordownload.html.
2. http://leftbrainmarketing.com/blog/2010/09/30/revising-our-demand-generation-definition-as-b2b-marketers.
3. Adapted from a comment by Jen Horton at http://blog.reachforce.com/sales-and-marketing-tips/lead-generation-vs-demand-generation-marketing-wtf.
4. http://www.youtube.com/watch?v=1st6Bjopm2o&feature=related.
5. IBM subsidiary Unica defines marketing automation as "the processes and technology which help to improve the effectiveness and efficiency of marketing work" and goes on to discuss this deceptively simple definition at http://www.marketingcentral.com/marketing-software/marketing-automation.html.
6. http://spearmarketing.com/blog/eloqua%E2%80%99s-%E2%80%9Cjuan-eloqua%E2%80%9D-campaign-email-creative-at-its-best.
7. http://jchernov.posterous.com/marketing-with-complications-grandeguide.
8. http://www.globalspec.com/wp/WP_BuyCycle_Maven.
9. Wesley V. Johnston and Thomas V. Bonoma. "The Buying Center: Structure and Interaction Patterns," *Journal of Marketing*, Vol. 45, No. 3, 143–156.
10. http://www.startwithalead.com/article.asp?ARTICLEID=1.
11. http://www.sethgodin.com/sg.
12. http://blog.hubspot.com/blog/tabid/6307/bid/4416/Inbound-Marketing-the-Next-Phase-of-Marketing-on-the-web.aspx#ixzz18D7w7c4t.
13. http://info.awarenessnetworks.com/rs/awarenessnetworks/images/Content-Marketing-Playbook-junta42-Awareness.pdf.
14. http://www.hubspot.com/Portals/53/docs/resellers/reports/state_of_inbound_marketing.pdf, p. 4.
15. http://www.pontiflex.com/download/Pontiflex_CPL_Report_Q3_2010.pdf.
16. http://www.hoovers.com/leads/build-a-list.
17. http://leads.infousa.com/MailingListsSalesLeads.aspx?bas_session=S15844277020685&bas_vendor=190000.
18. http://chiefmarketer.com/images/ProspectingSurvey.pdf.
19. http://realtimemarketer.com/how-to-generate-sales-leads-in-30-days-using-inbound-marketing.
20. http://diy-marketing.blogspot.com/2010/11/targeting-your-facebook-ads.html.
21. http://www.cloudmarketinglab.com/blog/marketing/social-media-sales-leads.
22. http://www.clickz.com/clickz/news/1866387/b2b-firm-pushes-facebook-page-qr-codes.
23. Adapted from http://www.yourcrmteam.com/blog/2010/11/create-a-lead-scoring-system-to-drive-more-sales.

24. http://www.silverpop.com/blogs/demand-generation/marketing-automation/whats-the-difference-between-crm-and-marketing-automation-in-b2b-demand-generation.html.

25. http://www.silverpop.com/marketing-resources/case-studies/edgar-online.html.

26. http://media.eloqua.com/documents/AberdeenLeadScoringandPrioritization.pdf.

27. http://www.silverpop.com/blogs/demand-generation/lead-management/the-five-myths-of-b2b-lead-management.html#more-859.

28. http://www.emarketer.com/blog/index.php/case-study-ibm-drives-millions-dollars-worth-sales-leads-social-media.

29. http://www.futurenowinc.com/resources/pa.pdf, p. 31.

30. http://www.boxesandarrows.com/view/building-a-data.

31. http://outsideinnovation.blogs.com/pseybold/2006/06/best_practices_html.

32. http://www.slideshare.net/Paris_d/yellow-tail-wine-consumer-persona.

33. http://www.cio.com/article/162300/State_of_the_CIO_2008_What_Kind_of_CIO_Does_Your_Company_Need_.

34. http://www.findnewcustomers.com/buyerpersonas.

35. http://www.youtube.com/watch?feature=player_embedded&v=IcoMvaOFqtM#!.

36. Both quoted in Frank Buytendijk, Toby Hatch, and Pietro Michell, "Scenario-Based Strategy Maps," Kelley School of Business, Indiana University, 2010, p. 337.

37. http://www.grokdotcom.com/topics/persuasionscenarios.htm.

38. http://www.psgroup.com/detail.aspx?ID=698.

39. http://iqcontent.com/publications/features/article_77.

40. http://www.webopedia.com/TERM/M/microsite.html.

41. http://www.getelastic.com/17-ways-to-minimize-friction.

42. http://blog.kissmetrics.com/5-awful-landing-pages.

43. http://www.marketingexperiments.com/journals/3rd%20Quarter%20%282010%29%20-%20MEx%20Research%20Journal.pdf, p. 81.

44. http://www.marketingexperiments.com/journals/3rd%20Quarter%20%282010%29%20-%20MEx%20Research%20Journal.pdf, p. 83.

CHAPTER 11

Customer Relationship Development and Retention Marketing

Chapter Outline

The Importance of CLV

Strategic CRM
A Word about Semantics
The Elements of CRM
The Transactional versus the Relationship Perspective
The B2B Foundations of CRM

Developing CRM Strategy
The International Speedway Corporation
The Customer Lifecycle

The Processes of CRM—Operational and Analytical
The ASPCA and the MSPCA
Targeting and Personalization
Personalized Email and Site Content
Customer Loyalty Programs

Emerging Issues—Apps and Social CRM
The Power of Apps
Social CRM

The Costs and Failure Rate of CRM Systems Projects

The CRM Vision—Seamless Customer Experience

SUMMARY
DISCUSSION QUESTIONS
INTERNET EXERCISES
NOTES

Key Terms

LEARNING OBJECTIVES

By the time you complete this chapter, you will be able to:

- Explain the importance of customer retention and CLV.
- Describe the difference between relationship and transactional marketing.
- Discuss the concept of CRM and the marketing functions on which it is based.
- Explain the elements of CRM strategy.
- Discuss operational and analytical CRM and why the customer database is essential to both.
- Describe tools for targeting customers.
- Explain the importance of apps in CRM programs.
- Discuss the nature and importance of social CRM.
- Understand what is necessary to make CRM work.

In 1996, Frederick Reichheld published a seminal volume entitled *The Loyalty Effect*.[1] The book's chief argument was that businesses were paying too much attention to—and spending too much money on—customer acquisition. In the process they were overlooking the greater profitability to be gained from maximizing the value of their customer base. The book struck a responsive chord among managers who found the prospect of more cost-effective, more accountable marketing extremely appealing. It launched the marketing mantra of the late 1990s, "It costs seven to ten times as much to acquire a new customer as it does to maintain an existing one." The argument was compelling since it was based on empirical data about customer value across industries, both consumer and business-to-business.

In addition to the high cost of customer acquisition, the advocates of relational approaches point to additional positive outcomes:

- The average company loses half its customers every five years.
- Reducing defections by 5 percent can increase profits by 25 to 85 percent, depending on the industry.
- As many as 85 percent of customers who defect say they were satisfied with their former supplier.
- Customers who are extremely satisfied are six times more likely to repurchase than customers who are merely satisfied.
- A satisfied customer will tell five people, while a dissatisfied customer will tell nine.[2]

The Importance of CLV

The relationship argument relies on the concept of customer lifetime value (CLV), which was discussed in Chapter 4, to demonstrate the profit impact of relationship strategies. Figure 11.1 documents the importance of relationship maintenance in the online apparel industry. After accounting for acquisition costs, the consultants identify three revenue streams associated with each customer—each one's *base* spending amount, the *growth* of spending as the customer persists with the marketer, and the revenue generated by customer *referrals*. In this example,

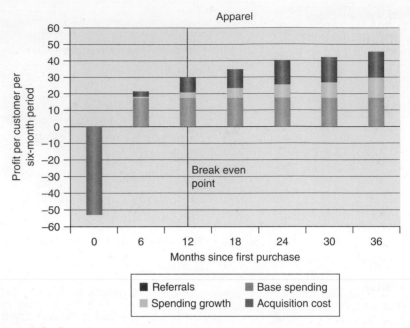

FIGURE **11.1** Components of Customer Lifetime Value for Apparel Purchases

Source: Adapted from Bain & Company Mainspring Online Retailing Survey, December 1999. Copyright © 1999 by Bain & Company, Inc. All rights reserved. Reproduced with permission.

breakeven on acquisition costs occurs after one year; in other industries it tends to be longer because of higher acquisition costs and/or longer purchase cycles. The general pattern, however, holds true across industry sectors in both consumer and business markets.[3] It emphasizes the importance of caring for customers in a way that causes them to return, to concentrate more of their purchases with the marketer and to refer new customers.

Each of the revenue streams makes a contribution to CLV as the customer persists. In the case of the apparel industry, the data indicate that

- The average repeat customer spent 67 percent more in months 31 through 36 of the relationship than in the initial six months.
- An average apparel shopper referred three people to the online retailer's site after the first purchase. After ten purchases, the shopper had referred a total of seven people.
- Loyal online customers also expressed willingness to buy other product lines from the online retailer. "For example, almost 70 percent of Gap Online customers said they would consider buying furniture from the Gap. And 63 percent of online grocery shoppers would buy toiletries and OTC (over the counter) drugs from their online grocers."[4]
- Customers who interact with the company or brand on Facebook, the major social network for brand interaction, are likely to already be customers and to buy more and to recommend more often after becoming fans.[5]

Although the economics of the relational concept are persuasive, implementing it requires a complete reversal in the way traditional marketers think about and perform their jobs. Change of this magnitude is always difficult, and such has been the case with relational strategies. In order to understand the issues, we need to contrast the older transactional model to the relationship model.

Strategic CRM

Before we discuss the process of developing CRM strategy, we need to comment on the changing definition of the familiar acronym.

A Word about Semantics

From its earliest days, CRM has stood for customer relationship management. The discipline focused on acquiring and managing data that provided insights for marketing programs that led to successful customer relationships. In that context, CRM made sense. However, the world has changed in many ways since the advent of data-driven marketing sometime in the mid-1970s. Improved hardware, software, and data storage capabilities materially altered the practice of CRM in the 1980s and 90s, allowing marketers to carry out strategies they had previously only envisioned. Important as these changes have been, they are dwarfed by the impact of social media marketing (SMM) in this space as in so many others. The advent of SMM has allowed marketers to listen to what customers are saying and to engage in real-time dialog with them. Many marketers have adopted the terminology "customer relationship marketing," or sometimes "customer retention marketing," considering that more appropriate to the current environment. As we use the CRM acronym throughout this chapter, we encourage you to translate it as "customer relationship marketing."

The Elements of CRM

CRM has three basic elements. The *strategic* process identifies CRM goals and objectives within the framework of overall marketing and business objectives. The strategy development process is the focus of this section. In a later section, we will discuss the *operational* or tactical program element and the *analytical* element. Each of the three elements requires different activities and expertise and needs individual attention. However, in practice, they are less distinct and may all be required at one point or another in order to carry out a CRM initiative.

The Transactional versus the Relationship Perspective

Consumer marketers in the traditional mass media environment have really had no choice except to pursue a transactional approach. These marketers ordinarily did not have direct contact with their customers. Consequently, they could not identify their customers as individuals and attempt to develop an ongoing relationship with them. The mass media did not facilitate identification and tracking of individual customers and prospects. The customer relationship, if there was one, was owned by an intermediary in a channel of distribution. These two factors created a powerful barrier to the establishment of direct relationships by marketers who produced the products and services. In addition, the large up-front investment required to build a product-specific customer database could not be justified by the small gross margins provided by many frequently-purchased consumer products.

B2B marketers had different but no less serious issues. They typically dealt directly with their customers through field sales forces. Sales representatives tended to feel that they had ownership of the customer relationship and to be reluctant to provide detailed data to a centralized customer database. Even if that reluctance did not exist, contact with customers often took place in various units including field sales, the telephone call center, field service, and technical support. To make the situation even worse, if the customer purchased items from more than one division or product line within the company, multiple and confusing customer contact points existed. What did not usually exist, however, was a data repository which permitted a complete view of the customer relationship with the firm. On the positive side, however, sales reps were often able to recognize customers who were transactional in nature, usually because they were price sensitive. Relationship customers had stronger ties with the firm, perhaps since they required customized products or specialized services. Reps who recognized the difference could, on an individual basis, allocate their time and effort according to the value of the customer relationship.

As long as customer relationship knowledge was the property of individual sales reps, attempts to develop strategic CRM programs floundered. What was lacking was centralized collection and management of customer data that could be analyzed to produce customer insights and translated into strategy. The importance of data was highlighted in a study by Zahay, Peltier, Schultz, and Griffin. They studied both traditional business outcomes data like sales and net income and also a type of outcome they called marketing-oriented customer performance. They operationalized the later as retention rate plus share of wallet, CLV, and return on investment (ROI). In a broad sense, they found that relational data collected at multiple customer touchpoints were more important than transactional data in predicting both business and marketing performance outcomes.[6] It could be hypothesized that relational data are important since it is used to develop strategies that affect business outcomes.

Nonprofit organizations also need robust CRM data and strategies. They need to retain and upgrade both members and donors. Some have extensive member databases built from their direct mail marketing efforts. Others have little in the way of member data beyond name and address. Many have members and donors that predate the Internet who still have never been asked for addresses. Moving to Internet-based member retention programs has been difficult for many. However, as more nonprofit organizations become adept at the use of the Internet, and especially as they acquire new prospects or members from web-based contacts, online CRM efforts are becoming a major part of nonprofit marketing strategies as well.

Whether in the B2C, B2B, or nonprofit marketplaces, the essentials of the two basic marketing approaches—**transactional** and **relational**—do not differ (see Figure 11.2). Traditional transactional marketing is centered on products and single economic exchanges. Marketers engage in one-way communication in the mass media, targeting market segments identified by conventional marketing research. This type of marketing is associated with traditional mass media, but online marketers can also be focused on their products at the expense of their customers.

When the marketing process moves to a relational approach, the focus shifts to customers and their relationship cycle with the organization. Customer needs and expertise in meeting them become key. Communications are targeted to individuals or carefully defined segments and contain personalized content. Goals are focused on growing customer value, not market share. CLV, which incorporates both revenue and cost to serve the customer, becomes a key metric as do customer satisfaction, loyalty, and employee satisfaction. In implementing the CRM strategy, two-way communication in any channel becomes the norm with project-based marketing research taking a back seat to meaningful, ongoing dialogue with the customer. Seamlessly satisfying customer experience becomes the vision that guides all marketing activities and permeates the entire organization.

The B2B Foundations of CRM

While there is much inconsistency in the definition of the term "CRM" today, there is little disagreement on how the discipline originated. By the early

Product-Centric vs. Customer-Centric

Marketing		Marketing
Product focus	⟶	Customer focus
Transactions	⟶	"Relationships"
Acquiring customers	⟶	Retaining customers
Product profitability	⟶	Customer profitability
Trial and error	⟶	Test, measure, and refine

FIGURE **11.2** Product-Centric versus Customer-Centric Marketing
Source: © Cengage Learning 2013

1980s, there was growing recognition among business marketers that the cost of a single sales call was spiraling out of control. Figures quoted were typically in the hundreds of dollars for one sales call. Marketers needed a way to make their field sales forces more efficient without risking their ability to grow sales. They turned to **sales force automation** in an attempt to offer more cost-effective service to customers while decreasing their overall sales costs. According to Moriarty and Schwartz, some of the sales force automation tools are:

- Sales force productivity tools such as call reporting and checking order and inventory status.
- Direct mail sales lead generation campaigns that included mail fulfillment of product information.
- Telemarketing, often to follow up the sales leads generated by direct mail.
- Sales and marketing management tools, including sales forecasting and reporting.[7]

In the intervening years, email has taken the place of some but not all direct mail, and online channels have added additional ways of reaching customers. This transition has not decreased the need for automating repetitive, often event-triggered, marketing activities. It has simply increased the number of activities to automate.

This is another information-driven marketing application. In the case of sales force automation, lower-cost media are used to generate (online advertising and events like webinars, and direct mail) and qualify (telemarketing and webinars) sales leads, as we discussed in Chapter 10. Field sales people are given access to a comprehensive customer/prospect database, which is also used for sales and marketing management applications. The result should be higher sales, better customer service, and lower cost to the enterprise.

Early systems focused on the sales force, with marketing developing and executing direct mail campaigns, and sophisticated call centers using the customer/prospect database to qualify leads and provide customer service. This has led to the "three-legged stool" concept of CRM portrayed in Figure 11.3. The sales force productivity "leg" has little application in the B2C marketplace, but the concept itself and the marketing and customer service components are entirely applicable. Types of software that support B2B CRM are identified and described in Table 11.1. The term CRM has been adopted to describe relational marketing in both the B2B and B2C spaces in spite of the differences just described. It also has the same meaning in the nonprofit space.

FIGURE **11.3** The B2B Foundations of Customer Relationship Management

Source: © Cengage Learning 2013

TABLE 11.1	Software to Support Customer Relationships
Contact Management	Software with multiple modules that emulate the salesperson's address book, daily appointment log, and customer files. Key components are contact information, including name, title, address, telephone(s), email, and fax, both work and home; a daily calendar, a tickler (reminder) file, and usually an electronic notepad of some sort. Firms can have the software customized to include routine forms such as sales call and expense reports.
Sales Force Automation	Takes contact management a step forward by integrating various modules and linking them to a central customer database. This lessens the bookkeeping requirements for the field sales force and permits the timely updating and transmission of customer information. For instance, sales leads can be transmitted directly from the central database to the field rep's laptop allowing immediate followup by the rep and monitoring by sales management.
CRM	Software that is integrated on an enterprise-wide basis. The objective is to centralize all customer data and to make a 360° (complete) picture of the customer available at each contact point within the firm. Information provision can be highly automated as when a telephone number triggers a "screen pop," making the customer record available to the call center representative by the time the call is answered. Integrated CRM software makes customer and product support data available to any authorized user anywhere in the world at any time. It also integrates all customer touchpoints into a complete view of multiple channels of communication. Integration is the precursor to marketing automation.

Source: © Cengage Learning 2013

Developing CRM Strategy

CRM consultants Don Peppers and Martha Rogers have long espoused a model that captures the essence of CRM (see Figure 11.4). Their view is an information-driven one, with every step in the process adding to the customer database that is essential to drive CRM strategy and programs. The steps are:

- *Identify* your customers by individual or household name and address and/or address.
- *Differentiate* them according to their needs and their actual or potential value.
- *Interact* with customers based on their own needs. From the organization's perspective, the interactions should become more cost effective. Each interaction should be used as an opportunity to increase the store of data about the individual or household.
- *Customize* at least some aspects of the organization's dealings with the customer. This could be things like tailored communications and specialized offers that allow the enterprise to recognize the customer as a valued supporter and that present opportunities for growing the value of the individual customer.

Data are the engine that drives CRM strategy forward to an ever-deepening relationship with the customer. Thoughtful use of data facilitates:

- Differentiated messages and offers that lead to effective communications channel choices.
- Customer segmentation by all the usual methods, including socialgraphics, and especially by customer value and the opportunity to grow value.
- Lifecycle communications that depend on the customer's position in the relationship cycle, from new through very active to ultimate trust in the brand.
- Active management and monitoring of performance, using KPIs throughout.[8]

The importance of all these activities, especially active management and monitoring, has been heightened by the potential of SMM in CRM. SMM expands the number of communications **touchpoints** and makes it imperative to integrate communications across channels.

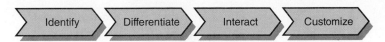

FIGURE **11.4** The Peppers and Rogers Model of CRM
Source: © Cengage Learning 2013

The International Speedway Corporation

The International Speedway Corporation (ISC) and its 13 regional racetracks already had what is arguably the world's most loyal sports followers—the NAS-CAR fans. They were not, however, satisfied that they were communicating with these fans and nurturing the relationship in the best possible way. They had transactional data from all the tracks, but they were not being used to develop strategic CRM insights. It was deemed important that all 13 tracks work collaboratively to focus on the customer and committing to the final program. The goal was to provide each visitor to the track an experience that was perceived as designed for him exclusively.

The customer database dated back to 2002. It contained more than 3 million customer records and over 10 million order records. They improved the data collection so that all new transactions data were fed directly into the CRM software. ISC spent all of 2009 analyzing a mountain of data. The analysis allowed them to develop many market segments based on behavior patterns and strategies for each of them that ranged from loyalty programs to up-sell programs. With better availability of transactions data, ISC was able to communicate with each ticket purchaser in accordance with the experience the individual buyer was seeking.[9]

Different tracks have approached the customer experience in different ways. Examples are:

- The Daytona International Speedway found that its patrons wanted a more in-depth look at behind-the-scenes operations. The Daytona 500 Experience is made up of an existing limited tour of the facilities and a new one-hour long tour that includes areas never before open to the public.[10]
- The Michigan International Speedway implemented new software that allows them to sell tickets directly in many channels and to retain customer data that had previously been the property of ticket agencies.[11]
- The Watkins Glenn International Speedway created personalized pages at MyTrackSchedule.com that allow the user to select relevant information, engage in discussions, and start new discussion groups.
- Several of the tracks have the customer experience manager in their managerial ranks.

The volume of activity and positive reactions on the Daytona Facebook page, as one example, suggest that the enhanced customer experience is pleasing to its many fans.[12]

INTERACTIVE EXERCISE 11.1   **Data-Driven Mindset**

The ISC has received several awards for CRM excellence. After receiving an award as "Innovator of the Year," Senior Director of Consumer Marketing, Jim Cavedo, was interviewed about the importance of data and how they used it. Watch the brief video. Do you agree with his perspective on the importance of data in CRM?

Visit http://bit.ly/rKVjq4.

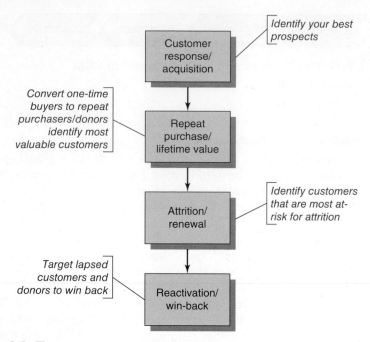

FIGURE **11.5** Mining the Customer Lifecycle
Source: © Cengage Learning 2013

The Customer Lifecycle

The concept of the **customer** (not the product) **lifecycle** is illustrated in Figure 11.5. It starts with strategic customer acquisition—acquiring more customers like your best customers. The next step is conversion and the concept is specific in stating that conversion means a repeat customer, not a one-time purchaser. The continuing objective is to grow customer value. The other requirement of the relational approach is to identify customers who are at risk of attrition and target them for retention or for migration to a different product in the line. A classic consumer example is baby food. When the child grows too old for baby food, attrition from that product class is naturally going to occur. The wise marketer has a line of toddler foods and snacks in the wings and has the data to know when it is time to market them to a household. Capturing and using that kind of data at the individual household level is the essence of relational marketing.

The attractiveness of the CRM concept quickly became apparent to marketers. After all, they had been preaching the virtues of customer orientation for many years. As a result, marketers of all kinds have taken many different paths in their search for strong and lasting relationships with their customers.

Customizing M&Ms

Mars' customized M&M candies have been a success story in a product category where innovation is hard to come by and repeat sales are essential. Customized M&Ms met both needs, especially that of giving consumers reasons to buy more candy than they ordinarily would. The My M&Ms site offers all kinds of customization—colors, text, images, and packaging for events like parties and weddings. The R&D team developed the concept and tested it internally in mid-2003, offering printing on white candy only. Employees ordered 800 pounds of candy the first day. They loved it but they requested choice in colors and packaging. Those requirements were met and the candies were first offered on the M&M site in 2004.

The team used the success of the initial offering to get information from their customers. According to Jim Cass, general manager of Mars Direct, "We reached out to every [My M&Ms] customer, and roughly 25% responded, providing detailed demographics as well as information on why they had made the purchase." *Bloomberg Businessweek* points out that they tested a product

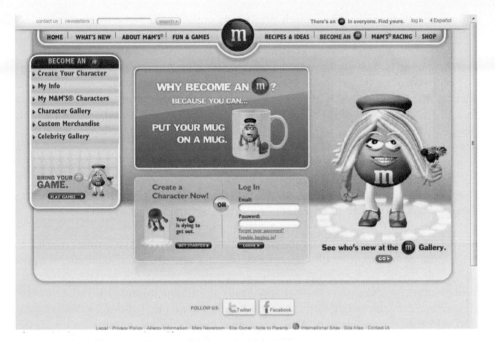

FIGURE **11.6** Become an M&M Character

Source: Mars Inc., http://www.mms.com/us/becomeanmm.

concept internally and used feedback from actual customers to refine it. This type of feedback is relatively fast and inexpensive on the web as compared to conventional marketing research, and it gets feedback from actual customers, not purchase intention data. Mars did not release detailed sales data, but one observer estimated that the product had sales in excess of $10 million within three years.[13] That is a lot of M&Ms and a lot of customers who return to purchase them!

The most recent effort at customer engagement is the "Become an M" character site. It allows customers to create an M avatar and put it on a product like a coffee mug or screen saver. There are free games on the site and free ecards on which the M avatar can be placed. Note in Figure 11.6 that there is also a tab that features M&M's sponsorship of a NASCAR racing team.

The brand also has an active Facebook page hosted by the blue M&M character. The page has over 2.5 million fans. It actively encourages visitors to "Like" the page which offers frequent contests and promotions. It also encourages fans to share these promotions with their own friends.

All this is engaging. It keeps customers coming back to buy more candy and even some coffee mugs. It probably results in referrals. These are objectives of good CRM and both the interactivity of the Internet itself and the pull of SMM can offer strong support.

The business case is clear for the use of relationship marketing in businesses and nonprofit organizations of all kinds. However, it is not easy to establish and perpetuate an effective CRM program. Achieving relationship marketing success requires a disciplined process and organizational buy-in. Let us turn to an overview of the tactical and operational processes necessary to make relationship marketing work in any organization.

The Processes of CRM—Operational and Analytical

The reason that CRM requires considerable discipline is twofold. First, emphasized in the preceding section, relationship marketing requires significant changes in the way marketing is done. The emphasis must move from promotional campaigns and marketing research projects to ongoing dialogue on multiple platforms, much of which can be captured and stored in a customer database. Second, it must be treated and managed as an ongoing process, not as a series of discrete events. It has often been described as "A Journey with No End." This is the antithesis of the way most marketing managers are measured, using short-term metrics, such as market share, sales growth, and expansion of customer base. The result is that, for CRM to succeed, changes in organizational thinking and action must go beyond the marketing department to the highest levels of the corporation. This degree of change is not easy and it requires a clear vision of the requirements and potential achievements of CRM.

Figure 11.7 represents the process.[14] It is a closed-loop process in which all possible customer contact data are captured and represented in the customer database and in which all marketing programs are information-driven.

Successful CRM cannot exist outside the context of the business unit's overall marketing strategy. The economics simply will not work unless the business identifies high value customers (initially based on marketing research if no database is available), individually or by market segment, targets those customers, and develops marketing strategies and programs that specifically meet their needs. This is a genuinely customer-centric approach; target customers are identified first and the value proposition, encompassing all aspects of the marketing mix, is then developed. It, too, is the antithesis of the traditional marketing model in which products are developed and it becomes the job of the marketing department to market and sell those products.

The customer database is the focal point of both **operational** and **analytical CRM**. The database is developed and used to conduct segmentation analysis and to develop customer profiles that drive both outbound programs like email newsletters and inbound programs like display advertising. Analytical models include

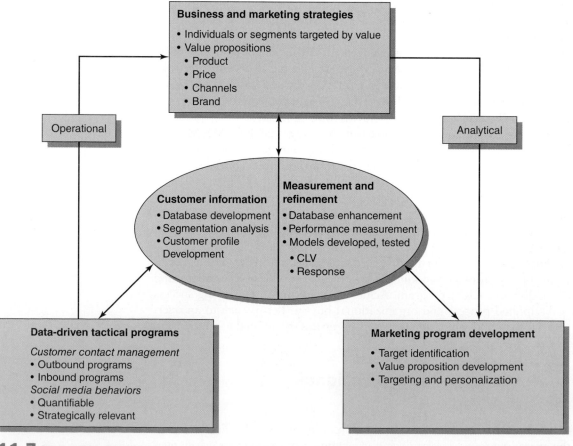

FIGURE **11.7** The CRM Process

Source: © Cengage Learning 2013

CLV and response models that predict response to future marketing programs on the basis of past response to similar programs. As programs are developed and executed, additional data are captured to enrich the database, to allow performance measurement of individual programs or customers, and to continually refine critical marketing models.

Marketers are beginning to include limited social media behavior in their databases. The data are limited because it must be usable in its raw form or quantifiable. This does not include the majority of brand-related conversations on social networks, although they have an important role in CRM. That will be discussed in the section on Social CRM.

Examples of data from social networks that can be usefully added to the database include:

- In B2B, it is possible to build apps that monitor the social conversations of a specific sales prospect on platforms like LinkedIn, Twitter, and Facebook. This gives the sales person valuable information about what the prospect is saying and often allows him to gauge how close the prospect is to a purchase decision. Be aware of three things. First this is social media listening data. It is ephemeral and not easily quantifiable, but it adds a useful dimension to quantitative prospect information. Second, it involves identifying individual customers in a way that probably would not be acceptable in B2C markets. Third, while this kind of data can contribute to customer qualification, it is likely to be accessed by a desktop or mobile app that lets sales reps follow customers of interest as they interact on social networks, not by entries in the customer database.[15]

- It is difficult to link consumer social network data to identified consumers without violating privacy restrictions. On a small scale, however, there may be social data that are worth adding to consumer profiles. Marketers are always on the lookout for influentials (*opinion leaders*) who can influence others in social space. One tool is the Klout score, which measures the influence of an individual on social networks. Any individual can sign up and receive a personal Klout score.[16] Developers can create tools that filter social media messages by Klout score. In CRM, this can be used to understand how influential customers are and what topics are relevant to their sphere of influence.[17] There is also identifiable data from sources like top blogs listings. For example, if mommy bloggers are strategically important to the brand, Babble's annual list of top 50 mommy bloggers[18] could be entered (manually) into the blog owner's database record. If the brand needs to reach out to influential mommy bloggers, the effort could be worthwhile. There are tools for measuring influence of identified persons on various platforms. For example, there is Twitalizer for Twitter[19] and Booskaha, which aims to help small businesses identify and reward their most valuable Facebook fans.[20] Including any of these data in databases presumes the influential individual is already a customer and has a record in the database.

Integrating social media data into tactical CRM programs and potentially adding it to the consumer database is a subject of great interest to marketers. However, the privacy challenges at present are huge. For now, *the best marketing advice for including social media fans and participants in the database is to drive them to the website and persuade them to register, thereby collecting email addresses and other useful data.*[21]

Social networks do offer opportunities in CRM programs, as evidenced by the ASPCA and its state affiliates.

The ASPCA and the MSPCA

The nonprofit American Society for the Prevention of Cruelty to Animals® (ASPCA) has become an adept user of the Internet in carrying out its mission of

FIGURE **11.8** The ASPCA Home Page

Source: ASPCA, http://www.aspca.org.

"providing effective means for the prevention of cruelty to animals throughout the United States."[22] The ASPCA is a venerable organization, founded in 1866 by Henry Bergh and modeled on England's Royal Society for the Prevention of Cruelty to Animals, which dates back to 1840.

Like many nonprofits, the ASPCA® saw the potential of the Internet to extend its reach and impact, but early efforts were tentative. In 2002, the society revamped its website (see Figure 11.8 for the home page as of late 2011) and strengthened its marketing program.

The website has extensive content to support responsible pet adoption, "parenting," and care, in addition to its work to prevent cruelty. It urges visitors to join its efforts by becoming a member, donating online, acquiring its affinity credit card, purchasing pet insurance, and signing up for communications. Incentives for providing an address include:

- Ability to send ecards
- Weekly newsletters
- Information relevant to animal protection in the registrant's state
- Access to the archives of ASPCA *Animal Watch* magazine
- ASPCA rewards program
- Special offers from the ASPCA online store[23]

The list of addresses had grown to over 250,000 by 2003. It consisted of members and visitors who registered on its website.[24] Online donations also increased with the new website, averaging about $62 as compared to $19.20 by mail.[25]

Visitors who register on the site are required to provide name, address, and whether they currently parent a cat, dog, or other pet. They are also asked whether they are an animal shelter professional, an educator, or an animal health or behavior specialist. Providing mailing address and telephone number is optional. Using this profile information, ASPCA is able to target messages to cat or dog owners or to animal health professionals. Its relationship marketing agency Convio reports on the results of a personalized fund-raising campaign in November 2003 and a later renewal campaign.

The 2003 virtual adoption appeal was to sponsor a pet by sending a donation to the organization. It was sent to both past donors and nondonor registrants who had provided profile information. According to Convio, "An overall 'Help us find safe homes for the holidays' message was altered slightly in the subject line to personalize it for the dog people and the cat people, and the order of appearance of dogs or cats on the message was different based on which category of recipient was receiving the message." They also tested a neutral message, targeting neither cat nor dog owners. The response rate averaged 230 percent higher among donors (see Figure 11.9a) for the personalized message. Among nondonors, the personalized message achieved an 85 percent higher response.[26] This is a simple profile, but the power of relevant personalization is great in the nonprofit arena, just as it is in the for-profit one.

Based on the success of that campaign, a similar strategy was used in a membership renewal program. The membership renewal notice followed a similar content strategy and engaged in a somewhat more complex test. They divided their list into dog only and cat only segments. People who owned both dogs and cats were not included in the test. Three messages were developed—one focusing on cats only, the second focusing on dogs only, and the third including both cats and dogs in the text and visuals of the message. Half the dog list received the dog only message, while half received the cat and dog message. Half the cat list received the cat only message while half received the cat and dog message. Both open and response rates were higher for the dog only and cat only messages (see Figure 11.9b). Again, the cat only message pulled a stronger response. Convio says that ASPCA raised 103 percent more from people who responded to one of the personalized messages than to the more generic cat and dog message. The agency reports that:

> Because this renewal campaign demonstrated significantly improved results through messages based on constituent preferences, the ASPCA plans to use targeted messages on an ongoing basis. The organization will not only continue to see stronger response rates, but also will deepen its relationships with constituents by showing them that the organization understands and cares about each individual's interests.[27]

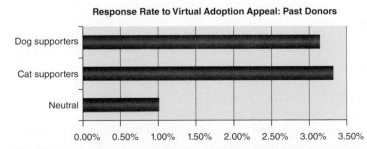

Response rates of past donors who provided dog or cat preferences and received the personalized message, compared with those receiving a neutral message

(a)

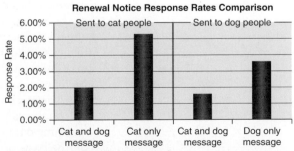

Renewal notice response rates for standard vs. targeted dog-only and cat-only messages

(b)

FIGURE **11.9** Response Rates to Adoption Fund-raising and Renewal Appeals

Source: Convio, "Using Constituent Information for Effective Fundraising and Marketing," pp. 5, 7.

The Convio platform also supports personalized fundraising and many of the state affiliates use that functionality to further engage their members and supporters by asking them to help raise money. Each year the Massachusetts chapter, the MSPCA, and its affiliate, the Angell Memorial Animal Hospital, sponsor an animal walk in multiple Massachusetts cities. Members who want to participate in fund-raising create a personal fund-raising page[28] from a template provided by the organization. It can be customized with their own image and message. Each participant sends it to her list and posts in on social networks of choice. Donors are acknowledged by automated email and, with their permission, donor names are posted on the personal page. The participant is kept informed of donations and encouraged to write personal thank-you emails. Donations come in right away, not after the event, and they are received automatically, relieving the participant of the responsibility of collecting the donations. This event raised over $160,000 in Boston alone in September 2011. Receiving a donation online allows the organization to capture the email address of the donor, and consequently acts as an effective acquisition tool.

All this activity does not take place without careful planning, disciplined execution, and constant monitoring. MSPCA-Angell starts contacting its list in early summer, encouraging members and nonmembers alike to fundraise. It sends reminders, both to acquire more fundraisers and to encourage participants to recontact their personal lists to solicit more donations. These reminders are sent on a careful schedule leading up to the event itself and thanking participants when it is over. It also hosts a Facebook page for each walk city location on which participants can post pictures and comments and it has an active Twitter page. It is easy to assume that many of the participants were Tweeting during the walk but there is no evidence of a **hashtag** on the MSPCA-Angell account that would assemble all the Tweets. They cross-promote the social network sites—all to make the best use of social networks and to keep their members engaged.

Operational (tactical) CRM program execution emanates from the database as in the ASPCA example. Outbound programs, which could be email promotions or marketing programs supported by physical world promotional media such as direct mail, are planned and implemented based on data from the database. One of the disciplines necessary to make CRM work is to compel programs to rely on the database. Often the pressure to get programs out the door causes marketers to want to forgo the front-end analytics and simply blast the entire list. The economics of the Internet, as we have frequently noted, makes that a seductive argument. It is fast and inexpensive compared to any other channel. However, damage to the relationship can be caused by an onslaught of untargeted, irrelevant marketer-originated communications. Airlines, for example, know the residential location of their frequent flyers and, if they have mined their data warehouses intelligently, they may have been able to ascertain clear flight patterns for individual customers. Why then do airlines contact their frequent fliers with promotional offers that originate in cities in which they do not live and to which they do not travel? Has your bank or credit card company recently sent you a promotion for a service or card to which you already subscribe? The cost of sending these messages may not be high, but the longer-term damage to the customer relationship and the perception of the brand may be significant. How can a customer trust a company that appears to know nothing about him, even though he has transacted with that company?

It is essential that inbound programs also depend on the customer database. Telephone call centers and Internet-based chat rely on the customer database for real-time data that allow representatives to provide seamless service to customers on the basis of knowledge about their dealings with the firm, both past and present. Social media data can be a useful addition to that knowledge if it can be made visible to the service rep.

Operational and analytical CRM work from the customer database. CRM strategy development should also be driven by knowledge and insights gleaned from the customer database. Strategies that revolve around customer value are the core of CRM. High value customers are targeted with value propositions developed on the basis of a deep understanding of their needs and behaviors. Care is taken to identify all customers who can be profitably upgraded, whether their current value is high or moderate. Resources are not dissipated on the attraction or even retention of low value customers.

None of these data-driven programs or strategies is viable, however, unless we can selectively reach identified targets with content and messages custom-tailored to each. The Internet provides an especially powerful medium for targeting customers with personalized content.

Targeting and Personalization

Direct marketing, again, provides the foundation concepts for *targeting* on the Internet. Direct marketers in the physical world have long used mailing or telephone lists as their primary targeting mechanism. As we noted in Chapter 7, email lists are now available and are likely to grow in both size and number in the coming years. For the present, however, good lists (translated as opt-in lists) are expensive and short. If the right type of rental list is available, it can be useful to the Internet marketer in the acquisition process, although building an opt-in list is recommended.

For retention purposes, however, the issues are different. The process that supports relationship marketing in either the physical or the online worlds is represented in Figure 11.10. The chief difference between the two is that Internet marketers are able to capture more data faster and to revise their content on a more frequent, even real-time, basis.

Targeting in CRM programs is most often accomplished by developing *customer profiles* and using them to identify either customers who are appropriate to receive a particular offer (the more traditional approach) or customers who represent sufficient value, either as individuals or as a segment, to warrant the development of a unique value proposition (a CLV-based approach).

There are two types of profiles available to marketers. *Anonymous* profiles are created without knowledge of the identity of the prospective customer. They are developed from clickstream data and perhaps enhanced with other data that belong to the marketer or are purchased from a third-party supplier. Cookies, as discussed in Chapter 6, are the most common way to develop anonymous profiles. A cookie can be used for tracking movement on the site after the click-through, for creating a user profile, or to manage the serving of ads to the user (see the discussion of behavioral advertising in Chapter 6). A cookie is also set when a user selects personalization options on a web page. However the cookie is set, when the user contacts the website again, the cookie is automatically activated. In general, a cookie can be read only by the server that sends it and can track activity only on one website, including where visitors come from and where they go as they exit. Cookie files can be located by the user and disabled, but that may prevent access to some websites. It will also erase any personalization the user has done.[29]

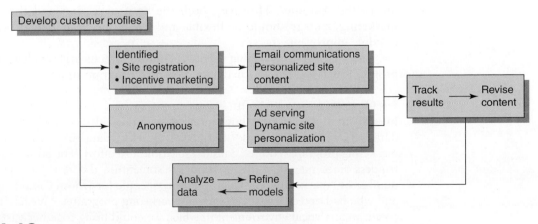

FIGURE **11.10** The Targeting and Personalization Process

Source: © Cengage Learning 2013

Identified profiles are compiled from data that are explicitly provided by a known prospect. This is often done by asking the visitor to register on a website and to provide profile information in the process. There are also infomediaries that offer incentives in return for customer information which they then sell to marketers. Companies that offer coupons from participating manufacturers over the web are an example of this type of information product.

The fastest way for a firm to build its own house list and to create its own identified profiles is *registration* on the website. This sounds simple, but it has to be done carefully. The process itself must be carefully thought out. And, of course, people must first be attracted to the site using acquisition techniques described in previous chapters.

The registration form must be carefully designed for ease and speed of completion, as discussed in Chapter 10 in the context of landing pages. A new registrant may have little, if any, existing relationship with the organization and will divulge only minimal information. Techniques that prevent error, like pull-down lists, are desirable. Even so, the form may not be completed unless there is an incentive. The incentive may be tangible, as on the many B2B sites that require visitors to register in order to get information of some type, perhaps to download a white paper. It may be intangible, as when the nonprofit offers the ability to "customize our newsletter to reflect your interests." There may be services offered to the registered visitor that are not available to the general public, as in the ASPCA case.

Note two things about the common strategy of providing an information incentive. First, the registrant should receive instant gratification, either by clicking on a link to download or by automatic email provision of the report. Making the person wait for something to arrive invalidates many of the special advantages of the Internet. If the information comes on a scheduled basis, not on demand, automate the process to send a "thank you" email (for an email newsletter subscription, for example) immediately. Second, this is a classic direct marketing lead generation process. Consequently, enough information should be gathered to begin to categorize the desirability of the prospect. At the same time, the information should not be so detailed or complex that the visitor does not complete the form. Abandoned forms can be tracked. If there is a consistent point at which the form is being abandoned, it signals a problem with the information gathering that should be corrected immediately.

The basic rule is to gather only the information genuinely needed by the marketer to make the next communication effective. As the relationship strengthens, more information that is more detailed and more personal can be collected. Just like politeness in the physical world, do not presume too much on a brief acquaintance! There should be a relationship program plan from the beginning that specifies the data needed and the customer lifecycle stage in which it will be collected. In the absence of a plan, data collection is just a "fishing expedition" which is unlikely to be valuable to the marketer and is highly likely to be annoying to the customer. However, both the data collection and the relationship marketing strategy should be flexible and should be examined at every step for possible improvements.

The database marketing bones of CRM are clearly evident in a recent program used by Cisco to make its sales lead program more effective.

Cisco Reactivation Program

In early 2010, Cisco had a huge number of names, titles, and addresses in multiple databases all over the world. Extracting the right data to use for an operational marketing program required considerable time and effort. The effort was sometimes fruitless since the stand-alone databases sometimes did not provide a sufficient number of "marketable contacts"—businesspeople for whom Cisco had an address and who had opted-in to Cisco's digital marketing programs. "We had to be able to create an analytical environment in which we could bring together vast amounts of data and cut down on how long ad-hoc queries or segmentation would normally take," said Mike Bull, Global Database Marketing Manager at Cisco.[30] His team evaluated various products and decided on a solution from Alterian.

One of the first insights produced by the Alterian CRM tool was the fact that only about 25 percent of their addresses worldwide were classified as actively marketable. The urgent need was to find out how many of the addresses represented qualified leads and to develop an interactive relationship with them without incurring an unreasonably large cost.

In order to develop a reactivation strategy, they developed a test for their U.S. addresses. They chose about 14.5 percent of the unmarketable U.S. addresses—a number large enough to justify a strategy decision and small enough not to do substantial damage to the potential value of their database if the test failed. The latter is important because the marketer *has only one chance* to ask a consumer or business customer to opt-in for marketing purposes. After that initial offering, customer contacts would be classified as spam and Cisco does not spam.

The database marketing team segmented the test group by high- and low-level corporate titles. They decided on three test cells composed of segments and offers:

Cell 1. High-position group: Get a Starbucks card by updating your profile.

Cell 2. Low-position group 1: Get a collaboration white paper by updating your profile.

Cell 3. Low-position group 2: Update your profile to stay current.[31]

The actual messages were as similar as possible and all resembled the winning version in Figure 11.11.

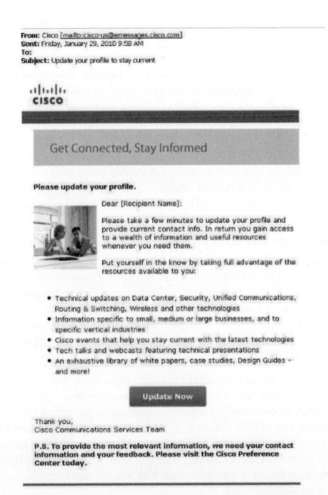

FIGURE **11.11** Cisco Reactivation to Low-Position Group 2: No Incentive

Source: Marketing Sherpa, https://www.marketingsherpa.com/article.php?ident-31805.

The results of the campaign were:

Cell 1

- Open rate: 17.10 percent
- Click-through rate: 7.60 percent
- **Conversion rate: 6.10** percent

Cell 2

- Open rate: 12.10 percent
- Click-through rate: 2 percent
- Conversion rate: 1.40 percent

Cell 3

- **Open rate: 18.30** percent
- Click-through rate: 6.50 percent
- Conversion rate: 3.90 percent

So which was the winner? Cell 3 "no offer" was the winner, which might be counterintuitive. The high-position cell 1 had a higher conversion rate, but it cost $25 for each opt-in (the definition of conversion for this program). The open rate for the low-position, no offer cell 3, was higher, but the conversion rate was lower, and conversion was the goal. However, the lower conversion rate with no incentive for cell 3 was deemed more desirable by management because it was more cost effective. The overall conversion rate across all three versions was 2.3 percent, higher than expected.

In line with direct marketing best practices, Cisco used the success of the U.S. program to guide similar programs in other English-speaking countries, including the U.K., India, Australia, New Zealand, and South Africa. They had similar results in each of the other countries, finding that contacts responded favorably to the direct approach to update their profile and to reengage with Cisco.

Overall, Bull was pleased that "the reactivation tactic has re-opened marketing dialogue with a large number of contacts previously deemed as unmarketable, and at a very low cost."[32]

At least part of the reason this program worked was that Cisco could contact these business people as individuals and indicate that they knew something about each one and valued her business. That is the goal of good personalization.

Personalized Email and Site Content

Personalized email can be a useful part of CRM as the Cisco case history illustrates. Done correctly, email personalization is an important marketing tool, as discussed in Chapter 7. Email is one tool in an outbound marketing program in which the marketer reaches out to customers.

If, however, the marketer chooses *personalized site content* part of the relationship program, the communication must await the visitor's return to the site. There are three basic types of personalized site content in use at present:

1. Rules-based personalization that chooses content on the basis of known characteristics, either from current information or from previous user information stored in cookies. Weather.com provides geographically appropriate content when the visitor enters a Zip code and remembers the Zip code for later use; both Amazon and Netflix have recommendation engines that infer additional product choices from items previously purchased. Rules-based algorithms can be quite complex and link many characteristics, but the concept is straightforward.
2. User-controlled personalization in which the user chooses the content elements to be displayed. This is the approach often used in opt-in where the subscriber is

asked which newsletters she wishes to receive or the bargain hunter is asked the product categories for which he wants to receive offers.

3. Information-driven personalization uses complex profiles and models to assign content instead of simpler decision rules.[33]

User-controlled personalization remains unchanged until the user decides to modify it. Rules-based personalization can also be relatively static, with rules and associated actions being established in advance and merely executed at the time of the visitor's arrival on the site. Information-driven personalization requires sophisticated quantitative models but it can be executed in real time for an inbound contact or as part of an outbound communication. The software builds a profile almost instantaneously when the visitor hits a site. It can use many types of data, depending on what is available and the level of identification of the visitor—everything from clickstream data to transactional data from the customer database. As the visitor moves around the site, the profile is updated. It also stores information, perhaps in the customer database and perhaps on a cookie on the visitor's own computer, in preparation for the next visit. Virtually any aspect of site content can be served to the visitor on the basis of the profile—the products to be displayed, incentives to be offered, and characteristics of the offer itself including price.

CRM itself and the tools of targeting and personalization all imply a continuous, closed-loop process of data capture, information-driven programs, and knowledge refinement. There is one additional technique that is widely used to increase the momentum and power of relationship marketing. That important technique is the loyalty program.

Customer Loyalty Programs

Loyalty programs are familiar and ubiquitous. Businesses from the corner pizza parlor to the urban department store to the international hotel chain have loyalty programs. Consumers and business travelers have wallets full of their cards. Incentives range from "Buy 9 get the 10th pizza free" to free airline tickets to rental car upgrades and many others.

Keep in mind, though, that loyalty programs are a part of CRM strategies. Loyalty programs alone do not represent a strategy. The key issue is that loyalty programs focus on changing behavior and their effects may not last past the reward. Strategic CRM focuses on long-term relationship and brand building and may have more long-term impact. In spite of their potential to have only short-term effectiveness, loyalty programs have become a staple of the marketing strategies of firms like Britain's Tesco supermarkets. Their loyalty program goes back over two decades and has been refined over the years. It has enjoyed disciplined execution, another reason for its effectiveness.

The Tesco Loyalty Program Increases Its Effectiveness

Tesco began its loyalty program in 1995 when, as Britain's second-largest food retailer, its growth had plateaued. By 2005, the program covered 10 million households in the U.K. and Asia. It captured data on store sales and linked them to individual household profile data. All these data are captured in a data warehouse and analyzed with sophisticated data mining tools as discussed in Chapter 4. Using the customer insights from these data, Tesco has branched out into nonfood retailing, offering everything from DVDs and games to travel, optometrist, and legal services. They also offer a broad array of financial and telecommunications services.

From the beginning of the Club Card program, Tesco used the data for segmentation analyses. Over time, the data have produced more detailed and actionable segments. Segments include cost conscious, mid-market and up-market demographic groupings. From a lifestyle perspective they have identified healthy, gourmet, convenience-oriented, family living, and other similar segments. By 2010, Tesco had made additional investments in metrics that allowed it to track which stores customers patronized, what they buy, and how they pay. These data are used to tailor merchandise selection to individual stores from its huge hypermarts to neighborhood convenience shops. According to Rust, Moorman, and Bhalla, "Shoppers who buy diapers for the first time at a Tesco store, for example, receive coupons by mail not only for baby wipes and toys but also for beer, according to a *Wall Street Journal* report. Data analysis revealed that new fathers tend to buy more beer because they can't spend as much time at the pub."[34]

Tesco tailors offers to the known interests of segment members, sending millions of customized print publications each quarter and customized emails on a more frequent basis. Coupons distributed in the print magazines are redeemed at a rate of 20 to 40 percent, a rate much higher than the industry norm. Tesco attributes this to the relevance of the coupons to each individual customer, not to higher-value coupons.

Tesco also runs special promotions, often on a seasonal basis. In August 2010, Tesco launched a back-to-school promotion that expected to see 16 million customers receive £140 in rewards. For each £5 in Club Card vouchers, they could receive £10 in reward tokens to spend on merchandise throughout the store.

In one five-year period in the 1990s, Tesco sales increased by 52 percent, a rate higher than the industry average. Tesco is now the number-one food retailer in Great Britain with a market share that has increased from 16 percent at the time of the Club Card introduction to over 30 percent at the end of 2010. According to Professor Don Schultz, "They are way beyond rewarding customers and retention; they are using data to drive business decisions."[35]

Tesco has not fared as well, however, in its SMM efforts. In early 2011, Tesco had only 6,100 Facebook fans, and was dwarfed by Sainsbury's 86,250 fans,[38] even though the latter is number three in market share at over 16 percent. [39] Part of the reason for its poor showing on Facebook may be that Tesco did not have one official fan page until March 2011. It had specialty pages for categories like clothing, beauty, pets, green living, and its Race for Life philanthropy program.

INTERACTIVE EXERCISE **11.3** Linking Mobile and Retail at Tesco

Tesco has multiple mobile apps, including one that has over 1 million users,[36] in which the customer can manage her Club Card account. It has another for its private branded wine, Tesco Wine by the Case. According to Tesco.com CEO Laura Wade-Gery, "All you need to do is take a picture of any wine bottle label from your iPhone and if it is one of the 1,000 that Tesco Wine by the Case stocks you'll see all the tasting notes and information about that wine, including the guide price."[37] In this topical video, the Reuters news agency tests the barcode scanner app introduced in late 2010 and speculates on the value of this type of app to retailers.

Watch the video at http://bit.ly/vM3g6g.

Internationally, Tesco has an even more powerful vision for creating loyal customers through its Home Plus operation in South Korea.

See this unique program at http://bit.ly/tb8i8q.

The official fan page now serves as a hub for all these specialty pages. Tesco expects data from Facebook pages to help it tailor offers to individual customers instead of to segments.[40] The official page links to Tesco Direct to facilitate access to online shopping, and now has topped over 340,000 fans, as of late 2011.

Tesco is good at reacting to current developments in CRM, including its use of apps and its activity on social networks. Let us look specifically at those two important developments.

Emerging Issues—Apps and Social CRM

The basic concepts of CRM have changed little over the years, but two new developments are changing the way it is executed. The changes to CRM programs that result from apps and social CRM are in their infancy, but they have already had a powerful impact.

The Power of Apps

It is no surprise to readers of this text that apps are popular and ubiquitous. Most of us have a smart device full of them. However, it may be a surprise that time spent on mobile apps has surpassed time spent on the traditional Internet (see Figure 11.12a). That is one measure of the growing importance of mobile marketing, a subject that is discussed in Chapter 16.

Figure 11.12b shows the types of apps used. Games, music, and entertainment are all popular. Practical services like maps and weather are also favored by many smartphone users. Social networking apps are near the top of the list with Facebook, the most downloaded across all operating systems, while Twitter is the number-five app for BlackBerrys, the mobile device of choice for many business users.[41] The Tesco case illustrates one popular use of a branded app, as do other examples throughout this text.

Speaking specifically to the role of apps in broadening media channels, Sir Martin Sorrell, chairman of the WPP agency, said:

> Apps are a classic example of this shift from broadcast to multifaceted engagement.... They enable brands to connect with consumers at numerous touchpoints, whether at home or in the shops.... It opens a lot of opportunities for our clients, but also challenges.... Location targeting is the holy grail that we as advisers on behalf of our clients are looking for."[42]

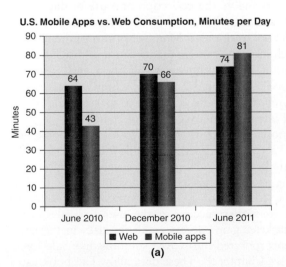

(a)

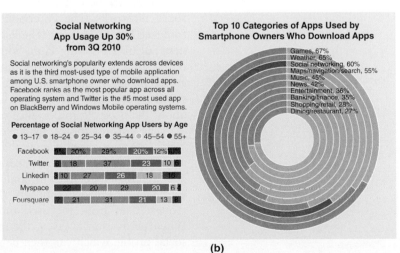

(b)

FIGURE **11.12** (a) Time Spent on Mobile Apps Exceeds Time Spent on Web (b) Types of Apps Downloaded by Smartphone Users

Sources: Charles Newark-French, "Mobile Apps Put the Web in Their Rear-view Mirror," June 20, 2011, Reprinted by permission of Flurry; and "The State of the Media: Social Media Report: Q3 2011," page 8, Copyrighted information of The Nielsen Company, licensed for use herein.

Location-based marketing is one of the mobile marketing topics discussed in Chapter 16.

Marketers should be mindful of the fact that although apps are popular and useful, it is not a case of "build it and they will come." Apps represent a marketing communications—and perhaps an ecommerce—program that needs to be targeted and executed with all the care of any other marketing program. We will discuss the issues in developing and marketing successful mobile apps in Chapter 16. When we do, remember that apps are primarily a CRM initiative. Downloading can be done on impulse, but it generally implies some level of brand familiarity and favorability.

Social CRM

There is no common agreement on a definition of social CRM. This definition has been widely adopted; it has also been widely criticized:

> [Social] CRM is a business function supported by a system and technologies whose aims are to improve a company's ability to derive insights into customer needs and behaviors by adding to their transaction data the lifestyle data they share online.[43]

The criticisms can generally be summarized as, "for what?" The argument, of course, is that the overall objective is sales and social CRM needs to make a clear contribution to that goal. That is true, but in the infancy of the approach, clear attribution of sales to social media data is difficult, so this definition works for now, although it will surely change over time.

In spite of the arguments, there are two things the proponents of social CRM agree on:

1. It adds two elements to our understanding of CRM. Figure 11.13a uses B2C terminology but the meaning is the same as our B2B terminology illustrated in Figure 11.13b. Traditional CRM is built around marketing and public relations, customer service and support, and transactions. Social CRM adds the role of satisfying customer experience and the impact of customer advocacy.
2. Social CRM is the result of an evolution in the discipline, not a revolutionary change. Additional tools, including listening and engaging, have become available to marketers and wise marketers have begun to take advantage of them. Figure 11.13b illustrates the expansion of customer insight that is possible with the addition of social media tools to the CRM toolbox.

Tools are becoming available to enable the collection and use of data from social networks. The Facebook Campaign Manager from Awareness is such a tool (see Figure 11.13b). The Facebook Campaign Manager is part of the Awareness Social Marketing Hub, which facilitates the management and measurement of multiple social marketing channels and supports publication and customer engagement on them. The Facebook Campaign Manager is not available as a stand-alone software product, and that should cause you to stop and think about the growing importance of integrated management of channels.

The core of the campaign effort is the creation of a custom Facebook tab, which is a specialized page in the Facebook profile.[44] Tabs allow marketers to create customized, interactive pages that can take advantage of Facebook options like geotargeting and can act as landing pages for marketing campaigns. The Facebook Campaign Manager supports the creation of tabs, allowing the marketer to request data from the user and to request access to the user's social profile. When permission is given, the marketer gains access to all the data in the users social profile which can then be incorporated into CRM solutions like Salesforce. com (see Chapter 1) and Eloqua (see Chapter 9). These data allow Facebook users to be integrated into marketing activities such as lead scoring and management, email follow-up offers, and additions to email lists including event-triggered programs. Remember that the marketer must provide an incentive that makes it worthwhile for the user to provide data, just like any good landing page.

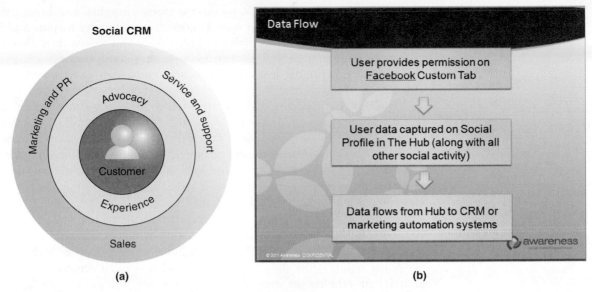

FIGURE **11.13** (a) The Elements of Social CRM (b) Integrating Permission-Based Social Profile Data into CRM Applications

Sources: Figure from Jacob Morgan, "What is Social CRM?" November, 3, 2010, Copyright © 2010 Chess Media Group, Reprinted with permission; and "Facebook Campaign Manager," p. 16, © 2011 Awareness, Inc. Retrieved from http://www.slideshare.net/bostonmike/facebook-campaign-manager. Reprinted with permission.

Another approach is a B2B application offered by Radian6. Radian6 has an analytics platform "to view their website activity and performance through the lens of social media."[45] It does this by importing data *from* the client's Google Analytics, WebTrends, or Omniture metric platform and combining it with relevant social media metrics. That allows marketers to see, for example, which of their content marketing activities are generating social media activity that results in website traffic, leads, or sales conversions. That is a first step and a useful one that we can expect to develop over the next few years. However, it is a long way from putting social media *data items* from *identified customers* into a database.

Best Buy is another business that is good at responding to developments in the social media space.

The Best Buy Community

In early 2008, Best Buy began to engage customers outside the traditional channels of retail stores, call centers, email, and direct mail. Best Buy searched social networks for its customers who needed service or support and helped them resolve their issues. Later in 2008, it established an online community to act as the focal point for this activity. Best Buy Unboxed is organized around product-category discussion boards in which customers can interact with Best Buy agents and one another. They can also access the Geek Squad and Blue Shirt service experts.[46] The community forum page on tablets and ereaders, for instance, has active ongoing conversations, with access to self-help resources and a tool that shows the Tweet stream from a Best Buy Twitter account.[47] Best Buy's community platform supplier, Lithium, says:

> Best Buy's community is thriving. In an average quarter the team sees activity in the region of 600,000 customers visiting the community and posting 20,000 messages (over 77,000 messages and counting) and looking at over 22 million pages of content.

Gina Debogovich, the Best Buy community manager, calls it "The Power of Unfiltered Communication." She says the community forums decrease support costs, drive product discussions, produce customer insights, and bring the power of Best Buy's employees to the web. Besides the community forums and Twitter accounts, the social CRM initiative includes blogs and videos. It is also multilingual, with communities and Twitter accounts in Spanish and French, as well as in English, and includes a community where employees can connect and share experiences and expertise.[48]

The Best Buy social CRM initiative is supported by other online activities like display advertising, online coupons, and email newsletters. It has even been supported by TV advertising, most famously the Twelpforce Mary commercial.[49] Best Buy also added other media channels, including an online magazine, and installed a video network in retail stores that allows them to show relevant content in departments throughout the store. It sells advertising on this instore network, seeming to have come full circle in its media efforts.[50]

In the end, it is all about customer experience. In 2011, Best Buy won Internet Retailer's top award for cross-channel shopping experiences that integrate the retail stores and the Internet. Criteria included store pickup of web orders and providing online order data to representatives at its call centers. The study suggested that retailers in general have a long way to go to provide a totally satisfactory multichannel experience for its customers.[51] Best Buy's continued innovation in customer communications has them leading the pack. There are, however, other good examples. Jerimiah Owyang of Altimeter has a discussion on the uses of social CRM in six different types of marketing activities that is supported by 18 brief case histories.[52]

Each of the tools and techniques we have discussed throughout this chapter can be a useful part of a comprehensive CRM strategy. The real difficulty, however, is putting them together into a successful, ongoing CRM process. At present, many enterprises are working to implement successful processes, but few have yet achieved the full potential of CRM.

In search of successful ongoing CRM, many firms have installed CRM systems that require hardware, software, and trained personnel—both technical and marketing. This has proven to be a large undertaking that has many opportunities, if not for total failure, at least for suboptimization.

The Costs and Failure Rate of CRM Systems Projects

Installing a CRM system in a large enterprise can be expensive. In 2004, International Data Corporation (IDC) interviewed representatives of over 30 large corporations in the United States and Europe. It found that the median investment in a CRM application prior to start-up was $426,000 and that the median total cost of the system over its first five years was $1.2 million. The majority of its respondents reported recouping its initial investment in CRM. Fifty-eight percent experienced a pay-back period of one year or less, 35 percent paid back the investment in one to three years, and 8 percent achieved payback in three years or more.[53]

The cost of a CRM system includes hardware, software, and training of both IT and marketing personnel. Costs can also include the engagement of a *systems integrator* to help install and customize the system. In 2011, consultant Arthur Hughes said that companies can spend as much as $20 million on the hardware, software, and data integration for an integrated data warehouse.[54] Software for CRM is licensed for the number of people who use it (per seat). Those costs can range from a few hundred dollars to a few thousand dollars per seat.[55] There is a wide range in all cost estimates for CRM systems and actual costs depend on many elements of the program. Costs may be impacted materially in the years to come by cloud computing and usage-based pricing, still in their infancy. All that said, implementing a CRM program can be both expensive and time consuming.

The same wide variance applies to estimates of the failure rate of CRM programs. The statistic often quoted is that as many as 70 percent of CRM programs fail to provide the expected ROI. In 2009, Michael Krigsman of ZDNet reviewed studies of CRM failure rates since 2001. He was unable to document the 70 percent figure. He found estimates of catastrophic failure, failures that kept the CRM system from going live, from 18 to 31 percent. With a looser definition of failure, failure to meet ROI expectations, he found relatively recent studies that reported rates of 47 and 56 percent. On the basis of the studies he reviewed and his discussions with experts in the field, Krigsman concluded that "many organizations do achieve acceptable ROI from their CRM implementations." He further states, "Still, the data clearly states that substantial numbers of CRM customers are dissatisfied with some significant aspect of their implementations."[56]

Why is there a significant failure to perform when the necessity of CRM is not in doubt? The simple answer is that CRM systems are not easy to implement. The data requirements and the technology can be daunting, but that is only a small part of the reason that many CRM projects fall short. The overriding reasons fall under the general heading of "organizational issues," ranging from lack of strong and consistent leadership from top management to failure to achieve buy-in from people throughout the organization.

There have been many studies of under-performing CRM systems over the years. While they may use different words, the reasons given tend to fall into three basic categories.[57] They are:

1. Lack of clear strategy and objectives
2. Lack of organization-wide buy-in and commitment
3. Focus on technology instead of on marketing and business requirements

CRM does change the way marketers, and indeed the entire business, think about interacting with their customers. Implementing a CRM system should be seen as a process of change management with organization-wide ramifications. That is a sizeable challenge, and many businesses have fallen short.

Keeping CRM focused on the enterprise's vision of how it wishes to interact with and to be perceived by its customers is necessary to overcoming barriers and avoiding failure drivers. The generic vision for CRM can be described as "seamlessly satisfying customer experience."

The CRM Vision—Seamless Customer Experience

The CRM vision is to provide the customer a totally satisfactory experience—through every distribution channel the enterprise employs, by means of any communications channel the customer chooses to use, 24/7/365. In an era of multichannel marketing, that is a tall order indeed!

Figure 11.14 suggests the nature of both the problems and the opportunities. Merchants can offer access to information and transactions through their retail stores, websites, telephone call centers, direct mail and catalogs, self-service kiosks like ATMs, and social networks like Facebook. Field service technicians, the person who repairs your refrigerator at home or copier at work, also represent the enterprise and can, in fact, present up-sell and cross-sell opportunities if they are properly trained and motivated. B2B marketers also have field sales forces as another important channel. No one marketer, B2B or B2C, is likely to use all these channels of distribution. However, most now offer a set—branch banks, a website, a telephone customer service center, and ATMs, supplemented

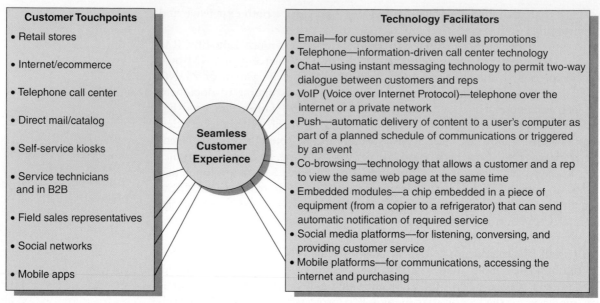

Customer Touchpoints	Technology Facilitators
• Retail stores	• Email—for customer service as well as promotions
• Internet/ecommerce	• Telephone—information-driven call center technology
• Telephone call center	• Chat—using instant messaging technology to permit two-way dialogue between customers and reps
• Direct mail/catalog	• VoIP (Voice over Internet Protocol)—telephone over the internet or a private network
• Self-service kiosks	• Push—automatic delivery of content to a user's computer as part of a planned schedule of communications or triggered by an event
• Service technicians and in B2B	• Co-browsing—technology that allows a customer and a rep to view the same web page at the same time
• Field sales representatives	• Embedded modules—a chip embedded in a piece of equipment (from a copier to a refrigerator) that can send automatic notification of required service
• Social networks	• Social media platforms—for listening, conversing, and providing customer service
• Mobile apps	• Mobile platforms—for communications, accessing the internet and purchasing

In the center: **Seamless Customer Experience**

FIGURE **11.14** The CRM Vision
Source: © Cengage Learning 2013

with occasional direct mail promotions, would be typical for a retail bank, for example. Most nonprofits have mail, telephone, website, as well as a Facebook page and personal contacts of various types. An industrial concern would be likely to have a field sales force, a website, printed catalogs, a telephone call center, field service technicians, a blog, and one or more brand communities for customer communication and support. Each of these channels represents a "customer touchpoint." Each of these touchpoints provides an opportunity to serve the customer well—through information, transactions, or service. Each customer contact sends a message about the brand—positive or negative. Technology can assist on both these dimensions.

Figure 11.14 also lists the technologies that are in most common use in CRM applications today. The technologies have been discussed in various contexts throughout this text. They all can be applied in B2C, B2B, and nonprofit environments.

The challenge to CRM is that the customer may contact the enterprise at any time, through any of the channels, using any of the available technologies. The marketer's job is to deliver the right product, service, or information—consistently and correctly—no matter when, where, or how the customer makes contact. Further, the product, service, or information should be delivered by the agent—anyone from a call center representative to a field service technician—with whom the customer makes the initial contact. Referring the customer from one person to another in the organization in order to try to get information or settle an issue is the antithesis of "seamless customer experience." The responder on social networks may be an anonymous administrator, but quick and relevant response is essential.

In this context, it is important to recognize technology as a means to an end, not an end in itself. Jeremiah Owyang coined a phrase that has been much repeated. Superimposed on a large sledgehammer it says, "Don't Fondle the Hammer."[58] His message? Do not emphasize the technology; focus on the customer.

Writing in the *Harvard Business Review*, Bain consultants Rigby, Reichheld, and Schefter say, "Executives often mistake the easy promise of CRM software for the hard reality of creating a unique strategy for acquiring, building relationships with, and retaining customers."[59]

Their solutions, as all the perspectives presented in this chapter, are centered around acquiring and retaining high value customers, developing the right value proposition, ensuring that all business processes are functioning properly, and motivating employees at all customer touchpoints. These are organizational and strategy issues; CRM systems can support strategies, but they cannot devise them. The enterprise must do the demanding work that goes all the way from identifying high value customers and learning how to increase their value to reengineering processes, if necessary, to learning how to keep customers from defecting. At that point, the enterprise knows what it needs to do and it has a foundation for choosing suppliers of CRM software, systems, and integration services to assist the company in implementing its strategies.

SUMMARY

Practitioners of CRM are often heard to say that, "CRM is a journey, not a destination." The process of learning about the customer is never ending; so are the marketing activities that make use of customer knowledge. In addition, new technologies and channels are frequently added to the menu of options. CRM is not only one of the most important aspects of contemporary marketing, it is one of the most challenging.

The discipline of CRM focuses on customer retention and the reactivation of lapsed customers on the premise that it is less expensive to maintain existing customers than it is to acquire new ones. Acquiring the best customers and growing their value is the essence of CRM strategy. CLV is a guiding metric throughout. It requires the business to move from a traditional, product-oriented perspective to one in which the customer is the central focus and the establishment of an ongoing relationship is the overall goal of strategy. Strategy development can be characterized by the steps of identification, differentiation, interaction, and customization. The customer lifecycle is used to establish the types of messages that will be most effective as the customer moves through relationship stages.

In order to implement either operational or analytical CRM programs on the web, a substantial amount of customer knowledge is necessary. This knowledge is embedded in profiles of individual customers or visitors to the website as part of operational CRM. Profiling is done either anonymously or for identified customers. While anonymous profiling has obvious relevance in the early stages of a potential customer relationship, it also has important privacy implications that should not be overlooked by the marketer. One way to avoid privacy issues is to develop value-added programs like frequent customer reward plans that deepen relationships over time and lead to willing revelation of additional information on the part of loyal customers. Identified profiles can be developed when the visitor or customer provides personal information, usually through registration on a site or making a purchase from it. This permits personalization of content that can be targeted to identified customers by email or at other touchpoints. This ability to reach identified customers with personalized content is a key reason for marketers to encourage social media followers to register and provide data for the database. Moving beyond simple profiles, marketers can develop models that target customers whose value can be grown or who are likely to be responsive to a particular offer.

Apps, both mobile and desktop, have become an important element of many CRM programs. Another important development is social CRM, which adds monitoring of social networks for marketing insights. It also permits response to individual customers for service and support and can be a useful brand development tool.

Marketers have a menu of options in terms of the channels they will use and the technologies they will implement. The CRM vision is to integrate the chosen channels and technologies in such a way that customer can make contact whenever he pleases, through that channel he prefers at that particular time (the customer touchpoint) and receive the information or service he desires without delay, errors, or being transferred from one enterprise agent to another. This is the "seamless customer experience." It represents both the opportunity and the challenge facing CRM programs of all types.

DISCUSSION QUESTIONS

1. Explain, in your own words, the importance of customer-focused relationship marketing and how it differs from traditional transactional marketing.
2. What is the role of CLV in relationship marketing?
3. Customer Relationship Marketing is generally considered to have its foundations in three B2B marketing functions. Explain what the functions are and what each contributes to a CRM program.
4. Explain the steps in the Peppers and Rogers model of CRM and the importance of the customer database in the process.
5. Explain what is meant by the customer lifecycle, and how CRM strategies and messages can be crafted for its various stages.
6. Discuss the differences between operational and analytical CRM and how they make use of the customer database.
7. Explain the difference between a customer profile and a model.
8. True or False: It is easy to include customer data from social networks in the database. Why or why not?
9. Targeting and personalization are different but related CRM concepts. Be prepared to define each, clearly explaining why they are different from one another and giving an example of each.
10. True or False: Personalization is a simple process of including the recipient's name in the subject line or body of the message. Why or why not?
11. Why have apps become an important part of CRM programs for many companies? Do you believe that apps you use are helpful in building relationships with brands? Sales?
12. Explain your understanding of "social CRM."
13. What are some of the major reasons that the implementation of large CRM systems may be prone to failure?
14. What do we mean by "seamless customer experience in multiple channels?"
15. Explain why CRM is a process, not a journey with a final destination.

INTERNET EXERCISES

1. Internet Career Builder Exercise
   a. These are some of the jobs that are available in CRM, not including technical positions that require specialized training. You can find others on sites recommended by your instructor or through search.

   Call center representative

   Inside sales representative

   CRM campaign analyst

   Marketing campaign analyst

   CRM database manager

   CRM campaign coordinator

   Sales professional, consultant

   CRM marketing manager

   CRM specialist

   CRM consultant

   Manager, director customer experience

   Director loyalty programs

   and many more

   b. Select a CRM job from the previous list or from your own search. Be careful to screen out the many technical positions unless you have the necessary skills. Outline the responsibilities of that position. You may find it useful to locate job postings on the web in order to understand the job requirements.
   c. Outline knowledge and experience from classes, internships, full- or part-time jobs, and volunteer work that prepare you for this specific position.
   d. Prepare five questions you could ask at a job interview. The questions should exhibit your understanding of the position requirements without lecturing the interviewer about what he or she already knows.
   e. Update your VisualCV® or LinkedIn Profile with this information.

2. Visit one B2C, one B2B, and one nonprofit website. Examine each carefully, identifying as many relationship building techniques as possible. Do you find extensive differences between them? Be prepared to discuss your findings, and the similarities and differences between programs on the two sites, in class.

3. By now you are probably receiving communications from at least one of the websites you are tracking.

Are they doing it well or not? How would you assess the effectiveness of this part of their CRM program?

4. If you are not one already, become a fan of a Facebook brand page and study the types of marketer-generated communications that appear there. What do you see in the way of customer contribution to the content on the page? What do you make of customer activity, or lack thereof, on the page?

NOTES

1. Frederick F. Reichheld, *The Loyalty Effect* (Boston, MA: Harvard Business School Press), 1996.

2. Joe Giffer, "Capturing Customers for Life," Capbridge Technology Partners, nd, www.cpt.com.

3. For a discussion of customer value in services markets see Valarie A. Zeithaml, Roland T. Rust, and Katherine N. Lemon, "The Customer Pyramid: Creating and Serving Profitable Customers," *California Management Review*, Vol. 43, No. 4, Summer 2001, pp. 118–42.

4. Sarabjit Singh Baveja, Sharad Rastogi, Chris Zook, Randall S. Hancock, and Julian Chu, *The Value of Online Customer Loyalty*, Bain & Company, April 1, 2000, http://www.bain.com/publications/articles/the-value-of-online-customer-loyalty-and-how-you-can-capture-it.aspx.

5. http://www.slideshare.net/ConstantContact/10-quick-facts-you-should-know-about-consumer-behavior-on-facebook.

6. Debra Zahay, James Peltier, Don E. Schultz, and Abbie Griffin. "The Role of Transactional vs. Relational Data in IMC Programs: Bringing Customer Data Together," *Journal of Advertising Research*, March 2004, pp. 3–18.

7. Rowland T. Moriarty and Gordon S. Schwartz, "Automation to Boost Sales and Marketing," *Harvard Business Review*, January–February 1989, pp. 100–108.

8. http://www.1to1media.com/View.aspx?DocID=31889&on24=SponsoredContent.

9. http://lisaarthur.wordpress.com/2011/05/26/international-speedway-corporation-races-ahead-with-integrated-marketing-management/ and http://www.aprimo.com/Secondary_.aspx?id=2109.

10. http://www.daytonainternationalspeedway.com/Articles/2010/10/Daytona-500-Experience.aspx.

11. http://crmsoftwarereview.org/blog/vertical-alliances-fantracker-ticketing-application-implemented-at-michigan-international-speedway.

12. http://www.facebook.com/DaytonaInternational Speedway#!/DaytonaInternationalSpeedway?sk=wall.

13. http://www.businessweek.com/innovate/content/dec2009/id20091217_120646.htm.

14. For a more detailed discussion see Russel S. Winer, "A Framework for Customer Relationship Management," *California Management Review*, Vol. 43, No. 4, Summer 2001, pp. 89–105.

15. http://www.radian6.com/what-we-sell/analysis-dashboard/integration.

16. http://klout.com/corp/kscore.

17. http://developer.klout.com.

18. http://www.babble.com/babble-50/mommy-bloggers/mom-bloggers-top-50-full-list.

19. http://6thfloor.blogs.nytimes.com/2011/03/24/a-better-way-to-measure-twitter-influence.

20. http://www.allfacebook.com/booshaka-will-battle-klout-for-facebook-influence-metrics-2011-09.

21. http://www.dmnews.com/eureka-turning-social-data-into-golden-customer-relationships/article/211407.

22. http://www.aspca.org.

23. Ibid.

24. "Using Constituent Information for Effective Fundraising and Marketing," February 2004, http://www.convio.com.

25. Kristin Bremner, "ASPCA Puts Some Bite into Its Online Fundraising Efforts," *DM News*, April 29, 2002.

26. "Using Constituent Information for Effective Fundraising and Marketing," February 2004, http://www.convio.com.

27. http://artsandsciences.virginia.edu/kipps/documents/ASPCAWhitepaper0604.pdf.

28. http://diy-marketing.blogspot.com/2007/09/its-always-pleasure-to-receive-.html.

29. For more information on cookies, primarily from the user perspective, see http://www.cookiecentral.com.

30. http://www.alterian.com/engagement/customers/case-studies-pdfs/346891.

31. https://www.marketingsherpa.com/article.php?ident=31805.

32. Ibid.

33. David Smith, "There Are Myriad Ways to Get Personal," *Internet Week*, May 15, 2000, http://www.techweb.com.

34. http://hbr.org/2010/01/rethinking-marketing/ar/pr.

35. Betsy Spethmann, "Loyalty's Royalty," *Promo*, March 1, 2004, http://promomagazine.com/mag/marketing_loyaltys_royalty/index.html. Other sources for the Tesco Club Card program include Bill Millar, "Is Customer Loyalty in the Cards," Peppers & Rogers Group, October 1, 2001, http://www.1to1.com/View.aspx?DocID=20021; "Tesco Has Links with the Corner Shops of England's Past," *Seklemian & Newell*, March 2005, http://www.loyalty.vg/pages/CRM/case_study_14_Tesco.htm; http://www.marketingweek.co.uk/sectors/retail/tesco-launches-%C2%A3140m-clubcard-promotion/3016529.article; and http://www.telegraph.co.uk/finance/newsbysector/retailandconsumer/8187435/Tesco-increases-market-share.html.

36. http://www.internetretailing.net/2011/03/tesco-steps-up-social-marketing-with-new-facebook-page.

37. http://www.24-7pressrelease.com/press-release/tesco-wine-app-on-iphone-makes-everybody-a-wine-buff-129950.php.

38. http://www.4psmarketing.com/blog/facebook-tesco-pages-and-data.

39. http://www.betterretailing.com/2011/01/money/tough-benchmarks-as-sainsburys-market-share-increases.

40. http://www.internetretailing.net/2011/03/tesco-steps-up-social-marketing-with-new-facebook-page.

41. http://blog.nielsen.com/nielsenwire/social.

42. http://www.guardian.co.uk/technology/appsblog/2011/feb/15/wpp-sir-martin-sorrell-mobile-apps.

43. http://thesocialcustomer.com/scorpfromhell/41148/social-crm-hiring-right-definition.

44. http://www.facebook.com/note.php?note_id=501377617203.

45. http://www.radian6.com/what-we-sell/analysis-dashboard/integration/web-analytics.

46. http://www.youtube.com/watch?v=RbkS8AnqNGU.

47. http://forums.bestbuy.com/t5/Tablets-eReaders/bd-p/tablets.

48. http://www.slideshare.net/gina.communities/best-buy-community-20-conference.

49. http://www.youtube.com/watch?v=6gN41STo4TM&NR=1.

50. http://www.marketingpilgrim.com/2011/01/best-buy-gets-friendly-with-online-and-instore-magazine.html.

51. http://www.internetretailer.com/2011/08/19/best-buy-tops-linking-stores-and-web-survey-says.

52. http://www.web-strategist.com/blog/2010/03/05/altimeter-report-the-18-use-cases-of-social-crm-the-new-rules-of-relationship-management.

53. "New IDC Study on Implementing Customer Relationship Management Applications Reveals Impressive ROI," February 2, 2004, http://www.idc.com/getdoc.jsp?containerId=pr2003_12_22_135532.

54. http://www.dbmarketing.com/articles/Art204.htm.

55. http://www.youtube.com/watch?v=I7RfTnMg-ys; and http://www.crmsearch.com/rightnow-review-pricing.php.

56. http://www.zdnet.com/blog/projectfailures/crm-failure-rates-2001-2009/4967.

57. http://media.techtarget.com/searchCRM/downloads/CRMUnpluggedch2.pdf; http://crmsearch.com/crm-failures.php; http://www.crm-resources.net/CRM-Software-Failure.php; http://bryanfoss.com/Images/CRMfailure-2008.pdf; and http://www.zdnet.com/blog/projectfailures/three-big-reasons-crm-initiatives-fail/5143.

58. http://www.slideshare.net/jeremiah_owyang/social-media-trends-for-2010?src=embed.

59. Darrel K. Rigby, Frederick F. Reichheld, and Phil Schefter, "Avoid the Four Perils of CRM," *Harvard Business Review*, February 2002, p. 9.

CHAPTER 12

Developing and Maintaining Effective Websites

Key Terms

accessibility (320)
AIDA (321)
alt tag (328)
breadcrumb (328)
CSS (Cascading Style
  Sheets) (335)
customer experience (329)
heat map (325)
stickiness (318)
usability (318)

LEARNING OBJECTIVES

By the time you complete this chapter, you will be able to:

- Understand the role websites play in customers' decision-making processes.
- Explain each step in the website development process.
- Identify important issues in website design.
- Discuss ways in which overall customer experiences with websites can be measured.
- Explain the concepts of usability and customer experience.
- Understand what is involved in the redesign of a major website.
- Identify major cost elements involved in initial development of a site or redesign and relaunch.

As Internet marketing has entered the economic mainstream, websites have attained new status and maturity. In the beginning of Internet marketing, companies rushed to create a website just to have one. Gradually, the potential of the Internet meant a movement from the idea that "everyone must have one," toward carefully crafted objectives, execution for **usability**, and measurement of effectiveness. Companies want their customers to stay on their sites as long as possible, navigate as many paths as possible, and return again and again, a concept often known as site **stickiness**. Getting the site to be "sticky" is a complex task involving the graphical design of the website, its content, the degree of personalization and interactivity, and the customer's experiences on the website.[1] In addition, in today's world, the web and other channels work together, as is stated in the title of this book. Today, customers assume that a company has a website and might go to the website first to gather information before ever going to a store or contacting a firm. The marketing aspects of creating and maintaining customer-effective sites will be covered in this chapter. Measurement is the subject of Chapter 14.

The Role of Websites

There are two key, but not mutually exclusive, roles a website can play in marketing strategy. A website can be a channel for providing information or a channel for generating sales or both. In the 15-year plus history of the commercial Internet, the use of websites as an "electronic brochure" has faded, and marketers have come to understand—and generally to take advantage of—the reach and interactivity of the Internet to meet a variety of marketing objectives. Some of the generic objectives that justify the existence of an enterprise website include to:

- Increase sales revenue
- Increase the visibility of the enterprise
- Advertise products and services
- Aid in brand development
- Provide customer service
- Generate sales leads
- Retain and grow customers
- Build an online community
- Provide cost savings, especially in promotion and customer service

Most firms are looking for tangible returns from their websites, either in cost savings or revenue enhancement, and are also looking for the site to reinforce their company strategy and to work in conjunction with other communications and marketing channels. Smart companies develop specific objectives for their website in terms of the stage of customer development, nurturing prospects until they become loyal customers through a series of targeted communications.

On the customer side of the equation, uses of the Internet have become more varied and a more integral part of the lives of B2C and B2B customers alike, as discussed in Chapter 5. Further evidence is found in the growth of online retail sales. U.S. online retail sales, while slowing during the Great Recession, are now back to double-digit levels. According to Forester Research, online retail sales grew 12.6 percent in 2010 to reach $176.2 billion. U.S. ecommerce, which includes B2B sales, is expected to reach $278.9 billion in 2015, an expected 10 percent compound annual growth rate (CAGR) from 2010 to 2015.[2] Further fueling growth is mobile commerce, which is expected to reach $31 billion by 2016. This figure represents a CAGR of 39 percent from 2011 to 2016, indicating mobile commerce is in a high growth phase similar to the high growth of the early days of the Internet. Even with this high growth rate, mobile commerce is only expected to be 7 percent of overall ecommerce sales by 2016.[3] Growth is not confined to the United States. Goldman Sachs, as reported by Internet Retailer, predicts that global ecommerce will reach the $1 trillion mark by 2013.[4]

Harris Interactive reported in December 2009 that 184 million of U.S. adults were online (80 percent). In fact, half of all those online bought something on the Internet in the last month, including 62 percent of those ages 30 to 39 and 56 percent of those ages 40 to 49.[5] In a research article in the *Journal of Interactive Marketing*, V. Kumar notes that his research supports the idea that "customers who shop across multiple transaction channels provide higher revenues, higher share of wallet, have higher past customer value, and have a higher likelihood of being active than other customers."[6]

The web is also an important source of product research, often surpassing that of retail stores. *Marketing Daily* reports that 40 percent of customers now say they will not buy a brand if they cannot find information they are looking for online and that the percentage leaps to over half of consumers for more expensive items like cars and computers.[7] According a PowerReviews webinar in May of 2010 entitled "5 Social Shopping Trends Shaping the Future of Ecommerce," although the majority of shoppers researching a branded product (57 percent) begin their research with a search engine, one-fifth (20 percent) choose the brand's site to begin their research. This trend toward web searching before purchase is an international trend, as the previous information comes from a consumer survey by Initiative, the Interpublic Group media agency, who surveyed over 4,000 consumers in five markets: the United States, Australia, China, Germany, and Spain.

The importance of multichannel shoppers is even greater than in the past, with research suggesting that multichannel shoppers purchase more frequently and in greater amounts than single channel customers. One study found that shoppers at J.C. Penney who purchased only on the Internet averaged $157 each year, while those who purchased only in stores averaged $195. Customers who purchased both at retail and on the Internet averaged $485, while those who purchased on all three channels—store, Internet, and catalog—averaged $887.[8] In fact, in 2008, the web surpassed the store as the preferred purchase method for multichannel shoppers, with nearly half of shoppers (49 percent) preferring the ease of usage and the ability to find difficult items that the web provides.[9]

More and more, consumers are responding to both for-profit and nonprofit direct mail by going to the organization's website and destination URLs or personal URLs (PURLs) that drive traffic from both mail and email to the site.

Websites are playing a key role in marketing strategy. However, if the website does not work well, does not give visitors what they want, or is not easy to use, its failure may nullify the best-designed strategy. Marketers therefore need to have a clear understanding of what makes a website effective for its users—consumer, business, or nonprofit.

Marketing managers must establish clear marketing and communications objectives for the site, identify the target market and its needs, monitor site planning and development, see that the site is meticulously tested for both technical quality and visitor usability, and ensure that it is updated frequently and accurately. Marketers must, in other words, treat it as they would any other critical marketing activity. The website is not a tool of the IT department; it is a tool of marketing and organizational communications.

None of this is meant to diminish the importance—and the difficulty—of designing and building a first-class website. The technical issues are numerous, complex, ever-changing—and mostly beyond the scope of this chapter. It is, however, highly recommended that marketing students acquire some first-hand knowledge of web development tools, either through formal classes or by using some of the many excellent free sources available on the web itself. Marketers who have even a rudimentary knowledge of technical issues will be more competent to deal effectively with the technicians responsible for web development and maintenance. The work of the technical specialists is demanding, but marketing must lead the way to a website that achieves marketing objectives. Otherwise the website will be full of technical sound and fury, but accomplish little of commercial value.

In addition to technical challenges, there are challenges involving the legal environment of marketing to website development. For example, in 2007, a federal district court allowed a class action against Target Corporation under the Americans with Disabilities Act (ADA) and held that California law requires these sites such as Target.com to be accessible to the blind.[10] The issue was the lack of "alt" tags in the site, which are used by screen-reading technology to help visually disabled users navigate websites. Target eventually settled this suit with not only a financial settlement, but by agreeing to make its website accessible to the blind.

Designing sites for **accessibility** by the physically challenged is good business practice. Some sites, such as the New York Public Library site (www.nypl.org), provide the ability to change the font size of the site by a click of a button. Sites such as the National Public Radio (NPR) have special links to a text only version of the site (http://thin.npr.org). These sites are important for those who use certain types of mobile phones or older versions of web browsers. Text-only sites are also important to those with physical challenges who may have special types of site readers or browsers.

Such accessible design is also required for the sites of all federal governmental agencies, of organizations that are created with federal funds, and the websites of public universities. Your school's site may have a page describing accessibility accommodations.[11] The issue of website accessibility to all those who have disabilities is not going to go away, and there continue to be lawsuits filed in other states and arenas making websites available to all consumers.

This chapter will deal with the general process of developing a site and the characteristics that make it attractive and useful from the customer's perspective. As you read this chapter, bear in mind that this is a discussion of marketing strategy as it relates to websites, not one about "cool" or "favorite" sites. It is about what works, and that is often a different issue—as we will make clear later in this chapter—from what is "cool" from a technical or aesthetic point of view. The perspective of "what works" is so important that Chapter 14 considers in detail the issues involved in measuring and evaluating site effectiveness on an ongoing basis.

Let us start the discussion of sites that accomplish business objectives by taking a look at the steps involved in the site development process.

The Website Development Process

Figure 12.1 summarizes the steps that are essential to the establishment of an effective website. It begins with the establishment of site objectives, which, in turn, should flow directly from the marketing objectives and the corporate objectives of the enterprise.

Establishing Website Objectives

The nature of the objectives will be dependent on whether the site is intended to be primarily informational or whether it is transactional in nature. There are many possible generic objectives, as discussed at the beginning of this chapter. The individual enterprise must take these generic objectives and develop them into specific, measurable objectives for the particular website. It is also important for the company to have a clear strategy so that website objectives and target markets can be well delineated.

If a site is informational in nature, objectives might be based on the **AIDA** hierarchy that is familiar in the mass media advertising environment:

Attention ⟶ Interest ⟶ Desire ⟶ Action

The argument would be that the website could be used to make potential customers aware of the product and service offerings of the business, to convey detailed knowledge about product use, and to develop an intent to purchase. The website might then connect the prospect with the party, then leading to a transaction. Some retail chains follow this model by providing basic information and store locator services that drive visitors into the retail store. Some manufacturers of business products choose not to create channel conflict by having a

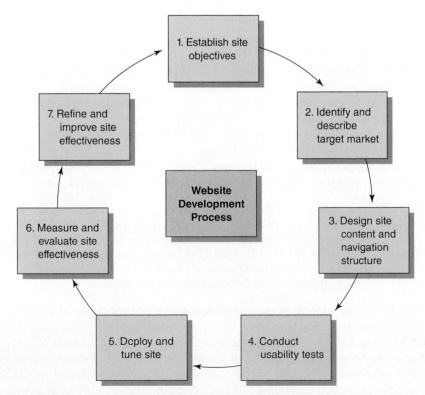

FIGURE **12.1** The Website Development Process

Source: Adapted from marketing materials of Accrue Software, Inc.

transactional website. They present product information and direct potential customers to the nearest dealer or distributor.

Characterizing a website's objective as a communications hierarchy process, however, has a major drawback—whether the market space is B2B or B2C. This approach overlooks the fact that the Internet is inherently a direct-response mechanism and risks ignoring important functions that can be included in Internet marketing activity that are difficult to carry out in the traditional mass media.

First, mass media communications do not ordinarily include a call to action. The interactive nature of the Internet makes it highly desirable to ask the prospect to take some action. If it does not appear reasonable to close a sale—a consumer shopping for automobiles or a business person gathering information on enterprise software applications, for example—an effort should be made to obtain the visitor's name and email address for further promotional activity. This makes an informational website into a sales lead generation process which is an accountable type of marketing activity that can help provide return on investment (ROI) justification for the expense of having a website.

Second, a communications hierarchy approach is likely to overlook the desirability of obtaining information about the prospect. Offering an incentive in return for information about the prospect or requiring registration to enter some of the deeper pages in the site are two ways of accomplishing this. On the web, informational incentives often work well and have little incremental cost. The *New York Times* has done a good job of packaging content in various ways—from newsletters called "Your Money" and "Movie Update" to offers for "Great Getaways" or for the "Sophisticated Shopper"—that it uses to persuade people to register on the site. The white papers and webcasts that are a prominent feature of the marketing efforts of many B2B marketers act as informational incentives to get people to register for the site. Whatever the tactic used to obtain information that identifies visitors to the site, the ability to do so is one of the important characteristics of the Internet.

Finally, the communications hierarchy approach ignores the very nature of the Internet, in which the customer chooses the content to which he wants to be exposed instead of having it presented to her by mass media. As a result, the task of creating awareness on the Internet is quite different from the situation mass media advertising faces in the physical world. As discussed in Chapters 5 and 6, there are many ways of bringing prospects to a website for the first time, some of which are online methods and some of which occur offline. The common theme is that few visitors just stumble onto a website by accident; most are brought there by some planned marketing or search technique. That implies that initial awareness is most likely to be created off the website, with provision of information taking place on the site itself.

As stated above, different objectives lead to different types of websites, often visually as well as operationally. An informational website is shown in Figure 12.2a, the site from Lipton, a division of Unilever. Lipton redeveloped its site to align with its positioning several years ago. According to the agency that developed the site:

> Real Branding worked closely with Lipton and its agency partners to create an integrated strategy that would reposition and enable Lipton.com to serve as the seamless online hub for all Lipton marketing efforts. Under this strategy, all Lipton marketing efforts are wrapped in the "Tea Can Do That" positioning and drive users online. Once directed to Lipton.com, the promise of "Tea Can Do That" comes to life in the form of experiential content that demonstrates Lipton's promise.[12]

These strategic objectives make a strong case for the website of a traditional consumer products company being key to positioning while providing a great deal persuasive informational content. Site visitors have a chance to play an interactive game to test knowledge of tea and its health benefits and other facts of health and well-being. The website now includes links to social media sites such as Twitter and Facebook so consumers can engage with each other and the brand. Although the primary purpose is informational, the site has a store locator service and offers the opportunity to purchase online. According to

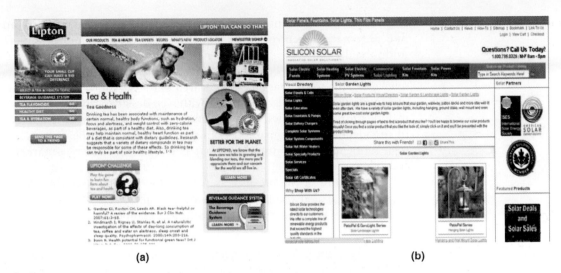

(a)   (b)

FIGURE **12.2** (a) Lipton Tea—A Branding Site (b) Silicon Solar—A Transactional Site

Sources: Lipton, http://www.liptont.com/tea_health/index.aspx; and Silicon Solar, http://www.siliconsolar.com/solar-garden-lights.html.

Alexa.com, Lipton.com is the top ranking tea site in the beverage category. About 30 percent of its search results come from the queries "lipton" or "lipton tea," indicating the strong brand itself drives traffic to the site. The company's new positioning tag line, "Drink Positive" continues to reinforce the same brand image established by the "Tea Can Do That" campaign.

On the other hand, an example of a transactional website is that of Silicon Solar Inc., a multichannel retailer of environmentally friendly solar products, including lighting, solar panels, and water heaters. It serves consumer and wholesaler markets and has an active affiliate program. Its site is designed to facilitate ecommerce transactions from each of its channels and this primarily objective determines its website design. Figure 12.2b shows one of the product pages from the garden lighting section. The thumbnail visuals on the main product page offer pop-ups with additional product details and the opportunity to purchase directly from the product detail page. The site supports easy navigation with a detailed product directory in the left-hand column on all pages. While primarily designed to facilitate transactions, like Lipton, Silicon Solar also fosters its positioning. The site is in the fast-growing renewable energy market and sponsors a Solar Power Forum where customers can connect with other users, product specialists, and industry experts. This type of virtual community helps newcomers make product decisions, provides educational opportunities, and gives Silicon Solar continuing insight into the interests and activities of its customers.

Good website objectives take into account the overall marketing objectives of the enterprise and provide a strong foundation for measuring site effectiveness. These sites also take into account the special capabilities of the Internet to provide information or to make shopping easy. In establishing objectives, marketers also need to be keenly aware of the needs and preferences of the target market. As a result, a concurrent task is identifying and describing the target market.

Identifying and Describing the Target Market

Marketing is clearly responsible for this important step in the web development process. The marketing function understands how the objectives relate to a specified target market. Marketing is also the location within the firm of detailed knowledge about the needs, attitudes, and shopping behaviors of market segments targeted by the business.

It is important that marketers share this information with all who are involved in designing and building the site. Think about it. Should a site, say an entertainment-oriented one, that is targeted to teenagers look and interact like an entertainment-oriented site that is targeted to older adults? You will undoubtedly agree that it should not and that content, visual appearance, and interaction should all be designed with a specific target market in mind. It is the marketer's job to see that the site is geared to the identified target market by sharing information about the target market with web designers and developers. These data include the demographics, lifestyles, and—very importantly—the web use behaviors of the identified target market. Both the marketers and the web technicians must then work together to translate what is known into a target-market-appropriate website.

The nature of the product as well as the specific target market also makes a difference. The marketing director of a hospital in Southern California reports on the results of using a focus group to test competing approaches to site design as follows:

> My colleague had focus-group tested the four color extravaganza against a much simpler, content-rich two-color document.... The group participants liked the simpler, content-rich stuff. "With all the fancy pictures and glossy design, you look as if you've just got money to burn," they said. "It's not very responsive to the consumer's need for information."[13]

Members of the target market for any health care application are probably looking for information with a serious purpose in mind. The site must be responsive to both the need for information and the attitude with which the target visitor enters the site. This approach implies that content should not be chosen on a whim or even on the basis of what is readily available. The site content should, instead, be chosen with a deep understanding of what the target market wants and expects. The same is true of the design and visual appearance of the site. It should be entirely appropriate to the objectives of the site as well as to the target market and its purpose in visiting the site.

A special landing page was created by Office Depot to market its products in business and government. The website (https://business.officedepot.com) shows the home page for business customers of Office Depot. The site is accessible not only by its own URL but also through the Office Depot home page for consumer marketing. The site offers customers the chance to choose solutions based on the size of their business; home business; small, medium, or large business; or national or global firm. Customers can also choose to look at solutions based on their particular industry, such as federal government, state and local government, health care, or education.

The business solutions division is specifically targeting firms of at least 15 employees who spend at least $6,000 per year on office and technology supplies. Companies not in this target market are invited to purchase on the company's regular site (www.officedepot.com). To get this specialized knowledge and help requires a login name and password, but the offered benefit for registration is solutions targeted to the B2B customer's specific business. Each level of business or type of industry has targeted benefits and support services. The design of the site is straightforward and easy to understand and well suited to a business customer.

Once the target market, its profile characteristics, and its reasons for visiting the website are determined, the next step is to design site content and the navigational structure. This step will guarantee optimum accessibility of the content to the target market.

Designing Website Content

Identifying the necessary content and the appropriate manner of presentation are other marketing tasks. The content of the site is something that, at first glance, appears quite straightforward. Marketers, after all, in every business except a start-up have experience in developing mass media advertising and marketing support material, such as brochures and catalogs. However, content on the web is not that straightforward. For one thing, Internet marketers believe that most viewers skim instead of reading word by word. This means that copy must be laid out in short blocks, preferably in columnar fashion. When the copy is long, the marketer should assume that many visitors will not scroll down far or will not jump to a continuation page, and should place key content accordingly.

A recent trend in web design has been the use of "Web 2.0" elements such as eye catching graphics, strong visual metaphors, and clean, clear fonts for text. The goal is to simplify the site's message and improve its visual appeal. Whatever we call these web design elements, the goal is to engage the website viewer and get them to take the next step for that site.

Even more provocative are a series of studies that focus on content pages conducted by the Poynter Institute, the Estlow Center at the University of Denver, and Eyetools, Inc. The carefully designed studies use eye-tracking cameras in the ongoing study of how consumers read news on websites. The cameras allow the researchers to record with precision the movement of a respondent's eyes on a web page (see Figure 12.3a). Results from a series of studies indicate that, in the absence of specific design elements:

- Eyes first land in the upper left of the page, especially if attracted by a headline.
- Users usually look at only the first few words of headlines.
- On these news pages, respondents tended to look at five headlines before clicking.

That information has led to dividing a web page into 16 quadrants, with the upper left being highest priority for content placement, roughly the middle being second priority, and roughly the right and bottom being lowest priority (see Figure 12.3b).[14]

The technology has also led to the development of **heat maps**, visual representations of eye activity on a web page. The red to orange areas in Figure 12.3c indicate the most activity and the blue to black the least. The upper left-hand corner of the page is often called the "Golden Triangle" because it forms a triangle shape. Others refer to this area as the "F" section since the user's eyes move backward and forward in that triangle area as they examine the content. The visual also shows the page break on the viewer's browser—often referred to as "above the fold" (see Chapter 7). It also slows a mouse click, which identifies the area on which the viewer's eye was focused when he left the page.

The unexpected finding of the early eye-tracking studies was that when entering a web page, more than half the readers included only text (no graphic elements) in their first three eye fixation clusters. The researchers also indicated that when the first three glances on a page included a graphic element, the element was more likely to be a photograph or a banner ad, not an informational graphic or other type of artwork.[15] This work contradicts conventional wisdom which says that graphics are first to attract the viewer's attention and supports those who argue for the primacy of content in web applications.

Today, this approach to web design is now more widely available. Tools such as AttentionWizard.com (www.attentionwizard.com) use an algorithm to create a simulated eye movement heat map based on their best guess of where the customer's eyes would move on a page. These are an excellent low-cost alternative to a full heat map study or can be used to complement other tools. Crazy Egg (www.crazyegg.com) uses web clicks to develop heat maps that are used as a surrogate for eye-tracking studies. ClickTale (www.clicktale.com) is another company that also includes comprehensive analytics on how users interact

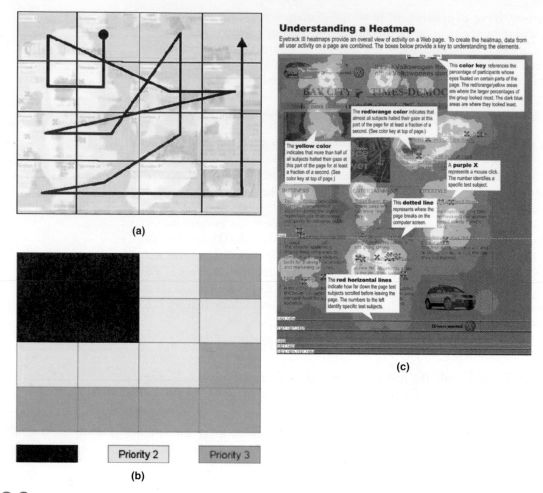

FIGURE 12.3 (a) An Eye Track Map (b) The Priority Grid (c) A Heat Map
Source: Copyright © The Poynter Institute, http://www.poynterextra.org/eyetrack2004/viewing.htm#1.3, and http://www.poynterextra.org/eyetrack2004/viewing.htm#1.2.

with the page, including time on page, page views, and both mouse movement and clicks.

The use of heat maps and the tracking of mouse clicks also argue for the importance of well-written copy on websites. The more task-oriented the viewer is and the more in a hurry he is, the more likely he is to leave as a result of poor content or poor navigation. It is also important to recognize that visitors enter the site at different times and on different pages—not necessarily the home page. Content must be relevant, make sense even if it has been archived for a long time, and repeat key points without sounding repetitive. And—of critical importance—visitors must be able to find it easily. This is the job of the content design and the navigation structure.

Designing the Navigational Structure

The first step is to design the content structure. The grammatically questionable but meaningful term "architect the information structure" is increasingly used to describe this process.[16] The implication is that there must be a coherent structure to the content of a site, usually one that is hierarchical in nature. This enables visitors to move around the site in a manner that fits each person's individual need to merely examine summary information or to drill deeper into the site in search of detailed information about a specified topic. At the same time the site designer or information architect plans a careful and comprehensive structure, they should adhere to a simple premise often referred to as KISS—Keep It Simple Stupid! One way of implementing the KISS rule is to try to see that the visitor is never more than three mouse clicks away from desired information. A frequent reason that visitors leave a site is that they cannot find the information they want with what they consider reasonable effort. Enabling them to do that is the job of the navigation structure.

The navigation structure defines the manner in which visitors move around the site. Or, quite simply, the navigation structure determines how easy it is to get from one place to another on the site and for the visitor to find what she needs. It may well determine whether she stays on the site or leaves, perhaps never to return.

Figures 12.4a and 12.4b show two highly recommended steps in developing the navigational structure of a website. The first is to develop a simple graphical flow chart that shows the structure of the site. It shows the home page or parent page, second-level pages (also called "child pages") which are the entry points to major content areas of the site, and the succeeding levels that provide more detailed types of content. There may be more levels than shown here, but going beyond three or four levels creates a complex site that may be difficult for visitors to navigate. Even though the graphical hierarchy appears deceptively simple, it ensures that the connections are logical and it gives an overview of the navigational task that will face visitors. It is a step that must not be overlooked.

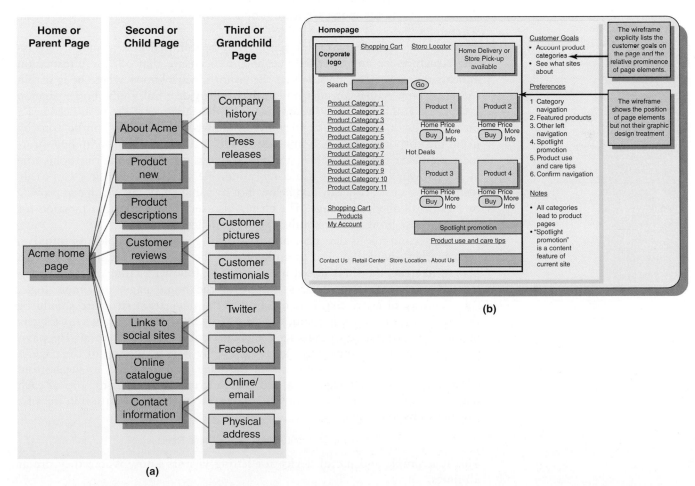

FIGURE **12.4** (a) Sample Plan of Website Hierarchy (b) "Wireframe" for Hypothetical Site Redesign

Source: © Cengage Learning 2013

INTERACTIVE EXERCISE **12.1**   Wireframe Technology

Visit http://www.hotgloo.com.

HotGloo is a wireframe technology site that allows for a free trial without a credit card. Set up an account and develop the home page of a website using the tool. You might want to redesign your university's website or the website of the company where you work. YouTube also has some HotGloo training videos. You may also find another site that provides a free wireframe service.

HotGloo

The next step is to develop mockups of pages. A detailed mockup called a wireframe is shown in Figure 12.4b. This shows the type, placement, and size of each piece of content on the page. It also provides notes to guide the technical part of the development process. Wireframes can be developed by sketching out the ideas on paper and using a whiteboard in PowerPoint, Word, or one of the many software products available that allow users to create wireframes.[17]

There are at least two rules that need to be followed in designing a navigation structure for any website. The first is to ensure that all key information appears on every page. Be sure that the visitor always knows where he is within the site. Many people consider it desirable to provide a link to the home page on every page within the site so visitors can simply start over if the path becomes a bit torturous or if they realize they are on the wrong path. This can be done by using the corporate logo as a link which fulfills two functions—branding information and the return to home page link. If that is done, the same rule holds true as it does when any icon is made into a link. Be sure that the visitor can easily identify it as a link, either by text below it or by using an **alt tag** which can provide further detail about an image. The alt tag also serves an important function for visitors whose browsers cannot display the graphics.

The second rule is that navigational structures must be simple and intuitive. That is, they should be clear and obvious to the visitor. The visitor should be able to navigate the site without instructions by following familiar web conventions (like the corporate logo as a link to the home page) or simple logic. Another way of expressing it is to say that the navigation structure should be designed with the visitor in mind, not necessarily according to the way managers and marketers are used to thinking about their corporate information. The navigational structure is commonly expressed by nav bars at the top of the page, a navigation menu in the left column of the page, and text links at the bottom of the page. Another navigational aid is **breadcrumbs**, a bar at the top of each page showing the path the visitor has followed to reach this location in the site. Breadcrumbs look like:

Home > About Acme Corp > Press Releases

This is a simple and useful device for letting visitors know where they are at all times.

If all else fails, the visitor should be able to do two things. The first is to refer to a site map, one of the text links that should be at the bottom of every page. The site map performs another important function, making it easier for search engines to index the site. The second thing is that there should be one or more links to the home page on every page in the site. It should be recognized, however, that having to resort to the site map or return to the home page is a failure in terms of customer-friendly websites.

Overstock.com—A Leader in Customer Service

Overstock.com, Inc. (shortcut: O.co) operates exclusively as an online retailer and offers brand-name merchandise at discount prices to its customers. The company not only offers a convenient way to shop for bargains, but it has shot to the top of the list in terms of customer service.

According to rankings published in the 2011 National Retail Federation Foundation/American Express Customer Service Survey, the company earned the number four spot in customer service rankings among all U.S. retailers.[18] Overstock rocketed to the top from nowhere (they were not even ranked) in a few short years.[19] "We're very happy that Overstock.com has been recognized for its fantastic customer service," said Katherine Mance, Executive Director, NRF Foundation. "Today's consumers have high expectations when it comes to Overstock.com's efforts are being rewarded in this way."[20]

The company has achieved this success by integrating its customer service across all channels, including web, phone, and email. Customer interactions are managed across channels and customer service agents can see if there has been any prior interaction, since customers often resort to multiple channels to get results.[21]

On the website itself, the registered customer can get recommendations based on preferences and prior purchases. The company also lets the customer set communication frequency preferences and see not only order history but the history of her customer service requests and responses. In addition, the company operates a customer loyalty program online that provides free shipping and 5 percent cash back to its members. The website also offers an active web community, where participants can exchange experiences with the company, record reviews, and otherwise engage with each other and the company.

As a result of its focused efforts in customer service, the company continues to see an improvement in not only in its customer service rankings, but also its Net Promoter score, which measures the extent to which customers would recommend a product. This score has increased nearly 7 times and customer satisfaction scores have increased 10 percent. The company has been able to manage its customer service more cost effectively and has reduced its email volume by 72 percent. A multichannel approach has worked for the company.

This information confirms the importance of websites that work well, providing a satisfactory **customer experience**, often integrating customer experiences across channels within the website's design. Only when usability testing confirms the ability of the site to provide a satisfactory experience should the company *deploy and tune* the site.

Netflix—Customer Service and Retention, The Ups and Downs of Web Marketing

One site to which consumers have reacted well in the past is Netflix—partly because of the popularity of its underlying business model, but also a result of the way the website serves its members. In fact, in early 2011, Netflix was a customer service darling. When a marketing research firm in 2005 surveyed online consumers, it found Netflix at the top of the satisfaction list, ahead of eretailers like Amazon, QVC, NewEgg, and L. L. Bean. The survey considered a number of factors like price and selection of merchandise. It also questioned respondents about overall experience, which included the look and feel of the website, navigation, functionality, performance, and other capabilities.

The study reported that satisfaction with the site was correlated with the likelihood of purchasing, loyalty to the site, and the possibility that the respondent would recommend the site to a friend. It also noted that Netflix users were highly likely to return to the site in spite of the fact that other online rental companies offered lower prices.[22] For the next six years, Netflix continued to be a top rated site, ranking second only behind Amazon in the Internet Retail category 2010 rankings according to the American Customer Satisfaction Index as reported by the University of Michigan.[23] According to Alexa.com in August of 2011, Netflix was rated in the top 100 websites worldwide in terms of traffic (as measured in terms of the highest combination of page views and visitors) and in the top 25 in the United States.

The Netflix business model, with which many of you are likely familiar, offers rentals of videos, DVDs, and games in a way that many consumers find quite appealing. Initially, with a small membership fee per month, consumers created their own movie queue. Consumers would then receive one to three DVDs at a time by mail, free of shipping costs. The rentals came in a postage-paid return envelope, so when members returned the DVD, they then received others from their queue. There were no shipping fees or late fees. The basic business model itself is attractive to people who prefer not to go out to the video store when they are ready to view a movie, or who are tired of paying late fees, or both.

The Netflix's website supports its basic business model in many interesting and consumer-friendly ways. It offers many ways to search the site, which has tens of thousands of movies available for rent. The member can search the collection by movie genre, by actor, or by director, or they can access new releases or the top 100 rentals. The website opens on a personalized member page that shows some recommendations for that household. Netflix engages the customer by actively encouraging members to review movies they have watched and the more reviews the customer writes, the more recommendations will be made. This member-generated content is available on the site, but its primary use is to improve the personal recommendations list for the individual household.

However, not everything is rosy. The firm faces tough competition from other companies such as satellite dish companies and websites like hulu.com that offer streaming video. Netflix has since changed its delivery mechanism and pricing from its initial launch and success. Movies are now available to stream over the Internet to devices like gaming consoles (Wii or Xbox) or directly over the Internet to the consumer's computer.

As a result of a failed attempt to create a separate brand name and login for streaming video versus DVDs, requiring a separate login and a higher price, the company has lost many customers and its earnings have suffered.[24] Netflix recently announced the intention to offer unlimited streaming video for $7.99 a month and charge $15.98 per month for both DVD and streaming services. Many factors will determine whether Netflix can stay on top of the pack in this business. This story outlines the dangers of not involving the customer in web service redesign. No matter how user-friendly the website, if the customer has

INTERACTIVE EXERCISE 12.2   Netflix

Visit www.netflix.com.

Go to the website and see what the company's current offerings are. Do these offerings and their pricing appeal to a broad enough audience to help the company maintain its long-term viability and profitability?

Can the company survive its customer service mistakes?

Create an account and write some reviews. Track the movies you are offered over time to see how well the company is taking into account your preferences.

not been consulted in major changes to the offering, the website will not survive. It remains to be seen if Netflix can weather this storm and continue to be a leading website. In fact, Netflix added 600,000 customers—of the some 800,000 customers it lost earlier in the year—in the fourth quarter of 2011, and the stock price soared 16 percent.[25]

Deploying and Tuning the Website

This stage is essentially a technical one. The site itself should be fine tuned, compressing images to make them load faster, checking links, and in general making sure that the site works as quickly and smoothly as possible. It is then ready to be uploaded to a host server (a computer that manages requests from browsers and returns HTML pages from the website in response to those requests) on the Internet. Uploading requires working closely with the ISP or hosting service to ensure that the site meets all its technical requirements. The host will deal with technical issues like load balancing and distributing content for faster access, but the company must continually monitor site performance.

Measuring, Evaluating, and Improving Website Effectiveness

Technical monitoring will be conducted by the IT department. Marketing is responsible for measuring and evaluating *the business effectiveness* of the site, a topic discussed in detail in Chapter 14. The evaluation metrics will provide information that points to areas in which it is possible to refine and improve site effectiveness. Possible improvements that surface as a result of site evaluation range from infrequently accessed pages to abandoned shopping carts to navigation paths that indicate difficulty in locating content. Continuous improvement should be the motto for websites. If improvements can be made without radically revising the site, they should be implemented immediately. When the burden of proof generated by the evaluation metrics and various kinds of user satisfaction measures warrants it, a full-scale redesign and relaunch of the website should be undertaken.

Looking back over this process, it should be abundantly clear that the initial steps in website development rely heavily on marketing for structure and guidance while technical design, function, and usability concerns tend to predominate in later stages. One of the worst mistakes Internet marketers can make is to simply turn the process over to the technical experts and say "design us a website." The result is almost certain to be a website loaded with technical bells and whistles but without a marketing objective in sight. Yet, this is what happens all too frequently in companies of all types and sizes.

The entire website development process, then, should focus on the marketing objectives of the site and the usability and user satisfaction required for the accomplishment of the objectives.[26] The process should be seen as an iterative one, with usability tests at various stages signaling either need for more work or readiness to proceed to the next stage. A research-based approach tends to exhibit the following set of steps.

- *Exploratory research* (most often qualitative research as discussed in Chapter 5) to determine how customers want to use the site should come first, before the development of site strategy and objectives. This may lead to the construction of personas, which will be described in a later section of this chapter.
- *Concept testing* should be used to refine design and navigation concepts and the design of individual pages. Respondents are questioned about the tasks they expect to perform on the site and whether concepts like navigation bar structure will facilitate task accomplishment.

- *Prototyping*, the creation of page mock-ups, should be done before design concepts are finalized. We further discuss concept testing and prototyping in Chapter 14 in the context of usability testing. A prototype will generally have some of the main functionality in place, for example, links to other pages, but will not have all functions like search bars and shopping carts actually working.

- *Beta testing* should be done before a new site or major component redesigns are released to the public. Beta testing is the process of asking experts and existing customers to try a product before it is offered commercially. In the web development process, this is done by putting the site on a server that does not have an Internet address. For the test, beta subjects can then be directed to a site that is not publicly available but is complete and fully functional.

- Once the site is deployed on the Internet, *customer feedback and usage statistics* should be used to continually monitor and improve site performance. The example of eBay's ability to listen to and act on feedback from its customers discussed in Chapter 3 provides an excellent model for this important activity. We discuss usage statistics in Chapter 13. Customer feedback and usage statistics provide the knowledge required for continuous improvement of the site.

- *Ongoing exploratory research* that serves to document how visitors are using the site and possible changes in customer requirements brings the knowledge-gathering process full circle and may, at some point, suggest that major site revisions are in order. Likewise, as new technology becomes available, sites may be redesigned to do things that were not previously possible.

Website Usability Criteria

Qualitative research where users interact with the site and then provide their feedback in a structured setting is invaluable in investigating the needs and behavior patterns of the target market of a specific website. Analyzing feedback on the site in social media sites can also provide valuable insight. In addition, customer satisfaction surveys are important to determine if a website is meeting its objectives. Finally, transactional measures of usability can be obtained by analyzing patterns on the site, retention rates, and return visits.

Another approach is to develop a set of questions or criteria that can be used to rate sites and to compare sites against each other. Forrester Research has developed a set of criteria that describe the effectiveness of the user experience on a given site. They have tested it on both B2C and B2B sites. The 25 criteria are listed in Table 12.1.

The criteria were factor-analyzed into four dimensions. The first factor is the *value* of the content to the user. The second is the effectiveness of the *navigational structure*. The third factor is the *presentation* of the site—details that range from the wording and graphics of the site to the effectiveness of the icons and clues like breadcrumbs that help visitors interact with the site. The fourth dimension is *trust*, which identifies elements of site functioning that make it dependable in the eyes of users. Rationale for the importance of some of the items is given in the right-hand column. It all boils down to making it easy for visitors to use the site and accomplish the tasks that brought them there.

The Forrester methodology uses carefully trained experts to rate sites on a five-point scale on each of the 25 criteria (see Table 12.1). The criteria have changed slightly over the years, with two more criteria added to the value category and two trimmed from some of the others. The initial study in 2003 found a great deal of variance between the customer experience provided by a sample of B2C sites. Some of the well-known sites generally performed well, however all had some areas in which they failed to provide a satisfactory experience, and in

TABLE 12.1	Forrester Research Criteria for Website Usability

Value	1. Does the landing page(s) provide evidence that user goals can be completed? 2. Is essential content available where needed? 3. Is essential function available where needed? 4. Are essential content and function given priority in the display?
Navigation	5. Are category and subcategory names clear and mutually exclusive? 6. Do menu categories immediately expose or describe their subcategories? 7. Are items classified logically? 8. Is the task flow efficient? 9. Is the wording in hyperlinks and controls clear and informative? 10. Are keyword-based searches comprehensive and precise?
Presentation	11. Does the site use language that's easy to understand? 12. Does the site use graphics, icons, and symbols that are easy to understand? 13. Is text legible? 14. Do text formatting and layout support easy scanning? 15. Do layouts use space effectively? 16. Are form fields and interactive elements placed logically in the display? 17. Are interactive elements easily recognizable? 18. Do interactive elements behave as expected? 19. Does the site accommodate the user's range of hand-eye coordination?
Trust	20. Does the site present privacy and security policies in context? 21. Do location cues orient the user? 22. Does site functionality provide clear feedback in response to user actions? 23. Is contextual help available at key points? 24. Does the site help users avoid and recover from errors? 25. Does the site perform well?

Source: Best and Worst of B2C Site Design, 2009, Forrester Research, Inc., April 2009.

fact, 18 out of 20 sites failed the usability test.[27] Just over a year later, Forrester compared 139 B2C sites with 31 B2B sites. The performance of the B2C sites consistently surpassed that of the B2B sites. Forrester recommended, among other issues, that B2B sites needed to make better use of web analytics to evaluate the effectiveness of their sites and assign priorities to improving the most glaring problems.[28] However, in 2009, Forrester examined 18 top B2C sites and found that 16 failed their usability test and all sites found it difficult to meet even one of the four categories of evaluation.[29] Usability testing has been around for over a decade, but companies often lose sight of its importance as the website develops.

A different approach is taken by Bizrate, which is owned and operated by Shopzilla, Inc. This company administers online surveys following ecommerce purchases and publishes reviews and ratings for emerchants. It uses these data for two purposes. When it has a sufficiently large sample of ratings for a particular eretailer, it rates their services on the site. It also shares the research collected from these surveys with the emerchant to help them improve its online shopping experience. Their sixteen quality factors are shown in Table 12.2. Eight of the items are measured immediately upon checkout by the pop-up and the other eight are measured by email after a sufficient time has elapsed for fulfillment to take place.

Their items are typical retail satisfaction measures that include ease of finding the products and prices, ecommerce issues like shipping costs and options, and fulfillment issues like delivery and customer service. For ecommerce sites shopping cart abandonment and other metrics like time on the site and the number of cross-sales can also be useful.

TABLE 12.2 The Shopzilla Quality Factors

What Are the 16 Quality Ratings and What Do They Mean?

Eight of the 16 quality ratings are determined at the point-of-sale or "checkout." These are collected by asking a store's customers to evaluate their purchase experiences immediately after completing the online transaction. The remaining eight quality ratings are determined when the purchase is expected to be received as an "after delivery" follow-up. Explanations of each ratings attribute are found below:

Source	Rating	Explanation
At checkout	Ease of finding what you are looking for	How easily were you able to find the product you were looking for
At checkout	Selection of products	Types of products available
At checkout	Clarity of product information	How clear and understandable was the product information
At checkout	Prices relative to other online merchants	Prices relative to other websites
At checkout	Overall look and design of site	Overall look and design of the site
At checkout	Shipping charges	Shipping charges
At checkout	Variety of shipping options	Desired shipping options were available
At checkout	Charges stated clearly before order submission	Total purchase amount (including shipping/handling charges) displayed before order submission
After delivery	Availability of product you wanted	Product was in stock at time of expected delivery
After delivery	Order tracking	Ability to track orders until delivered
After delivery	On-time delivery	Product arrived when expected
After delivery	Product met expectations	Correct product was delivered and it worked as described/depicted
After delivery	Customer support	Availability/ease of contacting, courtesy and knowledge of staff, resolution of issue
After delivery	Would shop here again	Likelihood to buy again from this store
After delivery	Overall rating	Overall experience with this purchase
After delivery	Likelihood to recommend	How likely are you to recommend this merchant

Source: Bizrate, http://about.bizrate.com/ratings#10.

Whatever the measures that are used—and we will cover more options in Chapter 14—it is important to meet or to even exceed customer expectations. If the website does not satisfy expectations, visitors will leave, and many will never return. Even if that has become a trite statement, it is true, and there is no reason to doubt that it will continue to be true. There is simply too much competition on the Net both in terms of products and services and in terms of competition for the user's attention. Second chances are rare in Internet marketing; the pressure is great to do it right the first time. Marketers have turned to the concept of customer experience to provide an overall framework to guide their efforts.

Other Website Design Tips

Some other tips for effective website design include:

- *Use several search options.* A general search box is appropriate, as well as the ability to search the site's specialized content. It is possible to arrange to use the Google search engine on your site, if appropriate.

- *Avoid flash* (highly animated) introductions as they date your page and can result in a loss—as much as 30 percent—of your website visitors who do not wish to click on the flash intro page to continue to the site.
- *Avoid videos* that load automatically for the same reason as flash above. Let visitors decide about their own customer experience.
- *Set the home page up in columns*, basically a three-column structure on the home page. Columnar organization makes it easier to engage in the skimming that is characteristic of viewers of web pages. It also makes it essential to chunk content into short paragraphs or blurbs (like the Staples home page example in Figure 12.6). Without this kind of organization, the page becomes a dense mass of text, unlikely to be read by visitors. An easy way to create columns is to use a tabular structure to the site, although most web designers recommend using **Cascading Style Sheets (CSS)**.[30]
- *Invest in CSS* because they are worth the investment in time. CSS is a way to use a style sheet language to separate the content of the site from the presentation style elements, such as layouts, colors, and fonts. Presentation details are handled by a merger (or "cascade") of site-specific style sheets. Benefits include visual continuity and brand cohesiveness. Links to style sheets are preferable to embedded code because updating the site means simply making changes to the linked style sheets used by each page.
- *Use web content management system (WCMS)* so that your site users can easily upload content to the site without going through the tech folks. Content is king now as visitors look for a reason to come back to your site.
- Make it *easy to navigate* the page:
  - Use a "breadcrumb" bar at the top of each page.
  - Link back to the home page on each page.
  - Include text links at the bottom of the site to support pages, including a site map.
- *Use color wisely*. Designers recommend a plain white background for readability and fast downloading. Borders can highlight site branding and navigation tools. Color preferences vary by national origin and by ethnicity and the preferences of the target market should be taken into account.
- *Use large, readable fonts*. The font used should be a contemporary sans serif font, perhaps Arial or Verdana. Sans serif fonts lack the little lines at the tip of letters (A) as opposed to fonts with serifs (T). Sans serif fonts give a clean, crisp look and are generally recommended for web pages. The font size should be large enough to be easily read with normal browser settings.
- *Avoid scrolling* whenever possible. A home page and second- and third-level pages should not be long and require only a little scrolling to see the entire page. The site should be sized to fit horizontally into any monitor that is set to normal pages, no matter what the size of the monitor itself.
- *Test on multiple platforms* such as different types of mobile operating systems (iPhone, Android, etc.) and table devices, such as the iPad. Make your site readable by everyone.

Good site design and navigational structure should be developed in a manner appropriate to a site's objectives and target market. However, no set of rules can capture the gestalt of what makes a website work in the eyes of its target customers. So here comes another "trite but truism"—the only way to find out what customers and prospects think is to ask them! That is the nature and purpose of a *usability test*. We discuss the process for conducting usability tests in detail in Chapter 14.

Providing a Rewarding Customer Experience

The concept of customer experience is not new to service marketers. Valarie Zeithaml and Mary Jo Bitner point out that customers evaluate products and services according to the properties of their offering. One category of properties

is *search qualities*, attributes, such as color, style, and price, that lend themselves to evaluation prior to purchasing. *Experience qualities* can be discerned only during the use of the product or service. Airline travel and restaurant meals are examples of service products that must be purchased and consumed before their characteristics can be evaluated. Goods may also have *credence qualities*, properties that cannot be accurately evaluated even after consumption. Services like repairs on your computer can be evaluated only indirectly—does it work or not—but there are often lingering doubts about the quality of the repair and its cost. Zeithaml and Bitner point out that most tangible products are high in search qualities, while services are more likely to be high in credence qualities. Both products and services can be high in experience qualities. Automobiles, for example, have a high component of experience qualities, and, in their image-building efforts, automobile marketers tend to play up the experiential components. Many services like vacations are inherently experiential. The quality of the customer's experience with the product or service is a key determinant of satisfaction with it.[31]

That makes it important to understand the nature of customer experience and what marketers can do to engineer satisfactory experience. Rayport and Jaworski, whose basic reference point is the physical world, suggest that there are four dimensions of a customer interface that work together to create customer experience. They are:

- *Physical presence and appearance.* Physical presence is an attribute of products and services in the offline world, but appearance is a characteristic of websites. Note how different the appearance is between the branding site and the transactional site portrayed in Figure 12.2. Each promised a different experience, one based on the nature of the target market and the task it expects to complete on the site.
- *Cognition.* This is the thinking/knowledge aspect of the experience. It may be driven by information, as when information in the customer database allows the service rep or the website to provide a personalized and satisfying experience.
- *Emotion or attitude.* Emotional or attitudinal aspects are characteristics of human beings, but a website can convey some of those aspects visually.
- *Connectedness.* This dimension implies the ability of all people or elements to work together to provide satisfactory experience for the customer. Effective teamwork can also be enabled by information that keeps everyone moving in the same direction.[32]

Often a website, such as Amazon.com, can outperform human beings at the customer interface by being available 24/7/365 and maintaining an encyclopedic knowledge of customer preferences. Berry, Carbone, and Haeckel describe the role of the website in the customer experience as one of giving off clues of various kinds. One set of clues relates to functionality. Can a website that is frequently down or that provides outrageous information when you conduct a search be trusted with your credit card number? Their second set of clues relates to the sensory experience—sights, smells, voices. In the multichannel environment, the site can drive customers to a retail store in which sensory experiences can be provided. The site can suggest some of the experiential characteristics with logos, pictures, and other visuals that evoke the store experience. These authors say:

> To fully leverage experience as part of a customer-value proposition, organizations must manage the emotional component of experiences with the same rigor they bring to the management of product and service functionality. The way to begin that effort is by observing customers and talking to them about their experiences in order to gain a deeper understanding of the clues they're processing during their encounters with the company.[33]

TABLE 12.3	Top Organizations in Terms of Customer Experience

Top Half of Organizations in the 2011 Temkin Web Experience Ratings

Rank	Company	Industry	Rank	Company	Industry
1	Amazon.com	Retail	28	Hampton Inn	Hotel
2	Regions	Bank	28	JCPenney	Retail
3	USAA	Insurance	28	TD Ameritrade	Investment firm
4	Discover	Credit card	33	Barnes & Noble	Retail
4	USAA	Bank	33	Marriott	Hotel
6	Vanguard	Investment firm	33	Rite Aid	Retail
7	eBay	Retail	33	Walgreens	Retail
7	Southwest Airlines	Airline	37	Apple	Personal computer manufacturers
9	A Credit Union	Bank			
10	Fidelity Investments	Investment firm	37	Hyatt	Hotel
10	Kohl's	Retail	37	Macy's	Retail
10	TD Bank	Bank	40	A Credit Union	Investment firm
13	ING Direct	Bank	40	Capital One	Credit card
13	JetBlue Airlines	Airline	40	Comfort Inn	Hotel
15	Chase	Credit card	40	Staples	Retail
15	ING Direct	Investment firm	40	Target	Retail
17	Charles Schwab	Investment firm	40	Wal-Mart	Retail
17	Wells Fargo	Credit card	46	Fifth Third	Bank
19	Chase	Bank	46	GEICO	Insurance
19	Continental Airlines	Airline	48	Best Buy	Retail
19	Courtyard by Marriott	Hotel	48	Citibank	Bank
			48	Kaiser Permanente	Health plan
19	SunTrust Bank	Bank	48	Old Navy	Retail
19	Wells Fargo/ Wachovia Bank	Bank	48	Sam's Club	Retail
			48	Toys 'R' Us	Retail
24	American Express	Credit card	54	Best Western	Hotel
24	Bank of America	Bank	54	Hilton	Hotel
24	PNC	Bank	54	Holiday Inn Express	Hotel
24	US Bancorp	Bank	54	Lowe's	Retail
28	Capital One	Bank	54	MetLife	Insurance
28	Costco	Retail	54	TracFone	Wireless

Source: Temkin Group, "2011 Temkin Web Experience Ratings Overview Of Results," p. 2. Copyright © 2011 Temkin Group. All rights reserved. Reprinted with permission.

As these two sets of concepts suggest, the importance of customer experience and the activity of staging consumer experiences is not new or unique to the web. Many good service marketers practice elements of experience marketing—the chocolate on the pillow of the turned down bed in the Ritz-Carleton Hotel or the greeter at the door in a Walmart store are both examples. Some retailers have incorporated experiential marketing into their operations in innovating and entertaining ways. The Temkin Group recently created a list of companies that provided the best consumer web experiences, according to the 6,000 consumers interviewed (see Table 12.3).

Many of the companies ranked by Temkin's survey are sites that consumers use to complete their everyday transactions, such as banking retailing, hotel, and investment sites. These sites are transaction-based and a smooth customer experience is based in effective transaction processing, such as Amazon's streamlined order process. Another objective of informational websites is often reinforcing the company brand image. An enterprise renowned for its ability to stage compelling customer experience in the physical world and reinforce its branding in an effective portrayal of experiential characteristics on the web is Disney.

INTERACTIVE EXERCISE 12.3   A Splash of Disney Memories

Visit http://bit.ly/tVzQEg.

Examine the shared content on the channel. There is often a "Best of the Month" award where users vote on each other's content. How does this shared experience reinforce the Disney brand and enhance the customer experience? Is the customer experience expanded beyond the park visit and, if so, how?

Multichannel Customer Experience at Disney

Surely in the physical world, the company that epitomizes the customer experience has to be Disney. Disney's theme parks are the best and most visible example of its attention to the quality of the customer experience. The experience begins with the physical design of the parks, which ensures that the visitor is transported into a controlled environment where jarring notes can be kept to an absolute minimum. The grounds are meticulously maintained, as you know if you have even thrown down a candy wrapper there and seen a worker snatch it up immediately. The concern with maintenance and physical appearance extents to extensive plantings which are changed regularly to keep them fresh and in bloom. The customer experience even extends to the design of the entrance, which is slightly uphill as visitors enter, creating a towering vision of the enchanted castle. Coming out at the end of the day, the incline creates an easy walk for weary visitors.

The concern with total customer experience continues with careful employee selection and intensive training—except that these individuals are not considered employees; they are "cast members." Training includes elements beyond customer service basics, including topics like staying in character and drawing visitors into the experience of rides and other activities. There is another exception to common practice here, however. Consumers who come into the park are not considered customers or even visitors; they are guests. Cast members begin the day with the rallying cry, "Showtime!"

Disney makes an intensive, and largely successful, effort to incorporate some of the "magic" into its website. The site is very large, covering Disney movies, videos, television programs, and information on the Disney Fan Club. Pull-down menus at the bottom of the site help the visitor navigate through other major portions of the site. The visitor is given a great deal of assistance in navigating a complex site and also is allowed considerable control over the nature of her experience on the site. Disney also understands that every vacation experience is unique and co-created by the customer, so the site also allows for sharing of the Disney experience. There is a video channel similar to YouTube where customers can share their unique experiences of the Disney vacation. In the Splash of Disney Memories Channel section of the site, customers have a chance to share videos, photos, or stories. In one such example, Bridget shares her family's unique experience in taking each of their sons to Disney for their first birthday. There is no better way to convey the customer experience than to have customers tell others about it. This Channel also ensures that the customer experience lasts beyond the visit to the park and all the way up to the next Disney experience!

Direct Experience at the San Diego Zoo

Another site that offers many experiential elements is that of the San Diego Zoo (see Figure 12.5). At the "fold," it has a series of banners—in this case, its own house advertising. Attracting members is important, as is increasing revenue from the Zoo store. The final banner offers opportunities to book travel and hotels through the Zoo site, which provides affiliate revenue for the Zoo. In Figure 12.5, visitors are encouraged to print their own admissions tickets online, thereby avoiding the often-long lines at the Zoo gates.

FIGURE **12.5** The San Diego Zoo Entry Page
Source: San Diego Zoo, http://www.sandiegozoo.org/zoo/index.php.

The San Diego Zoo is adroit at taking advantage of its current animal stars, creating interactivity with webcams and videos of the animals. The "Panda Cam" provides 24/7 coverage of the world of the Zoo Pandas, with time-lapse features. Polar bears are another consistent crowd-pleaser at the Zoo. The bears are also featured in their own webcam and video clips, and are introduced to the website visitor by name with a personal description: described as Kalluk, "The Athlete"; Tatqiq, "The Princess"; and Chinook, "The Stalker." The "Home" page features links to practical information a visitor needs—directions, hours, and maps of exhibits. Special programs are highlighted, such as an opportunity to see the Zoo at night during the summer, featuring a celebration of China. Other visitor information, like dining opportunities, are also included. The main navigation bar, which has drop-down listings of second-level pages, is the same one seen at the top of the introductory page. Below the main navigation bar there is a second navigation bar containing specifics for visitors.

The website's blogs are also an interesting feature. The Zoo uses a single blog structure, but with different paths. The visitor can narrow the blog entries seen to his particular interest, choosing from categories that range from conservation to insects, with topics such as pollination being covered in the spring season. The blog entries are written by Zoo experts and comments and questions from readers are solicited and are answered when possible. Links to more detailed information, to videos, and to webcams are frequently seen. The only complaint is that the weblogs are hard to find, not being intuitively included in any of the navigation aids on the home page. Overall, however, this website is a virtuoso performance in terms of structure, content, and performance.

Take a moment to think about the different sites that have been used to illustrate topics in this chapter. They may have different objectives, different appearances, and give their visitors different experiences. The nature of each experience is based on the tasks the visitor expects to perform on the site and the reason for the site visit. However, all sites need to provide their visitors with satisfying experiences, ones that make them likely to return, and maybe even to recommend the site to a friend.

Resources for Website Development

There are few roadmaps for the Internet marketer in search of ways to create a satisfying, rewarding, and even exciting experience for the website visitor. Four things that you need to do on a regular basis will be helpful:

- Think carefully about the marketing objectives for the site; is the visitor experience contributing to the attainment of the objectives? Even better, think about it from the visitor's point of view. What should a visitor "take away" from the site—not just in terms of information obtained but also in terms of the feeling and overall attitude with which the visitor leaves the site?

- Be alert for marketing activities that focus on experience and learn from them, whether they are competitors or in a totally unrelated business sector. The San Diego Zoo and Disney examples in this chapter are cases in point.

- Track some websites on a regular basis. These should include not only your direct competitors but also some "idea" sites. You may learn a great deal from totally unrelated sites, for example, a B2B marketer who follows some entertainment sites like Sony.com or a fantasy football league like ESPN's.

- Talk to your customers, frequently and comprehensively. Do not, however, expect that they will simply present you with great new ideas for improving the experience on your website. They will be able to tell you what they like, what they do not like, and other things you might do. The latter will usually be things they have seen elsewhere that could be adapted to your site. While this feedback can be useful, it is not likely to produce really new ideas. You must develop the truly innovative ideas from a deep understanding of customer likes, dislikes, and expectations.

Some of the suggestions for change that come from customer feedback and monitoring may result in incremental improvements to the website. These improvements can be made as their desirability is confirmed and may or may not be announced to consumers. As long as the improvements and refinements simply improve the customer experience and do not change the way the customer uses the site, they probably can be done without fanfare. At some point, however, websites may deem it necessary to do a complete redesign and relaunch. Even successful sites like that of Staples may opt for a complete remake of its site.

The Relaunch of Staples.com

Corporations are not often forthcoming about the reasons they have chosen to do a major site relaunch or how much it costs. There are, however, two basic reasons for an extensive site redesign. One is site metrics, the voice of the customer, or both, that point to major difficulties in using the site. For example, if the site metrics discussed in Chapter 14 show that many people are leaving from the product pages without making a purchase, the firm should question customers to find out why. The answer will often be, "We can't find what we want." That is a strong indicator that the site needs to be redesigned. The second possibility is that new technology has become available that enables functionality on the site that was not previously available. An example is the "print your own admission ticket" function on the San Diego Zoo site. At first glance, printing something like an admission ticket or a manufacturer's coupon to be redeemed in a retail store does not seem like a major technological issue. However, extensive security systems are necessary to let you print valid zoo or concert admissions tickets and keep the hackers from printing invalid ones that are indistinguishable from real. Marketers want to offer functionality like printing tickets that makes purchasing easy and convenient for their customers.

Staples did not say precisely why it decided on a major website redesign, but it was clear about the strategy it was pursuing. The basis of the strategy is

(a)   (b)

FIGURE **12.6** (a) The Staples Entry Page (b) Staples Back to School Center

Source: Staples the Office Superstore, LLC, http://www.staples.com, and http://www.staples.com/sbd/cre/marketing/back-to-school/index.html.

seen in its brand promise "Easy" and the "that was easy!" slogan used in all its channels—store, website, telephone call center, and catalog, and is still featured on the main entry page (see Figure 12.6a). The redesign was focused around three themes:

- Easy to find
  - Through usability research with customers, Staples reduced the number of product categories from 24 to 17. The site handles over 40,000 items, so categorizing them in a customer-intuitive way is not easy.
  - Information was furnished in a functional format. For example, the "Back to School Center 2011" page (see Figure 12.6b) allows for shopping by grade level or by specific item and includes links to suggested back to school lists for specific grades.
  - The navigation structure was revised to focus more on the products and information that customers access most frequently.
  - Users could access the "show all products" drop-down menu from pages other than the home page.
- Easy to order
  - An Easy Reorder feature lists a record of customer past purchases. The functionality made it easier to select multiple items from a list and add them to a shopping cart.
  - When products are ordered, other "Necessary and Recommended" suggestions were presented.
- Easy to check out
  - An Easy Rebates feature let customers submit rebates online with no paper processing or mailing. A tracking number is returned by email so the customer can keep track of the rebate as it is processed.
  - The information available for tracking orders was increased.[34]

Taken individually, most of these features are not unique; other sites have one or more of them. What sets a relaunch like this apart is the careful research and planning. Staples is known to have a usability laboratory in which it continuously tests and refines the design and operation of the site. For example, for the relaunch, it conducted card sorting research with over 5,000 customers in order to reduce and refine the product categories listed on the home page.

The Staples research team used other tools, both qualitative and quantitative, to segment customers. They rode on delivery trucks, visited customer job sites, monitored telephone service reps, and conducted focus groups. They have a customer panel that was used to produce samples for surveys. The result was a set of seven customer segments. Two of those became the focus of the site

INTERACTIVE EXERCISE **12.4**   **What Is Your Office Supplies Persona?**

Would you like to know whether you are more like Lisa Listmaker or Sammy Specific or Sally Sales-sleuth? Take the brief survey posted as "quiz" at the bottom of the Staples multimedia press release at http://prn.to/tjJLYs.

Do you think that you fit one of the personas? Do you think personas can help Internet marketers or do you just think this is a bit silly?

redesign. Personas, a way of describing different groups of customers by giving them a unique personality, were built around these two key segments—Lisa Listmaker and Sammy Specific.

Lisa Listmaker is an office manager whose goal is to get the purchase done as quickly as possible. She has a standard order list complete with item numbers. She shops most often at Staples.com but also uses the catalog and the nearest retail store. The Easy to Order features are important to Lisa, who wants to get everything done at once, quickly and efficiently.

Sammy Specific runs a small business and does not plan carefully for office purchases. He does not shop by item number but he does know the products he needs by brand or type. The "Learn More About" and "Help Me Decide" informational pages make his purchasing easier. Both Lisa and Sammy use the "My Account" functionality to list previous purchases, to keep track of favorites, and to do things like sort them by product, date, or total amount.[35] A third persona that Staples includes in its quiz, although not as key, is Sally Sales-sleuth who is coupon and promotion-driven and loves to shop for a bargain.

The use of personas is considered one of the advanced web design techniques. It gives guidance to designers: "Would Sally like this function?" and "What would she use it for?" It also gives the technical personnel—programmers and others—the sense of real persons for whom they are creating web pages. One positive outcome is to keep designers and programmers from filling a site up with aspects that are not used by many visitors and that make site functioning slower or navigation more difficult or both.

Careful, thorough customer research, an umbrella strategy, and clear objectives are the marks of a site design or redesign that has a high probability of providing satisfactory customer experience. The Staples.com site ranks among the top 40 of consumer site in the Temkin survey and in the top 200 sites in the United States according to Alexa.com. In 2011, the site experienced a 30 percent increase in international traffic. The company continues to grow and develop its site, with about 6 percent of site traffic now coming from its weekly ad offer, an online version of its newspaper insert. That portion of the site also includes other "hot deals" that can be delivered directly to the customer by email.

Staples is not alone in its approach. More recently, RailEurope, Inc., which is the largest distributor of European rail products in North America also made use of personas, site hierarchies or mapping, wireframes, and usability testing to get feedback from its users. The company worked with BusinessOnline to create the Travel Comparator™ so that RailEurope's customers in North America could understand the differences in travel times and connections between different modes of transport. The result of the redesign was that 41 percent of the users found the site easier to use and the number of travelers and bookings to the site also increased. The site also was redesigned for improved engagement through social media networking sites and discussions on the RailEurope site.[36]

How Much Does It Cost?

This is a question everyone would like to have answered. Current data are not readily available, but there are a number of generalizations that can be made. First, you are probably aware that there are many sources of free website templates and free or inexpensive web templates. Web hosting applications such as Adobe Corporation's Dreamweaver include packaged templates as well as an easy, visual approach to web design that does not require knowledge of HTML. As far as the web hosting is concerned, if it is free, your site will undoubtedly be subjected to ads served by the host. Depending on your purpose that may be acceptable, but it should be expected. Unique domain names are not free, but they are available at low cost.

If free site templates are provided by a reputable supplier, they usually work pretty well and may meet the needs of individuals or small businesses. Wordpress provides a number of free templates for web and blog design and over 25 million people have used these capabilities to create their own websites and blogs.[37] The free templates available from various sources, however, may not be very flexible and you may soon find yourself wanting to do something that is only available as a purchased service. Do you see a marketing strategy there? There are also paid solutions such as Squarespace (www.squarespace.com) that allow the consumer to take control over a large portion of the website design in terms of developing and adding content to easily created templates. More formal web content management systems (CMS) also allow users to maintain their own content even in large, sophisticated websites. There are also sites now that can provide offshore or crowdsourced solutions to web design needs at a fraction of the cost of hiring an expensive design firm, although quality varies greatly with these alternatives.

At the other extreme, websites can cost hundreds of thousands of dollars to develop, and a million or more if major hardware purchases like high-volume servers are required. Costs can, in general, be broken down into design, programming, specialized software, dedicated hardware, consultants, and systems integration. One reason that costs are hard to come by is that most sites are built using a mix of purchased services and in-house labor. Each firm needs to take a hard look at its in-house capabilities and how much time the necessary specialists will be able to devote to site development. Then it can begin to identify the purchased services it will need and to develop estimates of costs.

Careful attention to all the details can result in an acceptable website for a few thousands or perhaps a few tens of thousands of dollars. There is, however, one rule of thumb that has existed since the beginning of the commercial Internet and appears to be as true today as it was in the mid-1990s. *Maintenance of the site may cost from three to five times as much each year as the original development costs.* That is a daunting figure to many managers. However, if the website is not well maintained and continuously improved, it may do more harm than good to the reputation of the organization.

Whatever manner the marketer uses to establish a web presence, it is imperative to remember that the expectations of customers are constantly increasing. Whether B2C, B2B, or nonprofit, they expect a quality site in terms of both

---

INTERACTIVE EXERCISE 12.5   **Website Redesign**

The site designquote.net has a wizard that allows you to determine how much it will cost to develop a website at http://bit.ly/spw4yk.

Develop some criteria for a site redesign and enter them into the wizard. What are the prices for the website solution and how do the prices vary depending on the choice to use a student or offshore developer versus a professional? What would determine which choice you would make in terms of selecting a web developer? You may also try another, similar site if you find one on your own.

usability and aesthetic appeal. In order to be part of the Internet economy, the marketer must find a way to meet customer expectations about the site itself and the fulfillment and customer service that supports it. Anything less may do fatal damage to an Internet business or lasting harm to a brick-and-mortar brand.

SUMMARY

This chapter sets forth a marketing perspective on building and maintaining websites without understating the effort and expertise needed for successful technical design, programming, and implementation. Marketers are primarily responsible for the initial stages of website development in which objectives are established, the target market is identified and described to all participants, and the information architecture and navigational structure of the site are laid out. Web personas are usually developed by marketers and are a good way to understand customers and how they might interact with the site.

Marketers are also responsible for working closely with technical professionals during actual site development and closely monitoring the site for visitor usability and consistency with business and marketing objectives. In today's world, the website may play many roles and be used by marketers for everything from getting sales leads to developing online communities. In addition, customers shop across multiple channels and increasingly rely on the web for product research. As the distinction between online and offline blurs, the website must meet the needs of multichannel shoppers, as well as be concerned about the overall functioning of the website. So web design and implementation has increasingly become a difficult task and one that is not just technical in nature but involves the understanding of the customer that a marketer can posses. Sites must also be designed for all types of consumers, including those with physical disabilities.

The first step in ensuring that the site meets visitor expectations is technical usability—does the site work smoothly and are visitors able to find the information they want? This is a behavioral measure and it is measured by usability testing, eye-tracking studies, and mouse-click analysis. The site's navigational structure and content must meet the needs on the target market. A website development process will help ensure that the site as delivered is the one envisioned by the firm to meet the market need.

The second step in making sure the website meets expectations is visitor satisfaction. As a purely attitudinal measure satisfaction can be measured by conventional marketing research techniques such as user satisfaction surveys. As a transactional measure, expectations can be measured by retention rate and return visits to the site. The most comprehensive level is the overall customer experience. The aim should be to move visitors through a series of stages that begin with functionality and progress through to a truly interactive, personalized, and customized site experience which also involves users sharing their experiences with each other. A variety of measures, monitored on a regular basis, will be necessary to understand the dimensions of experience on a particular site and to continuously improve the experience for the target visitor. Taken all together, effective website development and adequate ongoing maintenance is a complex and difficult task.

At some point, market development or the availability of new technologies may make the complete redesign of the site desirable or even necessary. Web 2.0 design trends will be overtaken and improved upon and marketers will change their websites to improve usability and the customer experience where appropriate. These occurrences will initiate the website development process once again and the process will be no less demanding than the original development of the site. As the Staples example suggests, redevelopment itself can be time-consuming and expensive. A complete site redesign may be taken as a marketing opportunity to stage a highly visible relaunch, one that draws attention to the improved customer experience available on the site.

There are alternative ways in which a firm can establish and maintain its web presence. The option should be chosen which provides the best long-term fit with company objectives, availability of necessary resources, and the firm's level of commitment to a meaningful website.

DISCUSSION QUESTIONS

1. True or False: It is imperative that marketers play the leading role in all stages of the website development process. Take a position on this statement and be prepared to defend your answer.
2. What are the steps involved in developing a website? What should be the marketer's role in each step?
3. This chapter makes references to both testing and conventional marketing research. What testing and research techniques are appropriate in the website development process and what is the role of each?

4. What is the best way to assess customer satisfaction with a website?
5. Explain the concept of "consumer experience." What is its relevance to Internet marketing? Contrast that with the role of the consumer experience in the offline retailing environment.
6. How does a marketer know when a site should simply be improved upon and when it should be completely redesigned and relaunched?

INTERNET EXERCISES

1. Internet Career Builder Exercise
   a. Website design and usability testing continue to be strong career paths. You may choose the level of technical background you wish to obtain and therefore further define your chosen career path, but not all jobs in this field require a strong coding background. Many companies want people just like you with some technical knowledge but the ability to evaluate a website from the user's perspective. Here are some potential entry-level job titles:

   Junior web master

   Usability specialist

   Usability architect

   Customer experience architect

   Website usability analyst

   Marketing website coordinator

   b. Select a web design and testing job title from the preceding list or from your own search. Outline the responsibilities of that position. You may find it useful to locate job postings on the web in order to understand the job requirements.
   c. Outline knowledge and experience from classes, internships, full- or part-time jobs, and volunteer work that prepare you for this specific position.
   d. Prepare five questions you could ask at a job interview for this type of job. The questions should exhibit your understanding of the position requirements without lecturing the interviewer about what she already knows.
   e. Update your VisualCV® or LinkedIn Profile with this information.

2. Think of some specific ways in which a website can support the marketing strategy of an existing business. In the retail space, Walmart, Target, Kmart, and Nordstrom each have specific strategies. Examine the sites and outline the extent to which the website illustrates that particular strategy. Be prepared to discuss the points of strategy integration between the offline and online marketing efforts.
3. Identify a website that you judge to have major experience components. Spend some time on the site and be prepared to discuss your experience in class. Pay special attention to whether or not you feel the experience components contribute in a meaningful way to achievement of site objectives and whether the experiences provided are in line with the needs of the target market.
4. Examine the list of companies rated by Temkin in Table 12.3. How many of them have you used and what has been your overall impression? Using your own website evaluation criteria that you develop from the readings, your experience and other sources, rate one of the sites in terms of usability.
5. Choose one of the sites you are tracking and do a careful assessment of the degree to which it is either easy and pleasant or difficult and frustrating to navigate. Develop a set of criteria that you consider important in assessing whether a site provides good navigation or not.
6. Choose a specific culture within the United States, such as Hispanics or African-Americans, and find some sites that are targeted toward those cultures. Some ideas might include: Allstate's Spanish language site (www.miallstate.com), the history channel's

Spanish langue site (www.historyenespanol.com), or blackplanet.com. Do some research and find some case studies and examples of good web design for sites targeted for that culture. What are the values of that particular culture? How does website design differ for that particular culture than for mainstream websites?

7. Choose a specific country other than the United States, such as China, and find some sites that are targeted toward that country. Some ideas might include: a Chinese chat site that also offers games and other features (http://qzone.qq.com). Do some research and find some case studies of web design for that country. What are the shared values of that particular country? How does website design differ for that particular country than for websites targeted for the United States?

8. Think about the "digital divide" from Chapter 13. Are there differences in how the affluent versus nonaffluent use the web? Find out how those making $500,000 plus use the web versus those making less than $50,000 per year. What implications does your research have for marketers seeking to target those segments?

NOTES

1. Holland, Joanna and Stacey Menzel Baker, "Customer Participation in Creating Site Brand Loyalty," *Journal of Interactive Marketing*, Vol 14, No. 4(2001) pp. 35–45.

2. Sucharita Mulpuru with Vikram Sehgal, Patti Freeman Evans, and Doug Roberge, "US Online Retail Forecast, 2010 to 2015: eCommerce Growth Accelerates Following 'The Great Recession'," Forrester, February 28, 2011.

3. Sucharita Mulpuru with Patti Freeman Evans, Vikram Sehgal, Julie A. Ask, and Doug Roberge, "Mobile Commerce Forecast: 2011 to 2016," Forrester, June 17, 2011.

4. http://www.internetretailer.com/2011/01/04/global-e-commerce-sales-head-1-trillion-mark, retrieved August 15, 2011.

5. http://www.marketingcharts.com/interactive/internet-users-now-spend-13-hoursweek-online-11471, retrieved August 17, 2011.

6. V. Kumar and Rajkumar Venkatesan, "Who Are the Multichannel Shoppers and How Do They Perform?: Correlates of Multichannel Shopping Behavior," *Journal of Interactive Marketing Special Issue: Multichannel Marketing*, Vol. 19, No. 2 Spring 2005 pp. 44–62.

7. http://www.mediapost.com/publications/?fa=Articles.showArticle&art_aid=156230, retrieved August 22, 2011.

8. "The Changing Role of the Catalog for Multichannel Retailers," DoubleClick, 2004.

9. http://www.marketingcharts.com/direct/draft-first-time-ever-multi-channel-holiday-shoppers-prefer-Web-to-in-store-6380, retrieved August 17, 2011.

10. http://www.nfb.org/nfb/NewsBot.asp?MODE=VIEW&ID=221, retrieved August 22, 2011.

11. The federal accessibility guidelines can be found on the on the Usability.gov site at http://www.usability.gov/pdfs/chapter3.pdf.

12. "Tea Time," August 30, 2005, http://www.imedia connection.com/content/6628.asp.

13. Susan Solomon, "Hey Marketers, Content's Back in Style," *Click Z Network*, December 5, 2000, http://www.clickz.com.

14. "Viewing Patterns for Homepages," nd, http://www.poynterextra.org/eyetrack2004/viewing.htm#1.3.

15. Marion Lewenstein, "Study Snapshot Suggests Serendipity Lives Online," Poynter Institute, August 18, 2000; and

"A Deeper Probe Confirms Findings," July 12, 2000, http://www.poynter.org.

16. A useful reference can be found in the Information Architecture Tutorial at http://hotwired.lycos.com/webmonkey/design/site_building/tutorials/tutorial1.html.

17. http://www.webdesignshock.com/best-online-wireframe-tools, retrieved August 30, 2011.

18. http://www.prnewswire.com/news-releases/overstockcom-4-in-customer-service-as-ranked-by-the-national-retail-federation-and-american-express-113296244.html, retrieved November 12, 2011.

19. http://www.overstock.com/excellent-customer-service/21333/static.html, retrieved November 12, 2011.

20. http://www.prnewswire.com/news-releases/overstockcom-4-in-customer-service-as-ranked-by-the-national-retail-federation-and-american-express-113296244.html, retrieved November 12, 2011.

21. http://www.rightnow.com/files/casestudy/Overstock.com-Case-Study.pdf, retrieved November 12, 2011.

22. Shankar Gupta, "Study: Online Shoppers Consider More Than Price," June 1, 2005, *Online Media Daily*, http://www.mediapost.com/publications/article/30725.

23. http://www.theacsi.org/index.php?option=com_content&view=article&id=206:acsi-scores-february&catid=14&Itemid=259.

24. http://www.reuters.com/article/2011/10/20/us-Netflix-idUSTRE79J6UC20111020, retrieved October 20, 2011.

25. http://abcnews.go.com/Technology/wireStory/netflix-regains-600k-us-subscribers-4q-15442286#.Tyki0ly6YsI, retrieved February 1, 2012.

26. For a detailed manual on designing and developing websites from a customer usability perspective see http://www.usability.gov.

27. The Best and Worst of Site Design, 2003, Forrester Research, Inc., September 2003.

28. B2B Web Sites Fail The Usability Test, Forrester Research, Inc., January 2005.

29. Best and Worst of B2C Site Design, 2009, Forrester Research, Inc., April 2009.

30. Jakob Nielsen, *Designing Web Usability* (Berkeley, CA: New Riders, 2000).

31. Valarie A. Zeithaml and Mary Jo Bitner, *Services Marketing* (New York: The McGraw-Hill Companies, Inc., 1996), pp. 57–59.

32. Jeffrey F. Rayport and Bernard J. Jaworski, "Best Face Forward," *Harvard Business Review*, December 2004.

33. Leonard L. Berry, Lewis P. Carbone, and Stephan H. Haeckel, "Managing the Total Customer Experience," *Sloan Management Review*, Spring 2002, pp. 85–89.

34. "Staples Launches New Staples.com for Easy Online Ordering," Press Release, July 27, 2005, http://investor. staples.com/phoenix.zhtml?c=96244&p=irol-news Article&ID=735662&highlight=.

35. "Staples Launches New Staples.com for Easy Online Ordering," Press Release, July 27, 2005, http://investor. staples.com/phoenix.zhtml?c=96244&p=irol-news Article&ID=735662&highlight=; and Susan Kuchinskas, "A Staples.com Even 'Lisa Listmaker' Could Love," InternetNews.com, February 28, 2005, http:// www.internetnews.com/ec-news/article.php/3486026.

36. http://www.businessol.com/work/case-study/raileurope-cs, retrieved August 30, 2011.

37. http://wordpress.org, retrieved October 22, 2011.

CHAPTER 13

Customer Service and Support in Web Space

Key Terms

agent (367)
artificial intelligence (367)
call center (358)
call routing (366)
embedded service module (366)

ERMS (email response management system) (366)
help desk (366)
IVR (interactive voice response) (366)

rule (359)
virtual agent (367)

LEARNING OBJECTIVES

By the time you complete this chapter, you will be able to:

- Explain the evolutionary stages of customer service provision.
- Understand the role of customer service in creating sustainable competitive advantage.
- Explain the importance of integrating customer service with other customer-facing enterprise activities.
- Identify themes that recur in discussions of providing exceptional customer service.
- Describe the various technologies and channels used to deliver customer service.
- Discuss the steps involved in developing a strategic customer care program.
- Distinguish between customer service and customer experience.

"It's not getting better; it's getting worse." That is the conclusion from a number of recent studies of customer service.

- In 2011, *Consumer Reports* found that during the previous 12 months, 64 percent of respondents had left a store because the service was poor and 67 percent had concluded a customer service call without having their problem resolved.[1]
- A 2011 study by Customer Care Measurement & Consulting and Arizona State University (ASU) was headlined "Fewer customers satisfied than ever before." According to Professor Mary Jo Bitner, executive director of the Center for Services Leadership, good customer service leads to customer loyalty and enhances profitability. However, many firms do not execute their consumer complaint-handling policies well.[2]
- The original study in the "customer rage" series, conducted by ASU in 2004, found that 73 percent experienced rage in their customer service encounters. That was an 11 percent increase over 1976 when the first study was conducted by the White House.[3]

Marketers know that customer service is a cornerstone of customer loyalty and retention. How could they allow the quality of customer service to decline? There seem to be multiple reasons, and certainly, one is the economic recession and accompanying efforts by businesses to cut costs. On the customer side, people may be facing more frustrations as a result of economic conditions and therefore be quicker to anger. Many businesses have placed technology between customers and a human customer service representative and this may be another reason for service that is perceived as unsatisfactory.

The Importance of Customer Service and Satisfaction

For a number of years, consulting firm Accenture has surveyed consumers around the world about their experiences with service in various industry sectors. One of its conclusions echoed the refrain about the pervasiveness of poor services: "No set of industry providers managed to deliver a very satisfying experience to more than half of their customers—hotels and retailers came closest." It also concluded that customers are more demanding than ever. This creates a volatile combination, and it results in both customers switching products or providers, and in posting negative reviews and comments online. In its global sample, it found that 69 percent of customers switched to another provider as a result of poor service in 2009 versus 59 percent in 2007. Damage is also done to the brand's image. Eighty-nine percent of all respondents shared their negative experiences with family and friends and 25 percent of them posted these experiences online. Interestingly, customers in emerging markets were even more likely to share by word of mouth (96 percent) and to post online (40 percent). The study covered ten industry sectors and found differing levels of satisfaction among them. Hotels and retailers provided the best service; life insurers, cable companies, utilities, and phone companies provided the worst.[4]

Lack of satisfaction is costing companies that do not provide a satisfactory customer experience—including customer service. Burke Research used data based on industry studies to illustrate the size of the problem. Its studies of the insurance industry indicate that as many as 40 percent of policyholders may experience a service problem or failure in a given year. Look at the results shown in Figure 13.1. As is typical in customer service and satisfaction studies, some of the customers (in this case, 20 percent) who experienced problems did not report them. Only 10 percent of those *unreported* will not repurchase; but keep in mind that the insurance provider has lost hundreds of opportunities to identify problems and, presumably, to correct them. Notice that if the customers were *satisfied*, they intended to repurchase. Of those who were *mollified* (only partially satisfied), only 5 percent will not repurchase, while 40 percent of those who were *dissatisfied* declared their intent not to repurchase. The result was 274 lost customers out of a total of 6,000. The study did not estimate the dollar value of the lost customers, but insurance customers represent a continuing stream of revenue, so you can imagine that their customer lifetime value (CLV) is high. This analysis also shows something else that is noteworthy about customer satisfaction: *it is not the fact that customers experience a problem that is critical to their defection; it is the fact that their problem is not satisfactorily resolved.* This places the onus for customer retention squarely on the customer service function.

On a macro level, the cost of customers lost as a result of poor service is described as a 338.5-billion-dollar problem globally by telecommunications firm Genesys. In the United States alone, the annual cost of business lost through poor service is $243 billion. Its study of customer service experiences in 16

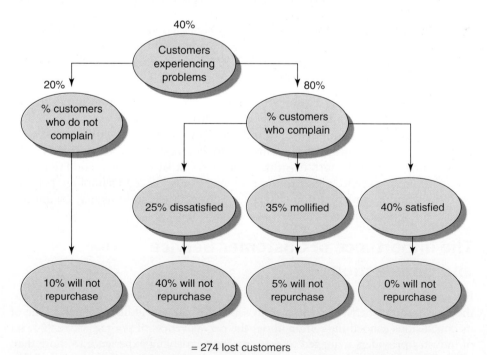

= 274 lost customers

FIGURE **13.1** The Financial Impact of Customer Service Problems

Source: "Linking Measures of Customer Satisfaction, Value, and Loyalty to Financial Performance," White Paper Series, 5(3). p. 2. Copyright © 2004 Burke, Inc. Reprinted with permission.

TABLE 13.1 Monetary Losses Due to Poor Customer Service

Key Findings	By the Numbers
The cost of poor customer service in 16 key economies	US$ 338.5 billion
Average value (in one year) of each customer relationship lost to a competitor or abandoned	US$ 243 billion
Greatest satisfier across all countries was competent people to assist in any channel	#1
Percentage of consumers who would welcome proactive engagement to improve their experience through extended offers or help during self-service transactions	86.4%

Source: "The Cost of Poor Customer Service: The Economic Impact of the Customer Service and Engagement in 16 Key Economies," Genesys Telecommunications Laboratories, Inc., November 2009. Reprinted with permission.

different countries found that competent personnel were the most important satisfier although almost 90 percent of respondents were willing to engage in self-service (see Table 13.1).[5]

The Impact of Improved Customer Service

Do all these dreary statistics mean that businesses do not know how to provide good customer service? No, it does not. The knowledge is available; it is the business will that is often lacking. The experience of Harrah's Casinos shows both the possibilities and some of the issues.

At Harrah's Casinos

One business that can demonstrate the financial impact of improved customer service is Harrah's. We discussed its information-driven program to increase customer value in Chapter 4. Improving customer service was an important part of the program. According to CEO Gary Loveman:

> Casino service generally is disappointing all around. Service is hard to deliver in a casino. Employees are under strict rules to ensure there is no corruption. For example, dealers might want to give you a hug but can't, because you might slip something into their pockets. It's not like a hotel.

Proactive measures were taken to improve customer service at all the properties. Loveman continues:

> beginning in 1999 we started paying out a bonus to every nonmanagement employee of the casino if his or her property improved its customer service scores by 3 percent over the same period a year earlier. And as long as the property is at 80 percent of its operating-income plan or higher, everyone gets a bonus. We've paid out $40 million in bonuses to employees across the system—anywhere from $75 to $300 each, each quarter. In the employee areas there are graphs to let them know their service numbers, which are based on customer satisfaction surveys. The data come in each week, and employees check to see how they're doing.

The customer satisfaction surveys are important, both as overall measures of satisfaction and also as a driver of customer value. Harrah's was able to directly attribute increase in customer value to the improvement in customer service. Loveman says:

> We can track the customers who fill out surveys. We can track their gaming behavior, so we can assess whether a player who rates us better this year than last year also plays more. And the answer is remarkably positive. The people who get happier with our service play much more with us, and the people who become unhappy play much less with us. *Market by market, where our profitability and revenues greatly exceed our relative market position, there's no question but that the results are largely service driven*" [emphasis mine].[6]

The importance of customer service to the success of the enterprise has continued through Harrah's acquisition of rival Caesars Entertainment in 2004, a leveraged buyout that took the company private in 2008, the stresses that followed the financial collapse beginning in late 2008,[7] and the rebranding to Caesars Entertainment in 2010. The reaction of an industry executive in early 2012 testifies to the durability of the customer service strategy. While he had often stayed at other properties in the chain, he had never visited this particular location. In his blog, he wrote:

> To being greeted with a welcome and a smile from Valet, to the same greeting and welcome from the bellman, the professionalism and greeting at the front desk and the welcomes and smiles from the entire staff, "kudos" need to go out to the management at this property for practicing what they preach at Caesars Entertainment, "Customer Service".
>
> The cocktail servers would come up to you, introduce themselves by name, welcome you and take your order via an iPad and then another server would bring your drink. Great concept. And it works with ease.[8]

The guest adds that staff told him that this bar service system was being tested at this location and if successful, it would probably be rolled out to other properties.

This is one of a number of case histories we will cite in this chapter that point out that achieving customer service excellence tends to take years, even decades, to accomplish. The ongoing commitment to exceptional customer service is, therefore, difficult for competitors to emulate and it provides a sustainable competitive advantage to companies that achieve it.

In B2C Markets

Is excellent customer service really worth the cost—across industries and markets? The answer is yes!

American Express conducts annual studies of customer service experience. The samples are global and can be broken out for the United States only and for specific market segments, which vary from year to year. The 2010 survey report broke out two segments of particular interest to many marketers: young professionals and affluents. It defined the young professionals as being less than 30 years of age, having a college degree, and having a minimal household income of $50,000. Affluents have a household income of $100,000 or more.

The Amex study (see Figure 13.2) indicated that 58 percent of customers will spend more (about 9 percent more) on a company they believe provides excellent customer service. Perhaps even more important, 79 percent of the affluents in this study say they have spent more, with an average spending of 11 percent more.

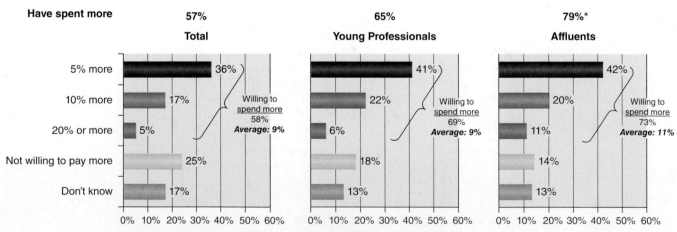

*Significantly higher than (Affluent/Young Professional) segment at the 95% confidence level

FIGURE **13.2** Increased B2C Spending as a Result of Good Customer Service

Source: 2010 American Express Global Customer Service Barometer: Findings in the United States. Reprinted with permission.

In B2B Markets

An older study of the impact of CRM on the profitability of high technology firms provides additional detail and insight into the importance of customer service in the B2B (business-to-business) space. Another study by Accenture found that excellent CRM performance could improve a company's return on sales by as much as 64 percent over merely average performance. Ten CRM capabilities accounted for fully half the improvement in return on sales. Of those, five are clearly customer service capabilities:

- Strategically manage large account customers (ranked number 4).
- Develop effective customer service systems (ranked number 6).
- Proactively identify customer problems and communicate resolution options (ranked number 7).
- Leverage customer information from the service process (ranked number 8).
- Prevent customer problems via customer education (ranked number 9).

For each billion dollars in sales, Accenture estimated impact on increased profitability as follows:

- Customer service—$42 million
- Sales and account management—$35 million
- Marketing—$34 million.[9]

While the importance of customer service seems irrefutable, technology in general and the Internet in particular have made enormous changes in the way customer service is delivered. It has become more than a pleasant smile and a cheerful answer to a question. Customers demand more comprehensive customer service and support at the same time technology enables companies to provide them in a cost-effective manner. The Internet may also have contributed to increasing customer expectations about service quality. Throughout the global economy, the enduring chorus of complaints about customer service suggests that most companies either are not getting the message or have not mastered the techniques.

Who Are the Customer Service Champions?

One of the most widely followed lists of businesses with excellent customer service is the one from *Bloomberg Businessweek*. The 2010 list (see Table 13.2) shows L.L.Bean as the winner. Coming in second is the specialty insurance firm USAA. They are both "usual suspects" in any list of top customer service. So are many of the others on this list.

The notable issue is what is missing from the list. Do you see any B2B firms on the list? Certainly some of these, hotels and rental cars for instance, serve business customers, but they are basically retailers or service firms. There are no B2B firms on the list. Dell is the closest, but its markets are broader than B2B.

This lack of B2B firms on the list is not because the raters, *Bloomberg Businessweek* and the J. D. Powers data on which the BBW ranking was based, B2B firms. These firms simply did not make the list. There has not been a recent published rating of B2B firms in general. *CRM Magazine* does compile a list each year by industry sectors that are relevant to CRM. Figure 13.3 shows a portion of its ranking.[10] You will note that it includes more than just customer service

TABLE 13.2	Top U.S. Firms Ranked by Quality of Customer Service				
Rank	Brand	Industry	Quality of Staff	Efficiency of Service	Total Score
1	L.L.Bean	Online/Catalog Retail	A+	A+	1055.95
2	USAA	Insurance	A+	A+	1042.76
3	Apple	Computers & Electronics	A+	A+	1016.55
4	Four Seasons Hotels and Resorts	Hotel	A+	A+	1000.9
5	Publix Supers Markets	Supermarket	A+	A+	992.02
6	Nordstrom	Department Store Retail	A	A	974.71
7	Lexus	Automotive	A+	A+	966.44
8	The Ritz-Carlton	Hotel	A+	A+	950.74
9	Barnes & Noble	Big Box Retail	B+	A	944.32
10	Ace Hardware	Home Improvement Retail	A	A	939.69
11	Amazon.com	Online/Catalog Retail	A+	A+	933.55
12	Wegmans Food Markets	Supermarket	A	A+	923.85
13	Starbucks	Restaurant	A−	A−	923.77
14	America Mutual Insurance	Insurance	A+	A+	920.8
15	Charles Schwab	Brokerage	A−	B+	918.68
16	Jaguar	Automotive	A+	A+	916.34
17	WestJet	Airline	B+	B+	909.6
18	American Express	Credit Card	B+	B−	900.46
19	Enterprise Rent-A-Car	Rental Car	B	B	900.02
20	Branch Banking & Trust	Banking	B+	B−	895.91
21	Panera Bread	Restaurant	B+	B+	892.45
22	True Value	Home Improvement Retail	A−	A	879.02
23	Dell	Computers & Electronics	B+	A−	872.64
24	Southwest Airlines	Airline	B	B+	871.84
25	Fairmont Hotels & Resorts	Hotel	A+	A+	871.65

Source: From "USSA's Battle Plan," Bloomberg Businessweek (February 18, 2010). Used with permission of Bloomberg Businessweek.com (http://Businessweek.com). Permissions Copyright © 2010. All rights reserved.

excellence. These are firms that serve the CRM industry—primarily software firms—so the depth of the functionality their software products offer is important. This industry changes quickly, so the firm's ability to correctly predict the direction of change and respond to it is also important. However, it does mean that this is not exclusively a customer service ranking.

An example of good customer service in B2B comes from Portakabin, a manufacturer of modular and portable buildings in the United Kingdom. Its approach shows how important it is to cultivate an organizational culture of customer service.

"Modular Buildings on Time and on Budget"

Portakabin, headquartered in Huntington, York, was established in 1961 and now does business throughout Europe. It manufactures a broad line of portable and modular buildings ranging from the Lilliput nurseries line to its Portaloo line (that is a "Porta-Potty" in the United States).

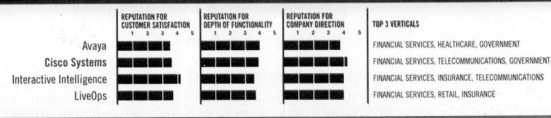

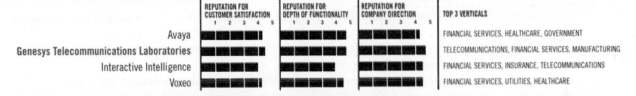

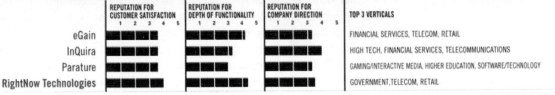

FIGURE **13.3** Leaders in B2B Customer Service

Source: "The 2011 Service Leaders," by the Editors of CRM Magazine, March 2011. Reprinted with permission of CRM Magazine. (http://www.destinationcrm.com/Articles/Editorial/Magazine-Features/The-2011-Service-Leaders-73783.aspx).

Its home page is full of promises. They include:

- "Quality service—for your peace of mind"
- "A proven track record of delivering 99.9% of our modular buildings on time and on budget"
- "If we should ever fail to meet your contract start date, we'll give you a week's free hire [rental] for every day we're late."[11]

Ok, anyone can make promises, but there is much evidence that the company is serious. Service promises appear on all the product pages. Even more important, the company established a Customer Charter in 2004. It makes explicit promises in the areas of delivery time, meeting budget, customer service, quality, and safety. It backs up the promises with case histories of satisfied customers. More important, it guarantees monetary compensation if its promises are not met.

The company points with pride to the fact that it does multiple-item customer satisfaction studies and uses them to improve the quality of its service.[12] It also uses the Net Promoter Score, which is a single measure of how likely customers are to recommend the product.[13]

Portakabin is one of many B2B firms that understand the issues in providing excellent customer service. It does not happen overnight; the company first published its customer service charter in 2004 and its customer service initiative goes back even further. It has also obviously followed the quality management literature that says that "what gets measured gets managed." The quality literature also points out the importance of "walking the walk" over "talking the talk." It is true that anyone can make promises. It takes company-wide effort and persistence to keep those promises, but that is the essence of good customer service.

What Do Consumers Want?

While developing a customer service strategy, it is important to focus on what customers really want. Earlier data from the CCMC/Arizona State University Consumer Rage studies[14] showed that, first and foremost, consumers wanted their product or problem fixed. In the 2011 survey (see Figure 13.4), the researchers added a new question and it rose to the top of desired consumer remedies; an overwhelming 90 percent of customers want to be treated with dignity. Marketers and customer service professionals need to read and heed; notice that only 40 percent of respondents felt they got the treatment they deserved. In fact, if you compare the two columns, what they wanted versus what they got, there is a huge gap between them on all issues.

Equally compelling is the degree to which non-monetary remedies (shaded) are most desired. In addition to being treated with dignity, customers want an explanation, assurance that the problem will not be repeated, and a chance to vent. They rarely get the two things that are easy and cost-free to the firm—a simple thank you for the customer's business and an apology. Other data from this study reveal that 47 percent of the respondents felt they got nothing at all in the way of remedies for their complaints. That is down slightly from the average 51 percent in earlier versions of the survey,[15] but it is still a sad commentary on the state of customer service in the United States.

The American Express annual studies of customer service can be broken out to show only the United States sample. The data in Figures 13.5 and 13.6 apply only to the U.S. Looking at the U.S. data in Figure 13.5, one can see a slight change in what customers want over a year's time. The preference is to resolve issues by speaking with a real person over the phone or in person. The degree to

Remedy**	% Wanted	% Got
To be treated with dignity*	90%	40%
My product repaired/service fixed	77%	32%
An explanation of why the problem occurred	73%	23%
An assurance that my problem would not be repeated	72%	19%
Just to express my anger/tell my side of the story	71%	42%
A thank you for my business	70%	32%
An apology	62%	38%
My money back	49%	17%
A free product or service in the future	32%	10%
Financial compensation for my lost time, inconvenience or injury	22%	2%
Revenge	16%	3%
Other	10%	2%

*New question in 2011
**Shading indicates non-monetary remedy

FIGURE **13.4** What Complainants Wanted Vs. What They Got

Source: 2011 National Customer Rage Study, conducted by Customer Care & Measurement & Consulting in collaboration with the Center for Services Leadership in the W.P. Carey School of Business, Arizona State University; data furnished by Scott M. Broetzmann, CCMC.

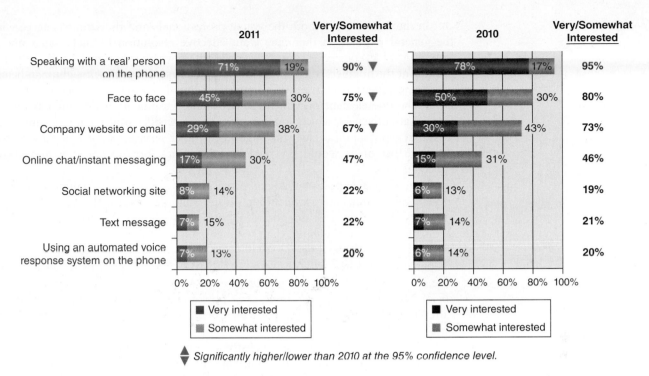

FIGURE **13.5** What Service Channels Do Customers Prefer
Source: 2011 American Express Global Customer Service Barometer: Findings in the United States. Reprinted with permission.

which these elements, and that of resolving problems on the company website, were considered very important declined between 2010 and 2011. Online chat is only moderately popular and remains about the same over the one-year period. The less personal resolution methods of social networking, text messaging, and interactive phone service were low in the respondents' preferences and remained that way from one year to the next.

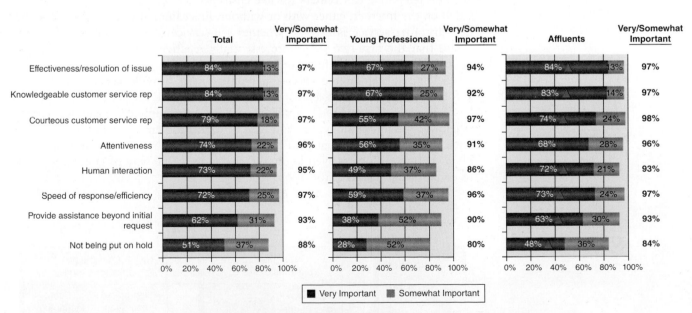

FIGURE **13.6** What Elements of Service Are Most Important, by Segment
Source: 2010 American Express Global Customer Service Barometer: Findings in the United States. Reprinted with permission.

In the 2010 survey, both the young professionals and the affluents agree with the general population that they want effective resolution of their issues and a knowledgeable, courteous customer service rep above all (see Figure 13.6). Actually, looking at the numbers, they want it all: attentiveness, to speak with a human being, speed and efficiency, assistance beyond their initial request, and not to be put on hold. The one element on which the two market segments really differ is on the issue of attentiveness, which young professionals consider somewhat less important. Yes, they want all these elements of good customer service, but are they asking too much? Most of us would say these are the basics, not service over and above expectations.

Would you expect the young professionals to be more willing to accept impersonal channels of service than, presumably older, affluents? The 2010 survey says the differences do not reach statistical significance (see Figure 13.6). Affluents are more willing than young professionals to use text messaging (28 percent to 27 percent), less willing to use interactive phone (21 percent to 32 percent), and less willing to use social networks (28 percent to 34 percent). The increased willingness of young professionals to access customer service on social networks and to use interactive phone channel is what the assumed age differential would predict, but the willingness is low to begin with and the differences are small.

There are some differences in customer service expectations across countries, but they, too, tend to be small.[16] They are, however, a reminder that global marketers must be sensitive to the cultural context of the various countries in which they do business.

The Evolution of Customer Service Strategy

The Internet is not only a key reason why the expectations of both B2C and B2B customers are rising, but also can be a way in which their expectations can be met in a cost-effective manner. Figure 13.7 suggests an evolution in the way customer service is delivered that has the potential to improve service without increasing the cost of providing it. It involves, first, moving away from total reliance on telephone **call centers** for live customer service to customer service provided on the Internet, either with or without direct human intervention. Whether live customer service is used or whether self-service over the web is the norm, notice that the first two stages are essentially reactive. The customer must ask; only then service will be forthcoming.

The final step in the evolution would be to provide service proactively, before the customer even asks, perhaps even before he knows he needs it. This has variously been called "anticipatory" or "preemptive" customer service. Whatever the terminology, the aim is to prevent problems, not just resolve them once they occur. The intent is to provide information that resolves potential problems before customers even know they have one. One way of going about it is to employ rules-based automation.

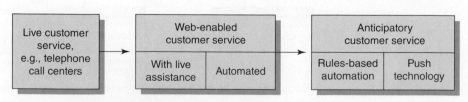

FIGURE **13.7** Customer Service Evolution

Source: © Cengage Learning 2013

Rules-based automation involves routines like, "*If* the customer has purchased Model Y, *then* send Update Y2." The business may notify the customer by email that an update is available. This is usually done with software to ensure that the customer is aware of and agrees to the modification of the software. The other way is to push content to the user. Many sites now offer the option of notices or alerts when something relevant to the customer happens. For example, the *Wall Street Journal Online* offers desktop alerts on subjects selected by the subscriber. These appear on the subscriber's desktop without any action being taken by her.

As we will see throughout the chapter, firms of all kinds are moving to provide more service over the web. Few, however, are anywhere close to taking full advantage of the opportunities offered by the Internet to deliver satisfying customer service at a reasonable cost. Even fewer are robust anticipatory customer service and support.

Remember that the first two stages of customer service evolution are reactive. The customer asks for service or support and the business is expected to provide it, which alone is a large order. To recognize potential problems before they occur and provide anticipatory service is a major undertaking.

Cost of Customer Service by Channel

Reasons for offering customer service on the web include pleasing the customer by 24/7 availability and consistency of information. There is no doubt that economics is also an issue, especially in recessionary times. The cost of providing customer service varies significantly by channel.

Peppers and Rogers quote a study by Forrester that listed average costs by channel. From most to least expensive they are:

- Call center with live agent $9
- Click-to-call $7.75
- Click-to-chat $5
- Email $2.50
- Virtual agent $1
- Self-service $0.10

Peppers and Rogers add that a few years ago 90 percent of customers accessed service by phone or email. In 2011, more than 50 percent of service requests came through online channels. They use these data to argue that "B2C-based social CRM could be considered the Internet's next killer app. Social CRM is all about delivering customer delight while monetizing the channel as part of an integrated customer strategy."[17] We discuss social CRM in Chapter 11.

The marketer must walk a fine line between pleasing customers and keeping costs in line. It makes sense to make live service accessible for high-value transactions and transactions that have a bearing on customer retention and consequently CLV. As the most cost-effective type of interaction online, self-service, including virtual agents, has a welcome role in activities like verifying account, order, and shipment status and other activities that simply require accessing information. When customers have a serious or time-sensitive issue they want to reach a live person by phone or chat. Email is somewhere between live and self-service. It is satisfactory for problems that are not time-sensitive as long as it receives a prompt and helpful response. With that in mind, marketers can attempt to direct customers to the most cost effective channel for a particular need. Customers, however, always want to know that there is a live person available if other options are not satisfactory.

A Word about Self-Service

There may be more to the issue of when to use self-service technologies than incentives or charges. A study of over 800 service encounters that involved self-service technology revealed that there were instances when consumers actually preferred self-service. They included:

- Experiencing a sudden need: A consumer who recognized a need for cash and was able to fill it immediately at an ATM was satisfied with the encounter.
- When self-service performed better than alternatives: This included situations in which the self-service technology was easy to use, preferable to dealing with service personnel, when it saved time or money, and when it was found at the time and place the customer wanted it.
- When it simply did its job: Customers were satisfied with self-service when it fulfilled their need and let them go on about their business.

On the other hand, there were clear situations in which customers were not satisfied with the use of self-service technology. They were:

- When the technology failed.
- When the process itself did not work: It is nice to be able to fill out a credit card application online, but if something happens and the application does not get processed, the consumer is not happy.
- When the self-service technology or process was poorly designed: The customer who has already filled out an application online and is asked to fill out a second one on paper is definitely not happy.
- When the customer is responsible for the failure: Some of the technology is so complex that the customer simply cannot figure it out, resulting in a failure.

The overall impression left by this piece of research is that self-service technologies have a great deal of potential to deliver satisfactory customer experience if they are carefully designed and if customers are trained in or guided through their use.[18]

The experience of firms that have made customer service an integral part of their strategies shows that implementing customer-centric service provision systems is a major undertaking for corporations, no matter what their age, size, or business sector is. Let us look at an organization that has had customer service in its corporate DNA from the very beginning.

A Proud Tradition of Customer Service at Eddie Bauer

Eddie Bauer established his retail store in 1920 in Seattle. An avid sportsman, he called his store Eddie Bauer's Sports Shop. By 1922, he had a formal customer service creed with a delightfully old-fashioned ring:

> To give you such outstanding quality, value, service and guarantee that we may be worthy of your high esteem.

His business philosophy included an unconditional guarantee, which was relatively unusual at the time. This philosophy served him well when he began a mail order catalog in 1945. Successful mail order retailers have always understood that, lacking an in-store experience, which can have important social dimensions, top-quality customer service was essential to mail order success.

After Eddie Bauer's retirement in 1968, growth accelerated with the opening of new stores and the addition of specialty catalogs. The first international catalog was launched in Germany in 1993 followed by three stores and a catalog in Japan in 1994. By 1995, there were stores in Germany and other European countries. The company had also undergone ownership changes during this period of time, first being sold to General Mills and later to Spiegel. In spite of growth and management changes, the customer service philosophy of Eddie Bauer has been kept alive within the company and is featured on its website and in its catalogs (see Figure 13.8).

FIGURE **13.8** The Eddie Bauer Customer Service Page with Guarantee and Contact Options

Source: Eddie Bauer, http://www.eddiebauer.com/custserv/custserv.jsp?sectionId=296.

The 1996 website was also one of the early entrants into the eretail category. Today, the company features an easy-to-use website with catalog quick order and store locator features that emphasize the multichannel nature of Eddie Bauer's business. The customer service page in Figure 13.8, which is accessible from every other page in the site, lists many self-help options including order status and history, which allow customers to track their orders, delivery information, easy returns, size charts with instructions for measuring for a correct fit, gift certificates, watch repair, and monogramming services.

If self-help does not answer the question, contact information is provided. The left sidebar highlights the Eddie Bauer Guarantee and Creed. Most important of all, it offers access to a human representative, which is critical for customers who have tried self-help but not found the needed problem resolution.

The signs of customer service commitment visible on this website are impressive. Eddie Bauer is also well regarded for keeping its promises to customers. Providing good customer service should be just that simple. However, if customer service is poor, it is a difficult and lengthy process to turn it around. British Airways is one of the classic cases in this respect.

Using Technology to Provide Customer Service at British Airways

Instead of having a fortunate heritage of commitment to customer service like Eddie Bauer, British Airways (BA) had just the opposite. Consider the following quote from an employee:

> I remember going to parties in the late 1970s, and if you wanted to have a civilized conversation, you didn't actually say that you worked for British Airways, because it got you talking about people's last travel experience, which was usually an unpleasant one.[18]

BA's inattention to customer services issues was rooted in its history. The airline we know today as British Airways was formed when the British Airways Board assumed control of two separate state-run airlines, British European Airways (BEA) and British Overseas Airways Corporation (BOAC). Both airlines retained their own boards of directors and management structure, with the British Airways Board providing an extra level of bureaucratic policy control. Both BEA and BOAC saw themselves as government agencies that represented British pride and tradition, and both had management groups primarily made up of military veterans. Their sense of business mission was often described as being limited to getting the aircraft into the air and down onto the ground on time. Even profitability was secondary, and the recession of the late 1970s reduced revenues and increased costs to a point that the survival of the airline was threatened.

In 1981, Sir John King was appointed chairman with the expectation that he would reverse the financial fortunes of the airline. Among the management appointments he made was that of Sir Colin Marshall, the CEO of Avis Rent A Car, in 1983. Although he had no airline experience, Sir Colin understood customer service and its importance in the marketing of travel services. He quickly undertook a quality management program that generated increases in productivity throughout the business and was a key part of the airline's return to profitability by the late 1980s.

Customer service, however, was still an unresolved issue. According to Charles Weiser who was brought in to deal with the situation:

> When I joined British Airways' customer relations department in 1991, I found an operation virtually untouched by the quality revolution that had caused the airline's reputation and fortunes to soar. The department took more than 12 weeks on average to respond to customer correspondence, it lost 60% of calls from customers on any given day, and the cost of compensating customers with grievances was rising rapidly.[20]

The first step was to train employees to stop arguing with customers about the facts of the case and to set about resolving their complaints. The overriding goal was long-term customer retention, not short-term cost savings. The eventual outcome was a four-step process:

1. Apologize and take ownership of the problem.
2. Respond quickly. BA research showed that as many as 50 percent of customers defected if complaints were not resolved within five days.
3. Assure the customer that the problem is being resolved.
4. Do it by telephone. Remember the time was the early 1990s and the alternative was mail. Both the speed and the personal contact were deemed important in retaining the customer.[21]

There was ongoing investment in training and information systems to support customer service throughout the company. BA even made an effort to *generate customer complaints*, because it knew that many dissatisfied customers do not complain. Customer service did improve, and further research showed that for every £1 invested in customer retention efforts there was a return on investment of £2.

In 1995, Sir Colin Marshall discussed the airline's efforts and results up to that point with the *Harvard Business Review*. Some of the points he made were:

- The basic price of entry in the airline industry has five points; getting passengers where they want to go, doing it safely, having the desired routes, providing nourishment, and letting them build up frequent flier miles. These are things the customer takes for granted, not things that make them satisfied or loyal customers.
- In all customer segments, there are travelers who will pay a small premium in price for superior service.
- Customers do not buy an object; they buy an experience. BA tries to make the travel experience seamless, personal, and caring.
- In order to meet the service-driven standards that customers want, BA listens carefully to its most valuable customers.[22]

The airline also continues to invest in technology that improves customer service. This has included:

- Eticketing that eliminates paper ticketing and speeds airport check-in.
- Online check-in through the website.
- Self-service kiosks that operate in multiple languages in major airports. They allow customers to select seats, print receipts and boarding passes, and check luggage.
- More recently, BA has introduced apps for the various mobile platforms (see Figure 13.9). The apps provide information about schedules, flights, and so on, and allow the customer to download boarding passes to the mobile device.

FIGURE **13.9** British Airways' Mobile App

Source: British Airways, http://www.britishairways.com/travel/mobile/public/en_gb?link=main_nav.

The BA experience represents an odyssey lasting more than 30 years in search of exceptional customer service. As its foray into mobile applications illustrates, it is an odyssey that never ends. New technologies become available to improve the overall customer experience, and the customer becomes ever more demanding as time goes on. Customer experience should be the key focal point. Providing good customer service is a natural outgrowth of customer focus, whether the entity is a corporation, a nonprofit, or, as we see next, a government agency.

eGovernment: The State of New York Department of Motor Vehicles

Like other states and national governments, the State of New York offers many ebusiness services to citizens and companies that wish to do business with the state. According to its website, "From reserving a camp site to purchasing a MetroCard, it can be done online here."[23] One of the busiest pages is that of the Department of Motor Vehicles (DMV). It offers an extensive set of online services.[24] In 2005, automation software was installed to allow citizens to find answers to questions online and to reduce the number of emails that were manually processed. The page is called Find DMV Answers[25] and it provides information beyond the usual FAQs. Its automation software provider reported that benefits of the system included:

- At least 97 percent of users find the information they need.
- The volume of email inquiries has decreased by 80 percent.
- The easy-to-use and up-to-date knowledge base has reduced the number of telephone calls and visits to DMV offices.
- Much of the repetitive routine is handled online, allowing support staff to focus on customers who need individualized attention.

This type of success was achieved only after intensive effort to initially build a knowledge base and to continue to improve it on the basis of customer usage patterns. For example, Internet customer relations manager George Filieau found that many users were sending email even though the answers to their questions were available on the site. As a result, the DMV changed the navigation of the site so knowledge base items became visible before the customer was able to send an email. The number of visitors who found immediate answers to their questions increased from 94 percent to the current 97 percent. This high rate of self-service reduces customer service costs and eliminates email backlogs, giving citizens quick answers to their queries.[26]

Creating Strategies for Service Excellence

Each of these organizations described in the previous section has followed a different path to arrive at customer service excellence. Taken together, these case histories illustrate a number of aspects of providing exceptional customer service. These are some of the recurrent themes:

- Excellent customer service cannot be delivered by a single department acting in isolation from the rest of the organization.
- Providing superior customer service is a long-term endeavor. If a customer service culture must be built in an organization that does not have one, it takes time and effort plus a substantial infusion of corporate resources.
- The customer service culture should pervade the entire organization. Customer service skills and philosophy should not be limited to a narrowly defined customer service department.
- Creating a culture of customer service is virtually impossible in an organization that does not follow at least some of the tenets of quality management (or business process reengineering, if you prefer that term).

- Quality programs emphasize collection of data about processes ("what gets measured gets managed"). This is especially important for "softer" parts of the organization like marketing and customer service.
- Technology offers many opportunities to improve customer service, including allowing customers to access the services they want, when they want, and where they want.
- Technology also makes it possible to offer customers multiple channels for accessing customer service.
- Even in the Internet age, however, customers want to know that they can access a competent and caring human being when necessary.
- It is helpful when the provision of customer service is done with a clear objective in mind. Cost savings are a desirable outcome, but improving customer experience is a better long-term objective.

Above all, what case histories throughout this chapter illustrate is that it is difficult to build an organization that consistently delivers outstanding customer service. That is why customer service excellence can form the centerpiece of sustainable competitive advantage.

These examples also make it clear that developing, introducing, and continuing to execute a successful customer service strategy is an ongoing process. It is helpful to see the steps in the process laid out early in the journey. Consultancy PricewaterhouseCoopers (PWC) has been studying how enterprises achieve excellent customer care for a number of years. Its perspective goes beyond simply pleasing customers to making customer care an important component of good strategy and the profitability it achieves.

The Pillars of Strategic Customer Care

PWC concludes that there are three stages, each with substages, in the process of developing strategic customer care (see Figure 13.10). In Stage I, companies focus on customer acquisition and learning about their customer base. Stage II represents CRM strategies of ever-increasing intensity. Stage II companies place emphasis on segmenting the customer base and learning to serve each segment more effectively. In Stage III, companies are able to use technology to offer consistent customer care at all times and at all customer touch points. PWC describes organizations that have achieved customer care excellence as follows:

> Stage III organizations have realized that they cannot be all things to all people. While most customers are potentially profitable, some customers offer more long-term promise than others. The ability to predict who these customers are is a necessary skill on the upward path to strategic customer care. By wisely applying the right technology and information tools (remember, technology is not a solution in its own right), companies at the strategic level of customer care exercise a core level of service for *all* their customers and a distinctive, optimized level of care for their *best* customers.[27]

The first three steps—profiling, segmenting, and understanding customers' needs—should all sound quite familiar. Profiling and segmentation are discussed in Chapter 4 as a data-driven way of identifying segments of customers with the highest potential CLV. We continue to emphasize the importance of customer

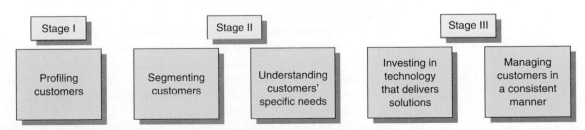

FIGURE **13.10** Pillars of Strategic Customer Care

Source: © Cengage Learning 2013

focus and customer knowledge. Putting it in the customer service context once again emphasizes the fact that customer knowledge is most valuable when it is acquired for specific, high-value customer segments.

Not until Stage III does this model specify the implementation of technology to meet customer needs. There are many technologies that offer potential in supporting customer service. The older ones support the telephone call center. More recent technologies support customer service provision on websites.

Telephone-Related Technologies

Technologies that are commonly used to enhance the productivity of telephone call centers include:

- *Interactive voice response (IVR).* All of us are familiar with the menu of choices presented to us when we dial into the main telephone numbers of most large organizations. This can be profoundly annoying and frustrating, but it also represents a type of automation that can deliver major cost savings. If the menu options are a good fit with the customer's needs in dealing with the business and if the number of first-level options is kept to no more than four to six, the annoyance factor can be minimized.
- *Intelligent call routing.* The software that controls telephone call centers can recognize incoming numbers and route calls to the most appropriate representative based on a set of user-supplied decision rules. When they are well executed, call routing systems are essentially invisible to the customer and provide specialized and personalized service
- *Call recording.* Recording calls permits real-time supervision in a call center environment and allows supervisors to review calls with reps at a later time as part of training activities. Recording also acts as proof of what has transpired during a call and can be especially important in situations like financial services where there are legal requirements for information provision prior to purchase.
- *Help desk/problem-tracking software.* **Help desk** is the generic term used to describe the technical services support group in a high-tech firm. A help desk is staffed by people who are trained to answer routine questions themselves and to refer difficult questions to the appropriate expert. Help desks are supported by software that can manage incoming requests and queue them, send automatic acknowledgements, maintain a knowledge management database that holds technical information and results of past requests, and provide a variety of management reports. Early help desks were telephone oriented. Today many of the queries come in by email.

Website Technologies

The Internet offers many technologies that can make customer service and support more accessible to the customer and more productive to the firm. They include:

- *Email response management systems (ERMS).* As the term suggests, this software helps organizations manage large numbers of email messages addressed to generic addresses like support@textbook.com. The software usually contains filters that route mail to reps based on keywords in the message content. Software modules can also perform functions like sending automatic messages or routing a stream of continuation messages to the same rep.
- *Embedded service modules.* Mainframe computers and servers, as well as many other electronics like medical devices, have long had embedded hardware and software that provide ongoing diagnostics. Some of these have been called "self-healing"; in other words, the equipment fixes itself, either by code embedded in it or by intervention by a remote operator.
- *Mobile applications.* Users have adopted the wireless Internet in large numbers as we discuss in detail in Chapter 16. Customer service apps from the BA app shown in Figure 13.9 to content notifications by news channels to severe weather alerts by weather channels have become part of daily life.

INTERACTIVE EXERCISE 13.2   **Virtual Agent of eBay**

eBay has developed a virtual customer service agent that has met with reasonable success. Introduce yourself to Emma in Australia and see how the interaction goes

Visit http://bit.ly/tc1IsQ.

- *Agent technology.* This is the contemporary manifestation **artificial intelligence**, or expert systems, that access knowledge banks, follow decision rules, and learn from experience.

Software firms have long tried to develop solutions that can interact with customers in the guise of a human being. The idea of being able to deliver customer service in a personal manner by means of an intelligent **virtual agent**, one that can make choices like answering customer questions, is attractive but perhaps even harder than it sounds.

- *Voice activation.* Finally, consider another technology that has been in existence for a long time but is just now coming into its own. Speech recognition has been expensive, hard to use, and not terribly accurate. Its primary use to date has been in disability services applications. It is probably wireless technology that has stimulated further development of voice recognition because the keyboards on wireless devices are small and difficult to use. Voice activation will greatly increase the ease of use of these devices.

Social Media as a Customer Service Channel

Many companies are tempted to use a social network channel for providing customer service. Customers are already using Twitter and Facebook, and besides, the platforms are free. What could be better? Of course, it is not as easy as that. The service page has to be monitored constantly by well-trained service personnel. It is a large commitment, but if it is made, the results can be positive.

In Chapter 9, Zappos is described as an avid user of Twitter across the corporation. It uses Twitter for many reasons, with customer service being first and foremost. It has a dedicated customer service page, @Zappos_Service.[28] Take a look at the page. Chances are good that you will see some chitchat, information being provided, and offers to help if the person will describe the problem. You will also generally see a steady volume of activity except perhaps in the wee hours of the night.

Best Buy's Twelpforce represents another active approach to customer service on Twitter. The page, @twelpforce, says that the force is with you "anywhere you need us."[29] It also points the user to the Best Buy knowledge base BBYFeed.com. The page is managed by a number of Best Buy employees with technical expertise. It is considerably more serious than the @Zappos_Service page, but both seem to work to satisfy customer needs.

Themes in Strategic Customer Management

Once the appropriate technology solutions have been implemented, the final phase of the process is to put a strategic customer management program in place. We have discussed that in the context of high-CLV customers and customer segments. The Tesco case history in Chapter 11 emphasized the importance of segmenting customers by value and developing individualized marketing and customer service strategies for each. BA is an example of a service business that interacts with individual customers and that can, with the proper data in hand, treat each one according to her value to the firm. Strategic customer management leads to a program of differentiated customer service. Differentiated customer service is one of the pillars of CRM as discussed in Chapter 11. It does, however, present a problem for low-value customers.

The Dark Side of Differentiated Customer Service

Business Week stated the issue succinctly in an October 2000 cover article, "Why Service Stinks." The article points to the consistent decline in customer satisfaction in most consumer sectors as measured by the University of Michigan American Customer Satisfaction Index. It quoted Len Berry, a Texas A&M marketing professor and one of the codevelopers of the ServQual index of service quality, who sees "a decline in the level of respect given to customers and their experiences."[30]

The article takes a dim view of the practice of strategic customer care that we have just described, pointing out that it leads to great differences in the way that high-value customers and low-value customers are treated.

The article uses examples including better service for frequent fliers on the airlines and ever-increasing fees for financial services customers who do not meet certain minimum revenue standards. The article ends with an advice to the individual consumer on improving his customer profile. It concludes, "These days, the best way to ensure good service is to make yourself look like a high-value, free-spending customer."[31]

More recently, Australian customer experience professional David Johnson wrote a detailed and thoughtful post about differentiated customer service. He asserts that differentiated customer service based on careful analysis of customer needs can be profitable. He adds that only if the difference of high- versus low-value customers is substantial—100:1 for frequent versus occasional flyers or 10:1 in some retail banking applications—it is worthwhile to develop differentiated service programs. His conclusion is that differentiated service programs must be kept simple, coordinated over multiple channels (web and retail, for instance), offered at important service encounter points, and be governed by a clear set of corporate policies.[32] This is a useful perspective even though there may still be conflicts, especially if customers recognize the difference in service levels.

Building Anticipatory Customer Service

The issues of the cost and effectiveness of customer self-service, important though they are, still do not make full use of the web's potential to deliver high-quality customer service at a lower cost to the marketer. The potential lies in the anticipatory service concept of being proactive, not simply waiting passively until customers request service. In order to do this, companies must anticipate potential problem areas before they become troublesome, develop solutions, and provide service that exceeds customer expectations.

Forrester Research says that a firm needs to do three things in order to implement anticipatory customer service. They must:

1. Build customer scenarios, using data including call center reports, email logs, chat transcripts, and website software that can report unusual volumes of activity and uncover patterns in day-to-day service queries. Use the scenarios to determine where intervention can prevent problems such as common customer mistakes in placing orders.
2. Make customer service pervasive by fulfilling common requests before the customer even asks and by ensuring that service is readily available throughout the value chain. Simple things like customer accounts that prevent people from having to fill out forms each time they purchase are important services. Retaining credit card information in these accounts is a security question that is discussed in Chapter 15.

3. Design the service process for "seamless escalation"; translated, guide customers to the service they need without having to move through frustrating layers of information that does not fit the needs of the customer. Be sure there is a real person at the end of the path.[33]

The Broader Issue of Customer Experience

In recent years, the concept of **customer experience** has not been replacing customer satisfaction, but adding a dimension. Customer experience is one of those things that every customer understands. Customers know that good customer service is one of the elements that is required for good customer experience, but there are more elements that make up the good experience.

While customer experience is recognizable, the definitions are hazy. Bruce Temkin of the Temkin Group is a long-time customer experience guru; he calls himself a customer experience transformist, because transformation is what most businesses require. His definition of customer experience is simple and straightforward, but it seems to cover all the bases. According to him, customer experience is:

the perception that customers have of their interactions with an organization.[34]

He goes on to say that creating a good customer experience requires three things:

1. Disciplined execution. It is not just sloganeering; it is disciplined execution of customer-centric policies.
2. Increase in customer loyalty. Good customer experience increases loyalty, retention, and the business bottom line.
3. Meeting customers' needs and expectations. Technology is often a component, but as we have described it in the context of customer service strategy, technology is only a means to an end.

He has six laws that guide the business transformation required for creating good experience. They are:

1. Every interaction creates a personal reaction.
2. People are instinctively self-centered.
3. Customer familiarity breeds alignment of policies and individual employee actions.
4. Unengaged employees do not create engaged customers.
5. Employees do what is measured, incented, and celebrated.
6. You cannot fake it.[35]

Notice that Temkin's laws have a lot to do with employees and creating positive interactions between them and the customers of the business. That is the core of the issue; technology can assist the process, but it cannot create it. The free ebook that sets forth these laws has plenty of food for thought. You are encouraged to download it and read it (http://experiencematters.wordpress.com/2008/07/22/free-book-the-6-laws-of-customer-experience).

The Importance of Good Customer Service and Experience

One theme that recurs throughout this chapter is the importance of good people and smoothly functioning organizations. Whether we are talking about good customer service or the broader concept of good customer experience, it is not quick or easy to develop. That is especially true if you have to turn around an organization that has poor customer service in its DNA. The example of BA, which has been working on customer service for decades, is a good example. It is much easier to be Southwest Airways and initiate a business based on principles of customer centricity and exceptional customer service. But either way, it is not easy to maintain it on a day-to-day basis. That is why customer service creates a sustainable competitive advantage.

If good customer service were easy, presumably everyone would be doing it. It is hard. It takes time and effort and, as we noted earlier in the chapter, investments in good customer service may be considered expendable in lean economic times. These are the reasons why relatively few organizations consistently deliver good customer service and make it part of an overall good customer experience. Providing good service and overall experience is clearly a competitive advantage. Because good service and experience are hard (and time consuming) to copy, the competitive advantage is sustainable. This makes customer service an important element of business strategy.

SUMMARY

Providing superior customer service is an important part of a CRM strategy. Data from various sources emphasize that service is important to both customer loyalty and profits in B2C and B2B markets. The data also point out that customer service is a multifaceted construct that includes not only service recovery but also issues like timely delivery and provision of information that makes it easier for customers to use the product.

Anecdotal evidence helps us appreciate the complexity of the customer service issue and the necessity to engage in a process of continuous improvement in order to develop and maintain excellent customer service. The process includes both making sure that business systems work and implementing technology to deliver service when appropriate. The examples also stress the key role of organizational factors in creating a successful customer service system.

Delivering good customer service has also become an information-driven activity. It requires segmenting and profiling customers, identifying and targeting high-CLV segments, developing differentiated service programs for different customer segments, and giving all segments seamlessly satisfying experiences appropriate to their values.

In order to make customer service cost-effective, technology must be part of the equation. One aspect of technology implementation is to offer customer-driven self-service opportunities. Self-service, when it works well, can be satisfying to customers and at the same time reduce the marketer's costs. There are a myriad of technologies in widespread use today and on the horizon that offer interesting opportunities for delivering customer service. None of the technologies is cheap, and marketers must make careful trade-offs between what customers need and the technology solutions they offer.

Offering superb customer service and targeting customer segments with the appropriate level of service are both essential to marketing success in the global Internet economy. The ability to deliver exceptional customer service has potential to produce sustainable competitive advantage that no other strategic marketing variable can match.

DISCUSSION QUESTIONS

1. Throughout the chapter, reference is made to exceptional customer service as the basis for sustainable competitive advantage. Do you agree with this perspective? Why or why not?
2. The Internet has the capacity to increase customer expectations about service levels and also to be the vehicle that delivers service that meets or exceeds those expectations. Take a position on this statement and discuss it.
3. Do you believe that good customer service has a direct impact on the profitability of a business? Can you provide evidence to back up your position?

4. True or false: Customer service is less important in B2B markets than in B2C. Why or why not?

5. Moving all service delivery to the web where customers can access it when they need it is the most important aspect of building a successful customer service program. Do you agree or disagree? Why?

6. What are the customer service channels people are most willing to use to resolve problems? The least willing?

7. What are the highest cost service channels? The lowest cost? What implications does that have for effective customer service strategy?

8. What is the concept of anticipatory customer service? What role can it play in successful customer service delivery?

9. *Bloomberg Businessweek* recently published a debate feature entitled "Virtual Agents Will Replace Live Customer Service Reps."[36] Would you take the pro or the con position? Why?

10. Can you identify industries or specific businesses for which mobile customer service apps seem especially desirable?

11. Can you find other examples, besides Zappos and Best Buy, of companies that are actively using social networks for customer service?

12. Can you identify any ethical issues that are inherent in sophisticated customer service programs?

13. How does customer experience differ from customer service?

14. Think about the issue of organizational issues and the impact on the delivery of exceptional customer service. Have you encountered any customer service instances in which people in the same organization seemed to be giving you different information or advice? Why do you think this happened?

INTERNET EXERCISES

1. Internet Career Builder Exercise
   a. These are some of the jobs that are available in customer service. You can find others on sites recommended by your instructor or through search.

      Call center representative

      Bilingual customer service representative

      Customer account manager

      Customer care representative

      Technical services representative

      Help desk

      Member services representative (nonprofit)

      Product support representative

      Call center supervisor

      and many more

   b. Select a customer service job from the list in 1a or from your own search. Outline the responsibilities of that position. You may find it useful to locate job postings on the web in order to understand the job requirements.
   c. Outline knowledge and experience from classes, internships, full or part-time jobs, and volunteer work that prepare you for this specific position.
   d. Prepare five questions you could ask at a job interview. The questions should exhibit your understanding of the position requirements without lecturing the interviewer about what she already knows.
   e. Update your VisualCV® or LinkedIn profile with this information.

2. Find a reason to contact a website or a social network service page (asking for information, searching for support for a previously purchased product or service, etc.) and make the contact. Keep track of the timeliness, correctness, and completeness of the responses. Describe them and characterize your overall experience.

3. Identify a website that has a significant customer self-help component. Websites for consumer software and consumer electronics companies are especially good candidates, but there are many others. Think of a specific problem or question that you might have in relation to this product. Visit the site and try to solve the problem or get answer to the question. Describe the nature of your experience and your degree of overall satisfaction.

4. Visit the websites you are tracking. Learn as much as you can about their customer service policies. Be alert to how easy it is to find the information you would need as a customer and how complete it appears to be. Note any aspects of the way the site provides customer service that look like they are particularly good or especially problematic. Establish several criteria that identify good service policies. Rank the sites according to your perception of their customer service policies and practices. Be prepared to discuss your criteria and rankings in class.

NOTES

1. http://www.consumerreports.org/cro/magazine-archive/2011/july/shopping/customer-service/overview/index.htm.

2. http://asunews.asu.edu/20111102_business_customerrage.

3. http://wpcarey.asu.edu/csl/knowledge/2004-National-Customer-Rage-Study.cfm.

4. http://www.accenture.com/SiteCollectionDocuments/PDF/Accenture_2009_Global_Consumer_Satisfaction_Report.pdf.

5. https://www1.vtrenz.net/imarkownerfiles/ownerassets/1076/Genesys_Global_Survey09_screen.pdf.

6. David O. Becker, "Gambling on Customers," *McKinsey Quarterly*, 2003, No. 2, http://www.mckinseyquarterly.com/article_page.aspx?ar=1299&L2=17&L3=104.

7. http://www.bloomberg.com/news/2010-08-06/loveman-plays-new-purely-empirical-game-as-harrah-s-ceo.html.

8. http://cjp-gaming.com/2012/01/14/harrahs-laughlin-customer-service-excellence/v.

9. "How Much Are Customer Relationship Capabilities Worth?" 2001, http://www.accenture.com.

10. For the complete list, go to http://www.destinationcrm.com/Articles/Editorial/Magazine-Features/The-2011-Service-Leaders-73783.aspx.

11. http://www.portakabin.co.uk.

12. http://www.portakabin.co.uk/customer-feedback.html.

13. http://www.netpromoter.com/np/calculate.jsp.

14. http://wpcarey.asu.edu/csl/knowledge/2004-National-Customer-Rage-Study.cfm; and http://www.consumerreports.org/cro/magazine-archive/2011/july/shopping/customer-service/are-consumers-too-whiny/index.htm.

15. 2011 National Customer Rage Study, conducted by Customer Care & Measurement & Consulting in collaboration with the Center for Services Leadership in the W.P. Carey School of Business, Arizona State University; data furnished by Scott M. Broetzmann, CCMC.

16. For cross-national comparisons, see http://about.americanexpress.com/news/docs/2011x/AXP_2011_csbar_market.pdf.

17. http://www.peppersandrogersgroup.com/view.aspx?docid=32987.

18. Matthew L. Meuter, Amy L Ostrom, Robert I. Roundtree, and Mary Jo Bitner, "Self-Service Technologies: Understanding Customer Satisfaction with Technology-Based Encounters," *Journal of Marketing*, Vol. 64, July 2000, pp. 50–64.

19. John P. Kotter, "Changing the Culture at British Airways," Harvard Business School, No. 9-491-009, 1990, p. 1.

20. Charles R. Weiser, "Championing the Customer," *Harvard Business Review*, November–December 1995, p. 113.

21. Charles R. Weiser, "Championing the Customer," *Harvard Business Review*, November–December 1995, pp. 113–116.

22. Steven E. Prokesch, "Competing on Customer Service," *Harvard Business Review*, November–December 1995, pp. 101–112.

23. "e-bizNYS," 2005, http://www.nysegov.com/e-bizNYS.cfm?displaymode=normal&fontsize=100&contrast=lod&content=about.

24. http://www.nydmv.state.ny.us/transact.htm.

25. http://nysdmv.custhelp.com/cgi-bin/nysdmv.cfg/php/enduser/std_alp.php.

26. "State of New York Department of Motor Vehicles," 2004, http://www.rightnow.com/news/article.php?id=724.

27. "The Route to Strategic Customer Care," PricewaterhouseCoopers, 1998, http://www.pwcglobal.com.

28. http://twitter.com/#!/zappos_service.

29. http://twitter.com/#!/twelpforce.

30. Diane Brady, "Why Service Stinks," *Business Week*, October 23, 2000, p. 120.

31. Diane Brady, "Why Service Stinks," *Business Week*, October 23, 2000, p. 128.

32. http://www.customerexperience.com.au/is-differentiated-customer-service-worthwhile-part-one.html.

33. Forrester Research, "Tier Zero Customer Support," December 1999.

34. http://experiencematters.wordpress.com/2008/08/06/what-the-heck-is-customer-experience.

35. http://experiencematters.wordpress.com/2008/07/22/free-book-the-6-laws-of-customer-experience.

36. http://www.businessweek.com/debateroom/archives/2010/07/virtual_agents_will_replace_live_customer_service_reps.html.

PART 4

Evaluating Performance and Opportunities

CHAPTER **14**

Measuring and Evaluating Web Marketing Programs

LEARNING OBJECTIVES

By the time you complete this chapter, you will be able to:

- Discuss the various types of Internet marketing metrics that are available.

- Explain the importance of usability testing.

- Identify the reasons why traffic and audience measurement are a central issue in Internet marketing.

- Understand the process of collecting data from server request log files, tagged pages, and user panels.

- Define key traffic, audience, and campaign metrics and the purpose of each.

- Discuss the role of objectives and key performance indicators in the identification and use of metrics.

- Discuss the importance of segmentation to an understanding of visitor activity.

- Identify issues involved in obtaining a complete picture of the customer buying process, both on and off the web.

Marketing Effectiveness

From the beginning of this book, we have discussed the important role that customer information plays in all aspects of Internet marketing. There are many types of and many uses for the vast quantity of customer information that is available from the Internet. One key part of that information is the **clickstream** of data that is produced by user activities on the web. While these data are essentially a by-product of Internet activity and therefore has little, if any, incremental cost of production, it is not in a form that is usable to marketers. They need to know what data are available, what metrics are needed, and how to obtain them. Those topics comprise the major part of this chapter.

Before dealing with the quantitative **metrics** that are available, we will look at a mostly qualitative approach to information about Internet marketing effectiveness. The subject of website usability was broached a number of times in Chapter 12. We will begin this chapter with a discussion of the methodology of usability analysis. Later in the chapter, we will discuss the manner in which metrics and usability studies interact.

In the meantime, however, consider the increase in marketing effectiveness that can be achieved in both B2C (business-to-consumer) and B2B (business-to-business) markets with a thoughtful approach to Internet metrics.

Improved Marketing at a Pizza Chain

According to a 2011 case study by metrics provider Cognos, New England–based pizza chain Papa Gino's was able to use an integrated metrics solution to improve both its marketing and its budgeting and financial operations. The company also wanted to introduce a customer loyalty program and increase online sales. It saw integrated metrics and business analytics as a key tool for implementing these strategies effectively.

Papa Gino's priorities included both operational and marketing issues. Marketing priorities were as follows:

- *Focus managers on analysis, not data collection.* When the project began, Papa Gino's was collecting point-of-sale data for its more than 275 restaurant locations and analyzing it on spreadsheets. It took district managers hours each day to aggregate data and examine it. The analytics project provided them with a single-page report at the beginning of each day that allowed them to immediately focus on problems at individual locations and begin the process of resolving them.
- *Improve customer service.* Delivery time is an important customer service issue for Papa Gino's. According to Martha Lieber, Director of Business Systems:

  > We found that, on average, we were promising to deliver pizzas within 45 minutes, but we were actually delivering them in less than 30 minutes. As a result, we started to adjust the promise time to reflect reality—setting our customers' expectations more accurately and potentially avoiding lost orders.

- *Improve promotions management.* Papa Gino's was using email, SMS, and direct mail to deliver coupons to customers. The new system allowed the company to track coupon usage and determine which offers performed better. It introduced a customer loyalty plan and found that members of that plan purchased 33 percent more often than customers who were not members of the loyalty plan. It also discovered that online orders were 40 to 70 percent larger than in-store orders. With this information in hand, the company was able to refine its coupon offers, promote its loyalty plan, and encourage online orders.

Recognizing the importance of social media, Papa Gino's was also able to monitor its Facebook and Twitter activity using the same integrated metrics solution. Future plans included introducing mobile apps and working on promotions with providers like FourSquare and Groupon, using data from the single metrics provider to measure the effectiveness of all channels.[1]

A Software Firm Focuses on Analytics

Enterprise software firm Sybase provides database, analytics, and mobile solutions for large customers all over the world. As such, it was natural for its analytics-oriented executives to work on improving their own marketing operations using their own analytics solutions. Like Papa Gino's, Sybase focused on specific aspects of its business in order to increase the effectiveness of its efforts.

The three areas it chose were:

1. Sales effectiveness
2. Marketing campaign effectiveness
3. Marketing expenditure optimization

For each sales region, an analysis of marketing activity and prospect response for all key accounts was performed on a bi-weekly basis. The company also analyzed the digital activity of accounts that were currently inactive, looking for signs those accounts were entering an active phase of the buying cycle. Both types of analysis allowed the company to deploy its field sales effort more effectively and to support it when necessary with marketing effort.

Each marketing campaign (e.g., a webinar or a telemarketing campaign) had its own specific marketing objective. Objectives might be number of registrants for a webinar or number of qualified leads for a telemarketing campaign, for example. The success of each individual marketing campaign was measured against its own stated objectives, and future campaigns were improved based on this information.

In addition to using industry **benchmarks**, Sybase analyzed all its marketing expenditures every two weeks. It used a matrix for comparison within each region and for each product that compared marketing expenditure and prospect interest levels. This detailed information allowed it to allocate marketing expenditures where it had the greatest likelihood of success.

These two brief case histories have common themes regardless of the fact that one is a regional restaurant chain (B2C) and the other is a global provider of enterprise software (B2B). Both focused on key areas of the business with desired business goals in mind. Both used metrics to understand the performance of each business area and to deploy marketing effort in ways that had the highest probability of success. In Chapter 4, we described how customer data, captured in the customer database, improves the quality of marketing decision making. These cases are examples of how marketing campaigns and operational data, captured on the web and in the real world, can improve marketing decision making.[2]

The Importance of Marketing Metrics and the Difficulty of Doing Them Well

In a world that is full of options and choices, where do metrics rank in the marketer's hierarchy of importance?

Figure 14.1a lists a number of types of customer behavior of importance to the marketer including items like offline behavior, social media behaviors, and behavior during a single website session. There are also performance measures like comparative channel performance, marketing campaign effectiveness, and display advertising performance. Some are difficult to measure; some are relatively easy. Offline is hard because marketing research or third-party data are usually required. Behavioral metrics are more easily collected online. Beyond that, what you see is that anything that represents an integrated view of various

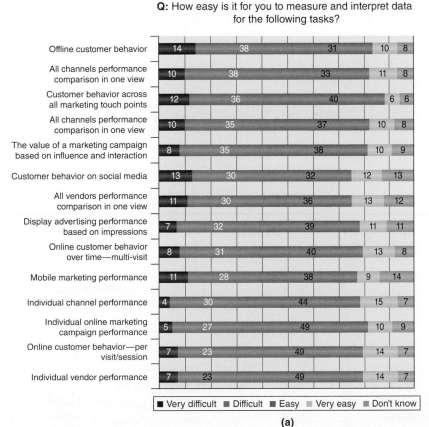

Q: How easy is it for you to measure and interpret data for the following tasks?

	Very difficult	Difficult	Easy	Very easy	Don't know
Offline customer behavior	14	38	31	10	8
All channels performance comparison in one view	10	38	33	11	8
Customer behavior across all marketing touch points	12	36	40	6	6
All channels performance comparison in one view	10	35	37	10	8
The value of a marketing campaign based on influence and interaction	8	35	38	10	9
Customer behavior on social media	13	30	32	12	13
All vendors performance comparison in one view	11	30	36	13	12
Display advertising performance based on impressions	7	32	39	11	11
Online customer behavior over time—multi-visit	8	31	40	13	8
Mobile marketing performance	11	28	38	9	14
Individual channel performance	4	30	44	15	7
Individual online marketing campaign performance	5	27	49	10	9
Online customer behavior—per visit/session	7	23	49	14	7
Individual vendor performance	7	23	49	14	7

(a)

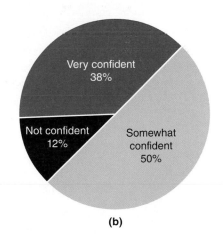

Q: How confident are you that you are tracking the right metrics for online marketing performance?

- Very confident 38%
- Somewhat confident 50%
- Not confident 12%

(b)

FIGURE **14.1** (a) Important Marketing Metrics (b) Marketers' Confidence That They Are Using the Right Metrics

Source: Forbes, "Bringing 20/20 Foresight to Marketing," May 2011, from Coremetrics, an IBM company. Courtesy of the IBM Corporation.

channels and multiple **touchpoints** is difficult. Anything that requires measurement of the effectiveness of a single channel or a campaign or the tracking of an individual visitor is relatively easy. That says a great deal about the current status of metrics—not just web metrics but the integrated metrics that marketers need.

Figure 14.1b presents a sobering perspective on the current perspective of marketers with regard to the metrics they actually track. Only 38 percent are "very confident" that they are tracking the right metrics. That means that most marketers have a lot of metrics work to do, and they must do it in an ever-changing Internet and mobile environment.

These charts taken together suggest that marketers must start with the metrics basics and add the more complex multichannel, multi-campaign issues as their expertise allows. We begin with one of the most basic of issues, "Does the visitor find it easy to use my website?"

Ways to Evaluate Website Effectiveness

In Chapter 12, we discuss the concepts of usability and customer experience, both of which lead to website effectiveness in a business context. It is important to take a high-level view of that term, because it can have different but equally important meanings. Figure 14.2 lays out the issue.

Unfortunately, the term "site effectiveness" is strategically appropriate when used in three different but related ways. The one is *site usability*, which is essential to good customer experience, and resultant business success. This usability is the way the visitor looks at the site, the way he gauges its ease of use and its value to him. If the visitor finds the usage experience satisfactory, the site has a greater chance to be successful in the long run. That is the purpose of **usability testing**, which is an important part of the web development process. In the next section, we will examine the methodology of usability testing.

The second perspective is "traffic," "audience," and "campaign measurement"—the terms used to describe metrics that provide effectiveness data vital to marketers. We will discuss those measurement techniques in detail in this chapter because they are measures of business performance. The third perspective is that of *site performance*. This is the data that are needed by site technicians to gauge and improve site performance. Even though it is the responsibility of the technical side of the web team, marketers should be familiar with the basic approaches, which we will cover along with other metrics.

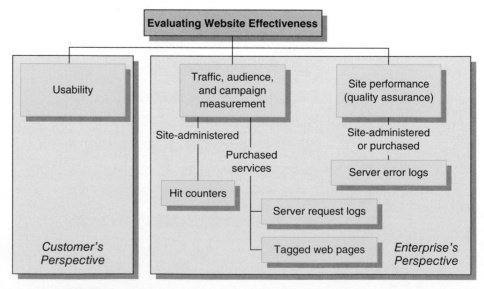

FIGURE **14.2** Perspectives on Website Effectiveness
Source: © Cengage Learning 2013

It is appropriate to look at usability testing first, since its greatest value comes prior to the actual deployment of a site or a redesign. In advertising terms, it is a pre-testing technique, before the site is opened to all visitors, that is used to ensure that the site functions according to user expectations. It also can and should be used on an existing site from time to time, especially if other metrics suggest site problems.

Usability Testing

First, it is important to be clear about what usability testing is and is not. It is not conventional marketing research, although it may incorporate focus group research techniques into the testing process. It is, in fact, more similar to the testing done by direct marketers or in advertising laboratories than to the marketing research survey approach typically used by mass media marketers.[3] In addition, usability testing should not be confused with the testing of communications appeals, which should be part of the enterprise's overall marketing communications program not of the website development process itself.

Usability testing is exclusively designed to see if the site works in a user-friendly fashion according to the expectations of members of the target market. Site performance (quality assurance is another frequently-used term), as portrayed in Figure 14.2, is a different issue that needs different metrics. Usability tests are essentially qualitative, and *they are performed by marketers interacting with target site users, not by technicians.*

There are many marketing services and agencies with expertise in usability testing, but the undisputed guru of web usability is Dr. Jakob Nielsen. Now a consultant, he was with the original Bell Labs and IBM before moving to Sun Microsystems where he was lead usability engineer for the establishment of the first Sun website in 1994. His personal website (www.useit.com) is filled with information about usability testing and is updated frequently. Nevertheless, some of the most instructive material on the site dates back to his early experiences with Sun in the mid-1990s. This supports the assertion that usability testing has strong foundations in basic testing approaches, many of them originating in psychology laboratories and adapted for specific uses in applications such as advertising evaluation and computer hardware and software design. Even a cursory inspection of Dr. Nielsen's site indicates that much of his current activity involves spreading the word about usability testing to managers around the world, railing against those who ignore (or are ignorant of) principles of good design for usability.

Stages of Usability Testing

Usability testing can be divided into general categories as follows:

- *Concept testing* is the earliest stage and reflects none of the actual site programming. In testing at this stage, one or more concept boards are shown to respondents who critique it from the perspective of how logical they perceive it to be and how easy they think it would be to use. Concept tests are useful at a very high level to prevent egregious design flaws and to give general guidance to the designers about what customers and prospects expect and what they think about the design concepts presented to them. This type of testing can be done relatively quickly in a focus group setting. Since it requires only the development of concept boards, it is also relatively cheap. Remember that the concept boards are testing the design of major pages on the site and the degree to which these pages communicate the desired corporate image and specific communications objectives, not the communications appeals themselves.
- *Prototype* testing is the second level. At this point in the development process, the site design is complete and at least some parts of the site are functional. Testing a prototype affords an opportunity to get reactions to

the appearance of the site and to get some information about the degree to which the site structure is consistent with customer expectations. The earlier prototype testing is conducted, the more visual appearance and structure can be changed without increasing the development time and cost of the site. Early testing, however, implies that much functionality is probably not operating and that the test will be somewhat artificial. The marketer must carefully assess the trade-off between early and more complete testing.

- *Full usability testing* indicates that the site has been uploaded to a server and is fully functioning, even though it is not accessible to the general public. Dr. Nielsen has a page on his site that shows a testing setup in detail.[4]

In viewing both the examples in Interactive Exercise 14.1, you can see similarities to a marketing research **focus group**. The two techniques have many of the same advantages and disadvantages, among them the opportunity to get a great deal of information from a few carefully selected respondents and the care that must be taken by the person conducting the test not to bias the responses of the test subject. Some basic training in eliciting qualitative data is desirable for the person conducting the test, but it is not beyond the resources of even a small company to conduct its own series of usability tests.

The main focus of a usability test is to ask test subjects to perform tasks that simulate what a visitor would want and expect to do on the site. In a more recent research project, Dr. Nielsen and his colleagues tested 20 ecommerce sites, and he explained the various types of tasks required in the test. First, test subjects were asked to simply explore the site for a few minutes to see what they believed the purpose of the site was. The second task was to ask them to locate a specific product on the site. For example, on one home-products site, they were asked to locate the cheapest toaster. For the third task, element test subjects were given a more open-ended task. An example was, "Pretend that you have just moved from Florida to a cold climate and that you don't own any winter clothes. Please buy what you will need to be able to go for a walk in freezing temperatures."[5] The fourth task was for the users to answer specific questions about customer service on the site, like whether the customer could cancel an order after placing it.

In this research project each website received attention for 35 to 40 minutes. This is considerably less than the one hour or more usually spent when a single site is being tested. Dr. Nielsen notes that after two hours, both the test subjects and the facilitators are sufficiently tired that further useful results are unlikely, no matter how many or how few sites are being tested.

Usability Testing and the Pareto Curve

Usability testing should not be considered an option or a luxury. Even the best-designed websites invariably have problems that are quickly detected by users. Even the so-called cosmetic problems will produce an inferior user experience.

INTERACTIVE EXERCISE **14.1**   Interactive Usability Testing

Visit http://bit.ly/u9Xk2k.

Look at how a simple conference room was set up in 1995 to perform a usability test and read Dr. Nielsen's explanations. Click along the interactive photo to see the room setup, the concept board, and a card-sort exercise in which respondents sort items into homogeneous sets.

Then fast forward to the present and see a similar setting in operation with an actual respondent participating in the usability test by viewing the video on this site.

Watch the video at http://bit.ly/tXEpw6.

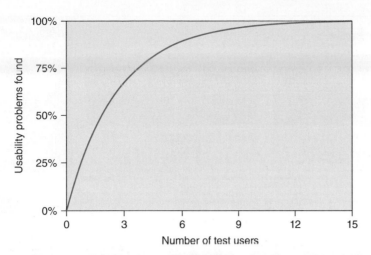

FIGURE **14.3** Pareto Curve for Usability Testing
Source: © Cengage Learning 2013

The need for testing is often questioned on the grounds of both time and expense. Dr. Nielsen makes a strong case for the affordability of user testing by constructing a **Pareto curve** (see Figure 14.3), which shows that over 75 percent of a site's usability problems can be identified with five user tests and that 100 percent will be found by testing 15 users.[6] He also states that, with experience, the tests can be completed in two workdays if user recruiting has been outsourced to a commercial marketing research firm.[7]

The message should be that eliminating or skimping on usability testing is a false economy. It should be a standard part of the launch of any new website, whether it is completely new or a redesign. It should also be done when other site metrics indicate usability problems, as will be explained in the next section.

One important decision the marketer will have to make is at which stage in the development process the usability testing should be done. The earlier it is done, the easier it will be to make fundamental changes. At the same time, the lack of prototype functionality in early-stage testing makes it somewhat artificial. On the other hand, if the functionality is nearing completion, considerable time and money have been invested in the site and it will be harder to make major changes. The issues involved in testing a prototype versus a fully functioning site suggest that several small-scale tests at various mileposts along the way might be more productive than any single larger-scale test.

Once a site is launched, qualitative metrics are essential for monitoring its ongoing progress and for identifying areas for improvement.

Enterprise Metrics for Evaluating Websites

Site metrics fall into two basic categories—measures of business performance and measures of site performance. These business effectiveness measures provide data by which marketers can judge the success of marketing programs both on and off the website. They are key to managing Internet marketing activities and demonstrating ROI (return on investment) on those activities.

FreshDirect has succeeded in the fresh-food delivery business where other, earlier entrants failed. It made its first deliveries in 2002, and by 2010, it had acquired 600,000 customers in the New York City metropolitan area[8] and anticipated sales of $300 million and expansion into other cities.[9] In order to compete with supermarkets, FreshDirect had to offer quality, on-time deliveries, and the brands that discriminating New York shoppers demanded. In addition, as the detailed "tour" information in Figure 14.4 suggests, it had to maintain a content-rich website to convince people of the desirability of shopping for food on the web.

FIGURE **14.4** Trust-Building Content on the FreshDirect Website
Source: FreshDirect, http://www.freshdirect.com.

According to Unica, its metrics vendor, FreshDirect needed an in-depth understanding of the best product categories for its clientele, which elements of its website were most popular, and how well its marketing campaigns and product promotions were working.

Analysis of metrics yielded the following insights:

- Like other retail sites, FreshDirect used a recommendation engine. For example, when a shopper orders a steak, a dialog box on the confirmation page recommends complementary items like potatoes, herbs, and steak sauce. Metrics showed that customers frequently purchased the recommended items, so the complementary items were given greater prominence on the site.
- FreshDirect segments its database by variables that include purchase history, order size, and geography. That segmentation enabled it to target a promotion for a new prime meat product line to customers who had previously purchased meat. For Valentine's Day, the company sent all customers an email offering meal suggestions and related specials. Metrics were able to relate purchases back to the email campaign and revealed that 50 percent of the recipients opened the email and 15 percent of them clicked-through to the site. Sales of the promoted products increased substantially, and the success of this seasonal email has influenced the company's email campaign planning.

- FreshDirect uses metrics on local keyword searches to add frequently searched products—organic produce or specific brands, for example—to guide the addition of products to its selection.
- FreshDirect monitors a wide variety of metrics related to check out including most frequent shopping time, most frequent checkout time, duration of shopping visits, time required to make a purchase, and how frequently and at what point shoppers drop out of the checkout process. The site has undergone many usability tests, so the rate of shopping cart abandonment is satisfactorily low.
- Using marketing research, FreshDirect found that 50 percent of its customers used iPhones, so in 2010, it introduced an app that allows users to purchase virtually all the items offered on the regular website; it has features like lists and frequently purchased items.[10]

New developments like mobile apps provide a continuing challenge for the suppliers of integrated metrics solutions.

There are many other metrics available to and used by FreshDirect. These examples highlight just some of the metrics and the direct impact they have on business decisions. It also suggests the importance of integrated metrics solutions that can provide views of not only the website, but also online advertising and email campaigns and related online activities like keyword searches.

While these kinds of measures of business effectiveness are vital to marketing managers, measures of site performance give directions to the technicians who maintain the site. In the words of the website development process, this means tuning the site to maintain and improve the manner in which it functions. Let us turn briefly to site performance. We will then devote the remainder of the chapter to discussing the source, nature, and use of detailed business effectiveness measures.

Website Performance

Figure 14.5 shows a report of the performance of a single web page—the page itself—and each file on it. Timing starts from the time the URL (www.alertsite. com) is translated into the IP (Internet Protocol) address—the **DNS (Domain Name System)** Lookup on the legend at the bottom of the chart. The more detailed printed report (not shown) indicated that it required 0.0024 seconds to look up the IP address on the network. Then the page starts loading, file by file. For each file, the webmaster can see how many seconds it took to connect with the file, how long it took for the first byte of information to load, and how long it took for content to load. Notice that many of the files are graphics—.gifs or .jpegs—and do not have significant text content. It took 1.3902 seconds for the page to load completely, which would be acceptable to most users. Reports like this are available in real time, that is, the webmaster can call up a status report for any page or many other elements of web functionality at any time.

AlertSite[11] is one of numerous firms that specialize in website monitoring. It offers monitoring and reporting services for mobile sites as well as conventional websites. It also offers tools like on-demand load balancing test to ensure that pages load properly under different usage scenarios. Other tools allow webmasters to create scripts that mimic user activity. The scripts are sets of instructions that allow technicians to test many aspects of site performance in a controlled laboratory-like setting.

This type of data is clearly of great use to the web technicians, but it provides little value to marketers. Marketers should be concerned about the smooth functioning of the site, but it is the job of the webmaster to make it happen. Marketers are concerned with the traffic and audience data because it has direct relevance to marketing campaign success.

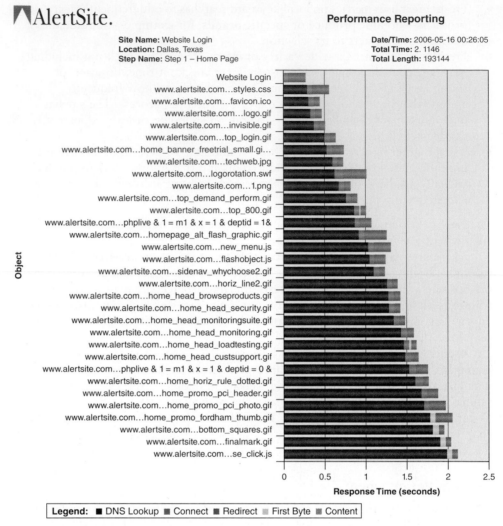

FIGURE **14.5** Sample Web Page Performance Report

Source: http://www.alertsite.com.

Collecting Website Traffic, Audience, and Campaign Data

An important measure of the business effectiveness of a site is the number and quality of its visitors. Site effectiveness can also, of course, be measured by sales if it is a transactional site. However, both content and transactional sites rely heavily on traffic and audience measurement for the reasons described at the beginning of the chapter: to manage and to improve the site, to establish advertising rates, and for other marketing purposes such as persuading other sites to link or to become affiliates. The relevant measures can be defined as follows:

- Traffic data describes *activity* on the site. It includes metrics such as number of visitors, sessions, and page views.
- Audience data describes both the *behavior* of people on the site—where they come from, what paths they take through the site, and whether they take desired actions—and the *people* themselves using both anonymous and identified profile data as described in Chapter 4.
- Campaign data describes the results of a specific marketing program like an online display ad or an email blast.

There are three basic ways of collecting those measures from the site itself—hit counters, server request log files, and tagged web pages. It is important to understand the basic technology they entail before looking at the statistics they generate.

Hit Counters

A **hit counter** is a small piece of software that can be added to a website to provide few basic metrics like number of visitors to a particular page. Website development tools have hit counters that can be inserted as part of the process of building the site. Others can be found free on the web. Older ones are visible meters on the site; newer ones may not be visible to the visitor. A hit counter is a few lines of HTML code that is placed on each page that the owner wants to measure. Many sites provide free hit counters in the hope that the website owner will purchase reporting services or more complex hosted counters.

Figure 14.6 shows a sample of one of the many reports that can be obtained from a hit counter. For each day of a specific week of a specific month, it shows the number of pages that have fully loaded (page views), the number of **unique visitors,** and the number of visitors who return. There are multiple ways in which sites can identify unique visitors, which will be discussed in a later section of the chapter. The figure also shows the main navigation bar of the site. It gives an idea of how many reports can be obtained from the relatively simple technology of a hit counter.

Whether the marketer chooses a simple hit counter or a more comprehensive web analytics application, there are two basic ways of collecting the clickstream data—server request log files and coded pages.

Server Request Log Files

As the name suggests, these files are created by the **server** that houses the website. Each time a browser requests a file in order to build a web page, the action generates an entry in the **server request log**. That sounds like a simple and straightforward statement, but it has enormous implications. Each graphic on a web page is a separate file and there can be several content files on a single page, as shown in Figure 14.5. So if, say, a simple web page has three graphics and one content block, each time that web page is accessed, four hits are registered on the server log. Yes, *a hit is counted for each file on the page*, no matter how many or how few.

Just to complicate the situation further, what the server registers is the requester's IP address. Every computer linked to the Internet, whether it is a server or recipient (client) of information, must have such an address. Some addresses are permanent, but if the user is linked by a dial-up connection, the address is dynamic, meaning that it is assigned only for the duration of that session. These addresses are made up of as many as 12 numbers separated by periods in a configuration like xxx.xxx.xxx.xxx. So think of a really big spreadsheet, with many rows, each representing a served file, and a number of columns that record the following data:

- The IP address of the requesting computer
- Date and time of request
- Code indicating whether request was successful or not
- Number of bytes of data transferred
- Referring site
- Type and version of web browser making request
- Operating system of computer making request[12]

Now think about how big that spreadsheet is going to get and how quickly![13]

No marketer wants to spend time understanding the arcane language of server log files, much less trying to make sense of the millions of requests a busy site gets each day. There are many software applications that will take

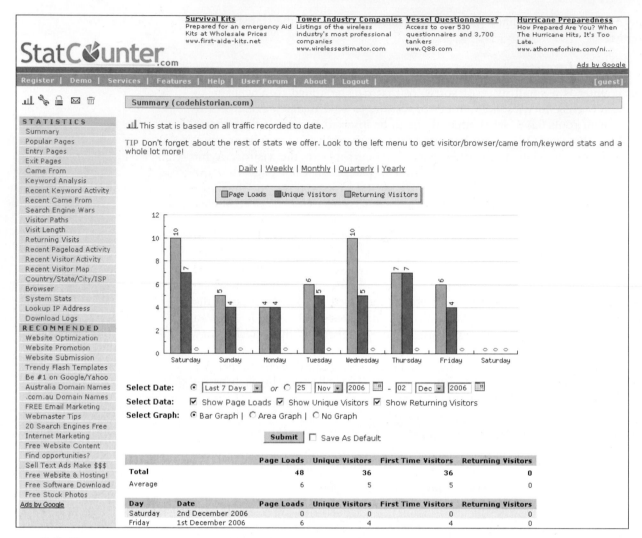

FIGURE **14.6** Sample Traffic and Audience Report

Source: StatCounter Limited, http://my5.statcounter.com/project/standard/stats.php?account_id=236678&login_id=1&
code=77e7066cb8b3c11b9722f4d088c18138&guest_login=1&project_id=234043.

the server log data and translate it into reports that are relevant to marketing decisions. Many hosting services provide basic web analytics as part of their package.

Server logs are maintained as part of running the site, so it is natural that these data are the first to be used to evaluate site effectiveness. If you stop and think about the earlier example, it is stated in terms of a single page. The server log file alone cannot report on more than one page at a time. Consequently, it cannot track the movement of a user through the site, a subject of great importance to marketers.

Tagged Web Pages

In order to provide marketers with this important information, another technique appeared in the 1990s. It has been given various names—web bug, beacon, **pixel** tag, coded page, and so on. More recently, the Internet community seems to have settled on the use of "tag" and "tagged pages." This term is a bit confusing because there are tags that are part of the site itself (meta tags and title tags, for example) and user-supplied tags (the tag you put on an image that you upload to the web, for example). However, we will stick with the term **tagged web pages.**

TABLE 14.1	Data Made Available by Tagged Web Pages

Information About the Visitor (often called "Dimensions" in the metrics literature)	Metrics Produced for the Marketer
• Page • Entry Page • Exit Page • Referrer • Browser • Platform • Geographic Data (Country, City, Time Zone, Organization, etc.) • Date • Time • Day of the Week	• Number of visitors • Number of views • Number of visits • Number of new visitors • Number of repeat visitors • Total time online • Average viewing time • Average visit duration • Views per visit

Source: Adapted from http://ems.eos.nasa.gov/NI82/UnicaNetInsight821PageTagGuide.pdf.

A **tag**, then, is a few lines of code that are placed on each page in the site that is to be tracked. It gives marketers access to numerous metrics that would not be available with server log data alone. Tagged web pages allow the marketer to track a visitor as he moves from one page of the site to another. It also allows tracking events that occur on the page, like changing a piece of data in a form or selecting an item from a drop-down menu.

Table 14.1 gives an example of the visitor data that can be captured using tagged pages, and the resulting metrics that are made available to the marketer. The metrics aggregate the data from many visitors into information that marketers need.

Tagged web pages are necessary in order to expand data capture beyond the server request log. In order to capture the data, a cookie must be set on the user's computer. And in order to collect detailed information about visitor activity, tags must be used in conjunction with cookies. Cookies themselves have become controversial (we will consider the user privacy implications in Chapter 15), although the general Internet public seems less aware of tagged pages in general.

Cookies Cookies are small data files that are stored on the user's computer that transmit data back to a web server. There are several types of cookies:

- *Session cookies* are effective for only one visit. They are placed when the visitor enters and expire when she leaves.
- *Persistent cookies* remain for a specified period of time, a year perhaps, and then they expire.
- *Third-party cookies* are set by an outside services provider like an ad serving firm or a metrics service.
- *First-party cookies* are set by the website itself.

Cookies can also be set to retrieve personal information or not, which should be controlled by the privacy options the user has selected.

Minus all the technical issues—and there are many—the process of capturing and using server log data is a simple concept. The concept is portrayed in Figure 14.7. The cookie—set on each visit or on first visit if a persistent cookie—stores data that makes the user experience easier like remembering user names and passwords for sites where the user has registered. The tags on web

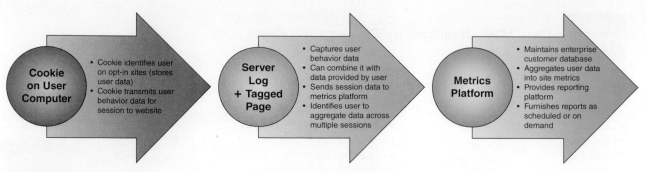

FIGURE **14.7** Interaction between Cookie, Tagged Web Page, and Metrics Platform
Source: © Cengage Learning 2013

pages allow the capture of user behavior and its attribution to the individual—identified or anonymous. Data are transmitted to the metrics platform, which stores enterprise customer data and maintains it for the sole use of that client and perhaps for purposes of model construction by the vendor. There is no movement of data between clients of a metrics service; that would be an egregious violation of client trust. Site metrics are aggregated from individual-level data and reported to the client according to the client's instructions.

Server log data is one of the primary ways to collect customer behavior data on the Internet. The other major type is panel data.

Panel Data

The process for using panel data to generate site effectiveness data is the same as using panels in the traditional marketing research process. The first step is to recruit a statistically representative panel of Internet users who agree to participate in the data collection. The size of the panel is determined by traditional statistical criteria including the size of the universe to be sampled and segments that are to be broken out of the aggregate data. Specialized software is downloaded onto the participant's computer to record the clickstream data. The software is polled at regular intervals to upload the data.

However, there are different approaches that can result in subtle differences in the metrics, which is exemplified by two of the largest vendors, comScore and Nielsen. Here are the basics of their methodology in their own words:

- *comScore's User Panel.* "Central to most comScore services is the comScore panel, the largest continuously measured consumer panel of its kind. With approximately 2 million worldwide consumers under continuous measurement, the comScore panel utilizes a sophisticated methodology that is designed to accurately measure people and their behavior in the digital environment … [comScore's Unified Digital Measurement technology] is unique to the industry and provides a superior solution by overcoming common methodological shortcomings, such as the inability to measure the actual person not just machine, over- or under-counting usage based on cookie deletion habits and misrepresentation based on a multiple usage devices or the same person using multiple browsers."[14]
- *Nielsen's Hybrid Panel.* "[Nielsen's] unique approach combines representative, people-based panels with, tag-based measurement to deliver a holistic view of the digital universe and its audience. The result is a Total Internet Audience metric that offers a sophisticated approach to understanding consumer behavior and provides comprehensive digital media measurement across all devices and locations, including mobile devices, tablets, secondary PCs and access points outside of home and work locations. In the U.S., Nielsen's online panel measures the activity of more than 200,000 Internet users across more than 30,000 sites, and extends to more than 500,000 panelists worldwide."[15]

The commonality is that both use panels, which are representative samples of the larger population, and project that data to the total population. comScore uses a large panel. Nielsen uses a smaller one and adds site-level data to it.

Which is better? Methodologists can argue endlessly about the merits of various sampling, data capture, and extrapolation techniques. What is clear is that they do produce slightly different data. The marketer needs to carefully examine the various metrics products in light of his own needs. He also needs to be disciplined and consistent in the metrics used.

Proponents of panel data argue that there are several benefits of this type of data as opposed to server request logs. First, the source of the data is unambiguous, as it often is not with server logs. For example, international IP addresses can be difficult to identify precisely in terms of their source. Second, a person who uses the Internet from both home and work is two separate people according to server request logs, but carefully planned and maintained panel data can overcome this issue. Third, the measurement firm can collect demographic and behavioral data from panel households that can be very useful in reporting and analytics. Since server request logs identify most users by dynamic IP addresses, it is not possible to use much third-party data to enhance it. Getting visitors to register on the site, however, can overcome this difficulty to some extent.

The marketer needs to have a basic understanding of the methods used to collect traffic and audience data, but her primary job is to select the metrics that can accurately evaluate the effectiveness of the website and Internet marketing campaigns. Let us turn now to a discussion of the metrics that are available.

Measuring Website Traffic, Audiences, and Campaigns

Whatever the method of data collection, the same set of variables can be measured. The definitions that follow are generally accepted within the Internet industry:

- Traffic measures simply document site activity. Some of the key traffic metrics are:
  - Hits: the number of files requested. The hits metric is of little use to the marketer, although it is important to the webmaster as previously explained.[16]
  - Impressions: the number of times an ad banner is requested by a browser.
  - **Page views** or deliveries: the number of times a web page is requested. Although you often see page views reported, they must be viewed with caution. Many sites use the Ajax technology to load multiple items on a page before the user requests them. Think of a retail ecommerce page with thumbnails that can be clicked on to get a larger image and text description. The entire page is loaded when the user requests it, although the user may choose to view none, all, or some of the full-size product images. What matters is which of the products are viewed, not the page view itself.[17] The various metrics platforms can handle this issue, but it requires special attention by the webmaster.
  - Sessions: the amount of activity on a site during a specified period of time.
  - Click-throughs: the number of times any link is clicked.
- Audience measures provide data about the people who visit the site. Key audience metrics include:
  - Visitors: the number of people who visit a site.
    - Total (includes multiple visits by the same user) or unique (different people) during a specified time frame
    - Unidentified (anonymous) or identified (registered or customer)
    - Unique (each visitor is counted only once during a specified time period)

- Behavior on the site
  - Number of page views
  - Session time
  - Path through the site
  - Shopping cart abandonment
  - Entry page (many visitors do not enter through the home page)

And there are many others. You should be aware that there is no clear dividing line between traffic and audience measures, but traffic always implies general information about site activity while audience always implies information about the demographics and behaviors of visitors to the site.

In addition, there are measures of marketing campaign effectiveness:

- Campaign measures provide data about the effectiveness of marketing efforts.
  - By communications channel: email, mail, online banners, and so on.
  - By offer: free shipping versus 25 percent off, for example
  - Search effectiveness by keyword

And, again, many others.

Campaign measures have the ability to integrate measures about offline activity (direct mail for example), or activity off the website (search keywords for example). Results are shown in terms of metrics like page views, number of visitors, number of unique visitors, and sales revenue. For **multichannel** marketers, the ability to see reports that cover all types of marketing activities across all their channels is essential.

In order to be meaningful, all these measures must be taken during a specified period of time. That leads to an almost endless set of metrics that can be produced, depending on the needs of the marketer. Some common metrics are:

- Average number of visits per day
- Number of page views per month
- Average visitor session length last month
- Number of hits for each hour of the day
- Paid search results for the most recent seven-day period

And so it goes—almost infinitely.

Choosing the Right Metrics

If there are an almost infinite number of metrics available, how does the marketer choose? There is only one way: matching marketing objectives to marketing metrics. An example of social media metrics matched to social media objectives was shown in Chapter 9. Figure 14.8 shows three typical marketing campaign objectives and some of the metrics that might be used to measure them. The objectives are SMART—that is, they are specific, measurable, achievable, and realistic, and they have a time frame.[18] The SMART rubric is one way of establishing managerially relevant objectives. Later in the chapter, we will present an example using key performance indicators (KPIs), which is another approach to establishing metrics that matter to business success.

Take, for example, the first objective listed; to increase the number of registrants for an email newsletter in the first quarter of the fiscal year. How many people come to the site and how many continue on to the registration page are clearly important. Where they come from (the referral source) is likely to reveal important data for planning future programs. Would you hypothesize that the longer a visitor remains on the site, the more likely he is to register for the newsletter before leaving? Probably so. Take a careful look at the drill-down to specifics about activity on the registration page. It is important to know how many registered as a percentage of total site visitors; that is essentially a conversion measure. It is equally important to know how many people started to register—they apparently were interested—but did not complete. Why did they abandon the registration page before completing it? The last box completed

Sample Campaign Objective	Corresponding Metrics
Increase Number of Email Captures by 5% in Q1	Number of unique visitors Referral source Length of visit Number of unique visitors to registration page • Number of completed registrations • Number of incomplete registrations • Last form box completed
Reactivate 10,000 Lapsed Customers in Q4	Number of emails sent • Reactivation message A/B Number of click-throughs A/B Bounces from reactivation landing page Number of incentive offers accepted A/B
Convert 2,000 Newsletter Recipients to New Customers in Last Six Months of FY	Number of emails sent Monday/Friday • Product offer A/B/C Number of click-throughs for each newsletter link Number of sales • By newsletter edition • By product Value of average sale by product Bounces from offer page A/B/C Heat map of offer page A/B/C

FIGURE **14.8** Matching Marketing Campaign Objectives to Program Metrics
Source: © Cengage Learning 2013

may suggest the reason. Did the following box ask for information that the potential registrant did not want to reveal? That is often the case. If many people terminated registration at that point, a redesign of the registration page is in order.

For both the reactivation objective and the conversion objective, it is obvious that alternatives are being tested—a simple A/B split for the reactivation objective, different incentives perhaps, and a three different product offers being tested in the conversion appeal.

There is a logic to each set of metrics beyond just arriving at a measure of campaign success. In each case, the metrics begin with a baseline of activity and drill down to the specifics that measure campaign success. In each case, the objectives guide the choice of metrics. *Mapping metrics to objectives, in a clear and explicit manner, is the only way to bring order to the mind-numbing array of metrics choices.*[19]

Using Google Analytics

There are many good metrics platforms; many of them offer at least part of their functionality for free. Why single out Google Analytics? In early 2011, it was estimated that over 12 million sites, including blogs and other platforms, used Google Analytics. By Alexa ranking, almost 50 percent of the top 1 million sites reported used the platform.[20] Is the heavy usage because Google Analytics is free? While that certainly does not hurt, Google Analytics provides robust analytics that many users need. Google gives good explanations of how to use it, and a small industry of marketing services firms and consultants offers assistance. A good piece of advice for most new users is to start small, with a free platform, and determine what is really needed in terms of metrics, reporting, and access by various individuals within the firm. It will be obvious when the business outgrows the free platform and needs a paid metrics provider.

As the Google Analytics product tour explains, the site owner has a dashboard and many options for accessing more detailed metrics. Figure 14.9 shows the **dashboard** in our example—this author's blog—for a specific month. (The time frame is a variable and the user can request comparisons; the current week to the same week last year, for example.) The overview on the dashboard shows some of the basic metrics we have just discussed (the number of visits and page views, for example). Most visitors appear to come for information on a particular subject because only a small number of them visit a second page. The pie chart says that most of them come from a search engine, the result of tagging and content designed for search (the good news). The bad news is that the bounce rate is high. Google defines "bounce rate" as the number of people who leave from the page on which they entered, further confirmation of the fact that few readers go on to a second page. Other metrics services define bounce rate by the amount of time readers remain on the page; for example 5 seconds or less would constitute a "bounce." This discrepancy is a warning that definitions vary between platforms, and the user must be certain of the interpretation of the metric.

In this example, by clicking-through on the bounce rate metric, I get a detailed chart that shows the bounces for this particular month by day, by week, or by month, as I choose. Google encourages me to use its Website Optimizer product[21] to test various content and lower the bounce rate. This feature would be very useful for someone who was trying to monetize a site or blog.

Continuing on through the dashboard, I see that the number of visitors do not vary much by day of the week. Most come from the United States and

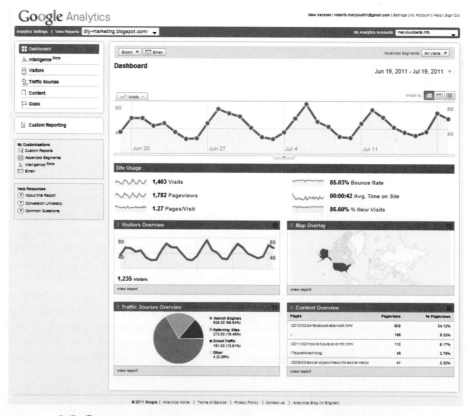

FIGURE **14.9** Dashboard for A Google Analytics Account

Source: Google, Inc., http://www.google.com/analytics.

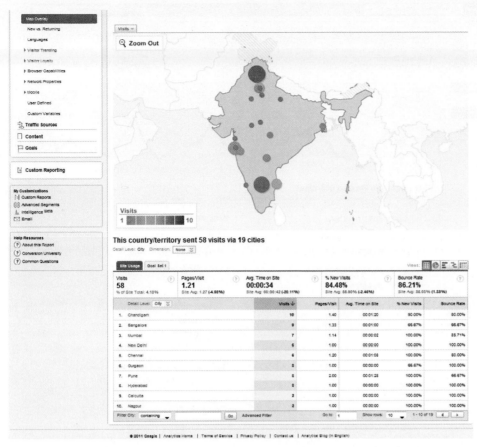

FIGURE **14.10** Blow-Up of Map Area on Analytics Dashboard

Source: Google, Inc., http://www.google.com/analytics.

Canada, although I have former students in Europe and Asia, especially India, who are loyal followers, as shown by the heat map in Figure 14.10. Another aspect of a metrics report is that just about any term or image is linked to more detailed data; the user simply clicks on the item to access it in greater detail.

The most skewed data on my dashboard summary is that more that 34 percent of the page views go to one post that is over a year old ("Do Facebook Ads Work?" from October 2010) and should not be getting that kind of traffic. I want to drill down in an attempt to find out why. First, I look at some other elements on the dashboard by simply clicking on the link or the image. When I click on the country map, I see that the Indian traffic comes from large cities, which makes sense because my former students there are working professionals.

At this point, I have looked at only overview (dashboard) data. Remember that I am focusing on a single question: why is there so much traffic on a single, older post? I have to visit pages with more detail (drill down) in order to try to understand the answer to that question. But unless I have a clear focus—an important marketing question—I will get lost in all the detailed data.

The process itself is like a detective story. The analyst follows clues, hoping to find an answer. Some of the clues lead to useful data; others are dead ends. The dead ends have been eliminated from this story, leaving only the data that aid in understanding the single marketing question. Still, it takes four more Google Analytics pages to understand the nature of this traffic (see Figure 14.11a–d). Each page has text beside it so you can match interpretation to data. While this creates a long figure, it is still important to review closely, and will be best understood after viewing the Google Analytics product tour (see Interactive Exercise 14.2). We start with one of the pages on the left navigation bar of the Dashboard, the Content page. From there we go to Traffic Sources and look at Search Engine referrals, and from there

Next, I click on Content > Top Content (left sidebar) in an effort to understand why the Facebook ads post is getting an inordinate amount of traffic. This page gives me a list of data, and while it is interesting that viewers spend over 3 minutes on this page as compared to only 42 seconds on the average for the site, the data do not indicate *how* they found the post.

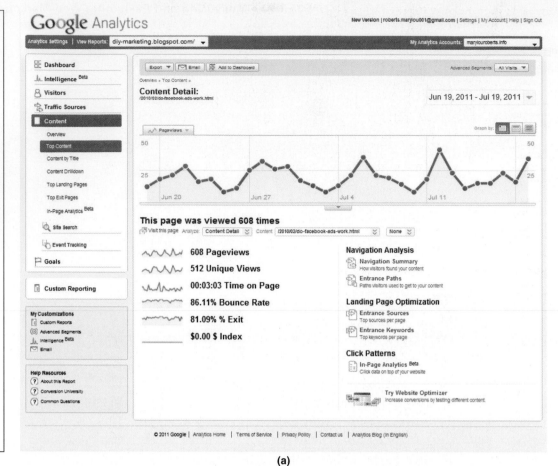

(a)

Next, I click to Traffic Sources > Search Engines, since the majority of the traffic is referred by search engines. Seven search engines sent traffic to the blog during that month, with Google far out in front.

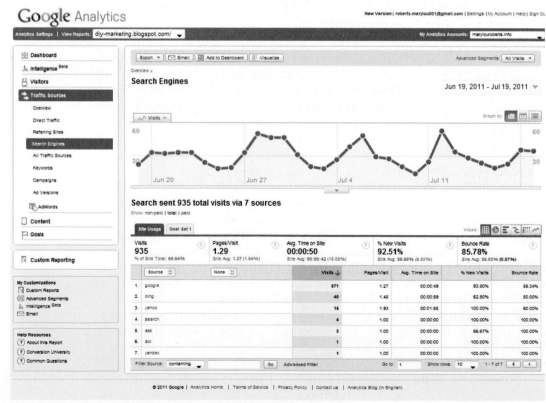

(b)

FIGURE **14.11** A Google Analytics Walkthrough

Source: Google, Inc., http://www.google.com/analytics.

Clicking on the Google link on that page leads to another page with the search terms (keywords) that led users to this post. The keywords have a lot of variations on the post title, "Do Facebook Ads Work?"

(c)

Finally, I check the In-Page Analytics screen that overlays data on the page itself. While it does not help me understand the traffic to that page, it does answer another question. There are two more posts on the effectiveness of Facebook ads that were added to this post later to try to take advantage of the traffic it gets. Those links are at the bottom of the post. The overlay data shows that 15 percent of the readers clicked-through to the later post on whether Facebook ads work while only 10 percent clicked-through on the targeting post. While the ratio makes sense, it is disappointing that so few of the readers were interested in the more recent data.

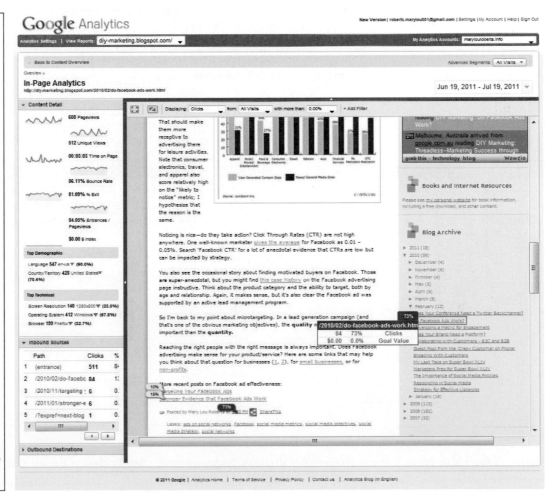

(d)

FIGURE **14.11** (*Continued*)

to Keywords. Finally, I look at an overlay called In-Page Analytics that shows click-throughs on the blog post I am researching. Each of these pages can be expanded into a number of subpages, as shown in Figure 14.11a, where the Content bar on the navigation pane is expanded to see a variety of content-related metrics options.

There is a little more to this story than simply writing a blog post for search visibility, although the keyword report (see Figure 14.11c) shows a number of different referrals. Note that these are not just "keywords." They are "search strings," the detailed phrases that searchers find more effective than single words. The search engines screen (see Figure 14.11b) shows that Ask.com referred three visitors to the page during that month. That is not much, but I do not see Ask.com on the referral pages for any of the other posts. A quick search on Ask.com reveals that this post has been linked to that site and usually shows up on the first screen when the question "Do Facebook Ads Work?" is entered on Ask.com. There are times when the marketer has to do some sleuthing above and beyond the metrics reports to understand what is occurring, and it is important to really understand the content, not just to look at a few numbers.

Segmentation and Conversion Metrics

Virtually all metrics platforms, including Google Analytics, provide the opportunity to segment data to uncover most and least profitable market segments and to provide data about what marketing approaches work best with the most profitable segments. The primary difference between segmentation of digital data and traditional market segmentation is that behavioral data is available to the Internet marketer. Conventional Internet marketing wisdom is that behavioral segmentation is more likely to reveal segment profitability, although conventional segmentation criteria like gender or geography may be necessary to understand how to reach segments.

With that in mind, let us look at a few of the types of segmentation and conversion analytics that are available from WebTrends, a metrics platform designed primarily for the enterprise user.

WebTrends offers what it calls "predefined segments" like new versus returning visitors and new versus repeat buyers. They are predefined because the coding and report formats have already been set up and are therefore quick and easy to use. The example that begins with Figure 14.12a focuses on new versus

Campaigns by New vs. Returning Visitors						Go To	Query
	New vs. Returning Visitors Campaign Drilldown	Visits ▼	Page Views ▼	Clickthroughs ▼	Orders ▼	Revenue ▼	Average Revenue per Order ▼
■1. ▽ Returning Visitors		47,273	489,783	38,129	2,761	$692,171.86	$250.70
	▽ Email Campaign	30,592	300,543	26,481	1,482	$364,707.08	$246.09
	▽ Zedesco	30,592	300,543	26,481	1,482	$364,707.08	$246.09
	▽ Free Shipping on Everything	18,816	183,543	16,408	935	$240,540.43	$257.26
	▷ Direct Email	18,816	183,543	16,408	935	$240,540.43	$257.26
	▷ Zedesco Anniversary Sale	8,454	83,686	7,085	400	$89,667.52	$224.17
	▷ Zedesco Take a Picture Week	3,322	33,314	2,988	147	$34,499.13	$234.69
	▷ Portal	11,595	129,037	7,900	877	$225,936.99	$257.62
	▷ Advertising Partner	4,627	52,301	3,325	354	$86,759.16	$245.09
	▷ Affiliate Network	679	7,902	423	48	$14,768.63	$307.68
■2. ▽ New Visitors		24,922	272,516	25,784	534	$77,292.93	$144.74
	▷ Portal	14,277	156,465	14,390	285	$40,080.32	$140.63
	▷ Advertising Partner	6,070	66,441	6,124	120	$17,640.43	$147.00
	▽ Email Campaign	3,793	40,500	4,442	113	$17,660.76	$156.29
	▽ Zedesco	3,793	40,500	4,442	113	$17,660.76	$156.29
	▽ Free Shipping on Everything	1,700	18,142	2,374	60	$10,545.85	$175.76
	▷ Direct Email	1,700	18,142	2,374	60	$10,545.85	$175.76
	▷ Zedesco Anniversary Sale	1,280	13,611	1,255	33	$4,667.00	$141.42
	▷ Zedesco Take a Picture Week	813	8,747	813	20	$2,447.93	$122.40
	▷ Affiliate Network	821	9,110	828	16	$1,911.40	$119.46
Total		-	762,299	63,913	3,295	$769,464.79	$233.52

items 1-2 of 2

(a)

FIGURE **14.12a** New Versus Returning Visitors Segmentation for Zedesco Email Campaign—Report Format

Source: Webtrends, http://product.webtrends.com/WRC/8.7/ResourceCenter/rc/library/pdf/hdig/How_Do_I_Use_WebTrends_for_Audience_Segmentation.pdf.

(b)

FIGURE **14.12b** New Versus Returning Visitors Segmentation for Web Pages—Overlay (WebTrends SmartView) Format

Source: Webtrends, http://product.webtrends.com/WRC/8.7/ResourceCenter/rc/library/pdf/hdig/How_Do_I_Use_WebTrends_for_Audience_Segmentation.pdf.

returning visitors. While you look at it, you should keep in mind that customers of sophisticated metrics platforms can develop customized segmentation approaches, using variables of their own choice, to meet virtually any marketing need.

Figure 14.12a shows the report for an email campaign carried out by hypothetical electronics supplier Zedesco. For returning visitors, it shows that average revenue per order—an important retailing metric—was highest for returning visitors who were referred by an affiliate network. While that is an important piece of information, the marketer must couple it with the fact that the affiliate network referred fewer visitors than any other referring source. The marketer can also see that the free shipping offer was more productive in terms of number of orders and average revenue per order than either of the other email campaigns. For the new visitor segment, the free shipping offer was also the most productive. It produced a higher average order size than affiliate referrals for the new visitors, which is different from the data for returning visitors. These data, and more that could be accessed by expanding the various lines on the report, provide the marketer with important information for planning future marketing programs of various types.

Figure 14.12b shows an overlay on the home page of Motorcycle Superstore for a one-month period. Beside the link to each of the site's product pages, the report shows the average revenue per order for each order placed after a click-through on that link. In terms of data, it shows a higher average order size for returning buyers than for new buyers. While this might be expected, it provides guidance for the marketer. In terms of metrics presented, New Buyer, Repeat Buyer, and month of September are all choices of the metrics user; there are other segmentations and time periods available. The tabs indicate that there are other data sets

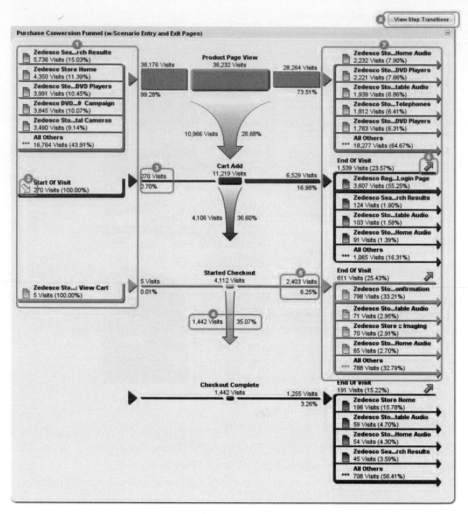

FIGURE **14.13** A Conversion Funnel Showing Paths Through the Website

Source: Webtrends, http://product.webtrends.com/WRC/8.7/ResourceCenter/rc/library/pdf/aug/Tracking_Conversion_and_Abandonment_through_Scenario_Analysis.pdf.

available for this site, so once again consider the huge number of metrics that can be chosen when evaluating the most profitable elements of a website.

As a final perspective on the analytics available from server log data, consider the conversion funnel in Figure 14.13. This is a graphic representation, complete with data, of the conversion concept discussed in Chapter 10. The steps in the funnel are user defined, that is, the user specifies which behaviors to show including, for example, viewing a product page and adding an item to the shopping cart.

The left pane shows the point at which visitors entered the process. Most came from sources like search or from various other pages in the site. The right pane shows when they left the process: many moved on to other pages in the site, a considerable number ended their visit instead of adding an item to their cart, and some started the checkout process but did not complete it. About 3 percent did complete a transaction (clicking checkout complete at the bottom of the figure), but what goes on in between is even more informative to the marketer.

Take just one path as an example:

- 38,232 visitors viewed the product page
  - 10,966 added something to their shopping carts
  - 28,264 visitors went somewhere else—many of them went to another Zedesco page; over 18,000 went to other sites

- Of those who added something to their shopping carts, 4,106 started the checkout process
  - 6,529 did not start checkout and went somewhere else—most went to another Zedesco page; 1,539 ended their visit by exiting the Zedesco site

Why did they leave without making a purchase? What can the marketer do to keep them on the site and persuade them to complete a purchase? These are the kind of questions marketers should be asking. If visitors went to another Zedesco page and purchased something there, then it appears they found what they were looking for and metrics provided the answer. If visitors added something to their shopping carts but exited after seeing the shipping charges (more detail than is on this chart, but available from metrics), then shipping charges seem to be a problem. What can the marketer do about that? If people simply looked at the product page and then left the site, where did they go (also available from another metrics report)? If they left and went to a competitor site, then they apparently did not like what they saw on the Zedesco site—which could suggest a product or maybe a pricing problem that should concern the marketer. If they left and went back to search, they did not find the product they were looking for and that may be of less concern to the marketer.

This path analysis and many other views can be very helpful to the marketer trying to understand what is happening on the website. The metrics do not answer all the questions. Sometimes that will require looking at other metrics, as just suggested. Sometimes, it may suggest that marketing research is needed, for example, to find if the product is not viewed as satisfactory by many potential customers. Whatever the situation, *metrics point the way*.

As we move on, remember that this is only a small sample of the metrics from server log data that is available to marketers. Even so, different perspectives may be gained by looking at customer panel data.

Metrics Based on Panel Data

Clickstream data based on server request logs and tagged web pages provides metrics for a single website's operations and traffic. On the other hand, panel data is obtained from the clickstreams of carefully selected panels of Internet users, and that permits comparisons of activity across websites. The use of panel data also allows the accumulation of background demographic, lifestyle, and activity data from panel members.

Nielsen is perhaps the best-known name in this space because it is descended from Nielsen Media Research, the source of the familiar television ratings. comScore was created specifically to measure Internet trends. Both use careful scientific sampling methodology to create their panels. However, there are differences in their approaches,[22,23] but the general process is the same.

Households are contacted using established random sampling techniques from the marketing research industry. Once an Internet user has agreed to become a panel member, a special piece of Java-based software is installed on his computer to record each click. This is similar in concept to the recording devices that collect television rating data. Not only does it give statistically representative data from a relatively small sample, it also creates a panel that is available for custom research studies. For example, if a client wants to study some aspect of senior citizens' use of the Internet that is not covered by commercially available reports, she may turn to a firm like Nielsen or comScore that maintains a user panel. The owner of the panel can identify members based on criteria supplied by the client, recruit them to participate in a special research project, and provide the custom data and usually a report to the client. This kind of segment-based data collection is prohibitively expensive except in a panel environment. Panels also permit longitudinal studies that provide trend data over time.

Collecting data about Internet use, however, faces a particular issue that is not found in the traditional marketing research environment. People use the

Internet at work for both work and personal purposes. Measurement of Internet traffic is not complete without data collected in the workplace. Collecting personal user activity in the workplace is difficult, however. Workers do not want their bosses to know that they are using the business network for personal activity. Network managers do not want outside software on their networks. Consequently, the panel firms have difficulty getting cooperation to track panel member activity at work and are not transparent about how they do it and how large their "at-work" samples actually are.

There are numerous panel metrics firms in addition to Nielsen and comScore. In general, they recruit convenience samples and base their metrics on those. The samples can be quite large, but they are not random nor are they necessarily statistically representative. They do, however, offer free or low-cost access to small businesses and individual users that is not available from the larger panel firms.

Two examples illustrate the possibilities. Quantcast specializes in audience measurement for websites. Users can obtain the profile for an individual site, like the profile for entertainment site Gawker shown in Figure 14.14. The profile includes traffic data for various geographic locales and selected time periods. It also provides demographic data and a section (not shown) called "Audience Also Likes." This shows affinity—similarity—data. In this case, users of Gawker also like to visit technology, auto, and gaming sites. For Gawker, because it is a heavily trafficked site, Quantcast is able to estimate what percentage of the traffic is made up of regular visitors, and how much of the access is from work and how much is from home.

Compete is a metrics supplier that emphasizes traffic data. Data freely available on their website show monthly traffic as measured by unique visitors, site

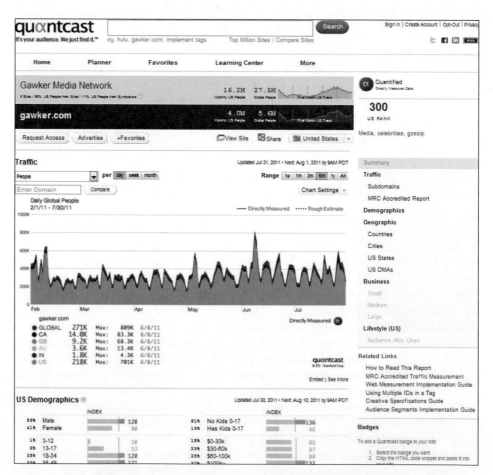

FIGURE **14.14** Site Profile of the Gawker Media Network

Source: Quantcast, http://www.quantcast.com/gawker.com, accessed August 1, 2011.

> **INTERACTIVE EXERCISE 14.3** | **Measuring Traffic**
>
> Visit Quantcast.com or Compete.com and obtain traffic data for one or more sites that interest you. Better yet, visit both and compare the data you get from the two different platforms and panels.
>
> Quantcast has a video that explains its service at http://bit.ly/u7xk0f.
>
> Compete has an overview of its Compete Pro product that explains its features at http://compete.com.
>
> Why would a business choose to use either or both of these services?

rank by unique visitors, and rank as compared to leading competitors. Depending on the amount of data Compete has, the visitor may be able to see other sites visited by this audience and top keywords. Compete offers more detailed data, including competitive data, to paid subscribers.[24]

Note that both these panel-based metrics sites also offer a huge amount of detailed data, allowing the marketer to drill down to the specifics he is interested in. They also offer many choices of time frame and report configurations, once again emphasizing how many metrics are available and the care that must be taken to select the right ones to meet stated marketing objectives. Traffic data is available from the firm's own analytics, but only third-party panel data can provide traffic and audience data about competitors.

How to Choose the Right Metrics

Throughout the chapter, we have emphasized the almost infinite number of Internet metrics available to the marketer and both the difficulty and the importance of choosing the right ones. One of the undisputed authorities on web metrics is Avinash Kaushik, who is Google's Digital Marketing Evangelist and founder of a firm that offers certification in web analytics. In April, 2010, he wrote a blog post called "Metrics 101" that is worth reading in its entirety. In it, he distinguishes between a metric, which is simply a number, and a KPI (key performance indicator), which is "a metric that helps you understand how you are doing against your objectives." There are more complex definitions of both concepts, but none that are more helpful to marketers who are attempting to make sense of the metrics issue.

The table in Figure 14.15 is the work of one of the metrics certification students. He focused on a presumably hypothetical bike company. The framework included high-level business objectives, marketing goals, the KPIs that will be reported, and the numerical target for each KPI. The implication is that the KPIs are the result of a conscious decision by management about what data are essential to the management of the business.

Kaushik's comment on the student's work points out another advantage of this type of framework:

> I really liked Matt's presentation for his motor bike company analysis. In less than half a page one could see the complete picture of what the business was solving for and what the expectations were.
>
> Particularly clever I thought was his inclusion of the segmentation in his framework presentation. At a glance for the most important goal for the quarter (build a robust customer database for future marketing) you can see how their campaign strategy worked.[25]

In other words, the choice of KPIs sets a long-term framework for management in controlling the effectiveness of, in this case, the marketing operation. All the KPIs are important, but one can be singled out for emphasis in one fiscal time period. In this example, Kaushik implies that building the customer database by

Bike Company X Web Analytics Framework							
1 **Business Objective**		**2** **Goal**		**3** **KPI**		**4** **KPI Target**	
Sell Bike Parts		More sales		Monthly revenue		$15,000/mo	
		Increase unique visits		Monthly unique visitors		13,000	
		Make a profit		Profit margin/sale		40%	
Effective Marketing		CRM–build a customer database		Number of new registrations/mo		300/mo	
Build Goodwill		Draw qualified customers		Conversion rate		3%	
		Serve as resource to riding community		Number of page views of resource pages		1500/mo	

5 Segmented KPI: (example) number of new registrations/mo		
Total Reg Goal = 300	**Result = 332 (110% of Goal)**	**Percent**
Paid Search	223	67%
Organic Search	67	20%
Referrals	17	5%
Direct	25	8%

FIGURE **14.15** Web Analytics Template

Source: Figure: Bike Company X Web Analytics Framework by Matt Smedley, appearing on Occam's Razor by Avinash Kaushik. Reprinted with permission.

increasing the number of new registrants was the key focus for the chosen time period. Consequently, the analyst drilled down into the segmentation figure to find out where the most registrants came from. The fact that paid search lead by a huge margin points the way to future strategy.

Kaushik makes another important point in his blog post, "In aggregate almost all data is useless (like # of Visits)."[26] The actionable data is found by drilling down—to where the visits came from or to the source of the new registrants, for example. *Metrics—numbers—alone do not meet marketing and management needs. Only when the metrics are carefully chosen and reported in sufficient detail to guide strategic choices are business needs met.*

The New Issues—Social Media and Mobile Metrics

Most of the material in this chapter assumes metrics from websites and online marketing campaigns—clickstream data. That is the easiest data to collect, but it is not the only data of importance to marketers. For several years, metrics suppliers have been working to integrate other communications channels, like direct mail and retail store interactions, into their platforms. It is now possible to include data from offline channels in metrics dashboards in order to get a more complete picture of customer activity. As that integration has been accomplished, other challenges have arisen.

Social networks represent one of those challenges. Social media metrics were discussed in Chapter 9 because they are unique to the social media space. Choosing the most important ones and integrating them into the overall metrics picture is important, and there is a long way to go before marketers can declare success on that front. Leading marketers and metrics providers are making progress, as suggested by the Papa Gino's example at the beginning of the chapter.

Mobile is the other exploding channel, to be discussed in Chapter 16. Mobile clearly represents another channel that marketers need to understand and integrate into their view of customer activity. While that also will be a challenge, there is one piece of good news here. Mobile users are accessing email, websites, and social networks and interacting with apps. The metrics for those activities already exist. A recent study by Forrester Research for WebTrends[27] indicates that key issues in the mobile marketing environment include developing a clear strategy, developing specific objectives, and selecting the right measures to justify ROI. That should sound familiar: It is exactly the challenge online marketers have faced from the beginning, and businesses with advanced understanding of online metrics should also be able to grapple successfully with mobile metrics. However, that level of success is currently not being achieved by many online marketers.

Marketers' Confidence in Their Metrics

At the beginning of the chapter, we pointed out that many marketers are not confident that their metrics are well chosen, although they are using various standard metrics. A recent survey conducted by Deloitte Consulting and Openet for the CMO Council makes the point in a slightly different way.[28] Marketing Charts reported that the study found that only one in five marketers rated their capabilities and the metrics that measured them as excellent or good (see Figure 14.16). That is not a very reassuring judgment on the part of people managing online marketing activities.

Why is their view so negative? The Forbes study referenced earlier in the chapter suggests some reasons. According to the report:

> While retention and acquisition are the top online marketing priorities of survey respondents, many indicated they were challenged to understand the influence of their campaigns beyond the basic key performance indicators (KPIs) of acquisition and conversion.[29]

Looking carefully at the data in Figure 14.17, we see that marketers want to understand the influence of each interaction with the customer, not just the acquisition or retention outcome. That implies they want to identify each stage in the conversion funnel, for example. The second-most important challenge is the need to understand the impact of all online interactions, whatever the channel

Online Marketers' Performance Capabilities, July 2011
(% of respondents)

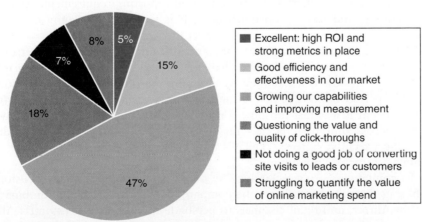

- Excellent: high ROI and strong metrics in place
- Good efficiency and effectiveness in our market
- Growing our capabilities and improving measurement
- Questioning the value and quality of click-throughs
- Not doing a good job of converting site visits to leads or customers
- Struggling to quantify the value of online marketing spend

5%, 15%, 47%, 18%, 7%, 8%

FIGURE **14.16** Online Marketers Rate Performance Capabilities

Source: Online Marketers' Performance Capabilities, July 2011. © 2007–2012 Watershed Publishing. All rights reserved. Reprinted with permission.

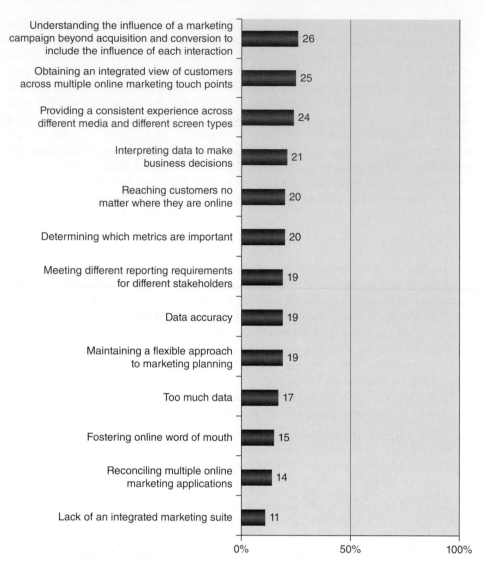

FIGURE **14.17** Key Online Marketing Challenges

Source: Forbes, "Bringing 20/20 Foresight to Marketing," May 2011, from Coremetrics, an IBM company. Courtesy of the IBM Corporation.

or device. Other metrics challenges include interpreting data for marketing action, identifying important metrics, meeting different reporting requirements, ensuring data accuracy, and having too much data. It is striking how many of the top challenges reported by these marketers reflect metrics issues.

These challenges, important as they are, still do not get to the heart of the online metrics matter. The ultimate challenge is understanding all buying influences and processes, whether they occur online or offline, and simultaneously or over a period of time. One consumer goods executive quoted in the study points out that it was just too time-consuming and expensive to capture buying patterns across multiple channels for the buying cycle of a specific product. A retailing executive agrees; "Today's multichannel consumer is neither offline or online," he said, "but all-line."[30]

His company is using technology by obtaining a complete view of customer purchasing activity. That allows the company to use the optimum combination of online, direct, and retail channels to persuade the individual customer. All of this comes from careful attention to metrics at each stage, over each channel, of the customer buying process. That is a tall order, but it is the metrics challenge for marketers going forward.

The ability to track and measure visitor activities is one of the unique capabilities of the web. If marketers are not using appropriate traffic, audience, and campaign metrics, they are missing out on a major benefit conferred by the Internet. However, the number of metrics is enormous and choosing the right ones and applying them to marketing decision making are huge challenges.

There are two different perspectives on the effectiveness of websites and Internet marketing programs. The user perspective is concerned with the usability of the website itself, which in turn leads to a satisfying user experience. Usability testing techniques are well established and should be made an integral part of the site development process. With planning, this can be done without massive expenditures of either time or money. Testing should also be done on established sites when the quantitative site metrics suggest there may be usability problems.

There are two basic types of data that chronicle Internet activity—data taken from website server logs and panel data taken from the computers of users themselves. Site performance metrics, obtained from server logs, are important to the technicians whose job is to keep the site working smoothly but have little direct relevance for marketers. Marketers focus on traffic, audience, and campaign metrics in order to provide information about site visitors and to measure marketing campaign effectiveness. These metrics are obtained from the appropriate combination of server request logs, tagged web pages, and cookies placed on user computers. Internet enterprises large and small usually outsource the collection and reporting of these metrics to marketing services firms that have the specialized platforms and consulting expertise required for this demanding endeavor.

The use of traffic, audience, and campaign metrics to gauge effectiveness presupposes that marketers have clear marketing objectives. These objectives may range from provision of information to customer service to sale of products. When the objectives are transactional in nature, behavioral measures in the form of traffic and audience metrics are needed. When there are branding objectives, marketing research may be required to measure the attitudinal variables that are used to assess the effectiveness of branding efforts, both online and offline.

Whether the marketer relies on SMART marketing objectives or the business has identified key performance indicators, mapping metrics to objectives is a key task. Then the marketing analyst must uncover the detailed metrics that point the way to marketing planning and strategy decisions.

All these must be done in a multichannel environment in which customers interact with various marketing touchpoints over a buying cycle that can last for days or weeks or even longer. That defines the challenge for both the analyst and the user of Internet marketing metrics.

SUMMARY

DISCUSSION QUESTIONS

1. The term "metrics" is commonly used by Internet marketers. Explain your understanding of the meaning of the term.
2. True or False: Internet marketers need to decide whether they will conduct measurement from a visitor usability perspective or from a traffic and audience measurement perspective. Defend your answer.
3. At what point in the site development or redevelopment process should usability testing be done?
4. The term "hit counter" implies that all this technology can do is to measure the number of people who enter a site. Based on the discussion in this chapter, is that an accurate perception? Why or why not?
5. Describe the similarities and differences between server request logs and panel data. Which do you think is most useful?
6. True or False: The webmaster and the marketer use the same metrics when assessing website effectiveness.
7. What are the uses of server log data, cookies, and tagged pages in the collection of website effectiveness data?

8. What are some of the specific metrics that measure Internet traffic, audiences, and campaigns? Which ones do you think are most important?

9. What are some of the special advantages of user panel data?

10. How should the marketer go about choosing the right metrics to measure website or campaign effectiveness?

11. What are SMART objectives?

12. What is the meaning and importance of the term "KPI"?

13. What are some of the main challenges facing the web metrics discipline at present?

14. Do you believe that most commercial websites are using metrics to improve customer experience and enhance marketing effectiveness? Do you have any personal experiences that support your view?

INTERNET EXERCISES

1. Internet Career Builder Exercise

   a. The entry-level jobs in metrics, and some of the ones that require experience, invariably include the term "analyst."

      Internet marketing analyst

      Search marketing analyst

      Social media marketing analyst

      Mobile marketing analyst

      You can substitute the area of Internet marketing you are interested in and likely find analyst jobs posted in that field. Advanced positions include:

      Web analytics director

      Web analytics manager

      and many more

   b. Select a metrics job from the given list or from your own search. Outline the responsibilities of that position. You may find it useful to locate job postings on the web in order to understand the job requirements.

   c. Outline knowledge and experience from classes, internships, full or part-time jobs, and volunteer work that prepare you for this specific position.

   d. Prepare five questions you could ask at a job interview. The questions should exhibit your understanding of the position requirements without lecturing the interviewer about what she already knows.

   e. Update your VisualCV® or LinkedIn Profile with this information.

2. Conduct a partial usability analysis of your school's website. Describe two tasks that you believe the target audience wants to perform on the site. Go to the site, and attempt to perform both tasks. Record your experience for each, noting the time it took to perform each task. What recommendations would you make to the webmaster of the site based on your test?

3. Using one of the sites you are tracking, prepare a careful summary of the objectives you believe that site has. In doing so, keep in mind that the objectives of the site may be a subset of the marketing and business objectives of the organization. When you are satisfied that the set of objectives is complete, list the corresponding metric or metrics that would be needed to measure each objective. Present this information in a table that shows objectives and the corresponding metrics.

4. Using a website with which you are familiar, develop a scenario that tells the story of how one user segment would behave on a visit to the site. When you are satisfied that your scenario represents behavior of one segment adequately, identify the metrics that would be useful in ascertaining if the segment's needs are being met and if the customer experience for this segment is satisfactory.

NOTES

1. http://www-01.ibm.com/software/success/cssdb.nsf/CS/STRD8HVM5F?OpenDocument&Site=cognos&cty=en_us.

2. http://media.eloqua.com/documents/eloqua_eBook_chapter9_final.pdf.

3. See "Chapter 10, Testing Direct Marketing Programs," in Mary Lou Roberts and Paul D. Berger, *Direct Marketing Management*, 2nd ed. available for free download at www.marylouroberts.info for a detailed description of the direct marketing testing process.

4. http://www.useit.com/papers/sun/usabilitytest.html.

5. Jakob Nielsen, Rolf Molich, Carolyn Snyder, and Susan Farrell, 2001, *E-Commerce User Experience* (Freemont, CA: Norman Group), p. 337.

6. The formula used is $N(1(1 - L)^n)$ where N is the total number of usability problems, L is the proportion of usability problems found by testing a single user, and n is the number of users tested. "Why You Only Need to Test with 5 Users," http://www.useit.com/alertbox/20000319.html.

7. "Cost of User Testing a Website," http://www.useit.com/alertbox/980503.html.

8. http://www.thedeal.com/newsweekly/dealmaker. php?slideshow=86&slide=551.

9. http://blogs.wsj.com/digits/2010/04/06/fresh-direct-goes-to-greenwich.

10. http://www.unica.com/documents/us/Unica_CaseStudy_FreshDirect_072109.pdf.

11. http://www.alertsite.com/index.shtml.

12. Richard Hoy, "Traffic Analysis Solutions for Small Business: Part 1," June 9, 2000, http://www.clickz.com.

13. See a sample server log file at http://www.jafsoft.com/searchengines/log_sample.html.

14. http://www.comscore.com/About_comScore/Methodology.

15. http://www.nielsen.com/us/en/measurement/online-measurement.html.

16. http://www.opentracker.net/article/hits-or-pageviews#.

17. http://www.clickz.com/clickz/column/1713395/ajax-counting-nightmares.

18. http://www.marketingteacher.com/lesson-store/lesson-objectives.html.

19. See http://www.marketo.com/library/Social-Media-Plan-Template.pdf for a sample social media marketing plan with program objectives for various media and the corresponding metrics. The sample is B2B but the principles are universal.

20. http://www.quora.com/How-many-users-or-websites-are-using-Google-Analytics.

21. http://www.google.com/websiteoptimizer.

22. http://www.comscore.com/About_comScore/Methodology.

23. http://www.com/us/en/measurement/online-measurement.html.

24. http://compete.com.

25. http://www.kaushik.net/avinash/web-analytics-101-definitions-goals-metrics-kpis-dimensions-targets.

26. Ibid.

27. http://www.webtrends.com/~/media/Webtrends_Mobile_Measurement_whitepaper.pdf.

28. Download the executive summary from this page http://www.cmocouncil.org/resources/forms/outlook-report/index.php?id=207.

29. http://www.forbes.com/forbesinsights/bringing_foresight_to_marketing/index.html, p. 8.

30. Ibid.

CHAPTER 15

Social and Regulatory Issues: Privacy, Security, and Intellectual Property

Chapter Outline

The Role of Trust in Facilitating Internet Activity

Data Protection and Privacy on the Internet
Consumer Attitudes toward the Privacy of Their Information
Regulation of Children's Privacy Issues
Regulation of Privacy in the Financial Services Sector
Regulation of Privacy in the Health Care Sector
Privacy Issues Going Forward
Response of U.S. Business to Privacy Concerns
The Fair Information Practices Principles
Privacy Organizations and Seals
Privacy Regulation in Various Internet-Using Countries

Consumer Data Security Breaches
Consumer Knowledge about Internet Security
Internet Security Threats

Protection of Intellectual Property in the Digital Age
What Is Intellectual Property?
The Digital Millennium Copyright Act
Publishing under Creative Commons

SUMMARY
DISCUSSION QUESTIONS
INTERNET EXERCISES
NOTES

Key Terms

LEARNING OBJECTIVES

By the time you complete this chapter, you will be able to:

- Discuss trust as a facilitator of Internet activity.

- List some of the concerns consumers have about the privacy of their personally identifiable information.

- Discuss the privacy issues that are especially applicable to users of social networks.

- Identify consumer concerns about privacy and security in the mobile space.

- Describe privacy protection efforts that affect children, financial, and health data.

- Identify actions being taken by businesses to protect personally identifiable information.

- Identify the Fair Information Practices Principles.

- Discuss self-regulation and regulatory action to protect privacy in countries other than the United States.

- Explain the significance of data breaches and other threats to the security of consumer data.

- Discuss significant issues related to the protection of intellectual property on the Internet.

From the origin of the Internet as a project sponsored by the U.S. Department of Defense to its current status as a global network, the relationships among Internet users, governmental agencies, and the public at large have often been strained. The Internet boasts a tradition of free speech and a "caveat emptor" attitude toward information and activities that take place there. However, as the Internet has evolved into a mass medium with users of all ages and degrees of technological sophistication, there has been greater concern over protection of users. Public policy makers all over the world have evidenced this concern.

There are a variety of consumer protection issues that have either arisen or become more urgent because of the Internet. This chapter will examine three key issues: the privacy of **PII (personally identifiable information)**, the security of data and transactions, and the protection of intellectual property on the Internet. It will consider customer attitudes and behaviors with respect to privacy and security issues. It will also consider both corporate and governmental reactions to the various issues.

The ability of business and government to assure citizens that their data are safe and being used properly affects the trust people have in those institutions. That is especially true on the Internet, where consumer power and access to information has reached an all time high.[1] We should therefore begin by briefly considering the importance and role of trust as a facilitator of Internet use and ecommerce activity.

The Role of Trust in Facilitating Internet Activity

The Edelman public relations firm conducts an annual study of trust in institutions in various countries. The 2011 study was conducted among a sample of "Informed Publics," a very specific subset of the population who are college-educated, upper income, media savvy consumers.[2] Each year Edelman has found differences, some of them substantial, among countries in the degree to which they trusted business, government, the media, and nongovernmental organizations (NGOs) to do the right thing. Looking at the trend over time in the United States (see Figure 15.1a), it is clear that the global financial crisis that began in 2008 damaged trust in all institutions studied. However, over time, the pattern remains the same: NGOs are the most trusted and media is at or near the bottom. Business retains a substantial level of trust among the public.

Businesses know that trust is important. What creates it? The most important factors at present according to Figure 15.1b are quality of product, transparency, projecting a trustworthy image, and good treatment of employees. Looking at other questions in the study, the Edelman report points a high level of agreement with the statement that "corporations should create shareholder value in a way that aligns with society's interests, even if that means sacrificing shareholder value." That notion is consistent with Figure 15.1b, which shows the public regards being a good corporate citizen as more important than financial returns to shareholders.

Overall conclusions reached by the 2011 Trust Barometer study are

- Businesses must align their mission and operations with the social good.
- The current media landscape is characterized by skepticism and that requires organizations to employ multiple voices (although CEOs were

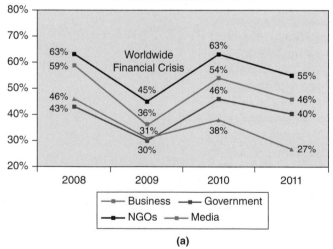

In U.S., 2011 Decline Mirrors 2008–2009 Drop Only Country to See Across-the-Board Fall

Trust in Institutions: 2008–2011

(a)

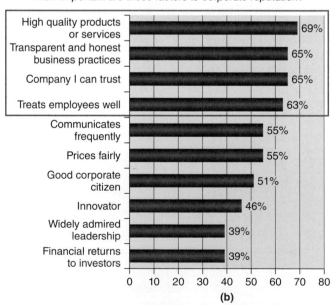

What Matters for Corporate Reputation: Quality, Transparency, Trust, Employee Welfare Most Important

How important are these factors to corporate reputation?

High quality products or services	69%
Transparent and honest business practices	65%
Company I can trust	65%
Treats employees well	63%
Communicates frequently	55%
Prices fairly	55%
Good corporate citizen	51%
Innovator	46%
Widely admired leadership	39%
Financial returns to investors	39%

(b)

FIGURE **15.1** (a) Trust in Institutions, U.S. Sample (Informed Publics Ages 25-64) (b) Importance of Trust in Corporate Reputation, 23-Country Global Sample (Informed Publics Ages 25-64)

Source: Results come from the report "2011 Edelman Trust Barometer Findings," pp. 11, 16. Copyright © 2011 Edelman. All rights reserved. Reprinted with permission.

found to be especially influential) and to use multiple communications channels.

- Corporations must respond to expectations for authority and accountability.
- Trust is a "protective agent," which conveys tangible benefits, while lack of trust is hard to change.[3]

There is evidence that the degree of trust consumers have in the Internet in general and in specific brands does influence their behavior. Milne and Culnan, in a study of who reads privacy policies, list privacy actions taken by readers after they read privacy policies:

- 87 percent refused to give information to a website because it was too personal or unnecessary.
- 84 percent asked to have their name and address removed from marketing lists.
- 81 percent asked a website not to share name or personal information with other companies.
- 66 percent decided not to use a website or to purchase because they were unsure of how personal information would be used.
- 32 percent set their browser to reject cookies.
- 32 percent supplied incorrect information to a website when asked to register.[4]

People are willing to take various actions to protect their PII. Those actions sometimes seem counter to the data needs of marketers.

On the other hand, writing about "The Trust Imperative," MIT marketing professor Glen Urban points out that there are positive advantages in building trust in the customer base. He identifies those advantages as

- *Reduced customer acquisition cost.* He argues that the advertising of trusted brands will receive greater attention. In addition, customers will be more loyal to trusted companies, reducing their need to acquire large numbers of new customers to replace defecting ones.
- *Higher profit margins.* Customers are willing to pay a premium for products or services from a trusted supplier.
- *Growth.* Trusted companies will be more successful in selling more to their existing customers and in converting visitors to customers.
- *Long-term competitive advantage.* A trusted brand and strong relationships based on understanding of customer needs will contribute to long-term success.[5]

Accenture, which has a page devoted to privacy and trust,[6] agrees, saying that "If companies are to use today's revolutionary technologies effectively to fuel economic growth, they must meet the privacy challenge head-on. Today, privacy and trust have become critical aspects of any business imperative."[7] Accenture identifies the dimensions of trust as

- *Security.* The protection of personal information against misuse or theft.
- *Data control.* The consumer has control over who has access to PII and when as well as what they are permitted to do with it.
- *Personal access.* The consumer has control over who can contact her and how.
- *Benefit.* The uses of the data provide value to the consumer as well as to the business.

Experts agree that trust can only be built, action by action, over a period of time. That emphasizes Professor Urban's contention that trust can provide long-term competitive advantage. That advantage would accrue to companies who pay immediate attention to the importance of being a trusted entity in both B2C and B2B markets. He adds that, "Trust is hard to earn—and easy to lose."[8]

INTERACTIVE EXERCISE 15.1   Trust in Social Media

Chris Brogan has a great deal to say about how to develop trust through blogging and other social media activities. Read a summary and view the interview video at http://bit.ly/tCNZ9H.

The rise of social media has added another dimension to the issue of trust in businesses and their brands. Social media guru Chris Brogan has written a book called *Trust Agents* and speaks often about the importance of trust issues to businesses and their brands. He defines a trust agent as someone who is working to put a human face on a business. In an interview with HubSpot he said:

> The trust agent is the kind of person who, inside an organization, is translating that organization's presence on the web, how to be human at a distance. The idea is that we have all this marketing speak, PR speak, etc. What a trust agent is, is somebody that you get the feeling that you're doing business with that company through that person.[9]

With an understanding of the importance of trust and the role of data protection and privacy in creating it, we can turn to an examination of the state of data privacy in the United States and globally.

Data Protection and Privacy on the Internet

Writing in the *Journal of Interactive Marketing*, Harvard professor John Deighton points to the increasing vulnerability consumers feel as a result of the way business is done on the Internet. According to Deighton:

> In the physical world, they (consumers) can choose to be anonymous, trading cash for goods and moving on with no trace of their identity left behind. When they trade in cyberspace, anonymity is not an option. They have to say who they are, how to get back to them, and what their credit record is worth, or the transaction falls apart. They will give this information only if they are confident that it will not be used against them. If they are not sure of that, they know full well that there are many other ways to do business, and they will cast their vote to defer the arrival of the digital age.
>
> Deeper insight into the human need for privacy, then, is perhaps as important to the blossoming of the interactive marketing industry as any single factor. We need to understand why so often people want to be let alone, and why sometimes they do not. Marketing fundamentally, of course, is about meeting customer needs. In the matter of privacy, what are the needs that are met and not met?[10]

In this section, we examine what is known about consumer privacy concerns in the United States and other Internet economies, and what responses have been made by business and regulatory agencies in the United States and the European Union (EU).

Consumer Attitudes toward the Privacy of Their Information

There have been studies of consumer attitudes about the privacy of personal information since the beginning of the Internet. In general, they have shown that consumers are concerned about the privacy of their PII, although their willingness to take action to protect it varies with issues and time. The 2010 Ponemon Institute study of trusted brands makes the following points:

- Consumers perceive loss of control of personal information. Only 41 percent feel in control and that percentage has been dropping consistently since 2006.
- Identity theft is a major concern. Fifty-nine percent of respondents cited identity theft as a major factor in decreasing trust of brands while 50 percent said that occurrence of a data breach was important.

- Privacy protection features contributed to brand trust. Sixty percent of respondents looked for substantial security protections while 53 percent cited accurate data collection and use. They also had a positive view on limits to the collection of PII and online anonymity.[11]

These general findings are important, but it is clear that three specific issues dominated the discussion of consumer data privacy by 2011. These issues are a long-held concern about being tracked online, and newer concerns related to use of social networks and mobile technologies.[12]

Behavioral Tracking

In 2008, Harris Interactive conducted a poll designed by privacy expert Dr. Alan Westin. In general, it found about 60 percent of respondents to be "uncomfortable" when major portals used information about online activities to target ads or tailor content based on a person's hobbies or interests. A quarter of the respondents were "not at all" comfortable with this practice. Only 7 percent were "very comfortable," while 34 percent were "somewhat comfortable."

The researchers then introduced four possible data safeguards based on 2007 Federal Trade Commission (FTC) recommendations. The issues covered were consumer control of their data; security and limited retention of data; express consent for changes in privacy policies; and special protection for sensitive data including data about children, sexual orientation, and health.[13] (The FTC issued revisions in 2009 that maintained these four principles but loosened the application to anonymous user data and contextual advertising.)[14]

Knowledge about the privacy safeguards caused a majority of the respondents (55 percent) to be more comfortable with corporate use of information about their online activities to target advertising or customize website content. Few, only 9 percent, were "very comfortable" while 19 percent were "not at all comfortable." However, both the "very" and the "not at all" responses were only slightly changed by the provision of knowledge, suggesting that respondents at both extremes of the scale were less likely to change their positions than those in the middle.

Differences were seen between the generations in both sets of data. Echo Boomers (aged 18 to 31) and GenXers (32 to 43) were initially more favorable to data use than were Baby Boomers (44 to 62) and Matures (63 and over). After they read the privacy safeguards, all age segments became more favorable, but a majority of Matures still remained opposed to these uses of PII.

The changes were not large; Echo Boomers increased their favorability from 49 to 62 percent, for example. Dr. Westin commented on the fact that the privacy safeguards did not cause a greater change saying:

> The failure of a larger percentage of respondents to express comfort after four privacy policies were specified may have two bases—concerns that web-companies would actually follow voluntary guidelines, even if they espoused them, and the absence of any regulatory or enforcement mechanism in the privacy policy steps outlined in the question.[15]

A more recent poll by the Gallup organization for *USA Today* presents a similar picture. Figure 15.2a indicates that a majority of Internet users are opposed to ad targeting based on online activity data, and this does not change much when it is pointed out that the advertising helps provide free access to content. Figure 15.2b suggests explicit user control and still only 47 percent of users would accept targeted advertising from sites they choose, with 37 percent preferring to accept no targeted ads. Again, age differences are seen with opposition to targeted advertising increasing with age. It might not be surprising that the highest percentage of users who would allow targeted advertising is seen at the lowest income level; that includes many young people and students. It is less intuitive that users in the higher income range were more accepting of targeted advertising than those in the middle income range.[16]

Internet Users' Views About Online Tracking for Ads

	Yes %	No %
Should advertisers be allowed to match ads to your specific interests based on websites you have visited?	30	67
Are these methods justified because they keep costs down so users can visit websites for free, or are they not justified because the free access is not worth the invasion of privacy involved?	35	61
(% Yes = justified; % No = not justified)		

(a)

If you had a choice, which would you prefer—to allow all advertising networks to target ads specifically to you, allow only those advertising networks you choose to target ads specifically to you, (or) to not allow any advertising networks to target ads specifically to you?

(by age and annual income)

	Allow all %	Allow only those advertisers I choose %	Allow none %
All Internet users	14	47	37
18 to 34	13	57	28
35 to 54	15	48	36
55+	14	37	45
$75,000 or more	16	49	33
$30,000 to $74,999	14	53	32
Less than $30,000	14	36	47

(b)

FIGURE **15.2** (a) Attitudes toward Online Ad Tracking (b) Attitudes toward Targeting Based on Degree of Consumer Control

Sources: Internet Users' Views About Online Tracking for Ads, USA Today/Gallup Poll, Dec. 10–12, 2010, and "If you had a choice, which would you prefer...", USA Today/Gallup poll, Dec. 10–12, 2010. Reprinted with permission.

Consumer sensitivity about use of their online activity data for behavioral advertising has not escaped the notice of Internet marketers. In 2009, the IAB, in partnership with five other national advertising and marketing trade groups, set forth principles for industry self-regulation of online behavioral advertising (OBA).[17] Of several principles, the three with the most impact are

- Education of consumers about OBA
- Transparency in the deployment of that adverting
- Consumer control over collection and transfer of data

Practically speaking, the program offers consumers more notice that behavioral data are being collected and more choices over what data are collected and by whom. The notice is displayed near behavioral ads and on corporate websites near the point where data are being collected. Consumers can exercise choice by opting out of some or all of the business's online behavioral ads. As of November, 2011, over 400 companies were participating in the DAA program,[18] entitling them to display the Advertising Option Icon shown in Figure 15.3. The participating companies include ten of the Top 20 global advertising brands and all ten of the Top 10 advertising networks, which together reach more than 85 percent of all U.S. Internet households.

Evidon, a compliance services company, is one of three "approved providers" of the DAA program (the others being DoubleVerify and TRUSTe).These companies have authorization from the DAA to distribute the DAA Icon to companies as well as provide resources for consumers, advertisers, and ad networks. Enforcement of compliance with the DAA Self-Regulatory Principles for OBA is

FIGURE **15.3** Advertising Option Icon
Source: Digital Advertising Alliance, http://www.aboutads.info.

handled by both the Council of Better Business Bureaus' National Advertising Review Council (NARC) and the Direct Marketing Association.[19]

Professor Alessandro Acquisti of Carnegie Mellon University has been studying the economics of privacy for many years and has an informative resources page on the subject. On it, he points out that the subject of privacy represents an economic trade-off for both business and consumer. As data storage has become cheap, businesses have been encouraged to collect more data about users. As the previous studies have indicated, consumers are not thrilled about the collection and use of their data. He points out the essential economic trade-off that affects both:

> The hunger for customization and usability has led individuals to reveal more about themselves to other parties. New trade-offs have emerged in which privacy, economics, and technology are inextricably linked: individuals want to avoid the misuse of the information they pass along to others, but they also want to share enough information to achieve satisfactory interactions; organizations want to know more about the parties with which they interact, but they do not want to alienate them with policies deemed as intrusive.[20]

A recent study by Harris Interactive shows that most consumers still do not believe that the majority of online display ads are relevant to their needs. Still, they are reluctant to share information with advertisers. Figure 15.4 shows the types of information they are most reluctant to share, with financial and contact information topping the list. A third of the respondents were definitely unwilling to share their online browsing data. In response to another question, over one half of the respondents said they would be or might be more likely to do business with marketers who allowed them to opt out of behavioral advertising. Since that is not an attractive solution to marketers, it is obviously important for them to try to find a way to make the Internet community more comfortable with the concept of online tracking for behavioral advertising.

Even before the behavioral advertising issue has been completely settled, the new Internet developments of social media and mobile have presented new privacy challenges.

Privacy, or Lack Thereof, on Social Networks

In 1999, Scott McNeely who was then CEO of Sun Microsystems famously said at an industry event, "You have zero privacy anyway. Get over it."[21] That statement received considerable attention at the time, but as the preceding section shows, many people are still concerned about lack of privacy. Just as famously, Facebook founder Mark Zuckerberg was quoted in 2010 as saying that people no longer have an expectation of privacy. At an industry conference he said:

> People have really gotten comfortable not only sharing more information and different kinds, but more openly and with more people. That social norm is just something that has evolved over time.[22]

Whether you agree with those statements or not, it is clear that the rise of social networks has added another dimension to the issue of PII privacy.

Volumes can be, and have been, written about the issue of privacy on social networks. To cut the issue down to somewhat manageable size, this section will concentrate on Facebook, which is the focus of much of the privacy controversy.

Types of Information that U.S. Internet Users Would Not Share with Advertisers, July 2011
(% of respondents)

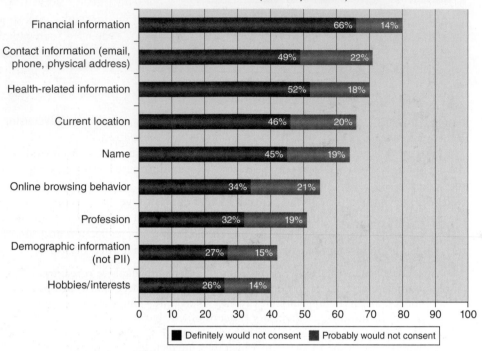

Note: n = 1,004

FIGURE **15.4** Types of Information That Consumers Do Not Want to Share with Advertisers
Source: eMarketer Inc., August 11, 2011.

However, the reader should keep in mind that to a greater or lesser extent, these issues do apply to all social networks.[23] The specifics are laid out in the privacy policy of each site, and you should consult them for more details.

Even the discussion of Facebook privacy issues can emphasize only some of the major issues confronted by the network over its lifetime. Here is a partial chronology:

• *2004: Facebook is founded as a closed network for students at Harvard.* According to the *Harvard Crimson*, Zuckerberg had already faced a privacy blowback from an earlier site, facemash.com. He told the *Crimson* that members were offered intensive privacy options:

> You can limit who can see your information, if you only want current students to see your information, or people in your year, in your house, in your classes. You can limit a search so that only a friend or a friend of a friend can look you up. People have very good control over who can see their information.[24]

• *2006: Facebook opens registration to the general public.* Later that year, it introduced the News Feed product, which showed all the activity of friends on an individual's page. Many users were vocally opposed to the new product because it cluttered their page and others were disturbed by the information it showed. Facebook responded by pointing out that privacy options had not changed, but it was only a few days before Facebook responded to the controversy by introducing new privacy controls and admitting that they erred initially.[25]

The author of a Facebook privacy timeline at the Electronic Frontier Foundation argues that you can see Facebook privacy protections eroding over time.[26] There is no doubt that Facebook privacy policies and options change frequently so any content you see on other sites is probably already outdated. You can see the current privacy options and find a link to Facebook's privacy policy and FAQs by clicking on the Privacy link at the bottom of your Facebook page.

- *2007: Facebook offers an advertising product called Beacon.* Essentially, it allowed subscribers to see what friends had purchased on numerous large sites who were participating in the program. As the controversy about the system built, Facebook changed the privacy option to allow users to opt out of the notifications, but it did not allow them to opt out of the system entirely, meaning that their data were still being collected.[27] A lawsuit in 2008 forced Facebook to allow members to opt out of Beacon entirely. In 2009, Facebook discontinued the product.

- Also in 2007, Facebook also began to allow developers to create their own apps.[28] It appears that a security flaw in the Facebook platform allowed apps to access member profile data and make it available to third parties. Facebook addressed the security problem in 2011 after it was exposed by Internet security firm Symantec.[29]

- *2008: Facebook Connect is introduced.* This service allows members to sign in to other websites using their Facebook username and password. Many of these other websites developed apps, some of which allowed members to post to Facebook. The privacy issue arose when privacy settings on the apps were more lenient than those on Facebook. Modifying them was initially difficult or impossible.[30]

- *April 2010: Facebook introduced the "like button" icon for websites.* The icon essentially makes a Facebook page for each product on a site that is liked by a visitor.[31] The icon also allows Facebook to collect browsing data even if the member has not liked the product.[32]

- *Late in 2010: Facebook introduced facial recognition technology that enabled automatic photo tagging.* Photos uploaded and tagged by users were matched with other photos using facial recognition software. The user was then was allowed to add the tag to the other photos. Users were allowed to adjust their privacy settings to opt out of automatic tagging and were notified after they had been tagged by another user, but many users still objected to the practice.[33]

  Alessandro Acquisti and his colleagues demonstrated the power of the software by taking pictures of Carnegie Mellon students (with their permission) and matching them with Facebook profile pictures. They were able to identify 31 percent of the students by name.[34] At this writing, controversy swirls around that site feature and Germany has become the first country to demand that the feature be disabled and all data about German citizens be destroyed.[35]

- *November 2011: Facebook reached what was described as "a broad settlement" with the FTC that requires the company to respect the privacy of users.*[36] In its announcement, the FTC listed a number of instances in which it alleges that Facebook did not keep privacy promises made to its users. The settlement also required that Facebook undergo regular privacy audits by independent auditors for the next 20 years.[37] In a blog post,[38] Mark Zuckerberg admitted that Facebook had made mistakes and said that many had already been corrected. The agreement is similar to one made between the FTC and Google earlier in 2011.[39]

For sure, this is a story that is "to be continued." Facebook continues to add features and users continue to find additional uses for it. For example, the *Wall Street Journal* predicts that Facebook as a recruiting tool could rival the traditional job boards by 2012.[40] Remember that this is also a story that is being played out on other social networks.[41] Google's announcement in mid-2011 of Google+ for individual users and its opening to business users late in the year is a good example.[42] Mobile, however, is a bit of a different story.

Security and Privacy on Mobile Networks

Previously, it appeared that security of data was the greatest concern for mobile users—both for laptop computers and for cell phones. Security of data is clearly an issue while data are being transferred back and forth over wireless networks. Other mobile security issues will be discussed in the next section.

Primary Concern When Using Mobile Apps

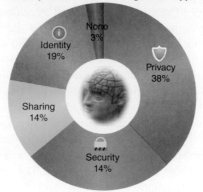

Total Qualified Smartphone Users (*n* = 1000)

FIGURE **15.5** Privacy a Greater Concern Than Security among Smartphone Users
Source: TRUSTe, http://www.truste.com/blog/?p=1456.

However, recently the picture seems to have changed. TRUSTe conducted a study of smartphone users in early 2011. It found that concern over data privacy has outstripped concern over data security among its sample of smartphone users (see Figure 15.5). In addition to highlighting the importance of privacy, especially among users of mobile apps, the study confirmed that respondents distrust targeted advertising and 85 percent want to be able to opt out of targeted mobile ads. They are also distrustful of location tracking; 77 percent do not want apps to be able to track their location. Virtually all (98 percent) want more control over how apps collect and use PII. They value strong passwords and privacy trustmarks, and they pay attention to privacy policies. Are consumers more aware of both privacy and security issues in the mobile environment? Possibly.

The mobile picture is full of contradictions, however; that is perhaps a sign of a maturing space. A study by KPMG calls the situation paradoxical and that seems to be an apt description. Their global sample is made up of owners of cell phones, PDAs, and smartphones. The paradox is shown in Figure 15.6. Concern over the accessibility of PII and credit card information increased between 2008 and 2010. So did annoyance over receiving unsolicited email. These concerns were shared by a large majority of the sample and were consistent over geographical regions.

At the same time, these respondents showed a greater willingness to provide PII with approximately 58 percent being either very or somewhat willing to share their personal information *if it resulted in lower costs.* The report comments that "if providers are willing to provide something of value in return—whether it be discounts, personalized offers and content, or new services—consumers may be willing to take a greater risk."[43] The report also points out that consumers continue to increase their use of mobile services; use of banking and other financial service, cloud computing, and online purchasing are all increasing in the mobile space.

Another 2011 study by security firm McAfee and Carnegie Mellon University deals with the blurring of the lines between personal and workplace use of mobile devices. The report says that "mobility is changing our lives on all levels—personal, professional, and political,"[44] and that the changes offer dazzling opportunities to organizations of many kinds, but they also present security issues. Workers tend to use corporate devices, both laptops and mobile phones, for both business and personal use. They use their own equipment for business purposes. Businesses need to provide data to their workers wherever they are, whenever they need it. Lost and stolen devices are as big a worry, as is hacking. All of these suggest a security nightmare for corporate IT managers who need to have strong policies in place and to ensure that workers are aware and observant of them.

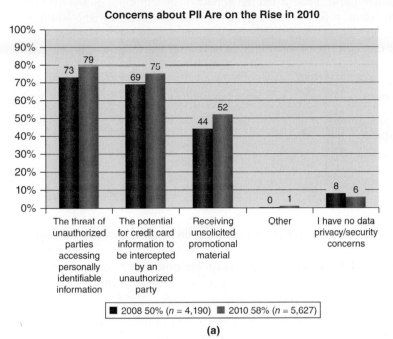

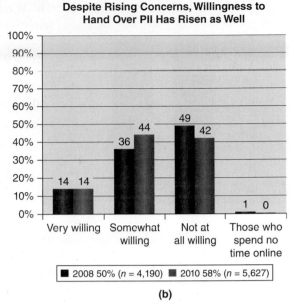

FIGURE **15.6** (a) Concern over Data Privacy Issues among Mobile Users (b) Willingness to Provide Personally Identifiable Information

Source: KPMG, Consumers and Convergence IV, "Convergence Goes Mainstream: Convenience Edges Out Consuer Concerns Over Privacy and Security, Copyright 2010 of KPMG International, pp. 6–7 (http://www.kpmg.com/Global/en/IssuesAndInsights/ArticlesPublications/consumers-and-convergence/Documents/Consumers-Convergence IV july 2010.pdf).

The conclusion is that in the current mobile environment, privacy is the chief concern of consumers while data security is the chief concern of businesses. That does suggest opportunity in both market spaces. Retailers who are seen as trustworthy, which includes providing needed security for data and transactions, have an opportunity to prosper in the mobile environment. Businesses who invest the required time and money in appropriate mobile security practices will lessen their own exposure to risk and contribute to their reputation for trustworthiness.

Before we leave the subject of the privacy and security of user data, we need to consider three especially sensitive subjects, data about children, financial data, and health data. In general, the United States has been unwilling to regulate Internet data practices, but the sensitivity of these types of data has led to regulation in the United Sates as well as in Europe, where there has been greater willingness to regulate data practices. The first regulation in the United States was COPPA, the Children's Online Privacy Protection Act.

Regulation of Children's Privacy Issues

Whether you call them "the MySpace generation"[45] or describe them as "Born Digital" (children born after 1980 who are accustomed to digital access),[46] children and teenagers are active on the web and encounter a variety of dangers there. Our concern is with the privacy of their data. The following two stories are illustrative.

1. The *Wall Street Journal* investigated the amount of data about children that is available online and found it to be substantial. It noted that the small sites that proliferate in the children's market had privacy policies that varied widely. However, Google placed the most tracking cookies of the 50 large sites analyzed. According to the journal's analysis:

   > Google accurately identified a dozen pastimes of 10-year-old Jenna Maas—including pets, photography, "virtual worlds" and "online goodies" such as little animated graphics to decorate a website.
   >
   > "It is a real eye opener," said Jenna's mother, Kate Maas, a schoolteacher in Charleston, S.C., viewing that data.[47]

2. The *Washington Post* investigated the impact of smartphones on the data pro-
    files of older teens. It focused on 13-year-old Scott Fitzsimones who had just
    gotten an iPhone. He immediately set up accounts with Facebook and Pandora
    and "went on an apps downloading spree." That involved using his parents'
    credit card and providing data. He told the *Post* that the first time a game asked
    for his location he stopped and wondered why. However, he gave it and nothing
    bad happened, so he has given it many times since. In fact, he "never says no."[48]

In the earlier discussion of privacy surveys, it was evident that attitudes
changed, usually becoming less concerned about privacy issues, as younger people were questioned. The Australian Law Reform Commission produced a report
in 2010 that contains a useful summary of generational differences in attitudes
toward privacy in Australia and a number of other countries, including the United
States.[49] It references the widely quoted Pew study of teenagers and their attitudes
toward online information.

The study of teenagers' information sharing on social networks gives insight
into attitudes and practices. The Pew study focused on profile information while
noting that many other kinds of data are available online. It found that teenagers
did actively manage their profiles, walking a fine line between protecting their
information and reaching out to others on the web. Specific findings include

-   55 percent of the online teens in their study had online profiles.
    -   66 percent of those did not make their profiles available to all Internet users.
    -   Among those who have public profiles, 46 percent say they give some or
        a lot of false data about themselves. They post false data both to protect
        themselves and to be playful.

In general, the findings suggest that teens are aware of the existence of data
about themselves and have reasonably proactive strategies for dealing with their PII:

-   Most teens are using social networks to stay in touch with people they
    already know and 46 percent use networks to find new friends.
-   Girls were more concerned about the release of their personal information,
    while boys and younger teens were more likely to post false information.
-   Older teens were more likely to share information than younger teens.

Overall, the picture is of children and teenagers who provide substantial data
about themselves, both implicitly and explicitly, on the web.[50]

There is a regulatory tradition of considering children a vulnerable group
in terms of marketing and advertising, and from the early days of the Internet,
special attention has been given to children as Internet users. In 1997, the FTC
brought the first-ever privacy complaint against the GeoCities website, which
alleged that the site had violated its own privacy policy. Its violations were alleged
to be especially serious in the case of its children's community. The issue was said
to be that GeoCities collected data from children in return for free website hosting,
and turned that data over to third parties who then used it in ways inconsistent
with GeoCities' posted privacy statements. The complaint was settled in 1999,
just after Yahoo! announced its acquisition of the site. The consent decree specified
a rigorous set of privacy practices that GeoCities agreed to follow for ten years.[51]

This move by the FTC was followed by the passage by Congress in 1998 of
the COPPA. The major provisions of the act required websites that knowingly
collect information from children under the age of 13 to

-   Provide parents notice of their information practices.
-   Obtain prior parental consent for the collection, use, and/or disclosure of
    personal information.
-   Provide a parent, on request, with the ability to review the personal information
    collected from his child.
-   Provide a parent with the opportunity to prevent the further use of personal
    information that has already been collected, or the future collection of
    personal information from that child.

- Limit collection of personal information for a child's online participation in a game, prize offer, or other activity to information that is reasonably necessary for the activity.
- Establish and maintain reasonable procedures to protect the confidentiality, security, and integrity of the personal information collected.[52]

The FTC is in charge of the guidelines for implementation of COPPA. It maintains a Children's Privacy page that provides information for websites that deal with children under 13 years of age. It also has links to information for parents and teachers as they attempt to protect and educate children on issues of privacy and safety on the web.[53] In late 2011, the FTC issued its first proposed revisions to COPPA in several years. Need for revisions stems from improved technology for parental control and technology that makes children more vulnerable, including GPS-based applications.[54]

Regulation of Privacy in the Financial Services Sector

An example of regulation with broad impact is the Gramm-Leach-Bliley Act (GLBA), which became law in November 1999 and took effect in July 2001. According to Robert Pitofsky, who was then chairman of the FTC, the GLBA

> requires a financial institution to disclose to all of its customers the institution's privacy policies and practices with respect to information it shares with both affiliates and nonaffiliated third parties and limits the instances in which a financial institution may disclose nonpublic personal information about a consumer to nonaffiliated third parties. Specifically, it prohibits a financial institution from disclosing nonpublic personal information about consumers to nonaffiliated third parties unless the institution satisfies various disclosure and opt-out requirements and the consumer has not elected to opt out of the disclosure.[55]

The law requires that each year consumers must be notified about the specific privacy policy of the institution and offered an opportunity to opt out of certain types of information collection and transmission. Anecdotal evidence in various settings suggests that few consumers read this information with care and even fewer take the opportunity to opt out of the specified data collection and transfer activities. It also requires that corporations take proactive steps to ensure the safety of consumer data.

Several years after its implementation, there is criticism of the GLBA. The Electronic Privacy Information Center (EPIC) says:

> First, the GLBA does not protect consumers. It unfairly places the burden on the individual to protect privacy with an opt-out standard ... Second, the GLBA notices are confusing and limit the transparency of information practices.[56]

EPIC argues for closing loopholes in the law and improving its enforcement. Most of all, it argues for consumer opt-in to practices that involve their PII and for privacy notifications in understandable layman's language.

The Dodd-Frank law, passed in the wake of the financial crisis of 2008, appears to do little to improve the situation described by EPIC. Called the Dodd-Frank Wall Street Reform and Consumer Protection Act,[57] it sounds as if data protection might be a component. That is apparently not the case; its coverage is limited to credit data. Quoting a presentation to the American Bar Association, it does cover "analyzing, collecting and maintaining credit report information" but not impact "data security, data disposal, and red flags."[58] The reference to **red flags** refers to corporate policies to detect and prevent identity fraud.[59] That means that GLBA is still the main law mandating the protection and privacy of consumer data.

Regulation of Privacy in the Health Care Sector

Health-related information is another area of special consumer concern. In 1996, Congress added a provision on privacy of medical records to the Health Insurance Portability and Accountability Act (HIPAA). The provision required that, if Congress did not pass a comprehensive law on the privacy of medical data within three years, the Department of Health and Human Services (HHS) would be required to develop a set of regulations to deal with misuse and disclosure of medical records. No law was passed, and in 1999, a set of rules was issued for public comment by the HHS, with a final revision issued in December 2000. The new administration, recognizing the public concern about this issue, agreed to let the rules take effect as scheduled in April 2001. The rules give patients greater control over their health information including access to their medical records, restrict the use and release of medical records, ensure the security of personal health information, and provide penalties for the misuse of personal health information.[60] One visible result has been the posting of data policies in the offices of health care providers and the requirement that each patient sign a statement asserting that he has read and understood the provider's data privacy policies.

The Office of Civil Rights of the Department of Health and Human Services is responsible for enforcing the law. It maintains a web page with information for consumers and for the health care providers, insurers, and health services providers who are covered by the law. It includes compliance mechanisms and training programs for health care providers.[61]

COPPA, GLBA, and HIPAA could have important ramifications as models for regulation of other industry sectors. In addition, they have a direct effort on marketers and services firms that serve the regulated sectors. They will affect database use throughout the industry as well as list brokers, who will be asked to certify that the lists they are renting are from organizations whose practices comply with the regulations. Had the attacks of 2001 and the financial crisis of 2008 not occurred and diverted attention from general consumer privacy issues, there might have been more regulatory attempts in the recent years. However, there have been developments that point the way to the future.

Privacy Issues Going Forward

Consumer concern coupled with well-publicized data breaches (discussed in the next section) cause data privacy and security to remain a concern for public policy makers around the world. Privacy expert Jay Cline suggests there are two main reasons for the recent flurry of regulatory initiatives about data privacy. They are

1. Marketing technologies including location data, online privacy, and smart grid technology. The first two are familiar to readers of this chapter. But what does the concept of a smart grid for distributing electricity have to do with consumer data privacy? According to the Future of Privacy Forum, "The many ways in which data about consumer demand will be used for smarter electricity provision have the potential to revolutionize the electricity industry and to benefit society. However, this very same information about consumers will create major concerns if consumer-focused principles of transparency and control are not treated as essential design principles from start to end of the standards development process."[62] That is something new to worry about!

2. "Bureaucratic momentum," which he describes as regulatory agencies around the world hitting their stride. Cline points to activities of a number of U.S. regulatory agencies, including a privacy framework issued by the FTC in 2010.[63] Canada has passed an email spam law and Mexico has established a well-funded data protection bureau. The EU continues to be aggressive in the area of data protection. The European Commission has issued notice of its intent to update the landmark 1995 Data Protection Directive.[64] The EU has also passed a far-reaching law that requires marketers to obtain consent from the user before setting almost all cookies, although that law has met with resistance in some European countries.[65]

Response of U.S. Business to Privacy Concerns

Businesses in the United States have argued strongly for self-regulation as the best approach to meeting consumer privacy concerns. They have been supported in their preference for self-regulation by trade associations and by the stated preference of the FTC for self-regulation. The FTC recently issued a report that includes a framework for businesses to use as they refine their approach to consumer data privacy (see Figure 15.7). Its principles are a comprehensive approach, which it calls "privacy by design," simplified consumer choice, and transparency.

As you can see from the FTC framework, U.S. businesses are expected to develop their own privacy approaches with only general guidelines. There are two types of privacy disclosures that can be enlisted in order to come up with a comprehensive privacy approach. They are

- A *privacy policy notice* is a comprehensive description of a site's privacy practices. To be acceptable, it must be located in a single, readily identifiable place on the site. It must be easily accessible by a single link or icon. The link should be present on the home page, and it is also desirable to have it in a visible location when information is being collected, for example on registration pages.

Protecting Consumer Privacy in an Era of Rapid Change:
A Proposed Framework for Businesses and Policymakers

Scope: The framework applies to all commercial entities that collect or use consumer data that can be reasonably linked to a specific consumer, computer, or other device.

Principles:

PRIVACY BY DESIGN
Companies should promote consumer privacy throughout their organizations and at every stage of the development of their products and services.

- Companies should incorporate substantive privacy protections into their practices, such as data security, reasonable collection limits, sound retention practices, and data accuracy.
- Companies should maintain comprehensive data management procedures throughout the life cycle of their products and services.

SIMPLIFIED CHOICE
Companies should simplify consumer choice.

- Companies do not need to provide choice before collecting and using consumers' data for commonly accepted practices, such as product fulfillment.
- For practices requiring choice, companies should offer the choice at a time and in a context in which the consumer is making a decision about his or her data.

GREATER TRANSPARENCY
Companies should increase the transparency of their data practices.

- Privacy notices should be clearer, shorter, and more standardized, to enable better comprehension and comparison of privacy practices.
- Companies should provide reasonable access to the consumer data they maintain; the extent of access should be proportionate to the sensitivity of the data and the nature of its use.
- Companies must provide prominent disclosures and obtain affirmative express consent before using consumer data in a materially different manner than claimed when the data was collected.
- All stakeholders should work to educate consumers about commercial data privacy practices.

FIGURE **15.7** Framework for Protection of Consumer Data Privacy

Source: Federal Trade Commission, http://www.ftc.gov/os/2010/12/101201privacyreport.pdf.

- The FTC framework takes this common approach a step further by recommending a comprehensive, corporate-wide approach to privacy. The framework specifically states that privacy policies should be shorter and more understandable. Since privacy policies are written, or at least cleared, by corporate attorneys, this recommendation is difficult to implement.
- An *information practice statement* is a discrete statement that describes a specific information practice from which a potential use of the information can be inferred. Examples include: "Click here if you want to be informed about future offers of this nature" or "We will not share your information with any other organization."
  - Information practices statements are short and specific. They can be useful both to identify the choices that consumers have and to provide information about what information is being collected and how it will be used in the interest of transparency.

With the exception of financial services, health care businesses, and those that market to children under 13, the burden of designing a privacy approach and seeing that it is properly executed is left up to the business itself. There is, however, a set of privacy standards that is accepted by most of the Internet-using nations, called the Fair Information Practices Principles.

The Fair Information Practices Principles

The Fair Information Practices Principles have become an important international standard in the field of data privacy. They have evolved over the last quarter century as a result of analyses by governmental agencies in the United States, Canada, Australia, and Europe, and are widely accepted in regulatory frameworks around the world. The principles, as listed by the FTC,[66] are

- *Notice/Awareness.* Customers should be given notice before information is collected in order to allow them to make informed decisions about what to divulge. Notification should include identification of the entity collecting the data, uses to which it will be put, with whom data will be shared, nature of data collection including voluntary or involuntary, methods of collection, data security measures, and consumer rights with respect to collection and use of data.
- *Choice/Consent.* Consumers should be given control over how information will be used for purposes beyond the current transaction. This includes both internal use of the information, such as putting it in a database, and external use, such as transferring it to a third party.
- *Access/Participation.* The consumer should be able to view data about himself or herself and to assure that the data is accurate and complete.
- *Integrity/Security.* Integrity describes the accuracy of the data; specifically that anyone who accesses the data at a given moment receives exactly the same data. Security refers to the managerial and technical measures that protect the data from unauthorized access and use.
- *Enforcement/Redress.* There should be a mechanism in place to enforce these principles of privacy protection and to provide remedies for injured parties.[67]

While these fair information principles provide a strong conceptual framework for privacy action by businesses, they do not provide sufficient guidance for the majority of firms who lack internal expertise in this area. In addition, businesses would benefit from greater understanding of privacy issues on the part of consumers while consumers would feel more confident if privacy approaches were sanctioned by a trusted third party. This has lead to the establishment of various industry-supported privacy organizations.

Privacy Organizations and Seals

As part of the industry effort to achieve effective self-regulation, a number of organizations have either been formed or have added a privacy initiative to the

INTERACTIVE EXERCISE 15.3   **Privacy Seals and Advocates**

The U.S. Chamber of Commerce has a list of organizations that award privacy seals:

http://bit.ly/sOCWes.

EPIC has a list of privacy advocates:

http://bit.ly/tkN2JE.

Visit one organization on each list, examine its offerings, and think about how they impact consumers and businesses.

services they offer. In general, these organizations can be characterized as non-profit organizations that specialize in the privacy arena or trade organizations that support the privacy actions of their members. Often, as in the case of TRUSTe and the Better Business Bureau Online, compliant organizations are allowed to display their seal on the organizational web page. There is no comprehensive listing of privacy-related organizations.

Most industry leaders and regulators in the United States still voice strong support for self-regulation. However, many other countries have taken a regulatory approach toward Internet privacy from the beginning, believing that self-regulation is insufficient to protect the public. In the next section, we will look at privacy activities in other major Internet-using countries.

Privacy Regulation in Various Internet-Using Countries

Privacy is a concern in countries around the world, but it is not safe to assume that the concerns are the same from one country to another. The marketer who is conducting business globally must be aware of consumer concerns and actions as well as of the regulations in each country. While the regulations are generally based on the fair information practices principles, their degree of severity varies from one country to another.

The legislation with the most widespread impact is the EU Directive on Protection of PII.[68] It was adopted in 1995 by the Council of Ministers and took effect on October 28, 1998. Unlike the United States, the EU has a declared preference for regulation in the area of PII privacy and has a record of action that dates back to the Council of Europe Convention in 1981. The 1995 directive was aimed at bringing the protection of PII into the Internet age. Its purpose was to ensure that data could move freely between the member countries of the EU while guaranteeing a stated level of privacy protection. Its basic principles are essentially the Fair Information Practices Principles.

For its time, the regulation mandated for EU countries by the 1995 directive was strict and reasonably comprehensive. However, since then new technologies like RFID, cloud computing, and mobile have introduced new dimensions to the privacy issue. The EU responded by submitting a comprehensive framework, which had not yet been enacted by mid-2011. The framework, among other issues is intended to deal with new technologies and to attempt more standardization of data protection globally.[69]

In the absence of consistency of privacy regulations around the world, it is impossible to summarize the global situation. In addition, privacy regulations change frequently. For example, India passed a strict law regulating personal data privacy in 2011.[70] The laws can also be quite complex. For example, different provinces in Canada have different privacy laws.[71] Marketers have to cope with different laws in every country, even in the countries of the EU.[72]

The map in Figure 15.8 shows a world map of surveillance and privacy protection. While it is interesting, be aware that it has a perspective different from that taken in our discussion. Privacy International is a United Kingdom–based privacy advocacy organization. In cooperation with EPIC in the United States, it conducts annual studies of privacy around the world. Its ratings focus on the

Map of Surveillance Societies Around the World

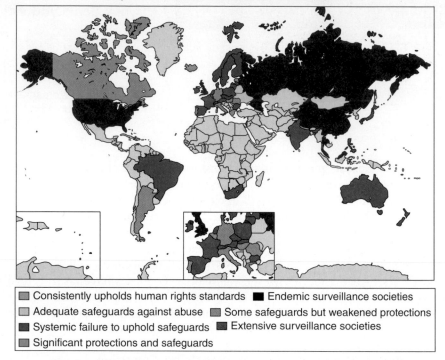

Legend:
- Consistently upholds human rights standards
- Adequate safeguards against abuse
- Systemic failure to uphold safeguards
- Significant protections and safeguards
- Endemic surveillance societies
- Some safeguards but weakened protections
- Extensive surveillance societies

FIGURE **15.8** Global Map of Surveillance and Privacy Protection

Source: Privacy International, https://www.privacyinternational.org/article/leading-surveillance-societies-eu-and-world-2007.

trade-off between surveillance (everything from closed circuit TV cameras to maintenance of databases about citizens) and the protection of personal privacy. When that trade-off is the standard, not many countries rank well, and most are tending toward more surveillance, not more privacy of PII.[73]

From the data presented in this section, it is clear that trust is important to the success of Internet business. It is equally clear that trust in the ability of institutions to protect PII is not high around the world, and that government and corporate efforts to protect personally identifiable data vary greatly from one country to another. The other issue of special important to the creation and maintenance of trust in Internet businesses is that of the security of PII. We will now turn to a discussion of the business and marketing issues that relate to the security of data and transactions.

Consumer Data Security Breaches

News about security breaches are reported on an almost daily basis. These breaches compromise the security of PII. Some are large and some impact only a few hundred consumer records. Some breaches reveal ingenious ways to obtain consumer data. For example, here is a summary of some of the largest and most widely covered data breaches:

- Beginning in 2005 and made public in 2007, TJX (parent company of T.J. Maxx and other retailers) suffered a massive data breach. Hackers accessed over 46 million credit card numbers and other transactions information.[74] The hack is generally attributed to weak encryption in an internal wireless database that allowed hackers to access data.[75] Urban legend has it that hackers sometimes sat in a parking lot and accessed data from their car using a laptop, a telescope antenna, and a wireless LAN adapter.[76] Estimates of the full cost to TJX vary widely, but it clearly ran into the hundreds of millions of dollars, maybe more.[77]

- In March 2011, Epsilon, a marketing services firm that maintains the email databases of over 2,500 corporate clients, announced a major data breach that allowed hackers to access email addresses. Epsilon said that about 2 percent of its clients were affected, so that could be as many as 50 large corporations, including retailers and financial services providers.[78] One expert estimates that as many as 5 million individual addresses might have been obtained, but there is no official estimate of the size of the breach.

- In April 2011, Sony announced a massive data breach in its PlayStation network. Data obtained included items like user names and passwords and could have included some credit card numbers. A second breach occurred on May 2, bringing the number of customers affected around the world to over 101 million users and 12 million unencrypted credit card numbers.[79] Sony was forced to close down the system for a period of time and to provide free usage to compensate for the downtime. Sony estimated the cost of the breach at $171 million.[80]

- In June 2011, the Privacy Commissioner of Canada announced that office supply firm Staples had failed to completely wipe out all personal information from computers that it renovated for resale. The commissioner gave Staples a year to prove it was able to wipe out all data from used computers before it sold them.[81]

A large number of breaches originate on college campuses, which is not particularly surprising. Data in recent years show many thefts of health-related information, which is disconcerting. The Privacy Rights Clearinghouse (PRC), which has maintained a chronological list since 2005, estimated that a total of 535,363,707 data records had been compromised in 2,625 breaches reported as of August 11, 2011.[82]

The cost of data breaches to the affected organizations continues to rise. The Ponemon Institute, a research firm specializing in privacy and information management, estimated that the cost per compromised record was $204 in 2009 compared to $202 in 2008, and that the average cost per breach was $6.75 million compared to $6.65 million in 2008. The larger the breach, the greater the cost.[83] The dollar costs, of course, do not measure the loss in consumer trust that results from a data breach. There has been considerable discussion in recent years of the importance of transparency; reporting a breach when it occurs and being accurate about the nature and possible consequences of a breach. It is important to notify customers on a timely basis and to give them all possible assistance in preventing or limiting financial damage to the consumer. Transparency may limit, although it will not prevent, damage to the consumer's trust in the organization.

Consumer Knowledge about Internet Security

Consumers appear to have a basic understanding of the importance of keeping their online activities secure. Finnish security solutions firm F-Secure conducted

---

INTERACTIVE EXERCISE 15.4   **Database of Data Breaches**

There are at least two major databases of data breaches.

The chronological list on the PRC site is updated daily. It has considerable detail and often links to more information:

http://bit.ly/tUePhd.

The Open Security Foundation has maintained a Data Loss Database by month since 2001:

http://datalossdb.org.

Visit one or both of these sites and scroll through a set of listings to see the number and diversity of data breaches.

Note: Neither database is easily searchable. If you want to locate a specific breach, you are advised to do a general search to find when it was announced, then find it in that time frame on the database.

surveys of Internet users in the United States, Canada, the United Kingdom, France, and Germany in 2008 and 2009. Findings from 2008 include

- 95 percent of respondents had security software on their computers.
- Only 18 percent were confident that they were completely protected from malware.
- Although most respondents were confident that their antivirus protection was up to date, only 10 percent were confident that they could open email attachments and 9 percent were confident that they could open email links without danger of being infected with malware. F-Secure commented that most respondents were not aware of how frequently antivirus software should be updated.
- 50 percent of respondents in the United States, Canada, the United Kingdom, and France felt their credit cards were safe while transacting online while only 15 percent of German respondents felt secure.
- 65 percent of respondents in the United States, Canada, the United Kingdom, and France felt their online banking transactions were safe, versus 28 percent in Germany.
- Only 37 percent of respondents were confident they could identify a phishing email and 27 percent were confident they could identify a phishing site.[84]
- 28 percent of respondents used their mobile phone to access the Internet, but 86 percent did not have mobile security.[85]

Their 2009 survey added respondents in Italy, India, and Hong Kong. Findings included:

- 50 percent felt safe when banking online but only 16 percent felt safe using a credit card to make a purchase online.
- 54 percent did not agree that their children were safe online while over a third could neither agree nor disagree, indicating that they were not sure.
- 54 percent felt confident they would not fall for a phishing email, but 27 percent were not sure they could identify a phishing email.[86]

Once again, we see a mixed picture with Internet users exhibiting a reasonable knowledge of threats but less confidence that they could deal with them successfully. With that in mind, let us look at a list of the most common types of security threats affecting both consumer and business computers.

Internet Security Threats

The ways in which cyber attacks can be carried out are myriad and seem to be growing every day. HP released a study in late 2011 that documented the costs to business and government. The head of HP's Enterprise Security division commented that, "Instances of cybercrime have continued to increase in both frequency and sophistication, with the potential impact to an organization's financial health becoming more substantial." Over the four-week period covered by the survey, responding organizations reported 72 cyber attacks in the form of malicious code, denial of service, stolen devices, and web-based attacks. That represented a 45-percent increase over the preceding year.[87] This is a huge problem for the corporate IT manager. In this section, we will concentrate on the kinds of threats and criminality that are most often directed at the individual Internet user, not the corporation.

Malware

Malware is literally "bad software," software designed to do damage. It is a generic term for much of the malicious software on the web including viruses, worms, Trojan horses, and spyware. Viruses attach themselves to otherwise legitimate software or documents and spreading across networks when their code is executed. Worms are similar, but they do not have to be attached to other software. They exploit weaknesses in the system or employ so-called social engineering, which is simply deceiving people in order to gain access to the system. Trojan horses are manually attached to legitimate software and rely on use of the host software to spread.

Spyware and Adware

Spyware and **adware** are both marketer-initiated actions. Spyware works in the background as consumers move around the web, tracking their movements and recording things like keywords used in searches. Adware is free, advertiser-supported software that includes toolbars and games. It includes software for pop-up and pop-under ads. When adware is installed on a computer without the user's permission, it becomes spyware.

In many cases, spyware is simply used to create anonymous profiles. In other cases, it may be much more intrusive, for example, repeatedly changing the consumers opening page to a specific website in spite of the consumer's efforts to specify another page or resisting all efforts to stop the advertising pop-ups. Spyware is often placed in the process of receiving a free download. The presence of spyware may, in fact, be specified in the service agreement the consumer must sign before the download begins. Based on all we know, it seems reasonable to assume that most consumers do not read the agreements carefully and consequently are unaware of the software and the fact it may be collecting and transmitting data without their knowledge.

Phishing, Pfarming, and Spoofing

Adware and spyware result from marketer-initiated efforts. A variety of other techniques are used by fraud artists to obtain the PII of consumers.

- **Phishing** is the practice of using fraudulent emails in an attempt to get information like consumer account numbers and passwords. These often come in the form of an email that purports to be from a recognized financial services provider. They might inform customers that there is a problem with their account and they need to provide information to clear it up. From the consumer standpoint, the rule is simple. *Never provide personal information in response to an incoming email.* That should be enough to protect the consumer, but unfortunately it is not.
  - **Spear phishing** is a newer and more sophisticated entry into the gallery of bad software. It is a highly targeted phishing scheme that aims to get access to an organization's entire computer system. Spear phishing is carried out by authentic-looking emails that appear to come from the organization or from an employee of the organization.[88]
- **Pfarming** also attempts to obtain PII, but it does so in a different way. Perpetrators hack into the DNS (domain name system) servers that provide the IP addresses for URLs and thereby allow users to access websites on the Internet. They hijack some of the pages and create a site that looks much like the original. Because they have gained unauthorized access to the DNS server, they can direct the user to the fake site and trick him into divulging personal information. Because the sites look real, this fraud is hard for consumers to detect. A similar technique has been widely used to scam charitable donations after disasters by using sites that resemble sites of legitimate charities.
- **Spoofing** is the general term that describes a situation in which a person, computer program, or website is able to masquerade successfully as another. Spoofing requires that the criminal first identify the IP address of the trusted website. Then it must waylay individual data packets and modify their identifying headers so it appears that they are coming from the trusted website. That sounds difficult to do, but there are apparently many poorly written Internet Protocols that make it possible for people with technical expertise to tap into the telecommunications stream that comprises the traffic of the Internet.

Whatever the method used to steal PII, the possible outcome is identify theft. Identify theft implies that a thief has obtained access to information that allows him to pose as another individual, doing things like using the other person's credit cards or bank accounts. It poses a direct threat to consumers' financial well-being and is a topic of considerable and growing concern.

Identity Theft

According to the Identity Theft Resource Center, "**Identity theft** is a crime in which an impostor obtains key pieces of personal identifying information (PII) such as Social Security numbers and driver's license numbers and uses them for their own personal gain."[89] Identify theft can occur online, but many instances occur offline as a result of theft of mail, loss of personal documents, and careless disposal of documents by a person or a business. The latter often goes by the descriptive term "dumpster diving."

Javelin Research and Strategy conducts an annual survey that is co-sponsored by a number of financial services firms. Their 2010 report contained both good news and bad. President James Van Dyke puts the bad news first:

> "The 2010 Identity Fraud Survey Report shows that fraud increased for the second straight year and is at the highest rate since Javelin began this report in 2003(2)... The good news is consumers are getting more aggressive in monitoring, detecting and preventing fraud with the help of technology and partnerships with financial institutions, government agencies and resolution services."

Data from the report illustrate the magnitude of the problem:

- 11 billion Americans were affected by identity fraud in 2009. Potential losses totaled $54 billion. There is good news here also; out-of-pocket costs for resolving thefts dropped to $373 per incident.
- Time to detect and resolve fraud has dropped, primarily due to use of technology, including mobile, by financial institutions and individuals.
- 18 to 24 year olds take nearly twice as long to detect and report fraud and therefore remain its victims for longer. This is because they monitor their accounts less frequently.[90]

There are also many ways in which corporate security can be breached and personal identity can be threatened. Individuals, corporations, government agencies, and nonprofit organizations all stand to lose financially from criminal activities that violate the security of their Internet activities. Organizations stand to lose even more if they lose the trust of their customers, their donors, and the citizenry in general. All organizations that hold any amount of customer data have a fiduciary responsibility for the protection of that data. It is a responsibility that organizations are taking with increasing seriousness, even as cybercriminals become more ingenuous in their attempts to breach security systems.

There is one additional type of activity we need to examine before concluding this chapter. It does not usually include breaches of security, but it does involve potential theft of a possession. The subject is the thorny one of intellectual property on the Internet.

Protection of Intellectual Property in the Digital Age

The right of persons and legal entities to protect nontangible property of importance has long been recognized. Copyright and patent laws provided reasonable protections for several centuries. Technology in the form of copiers and later computers made the protection of copyrighted material more difficult. The ease of sharing content on the Internet has exacerbated the problem.

What Is Intellectual Property?

Intellectual property is a broad concept, encompassing many areas of endeavor, beyond just the copyrights of books, music, and other published material that many of us confront on a daily basis. The World Intellectual Property Organization (WIPO) defines intellectual property as

- *Creations of the mind* [emphasis mine]: inventions, literary and artistic works, and symbols, names, and images used in commerce.

The WIPO divides intellectual property into two main categories:

- *Industrial property* includes legal constructs including patents and trademarks.
- *Copyright* applies to literary works, artistic works, and architectural designs. Literary works include not only written material from books to plays but also films and music.

The WIPO further explains the coverage of copyright laws as

Rights related to copyright include those of performing artists in their performances, producers of phonograms, and those of broadcasters in their radio and television programs.[91]

The Digital Millennium Copyright Act

The Committee on Intellectual Property Rights and the Emerging Information Infostructure of the National Academy of Sciences points out that from the time of Thomas Jefferson, access to information has been a cornerstone of American democracy and of the educational system. Public libraries have made printed material available to any citizen at virtually no cost. One hallmark of this system is that a published item is available to only one person at a time.

However, when that same content is published electronically, there is no theoretical limit to the number of people who can access it simultaneously. That leads to the worst nightmare of musicians and authors and their publishers— that electronic publishing will ultimately lead to the sale of only one book or recording. The rest would simply be copied.

After years of international discussion about intellectual property issues as they pertain to electronic products of all kinds, Congress passed and President Clinton signed the Digital Millennium Copyright Act in 1998. It has many provisions that affect Internet users, libraries, websites, and educational institutions. Among the provisions are to make it a crime to circumvent the antipiracy codes built into most commercial software or to make or sell code-cracking devices. Libraries and educational institutions receive certain exemptions that allow them to make copyrighted material available to authorized users. However, ISPs are required to remove material that constitutes copyright infringement from customers' websites and webcasters are required to pay licensing fees to recording companies.[92]

The issues are also difficult because the interests of various stakeholders clash with little obvious way of reconciling them. In addition, traditional practices and laws vary in different countries around the globe.[93] The EU maintains a page with links to legislation and deliberations about the protection of intellectual property in the countries of the union[94] and links to the laws of other countries are easily found by web search. Enforcement of laws also varies around the globe, so the situation is not easy to navigate.

The WIPO is a central resource for information about the protection of intellectual property around the world. In 2011, its director general discussed three main principles for copyright protection: neutrality toward technology, comprehensiveness and coherence, and simplicity. Mr. Gurry said, "We need a global infrastructure that permits simple, global licensing, one that makes the task of licensing cultural works legally on the Internet as easy as it is to obtain such works there illegally."

In the absence of a comprehensive solution in the form of copyright law, the Creative Commons offers a viable alternative.

Napster and Other Intellectual Property Controversies

Napster is clearly the poster child of the intellectual property controversy on the Internet. As most students know well, Napster was the home of software that makes it possible to download music over the Internet. It is the prime example of the consumer P2P (peer-to-peer) business model (see Chapter 3), first attracting media attention when it slowed the computer systems of several universities in the United States so severely that it was banned from many campus networks.[95] Napster not only drew media attention, it also attracted the ire of the recording industry. At the end of 1999, several record companies filed suit, essentially to prevent Napster from facilitating the distribution of copyrighted music.

At its height, it is estimated that 30 million people were registered with Napster. In 2000, Bertelsmann AG, a European media conglomerate, acquired Napster with the intention of turning it into a subscription service.[96] Under that business model, Napster continued to exist but failed to thrive. It no longer exists as a separate entity but as the streaming technology for Best Buy.

Its place has been taken by a host of other file-sharing products, with Kazaa the apparent leader in MP3 downloads and BitTorrent leading the way in downloading large files like videos. The latter is currently evolving into a software firm. Perhaps the closest successor to Napster was LimeWire. It operated as a purveyor of P2P file-sharing software, but it was, in fact, widely used for the illegal sharing of music. The Recording Industry Association of America (RIAA) brought suit against LimeWire in 2006 and in 2010, it was ordered to shut down permanently and to block the unauthorized sharing of music on the software it had distributed.[97] The RIAA continues to prosecute illegal music downloading and sharing.[98]

RIAA was one of the major supporters of the Stop Online Piracy Act, introduced in October 2011. If passed, the act would allow the Department of Justice to force U.S. businesses, including payment systems and search engines, to stop doing business with foreign websites accused of copyright infringement.[99] Supporters include publishers and broadcasters as well as music producers. Internet businesses like Google, Facebook, Amazon, and Twitter are strongly opposed to the bill, saying it would stifle Internet activities. Their opposition included a threat to temporarily suspend their sites in protest.[100] This is the most recent, and likely not the last, salvo in the continuing battle to protect the rights of content owners while allowing unfettered access to Internet content.

There tends to be considerable buzz around the issue of illegal peer-to-peer file sharing, especially because well-known artists continue to speak out against it. However, it is very hard to find credible statistics on the subject. Beware one post that says "consumer attitudes toward music downloads have changed dramatically."[101] The post has been reposted frequently without attribution, which is not acceptable blog practice by Internet intellectual property standards, but it is hard to find the original post and author. No credible studies are referenced.

The technology editor of the UK newspaper, *The Guardian*, affirmed the lack of statistics in 2009 but argued against the conventional wisdom that illegal downloading damages the music industry. His hypothesis is that money is being spent on DVDs and games instead of music.[102] Many others have suggested that Apple's iTunes model, because it focuses on inexpensive downloads of single tracks instead of expensive purchase of entire albums, is responsible for the presumed decrease in illegal music downloading. The thesis seems reasonable, but there is no definitive data to support it. It is also not clear how the new Apple iCloud service will affect the situation,[103] so the controversy continues.

The Digital Millennium Copyright Act was an attempt to deal with these issues in a way that protects consumer access to information; at the same time, it protects the interests of owners of intellectual property.

Publishing under Creative Commons

The basic meaning of copyright is best expressed by the "all rights reserved" phrase. That makes it difficult to do many things, from writing a textbook or a research paper to publishing a blog. The Creative Commons is a nonprofit organization that aims to maximize the productivity of the Internet. In its own words, it "develops, supports, and stewards legal and technical infrastructure that maximizes digital creativity, sharing, and innovation."[104] It does this by offering licenses that provide more flexible choices than the "all rights reserved." The basic idea is to let the individual or organization retain the copyright to their work but choose the conditions under which people may use and distribute the content without requesting explicit permission from the owner. This extends to how people may modify the work, as long as they provide appropriate attribution. It is important to point out that the person who obtains the license must be the owner, presumably the developer, of the content. You cannot license someone else's content.

Figure 15.9 is an example of one type of license, which Creative Commons calls "ShareAlike." In this case, the content can be used and modified as long as it is attributed as the owner has specified, it is used noncommercially, and any distribution is done under a similar license. In other words, the person who modifies the content cannot choose more stringent distribution terms than the original creator. When the owner applies for a license, Creative Commons

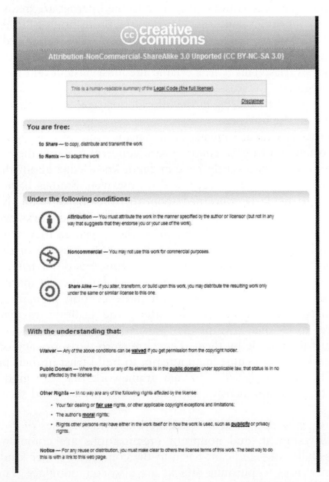

FIGURE **15.9** Example of a Creative Commons License

Source: Creative Commons, http://creativecommons.org/licenses/by-nc-sa/3.0.

provides a badge for the content that identifies it as licensed under Creative Commons and links to the attribution criteria the owner has chosen.[105] The site has a complete list of all types of licenses available in straightforward layman's language.[106]

Creative Commons operates globally through affiliates throughout the world. It is not a panacea for all the world's intellectual property woes, but it provides an easy and workable solution for some content creators like marketers and bloggers who actually want their content to be widely shared.

There are many companies around the world working on technological fixes to the intellectual property issue, and businesses do need to employ appropriate technology. However, from the corporate point of view, it will require management skill and vigilance to protect these important assets in an ever-changing world. From a broader social point of view, online intellectual property protection is a public policy issue that needs to be approached on several fronts. There are legal and regulatory issues that need to be dealt with while providing consumers with flexibility and control in the way they access content on the Internet. Finally, there is a need for better consumer understanding of the subject of intellectual property and the responsibility of consumers in helping to maintain a free and fair marketplace. All this takes place in the context of ever-changing technology, making it a challenge for public policy makers around the world.

SUMMARY

The social and regulatory issues that pertain to the Internet are many and varied. In this chapter, important concerns related to the protection of PII, data security, and intellectual property were reviewed. These issues are recognized in Internet-using counties around the world, although the reaction in individual countries to each issue often varies. This is true even at the most basic level of preference for industry self-regulation versus a regulatory approach.

Trust is essential to success in the information age, especially for businesses that are active on the Internet.

The Internet has caused intense focus on the issue of privacy of PII on the Internet. Consumers in many countries are concerned about their PII security, although they do not necessarily have in-depth knowledge about the subject or examine privacy policies that are posted on the web. Studies have shown that consumers are particularly concerned about the tracking of online behavior that is widely used by behavioral advertising. Users of social networks evidence some concern for the privacy of their information there even as they actively use the networks. Mobile users are also concerned about the privacy of their personal data but even more about its security. Privacy concerns differ from one country to another, creating a difficult situation for the global Internet marketer.

Businesses in the United States—with the exception of marketers of children's products, financial services marketers, and health care marketers—are essentially free to set their own privacy policies. Once they have published policies, they must then abide by them. There are third-party privacy organizations whose aid marketers can enlist in an attempt to build trust in their privacy practices. The FTC has published a privacy framework that can guide businesses as they develop a comprehensive approach to the privacy and security of consumer data.

There are many threats to data on the Internet. Breaches of data stored by businesses, government, and nonprofit organizations are common and many pose the possibility of significant harm to the consumer. Other kinds of threats ranging from viruses to phishing attacks are also commonplace. The specter of identity theft is ever-present, and it presents the possibility of significant damage to consumers who experience it.

The maintenance of intellectual property rights, especially those of copyrighted literary works, is of direct concern to marketers. Illegal copying and downloading of material, including, but not limited to music, has been an Internet issue almost from its beginning. The music industry, in particular, has been aggressive in pursuing legal action that has led to the shutdown of sites seen as promoting illegal downloading. Changing business models, including the ease and cost effectiveness of downloading single tracks of music, may also have affected consumer perceptions. In the absence of consistent intellectual property laws around the world, the situation is challenging. However, the presence of Creative Commons offers new options to publishers that may ease the situation for some of them.

Dealing with these concerns is an ongoing issue because new challenges continue to arise. Both business and policy makers must deal with these challenges in the face of an ever-changing technological environment.

DISCUSSION QUESTIONS

1. Explain why managers should be concerned about the trust customers have in their brand or company and what they can do to build trust.
2. Do you think consumers often take actions on the Internet that reflect lack of trust in websites or marketing practices there? What might some of those actions be?
3. Discuss concerns that consumers may have about the privacy of their PII. What do you think a business can and should do to alleviate these concerns?
4. The chapter highlights online tracking for behavioral advertising as a particular concern of many Internet users. Has anything you have learned in this course made you more wary of what sites you visit and what information you divulge on the Internet?
5. What are some of the special privacy issues faced by users of social networks?
6. Why do you think that security seems to be a greater concern than privacy for users of mobile devices?
7. What actions would you recommend to Internet users to protect the privacy of their PII?
8. What are the Fair Information Practices Principles, and why are they important?
9. Have you or anyone you know ever been informed that they had been affected by a data breach? If so, what actions were recommended for their protection? More generally, what actions should consumers take if they fear some of their data may have been compromised?
10. Have you experienced any of the other security threats discussed in the chapter? What was the result?
11. How has the Internet increased both the importance and the difficulty of protecting intellectual property?
12. What do you perceive to be the attitudes of your peers to sharing of intellectual property on the web?
13. Do you think that Creative Commons licenses offer value in the protection of intellectual property on the Internet?
14. Examine the complex issue of providing personal information in return for content or services and try to precisely define your own position on the issue.

INTERNET EXERCISES

1. Internet Career Builder Exercise
   a. These are some of the jobs that are available in the field of privacy and security policy making and compliance. In the field of privacy, some jobs require a law degree. In the field of Internet security, many require an information technology degree. These jobs, and others, do not require law training or extensive technological expertise. You can find others on sites recommended by your instructor or through search.

      Privacy analyst
      Privacy officer

   Privacy manager
   Chief privacy officer
   HIPAA privacy officer
   HIPAA compliance officer
   Project manager, data privacy
   GLBA compliance officer
   Trainer, HIPAA or GLBA
   and many more

   b. Select a privacy or security job from the given list or from your own search. Outline the responsibilities of that position. You may find it useful to locate job postings on the web in order to understand the job requirements.

c. Outline knowledge and experience from classes, internships, full or part-time jobs, and volunteer work that prepare you for this specific position.

d. Prepare five questions you could ask at a job interview. The questions should exhibit your understanding of the position requirements without lecturing the interviewer about what she already knows.

e. Update your VisualCV® or LinkedIn profile with this information.

2. Conduct your own privacy survey, using the websites you are tracking or others that you visit frequently. Do

they all have a privacy policy? Do the policies you find seem to meet the requirements of the Fair Information Practices Principles? Why or why not?

3. Conduct informal interviews with consumers in order to evaluate how much they seem to know about various Internet privacy and security issues. Evaluate the degree to which they seem to be taking actions to protect their own PII.

4. Research the privacy and security policies of your school. Do you think most students are aware of these policies and understand the reasons for them? Do you think most students agree with them? Why or why not?

NOTES

1. Glen L. Urban, "The Trust Imperative," MIT Working Paper 4302-03, http://ssrn.com/abstract=400421, 1.

2. All informed publics met the following criteria: college-educated; household income in the top quartile for their age in their country; read or watch business/news media at least several times a week; follow public policy issues in the news at least several times a week.

3. http://www.edelman.com/trust/2011/uploads/Edelman%20Trust%20Barometer%20Global%20Deck.pdf.

4. George R. Milne and Mary J. Culnan, "Strategies for Reducing Online Privacy Risks: Why Consumers Read (Or Don't Read) Online Privacy Notices," *Journal of Interactive Marketing*, Vol. 18, No. 3, Summer 2004, 22.

5. Glen L. Urban, "The Trust Imperative," MIT Working Paper 4302-03, http://ssrn.com/abstract=400421.

6. http://www.accenture.com/us-en/technology/technology-labs/Pages/insight-privacy-trust-summary.aspx.

7. "The Economic Value of Trust," *Accenture Outlook*, 2003, Number 3, 34.

8. Glen L. Urban, "The Trust Imperative," MIT Working Paper 4302-03, http://ssrn.com/abstract=400421, 4.

9. http://blog.hubspot.com/blog/tabid/6307/bid/9242/Becoming-a-Trust-Agent-w-ChrisBrogan-InboundNow-6.aspx.

10. John Deighton, "The Right To Be Let Alone," *Journal of Interactive Marketing*, Vol. 12, No. 2, Spring 1998, 3.

11. http://www.ponemon.org/news-2/26.

12. See a comprehensive and ongoing study of these issues in the *Wall Street Journal*, http://online.wsj.com/article/SB10001424052748703940904575395073512989404.html#articleTabs%3Darticle.

13. http://www.ftc.gov/os/2007/12/P859900stmt.pdf.

14. http://www.ftc.gov/opa/2009/02/behavad.shtm.

15. http://www.businesswire.com/news/home/20080410005107/en/Majority-Uncomfortable-Websites-Customizing-Content-Based-Visitors.

16. http://www.marketingcharts.com/direct/2-in-3-online-americans-oppose-ad-tracking-15448/gallup-online-tracking-selective-dec-2010jpg.

17. http://www.iab.net/behavioral-advertisingprinciples.

18. http://www.aboutads.info/participating.

19. http://www.iab.net/media/file/OBA_OneSheet_Final.pdf.

20. http://www.heinz.cmu.edu/~acquisti/economics-privacy.htm.

21. http://www.wired.com/politics/law/news/1999/01/17538.

22. http://www.guardian.co.uk/technology/2010/jan/11/facebook-privacy.

23. http://www.mediapost.com/publications/?fa=Articles.showArticle&art_aid=139417.

24. http://www.thecrimson.com/article/2004/2/9/hundreds-register-for-new-facebook-website.

25. http://www.guardian.co.uk/technology/2006/sep/08/news.newmedia1.

26. http://www.eff.org/deeplinks/2010/04/facebook-timeline.

27. http://www.ft.com/cms/s/0/f66e1f9e-9eec-11dc-b4e4-0000779fd2ac.html#axzz1URwCj7zf.

28. http://www.facebook.com/press/releases.php?p=3102.

29. http://online.wsj.com/article/SB10001424052748703730804576315682856383872.html?KEYWORDS=symantec+facebook+security+flaw.

30. http://news.cnet.com/8301-13577_3-10419950-36.html.

31. http://diy-marketing.blogspot.com/2011/09/discovering-facebook-like-button.html.

32. http://online.wsj.com/article/SB10001424052748704281504576329441432995616.html.

33. http://nakedsecurity.sophos.com/2010/12/17/facebook-friendships-get-creepier.

34. http://latimesblogs.latimes.com/technology/2011/08/facebook-photos-facial-recognition-puts-names-to-faces-at-black-hat-conference.html.

35. http://www.pcmag.com/article2/0,2817,2390440,00.asp.

36. http://www.nytimes.com/2011/11/30/technology/facebook-agrees-to-ftc-settlement-on-privacy.html?_r=1.

37. http://www.ftc.gov/opa/2011/11/privacysettlement.shtm.

38. http://blog.facebook.com/blog.php?post=10150378701937131.

39. http://online.wsj.com/article/APfc8ffb68f4374e238cda0636a7faec90.html.

40. http://online.wsj.com/article/SB10001424053111903885604576490763256558794.html?mod=WSJ_hp_LEFTWhatsNewsCollection.

41. The case of British football star Ryan Giggs is instructive. His marital woes were aired on Twitter leading to a court

injunction forbidding people to talk about it and heated discussion in the British Parliament, http://www.guardian.co.uk/politics/2011/may/23/ryan-giggs-named-footballer-injunction-row.

42. http://googleblog.blogspot.com/2011/06/introducing-google-project-real-life.html.
43. http://www.kpmg.com/RU/en/IssuesAndInsights/ArticlesPublications/Documents/Consumers-and-Convergence-IV.pdf, 7.
44. http://www.mcafee.com/us/resources/reports/rp-cylab-mobile-security.pdf, 3.
45. http://www.businessweek.com/magazine/content/05_50/b3963001.htm.
46. http://www.borndigitalbook.com.
47. http://online.wsj.com/article/SB10001424052748703904304575497903523187146.html.
48. http://www.washingtonpost.com/business/technology/parting-with-privacy-with-a-quick-click-for-adolescents/2011/04/28/AF2gSjTG_story.html.
49. http://www.alrc.gov.au/publications/67.%20Children%2C%20Young%20People%20and%20%20Attitudes%20to%20Privacy/introduction.
50. http://www.pewinternet.org/~/media//Files/Reports/2007/PIP_Teens_ Privacy_SNS_Report_Final.pdf.
51. Mary L. Roberts, "Geo-Cities (A) and (B)," *Journal of Interactive Marketing*, Winter 2000, 60–72.
52. "Children's Online Privacy Protection Rule: Notice of Proposed Rulemaking," *Federal Register Notice*, nd, http://www.ftc.gov.
53. http://www.ftc.gov/bcp/menus/consumer/data/child.shtm.
54. http://www.ftc.gov/opa/2011/09/coppa.shtm.
55. Prepared Statement of the Federal Trade Commission on "Recent Developments in Privacy Protections for Consumers, October 11, 2000, http://www.ftc.gov.
56. http://epic.org/privacy/glba.
57. See a explanation that is in laymen's terms but biased toward the positive from the Senate Banking Committee at http://banking.senate.gov/public/_files/070110_Dodd_Frank_Wall_Street_Reform_comprehensive_summary_Final.pdf; and a careful, ongoing study of the implications of the law by consulting firm PWC at http://www.pwc.com/us/en/financial-services/regulatory-services/publications/closer-look-series.jhtml?WT.mc_id=cpc_Google_financial+services+regulatory+services+publications&WT.srch=1.
58. http://apps.americanbar.org/buslaw/committees/CL230000pub/materials/2011/winter/2011_confin_winter_privacy_and_data_sec_after_doddfrank.pdf.
59. http://www.ftc.gov/bcp/edu/microsites/redflagsrule/index.shtml.
60. "Protecting the Privacy of Patients' Health Information," Department of Health and Human Services, May 9, 2001, http://www.hhs.gov.
61. http://www.hhs.gov/ocr/privacy/index.html.
62. http://www.futureofprivacy.org/leading-practices/smart-grid-privacy.
63. http://www.ftc.gov/os/2010/12/101201privacyreport.pdf.
64. http://europa.eu/rapid/pressReleasesAction.do?reference=IP/10/1462&format=HTML&aged=0&language=EN&guiLanguage=fr.
65. http://www.pcworld.com/businesscenter/article/235985/eu_orders_member_states_to_implement_cookie_law_or_else.html.
66. http://www.ftc.gov/reports/privacy3/fairinfo.shtm.
67. Federal Trade Commission, "Privacy Online: A Report to Congress, Part III," June 1998, http://www.ftc.gov.
68. http://eur-lex.europa.eu/LexUriServ/LexUriServ.do?uri=CELEX:31995L0046:EN:HTML.
69. http://www.statewatch.org/news/2010/oct/eu-com-draft-communication-data-protection.pdf.
70. http://www.informationweek.com/news/government/policy/229402835.
71. http://www.pillsburylaw.com/siteFiles/Events/F1F60C7E25AC560FFD55F268A477DD84.pdf.
72. http://www.informationshield.com/intprivacylaws.html.
73. https://www.privacyinternational.org/article/leading-surveillance-societies-eu-and-world-2007#summary.
74. http://www.computerworld.com/s/article/9014782/TJX_data_breach_At_45.6M_card_numbers_it_s_the_biggest_ever.
75. http://www.msnbc.msn.com/id/20979359/ns/technology_and_science-security/t/encryption-faulted-tjx-hacking.
76. http://www.informationweek.com/news/201400171.
77. http://www.informationweek.com/news/199203277.
78. http://www.databreaches.net/?p=17374.
79. http://www.reuters.com/article/2011/04/26/us-sony-stoldendata-idUSTRE73P6WB20110426.
80. http://www.zdnet.com/blog/btl/sonys-data-breach-costs-likely-to-scream-higher/49161.
81. http://news.cnet.com/8301-17938_105-20073515-1/canadian-staples-in-customer-privacy-hot-water.
82. http://www.privacyrights.org/data-breach.
83. http://www.ponemon.org/news-2/23.
84. http://www.f-secure.com/en_EMEA-Corp/pressroom/news/2008/fs_news_20080228_01_eng.html.
85. http://articles.yuikee.com.hk/newsletter/2008/03/f.html.
86. http://www.f-secure.com/en_EMEA-Corp/pressroom/news/2009/fs_news_20090305_01_eng.html.
87. http://www.thenewnewinternet.com/2011/08/02/hp-study-cyber-criminals-are-reaching-into-your-companys-pocket.
88. http://www.microsoft.com/canada/athome/security/email/spear_phishing.mspx.
89. http://www.idtheftcenter.org.
90. http://www.prnewswire.com/news-releases/javelin-study-finds-identity-fraud-reached-new-high-in-2009-but-consumers-are-fighting-back-83987287.html
91. http://www.wipo.int/about-ip/en.
92. The UCLA Online Institute for Cyberspace Law and Policy, "The Digital Millennium Copyright Act," http://www.gseis.ucla.edu.
93. For a detailed examination of the issues from a global perspective see the *Primer on Electronic Commerce and Intellectual Property Issues*, World Intellectual Property Organization, nd, http://ecommerce.wipo.int/primer/primer.html.
94. http://europa.eu/legislation_summaries/internal_market/businesses/intellectual_property/index_en.htm.
95. http://www.sfgate.com/cgi-bin/article.cgi?file=/chronicle/archive/2000/03/03/MN97266.DTL&type=tech_article.

96. "Napster Audience Surges Ahead of Appeal," Reuters, October 2, 2000, http://www.techweb.com.

97. http://online.wsj.com/article/SB100014240527023033 41904575577192244735152.html.

98. http://www.riaa.com/faq.php.

99. http://www.pcworld.com/businesscenter/article/244011/ the_us_stop_online_piracy_act_a_primer.html.

100. http://articles.cnn.com/2012-01-06/tech/tech_web_sopa-web-piracy-act_1_foreign-websites-netcoalition-sopa?_s=PM:TECH.

101. http://www.articlesbase.com/music-articles/legal-music-download-vs-filesharing-47594.html.

102. http://www.guardian.co.uk/news/datablog/2009/jun/09/games-dvd-music-downloads-piracy.

103. http://www.syracuse.com/news/index.ssf/2011/06/apple_icloud_vs_music_piracy_w.html.

104. http://creativecommons.org.

105. http://search.creativecommons.org/?q=license chooser.

106. http://creativecommons.org/licenses.

CHAPTER 16

Mobile Marketing and Related Developments

Key Terms

LEARNING OBJECTIVES

By the time you complete this chapter, you will be able to:

- Identify important concepts that apply to the adoption and diffusion of technological innovations and the accelerating speed of their adoption.

- Describe the environment described as pervasive computing and explain changes it could make in the way we live and work.

- Discuss the current status of mobile adoption in one or more countries around the world and explain why penetration rates and usage behaviors differ between countries.

- Identify the strategic drivers of mobile technology and why they contribute to the adoption of mobile.

- Discuss the channels of mobile marketing with special emphasis on the ones that are unique to mobile.

- List the steps in developing a mobile marketing campaign.

- Discuss the role smartphones and mobile apps are playing in the world of mobile marketing.

- Describe the uses of location-based and barcode marketing with special emphasis on their relevance to small, local businesses.

- Explain the meaning and implications of digital convergence with emphasis on media convergence.

In 1996, the Internet burst on public consciousness and ignited a firestorm of activity. In the intervening years, both pure-play Internet firms and traditional mass media marketers have made the Internet a key element in marketing strategies. They have done so, not because the Internet is interesting technology, but because it has become part of the everyday life of consumers and businesses around the globe. This is especially true of the mobile phone and the role it is playing in the lives of people and in the marketing of brands. There is every reason to believe that mobile will be the dominant force in the Internet going forward. This chapter will examine the actions that marketers are taking to be part of the mobile space.

In evaluating these developments, we need to keep in mind that this is an ongoing process of developing innovative new products and services and facilitating their diffusion in the marketplace. There are three key concepts from innovation and diffusion theory that we should keep uppermost in our minds as we cover this material: the adoption process, the diffusion process, and the characteristics of a product that encourage adoption.

Consumer Adoption of Technology Innovations

The consumer adoption process is a generally accepted conceptualization of the stages a consumer goes through when confronted with a new product or service (see Figure 16.1a). According to the adoption process, the consumer must first become aware, then develop an interest, perform some prepurchase evaluation, and then try the product, either as a consequence of a purchase or of a marketer-sponsored promotion or incentive. Two important stages follow trial. First, the consumer must decide to purchase/continue purchasing the product, which can be behaviorally identified as adoption. A harder to discern stage is that of internalization in which the product has become an integral part of the

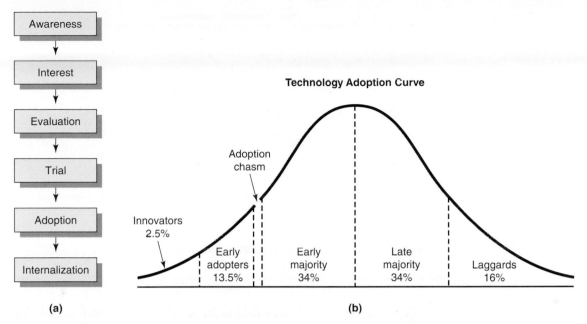

FIGURE **16.1** The Consumer Adoption and Diffusion Processes

Sources: © Cengage Learning 2013; and Chris Pinter, "Google Captures 28% of smart phone market share. – A technology adoption case study," February 4, 2011. © Copyright 2011 Pinter Electronics Consultants. All rights reserved. Reprinted with permission.

consumer's lifestyle. The internalization stage is particularly important in the case of technology. Products or services with a high component of technology often require that consumers undergo a substantial learning process in order to be used successfully. Only if consumers are willing to undertake the learning process, and only if that process is successful, is the product internalized and becomes an integral part of the consumer's life.

Closely associated is the concept of the diffusion process, which is familiar to students of marketing, communications, and sociology. With time on the horizontal axis and number of adopters (defined as first-time purchasers) on the vertical axis, the concept shows a process that is normally distributed around a population mean.

Figure 16.1b shows the traditional adoption curve as it is seen by technology marketers.[1] It includes the concept of "the chasm," a term popularized by Geoffrey Moore in 1991.[2] Moore points out that technologies may have initial success among the innovators and early adopters, but it is their ability to "cross the chasm" and penetrate the mainstream market that separates the successful from the unsuccessful technology products.

The third concept describes product characteristics that affect the ease of generating trial and adoption. These are widely accepted in the marketing literature as having:

1. *Relative advantage*: the degree to which product benefits are perceived to be superior to those of existing products.
2. *Compatibility*: the degree of consistency between the new product and consumer's perceptions of and behaviors toward existing members of the product category.
3. *Complexity*: the extent to which the new product is difficult to learn to use.
4. *Trialability/divisibility*: the extent to which the new product can be tried on a limited or modular basis.
5. *Observability/communicability*: the degree to which the new product's benefits are evident to or can be communicated to the prospective customer.

The degree to which an innovative product or service possesses these characteristics determines the ease with which it is adopted and diffused throughout the population.

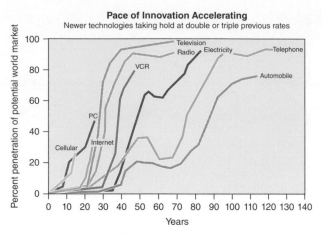

FIGURE **16.2** The Increasing Pace of Innovation

Source: Figure "Pace of Innovation Accelerating," by Joseph Jacobsen, printed in the "IBM Global Innovation Outlook" report. Reprinted with permission of Joseph Jacobson.

Reporting on a global conference held in 2004, IBM suggests that innovating in the Internet age is different in three important ways. They are:

1. Innovation occurs with greater rapidity across product types and national boundaries.
2. It requires collaboration across scientific and technical disciplines.
3. The traditional concept of intellectual property is being questioned. It needs to evolve from being a possession that is hoarded to being a productive asset that is invested or even shared to encourage further progress.[3]

Figure 16.2 shows the shape of adoption curves for a number of modern innovations. Older innovations like the automobile and telephone were slower to diffuse through the population than newer ones. The speed of adoption increased with radio and especially television, and then picked up speed with the VCR, the PC, and the Internet.

Using United States sales data, it appears that the pace of adoption of electronics products continues to accelerate. The DVD was launched in the United States market in 1997 and sold over 350,000 units its first year, making its growth the fastest ever for a non-phone product. The iPhone demonstrated that issue by selling one million units in the first quarter after its launch in 2007. In 2010, the iPad blew through all forecasts by selling three million units in just 80 days after its launch.[4] The take-up of services can be even faster with a forecast based on marketing research estimating that 76 percent of iPhone users would be using iCloud services "soon" after their launch in October 2011.[5]

Retail analyst Colin McGranahan of Bernstein Research summarized the situation by pointing out that it took five years for the DVD to reach the unit sales rate reached by the iPad in a single fiscal quarter.[6] While it is clear that the iPad benefited from the success of the iPod and the iPhone, the accelerating pace of adoption of successful product categories as shown in Figure 16.2 sets a high standard for marketers.

Let us begin our look at mobile marketing by looking at the environment in which it is taking place. The state many technologists have been looking forward to for many years is most often called *pervasive*, sometimes ubiquitous, *computing*.

Pervasive Computing

The pervasive computing concept existed long before the commercial Internet. This powerful concept implies that a single person has access to a myriad of computing devices to assist in performing all sorts of daily tasks.

Computing pioneer Mark Weiser of Xerox's PARC research laboratory has been working on the concept since the early 1990s. His vision is based on the idea of making computing power available in virtually every aspect of everyday living and making the computers themselves invisible to the user. This is different from the environment that surrounded either mainframe or desktop computers. There the focus was on the computer itself and on making it do the task the user wanted to accomplish.

The focus of the early pioneers was to enhance the world of everyday activities by using **embedded devices** that perform without human intervention. In a 1991 article for *Scientific American*, he described a world in which, "doors open only to the right badge wearer, rooms greet people by name, telephone calls can be automatically forwarded to wherever the recipient may be, receptionists actually know where people are, computer terminals retrieve the preferences of whoever is sitting at them, and appointment diaries write themselves. No revolution in artificial intelligence is needed—just the proper imbedding of computers into the everyday world."[7]

A few years later, IBM elaborated on the vision, using the synonymous term "**pervasive computing.**" According to IBM:

> Pervasive computing aims to enable people to accomplish an increasing number of personal and professional transactions using a new class of intelligent and portable devices. It gives people convenient access to relevant information stored on powerful networks, allowing them to easily take action anywhere, anytime.
>
> These new intelligent appliances or "smart devices" are embedded with microprocessors that allow users to plug into intelligent networks and gain direct, simple, and secure access to both relevant information and services. These devices are as simple to use as calculators, telephones or kitchen toasters.[8]

The word that gives most people pause in descriptions like this is "simple." We are all familiar with devices that are difficult to learn to use, complex software applications that require extensive study, and ancillary devices that are difficult to connect to the system or network. Some of us have never even gained confidence in our ability to program our DVR to record a program that we want to watch later or to successfully program all the functions on our cell phone. In other words, we have a great deal of experience to suggest that new technologies are usually not simple, especially in the early stages of their development or user adoption. Complexity can retard the diffusion of an innovation.

Table 16.1 lists six dimensions, often referred to as the "6 A's," of pervasive computing and their implications for the marketplace and for

TABLE 16.1 Dimensions of the Pervasive Computing Environment

Dimension	Marketplace Implications	Marketer Requirements
Access	Information instantaneously available, either through actively accessing the network or through passive provision by embedded devices	Large and constantly updated databases of content
Anyone	Inexpensive and/or embedded devices make pervasive computing readily available to most people around the globe	Increased market size; may also increase the number of small transactions
Anytime	Users able to access data and communications at any time, not just when they are seated at their desks	Be prepared to respond to customers instead of initiating customer communication
Anywhere	Wireless networks blanket first urban areas and then outlying regions, bringing access to residents and travelers	Increasingly high customer expectations for content and service
Any Internet-enabled device	Communications and data no longer limited to fixed desktop machines but available on a large number of small portable devices	Different display and revision of content necessary for mobile devices
Authorized	Networks able to provide secure access when required for communications and transactions	Security and authentication that are understood and trusted by customers

Source: © Cengage Learning 2013

marketers who seek opportunity in mobile. For the marketplace, and for both consumers and business users, the implications can be summarized as instant gratification of their desire for content of many kinds. Marketers will be required to develop more user-centric systems that deliver content and allow anyone with the appropriate device to make transactions *anywhere, anytime*. That is a tall order and it should be the driving force behind mobile marketing programs.

There are several examples of devices that could be considered the forerunners of pervasive computing as it was envisioned by the computing forefathers. One prime example is the multi-touch screen technology that has come to be known as *CNN's Magic Wall*. This technology was first used to aggregate election results onto a national map and has progressed to other applications like weather reporting and following CNN social media accounts for on-air reporting.[9] See another example in Interactive Exercise 16.1.

Impressive as both these new technologies are, they do not represent the full vision of pervasive computing. That vision appears to be developing in a way that is different from the concept that has been popular for many years. It can be summarized in a single word, *mobile*!

Cell Phones and Other Mobile Devices in the Global Market

Factoids about the sheer size and rapid growth rate of mobile from mobiThinking .com include:

- 5.3 billion mobile subscribers (77 percent of world's population) in 2011.
- Growth lead by China and India.
- Smartphones led the growth in 2010 and Android was expected to be the leading platform by 2011.
- Half a billion people accessed the mobile Internet in 2009, 277 million in China alone.
- Many of these users are mobile only, rarely using any other device to access the Internet.
- Mobile advertising spending worldwide is expected to reach $3.3 billion in 2011 and $20.6 billion by 2015.
- Search and local ads are especially important in the mobile space.[10]

Mary Meeker of Kleiner Perkins Caufield and Byers argues that social networking and search are helping to accelerate growth in the mobile space. She also points out that the rate of adoption for popular games is spectacular. FarmVille reached over eight million in the first 60 days after launch while CityVille reached well over 16 million in the same time frame. That dwarfs the adoption rates for even the iPhone and iPad.[11] No wonder marketers have invented the word "gamification" to describe the incorporation of game-like elements into products and promotions.

The most important point of all is that mobile is expected to be the dominant way to access the Internet by 2015.[12] That situation may already exist in Europe and Asia where mobile adoption has been ahead of the United States. For example, one analyst said that mobile phone penetration was 130 percent in Western Europe and 123 percent in Eastern Europe in 2010.[13] If you wonder how that is possible, it is because many people have more than one connection. It is even more the case in Hong Kong where market saturation was reached in 2002. The mobile phone market continues to grow with penetration at 175 percent in Hong Kong and nearing that in Singapore, Macau, and Taiwan.[14] The maturity of those mobile markets has lead to a great deal of activity on the mobile marketing front.

Mobile Marketing Campaigns

Mobile marketing campaigns in developed mobile markets demonstrate their ability to reach desirable target markets, open new market segments, deliver rich media, create partnership opportunities, and integrate into both online and offline marketing efforts. Three examples show this potential.

The Discovery Channel in Australia partnered with Tourism Australia to promote the new season of its popular motorcycle program, American Chopper. The Australian branch of the agency, Communicator Interactive, described its charge from the client as follows:

> We had to give these custom-made choppers a dinky-di experience and take fans of the show on a unique virtual tour around Australia. It sort of sounded like a bike-only Mad Max II, so we were all for it.

The campaign centered around a road trip from Sydney to Queensland and back to Melbourne. A virtual environment mirrored the ruggedness of the terrain and of the riders. Paul Senior, Paul Junior, and Mikey had a trip blog with posts, pictures, and videos. The bikes they ride in the show are fully customized and the campaign website allowed users to create their own customized chopper. The site also featured a contest for the best design. None of this sounds particularly new or revolutionary until you remember that it is all being done on mobile!

The campaign tied into Australia Tourism's Global Programs branding effort that showcases the unique culture and lifestyle of Australia.[15]

Johnson & Johnson chose mobile to launch its new Define contact lens in Hong Kong. Its target audience was young Chinese women and the company wanted the brand message to reach them in a fun and exciting way.

For the campaign, the company created:

- A branded WAP (wireless application protocol) site for 3G phones (see Figure 16.3a)
- Banner ads placed on mobile sites frequented by the target audience
- Outbound multimedia messaging service (MMS) messages to a database that was in existence at the beginning of the campaign and supplemented by new opt-ins as the campaign progressed

The campaign ultimately reached over 70 percent of Hong Kong 3G users. Highlights of the results were:

- Over 50 percent of the total Hong Kong 3G population viewed the mobile banner ads.
- It achieved a 10 percent click-through rate and completion of the opt-in registration form.
- Over 75 percent of all viewers visited the branded game site (see Figure 16.3b).
- 31 percent of all visitors were between the ages of 36 and 45.

(a)   (b)

FIGURE **16.3** The Acuvue Define Mobile Campaign and WAP
Site with Game

Source: Johnson & Johnson, 1-DAY ACUVUE DEFINE Brand Contact Lenses, http://blog.karentsui.
com/johnson-johnson-mobile-marketing-campaign.

The campaign was considered the most successful mobile campaign ever run
in Hong Kong, although no sales figures were made available.[16]

The ENO goes mobile. The venerable English National Opera endured years of
artistic and management turmoil that culminated in cancellations and large losses
for the 2002 season. In 2004, the worst of those problems were behind it,[17] but
it was still averaging only 70 to 80 percent of audience capacity, leaving its operations at barely break even.

Many arts organizations have turned to the Internet for last-minute ticket
sales in recent years, but the ENO took it a step further and turned to text
messaging. It used mobile agency Txtlocal, which returns 100 percent of donations to its charity accounts instead of taking a processing fee as most agencies
do. In two campaigns using simple 160-character text messages, the ENO spent
£500 and realized £8,000 in ticket profits by messaging opera attendees in its
own database.[18]

The ENO has also turned to mobile to boost its fund-raising. The insta-
Giv agency conducts the mobile donation program and promises at least
£4.45 to ENO from each £5 donated by mobile.[19] It also developed a mobile
opera guide app that provides information and access to tickets in a user-
friendly manner. As a result of the app and other online initiatives, online
ticket sales have gone from 10 percent to 50 percent in less than three
years.[20] Another key indicator of success is that 30 percent of ENO's audience is
now under 44 years old—a signal achievement for an opera company.[21]

Each of these campaigns had its own strategy that was part of the organization's overall marketing strategy. While the development of mobile marketing
strategies follows the basic template of developing a marketing campaign in any
channel, there are considerations that are unique to mobile. In particular, mobile
campaigns will make use of three critical components—apps, local marketing,
and the integration of social media into mobile. This is the SoLoMo (SOcial
LOcal and MObile) marketing phenomenon widely discussed in the mobile marketing literature. We will consider the development of mobile marketing strategies and
campaigns and discuss each of the three elements in turn.

Strategic Drivers of Mobile Marketing

The global rollout of broadband network availability is increasing the speed of cell phones and other mobile devices. There are, however, special considerations that marketers must keep in mind as they develop mobile marketing programs. Download speeds do not equal those of desktop computers. Content must be viewed on small screens. The extent to which mobile users will accept advertising in return for free content is as yet unclear.

Marketers will only be successful to the extent that they take into account the strategic drivers of mobile marketing. They are:

- *Context.* This means providing necessary information when and where the customer needs or wants it. The content trigger is in the hands of the customer, not of the marketer. Context in the wireless environment has two dimensions:
  - *Localization.* Through various geographical systems, the location of the user can be identified and information specific to that location can be provided. Location-based marketing programs are discussed later in the chapter.
  - *Personalization.* The customer expects to select not only the type of information desired but also the frequency of information provision. Unwanted content pushed to a mobile phone is especially annoying to users.
- *Growth of social networks.* People are accessing social networks on their mobile phones in large and increasing numbers. This provides a communications opportunity for the user and a marketing opportunity for businesses.
- *Time sensitive.* Screens are small and storage is limited on many devices, so information must be provided at the time appropriate to the customer, not the time convenient for the marketer. As a customer passes a store in a shopping mall, he may be willing to receive a coupon for a purchase in that store, which he can save or retain on the screen until he redeems it.
- *High-value.* The coupon will have to have a reasonable value in order to make it welcome in the wireless context.
- *Voice activation.* There are many situations, driving in particular, in which it is not safe—and in many locales, legal—to use the keyboard of a mobile device. Voice activation is one solution in these situations.
- *One-click payment mechanisms.* Consumers are not willing to enter credit card information on mobile keyboards and may be uncomfortable with the idea of their credit card data being transmitted wirelessly. They are not likely to be willing, either, to have numerous vendor-specific accounts, especially for micropayments. Amazon Payment Systems offers consumers the ability to pay at many other websites using their Amazon accounts. Its Checkout with Amazon service offers businesses the opportunity to accept payments through Amazon's 1-click system.[22] Google Checkout also offers consumers the ability to pay and businesses the opportunity to accept payments.[23] In the spring of 2011, Google was reported to be in discussions with Visa and Mastercard that could lead to a mobile wallet payment system.[24]
- *Security.* Users must be assured that data transmissions are secure, and authentication services must be provided in a way that is suitable for the devices. Embedded devices that identify the owner are one possibility. **SIM (Subscriber Identity Module) cards** that can be inserted and removed to protect encoded information are a widely used solution.
- *Privacy.* In addition to protecting personal data, providers of content and services will have to be sensitive to download times, lack of storage, and the fact that users are paying for airtime. They must not abuse technological capabilities like geographic location services.

- *Expanded permission marketing.* Marketers will have to extend the concept of permission marketing beyond simple opt-in. They must find out what kind of information consumers are willing to receive, how often they are willing to receive transmissions, and where they are willing to receive it. This means an accurate customer database that is updated in real time.

The inherent limitations of small screens and transmission times also mean that marketers must be vigilant in trying to stop mobile spam before it gets a major foothold in the marketplace. Earlier chapters described the ire of consumers who receive spam on their conventional systems. Although email sent to desktop systems does not cost the consumer, nor is it a significant use of scarce computing resources in most instances, consumers still hate spam email. Therefore, it does not seem unreasonable to predict that such consumers will hate unsolicited wireless advertising even more, because it is even more intrusive.

Developing Mobile Marketing Campaigns

The mobile space is sufficiently complex that a formal plan is needed for each campaign. It is important that the campaign be part of Internet marketing and marketing communications strategies as a whole, but planning and carrying out mobile campaigns require all the planning and monitoring steps required in any marketing communications activity.

Mobile Marketing Channels

There are many communications channels that can reach the mobile user. Some are channels that are heavily used on the wired Internet; others are relatively unique to the mobile space. At this time, there are specific types of communications that can reach only specific mobile devices—for example, the Martha Stewart emagazine for the iPad described in Chapter 5—but much content is available on most broadband-enabled devices, and device-agnostic access will continue to increase.

The basic channels of marketer communications are shown in Figure 16.4. The channels—from email to barcodes—are all familiar. The difference is that the content they carry is pushed to the mobile device once permission is given by the user.

Email, display advertising, search, and content marketing are similar in the mobile setting to their desktop counterparts. The primary difference in email, search, and content marketing is that existing textual content needs to be reconfigured for small screens. Streaming of music and video needs to be optimized for mobile, and the display of video also needs to be optimized for small screens.

Display advertising, in particular, has to be reconfigured for mobile. According to the Internet Advertising Bureau (IAB), the 350 pixel by 250 pixel banner is

FIGURE **16.4** Mobile Marketing Communications Channels

Source: © Cengage Learning 2013

currently the most popular in the United States, with 320 × 50 and 300 × 50 banner sizes also being used for smartphones.[25] The Mobile Marketing Association, which serves global mobile marketers, has a detailed set of standards for display ads, text messaging, multimedia messaging, video, and apps.[26] Mobile display ads arc small, and content has to be carefully considered.

Mobile apps, bar codes, **text messaging** in its various formats, and podcasts are the tools that are the most specific to the mobile space. Later in the chapter, we discuss each of these tools, illustrating its use with case studies.

Mobile Marketing Campaign Planning

U.K. mobile agency Aerodeon has an approach to developing mobile programs that reflects typical elements of any marketing campaign strategy and adds emphasis on mobile issues. Its approach is portrayed in Figure 16.5.

Each brand that contemplates a mobile campaign must answer the questions in Figure 16.5 for itself as it plans each campaign. Industry data do however, provide interesting indicators of possible answers to the initial question of how to target mobile campaigns to identified groups of target customers.

1. *Who are the customers and where are they accessing content?* The generic answer is that younger consumers, ages 18 to 34, are generally believed to be the heaviest users of mobile. Pew data for the U.S. market shows that fully 95 percent of them own cell phones (see Figure 16.6).

   Social networks, however, are a special case. The 2010 data from Nielsen showed that women and users aged 35 to 54 were the most active mobile users of social networks.[27] Pingdom statistics show differences in use of social networks by age across some of the popular networks:

   - The average social network user is 37 years old.
   - LinkedIn, with its business focus, has a predictably high average user age: 44.
   - The average Twitter user is 39 years old.
   - The average Facebook user is 38 years old.
   - The average MySpace user is 31 years old.
   - Bebo has by far the youngest users, with an average age of 28.[28]

   These data clearly show that different networks have different user groups and sometimes different reasons for usage. The marketer must understand the usage patterns of all mobile channels, including social networks, in order to reach the desired target audience.

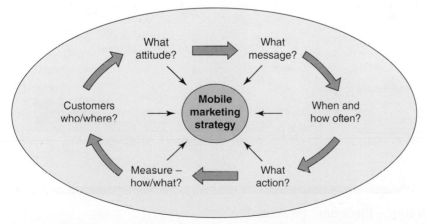

FIGURE **16.5** Essential Considerations in Developing a Mobile Marketing Campaign

Source: Adapted with permission from Chris Bourke, (July 2006) "How to Develop a Mobile Marketing Strategy: Integrating mobile into the mix to increase brand awareness, generate leads and win sales," figure 3, p. 10, Aerodeon.

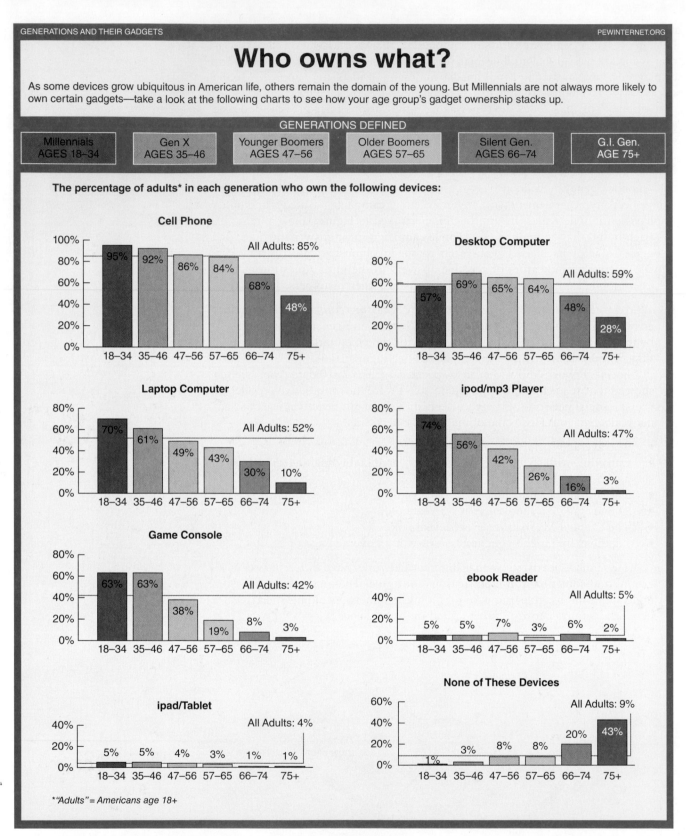

FIGURE **16.6** Generational Use of Various Electronic Devices

Source: Kathryn Zickuhr, "Generations and their gadgets," Pew Internet & American Life Project, February 3, 2011. From http://pewinternet. org/Infographics/2011/Generations-and-gadgets.aspx, retrieved 10/20/2011.

Even though there is great variance in the pattern of use by channel, the impact of the mobile Internet on younger demographic groups cannot be understated. Norwegian mobile operating system provider Opera produces a continuing series of global studies of mobile use. One of its executives commented on a 2010 study of Gen Y users:

> "We have often said that the next generation will grow up knowing the web mostly through their mobile phones," said Jon von Tetzchner, Co-founder, Opera. "We see this trend already emerging in different regions around the world. The mobile Web will bring a profound change in how we connect with one another. I think the results from this survey already show that change taking place."[29]

The key point is that marketers cannot generalize about the receptivity of any target audience—by age or any other demographic—to their message. It will depend on various brand, audience, and marketing factors.

2. *What attitudes do members of the target audience hold about our brand?* Another way of putting it is "Where are they on the branding hierarchy?" that we discussed in Chapter 5. A new brand, or a brand communicating to a new segment, needs to create awareness and might use videos to create awareness and favorable attitudes. A marketer with an established brand and following may simply need to provide a call to action, and might choose to offer an incentive by email or SMS that can trigger purchase.

3. *What message will be compelling?* The marketer should have an established brand promise and related messages that need to be conveyed, depending on the readiness stage of the target audience. As seen in Figure 16.4, there are robust options for conveying the message through channels that vary in their ability to convey in-depth information or to create an engaging customer experience or to execute any other message and creative strategy that is appropriate.

4. *When to send messages and how often both refer to important strategic drivers of mobile marketing?* Sending messages when users are in an appropriate mood and location (shopping in a mall, for example) has a much better chance of being effective than simply sending them randomly. How often users wish to receive message is an appropriate question to ask when they opt in to receiving the messages.

5. *What action do we want the mobile user to take?* That will depend on the objectives of the mobile campaign itself. Desired actions should be clearly specified as part of the planning process. The action should be specified—and encouraged, perhaps by an incentive—with equal clarity to the user.

6. *What metrics will be used to measure the success of the campaign?* As in all the measuring and monitoring efforts we have discussed in this text, the appropriate metrics are completely dependent on the objectives of the campaign. As discussed in Chapter 14, mobile metrics are readily available from platform suppliers and third-party metrics agencies.

This approach to developing a specific plan for each mobile marketing program makes it clear that determining which marketing channel to use is part of a series of decisions that stem from the choice of program objectives and target market segment.[30] Only when objectives have been established and the target audience profiled in detail can the mobile marketer choose channels and messages.

The Mobile Tools in Action

There are no comprehensive data that compare the use of the various mobile marketing tools. There is no doubt, however, that **mobile apps** have exploded on the scene with a force that seems likely to permanently change how we market to users—both businesses and consumers.

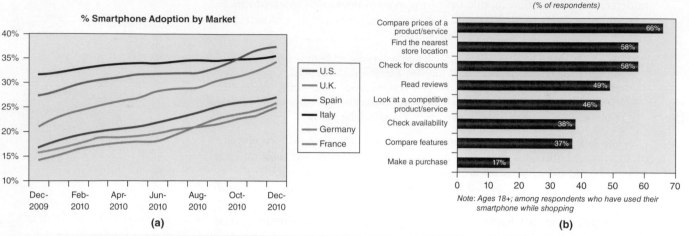

FIGURE 16.7 The Explosive Growth of Smartphones

Sources: http://www.comscore.com/Press_Events/Presentations_Whitepapers/2011/2010_Mobile_Year_in_Review, p. 13; and eMarketer, Inc., March 25, 2011.

What Is Behind the Explosion in Mobile Apps?

The enabling factor in the growth of apps was originally the smartphone with tablets later becoming important. The penetration of smartphones differs between countries, as shown in Figure 16.7a. That chart also points out the fact that the United States has generally been late to the party when it comes to the adoption of mobile, including smartphones. However, the users of smartphones are using them with a vengeance. Shopping is one category in which they find multiple uses for their phones, and **location-based services** are another (see Figure 16.7b).

Mobile Applications Are a Media Force

With smartphones and tablets assuming a dominant position in the lives of consumers, especially younger ones, a rush is on to make content available on various devices. The "app" is the driving force in this movement. Apps appeal to a wide variety of interests, lifestyles, and demographic groups. There are many apps for fashion and entertainment that particularly appeal to young women. And sports content is an excellent way to reach young male, as well as female, sports fans.

The National Hockey League's Blackberry Channel

Video content is an important component of sports marketing and it drives a "significant proportion" of the NHL's website advertising revenue according to the league's SVP-Digital Media.[31] The program used a free Blackberry Messenger app (see Figure 16.8b), driving awareness for the Blackberry platform and engagement with content on the NHL site among its target audience, 18- to 34-year-old hockey fans.

The initial campaign took place during the 2010 playoff season,[32] and resulted in over 1 million video starts with noticeable improvement in all metrics cited (see Figure 16.8a). The NHL made several adjustments to content in order to achieve the high access rate. It introduced content earlier in the segments, shifted the focus from the segment hosts to game action, and made the videos shorter. It also lengthened the window of time in which each video was accessible.

Both the NHL and Research in Motion (Blackberry) were pleased with the initial campaign and renewed it for the 2011 playoffs with content available

Metrics for BlackBerry All-Access Pregame Show on NHL.com, April–June 2010

153% increase in starts per show
89% increase in starts per segment
4% increase in completion rates
188% increase in % of average daily video watchers who started a show segment
145% increase in % of all NHL. com daily unique visitors who started a show segment

(a)

(b)

FIGURE **16.8** (a) Blackberry Video Metrics for 2010 NHL Channel (b) Channel for the 2011 Playoff Season

Sources: eMarketer, Inc., as cited by NHL and Omniture, March 4, 2011; and NHL, http://video.nhl.com/videocenter/console?catid=40&intcmpid=hp-promo-mod.

from October 2010 through the playoffs beginning in April 2011. By March 4, 2011, the campaign had already achieved "several million video starts" according to eMarketer.[33]

Backstage at the Oscars

The Oscar telecasts have been experiencing declining viewership for a number of years, and for the 2011 awards ceremony, numerous apps were available in the effort to increase engagement and viewership. The academy's official app was titled "Backstage at the Oscars" and allowed viewers their choice of camera shots not available on TV. If the viewer was still awake, she could watch shots from the Governor's Ball after the ceremony. This 99 cent app was available for iPhone, iPod Touch, and iPad. At least two apps were available for Android users—"Live from the Red Carpet" and the "Oscars Trivia Challenge."[34]

The most comprehensive coverage appeared to be from the Awards Hero: Oscars® Edition app, which was also offered for the iPhone, iPod Touch, and iPad. It featured all the nominees, related film trailers, deep content about Oscar history, and current entertainment news feeds. It not only allowed individuals to vote on their own award choices, but also had social features that allowed them to share their votes with friends on Facebook and Twitter. Users could create an Oscar pool to vie with friends for picking the most winners.[35] A few days before the 2011 Oscar awards about 10,000 people had purchased this 99 cent app.[36]

Media observers suggest that television viewership of live events has increased as a result of social media.[37] That did not work for the 2011 Oscars, a show for which numbers go up and down depending on the popularity of the films and actors nominated. The overall viewership declined by 10 percent, according to Nielsen. However, viewers in the prime demographic of 18 to 34 declined by only 5 percent, which attests to the power of mobile and social media to support traditional media.[38]

Apps Are Not Just for Young Sports and Entertainment Fans

The Martha Stewart domestic empire is a good example of that. Chapter 5 discussed her initial foray into iPad content—one of the early ventures into that new media space. For the Christmas season 2010, Martha Stewart Living Omnimedia

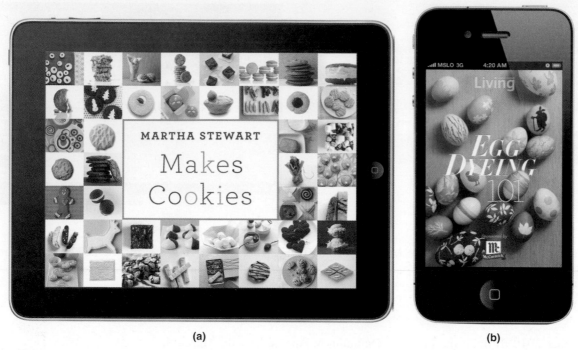

(a)   (b)

FIGURE **16.9** Martha Stewart Living Omnimedia Cookie and Egg Dyeing Apps

(MSLO) introduced a content-rich Martha Stewart Makes Cookies app for the iPhone, iPod Touch, and iPad (see Figure 16.9a). The iPad version was pricey at $7.99,[39] but it appeared to enjoy considerable success. In the spring of 2011, the Eye Dying 101 app (see Figure 16.9b) joined the growing gallery of mobile applications at MSLO.

MSLO has a large and devoted following, many of whom are well over the "young" demographic that is generally assumed to be the target for mobile apps.[40] This audience, however, is a heavy user of both mobile phones and family and home information. That is demonstrated by the fact that 190,650 followers downloaded the initial Martha's Everyday Foods app in just eight months following its introduction.[41] This proves that older consumers will use mobile apps, and like younger users, they will also pay for apps that offer relevant content.

The success of the MSLO apps illustrates once again the importance of understanding the target audience and its needs and usage patterns. A study by BabyCenter called "21st Century Mobile Mom Report" finds that 53 percent of the young mothers in its survey adopted the smartphone as a direct result of becoming a mom. The camera is their favorite feature; the video cam is the second favorite; and apps are third. Many of the apps relate to their children, and they are active users of apps while shopping.[42]

Location-Based Marketing

Does any young person pick up the telephone to find out what his friends are doing tonight? That is likely only if we are referring to the mobile phone, and the preferred method of communication may be text messaging, not voice conversation. If the user has a smartphone, it may be an app that allows him to locate friends. Alternatively, he may visit one of the social networks that uses GPS (Global Positioning System) technology to locate a predetermined group of friends.

If he uses a **location-based service**, he is one of only 7 percent of all online adults (8 percent of adults aged between 18 and 29) who use these services. And yes, it is likely to be "he"; 6 percent of online men use them as compared to only 3 percent of women.[43] That is enough to interest marketers; however, they continue to "follow the eyeballs." Keep in mind that this phenomenon is quite new and that the location-based marketing space is likely to undergo many changes before it reaches maturity. Let us briefly look at three companies that are currently major players in the space. Two are familiar names; one is a specialized newcomer.

1. In Google's often-bewildering array of products, there are several that have to do with location. You are probably familiar with Google Maps, which can be used on either the desktop or a mobile phone. The Google Maps mobile app[44] has a variety of features. The feature of most interest to marketers is the Place Pages, on which users can search for nearby businesses by keyword.

   This element is obviously a business-oriented feature, and once again it is especially appealing to small or local businesses that need to reach potential customers when they are in the neighborhood.[45] Businesses are often surprised to find that they are already visible on Google Maps, but that the information is often either wrong or incomplete, even though Google uses some basic services such as telephone directories to compile it. The business needs to sign on to Google Places and claim its business (i.e., prove it owns the business). It can then correct any wrong information, including its exact placement on the map, construct a profile, upload pictures and videos, and choose keywords. Once the page is established, the business owner can post information about upcoming events and can even offer coupons.

   Each page has a dashboard that gives basic metrics like number of impressions and click throughs. It also shows the keywords that have brought visitors to the site and the locations from which they have requested directions to the retail establishment. The coupons page also shows the number of coupons downloaded, but the establishment has to keep track of how many are actually redeemed. Google appears to place emphasis on this activity because it has recently begun to send page owners a monthly email with a summary of its results. That is a good reminder and especially appropriate in the small business environment where the social media marketer is probably the owner!

   Yahoo! Local works in the same way, and a local retailer should be sure to claim ownership and see that correct information is on both these local search resources.

2. The largest of the specialized services appear to be Foursquare[46] and Gowalla,[47] both of which were launched in 2009. Each uses a mobile app that allows users to check in from their current location. Foursquare offers badges that users can earn by checking in a specified number of times.[48] For the most part, this seems to be friendly competition, although the mayor of a location may get special prices from the owner of the business location. Foursquare's business page gives a listing of business near the viewer's location, assuming she is signed into an account that has GPS associated with it—nice touch!

   Gowalla offers the same sort of check-in functionality. It also allows users to create location-based events with a 12-hour duration, and also offers a passport to be "stamped" and prizes given at certain locations.[49]

Google Places, and the Foursquare and Gowalla location-based marketing functions all offer businesses large and small an opportunity for local visibility and the ability to offer promotions to attract customers, again on a purely local basis. The appeal this functionality has to retail businesses is hard to overstate.

Groupon was launched in Chicago in late 2008 and has steadily expanded into other major market areas around the world. Groupon focuses entirely on local marketing by featuring a "Deal of the Day" for each area.

Members can sign up for email alerts each day or can visit the Groupon site where they will find various promotions in their local area. There is a big incentive to share with friends; a certain number of sales are required to make the deal operational. Members purchase the coupon, and then print it out or save it on their mobile phones. The GPS feature of the mobile app allows users to search for nearby Groupon deals.

In addition to choosing a city, which is required since these are local promotions, the user can also personalize by gender, age, and zip code. As of late 2010, Groupon had 15 million active users in North America and also operated in Europe, Latin America, Japan, and Russia.[50] By early 2011, it had rolled out to additional cities and countries and the website said the service had sold over 38 million coupons and saved its members almost $2 billion.[51]

With its huge reach, it is not surprising that Groupon experimented with an offer for a national retailer. On August 19, 2010, Gap offered a 50 percent off coupon that resulted in $11 million in sales for the retailer and a huge surge in traffic for Groupon. According to blogger Tom Funk of Timberline Interactive, the coupon offer was heavily supported in social media. The day's social media timeline looked like this:

- 15 million Gap and Groupon email subscribers receive the offer, starting at midnight and in staggered fashion throughout the day.
- The offer was first tweeted to the 180,000+ followers of Twitter's @earlybird promoted tweet stream, a promotional channel that offers deals to followers.
- Gap tweets the offer to its 30,000+ followers.
- Groupon manually tweets and creates Facebook posts on its pages dedicated to each of the 85 geographical markets where Gap's offer was valid.
- Gap posted the offer to its 606,000 fans on Facebook.
- Groupon's 1,500 affiliate partners post Gap's offer on their websites.
- A sponsored post appears above the fold on the Digg social bookmarking site.[52]

That is a great deal of activity for a single day and it required careful coordination. The planning was essential to the success of this campaign, which integrated several marketing channels.

Since these services offer deals that are easy to access and may not be available elsewhere, they are wildly popular with consumers. eMarketer quotes a study by Yahoo! and Ipsos that found that 22 percent checked deal emails more than once every day, another 38 percent checked them once each day, while 23 percent checked them several times a week.[53] That is a huge 83 percent of the Ipsos Internet panel that checks email deal offerings at least several times each week!

Groupon's rapid growth has not been without controversy, however. Merchants have complained about the terms of its offers and charge that few of the customers who get the deals return. Pundits have questioned whether consumers are suffering from "deal fatigue." Groupon's difficulties suggest that the business models that will be most successful in the location-based marketing space are yet to be determined.[54]

Barcode Marketing

Barcode marketing is also used in local retail marketing, but in a different way using different technology. We all are familiar with the series of lines that make up Universal Product Codes; they have been used to track products in the supply chain and to maintain inventories for many years. However, as the demand grew for data to be embedded in the codes, the original codes became too small and 2D **barcodes** were introduced. They store information in a matrix pattern both horizontally and vertically and can store a large amount of data. They can be created in a variety of formats.[55] Barcodes can also be created as artwork.[56] Custom clothing site Zazzle offers a zebra barcode (see Figure 16.10) or allows you to create your own and have it printed on clothing or other items.[57]

FIGURE **16.10** Zebra Barcode Art

Source: Zazzle Inc., http://www.zazzle.com/zebra_barcode_art_poster-228676777407812710.

The 2D barcodes have become known as quick response, or QR codes. They can be printed on anything from a newspaper to a business card and just about anything in between. They can be read with a special barcode scanner, but they are easily readable by smartphone apps, opening a whole new world of promotional possibilities for the mobile marketer. QR codes were invented in Japan in 1994 and quickly adopted by Japanese and South Korean marketers. The rest of the world followed more slowly, but starting around 2010, QR codes have sprung up all over the world.

A trend report by mobile marketing services agency Scanbuy shows the size of the market and speed of its growth in the first quarter of 2011. According to the report:

- Scanning traffic grew over 800 percent over Q1 2010.
- 2D barcodes saw more scans than 1D (UPC) codes.
- Brands in the retail and media industries generated some of the most popular 2D campaigns.
- The Android operating system generated the most scans while the iPhone generated more than any other device.[58]

The promotions that can be developed by a creative marketer using 2D codes seem to be virtually limitless. However, there seem to be two basic uses at present. One is to take the shopper to a website for additional information. The other reads barcodes on products in stores, offering services like price checking and promotions.

Ralph Lauren Goes Mobile with Barcodes. As early as 2008, Ralph Lauren established a mobile website that made extensive use of barcodes. Advertising SVP David Lauren, son of the legendary designer, said it was important for its fashion-forward brand to lead trends. "This is about someone who's interested

INTERACTIVE EXERCISE **16.2** **QR Code Generator**

QR codes are quickly showing up everywhere! Would you like to make your own QR code? There are a number of sites where you can do so for free. Try the one at Kaywa and make your own!

Visit http://qrcode.kaywa.com.

in our brand and interested in technology, and wherever the two meet, that's what's appropriate," he told a reporter. The launch coincided with the company's sponsorship of the U.S. Open Tennis Championships and its app allowed users to watch the tournament on their phones. QR codes in print ads, direct mail pieces, and retail stores linked the shoppers to the mobile website (http://m.ralphlauren .com) where they could purchase merchandise and access content.[59] By 2011, the original app had been updated to allow viewing of runway shows and numerous other apps had been offered, including apps for iPad and Android phones.[60] QR codes continue to be an important part of the marketing strategy appearing in stores and publications around the globe.

Home Depot Introduces Barcodes in Stores. In spring 2011, Home Depot debuted a barcode promotion for MSLO kitchens, placing the codes on print ads and direct mail pieces and featuring them on store shelves (see Figure 16.11). The codes

FIGURE **16.11** Home Depot QR Code Promotion

Source: Shop Savvy, http://shopsavvy.mobi/2011/03/22/home-depot-barcodes-now-in-shopsavvy.

allowed customers to access content, including video demonstrations, and to purchase online from inside or outside the store.[61]

According to the promotional agency Scanbuy, the codes can easily be updated without having to print new material. Scanbuy is tracking clicks for this program that will allow Home Depot to track "which products customers are interested in, the location of interactions and representative demographics."[62]

Shopping Apps Provide Price Comparisons at the Point of Purchase

A different type of service permits consumers to read barcodes in retail locations to obtain pricing and promotional data. Shopping app provider ShopSavvy explains that its app aggregates data from over 22 million products. It does this by building a database that provides data on where a given product is sold, its price at each location, and current promotional deals. The data come from manufacturers who have signed up as clients, retailers who have joined the system, other partners such as distributors, and the web itself. As a result of the multiple data sources, if manufacturers and retailers want to control the quality of the data, they must become part of the system.[63]

ShopSavvy reports that its app has been downloaded over 64 million times. Since many of those are updates, there appears to be about 16 million unique users of the app.[64] That makes it and similar shopping apps a powerful force in today's retail marketplace.

An Alternative to Barcode Marketing: Near-Field Communications

NFC is generating huge buzz in the trade literature as the next great mobile technology. What is NFC? According to *PC Magazine*:

> NFC, or **near-field communications**, is a way for two devices to communicate small amounts of data when they're placed about four inches apart.

It goes on to explain what NFC can do in a way that tied back to our discussion of RFID chips in Chapter 2. It says:

> One way to look at NFC is that it's like RFID, but smart on both sides. RFID chips like those in Mastercard's PayPass credit cards, Visa's PayWave cards, and San Francisco's Clipper transit cards are dumb chips that store data which can be read or altered by card readers. When you tap the chip on a reader, it performs a transaction. NFC takes this a step further by putting the RFID chip in something that can do its own computing, like a mobile phone. So the phone itself can download coupons, for instance, and put the coupon data onto the RFID chip before it's tapped.[65]

Proponents of NFC technology are understandably enthusiastic, saying it opens up a new era in shopping. It is likely to begin with mobile payments but will expand to advertising, couponing, and other loyalty programs. One of those proponents is quoted this way:

> "NFC mCommerce is going to be huge. It will much bigger and grow much faster than ecommerce ever did," writes Michael Mullagh, CEO of ViVOtech. "Your smart phone is in some ways a much more powerful commerce device than your computer. It knows who you are. It knows when you are near or in your favorite stores. It can quickly access your search and purchase history. And best of all, it delivers instant gratification."[66]

Google surprised the tech world when it quietly dropped its use of QR codes on its Places service sometime in early 2011.[67] A local merchant's listing on Google Places had featured a QR code and the ability to print it out as a window poster. It was an interesting piece of technology, but it was not clear that many people even noticed when the QR code was removed. Industry supposition was that NFC technology would replace it.

FIGURE **16.12** The Google NFC Code Window Sticker
Source: Copyright Google, Inc., http://places.blogspot.com/2010/12/trailblazing-in-portland.html.

The tech forecasters were proven right when Google became one of the first to launch an NFC program with functions beyond mobile payments. From the consumer's perspective, the service allows her to use her mobile phone to rate local businesses and get personalized recommendations for similar local businesses. She can share recommendations and retrieve friends' reviews, also on her phone. From the business perspective, the early trials featured personal delivery of the NFC sticker to local businesses, which were encouraged to display it in the store window (see Figure 16.12). In the initial trial in Portland, Oregon, Google provided businesses with collateral material that encouraged their customers to rate the business and also promoted the product in the media. Marketing events included handling out co-branded Portland Trailblazers/Google t-shirts at a basketball game and running a contest to encourage users to share their reviews on social networks.[68] Google seems satisfied with the results judging by the fact that it continues to roll the service out to other urban markets.[69]

This lengthy odyssey into location-based marketing illustrates how intertwined the activities of SoLoMo marketing have become. That is why SoLoMo has become a rallying cry for mobile marketers. Growth in both local and mobile search has been high in recent years and the continued adoption of smartphones seems likely to continue that trend through at least 2015.[70] Add to that the ability to share content with friends and to receive marketer content on mobile social networks, and a powerful marketing force has emerged.

Podcasting

Only a few years ago, marketers were enthusiastic about opportunities for advertising and promotion that might be presented by **podcasting**. Like blogs, podcasts appear to have changed their focus. While it is hard to get precise information, a study by the Pew Internet Project in 2010 found teens moving from blogging to Facebook while older adults were heavier users of Twitter.[71] This parallels other data we have seen in this text and supports the observation that both blogs and podcasts have become tools of business, not a major occupation of consumers.

Apple's iTunes store has become a major distributor of podcasts, which also suggests that the tool is closely tied to the mobile environment. Observation suggests that podcasts are an important channel for some businesses, although even their video may be taking the place of audio-only content. It also suggests that media companies are heavy users of podcasts as another distribution channel for their content. Equally unscientific observation also suggests that many of the consumer podcasts available are for targeted markets—education and health often appear in search results.

Industry Self-Regulation

Marketers are concerned about preventing mobile spam and the damage it can do to consumer perceptions of the industry. In 2004, the Mobile Marketing Association (MMA) was formed, combining European- and U.S.-based trade organizations into one. The association has published a code of conduct for mobile marketing. As revised in 2008, that code includes:

- *Notice.* Marketers must provide users with an understandable and easy to locate description of the terms and conditions of a marketing program.
- *Choice and Consent.* Marketers are required to obtain opt-in consent for all marketing programs and to provide a simple opt-out mechanism. Consent cannot automatically be transferred to other marketing programs.
- *Customization and Constraint.* Marketers should target messages appropriately, using the data they collect for that purpose. They must take reasonable precautions to ensure that customer data are handled responsibly and in accordance with existing laws. They should limit mobile messages to those requested by the customer.
- *Security.* Marketers must implement reasonable procedures to protect customer data from all unauthorized use or users.
- *Enforcement and Accountability.* Members of the MMA are expected to abide by these guidelines. In the absence of outside regulation, they are expected to certify that they are abiding by the guidelines.[72]

Notice that these five categories are similar to the Fair Information Practices Policies discussed in Chapter 15. The implementation, described in the MMA's "Best Practices" publication, is more restrictive than the practices that are sanctioned on the wired Internet and that seems reasonable, given the difference in the two user environments. The MMA provides detailed implementation guidelines in its "Best Practices" publication[73] as well as standards for mobile advertising.[74]

The code of conduct is only binding on MMA members, but it is nevertheless an important step in the very early stages of mobile marketing. As stated, it applies to B2C (business-to-consumer) marketing only. However, it seems obvious that B2B (business-to-business) customers want the same kind of protection from unsolicited wireless advertising and that marketers who value their business will provide it.

The issue of customer data in the mobile environment became more prominent in early 2011 with the revelation that both Apple and Google were storing data on the location of mobile users.[75] While smartphones request permission to use location data, it is the knowledge that they were storing data that caused disquiet among many users and their elected representatives.[76] This aspect of consumer privacy[77] will continue to receive attention in the months and years to come.

Digital Convergence

Since the scientists at PARC and other early computing think tanks developed the concept of pervasive computing, the nature of the computing environment has changed in ways the founders could not envision. The concept of pervasive computing with its hub in a single piece of multifunction hardware has been replaced by the reality of media convergence. The Syracuse University Convergence Center offers this definition:

"Digital convergence" refers to the profound changes in the structure of media caused by the emergence of digital technologies as the dominant method for representing, storing, and communicating information. In the past, information and communication technologies were segmented into discrete economic and technical systems with minimal capabilities for **interoperability**.

They go on to say that the drivers of digital convergence are the coming together of content from many media channels, the ability of telecommunications networks to handle multiple media, and the "interactivity, interoperability, and connectedness" of networks and devices in both the home and office and, we could add, on the road.[78]

To put it simply, it appears that three things are converging—devices, networks, and media. Let us take a quick look at each of the three.

Device and Network Convergence

From the beginning of the computing era, hardware devices have become increasingly more integrated. Early mainframe computers mostly just computed; services like email were available, but they were cumbersome compared to today's versions. By the time of the laptop, computing and communications, including Internet access, were default expectations for all users. Device integration is even more obvious in today's mobile devices. Smart phones and tablets allow users to perform a wide array of tasks on the same device—from communications to playing games to watching videos. It is apps that open the way to a myriad of functions on smart mobile devices. This offers a myriad of opportunities to the marketer, as we have discussed throughout the text.

The concept that best describes the current state of device and network convergence is SoLoMo, referred to throughout this chapter (see Figure 16.13). Social networks provide the platforms for a variety of mobile devices. As social media continue to evolve, they will provide an even richer communications environment. It is the communications environment that is already preferred by younger consumers, and their elders are joining the move to social networks.[79] Search is a powerful integrating activity across networks and devices.

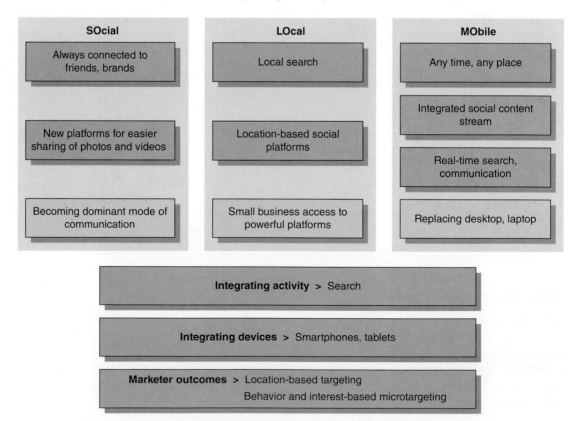

FIGURE **16.13** The SoLoMo Environment

Source: © Cengage Learning 2013

Search is the driving force in the emergence of localized marketing and it tends to be overlooked in the buzz surrounding constantly-changing platforms and devices. A late 2011 Pew study finds that the Internet has become the main source of local information with over half of all adults turning to the web for information about restaurants, bars, and clubs, with search being the most widely used access point.[80] Local search like Google Places and location-based platforms like Foursquare give even the smallest local business access to customers who are looking for information, which has a high probability of turning into a purchase. Increasingly, this search is taking place on mobile platforms at times and in locations that are close to the point of purchase. That provides a powerful impetus to purchase and a golden opportunity for savvy marketers.

To make the overall mobile experience satisfying, users are in the early stages of turning to integrated content streams. Early providers in this space include Flipboard, which provides a socially-influenced integrated stream of content.[81] That brings the concept full circle, with mobile content now having the capacity to be social.

Media Convergence

As far as marketers are concerned, **media convergence**—the convergence of multiple, often noncompatible, media into a seamless source of communication, information, entertainment, and marketing—is the biggest development of the Internet era and one that is likely to keep us occupied for years to come.

During the years preceding the Internet, and culminating in furious activity during the Internet bubble, media mergers and acquisitions occurred throughout the global media industry. This activity was fueled both by the need to compete globally and also by the desire to integrate activities across traditional and electronic media channels. Some of the major consolidations in the early Internet era included:

- The acquisition of CBS Records, a division of the Columbia Broadcasting Company Inc., by Japan's Sony Corp. in the late 1980s.
- During the 1990s, Canada's Seagram Company, formerly best known for leading brands of spirits, engaged in aggressive acquisition of media firms including Universal Studios and record companies in Europe and the United States.
- Seagram Company itself was acquired by French media conglomerate Vivendi in 2000.
- The history of media acquisitions by German media giant Bertelsmann goes far back. In the 1960s, it expanded into other European countries by purchasing print media. In the 1970s, it was music; in the 1980s, it was broadcasting. In 1995, it partnered with AOL to set up AOL Europe.[82]

The most significant event in this wave of consolidation was clearly the merger of AOL and Time Warner in January 2001. Like other media mergers chronicled earlier, this huge combination never produced the desired results,[83] and in 2009, Time Warner divested AOL.[84] In its search for new and exciting content, AOL purchased the Huffington Post, an Internet-only publication, in 2011.[85]

Huffington Post is itself an example of how media can converge under a single corporate umbrella. In the wake of the purchase by AOL, its business model received a lot of attention. One writer from a traditional media outlet characterized it as "a galley rowed by slaves and commanded by pirates."[86] One of Huffington Post's paid staffers took polite exception to this description. He identified some elements of the publication's business model as follows:

- Paid staff, who have the same expectations for attendance and productivity as staff at a traditional media outlet. They produce some of the content and do editorial and **curation** work for the site. Curation involves monitoring the flow of content that comes into Huffington Post, selecting what is appropriate for the site and editing it as necessary to conform to site guidelines.
- Other content, including text, videos, and images, comes from news feeds by traditional news aggregators like Reuters, the Associated Press, and Getty Images. Huffington Post, like all other users of this content, pays for it.

- Reporters and editors from many traditional and digital news media offer content to Huffington Post. The source of the content is identified but not usually compensated by Huffington Post. The benefit to the supplier outlet includes wider dissemination of its content and a link back to its own site.
- Then there are the bloggers who are not paid directly for their content. On a given day, you will see posts by prominent politicians, academicians, business people, and citizens who have something to say. Their contributions are many and varied.[87]

The way Huffington Post describes itself in Google search results reveals how it views itself and highlights another element of its business model. The one line description says: "Offers syndicated columnists, blogs and news stories with moderated comments." Reader comments are part of the site's content, and the company developed a unique approach to comments and their moderation. Readers have to be signed in to comment. In fact, when I open the home page, there is my picture, taken from my Facebook page. I am not overly taken with that type of personalization, but there it is. More important, readers can volunteer to become "superusers" and eventually moderators,[88] earning badges along the way.[89] Yes, it is free labor. But it is also a way of engaging with the publication and after several months of operation, the moderation strategy seems to be working.

One other insight into the Huffington Post business model comes from traditional media. A reporter used comments on posts as proxies for page views (which websites do not release in detail). Looking at just its politics page over three days, he found that:

- Huffington Post published 143 unpaid blog posts on the politics page. These posts received 6,084 comments, an average of 43 per article.
- It published 161 articles in its politics news feed, all of which were paid. These posts received 133,404 comments, an average of over 800 per post.
- During this time, a single post by staffer Sam Stein received almost 13,000 comments.[90]

The Huffington Post has a complex model in which various types of paid and unpaid content and rich media coexist in seeming harmony on a single site. Does this model point the way to the future? Only time will tell.

It is, however, clear that marketers will have to deal with a complex and ever-changing media environment for many years to come. This environment is full of risks, but it will reward marketers who assess it correctly and take innovative actions to reach highly targeted audiences in highly selective media.

SUMMARY

In the mid-1990s, the commercial Internet burst on the scene, creating revolutionary change in the way we all live and work. Before marketers had fully digested that change, the mobile Internet emerged. It creates revolutionary change in the way users deal with the traditional Internet and with traditional media. Those changes are still in early stages and are expected to continue for the foreseeable future. The challenge to marketers is heightened by the speed with which technological innovations are being adopted around the world.

The marketing challenge can be defined by the 6 A's of mobile marketing. This requires that marketers be able to deliver content to any authorized user *anywhere, anytime* on any enabled device. That puts stress on both content delivery systems and on the customer database. As devices that can receive mobile content proliferate, the challenge is magnified.

Mobile content has become another option in integrated marketing communications campaigns. It can reach users through many channels in ways that are increasingly powerful. Like other elements of Internet marketing communications, mobile is rarely successful in isolation from other elements. However, once a user has enabled a particular type of mobile communication, from email to an app, the marketer is able to push content to the user. The user will access it when convenient. That is the essence of permission-based mobile marketing.

Permission is one of the strategic drivers of mobile marketing. Others include personalization, sensitivity to time and location, and making it worthwhile, easy, and secure for the user to act in the mobile environment. Mobile marketing campaigns have special requirements that require separate campaign planning, even though the mobile campaign may be part of an integrated communications effort.

One of the primary drivers of mobile marketing is the mobile app. In order to reach the largest possible target markets, apps must be made available for various devices and operating systems. Apps open many opportunities, from delivery of specialized content to location-based marketing. Location-based marketing has become especially important because it allows small local retailers to participate in Internet marketing in an effective and cost-efficient way. That includes barcode marketing, utilizing technology like QR codes, and near-field communications.

From the beginning of the computer era, scientists have visualized a world in which computing power would be available anywhere, anytime. That vision has been realized with the advent of smartphones and tablets and the apps that permit virtually any kind of data activity whenever one is within reach of a wireless network.

It is likely that this is only one more stage on a journey without a defined ending. Marketers must be alert to new developments and quick to take advantage of them in their marketing programs.

DISCUSSION QUESTIONS

1. Explain your understanding of what mobile marketing is and what role it can play in marketing campaigns.
2. Discuss the concepts of the adoption and diffusion of technology products. Why is the diffusion process becoming increasingly rapid over time?
3. Do you believe that mobile will become the dominant type of Internet marketing? Why or why not?
4. What are the strategic drivers of mobile marketing? Why is each important?
5. Mobile marketing content is comprised of various types of media and the corresponding delivery channels. What are the channels by which mobile content can be delivered?
6. True or False: Receptivity to mobile marketing efforts can be effectively predicted by knowing the age of the target audience? Discuss your reasoning.
7. Why are smartphones and tablets such an important enabler for mobile marketing?
8. What is a mobile app? Why are mobile apps so important in mobile marketing?
9. What are some of the uses of location-based mobile marketing?
10. Why do you think couponing sites have become so popular? Do you use any of them? Why and for what purposes?
11. How can small local retailers participate in mobile marketing?
12. What is the difference between QR codes and NFC? Give an example of the use of each.
13. What is meant by digital convergence?
14. Do you expect media convergence to continue to become even more important over the next few years?

INTERNET EXERCISES

1. Internet Career Builder Exercise
   a. These are some of the jobs that are available in mobile marketing. You can find others on sites recommended by your instructor or through search.

   Manager of mobile and/or text marketing

   Mobile site designer

   Director of mobile usability

   Mobile account manger

   Mobile project manager

   App developer

   Mobile marketing analyst

   and many more

   b. Select a mobile marketing job from the list in 1a or from your own search. Outline the responsibilities of that position. You may find it useful to locate job postings on the web in order to understand the job requirements.

c. Outline knowledge and experience from classes, internships, full or part-time jobs, and volunteer work that prepare you for this specific position.

d. Prepare five questions you could ask at a job interview. The questions should exhibit your understanding of the position requirements without lecturing the interviewer about what she already knows.

e. Update your VisualCV® or LinkedIn Profile with this information.

2. Three mobile marketing campaigns—Discovery Channel, Johnson & Johnson, and ENO—are discussed in this chapter. Dissect the use of media in these campaigns. Discuss the way in which other Internet and traditional media can be used to enable and support mobile marketing campaigns.

3. Select a B2C, B2B, or nonprofit organization, business, or brand of your choice. Outline a mobile marketing campaign following the process portrayed in Figure 16.5. (Hint: you will find it difficult to specify what is to be measured for this campaign unless you establish specific and measurable marketing objectives for it.)

4. Take an inventory of the apps on your own smart device or someone else's. Even better do both. Discuss the use of the apps and the impact they have on your lifestyle and activities. Compare your usage to someone else's if you are able and draw marketing implications from the similarities and differences.

NOTES

1. http://www.pinterec.ca/google-capture-18-market-share-a-technology-adoption-case.

2. Geoffrey A. Moore, *Crossing the Chasm*, New York, Harper Business Books, 1991, revised 1999, 2002.

3. "Global Innovation Outlook 2004," IBM, http://t1d.www-306.cacheibm.com/e-business/ondemand/us/pdf/IBM_GIO_2004.pdf, 5.

4. http://www.geek.com/articles/gadgets/ipad-adoption-rate-faster-than-iphone-dvd-player-2010105.

5. http://www.tuaw.com/2011/06/21/76-of-iphone-users-will-adopt-icloud.

6. http://www.cnbc.com//id/39501308.

7. Mark Weiser, "The Computer for the Twenty-First Century," *Scientific American*, September 1991, pp. 94–10. Available online at his personal website http://www.ubiq.com/hypertext/weiser/SciAmDraft3.html, accessed November 11, 2005.

8. "What Is Pervasive Computing?" nd, http://www-3.ibm.com.

9. http://articles.cnn.com/2008-11-04/tech/magic.wall_1_multi-touch-technology-perceptive-pixel-cnns?_s=PM:TECH; http://www.washingtonpost.com/wp-dyn/content/article/2008/02/04/AR2008020402796.html; and http://www.huffingtonpost.com/2010/01/28/cnn-magic-wall-makes-twit_n_440627.html.

10. http://mobithinking.com/mobile-marketing-tools/latest-mobile-stats#mobile-internet-access.

11. http://www.slideshare.net/kleinerperkins/kpcb-top-10-mobile-trends-feb-2011?from=ss_embed.

12. http://www.morganstanley.com/institutional/techresearch/mobile_internet_report122009.html.

13. http://www.bbc.co.uk/news/10569081.

14. http://www.businesswire.com/news/home/20120105005948/en/Research-Markets-Hong-Kong—Mobile-Communications.

15. http://communicator.com.au/case-studies.html.

16. http://mmaglobal.com/studies/johnson-johnson-acuvue-define-3g-campaign-hong-kong.

17. http://www.guardian.co.uk/uk/2004/feb/19/arts.artsnews.

18. http://www.160characters.org/news.php?action=view&nid=2999.

19. http://instagiv.com/blog/2011/03/01/english-national-opera-britten-sinfonia-join-instagiv-platform.

20. http://www.figarodigital.co.uk/case-study/English-National-Opera.aspx.

21. http://www.washingtonpost.com/lifestyle/style/english-national-opera-redefined-itself--and-washington-should-take-note/2011/03/22/AFGjRLKD_story.html.

22. https://payments.amazon.com/sdui/sdui/home.

23. https://checkout.google.com.

24. http://www.readwriteweb.com/archives/Google_Joins_NFC_Forum_Ditches_QR_Codes.php.

25. http://www.iab.net/media/file/MobileAppFormats0311final.pdf.

26. http://www.mmaglobal.com/mobileadvertising.pdf.

27. http://blog.nielsen.com/nielsenwire/online_mobile/for-social-networking-women-use-mobile-more-than-men.

28. http://royal.pingdom.com/2010/02/16/study-ages-of-social-network-users.

29. http://www.opera.com/press/releases/2010/11/24_2.

30. See a more detailed planning presentation at http://www.slideshare.net/jeremiah_owyang/developing-a-mobile-strategy; and an accompanying video at http://www.youtube.com/watch?v=-Q6oHTtdNhQ&feature=player_embedded.

31. eMarketer newsletter, March 24, 2010, http://www.emarketer.com/Article.aspx?R=1008296.

32. You can view the initial video on YouTube at http://video.nhl.com/videocenter/console?id=68430.

33. eMarketer newsletter, March 24, 2010, http://www.emarketer.com/Article.aspx?R=1008296.

34. http://articles.cnn.com/2011-02-25/tech/oscars.apps_1_free-app-app-users-android?_s=PM:TECH.

35. http://itunes.apple.com/us/app/awards-hero-oscars-edition/id354596368?mt=8#.

36. http://marketplace.publicradio.org/display/web/2011/02/24/pm-all-oscars-all-the-time.

37. http://www.medialifemagazine.com/artman2/publish/Broadcastrecap_64/All-signs-point-to-a-stellar-Oscar-night.asp.

38. http://content.usatoday.com/communities/entertainment/post/2011/02/official-2011-oscar-ratings-down-10-from-last-year/1.

39. http://www.padgadget.com/2010/11/01/martha-stewart-makes-cookies-for-ipad-app-review.

40. http://mslomediakit.com/index.php?/magazines/martha_stewart_living/demographics.

41. http://mslomediakit.com/index.php?/martha_stewart_living_omnimedia/audience_research.

42. http://momentum.bigfuel.com/2011/03/babycenter%C2%AE-21st-century-mobile-mom-report-is-out.

43. http://pewinternet.org/Reports/2010/Location-based-services.aspx.

44. http://www.google.com/mobile/maps.

45. http://www.inc.com/guides/2010/07/how-to-use-location-based-social-networks-for-business.html.

46. http://foursquare.com/businesses.

47. http://gowalla.com/business.

48. http://www.4squarebadges.com/foursquare-badge-list/active-badges.

49. http://www2.ljworld.com/weblogs/social-media-blog/2010/may/20/whats-a-gowalla-a-brief-guide-to-location-based-so.

50. http://adage.com/digital/article?article_id=146819.

51. http://www.groupon.com.

52. http://blog.timberlineinteractive.com/post/Gaps-Groupon-Campaign-Grosses-2411-Million.aspx.

53. eMarketer newsletter, March 3, 2011.

54. http://www.newenglandpost.com/2011/10/22/6291.

55. http://www.barcode-generator.org.

56. http://www.squidoo.com/barcode-art.

57. http://www.zazzle.com/zebra_barcode_art_poster-228676777407812710.

58. http://scanbuy.com/web/press-kit/154-scanbuy-trend-report.

59. http://moconews.net/article/419-polo-ralph-lauren-launching-mobile-shopping-site.

60. http://www.guardian.co.uk/technology/appsblog/2011/feb/28/ralph-lauren-app-review.

61. http://www.internetretailer.com/2011/03/22/home-depot-customers-get-quick-response-mobile-bar-co.

62. http://www.mobilecommercedaily.com/2011/03/23/the-home-depot-rolls-out-nationwide-mobile-bar-code-program.

63. http://shopsavvy.mobi/brands.

64. http://www.mobilecommercedaily.com/2011/04/12/shopsavvy-mobile-shopping-assistant-app-exceeds-16m-installs.

65. http://www.pcmag.com/article2/0,2817,2372849,00.asp.

66. http://venturebeat.com/2011/04/11/nfc-under-hyped-ready-to-over-deliver.

67. http://www.readwriteweb.com/archives/Google_Joins_NFC_Forum_Ditches_QR_Codes.php.

68. http://www.bizjournals.com/portland/morning_call/2010/12/google-debuts-hotpot-in-portland.html.

69. http://searchengineland.com/google-promotes-hotpot-places-in-austin-in-advance-of-sxsw-64486.

70. http://bostinnovation.com/2011/03/11/pr-newswire-for-journalists-welcome/?isalt=0.

71. http://www.aolnews.com/2010/02/04/teens-love-facebook-study-finds-blogs-twitter-not-so-much.

72. http://mmaglobal.com/codeofconduct.pdf.

73. http://www.mmaglobal.com/bestpractices.pdf.

74. http://mmaglobal.com/mobileadvertising.pdf.

75. http://online.wsj.com/article/SB10001424052748703983704576277101723453610.html.

76. http://news.yahoo.com/s/ap/20110511/ap_on_hi_te/us_tec_location_tracking_hearing_senate.

77. http://www.computerworld.com/s/articlc/9216088/Shock_iPhones_store_location_data_Gimme_a_break..._?taxonomyId=17.

78. http://ischool.syr.edu/research/researchcenters/convergence.aspx.

79. "History," http://www.bertelsmann.com/bertelsmann_corp/wms41/bm/index.php?ci=178&language=2.

80. http://www.nytimes.com/2010/01/11/business/media/11merger.html?pagewanted=1.

81. http://www.readwriteweb.com/archives/social_networking_now_more_popular_than_email.php.

82. http://pewinternet.org/Reports/2011/Local-business-info/Overview.aspx.

83. http://www.youtube.com/watch?v=v2vpvEDS00o&feature=BFa&list=ULv2vpvEDS00o&lf=mfu_in_order.

84. http://www.foxnews.com/us/2009/12/10/aol-time-warner-split-complete.

85. http://edition.cnn.com/2011/BUSINESS/02/07/huffington.post.aol.merger/index.html.

86. http://articles.latimes.com/2011/feb/09/opinion/la-oe-rutten-column-huffington-aol-20110209.

87. http://www.huffingtonpost.com/2011/02/10/huffington-post-bloggers_n_821446.html.

88. http://www.huffingtonpost.com/p/frequently-asked-question.html#moderation.

89. http://diy-marketing.blogspot.com/2010/05/do-your-community-members-deserve-badge.html.

90. http://fivethirtyeight.blogs.nytimes.com/2011/02/12/the-economics-of-blogging-and-the-huffington-post.

A

A/B split presenting one offer, creative execution, and so forth to one group of customers or prospects and another version of the same offer, creative execution, and so on to another group of customers.

acquisition the marketing activities needed to procure a new customer.

ad format the way an ad is displayed on the publisher's site; the specifications that cause an ad to be displayed properly.

Advertising Model delivers its message with content from sponsors.

Affiliate Model offers incentives to partner websites, wherein a website agrees to post a link to a transactional site in return for a commission on sales made as a direct result of the link.

analytical CRM mining the customer database and developing programs or predictive models based on the resulting insights and data discovery.

ARPANet stands for Advanced Research Project Agency, originally an arm of the U.S. Department of Defense, which in the 1950s developed a connected system of computers that formed the basis of the modern Internet.

B

back-end activities that are required to satisfy the customer after a sale is made, including fulfillment and customer service.

bar code the printed, machine readable set of black lines and white space that identifies products according to the Universal Product Code; 2D bar codes are represented by a matrix in order to store more information.

benchmark an industry standard against which a business can measure its performance.

bounce rate number of bounces divided by number of emails sent.

brand a name, term, design, symbol, or any other feature that identifies one seller's good or service as distinct from those of other sellers (American Marketing Association definition).

brand equity the value of a brand, measured in financial terms.

brand image advertising metric that measures the type and favorability of consumer perceptions of the brand.

brand recognition/brand awareness advertising metric that measures the ability of target consumers to identify the brand under different questioning scenarios.

branded content any type of content over which the business has total control of production and distribution; the corporate identification may be highly visible or low key, depending on purpose and audience.

breadcrumb navigational aid showing path user has followed.

broad match all search volumes for a keyword idea, including synonyms and related words.

Brokerage Model brings buyers and sellers together to exchange goods and services.

Business Model the operational processes by which a business creates value, provides value to its customers, and captures value in the form of profits.

buy(ing) cycle process a customer goes through in deciding to make a purchase.

C

call center department within an organization that handles telephone sales and/or service.

call routing automated telephone systems that route calls to appropriate service agents based on data such as caller's telephone number or data provided by an IVR system.

CAN-SPAM Act U.S. law regulating advertising and promotional emails.

channel of distribution intermediaries through which products and information about transactions move in the course of a single exchange.

clickstream the complete data record, made up of mouse clicks, of consumer activity on the Internet during a specified period, usually the duration of a visit to a single website.

click-through rate number of clicks divided by number of opens.

cloud computing use of a remote network to store, manage, and process data.

CLV (customer lifetime value) the net present value of a future stream of net revenue from an identified customer.

Community Model connects like-minded individuals and groups for sharing.

concept testing research performed on the idea behind a product or a communications program.

confirmed opt-in somewhere in between opt-in and double opt-in; the visitor actively acquiesces to receiving email, again probably by another email confirmation.

content marketing creating and distributing content across the web that users find valuable and relevant, driving visitors to the website.

conversion process of moving a prospect from consideration to purchase.

cookie a few lines of code that a website or advertising network places on a user's computer to store data about the user's activities on the site.

CPC (cost-per-click) the cost of a paid ad campaign divided by the number of clicks.

CPM (cost-per-thousand) the amount paid in purchasing advertising; in this case, means the cost per thousand impressions, or the cost divided by the total number of impressions.

CSS (Cascading Style Sheets) a style sheet language to separate the content of the site from the presentation style elements, such as layouts, colors, and fonts.

curation organizing and maintaining a collection.

customer experience how customers perceive all the interactions they have with a company or brand.

customer lifecycle stages in the development of the relationship between customer and brand.

customer service solving customer problems.

customization process of producing a product, service, or communication to the exact specifications/desires of the purchaser or recipient.

D

dashboard customizable display of summary data.

data raw, unprocessed facts and numbers.

data mining analytic process and specialized analytic tools used to extract meaning from very large data sets.

database set of files (data, video, images, etc.) organized in a way that permits a computer program to quickly select any desired piece of content.

demand generation entire process of developing customer demand for a product or service.

digital convergence changes in media that have been brought about by changes in computing devices and networks.

directory aid in finding Internet websites; list of sites are usually arranged by category, and the directory has a search function.

display URL displays in ad but has link to another page.

DNS (Domain Name System) the process for converting the name of a website into its IP address.

domain name authority the extent to which a domain name is considered to be a reputable website in a particular category.

double opt-in a technique by which visitors agree to receive further communications but must perform two actions, usually checking an opt-in box on a site, and then responding positively to a sent email asking for confirmation.

E

ecommerce buying and selling goods and services online.

EDI (electronic data interchange) general term used to describe the digitizing of business information like orders and invoices so that they may be communicated electronically between suppliers and customers.

email marketing the process of developing customer relationships through offers and communications contained in email messages.

embedded device a device, often a microchip, that becomes part of another device, rendering various services, often doing so without human intervention.

embedded service module a device, usually a chip, that is part of a product and that is used to provide remote monitoring and diagnostics of the product's performance.

ERMS (email response management system) set of applications that handles large volume of email from customers and prospects, ensuring that messages receive prompt responses and are distributed to the appropriate agent; provides other functions like metrics.

ERP (enterprise resource planning) implementation of processes and software that integrates all aspects of the business from manufacturing resource planning and scheduling through service functions like human resources.

exact match search volume for a particular keyword.

extranet a corporate information system linked together to share designated information.

F

focus group the qualitative marketing research technique in which a group, usually six to twelve people who fit a particular profile, are brought together to discuss an issue under the guidance of a skilled moderator.

front end all the marketing and promotional activities that occur before a sale is made.

fulfillment the business processes necessary to receive, process, package, and ship orders to customers.

G

GPS (Global Positioning System) a satellite-based system for accurate location of a signal anywhere on Earth.

greening adopting environmentally sustainable business processes.

H

hard bounce undeliverable, usually due to a bad email address.

hard lead highly qualified sales lead.

hashtag a Twitter tool that uses the # symbol to define and group Tweets according to user-defined meanings.

heat map visual representations of eye activity on a web page.

help desk group in an organization that provides support for both hardware and software; also used in connection with specialized software that supports help desk operations.

high involvement a purchase situation in which the consumer performs an information search and undergoes an extensive choice process.

hit counter a piece of software inserted onto a website that measures the number of visits to the site.

hosting storing a website on the servers that will make it available to the Internet; can be

done internally or by specialty suppliers that offer hosting and associated services such as web metrics.

HTML (HyperText Markup Language) one of the foundations of the common Internet platform; describes the structure of web documents using a type of coding called tags.

I

identity theft stealing key items of personal information with criminal intent, usually to cause financial harm.

inbound marketing marketing approach that is focused on being visible to potential customers and using the visibility to drive them to a website where they can transact.

inbound marketing creating visibility on the Internet that brings visitors to the website or blog.

index server stores the information index, which has categorized websites as a best fit to certain keywords.

infomediary intermediary in channels of distribution that specializes in the capture, analysis, application, and distribution of information.

Infomediary Model reselling useful data.

information data that have been processed into more useful forms using techniques that range from simple summary formats to complex statistical routines.

infrastructure stack term used to describe the various layers of hardware, software, and purchased services that make up the network on which the Internet runs.

inquiry customer request for information that identifies the person or firm as a potential purchaser.

interactive presenting choices to or allowing input from the user.

interoperability the ability to exchange information between different operating platforms.

intranet corporate network accessible only to employees and outsiders with authorization.

IVR (interactive voice response) automated telephone systems in which customers key in or speak data and responses and the system responds with a combination of recorded voice messages and real-time information from databases.

K

keyword density percentage of times a particular word is used on a website page in comparison to the number of words on that page.

keywords search terms, words, or phrases that are selected by the user when making a search in a search engine; also refers to terms that are bid on in a PPC system, or a section in the HTML code for a website where site developers put terms that they hope search engines will classify the site when users search for those terms on the web.

KPI (key performance indicator) a metric that has been identified as an important measure or benchmark of business performance.

L

landing page a web page designed to receive visitors who are coming to the site as a result of a link from another site.

lead distribution dividing leads into categories based on their purchase readiness stage.

lead generation identifying sales prospects.

lead qualification determining whether a prospect has the characteristics necessary to make a purchase.

licensing legal permission to own or use a product or piece of content.

local search using a local search term in a search query.

location-based service content that is delivered based on the user's current location.

low involvement a purchase situation on which consumer spends little time or thought.

M

malware malicious software developed for the purpose of harming or taking control of certain actions on a computer or computer system.

Manufacturer (Direct) Model reaching buyers directly.

media convergence several types of media or media channels (text and images, for example) working together in a fashion that is seamless to the user.

Merchant Model providing goods and services.

meta tag a section in the HTML header section of a website that can be used to describe the site in more detail, including content and keywords; also known as meta name, or meta element.

metric a number used for evaluation or assessment of business success.

microsite (or minisite) a collection of web pages, often created for a particular subject or for a temporary period of time that has a URL different from that of the parent site.

mobile app a software application that runs on a smart mobile device.

multichannel using more than one channel of distribution or communications to reach the customer.

N

near field communications (NFC) a type of wireless connectivity that enables communication between enabled devices over short distances.

negative match key term that users do not want to be considered in their search.

NPV (net present value) current value of a discounted stream of future revenues.

O

open rate number of opens divided by number of emails delivered (sent minus bounces).

operational CRM designing and executing tactical CRM programs on the basis of data items or customer profiles.

opt-in actively choosing to receive further communications, usually by checking a box on a registration form.

opt-out taking an action to prevent the receipt of further communications, usually unchecking a box on a registration form.

P

page rank a mathematical algorithm named after Google co-founder Larry Page to indicate how important a page is on the web; used as a metric when evaluating websites.

page view a page actually seen by a visitor; generally measured as a page being delivered to the visitor, which is not exactly the same thing.

paid search the paid aspect of SEM based on an advertising model where firms seeking to rank high in specific search categories will bid on certain terms or "keywords" in the hopes of a lucrative ad ranking; also known as PPC (pay-per-click).

Pareto curve a plot of number of occurrences against percent of total; the source of the 80/20 rule.

peer-to-peer (P2P) transmission of files directly from one user to another.

permission refers to gaining the customers agreement to market to them in a certain way.

permission marketing marketing to customers who have given explicit permission to be contacted.

persona a way of describing different groups of customers by giving them a unique personality.

personalization process of preparing an individualized communication such as a newsletter or web page for a specific person based on stated or implied preferences.

pervasive computing computing power embedded in devices that makes computing capabilities available to anyone, anywhere at any time.

pfarming creating fake websites that are similar to legitimate business sites.

phishing emails that attempt to obtain personal information by making fraudulent claims.

phrase match search volume that includes an entire phrase.

PII (personally identifiable information) any piece of data that can identify a person, alone or in combination with other data items; also sometimes called personally identifying information.

pixel short for picture element; a single point on a display screen or in a graphic image.

podcasting a service that uses RSS technology to download audio content to a user's device.

Predictive Model relevant variables and associated response factors or probabilities are used to estimate the likelihood of occurrence of a specific behavior, given the existence of a given level of the specified variables.

predictive modeling using relevant variables and associated response factors or probabilities to estimate the likelihood of occurrence of a specific behavior, given the existence of a given level of the specified variables.

profile summary of the distinctive features or characteristics of a person, business, or other entity.

proprietary system software or networks that are the exclusive property of the firm that developed them and that cannot be used by others without permission.

prototype a preliminary model.

Q

QR (quick response) code a scannable matrix that links to a location on the web.

R

red flag refers to the Red Flags Rule that requires certain U.S. businesses to develop and document plans to protect consumer data from identity theft.

retention (customer retention) preventing existing customers from defecting to another seller.

RFID (radio frequency identification) technology that allows the identification of tagged goods from a distance with no intervention by human operation.

rich media combination of text, images, video, and other interactive elements.

roadblock the purchase of all ad units on a page for a specific period of time.

rule a statement that takes the form "If … then," specifying an action to be taken, given the occurrence of a particular event.

S

SaaS (Software as a Service) software as a service; making software available on a fee for use basis instead of on a license or purchase basis.

sales force automation business processes, and the software that supports them, that permit salespeople to work more effectively both in and out of their offices by providing electronic access to important documents, customer data, and support tools like calendars.

sales promotion a marketing communication that encourages the customer to take specific action.

scalability the degree to which an information system can grow with demand without completely replacing the system.

scenario essentially a story about how a customer goes about purchasing a product.

search engine website that works to help users find the things they want to find on the Internet.

search engine algorithm displays the search engine's "best guess" at which pages are most relevant to the user's search and in which order they should be shown.

SEM (search engine marketing) process of getting listed on search engines.

SEO (search engine optimization) process of designing a site and its content whereby search engines find the site without being paid to do so; also known as organic search, natural search, or algorithmic search.

server a computer from which other computers request files.

server request log record kept at the server level that records each file requested from a website.

SIM (Subscriber Identity Module) card a removable chip for cell phones that stores personal data and makes it easy to switch from one phone to another.

Six Sigma quality management technique that results in near-perfect products; technically, results that fall within six standard deviations from the mean of a normal distribution.

soft bounce temporarily undeliverable, usually due to a system problem.

soft lead sales lead that meets few if any of the qualification criteria.

spam unwanted email communication.

spear phishing targeted phishing attacks that use apparently legitimate communications in an attempt to breach a secure website.

spider programs that "crawl" the web and follow every link or piece of data that they see and bring this information back to be stored; also known as robots.

spoofing creating false identities in order to evade rules for conducting business and communications on the web.

spyware programs installed on consumers' computers, without their permission, that assume partial control over the operating system.

stickiness getting customers to stay on the site as long as possible, navigate as many paths as possible, and return again and again.

Subscription Model delivering services and content for a set fee.

supply chain the downstream portion of the value chain, the channel from suppliers to producers.

syndicated sale of content to multiple customers, each of whom then integrates it into their own products.

T

tag a piece of code that identifies a page or an element on it.

tagged web page a technique in which a small image is placed on a web page; used in conjunction with a cookie on the user's computer, the image returns data about user activity on the web page.

tags user-supplied keyword or category name.

telecommunications network of copper landlines, fiber-optic cables, and wireless transmitters that allows voice, data, text, graphics, and video to be transmitted over long distances.

testing statistical process by which alternative marketing approaches are compared and the best is selected.

text messaging and electronic message sent from one cell phone to another.

title tag the title the user sees in the blue bar at the top of the web page; also known as the HTML title tag.

touchpoint marketing jargon for each channel available for customer interaction.

transactional marketing focuses on the individual sale of a product or service.

U

unique visitor an identifiably distinct, although not necessarily identifiable, visitor to a website within a specified period.

universal search the inclusion of search results from multiple content sources such as videos, images, news, maps, books, and websites into one set of research results.

usability the ability of a site to provide a satisfactory experience.

usability testing ensuring that it is easy for visitors to navigate and, in general, to find desired content quickly and efficiently on a website.

user intent what the user is actually searching for.

Utility Model delivering services or content "pay as you go."

V

value essentially the usefulness (economic utility) of the product less its price; also known as customer value or customer perceived value.

value proposition customer value delivered to a specific target market.

video marketing the creation and deployment of videos that help create brand awareness and favorability.

virtual agent a program that simulates the conversation of a human being and uses artificial intelligence components to learn from experience, in this case to better understand customer requirements.

virtual value chain term given to an integrated supply chain in which all transactions are conducted electronically.

W

Web 2.0 second-generation Internet that provides better interactivity, information sharing, and collaboration.

Web 3.0 third-generation Internet, which is expected to have semantic abilities that support learning and personalization of web experiences.

Web Services applications that allow enterprises to exchange information over the Internet using open (public) standards; this permits otherwise incompatible systems to interact with one another without human or programming intervention.